Dictionary of Literary Biography

Documentary Series

1 *Sherwood Anderson, Willa Cather, John Dos Passos, Theodore Dreiser, F. Scott Fitzgerald, Ernest Hemingway, Sinclair Lewis,* edited by Margaret A. Van Antwerp (1982)

2 *James Gould Cozzens, James T. Farrell, William Faulkner, John O'Hara, John Steinbeck, Thomas Wolfe, Richard Wright,* edited by Margaret A. Van Antwerp (1982)

3 *Saul Bellow, Jack Kerouac, Norman Mailer, Vladimir Nabokov, John Updike, Kurt Vonnegut,* edited by Mary Bruccoli (1983)

4 *Tennessee Williams,* edited by Margaret A. Van Antwerp and Sally Johns (1984)

5 *American Transcendentalists,* edited by Joel Myerson (1988)

6 *Hardboiled Mystery Writers: Raymond Chandler, Dashiell Hammett, Ross Macdonald,* edited by Matthew J. Bruccoli and Richard Layman (1989)

7 *Modern American Poets: James Dickey, Robert Frost, Marianne Moore,* edited by Karen L. Rood (1989)

8 *The Black Aesthetic Movement,* edited by Jeffrey Louis Decker (1991)

9 *American Writers of the Vietnam War: W. D. Ehrhart, Larry Heinemann, Tim O'Brien, Walter McDonald, John M. Del Vecchio,* edited by Ronald Baughman (1991)

10 *The Bloomsbury Group,* edited by Edward L. Bishop (1992)

11 *American Proletarian Culture: The Twenties and The Thirties,* edited by Jon Christian Suggs (1993)

12 *Southern Women Writers: Flannery O'Connor, Katherine Anne Porter, Eudora Welty,* edited by Mary Ann Wimsatt and Karen L. Rood (1994)

13 *The House of Scribner, 1846-1904,* edited by John Delaney (1996)

14 *Four Women Writers for Children, 1868-1918,* edited by Caroline C. Hunt (1996)

15 *American Expatriate Writers: Paris in the Twenties,* edited by Matthew J. Bruccoli and Robert W. Trogdon (1997)

16 *The House of Scribner, 1905-1930,* edited by John Delaney (1997)

17 *The House of Scribner, 1931-1984,* edited by John Delaney (1998)

18 *British Poets of The Great War: Sassoon, Graves, Owen,* edited by Patrick Quinn (1999)

19 *James Dickey,* edited by Judith S. Baughman (1999)

See also DLB 210, 216, 219, 222, 224, 229

Yearbooks

1980 edited by Karen L. Rood, Jean W. Ross, and Richard Ziegfeld (1981)

1981 edited by Karen L. Rood, Jean W. Ross, and Richard Ziegfeld (1982)

1982 edited by Richard Ziegfeld; associate editors: Jean W. Ross and Lynne C. Zeigler (1983)

1983 edited by Mary Bruccoli and Jean W. Ross; associate editor Richard Ziegfeld (1984)

1984 edited by Jean W. Ross (1985)

1985 edited by Jean W. Ross (1986)

1986 edited by J. M. Brook (1987)

1987 edited by J. M. Brook (1988)

1988 edited by J. M. Brook (1989)

1989 edited by J. M. Brook (1990)

1990 edited by James W. Hipp (1991)

1991 edited by James W. Hipp (1992)

1992 edited by James W. Hipp (1993)

1993 edited by James W. Hipp, contributing editor George Garrett (1994)

1994 edited by James W. Hipp, contributing editor George Garrett (1995)

1995 edited by James W. Hipp, contributing editor George Garrett (1996)

1996 edited by Samuel W. Bruce and L. Kay Webster, contributing editor George Garrett (1997)

1997 edited by Matthew J. Bruccoli and George Garrett, with the assistance of L. Kay Webster (1998)

1998 edited by Matthew J. Bruccoli, contributing editor George Garrett, with the assistance of D. W. Thomas (1999)

1999 edited by Matthew J. Bruccoli, contributing editor George Garrett, with the assistance of D. W. Thomas (2000)

Concise Series

Concise Dictionary of American Literary Biography, 7 volumes (1988-1999): *The New Consciousness, 1941-1968; Colonization to the American Renaissance, 1640-1865; Realism, Naturalism, and Local Color, 1865-1917; The Twenties, 1917-1929; The Age of Maturity, 1929-1941; Broadening Views, 1968-1988; Supplement: Modern Writers, 1900-1998.*

Concise Dictionary of British Literary Biography, 8 volumes (1991-1992): *Writers of the Middle Ages and Renaissance Before 1660; Writers of the Restoration and Eighteenth Century, 1660-1789; Writers of the Romantic Period, 1789-1832; Victorian Writers, 1832-1890; Late-Victorian and Edwardian Writers, 1890-1914; Modern Writers, 1914-1945; Writers After World War II, 1945-1960; Contemporary Writers, 1960 to Present.*

Concise Dictionary of World Literary Biography, 20 volumes projected (1999-): *Ancient Greek and Roman Writers; German Writers; African, Carribbean, and Latin American Writers.*

Twentieth-Century Eastern European Writers
Third Series

Twentieth-Century Eastern European Writers
Third Series

Edited by
Steven Serafin
Hunter College of The City University of New York

A Bruccoli Clark Layman Book
The Gale Group
Detroit • San Francisco • London • Boston • Woodbridge, Conn.

Printed in the United States of America

The paper used in this publication meets the minimum requirements
of American National Standard for Information Sciences—Permanence
Paper for Printed Library Materials, ANSI Z39.48-1984. ∞™

Library of Congress Cataloging-in-Publication Data

Twentieth-century Eastern European writers. Third series / edited by Steven Serafin.
  p. cm.—(Dictionary of literary biography: v. 232)
"A Bruccoli Clark Layman book."
Includes bibliographical references and index.
ISBN 0-7876-4649-0 (alk. paper)
1. Eastern European literature—20th century—Bio-bibliography. I. Title: 20th century Eastern European
writers. II. Serafin, Steven. III. Series.

Z2483.T883 2001
[PN849.E9]   00–059334
809'.8947--dc21   CIP

10 9 8 7 6 5 4 3 2 1

Contents

Contents

Authors by Nationality

Czech Republic

Václav Havel

Miroslav Holub

Bohumil Hrabal

Ivan Klíma

Milan Kundera

Arnošt Lustig

Vladimir Páral

Jan Skácel

Josef Škvorecký

Ludvík Vaculík

Estonia

Jaan Kaplinski

Jaan Kross

Kalju Lepik

Paul-Eerik Rummo

Mati Unt

Hungary

Sándor Csoóri

Péter Esterházy

György Konrád

Miklós Mészöly

Dezső Tandori

Latvia

Alberts Bels

Vizma Belševica

Regīna Ezera

Astrīde Ivaska

Ojārs Vācietis

Māra Zālīte

Imants Ziedonis

Lithuania

Sigitas Geda

Justinas Marcinkevičius

Kostas Ostrauskas

Judita Vaičiūnaitė

Poland

Stanisław Barańczak

Miron Białoszewski

Adam Czerniawski

Zbigniew Herbert

Tadeusz Konwicki

Sławomir Mrożek

Tadeusz Różewicz

Wisława Szymborska

Adam Zagajewski

Romania

Gabriela Adameşteanu

Ana Blandiana

Mircea Cărtărescu

Mircea Dinescu

Ştefan Aug. Doinaş

Ileana Mălăncioiu

Norman Manea

Mircea Horia Simionescu

Ion D. Sîrbu

Nichita Stănescu

Plan of the Series

The advisory board, the editors, and the publisher of the *Dictionary of Literary Biography* are joined in endorsing Mark Twain's declaration. The literature of a nation provides an inexhaustible resource of permanent worth. We intend to make literature and its creators better understood and more accessible to students and the reading public, while satisfying the standards of teachers and scholars.

To meet these requirements, *literary biography* has been construed in terms of the author's achievement. The most important thing about a writer is his writing. Accordingly, the entries in *DLB* are career biographies, tracing the development of the author's canon and the evolution of his reputation.

The purpose of *DLB* is not only to provide reliable information in a convenient format but also to place the figures in the larger perspective of literary history and to offer appraisals of their accomplishments by qualified scholars.

The publication plan for *DLB* resulted from two years of preparation. The project was proposed to Bruccoli Clark by Frederick G. Ruffner, president of the Gale Research Company, in November 1975. After specimen entries were prepared and typeset, an advisory board was formed to refine the entry format and develop the series rationale. In meetings held during 1976, the publisher, series editors, and advisory board approved the scheme for a comprehensive biographical dictionary of persons who contributed to North American literature. Editorial work on the first volume began in January 1977, and it was published in 1978. In order to make *DLB* more than a reference tool and to compile volumes

that individually have claim to status as literary history, it was decided to organize volumes by topic, period, or genre. Each of these freestanding volumes provides a biographical-bibliographical guide and overview for a particular area of literature. We are convinced that this organization—as opposed to a single alphabet method—constitutes a valuable innovation in the presentation of reference material. The volume plan necessarily requires many decisions for the placement and treatment of authors who might properly be included in two or three volumes. In some instances a major figure will be included in separate volumes, but with different entries emphasizing the aspect of his career appropriate to each volume. Ernest Hemingway, for example, is represented in *American Writers in Paris, 1920–1939* by an entry focusing on his expatriate apprenticeship; he is also in *American Novelists, 1910–1945* with an entry surveying his entire career, as well as in *American Short-Story Writers, 1910–1945, Second Series* with an entry concentrating on his short stories. Each volume includes a cumulative index of the subject authors and articles. Comprehensive indexes to the entire series are planned.

Since 1981 the series has been further augmented by the *DLB Yearbooks*, which update published entries and add new entries to keep the *DLB* current with contemporary activity. There have also been *DLB Documentary Series* volumes which provide biographical and critical source materials for figures whose work is judged to have particular interest for students. One of these companion volumes is devoted entirely to Tennessee Williams.

We define literature as the *intellectual commerce of a nation:* not merely as belles lettres but as that ample and complex process by which ideas are generated, shaped, and transmitted. *DLB* entries are not limited to "creative writers" but extend to other figures who in their time and in their way influenced the mind of a people. Thus the series encompasses historians, journalists, publishers, book collectors, and screenwriters. By this means readers of *DLB* may be aided to perceive literature not as cult scripture in the keeping of intellectual high priests but firmly positioned at the center of a nation's life.

DLB includes the major writers appropriate to each volume and those standing in the ranks behind them. Scholarly and critical counsel has been sought in deciding which minor figures to include and how full their entries should be. Wherever possible, useful references are made to figures who do not warrant separate entries.

Each *DLB* volume has an expert volume editor responsible for planning the volume, selecting the figures for inclusion, and assigning the entries. Volume editors are also responsible for preparing, where appropriate, appendices surveying the major periodicals and literary and intellectual movements for their volumes, as well as lists of further readings. Work on the series as a whole is coordinated at the Bruccoli Clark Layman editorial center in Columbia, South Carolina, where the editorial staff is responsible for accuracy and utility of the published volumes.

One feature that distinguishes *DLB* is the illustration policy—its concern with the iconography of literature. Just as an author is influenced by his surroundings, so is the reader's understanding of the author enhanced by a knowledge of his environment. Therefore *DLB* volumes include not only drawings, paintings, and photographs of authors, often depicting them at various stages in their careers, but also illustrations of their families and places where they lived. Title pages are regularly reproduced in facsimile along with dust jackets for modern authors. The dust jackets are a special feature of *DLB* because they often document better than anything else the way in which an author's work was perceived in its own time. Specimens of the writers' manuscripts and letters are included when feasible.

Samuel Johnson rightly decreed that "The chief glory of every people arises from its authors." The purpose of the *Dictionary of Literary Biography* is to compile literary history in the surest way available to us—by accurate and comprehensive treatment of the lives and work of those who contributed to it.

The *DLB* Advisory Board

Introduction

Designed to introduce the lives and works of the most prominent literary figures of Eastern Europe, the *Twentieth-Century Eastern European Writers* series surveys the national literatures of the Czech Republic, Estonia, Hungary, Latvia, Lithuania, Poland, Romania, and Slovakia. Exploring the evolution of Eastern European literature contrasted against the complexity of unprecedented social and political transition, the series serves to acknowledge the contributions of those authors who have played a significant role in creating as well as preserving the quality and integrity of contemporary literary tradition. The First and Second Series include authors whose careers were established primarily in the first half of the twentieth century, reflecting the literary as well as historical development of their respective countries within the modern era up to and during World War II. The Third Series continues this progression by including authors whose major contributions evolved in the second half of the century, extending from the postwar experience into the new millennium.

Situated geographically as a corridor separating Western Europe from the vast expanse of Russia and the independent republics of Byelorussia and Ukraine, Eastern Europe is a composite of peoples and languages defined by a broad perspective of social and cultural identity. Facing the Gulf of Finland and the Baltic Sea, Estonia borders Russia in the east and Latvia in the south. Both Latvia and Lithuania also face the Baltic, as does Poland in the north. Lithuania borders Poland and Byelorussia. The central region consists of the Czech Republic, Slovakia, and Hungary. Romania faces the Black Sea in the west and borders Bulgaria, Yugoslavia, Hungary, and Ukraine. Lithuanian and Latvian are the only surviving Baltic languages of the Indo-European group that also includes the Italic language of Romanian and the West Slavic languages of Polish, Czech, and Slovak. East Slavic languages include Russian, Ukrainian, and Belorussian, whereas South Slavic languages include Slovene, Serbian, Croatian, Macedonian, and Bulgarian. Both Estonian and Hungarian belong to the western branch of the Finno-Ugric language group.

The oral and written literature of Eastern Europe is embedded in centuries of struggle for self-determination and autonomy. Writing for *The New York Times Book Review* (22 January 1981), Czech novelist Milan Kundera acknowledged the importance and value of literary tradition and spoke metaphorically for all of Eastern Europe in stating that a nation is "born" from and through its literature, and that each nation is in essence "tied to the destiny of its literature and of its culture." Kundera was among the many Eastern European writers denied the full measure of their literary and artistic inheritance. Forced into exile at the height of his creative powers, Kundera observed as an émigré the emergence of Eastern Europe from more than four decades of political oppression to forge a new era of nationhood and independence. Positioned as it is between the imposing ideologies of East and West, Eastern Europe has, throughout the course of history, been the object of aggression and conquest, ravaged by war and exploitation. Extending into the twentieth century, the plight for survival has never been more perilous or convoluted, as occupation and dictatorship have threatened the essence and existence of national and cultural identity.

After the devastation of World War I, Eastern Europe was reconfigured, and its peoples faced the difficult and painstaking process of recovery. This process was compounded by the repercussions of social and political upheaval, economic instability, and ethnic dissension that perpetuated the vulnerability of the region to foreign intervention. Fueled with bitter resentment toward the West and the impact of the economic crisis of the Great Depression, expansionist nations such as Germany and Italy targeted Eastern Europe as a source for future acquisition. Opportunism and aggression escalated into a threat to political stability and coexistence. Attempting to appease Adolf Hitler as a means to divert another world war, Western powers at the Munich Conference in 1938 conceded territorial claims to Germany. As a result, Hitler dismembered Czechoslovakia and established Slovakia as a German protectorate while allowing former Czech lands to become occupied by Hungary and Poland. On 23 August 1939 Hitler and Joseph Stalin signed a nonaggression pact that provided for the German-Soviet partition of Poland and the Soviet occupation of the Baltic states of Estonia, Latvia, and Lithuania. Refuting the compromise reached at the Munich Conference, a defiant Hitler on 1 September ordered the German invasion of Poland, which propelled the Soviet invasion from the east and simultaneously marked the beginning of World War II. Divided by German and Soviet forces, a defeated Poland fell victim to reprisal and atrocities of epic proportions. The German occupation led to the extermination of Polish Jewry as well as nearly three million ethnic Poles. On the eastern front, more than two million Poles were deported to their deaths in Kazakstan, Siberia, and the Soviet Far East.

In June 1940 Stalin ordered the Soviet occupation of the Baltic States, initiating a campaign of political suppression and genocidal policies that virtually decimated the populace. The reign of terror unleashed by Stalin was circumvented only by Hitler's decision to break the nonaggression pact. Turning on Stalin as a means to further extend the domain of the Third Reich, Hitler ordered the invasion of the Soviet Union in June 1941, leading to the German occupation of eastern Poland as well as Latvia and Lithuania. In November of that year Hitler brought both Romania and Hungary into the Axis alliance, thus extending his sphere of influence over virtually all of Eastern Europe. Confident of an expedient victory, Hitler drove deep into Soviet territory as part of a bold and calculated strategy to lay siege to Moscow and to force Stalin to capitulate. However, the early momentum of the German offensive was halted by fierce Soviet resistance, as well as adverse weather conditions that culminated in the months-long battle of Stalingrad. Consequently, the failure to take Moscow and the German surrender at Stalingrad in February 1943 proved disastrous for Hitler and the German military campaign and, in effect, served as the turning point of the war.

As the remaining German forces retreated from the Soviet Union, the advancing Soviet forces pursued, systematically solidifying the Soviet position in newly liberated Eastern Europe. In July 1944 Soviet forces began to drive the German army out of eastern Poland, which led to the establishment of a pro-Soviet provisional government. In August the dictatorship in Romania was overthrown, and the former Axis nation reentered the war on the side of the Allies. With the annexation of Estonia and the reoccupation of Latvia and Lithuania, the Baltic states were again subjected to harsh Soviet rule that initiated forced collectivization and government-sponsored Russian immigration. In 1945, as the war in Europe drew to a close, agreements reached between the victorious Allied nations at Yalta and then later at Potsdam allowed for the Soviet Union to be given jurisdiction over those territories occupied by Soviet troops. As a result, the sphere of Soviet control was established over the whole of Eastern Europe, from the Baltic region to the Balkans. Following the collapse of anti-Communist resistance, Poland was reorganized as a Soviet satellite state, and the majority of Germans in western Poland were expelled, while the Ukrainian and Belorussian districts in eastern Poland were transferred to the Soviet Union. Czechoslovakia was reestablished with territorial concessions to Russia and likewise fell under Soviet control. Allied with Germany during the war, Hungary as well as Romania also were given over to Soviet jurisdiction. With opposition either eliminated or effectively undermined, postwar Eastern Europe emerged as a communist bloc formed under rigid and repressive allegiance to the Soviet Union.

The war and its aftermath had a profound and devastating impact on all aspects of Eastern European culture, but none more dramatically than literature. During the German occupation of Central and Eastern Europe, the literary and artistic communities were subjected to extreme measures of political censorship and reprisal. Many writers were arrested and imprisoned, some of whom perished in concentration camps or were executed by order of the German Gestapo. In the wake of the Soviet "liberation" of Eastern Europe, as a means to gain control of intellectual and creative activity, the Soviet-imposed doctrine of Socialist Realism was intended to harness the literary community into the service of the state. The "official" literature was mandated to profess loyalty to the Soviet Union and the cause of Marxism-Leninism and to take a revolutionary posture toward all issues of "progress." Literature was thus an instrument of propaganda to initiate both praise and glorification of the Soviet East while systematically reflecting animosity and hostility toward the discordant West. Consequently, the Soviet-imposed mandate divided literary communities throughout Eastern Europe into those who accepted the "official" purpose of literature and those who refused to conform. Dissident writers were subject to harassment and persecution and often denied access to publication. Many were either forced into silence or fled their native countries to live in exile. The East European émigré community was displaced throughout Central and Western Europe, Scandinavia, and to various locales in North and South America, and as a result the condition of exile informs a significant portion of Eastern European literature in the second half of the twentieth century.

Immediately following the German dismemberment of Czechoslovakia, writers in both Czech and Slovak were subjected to severe restriction and censorship. Publication by Jewish writers such as Egon Hostovský, Jiří Orten, and Karl Poláček was banned, and many writers were arrested, tortured, or imprisoned. Among those who perished during the occupation were Orten, Poláček, Josef Čapek (brother of the prominent dramatist Karel Čapek), Vladislav Vančura, Bedřich Václavek, and the editor and critic Julius Fučík. Following the war, Czechoslovakia regained its independence and was ruled from 1945 to 1948 by a coalition government. During this period, literature experienced a resurgence of activity, illustrated most significantly in the poetry of Vladimír Holan, writing in Czech, and the Slovak authors Rudolf Fábry and Vladimír Reisel. However, the revival was short-lived, abruptly curtailed by the Communist takeover in February 1948. As a result, the Soviet-imposed doctrine of Socialist Realism was instituted as the "official" literature, forcing writers to conform to the accepted ideology or retreat into silence.

Similarly, the joint German and Soviet invasion of Poland abruptly ended an interwar period in Polish literature marked by intense artistic expression and bold experimentation, illustrated in the poetry of such writers as Bruno Jasieński, Anatol Stern, Aleksander Wat, Julian Przyboś, Józef Czechowicz, and Jerzy Zagórski, as well as the prose of Stefan Żeromski, Sofia Nałkowska, Juliusz Kaden-Bandrowski, and Maria Dąbrowska. During the German occupation of Poland, literary activity was severely restricted, forcing many of the most prominent Polish writers into exile. Again, many writers were arrested, deported, or sent to concentration camps, while others were executed or perished in the Warsaw Uprising and other resistance activities. Included among those seeking refuge in the West were the poets Julian Tuwim, Kazimierz Wierzyński, Jan Lechoń, Antoni Słonimski, and Józef Wittlin, as well as the novelist and playwright Witold Gombrowicz. Early postwar literature was dominated by established writers remaining in Poland, such as Nałkowska, Dąbrowska, Czesław Miłosz, Teodor Parnicki, Jarosław Iwaszkiewicz, and Jerzy Andrzejewski, as well as emerging writers such as Miron Białoszewski, Tadeusz Różewicz, and Zbigniew Herbert. However, with the proclamation in 1949 of Socialist Realism as the "official" mandate, literary activity was severely curtailed, forcing several writers into self-imposed exile, most notably the celebrated poet and literary scholar Miłosz, who lived for a period in France before residing in the United States.

The Soviet annexation of the Baltic states and the German occupation of Latvia and Lithuania severely restricted literary activity throughout the region and forced many writers into exile: from Latvia, Arturs Baumanis, Veronika Strēlerte (pseudonym of Rudīte Strēlerte-Johansone), Velta Toma, Linard Tauns, Aina Zemdega, and Anšlavs Eglītis; from Lithuania, Kazys Bradūnas, Alfonsas Nyka-Niliūnas, Henrikas Radauskas, Antanas Škėma, Marius Katiliškis, Aloyzas Baronas, Bernardas Brazdžionis, Algirdas Mackus, Algirdas Landsbergis, and Kostas Ostrauskas; and from Estonia, Arved Viirlaid, Karl Ristikivi, Ivar Grunthal, Aino and Oskar Kallas, Alexis Rannit, Ivar Ivask, and Bernard Kangro. Writers remaining in the Soviet-occupied Baltic states were, as in the other bloc countries, subject to strict adherence to the "official" literature of Socialist Realism or targeted for reprisal either through imprisonment or being denied access to publication.

Postwar Romanian literature—shaped primarily by poets belonging to the Bucharest group, notably Dimitrie Stelaru, Constant Tonegaru, Geo Dumitrescu, and Ion Caraion, and to the Sibiu group dominated by Ştefan Augustin Doinaş and Radu Stanca—was likewise subjugated to harsh and uncompromising censorship. Many writers were imprisoned for political reasons, and while some—notably Caraion and Doinaş—were later rehabilitated and allowed to resume their careers, many others either perished or fell silent upon their release. Among the writers forced into exile were the literary and religious scholar Mircea Eliade and the poets Dom Pagis and Paul Celan. After a succession of coalition governments in Hungary, the Communists in February 1948 established a one-party dictatorship under the leadership of Mátyás Rákosi. Among the many writers silenced by the new regime were established authors such as Lajos Kassák, László Németh, József Erdélyi, Lőrinc Szabó, and the highly esteemed Gyula Illyés, as well as younger, emerging authors—Sándor Weöres, György Faludy, János Pilinszky, Mihály Váci, and László Nagy.

The cultural devastation of Socialist Realism continued throughout the late 1940s and early 1950s and was interrupted—if only for a short-lived period of resurgence—in the mid 1950s following the death of Stalin in 1953. The Soviet failure to meet the imposing social and economic demands of the postwar condition had resulted in growing animosity toward the political regime that escalated in the aftermath of Stalin's death. The "collective" post-Stalinist government soon yielded power to Nikita Khrushchev, then the first secretary of the Communist Party, whose denunciation of Stalin at the Twentieth Party Congress in 1956 and public revelation of Stalin's campaign of terror and repression resulted in massive dissension within the Soviet system. As a means to defuse the widespread disillusionment and escalating unrest, the Soviet leadership introduced a relaxation of Party doctrine, including adherence to the mandates of Socialist Realism. The imposed cultural thaw was seized upon by literary, artistic, and intellectual communities as an unprecedented opportunity for change, and throughout the Eastern European bloc there evolved an atmosphere that openly dismissed the "official" Soviet-imposed literature in favor of a literature rejuvenated by a broad range of creative expression and experimentation. This change was marked by the appearance of a new generation of writers determined to challenge the boundaries of publication, as well as by the reappearance of writers whose works were previously banned or censored by the authorities. For many, the post-Stalinist thaw was a rebirth of creative and nationalistic identity, but the early euphoria and optimism soon faded as the Soviet leadership resumed a hard-line position and systematically moved to regain control over cultural life.

From the late 1950s through the mid 1960s emerging authors writing in Czech included prose writers such as Ivan Klíma, Kundera, Arnošt Lustig, Jaroslav Putík, Josef Škvorecký, Ladislav Fuks, and Vladimír Páral, the poets Miroslav Holub and František Hrubín, and the dramatist Václav Havel, as well as poets Valentín Beniak, Ján Kostra, Ladislav Mňačko, Dominik Tatarka, Ladislav Grosman, and Jaroslava Blažková, and the dramatist Peter Karvaš writing in Slovak. In the late 1960s the Slovak Communist leader Alexander Dubcek and other party leaders joined with the literary and cultural community in an attempt to reform the Communist system in what came to be known as the "Prague Spring." However, in the wake of the Soviet invasion on 21 August 1968, Dubcek was ousted; rigid Party control was restored; and independent literary activity was either suppressed or eliminated. As a result, many writers sought refuge in the West, including such notable Czech authors as Kundera, Lustig, Škvorecký, Jan Benes, Pavel Kohout, and Jiří Gruša, and the Slovak authors Mňačko, Grosman, and Blažková. Dissident writers remaining in Czechoslovakia were denied access to publication and subjected to persecution and arrest. Whenever possible, their works were either brought out by émigré publishing houses or appeared in underground samizdat editions that circulated within the literary community.

The post-Stalinist period in Poland initiated a proliferation of literary activity in all genres by new and emerging authors such as the poets Różewicz, Herbert, Białoszewski, and Wisława Szymborska, the dramatist Sławomir Mrożek, and prose writers Marek Hłasko, Tadeusz Konwicki, Marek Nowakowski, and Tadeusz Nowak, as well as previously banned writers such as Dąbrowska and writers in exile such as Kazimierz Wierzyński, Gombrowicz, and Miłosz. The revised mandate imposed by the political regime was disregarded, and bold and innovative publication remained a consistent feature of contemporary Polish literature, supplemented by the appearance in the late 1960s and 1970s of several independent press venues in Poland, as well as émigré publishing houses in the West. As the once-dominant Soviet authority over Polish cultural life continued to depreciate, many writers, artists, and members of the intellectual community consorted to support the development of a reformed and revalidated national consciousness.

In the Baltic states the cultural thaw inspired a literary revival that brought to the forefront writers of artistic importance determined to revitalize the stagnant complacency of contemporary Baltic literature. Postwar Latvian writers such as Ēvalds Vilks, Visvaldis Lāms-Eglons, Harijs Heislers, and Zigmunds Skujiņš inspired a new generation of authors that included prose writers such as Regīna Ezera, Saulcerīte Viese, Aivars Kalve, and Alberts Bels, and poets such as Knuts Skujenieks, Vitauts Ļūdēns, Imants Auziņš, Jānis Peters, and, most notably, Vizma Belševica, Ojārs Vācietis, Imants Ziedonis, and Māris Čaklais. Likewise, the literary community in exile fostered an equally committed and talented generation that included the poets Velta Sniķere, Valdis Krāslavietis (pseudonym of Valdis Grants), Linards Tauns (pseudonym of Alfrēds Bērzs), Aina Kraujiete, Gunars Saliņš, Aina Zemdega, Rita Gāle, Astrīde Ivaska, Baiba Bičole, and Olafs Stumbrs, as well as prose writers such as Dzintars Sodums, Modris Zeberiņš, Andrejs Irbe, Richards Rīdzinieks (pseudonym of Ervins Grīns), Aivars Ruņģis, Guntis Zariņš, Ilze Šķipsna, and Tālivaldis Ķikauka. In Soviet-occupied Lithuania the poet Eduardas Mieželaitis preceded a host of writers emerging in the late 1950s and 1960s that included the poets Janina Degutytė, Justinas Marcinkevičius, Judita Vaičiūnaitė, and Sigitas Geda, the dramatist Kazys Saja, and prose writers such as Jonas Avyžius, Mykolas Sluckis, Juozas Aputis, and Romualdas Granauskas. Estonian writers of the same period included Paul-Eerik Rummo, Ain Kaalep, Artur Alliksaar, Bernard Kangro, Asta Willmann, Ilmar Külvet, and Mati Unt.

With the establishment in 1948 of a one-party state in Hungary, the political regime of Mátyás Rákosi imposed severe ideological restrictions on all aspects of creative endeavor, and by 1950 literary and cultural life was brought under the complete control of the government. Despite the liberalizing policy initiated in 1953 by the premier, Imre Nagy, there existed a harsh and repressive atmosphere toward literary and artistic expression that deviated from the "official" standard. In April 1955 Nagy was ousted from power—and later secretly executed in reprisal for his reformist policies. Nevertheless, opposition to the government continued to escalate, and progressive activists within the literary and intellectual community were instrumental in orchestrating a nationwide reform movement that culminated in the Hungarian Revolution of October-November 1956. The revolt was brutally crushed with Soviet military intervention, and a new regime was installed under the leadership of János Kádár, first secretary of the Communist Party. Demonstrating remarkable tenacity and determination, despite the implications of renewed restriction, the Hungarian literary community remained highly productive and innovative. The postwar *Újhold* (New Moon) group, which included Madga Szabó, Ágnes Nemes Nagy, Pilinszky, Géza Ottlik, Iván Mándy, and Miklós Mészöly, most of whom began writing during World War II, joined with other writers such as Illyés, Faludy, Weöres, Ferenc Jahász, and István Vas—as well as a new generation including Váci, László Nagy, Ferenc Sánta, and György Konrád—to create a literature of contemporary importance.

Inspired by the postwar generation of writers that included the poets of the Bucharest group and the Sibiu group, as well as prose writers such as Zaharia Stancu and poets such as Miron Radu Paraschievescu and Nina Cassian, the emerging Romanian writers of the late 1950s and 1960s included Nichita Stănescu, Nicolae Labiş, Marin Sorescu, Radu Petrescu, Mircea Horia Simionescu, Matei Călinescu, and notable women writers such as Constanţa Buzea, Ana Blandiana, and Gabriela Adameşteanu. Determined to creative a vibrant and innovative literature, writers experimented in all genres before the reemergence of harsh political oppression that severely restricted progressive literary activity. The re-Stalinization policy initiated in the late 1950s by Romanian party chief Gheorghe Gheorghiu-Dej was adopted and then exploited by the totalitarian regime of Nicolae Ceauşescu as a means to extend control over all aspects of literary and cultural life. Functioning independently from Soviet authority, the Ceauşescu dictatorship subjected the literary community to extreme measures of censorship and severe reprisal for dissident behavior.

In the late 1970s the infrastructure of the Soviet system continued to deteriorate under the increasing social and economic demands of a modern, technological society, and the escalating internal tension in the Soviet Union soon spread throughout the satellite states, resulting in an increasingly visible display of public protest. In the summer of 1980 the demand for reform spurred the establishment of the Solidarity labor union in Poland, which emerged as the first independent social and political movement in postwar Eastern Europe. Widespread support for Solidarity helped unite the populace against Soviet domination. The volatile situation was further inflamed shortly thereafter with the announcement that the émigré Polish author Miłosz was awarded the Nobel Prize for literature, which seemingly reaffirmed the spirited demand for self-determination. As a result, on 13 December 1981 the Soviet leadership declared martial law and disbanded Solidarity, forcing the outlawed opposition movement underground. Nonetheless, the success of Solidarity reverberated throughout the Eastern European bloc, unleashing a wave of nationalistic sentiment in all the satellite states aimed toward the restoration of independence.

The opportunity for change was realized in the aftermath of political transition in the Soviet Union with the appointment in March 1985 of Mikhail Gorbachev as the Soviet president. Attempting to rejuvenate the faltering Soviet system, Gorbachev initiated his policy of glasnost (openness) as the first step of his broader program of political and economic reform, perestroika (restructuring), intended as a means both to stabilize internal dissension and to restore political control within the satellite system. In effect, however, the reform effort generated a bold and defiant assertiveness that further divided the East European bloc from Soviet authority. Relaxing the strict adherence to the ideological doctrine of Soviet aestheticism, Gorbachev's glasnost policy also served as a catalyst to ignite an impassioned period of creative expression and experimentation.

Throughout the late 1980s the East European economy continued to deteriorate, resulting in escalating internal strife. Public opposition and protest became increasingly confrontational and widespread, and in May 1988 the Kadar regime in Hungary was replaced by reform Communists, who in the following year instituted multiparty government after nearly half a century of dictatorship. Shortly thereafter, labor strikes in Poland virtually paralyzed the country, forcing the government into negotiations with the outlawed Solidarity. As a result, Communist authorities were forced to legalize Solidarity and to surrender its monopoly of power. Additionally, the resurgence of nationalistic fervor in the deeply entrenched Baltic states further compromised the Soviet sphere of control, illustrated most symbolically in Lithuania, where the Soviets restored Lithuanian as the official language. In December 1989 the Lithuanian Communist Party separated from the Soviet Communist Party, and, as a result, Lithuania became the first Soviet republic to permit a multiparty system. In that same month the so-called "Velvet Revolution" in Czechoslovakia ended Soviet domination of the former republic and presented the responsibility of leadership to the dissident writer Havel—who had been harassed and persecuted throughout the decades of Communist rule. The nonviolent transfer of power in Czechoslovakia coincided with the violent overthrow in Romania of Ceauşescu's dictatorship, ending nearly twenty-five years of what many consider one of the darkest periods in Romanian history.

In 1990 Estonia began negotiations with the Soviet Union, seeking to establish independence; in the next year Estonian was restored as the official language, and the Communist monopoly of power was abolished. Following the example of Lithuania and Estonia, Latvia also began to move toward independence. In June 1990 the Soviet Union entered into negotiations with the Baltic states, seeking a compromise to circumvent the momentum toward separation. In the wake of general elections in Poland, Solidarity leader Lech Wałesa was elected president that December by an overwhelming majority. Determined to maintain control over the Baltic states, in January 1991 Soviet troops interceded in Lithuania in an attempt to stop the independence movement, but the confrontation failed to stem the tide of opposition and ended in a months-long stalemate. Further provoking the situation, in August 1991 Latvia declared its independence from the Soviet Union. In the aftermath of a failed coup against Gorbachev, the Baltic states declared their independence, which was recognized by the Soviet Union on 6 September 1991. Unable to reverse the momentum for unilateral independence, the Soviet leadership in December announced the dissolution of the Soviet Union.

Twentieth-Century Eastern European Writers, Third Series represents a collaborative scholarly effort to survey the development of contemporary literature in Eastern Europe. The series includes writers of international reputation—Kundera, Klíma, and Havel; Mrożek, Herbert, and Nobel laureate Szymborska; Norman Manea; Peter Esterházy and György Konrád—and writers of artistic importance with limited exposure to English-speaking readers. Emerging from nearly half a century of communist rule, Eastern Europe continues to experience the ramifications of political change and transition. Struggling to reconcile past and present, the literary and intellectual community is forced to reassess and evaluate the legacy of each national literature in contrast to the uncertain future of postindependence Eastern Europe. This assessment incorporates the works of writers long silenced by oppressive political regimes, as well as works published abroad by dissident writers, many of whom lived in exile. Most importantly, it also includes the contribution of a new generation of literary practitioners determined to restore the integrity of creative expression and to redefine both the role of the writer and the purpose of literature.

—*Steven Serafin*

Acknowledgments

This book was produced by Bruccoli Clark Layman, Inc. Karen L. Rood is senior editor. Tracy Simmons Bitonti, Philip B. Dematteis, and Jan Peter F. van Rosevelt were the in-house editors.

Production manager is Philip B. Dematteis.

Administrative support was provided by Ann M. Cheschi, Dawnca T. Williams, and Mary A. Womble.

Accountant is Kathy Weston. Accounting assistant is Amber L. Coker.

Copyediting supervisor is Phyllis A. Avant. The copyediting staff includes Brenda Carol Blanton, Allen E. Friend Jr., Melissa D. Hinton, William Tobias Mathes, Jennifer S. Reid, Nancy E. Smith, and Elizabeth Jo Ann Sumner. Freelance copyeditor is Rebecca Mayo.

Editorial associates are Michael S. Allen and Michael S. Martin.

Layout and graphics supervisor is Janet E. Hill. The graphics staff includes Karla Corley Brown and Zoe R. Cook.

Office manager is Kathy Lawler Merlette.

Photography editors are Charles Mims, Scott Nemzek, and Paul Talbot.

Digital photographic copy work was performed by Joseph M. Bruccoli.

SGML supervisor is Cory McNair. The SGML staff includes Frank Graham, Linda Dalton Mullinax, Jason Paddock, and Alex Snead.

Systems manager is Marie L. Parker.

Typesetting supervisor is Kathleen M. Flanagan. The typesetting staff includes Mark J. McEwan, Patricia Flanagan Salisbury, and Alison Smith. Freelance typesetters are Wanda Adams and Vicki Grivetti.

Walter W. Ross did library research. He was assisted by Steven Gross and the following librarians at the Thomas Cooper Library of the University of South Carolina: circulation department head Tucker Taylor; reference department head Virginia W. Weathers; Brette Barclay, Marilee Birchfield, Paul Cammarata, Gary Geer, Michael Macan, Tom Marcil, Rose Marshall, and Sharon Verba; interlibrary loan department head John Brunswick; and Robert Arndt, Hayden Battle, Barry Bull, Jo Cottingham, Marna Hostetler, Marieum McClary, Erika Peake, and Nelson Rivera, interlibrary loan staff.

The Holub, Hrabal, Klíma, Lustig, Paral, and Skácel entries were translated into English by Elizabeth S. Morrison.

The editor once again expresses his appreciation for the contribution of the associate editors, whose expertise and commitment to their respective national literatures was instrumental in the development of the series. In addition, he wishes to acknowledge the contribution of the invaluable assistance of the librarians and staff of the Hunter College Library, in particular Norman Clarius. Support for this project was provided by a grant from the PSC-CUNY Research Award Program.

Dictionary of Literary Biography® • Volume Two Hundred Thirty-Two

Twentieth-Century Eastern European Writers
Third Series

Dictionary of Literary Biography

Gabriela Adameşteanu
(2 April 1942 –)

Magda Carneci
Institute of Art History, Bucharest

BOOKS: *Drumul egal al fiecărei zile* (Bucharest: Cartea Românească, 1975);

Dăruieşte-ţi o zi de vacanţă (Bucharest: Cartea Românească, 1979);

Dimineaţă pierdută (Bucharest: Cartea Românească, 1983);

Vară–primavară (Bucharest: Cartea Românească, 1989);

Obsesia politicii (Bucharest: Clavis, 1995).

Edition in English: "A Common Path," in *The Phantom Church and Other Stories from Romania*, edited and translated by Georgiana Farnoaga and Sharon King, selection, introduction, chronology, and bibliographical notes by Florin Manolescu (Pittsburgh: University of Pittsburgh Press, 1996); "Dialogue," translated by Farnoaga and King, in *Anthology of Contemporary Romanian Prose*, edited by Manolescu (Pittsburgh: University of Pittsburgh Press, forthcoming).

PLAY PRODUCTION: *Dimineaţă pierdută*, Bucharest, Bulandra Theater, December 1986.

TRANSLATION: Guy de Maupassant, *Pierre et Jean*, translated into Romanian by Adameşteanu and Viorica Oancea (Bucharest: Eminescu, 1979).

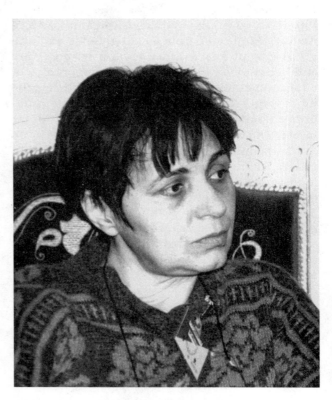

Gabriela Adameşteanu

Gabriela Adameşteanu is considered one of the most outstanding prose writers in contemporary Romanian literature. Her literary debut was in 1971; in 1975 she published her first volume. Her reputation was established by the publication of her mature piece of fiction *Dimineaţă pierdută* (Wasted Morning, 1983). Her career later changed directions when Adameşteanu turned to journalism in 1990, after the fall of communism.

Adameşteanu was born on 2 April 1942 in Tîrgu-Ocna, a small Moldavian town in eastern Romania. Her intellectual parents and her youth during the first hard decades of communist rule shaped her future writings, many of which consist of veiled biographical elements. Her mother, Elena (neé Predescu) Adameşteanu, came from a family of shopkeepers in Bucharest and was first a home economics teacher, but because of the communists' interdiction of her profession, she became a kindergarten teacher. She met her future husband, Mircea Adameşteanu, in 1938 in Kishinev, the capital of Bessarabia, a province regained by Romania in 1918 after World War I and lost again in 1940 to the Soviet Union during World War II. Adameşteanu's father was a passionate and dedicated high school teacher of history who had been the director of the high school in Tîrgu-Ocna. Because he had been a member of the Social-Democrat Party after World War II—one brother was also a political prisoner and another a refugee in Italy after the communist takeover of Romania—he had to take a lower position in Piteşti, a town in southern Romania. Mircea Adameşteanu came from an enlightened and progressive family that instilled in both Adameşteanu and her younger brother, Ion, the importance of education as well as the significance of their family heritage. Adameşteanu has always been proud of her family and was extremely attached to her father, who died in 1965 at age fifty-four.

Adameşteanu spent her formative years in Piteşti, where her parents had moved in 1946. In high school she began to demonstrate her literary talent and received a humanistic education despite the extremely politicized situation of the time, imbued as it was with Soviet values. From 1960 to 1965 Adameşteanu attended the Faculty of Romanian Language and Literature in Bucharest and was a part of the first generation of students who were no longer absolutely conditioned by the "social origin" of their parents. Through her own reading she also gained a solid background in modern Western literature. She made her literary debut in 1971 with a fragment of prose in *Luceafărul* (The Morning Star), a literary journal. In the same period, Adameşteanu contributed to several other literary magazines such as *România Literară* (Literary Romania), *Vatra* (The Hearth), and *Viaţa Românească* (Romanian Life).

In 1964 Adameşteanu married Gheorghe-Mihai Ionescu, an electrotechnics engineer with whom she had a son, Mircea Vlad, born in 1968. In 1965 she finished her studies with a thesis on the "Modifications in the Structure of Characters in Marcel Proust's Prose," an author just "rediscovered" in Romania in those years. In the same year Nicolae Ceauşescu became head of the

Romanian Communist Party (PCR) and inaugurated a period of political and cultural liberalization that lasted from 1965 to 1973. Adameşteanu described in some of her stories the effort she made for years to forget the political slogans learned at school and aesthetic cliches she was obliged to internalize, and the realist-socialist authors she had to study. After graduating from the university, she was offered a position as a publisher's reader of the department of encyclopaedias at the Editura Politică (Political Publishing House), Bucharest, in 1965. The department became a separate publishing house, The Scientific and Encyclopaedic Publishing House, in 1966, and Adameşteanu continued working there until 1984.

In 1975 Cartea Românească published her first novel, *Druml egal al fiecărei zile* (The Equal Way of Every Day). Adameşteanu's major themes and specific techniques are already present in this novel, which deals with the deep, distorted, and subtle echoes in psychology, language, and behavior that the communist political situation produces in the day-to-day life of people of various social categories. The novel describes the efforts made by a young provincial student from a bourgeois family to seduce her professor in order to start a scientific career and enter a superior social milieu. The seductress is an anonymous, poor, and timid adolescent girl, haunted by the history of her family destroyed by the communists; she discovers that even the new "high" life she enters by marrying the professor is as suffocating as the old one, a life in which she has to follow the same "equal way of every day" as before. The novel earned favorable critical responses from the literary magazines and received both the debut writer prize of the Union of Romanian Writers and the Ion Creangă Prize of the Romanian Academy.

Characteristic for Adameşteanu is a relatively long delay from one published book to another, and each novel is followed by a volume of short stories. In 1979 Adameşteanu published a volume of three short stories, *Dăruieşte-ţi o zi de vacanţă* (Offer Yourself a Day Off). In "Nelinişte" (Anxiety), the theme of incommunicability between a young married couple is interwoven with the theme of familial solidarity in the face of illness and death. In "Plimbare scurtă după orele de serviciu" (Short Walk after the Office Daily Program), a young woman and her older colleague try to dominate one another in conversation during several hours of walking. In the third piece, a novella that bears the title of the book, a couple's degradation caused by the strictures of society is seen in relationship with the degradation of the natural environment. The volume was favorably received by critics who noticed the "concise, austere style" and the "theme of the passive refusal, the silent, non-ostentatious resistance" with which Adameşteanu's characters defend themselves against a monstrous and aggressive daily existence.

In 1983 Adameşteanu became an editor at the Cartea Românească publishing house, where she succeeded in having many valuable books of Romanian literature published in spite of the increasingly severe censorship imposed by the Ceauşescu regime in the 1980s. In the year she was hired by Cartea Românească the most representative novel of her career, *Dimineaţă pierdută*, was published. The novel skillfully interweaves two levels of a complex narrative construction—the gossip between a poor old woman and an intellectual lady, and their memories of the history of a "high-life" family that lived in Bucharest between the World Wars. The tortuous but perfectly controlled play between exterior dialogues and interior monologues, between the present and the past, between the personal memories of the many characters and their general historical considerations, sharply contrasts a memorable, dense, and impressive image of Romanian society before World War II with the same society under the communist regime. As noted by scholar Valeria Cristea, *Dimineaţă pierdută* is a novel in which "an extraordinary feeling of history accompanies a strong, extraordinary feeling of life . . . in discreet, non-ostentatious, almost normal passages from one level to the other." Recognized by critic Nicolae Manolescu as "one of the best novels published in recent years," *Dimineaţă pierdută* was awarded the prize of the Union of Romanian Writers in 1984 and established Adameşteanu as a major Romanian prose writer. The novel enjoyed a special celebrity after its adaptation for the stage by director Cătălina Buzoianu in 1986 at the Bulandra Theater.

In the summer of 1989 Cartea Românească published Adameşteanu's second volume of short stories, *Vară–primavară* (Spring–Summer). This collection presents three categories of short stories that develop the author's preferred themes, already established in her previous books. In some of the stories, notably "Clădirea" (The Building) and "Testul" (The Test), the suffocating bureaucratic life of modest people and the theme of careerism in a totalitarian world are explored.

In others, such as "Dialog" (Dialogue), "Vară–primavară" (Spring–Summer), "Drum comun" (A Common Path), and "Scurtă internare" (Short Hospitalization), Adameşteanu describes the common, modest life of people living in poor conditions—peasants, workers, and commuters, for example—by using their specific language, transcribed in short, dramatic dialogues. The direct expression of the miserable, almost subhuman life endured by anonymous people in a totalitarian society reaches a high degree of authenticity in these stories. In the longest piece of the volume, "Scurtă întîlnire" (Short Meeting), Adameşteanu tells the story of an exile returning to his country after a long absence. The story, based on elements taken from the real history of one of the author's uncles, is expressed through the interior dreams and monologues of the exile—who fails to communicate with anybody from home—intermingled with the divergently expressed opinions of his recovered family. Appearing in the last year of Ceauşescu's regime, the volume was considered the sum of the "epic exercises of a mature novelist," as Cristea pointed out.

Adameşteanu's career was relatively undisturbed until 1989, for—as she later declared—she preferred to resist the totalitarian imposition of political and moral compromise on the prominent personalities of the time by leading the passive, modest existence that was reflected in many of her literary characters. During that year Adameşteanu, together with other writers, signed a letter of protest against the unbearable conditions of life in Romania and resigned as an editor at Cartea Românească. Like so many other Romanian writers, she became involved in the effervescent social political life of postcommunist Romania. In 1990 she became a member of the Group for Social Dialogue (GDS), a prominent group of previously dissident intellectuals that has been at the center of many important political and cultural actions following the Revolution of December 1989. In 1991 Adameşteanu became the editor in chief of *22* magazine, an influential weekly edited by the GDS that affirmed an independent and oppositional attitude toward the postcommunist regime, and sustained the candidacy of Emil Constatinescu, who became president of Romania in 1996. During her tenure at *22* magazine Adameşteanu wrote many highly provocative and insightful articles but has published only one book, *Obsesia politicii* (The Obsession of Politics, 1995), a collection of interviews she conducted with the most outstanding personalities of the new political elite of Romania. A volume titled *Cele de Romanii* (The Two Romanias), a collection of articles, studies, and memoirs is to be published by the European Institute Publishers in Iaşi in September 2000.

In Adameşteanu's own opinion, she has not abandoned her literary career, but has instead been enriched by her journalistic writing. Her earlier literary aim of testifying profoundly and truthfully against unbearable and absurd political conditioning is accomplished now by direct involvement in contemporary Romanian issues. Acknowledged as an important Romanian writer of the middle-age generation, Gabriela Adameşteanu is also considered an important and influential personality in Romanian social and cultural life.

Interviews:

Aurel Sasu and Mariana Vartic, *Romanul românesc în interviuri*, volume 1 (Bucharest: Minerva, 1985), pp. 4–9.

References:

Nicolae Ciobanu, *Intîlnire cu opera* (Bucharest: Cartea Românească, 1982), pp. 273–276;

Val Condurache, *Portret al criticului în tinereţe* (Bucharest: Cartea Românească, 1984), pp. 153–154;

Valerie Cristea, *Fereastra criticului* (Bucharest: Cartea Românească, 1987), pp. 201–215;

Mihai Dinu Gheorghiu, *Reflexe condiţionate* (Bucharest: Cartea Românească, 1983), pp. 46–49;

Ioan Holban, *Profiluri epice contemporane* (Bucharest: Cartea Românească, 1987), pp. 358–363;

Mircea Iorgulescu, *Scriitori tineri contemporani* (Bucharest: Eminescu, 1978), pp. 175–176;

Norman Manea, *Pe contur* (Bucharest: Cartea Românească, 1984), pp. 45–48;

Nicolae Manolescu, "Proza scurta," *România Literară*, 37 (1989): 7;

Laurentiu Ulici, *Literatura română contemporană* (Bucharest: Eminescu, 1995), pp. 337–339;

Ulici, *Prima verba*, volume 2 (Bucharest: Albatros, 1978), pp. 15–18.

Stanisław Barańczak

(13 November 1946 –   )

Roman Sabo

BOOKS: *Koretka twarzy* (Poznań: Wydawnictwo Poznańskie, 1968);

Jednym tchem (Warsaw: Orientacja, 1970);

Nieufni i zadufani: Romantyzm i klasycyzm w młodej poezji lat sześćdziesiątych (Wrocław: Ossolineum, 1971);

Dziennik poranny: Wiersze 1967–1971 (Poznań: Wydawnictwo Poznańskie, 1972);

Ironia i harmonia: Szkice o najnowszej literaturze polskiej (Warsaw: Czytelnik, 1973);

Sztuczne oddychanie (Poznań [samizdat edition], 1974; London: Aneks, 1978);

Język poetycki Mirona Białoszewskiego (Wrocław: Ossolineum, 1974);

Ja wiem, że to niesłuszne: Wiersze z lat 1975–1976 (Paris: Instytut Literacki, 1977);

Etyka i poetyka: Szkice 1970–1978 (Paris: Instytut Literacki, 1979);

Kątem u siebie / Under My Own Roof: Verses for a New Apartment. Poems, English translations by Frank Kujawinski (Forest Grove, Ore.: Mr. Cogito Press, 1980);

Tryptyk z betonu, zmęczenia i śniegu (Kraków: KOS, 1981);

Książki najgorsze 1975–1980 (Kraków: KOS, 1981); enlarged as *Książki najgorsze i parę innych ekscesów krytycznoliterackich* (Poznań: a5, 1990);

Czytelnik ubezwłasnowolniony: Perswazja w masowej kulturze literackiej PRL (Paris: Libella, 1983);

Uciekinier z Utopii: O poezji Zbigniewa Herberta (London: Polonia, 1984); translated as *A Fugitive From Utopia: The Poetry of Zbigniew Herbert* (Cambridge, Mass.: Harvard University Press, 1987);

Atlantyda i inne wiersze z lat 1981–1985 (London: Puls, 1986);

Przed i po: Szkice o poezji krajowej przełomu lat siedemdziesiątych i osiemdziesiątych (London: Aneks, 1988);

Stanisław Barańczak

Widokówka z tego świata i inne rymy z lat 1986–1988 (Paris: Zeszyty Literackie, 1988);

Tablica z Macondo: Osiemnaście prób wytłumaczenia po co i dlaczego się pisze (London: Aneks, 1990);

Zwierzęca zajadłość (Poznań: a5, 1991);

Biografioły (Poznań: a5, 1991);

Ocalone w tłumaczeniu: Szkice o warsztacie tłumacza poezji (Poznań: a5, 1992);

Zupełne zezwierzęcenie (Poznań: a5, 1993);

Podróż zimowa: Wiersze do muzyki Franza Schuberta (Poznań: a5, 1994);

Bóg, Trąba i Ojczyzna: Słoń a Sprawa Polska oczami poetów od Reja do Rymkiewicza (Kraków: Znak, 1995);

Pegaz zdębiał: Poezja nonsensu a życie codzienne. Wprowadzenie w prywatą teorię gatunków (London: Puls, 1995);

Pomyślane przepaście: Osiem interpretacji (Katowice: Uniwersytet Śląski, 1995);

Chirurgiczna precyzja: Elegie i piosenki z lat 1995–97 (Kraków: a5, 1998);

Geografioły: Z notatek globtrottera-domatora (Warsaw: Prószynski i S-ka, 1998).

Collections: *Wiersze prawie zebrane* (Warsaw: NOWA, 1981);

159 wierszy: 1968–1988 (Kraków: Znak, 1990);

Wybór wierszy i przekładów (Warsaw: PIW, 1997);

Zimy i podróże, edited by Antoni Libera (Kraków: Wydawnictwo Literackie, 1997).

Editions in English: "Report" and "This Palm Can Be a Handful It Can Be a Fist," translated by Adam Czerniawski, *Modern Poetry in Translation: Polish Issue,* edited by Bogdan Czaykowski, 23–24 (1975): 37;

"Empty," translated by Jolanta Raczko and Danuta Gabryś, in *Z nowej polskiej poezji / The New Polish Poetry,* edited by Milne Holton and Paul Vangelisti (Pittsburgh: University of Pittsburgh Press, 1978), pp. 103–104;

Where Did I Wake Up? The Poetry of Stanisław Barańczak, translated by Frank Kujawinski (Forest Grove, Ore.: Mr. Cogito Press, 1978);

"Browsing through *Homes & Gardens*" and "These men, so powerful," translated by Czerniawski, in *The Burning Forest: Modern Polish Poetry,* edited by Czerniawski (Newcastle upon Tyne: Bloodaxe Books, 1988; Chester Springs, Penn.: Dufour, 1988), pp. 180–181;

The Weight of the Body: Selected Poems, translated by Barańczak, Magnus J. Krynski, Richard Lourie, and Robert A. Maguire (Evanston, Ill.: TriQuarterly Books, Northwestern University / Chicago: Another Chicago Press, 1989);

Breathing under Water and Other Eastern European Essays (Cambridge, Mass.: Harvard University Press, 1990);

"The Three Magi," "Along with the Dust," "To Grażyna," "Don't Use the Word 'Exile,'" "A Second Nature," "After Gloria Was Gone," and "Setting the Hand Brake," translated by Barańczak, in *Polish Poetry of the Last Two Decades of Communist Rule: Spoiling Cannibals' Fun,* edited by Barańczak and Clare Cavanagh (Evanston, Ill.: Northwestern University Press, 1991), pp. 161–166;

"After Gloria Was Gone" and "Setting the Hand Brake," translated by Barańczak, in *Shifting Borders: East European Poetries of the Eighties,* compiled and edited by Walter Cummins

(Rutherford, N.J.: Fairleigh Dickinson University Press, 1993), pp. 284–285.

OTHER: *Poeta pamięta: Antologia poeji świadectwa i sprzeciwu 1944–1984,* edited by Barańczak (London: Puls, 1984);

Ryszard Krynicki, *Citizen R.K. Does Not Live: Poems of Ryszard Krynicki,* selected and introduced by Barańczak, edited by Robert A. Davies and John M. Gogol (Forest Grove, Ore.: Mr. Cogito Press, 1985);

Janusz Anderman, *Poland under Black Light,* translated by Nina Taylor and Andrew Short, introduction by Barańczak (London: Readers International, 1985):

Reginald Gibbons, ed., *The Writer in Our World: A Symposium Sponsored by Triquarterly Magazine,* contributions by Barańczak (Boston: Atlantic Monthly Press, 1986);

Tadeusz Borowski, *Selected Poems,* translated by Tadeusz Pióro, Larry Rafferty, and Meryl Natchez, introduction by Barańczak (Walnut Creek, Cal.: Hit & Run Press, 1990);

Witold Gombrowicz, *Trans-Atlantyk,* translated by Carolyn French and Nina Karsov, introduction by Barańczak (New Haven & London: Yale University Press, 1994);

Wiktor Weintraub, *O współczesnych i o sobie: Wspomnienia, sylwetki, szkice literackie,* edited by Barańczak (Kraków: Znak, 1994).

TRANSLATIONS: Dylan Thomas, *Wiersze wybrane* (Kraków: Wydawnictwo Literackie, 1974);

Osip Mandelshtam, *Późne wiersze* (London: Oficyna Poetów i Malarzy, 1977);

Joseph Brodsky, *Wiersze i poematy* (Warsaw: NOWa, 1979);

Gerard Manley Hopkins, *Wybór poezji* (Kraków: Znak, 1981);

Antologia angielskiej poezji metafizycznej XVII stulecia (Warsaw: PIW, 1982; enlarged, 1991);

E. E. Cummings, *150 wierszy* (Kraków: Wydawnictwo Literackie, 1983);

John Donne, *Wiersze wybrane* (Kraków: Wydawnictwo Literackie, 1984);

Tomas Venclova, *Siedem wierszy* (Warsaw: Wydawnictwo S: 1986);

Brodsky, *82 wiersze i poematy* (Paris: Zeszyty Literackie, 1988);

George Herbert, *Wiersze wybrane* (Kraków: Znak, 1989);

Venclova, *Rozmowa w zimie* (Paris: Zeszyty Literackie, 1989);

Emily Dickinson, *100 wierszy* (Kraków: Arka, 1990);

James Merrill, *Wybór poezji* (Paris: Zeszyty Literackie, 1990);

William Shakespeare, *Romeo i Julia* (Poznań: W Drodze, 1990);

Shakespeare, *Hamlet, książę Danii* (Poznań: W Drodze, 1990);

Shakespeare, *Burza, Zimowa opowieść* (Poznań: W Drodze, 1991);

Shakespeare, *Król Lear* (Poznań: W Drodze, 1991);

Philip Larkin, *44 wiersze* (Kraków: Arka, 1991);

Polish Poetry of the Last Two Decades of Communist Rule: Spoiling Cannibals' Fun, translated by Barańczak and Clare Cavanagh (Evanston, Ill.: Northwestern University Press, 1991);

Shakespeare, *Sen nocy letniej: Kupiec wenecki* (Poznań: W Drodze, 1992);

Robert Frost, *55 wierszy* (Kraków: Arka, 1992);

Hopkins, *33 wiersze* (Kraków: Arka, 1992);

Z Tobą, więc ze wszystkim: 222 arcydzieła angielskiej i amerykańskiej liryki religijnej (Kraków: Znak, 1992);

Shakespeare, *Makbet* (Poznań: W Drodze, 1992);

Shakespeare, *Dwaj panowie z Werony. Poskromienie złośnicy* (Poznań: W Drodze, 1992);

"Miłość jest wszystkim, co istnieje": 300 najsławniejszych angielskich i amerykańskich wierszy miłosnych (Poznań: a5, 1992);

Charles Simic, *Madonny z dorysowaną szpicbródką* (Poznań: a5, 1992);

Robert Herrick, *77 wierszy* (Kraków: Arka, 1992);

Brodsky, *Znak wodny* (Kraków: Znak, 1993);

Fioletowa krowa: 333 najsławniesze okazy angielskiej i amerykańskiej poezji niepoważnej od Williama Shakespearea do Johna Lennona: Antologia (Poznań: a5, 1993);

Od Chaucera do Larkina: 400 nieśmiertelnych wierszy 125 poetów anglojęzycznych z 8 stuleci (Kraków: Znak, 1993);

Shakespeare, *Juliusz Cezar* (Poznań: W Drodze, 1993);

Shakespeare, *Sonety* (Poznań: a5, 1993);

Shakespeare, *Jak wam się podoba* (Poznań: W Drodze, 1993);

Shakespeare, *Otello* (Poznań: W Drodze, 1993);

Andrew Marvell, *24 wiersze* (Kraków: Wydawnictwo Literackie, 1993);

Thomas Hardy, *55 wierszy* (Kraków: Znak, 1993);

Shakespeare, *Wiele hałasu o nic. Wieczór Trzech Króli* (Poznań: W Drodze, 1994);

Shakespeare, *Komedia omyłek. Stracone zachody miłości* (Poznań: W Drodze, 1994);

Seamus Heaney, *44 wiersze* (Kraków: Znak, 1994);

W. H. Auden, *44 wiersze* (Kraków: Znak, 1994);

Shakespeare, *Koriolan* (Poznań: W Drodze, 1995);

Elizabeth Bishop, *33 wiersze* (Kraków: Znak, 1995);

T. S. Eliot, *Koty* (Kraków: Wydawnictwo Literackie, 1995);

Shakespeare, *Król Ryszard III* (Poznań: W Drodze, 1995);

Dickinson, *Drugie 100 wierszy* (Kraków: Znak, 1995);

Thomas Campion, *33 pieśni* (Kraków: Znak, 1995);

Jan Kochanowski, *Laments,* translated by Barańczak and Heaney (New York: Farrar, Straus & Giroux, 1995; London: Faber & Faber, 1995);

Wisława Szymborska, *View with a Grain of Sand,* translated by Barańczak and Cavanagh (New York: Harcourt Brace, 1995; London: Faber & Faber, 1996);

77 Translations by Stanislaw Barańczak and Clare Cavanagh from Modern Polish Poetry, edited by Adam Dziadek (Katowice: Tow. Zachęty Kultury w Katowicach: Letnia Szkoła Języka, Literatury i Kultury Polskiej Uniwersytetu Śląskiego, 1995);

Shakespeare, *100 słynnych monologów* (Kraków: Znak, 1996);

Heaney, *Ciągnąc dalej: Nowe wiersze* (Kraków: Znak, 1996);

John Keats, *33 wiersze* (Kraków: Znak, 1997);

Herbert, *66 wierszy* (Kraków: Znak, 1997);

Shakespeare, *Tymon Ateńczyk* (Kraków: Znak, 1997);

Szymborska, *Nic dwa razy: Wybór wierszy / Nothing Twice: Selected Poems,* translated by Barańczak and Cavanagh (Kraków: Wydawnictwo Literackie, 1997);

Szymborska, *Poems, New and Collected, 1957–1997,* translated by Barańczak and Cavanagh (New York: Harcourt Brace, 1998);

Shakespeare, *Wesołe kumoszki z Windsoru* (Kraków: Znak, 1998);

Donne, *77 wierszy* (Kraków: Znak, 1998);

Shakespeare, *Henryk IV, cz. I i II* (Kraków: Znak, 1998);

Od Walta Whitmana do Boba Dylana: Antologia poezji amerykańskiej (Kraków: Wydawnictwo Literackie, 1998);

Edward Lear, Lewis Carroll, W. S. Gilbert, A. E. Housman, and Hilaire Belloc, *44 opowiastki* (Kraków: Znak, 1998);

Shakespeare, *Henryk V* (Kraków: Znak, 1999);

Henry Vaughan, *33 wiersze* (Kraków: Znak, 2000).

Barańczak and his wife, Anna, in 1991 (photograph by Joanna Hellander)

The poet, literary critic, and translator Stanisław Barańczak was born on 13 November 1946 in Poznań, Poland, to Jan and Zofia (née Konopinska) Barańczak. As a university freshman he was the literary director of the Theater of the Eighth Day, a group of nonprofessional actors who went on to create one of the most renowned dissident theatrical groups of the 1970s. After graduating in 1969 from Adam Mickiewicz University in Poznań with an M.A. in Polish philology, he took a position there as an instructor in Polish literature. He became an assistant professor in 1975, after completing his Ph. D. the previous year. He published his first poems in 1965 in the highly respected monthly *Odra*. His first volume of poetry, *Korekta twarzy* (Proofreading of a Face), appeared in 1968.

Barańczak's later poetry is renowned for its masterful use of poetic forms of great complexity; a propensity for intricate structural complexity can, however, already be detected in some of the sonnets in *Korekta twarzy*. The complexity is present both at the syntactic level in the form of inversions, enjambments, elaborate conceits, and intricate rhyme schemes, and at the semantic level in puns, unusual similes, far-fetched metaphors used to surprise, shock, or amuse, and an impressive, even excessive, vocabulary. Wit, in the sense associated with the English metaphysical poets of the seventeenth century—that is, the ability to construct a whole poem on just one conceit, forcing the reader to recognize surprising likenesses between apparently incompatible things— is also evident. These formal features enhance Barańczak's presentation of his ever-present metaphysical theme: the conflict between an individual's aspirations and the limitations imposed on him or her by both the human condition and by political systems.

Korekta twarzy was followed by *Jednym tchem* (In One Breath) in 1970 and *Dziennik poranny: Wiersze 1967–1971* (Morning Diary: Poems 1967–1971) in 1972. The world presented in these early poems, with its institutions and enforced human relationships, is not to be trusted. Real-life speech is incorporated into the poems only to be constantly scrutinized; the false overtones, imposed mostly by ideology, are held up to scrutiny. The lyrical "I" inhabiting this poetic world is extremely individualistic and critical of the surrounding reality. Like many "Romantic" and individualistic rebels before him, however, the speaker is unable to avoid turning his anger against himself.

Despite the tone of despair permeating his early poems, they constitute a solid foundation for Barańczak's subsequent poetic development. At this stage Barańczak begins to use body images as symbols of the state of society and the quality of human life. The pervading metaphor is that of a decaying, malfunctioning human body permeated by a skeptical human spirit that is constantly trying to escape total disintegration.

In his early critical studies *Nieufni i zadufani: Romantyzm i klasycyzm w młodej poezji lat sześćdziesiątych* (The Distrustful and the Overconfident: Romanticism and Classicism in the Young Poetry of the 1960s, 1971) and *Ironia i harmonia: Szkice o najnowszej literaturze polskiej* (Irony and Harmony: Essays on Recent Polish Literature, 1973), Barańczak identifies two opposite sensitivities found in the Polish poetry of the 1960s: the "romantic" trend, which is dynamic, distrustful, and questioning; and the passive, petrifying "classicism" of false platitudes. Accordingly, he divides poets into "active, ironic, dramatic rebels," who attempt to transform the source of their discontent, and "passive rebels," who are always willing to surrender to the inevitable. Since then, as a poet, a critic, and a translator, Barańczak has been interested in poetry that combines two contradictory concerns: what he calls in *Ironia i harmonia* the "desire for peace and acceptance [of reality] and the equally strong tendency to support truthfully conflicts and fears that this reality poses."

Język poetycki Mirona Białoszewskiego (The Poetic Language of Miron Białoszewski, 1974) was Barańczak's last book to be published by any state-controlled publishing house in Poland until the collapse of communism in 1989. On 5 December 1975 he signed an open letter in which fifty-nine respected intellectuals protested against arbitrary changes that the Communist Party proposed to introduce into the Polish constitution. In June 1976 he signed another letter, condemning the beating of a group of discontented Polish workers by the state paramilitary troops. On 4 September of that year he helped organize the Komitet Obrony Robotników (Committee for the Defense of Workers), or KOR, one of the elements that influenced the creation of the Solidarity movement in 1980 and led eventually to the collapse of communism in Poland. These actions resulted in a ban on Barańczak's publications and, in 1977, the loss of his position at the university. In the same year Barańczak was offered a position teaching Polish literature at Harvard University, but the Polish authorities refused him a passport. The only books of Barańczak's that were officially published between 1974 and 1989 were his translations into Polish of the works of English-language poets: Dylan Thomas (1974), George Herbert (1977), the metaphysical poets (1982), E. E. Cummings (1983), and John Donne (1984). Barańczak's original works were published either in samizdat editions in Poland or by publishing houses established in France and England by Polish émigré intellectuals. *Sztuczne oddychanie* (Artificial Respiration, 1974) was Barańczak's first book to appear in samizdat; it was followed by *Tryptyk z betonu, zmęczenia i śniegu* (Triptych of Concrete, Weariness, and Snow, 1981) and *Wiersze prawie zebrane* (The Almost Collected Poems, 1981), while *Ja wiem, że to niesłuszne: Wiersze z lat 1975–1976* (I Know It Is Not Correct, 1977) was published in Paris. Beginning in 1976 Barańczak helped to edit and publish the independent literary periodical *Zapis* (Record). In May 1977 he participated in a hunger strike in the Church of St. Martin's in Warsaw.

In *Sztuczne oddychanie; Ja wiem, że to niesłuszne;* and *Tryptyk z betonu, zmęczenia i śniegu* Barańczak expresses the state of national consciousness through an analysis of language, an approach that later came to be called "linguistic poetry." Polish linguistic poets were divided into two groups. The first—Tymoteusz Karpowicz, Miron Białoszewski, Witold Wirpsza, Zbigniew Bieńkowski, and Edward Balcerzan—saw language as a reality in itself and strove to explore its possibilities through poetry. The second—Barańczak, Ryszard Krynicki, and Adam Zagajewski—also saw language as reality, but one that had been deliberately degraded, enslaved, and mystified by ideologues.

In Barańczak's view, language, like the body, is under the pressure of decomposing forces: just as the body can break down, so can language. Barańczak's poems are perceptive studies of the uses of language in which juxtaposition of instances of political "newspeak" with a wide range of possible readings allows him to challenge the corruption, coercion, and brutality of the totalitarian state. This poetry, depressing and highly moral but never moralistic, is spoken by a suffocating, downtrodden, pessimistic, lyrical "I," an average human being who is forced to waste his or her life waiting in lines, living in a gray concrete cubicle, addicted to stupefying television shows and a deceitful press.

In the pieces collected in 1979 as *Etyka i poetyko: Szkice 1970–1978* (Ethics and Poetics: Essays 1970–1978) Barańczak argues that while the twentieth century is an age of despair and of institutionalized abuse of human rights, it is, at the same time, an age that calls for a dramatic reevaluation of cultural values. This situation poses a challenge to poetry, which, Barańczak agrees with the Polish poet Czesław Miłosz, is the only cognitive domain capable of carrying out a philosophical scrutiny of values. For Barańczak the poet's task is to discover the world's "hidden order," to elucidate the ramifications of the discovery, and to uphold the existence of this order in full awareness of the atrocities committed in the twentieth century. He regards Osip Mandelshtam and Joseph Brodsky as exemplary embodiments of this attitude and reveres them for remaining faithful to poetry against cruel odds. He lauds Miłosz for speaking on behalf of a poetic tradition that offers hope against despair. At its best, he suggests, twentieth-century poetry embraces both ethics and poetics.

In 1980, under pressure from the Solidarity movement, Adam Mickiewicz University restored

Barańczak and Clare Cavanagh, with whom he collaborated on poetry translations (photograph by Anna Barańczak)

Barańczak to his former position. He left Poland in March 1981 to become Jurzykowski Professor of Polish Literature at Harvard University. In 1983 the Polish government declined to extend Barańczak's passport, making him a political exile. That year he cofounded the quarterly *Zeszyty Literackie* (Literary Notebooks) as a meeting ground for Eastern and Central European intellectuals. He also became the editor of the American scholarly journal *The Polish Review*, from which he resigned in 1991.

Since his arrival in the United States, Barańczak has been one of the most prolific critics of contemporary Polish poetry and the most accomplished translator of poetry into Polish from English, Russian, and Lithuanian. The sheer volume of his translations towers over that of any other Polish translator except Tadeusz Boy-Żeleński. The sonnets and plays of William Shakespeare and the poems of Donne, Brodsky, Mandelshtam, Gerard Manley Hopkins, John Keats, Emily Dickinson, Robert Frost, James Merrill, Elizabeth Bishop, Philip Larkin, and Tomas Venclova read as naturally in his renderings as in the originals. Barańczak is not as successful in his translations of the Irish poets William Butler Yeats and Seamus Heaney, failing to convey the former's emotional and the latter's intellectual use of the English language. Barańczak has also translated works of Polish poets into English, collaborating with Heaney on the poetry of Jan Kochanowski (1995) and with Clare Cavanagh on that of Wisława Szymborska (1995, 1997, and 1998). He and Cavanagh also produced the anthology *Polish Poetry of the Last Two Decades of Communist Rule: Spoiling Cannibals' Fun* (1991).

Barańczak is at his best when he is tackling complex poetic structures, difficult rhymes, and richly orchestrated verse. His theory of translation, presented in *Ocalone w tłumaczeniu: Szkice o warsztacie tłumacza poezji* (Surviving Translation: Essays on the Translator's Workshop, 1992), is deceptively simple: he says that one should avoid rendering poetry as prose, carefully consider the poem's overall effect, and sustain at least the level of formal complexity present in the original. The real merit of the book, however, lies not in the enumeration of rules but in Barańczak's analyses of translations of the same poem by various translators.

Since moving to the United States, Barańczak has published four books of serious poems— *Atlantyda i inne wiersze z lat 1981–1985* (Atlantis and Other Poems from the Years 1981–1985, 1986), *Widokówka z tego świata i inne rymy z lat 1986–1988* (A Postcard from This World and Other Rhymes from the Years 1986–1988, 1988), *Podróż zimowa: Wiersze do muzyki Franza Schuberta* (A Winter Journey: Poems to the Music of Franz Schubert, 1994), and *Chirurgiczna precyzja: Elegie i piosenki z lat 1995–97* (Surgical Precision: Elegies and Songs from the Years 1995–97), which received the prestigious Nike Prize for the best book published in 1998—and five volumes of nonsense poetry: *Zwierzęca zajadłość* (Bestial Relentlessness,1991), *Biografioły* (Biographollies, 1991), *Zupełne zezwierzęcenie* (Absolute Beasts, 1993), *Bóg, Trąba i Ojczyzna: Słoń a Sprawa Polska oczami poetów od Reja do Rymkiewicza* (God, Motherland, and the Elephant's Trunk, 1995), and *Geografioły* (Geographollies, 1998). He has also published several volumes of essays. While in the past his essays almost always surpassed his poetry in their insights into the human condition, since his arrival in the United States his poetry has taken the lead in this respect. His American poetry volumes manifest his stylistic virtuosity at its best: each synthesizes several lines of development that are always present in his creative work while at the same time constituting a new stage in that work.

In the first of these volumes, *Atlantyda*, Barańczak casts a final glance at the civic preoccupations dictated for so long by the twists and turns of the Polish political drama. The Polish theme in this volume is restricted to two sentiments: paying tribute to friends and expressing nostalgia; significantly, this theme is introduced by a poem titled "Historia" (History) and closed by one titled "Nowy Świat" (The New World). The New World poses a wide range of problems, prompting Barańczak to write several poems exploring the limitations of his new role as an Eastern European in the America of "small talk" and "wine and cheese parties" who lectures on such esoteric topics as Polish Romantic poetry. His main theme, however, is the more profound one of confronting existence, searching for its hidden order, and learning how to cope with his inconclusive findings.

In *Widokówka z tego świata i inne rymy z lat 1986–1988* Barańczak uses the techniques of seventeenth-century English metaphysical poetry to explore existence in the next-to-last decade of the twentieth century. The speaker of the poems is placed between the actual world and the Great Unknown. The poet's function is to mediate, to pose questions, to name the basic predicament—

that the reason for existence will always remain unknown, and that it is the responsibility of the individual to carve some meaning out of the crude material of existence. Here Barańczak at last creates and sustains a style adequate to the predicament he is considering. The poems are little dramatic études, in each of which a theme is scrutinized from various angles and developed as a struggle of oppositions. Questions, illuminations, and insights exist in a momentary state of equilibrium that is always endangered by a total collapse of order. In the poetic world presented in *Widokówka z tego świata* it is too late to hope, not late enough to despair, and always timely to perceive.

Podróż zimowa: Wiersze do muzyki Franza Schuberta comprises twenty-four songs that follow exactly the tonalities of Franz Schubert's song cycle *Winterreise* (Winter Journey, 1827). Here Barańczak takes the metaphysical theme one major step further by depicting a journey into the heart of coldness: the coldness of human solitude in the world and in the civilization of the twentieth century. He also radically alters his poetics by striving for the utmost simplicity. These seemingly simple verses, however, acquire unexpected emotional intensity when they are juxtaposed with the tone of despair emanating from Schubert's music. Whether Barańczak overcomes the note of despair and reasons himself into accepting God's existence remains an open question; Barańczak is always eager to combine apparently incompatible options, only to open new perspectives.

Barańczak's literary awards include the Kościelskis Prize in 1972, the Jurzykowski Prize in 1980, and the Terrence Des Prés Prize in 1989. Since his relocation to the United States he has become the most prolific translator of his generation, the most formally accomplished poet among his peers, and one of the most insightful critics of Polish literature. He dedicated himself to the Orwellian task of analyzing communist newspeak for so long that his name became synonymous with "political," "civic," and committed poetry, while his main theme—the metaphysical exploration of the polarities of being, represented by "Fullness and Emptiness"—frequently gave way to more immediate concerns. Barańczak has, however, maintained a passionate steadiness in the pursuit of his metaphysical questions. He has developed a personal poetic language and a range of poetic techniques that enable him to express an existential vision, a vision that will survive changing social mores and collapsing political systems.

Interview:

Zaufać nieufności: Osiem rozmów o sensie poezji, edited by Krzysztof Biedrzycki (Kraków: Wydawnictwo M, 1993).

References:

Marcin Bajerowicz, "Język w stanie oskarżenia (o trzech tomikach poetyckich)," *Nurt,* 5 (1971): 16–19;

Bajerowicz, "Poezja skłóconych światów," *Nurt,* 12 (1969): 57–59;

Krzysztof Biedrzycki, "Na wszystko odpowiem, choć nie usłyszysz ani słowa . . .," *Znak,* 1 (1990): 100–105;

Biedrzycki, *Świat poezji Stanisława Barańczaka* (Kraków: Universitas, 1995);

Włodzimierz Bolecki, "Język jako świat przedstawiony: O wierszach Stanisława Barańczaka," *Pamiętnik Literacki,* 2 (1985): 149–174;

Grażyna Borkowska, "Wolny od doskonałości," *Tygodnik Powszechny,* 51–52 (1997): 17;

Janusz Drzewucki, "Stanisław Barańczak i ten drugi," *Twórczość,* 3 (1991): 82–95;

Krzysztof Dybciak, "Nowa fala w literaturze (1). Mowa cenna jak krew," *Tygodnik Powszechny,* 13 (1974): 3;

Jerzy Kempiński, "Na rogu Brattle i Mielżyńskiego," *Zeszyty Literackie,* 23 (1988): 114–120;

Krzysztof Koehler, "Kijanka czyli historia poezji ze wskazaniem na zwycięzcę: Merrill–Barańczak–Polski wiersz klasyczny," *bruLion,* 19a (1992): 148–155;

Tadeusz Komendant, "His Master's Voice," *Twórczość,* 5 (1989): 96–100;

Ryszard Krynicki, "Czy istnieje już poezja lingwistyczna?" *Poezja,* 12 (1971): 49;

Krynicki, "Kontynuacja i przezwyciężenie," *Poglądy,* 11 (1971): 12;

Jerzy Kwiatkowski, "Słowo Barańczaka," in his *Notatki o poezji i krytyce* (Kraków: Wydawnictwo Literackie, 1975), pp. 107–111;

Antoni Libera, *Stanisław Barańczak "Zimy i Podróże": Lekcja literatury z Antonim Liberą* (Kraków: Wydawnictwo Literackie, 1997);

Jan Józef Lipski, "Pajęczyna drętwej mowy i świat prawdziwy," *Zapis,* 7 (1978): 149–154;

Adam Michnik, "Wiersze Stanisława Barańczaka– zamiast przedmowy," *Kultura* (Paris), 5 (1977): 117–119;

Tadeusz Nyczek, "Jakieś Ty," *Zeszyty Literackie,* 27 (1989): 139–145;

Nyczek, "Strony obcości," in his *Emigranci* (London: Aneks, 1988), pp. 111–146;

Nyczek, "Wolność słowa (poezja Stanisława Barańczaka)," *Nowy Zapis,* 2 (1983): 23–40;

Dariusz Pawelec, *Czytając Barańczaka* (Katowice: Wydawnictwo Gnome, 1995);

Piotr Siemion, "Alchemia poezji," *Literatura na Świecie,* 12 (1985): 338–347;

Marian Stala, "Waga słów, niewygoda istnienia," *Tygodnik Powszechny,* 51–52 (1997):17;

Leszek Szaruga, "Szanse poezji," *Odra,* 10 (1971): 106–108;

Tadeusz Sznerch, "Próba samookreśleń," *Poezja,* 9 (1972): 98–106;

Adrianna Szymańska, "W kręgu *Orientacji,*" *Twórczość,* 12 (1971): 157–159;

Grzegorz Walczak, "Dwa wiersze (analiza wierszy *Pisanie życiorysu* Szymborskiej i *Wypełnić czytelnym pismem* Barańczaka)," *Poglądy,* 7 (1981): 16;

Witold Wirpsza, "Poeta okolicznościowy," *Kultura* (Paris), 7–8 (1977): 223–225;

Andrzej Zawada, "Korekta myślenia," *Odra,* 1 (1970): 113–114;

Jan Zieliński, "Lekcja anatomii i listy do Pana Boga," *Tygodnik Powszechny,* 7 (1989): 4.

Alberts Bels
(Jānis Cīrulis)
(6 October 1938 –   )

Ieva Kalniņa
University of Latvia

and

Kārlis Račevskis
Ohio State University

BOOKS: *Spēles ar nažiem: Stāsti un noveles* (Riga: Liesma, 1966);

Stāsti (Riga: Liesma, 1967);

Izmeklētājs: Romāns (Riga: Liesma, 1967);

"Es pats" līdzenumā: Stāsti (Riga: Liesma, 1968);

Robeža: Noveles, stāsti, romāns (Minneapolis: Tilts, 1969);

Būris: Romāns (Riga: Liesma, 1972); translated by Ojārs Krātiņš as *The Cage* (London & Chester Springs, Pa.: Owen, 1990);

Saucēja balss: Romāns (Riga: Liesma, 1973; Minneapolis: Tilts, 1973);

Pagrabā: Mākslas filma (Riga, 1974);

Poligons: Romāns (Riga: Liesma, 1977);

Sainis: Stāsti un noveles (Riga: Liesma, 1980);

Saknes: Romāns (Riga: Liesma, 1982);

Stāsti (Riga: Liesma, 1984);

Slēptuve: Romāns (Riga: Liesma, 1986);

Bezmiegs: Romāns (Riga: Liesma, 1987);

Sitiens ar teļādu: Romāns (Riga: Liesma, 1987);

Cilvēki laivās: Romāns (Riga: Liesma, 1987);

Cilvēki pilsētās: Romāni (Riga: Liesma, 1988);

Cilvēki pārvērtībās: Romāni (Riga: Liesma, 1989);

Saulē mērktie: Romāns (Riga: Preses nams, 1995);

Melnā Zīme: Romāns (Riga: Preses nams, 1996);

Latviešu labirints: Romāns (Riga: Daugava, 1998).

Collection: *Izmeklētājs; Būris: Divi romāni* (Riga: Liesma, 1977).

Edition in English: *The Voice of the Herald: A Novel; The Investigator: Stories,* translated by David Foreman (Moscow: Progress Publishers, 1980).

PRODUCED SCRIPTS: *Uzbrukums slepenpolicijai: Mākslas filma,* motion picture, adapted by Bels

from his novel *Saucēja balss,* Rīgas kinostudija, 1974;

Šāviens mežā: Mākslas filma, motion picture, adapted by Bels from his novel *Saknes,* Rīgas kinostudija, 1983;

Būris: Mākslas filma, motion picture, adapted by Bels from his novel, AVE, 1993.

SELECTED PERIODICAL PUBLICATIONS—
UNCOLLECTED: "Pagrabs: Kinoscenārijs," *Karogs,* 5 (1974): 72–78;

"Čempions: Traģikomēdija," *Literatūra un Māksla,* 24–25 (1988).

Alberts Bels is one of Latvia's most prominent contemporary writers. His novels and short stories are studies of human relationships that bring out the characters of time periods, as well as those of individuals. His narratives examine the fate of the Latvian people in a time of global transformation.

Bels was born Jānis Cīrulis on 6 October 1938 to Artūrs Konrāds Cīrulis and Alma Cīrulis in the family farmhouse, "Jaunmežplēpji," in the county of Ropāži near Riga. As a child he witnessed the radical changes brought about by World War II and the occupation of Latvia by the Soviet Union. In 1953 he completed his elementary schooling in Ropāži and enrolled in the Riga Communal School of Building Trades; two years later he moved to Moscow to attend the School of Circus Arts. The theme of circus life and its risks is a recurrent motif in his short stories. His nickname at the school was "Belka" (Little Squirrel), a term he turned into his pen name to avoid being confused with the writer Gunārs Cīrulis.

A fall in 1957 put an end to Bels's dreams of a circus career. A year later, following military service in the Soviet army, he began experimenting with various employment and career possibilities while completing his high-school studies. These experiences provided the material for future literary creations in which autobiographical strands are woven together with threads of history and journalistic and scientific motifs. On 5 January 1963 he wrote his first literary sketch, "Baltā cepure" (The White Hat); three days later he wrote his first published story, "Nakts etīde" (Nocturnal Etude, 1963; translated as "Eternal Etude," 1980).

Bels's first book, *Spēles ar nažiem* (Games with Knives, 1966), comprises eleven free-flowing, light, and occasionally lyrical short stories. Most are told in the first person; the narrators include an invalid, a small-time government functionary, and a student at a school for circus performers. The tone of the best known of these works, "Karš bija jauks" (translated as "The War Was Such Fun," 1980), stands in sharp contrast to the conventions of the military genre in Soviet literature, which demanded monumental figures enthusiastically engaged in epic struggles and performing heroic deeds. The hero of Bels's story is a boy who cannot accept the fact that his father has been killed in the war; he fantasizes about shooting sparrows with a howitzer and imagines an amputated human leg taking on a life of its own.

Each story in the volume revolves around a particular theme and a problem. In Bels's novels, on the other hand, the moral, historical, or philo-

sophical issues raised acquire multiple layers and branch out in unpredictable directions. His first novel, *Izmeklētājs* (translated as "The Investigator," 1980), was published in 1967; although it is flawed, the work has been appreciated for the impact its innovative treatment of form and character made on Latvian literature. The novel consists of the interior monologue of the sculptor Juris Rigers as he investigates the theft of some sculptures. Only at the end does the reader realize that the crime is imaginary: Rigers has actually been investigating his own personality. In this novel Bels inaugurates a procedure that became characteristic of his work: the conflation of time periods. The action of the novel spans a period of six hours, within which Rigers reviews the events of the preceding days, as well as the genealogy of his family.

In Latvian literature, this work marks a threshold in the development of the novel. According to the official Soviet standards of the 1940s and 1950s, literary works were expected to deal with the molding of individuals by their economic and social environment; it was deemed inappropriate to center a narrative on the normal human propensity for introspection. While the problematic status of personal identity had become a familiar theme in other literatures—including Latvian literature in exile—to Latvian readers in the Soviet Union such a perspective seemed a breath of fresh air, a harbinger of cultural change and political emancipation. Bels has specifically admitted to having been influenced by such authors as John Steinbeck, James Joyce, Marcel Proust, William Faulkner, John Updike, Mikhail Bulgakov, and Konstantin Simonov; moreover, in the early 1960s, a period of relaxed censorship in the Soviet Union, the influence of the New Novel and its principal representatives—Alain Robbe-Grillet, Michel Butor, Nathalie Sarraute—was widespread. Inevitably, the New Novel left its mark on Bels, who was always drawn to avant-garde movements.

Subjectivity is at the center of Bels's short-story collection *"Es pats" līdzenumā* ("I Myself" on the Plain, 1968). The "plain" or "open expanse" of the title alludes to the human need for a place where one can be "oneself." Human beings are depicted in two antithetical ways in the stories: either as cogs in a bureaucratic or institutional mechanism or as independent entities able to assert their will. The title story and "Ierēdņa augšāmcelšanās" (The Ascension of the Functionary) cast an ironic and satirical light on the monotonous, plodding, and unimaginative existence of the urban bureaucratic middle class. In contrast to these deadened souls,

Bels presents individuals who are able to take charge of the situations in which they find themselves: two such characters are the old teacher in "Augstākā matemātika" (translated as "Higher Mathematics," 1980) and the title character of "Zemūdenes komandieris" (translated as "The Submarine Captain," 1980). The theme of responsibility treated in these stories was a central motif in Soviet literature in the 1960s and 1970s.

At the 1968 plenary session of the Latvian artists and writers convention, Bels began his address: "Today, when the safest means of transportation is a tank, I nevertheless ran the risk of taking a plane to come to Riga." This sentence was understood as a criticism of the Soviet-led Warsaw Pact invasion of Czechoslovakia in August, which ended the liberalization movement that came to be known as the Prague Spring. Bels went on to bring up other forbidden subjects, raising the question of freedom of artistic expression in the Soviet Union and criticizing the Latvian Politburo member Arvīds Pelše for his dealings with Latvian writers.

From 1967 to 1969 Bels studied screenwriting in Moscow, but he was not allowed to defend his thesis, a script titled *Pagrabā* (In the Cellar); the work was published in 1974. Around the same time he completed the novel *Bezmiegs* (Sleeplessness, 1987); in 1970 he underwent several interrogations pertaining to the allegedly pornographic, anti-Soviet, and nationalistic aspects of the manuscript. The intervention of the Writers' Association and of several powerful members of the Communist Party put an end to the harassment. Critics have termed the novel, which finally appeared in serial form in 1986 and as a book in 1987, the "anatomy of an inert humanity" and an essay on "the morality of the era of paralysis." The main character, Eduards Dārziņš, is outwardly apathetic, as are most of the heroes in Bels's novels of the 1960s and 1970s; the novel is principally made up of his nighttime thoughts and emotions. One night Dārziņš hears a woman running outside his apartment and invites her in; in the morning, it turns out that she is a prostitute. In their lives both of them have sold out: she has sold her body, while he has sold his capacity to think for himself. Dārziņš's memories of the night in question are accompanied by an imaginary return to the thirteenth century, in which he relives the brutal colonization of Latvia by the Teutonic Order, and to World War II, another time of occupation by the Germans. In each of the periods in question the character with whom Dārziņš identifies is placed in a situation that forces him to choose between resistance and collaboration,

Title page for Bels's heavily symbolic novel about a huge sand dune that threatens the existence of a village in Courland during the nineteenth century

honor and betrayal. In the thirteenth century he chooses to fight the enemy, but during World War II his capacity for distinguishing friend from enemy is impeded by sentiment and family relationships. In his real life in the 1960s Dārziņš subscribes to a principle of noninvolvement and is content with the material advantages of a mediocre existence: an old car, a small room in a communal apartment, a television set. He is able to entertain ideas about change and hope for a better future for his country only at night; during the day such notions have to be suppressed, and paralysis takes over.

*Cover for Bels's 1996 novel, about political
repression in Latvia in the 1960s*

Bels was the first author in Latvian literature to evoke the power of material objects to create desire and suppress individuality. In this work he also treats the theme of betrayal and links the individual's destiny to that of his or her people. In this regard the novel echoes the concerns found in the work of such Latvian writers as Gunārs Priede, Ojārs Vācietis, Imants Ziedonis, and Imants Auziņš.

In the novel *Būris* (1972; translated as *The Cage*, 1990) the main character, Edmunds Bērzs, is an architect who has assimilated society's norms concerning work, family life, and material comforts such as a car, a house in the country, and so forth. The first half of the novel is a detective story: Bērzs disappears, and an investigator attempts to find him. Through interrogation of people who knew Bērzs, the investigator accumulates details about the architect's appearance, health, habits, and hobbies—facts that constitute a sociological profile of a middle-class existence. It takes forty days for the investigator to find Bērzs, who has been kidnapped

by a jealous rival for a woman's affections and locked in a cage deep in a forest. The second half of the novel details Bērzs's life in the cage and makes it clear that to survive such an ordeal one must keep alive the hope of being freed. When Bērzs is released, he realizes that the cage is also something he has interiorized: it is the cumulative effect of the societally imposed norms and habits that limit thought and create barriers to human relationships. Similarly, Bērzs's tormentor is trapped in a cage of his own fear and jealousy. *Būris* was the first of Bels's works to be translated into the languages of countries outside the Soviet Union (Czech and Finnish). When it was published in Finnish in 1976, Bels wanted to visit Finland but was denied permission to do so by the Soviet authorities.

Based on an actual event that took place during the revolution of 1905, *Saucēja balss* (1973; translated as "The Voice of the Herald," 1980) is the story of the daring and successful attack on a prison in Riga to free the revolutionary Jānis Luters, whom

Bels renames Ādolfs Karlsons. In recounting the arrest, interrogation, and liberation of the revolutionary, Bels shows Karlsons as not only a thinker but also a man of action—he is the first of Bels's characters to rise above his environment and influence events around him. Through metaphorical associations, Bels interweaves the detailed descriptions of events in the novel with meditations on such themes as freedom, betrayal, dishonor, and language. The reader hears many voices, including those of Karlsons, the interrogator, and the torturer, but dominating all is the voice of truth—a voice attesting to a people's right to freedom, growth, and hope in the future. The novel combines a prosaic presentation of historical facts and statistical information with motifs from Latvian folklore and the Bible. The style is characterized by changing rhythms and syntactical experimentation. The narrative seems to pulsate—to come alive—as it reminds the reader of the nation's past, draws parallels between czarist Russia and the Soviet Union, and urges the reader to seek the truth. The opinion of the critics and the reception by the readers place the novel among the highest Latvian literary achievements of the last quarter of the twentieth century. When it was made into a motion picture in 1974, Soviet authorities had to intervene several times to ensure the script was politically acceptable.

The novels that followed—*Poligons* (The Polygon, 1977), *Saknes* (Roots, 1982), *Slēptuve* (The Hiding Place, 1986), and *Sitiens ar teļādu* (Hit with Calfskin, 1987)—and the short-story collection *Sainis* (The Package, 1980) do not stand out among Bels's works, and the critical response to them was lukewarm. The philosophical and ethical issues raised seem shallow, and artistic concerns give way to didactic ones. One can only guess at the reasons for these shortcomings, which may have included increased censorship and surveillance of Bels's activities. Bels was also involved in a mysterious car accident and joined the Communist Party. In all, the period was a difficult one in Bels's life.

Love is the central theme of *Poligons;* it makes the world brighter and people more active. In contrast to those in love, the major part of society is self-indulgent and lazy. Bels shows that the source of most social ills is the individual's inability to overcome his or her egotism. The book also provides vague meditations on the meaning of life, death, friendship, and peace, among which the reader glimpses the author's skeptical attitude toward universal truths.

The stories in *Sainis* exemplify a variety of stylistic and thematic approaches. In these works Bels attempts to capture the variety and the beauty, as well as the strangeness, of life by treating such familiar topics as the circus and the state bureaucracy and occasionally, as in "Ilūziju zaļās būras" (The Green Sails of Illusion), by blending the real and the surreal.

Saknes takes up the theme of idealism that Bels had treated in *Saucēja balss,* examining it in a contemporary context. Bels chooses, for the first time, a rural setting for his novel. The central character is the forest ranger Liepsargs, who is killed while apprehending a poacher. The focus in the novel on the relationship between humanity and nature reflects a common theme in the media of the period. The title of the book and the story of the Liepsarga family history bring out the notion of a common destiny that binds individuals to their nation. The search for the nation's roots is also a dominant motif in the works of other writers of the time, notably those of Vācietis, Harijs Gulbis, Ilze Indrāne, Zigmunds Skujiņš, and Leons Briedis.

Slēptuve is a rather pallid account of the vulnerability and powerlessness of women in modern society. The heroine is a girl who is unable to exert any influence on the events that engulf her. *Sitiens ar teļādu,* on the other hand, is the story of a man who overcomes the inertia imposed by society and shapes his own destiny. Pēteris Urbāns embodies the traditional values of family and work that mark rural life.

In 1987, the year that marked the beginning of perestroika in the U.S.S.R., readers were treated to *Cilvēki laivās* (People in Boats), a work that is generally ranked among Bels's best. The main theme of the novel is the destiny of the Latvian people as it has unfolded over the centuries; a related theme is the powerful relationship that binds an individual to his or her ethnic or national community. The story is set in the nineteenth century in a small village in Courland whose existence is threatened by the inexorable advance of a vast sand dune. The dune becomes a multilayered symbol for the flow of time, the march of history, the might of nature, political despotism, and the discord that tears communities apart, as well as for the self-destructive tendencies of individuals. Just as the dune swallows up the hamlet, history has devoured the once prosperous nation of the Courlanders.

The causes of the disappearance of a people or a race vary, but surely one of the cruelest is forced incorporation into a larger and more powerful nation. Bels shows that this process has been facilitated by a lack of concern on the part of large nations for the fate of smaller ones. The lesson he wishes to impart is an understanding of the inherent importance of each people and, hence, the necessity of preserving the language, history, art, and traditions that are unique to each community. A people's survival, he suggests, is threatened by narrow-mindedness, apathy, and the rejection of one's cultural and linguistic identity. The vitality of a community can only be ensured by each member's diligence, dedication, and willingness to rise above selfish motives.

In 1989 Bels received the National Award of the Latvian Soviet Socialist Republic for *Cilvēki laivās*, a work that made a significant contribution to the movement for Latvian independence. His popularity was further underscored by the publication of two anthologies of his works, *Cilvēki pilsētās* (People in Cities, 1988) and *Cilvēki pārvērtībās* (People in Transformation, 1989).

In the late 1980s Bels became active in the independence movement Latvijas Tautas Fronte (Latvian People's Front). From 1990 to 1993 he was a member of the Latvijas Augstākā Padome (Latvian National Council). Following this political hiatus, he resumed writing and published the novel *Saulē mērktie* (Immersed in the Sun) in 1995.

Saulē mērktie focuses on the Latvian *leģionāri* who fought against the Russians during World War II. A second story line concerns the attempts of a soldier's wife to find her man when he fails to return from the war. In 1996 Bels published *Melnā Zīme* (The Black Mark), a novel re-creating the repressive atmosphere of the 1960s and evoking the author's frame of mind at the time he was writing *Bezmiegs*.

In *Latviešu labirints* (Latvian Labyrinth, 1998) Bels examines Latvian society in the period following the collapse of the Soviet system. The end of totalitarianism was accompanied by the disintegration of traditional values, and the challenge facing the central character of the novel is to find his way through the "labyrinth of democracy" and to preserve his identity in an alienating environment marked by selfishness and mistrust.

In addition to Finnish and Czech, the works of Alberts Bels have been translated into English, Estonian, Lithuanian, Bulgarian, Armenian, Romanian, and German. It is safe to say that these works have secured their author a distinguished place in the history of Latvian literature.

Interviews:
"Četri jautājumi Albertam Belam pirms trīs stāstu publicēšanas," *Literatūra un Māksla*, 9 (1979): 4;
Rimants Ziedonis, "Vietām jau var elpot," *Karogs*, 10 (1988): 134–138;
Ilgvars Spilners, "Jaunā laika ietekme uz rakstniekiem Latvijā," *Laiks*, 59 (1989).

Bibliography:
Laimonis Stepiņš, "Alberts Bels PSRS tautu valodās" and "A. Bels svešvalodās," *Karogs*, 10 (1988): 191–193, 199–200.

Biography:
Anita Rožkalne, "Alberts Bels," in *Latviešu rakstnieki biogrāfijās*, edited by Viktors Hausmanis (Riga: Latvijas enciklopēdija, 1992), pp. 41–42.

References:
Ildze Kronta, "Kā zemes lode griežas: Alberta Bela prozas diviem gadu desmitiem cauri ejot," in *Kritikas gada grāmata*, 16 (1988): 66–88;
Viktors Lagzdiņš, "'Es pats' līdzenumā un citur," *Lauku Dzīve*, 7 (1974): 7–23;
Artūrs Priedītis, "Alberts Bels," in *Mūsdienu latviešu padomju literatūra: 1960–1980*, edited by Viktors Hausmanis (Riga: Zinātne, 1985), pp. 187–198;
Anita Rožkalne, "Alberts Bels," in *Latviešu rakstnieku portreti: 1970s–1980s*, edited by Hausmanis (Riga: Zinātne, 1994), pp. 7–20;
Zigmunds Skujiņš, "Alberta Bela spēles ar nažiem," in his *Jātnieks uz lodes* (Riga: Preses nams, 1996), pp. 153–166;
Inese Treimane, "Cilvēki līdzenumos, būros, laivās . . . Parafrāze par A. Bela tēmu," *Grāmata*, 1 (1990): 47–51.

Vizma Belševica

(30 May 1931 –   )

Rolfs Ekmanis
Arizona State University

This entry originally appeared in Concise Dictionary of World Literary Biography:
South Slavic and Eastern European Writers.

BOOKS: *Visu ziemu šogad pavasaris* (Riga: Latvijas Valsts izdevniecība, 1955);

Zemes siltums: Dzeja (Riga: Latvijas Valsts izdevniecība, 1959);

Ķikuraga stāsti (Riga: Liesma, 1965);

Jūra deg (Riga: Liesma, 1966);

Gadu gredzeni (Riga: Liesma, 1969)—includes "Indriķa Latvieša piezīmes uz *Livonijas hronikas* malām," translated by Baiba Kaugara as "The Notations of Henricus de Lettis in the Margins of the *Livonian Chronicle,*" *Lituanus,* 1 (1970): 15–21;

Madarās (Riga: Liesma, 1976);

Nelaime mājās: Stāsti (Riga: Liesma, 1979);

Kamola tinēja: Dzeja (Riga: Liesma, 1981);

Ceļreiz ceļś uz pasaciņu: Divas lugas bērniem (Riga: Liesma, 1985);

Dzeltu laiks: Dzeja (Riga: Liesma, 1987);

Zem zilās debesu bļodas: Pasakas (Riga: Liesma, 1987);

Bille (Ithaca, N.Y.: Mežābele, 1992; Riga: Jumava, 1995);

Bille dzīvo tālāk (Riga: Jumava, 1996);

Lauztā sirds uz goda dēļa (Riga: Zvaigzne ABC, 1997);

Billes skaistā jaunība (Riga: Jumava, 1999).

Collections: *Ievziedu aukstums: Dzeja* (Riga: Liesma, 1988);

Baltās paslēpes: Mīlestības dzejas (Riga: Apgāds Artava, 1991);

Par saknēm būt: Dzejas izlase (Riga: Zvaigzne ABC, 1996);

Raksti, 4 volumes, 1 volume published to date (Riga: Jumava, 1999–).

Editions in English: "To Be Roots," "Don't Be Oversure," "That Was," and "Willow-Catkins," translated by Inara Cedriņš, in *Contemporary East European Poetry,* edited by Emery George (Ann Arbor, Mich.: Ardis, 1983), pp. 49–50;

Vizma Belševica

"Salome," "Snail in Inverted Goblet," "There in That Whirlpool," and "Don't Go, Women," translated by Cedriņš; "The Maple Blossom," translated by Juris Rozītis; "Painting Signatures," translated by Cedriņš and Astrida B. Stahnke; "Don't Be Oversure," "That Was a Polite Fish," "That Woman . . . ," "I Won't Knock," and "The Autumn Cobweb," translated by Cedriņš; "The Chestnut Tree," translated by Rozītis; "Night Indentations" and "Words about Words," translated by Cedriņš; and "In Fear," translated by Rozītis, in *Contemporary Latvian Poetry*, edited by Cedriņš (Iowa City: University of Iowa Press, 1984), pp. 89–102;

"I Carry My Love," "Silence," "Blessed Are the Poor in Spirit," "Relatives in Samarkanda," "An Argument between a Blossom and an Ax," and "Prometheus Speaks to the Eagle," translated by Stahnke, in *Shifting Borders: East European Poetries of the Eighties*, edited by Walter Cummins (Rutherford, N.J.: Fairleigh Dickinson University Press, 1993), pp. 98–103;

"The Black Time" and "The Well," translated by Māra Rozītis; "Words about Words," "I Knew It Well," "Goya's *Saturn Devouring His Children*," "Horses," and "I'm Really Not Asking for Much," translated by Ilze Kļaviņa Mueller, *World Literature Today*, 2 (1998): 283–286;

"The Black Time," "Death of the Nightingale," "The Wild Thyme," "Words about Words," "Forgive Me," "Nocturnal Digressions," and "To Be the Roots," translated by Māra Rozītis, in *Baltic Poets*, edited by Juris Kronbergs (Stockholm: Swedish Institution, 1999), pp. 60–71.

PRODUCED SCRIPTS: *Pieviltie*, motion picture, by Belševica and Janina Markulāne, Riga Film Studio, 1961;

Zemes atmiņa, motion picture, Riga Film Studio, 1961;

Dullais Dauka, motion picture, Riga Film Studio, 1968.

TRANSLATIONS: Konstantin Paustovskii, *Zelta roze* (Riga: Latvijas valsts izdevniecība, 1958);

Edgar Allan Poe, *Stāstu izlase* (Riga: Latvijas Valsts izdevniecība, 1960);

Aleksandr Grin, *Zelta ķēde* (Riga: Latvijas Valsts izdevniecība, 1961);

Grin, *Ceļš uz Nekurieni* (Riga: Latvijas Valsts izdevniecība, 1961);

Daniil Granin, *Pēc kāzām* (Riga: Latvijas valsts izdevniecība, 1961);

Jerome K. Jerome, *Trīs vīri laivā, nerunājot nemaz par suni* (Riga: Latvijas Valsts izdevniecība, 1963);

William Shakespeare, *Dots pret dotu* (Riga: Latvijas Valsts izdevniecība, 1964);

Dante, *Vita nuova*, translated by Belševica and Jānis Liepiņš (Riga: Liesma, 1965);

A. A. Milne, *Vinnijs Pūks un viņa draugi* (Riga: Liesma, 1967);

Mikola Vinhranovski, *Dārzi un likteņi* (Riga: Liesma, 1967);

Ivan Drach, *Ar tevu uz Tu*, translated by Belševica, Imants Ziedonis, Māris Časdais, and Viktors Zivzemniens (Riga: Liesma, 1968);

Rudyard Kipling, *Blēnu stāsti maziem bērniem*, translated by Belševica and Kārlis Egle (Riga: Liesma, 1969);

Axel Mұnthe, *Stāsts par Sanmikelu* (Riga: Liesma, 1971);

Ernest Hemingway, *Uzvarētājs neiegūst neko* (Riga: Liesma, 1971);

Hemingway, *Piektā kolonna* (Riga: Liesma, 1973);

Hemingway, *Sirmgalvis un jūra* (Riga: Liesma, 1973);

Hemingway, *Salas straumē* (Riga: Liesma, 1974);

Mark Twain, *Konektikutas Jeņķis karaļa Artura galmā* (Riga: Liesma, 1976);

Shakespeare, *Makbets* (Riga: Liesma, 1981);

P. L. Travers, *Mērija Popinsa* (Riga: Liesma, 1983);

Arthur Hailey, *Riteņi* (Riga: Liesma, 1987).

For most of her creative life Vizma Belševica, the most widely recognized Latvian poet of the second half of the twentieth century, lived in a society where freedom of expression was denied. But she produced a remarkable quantity and quality of lyric poetry, and her lyrical voice is also audible in her epic historical and philosophical poems and in her prose works. Her oeuvre comprises poetry, short stories, reminiscences, children's books, motion-picture scripts, and translations into Latvian of English, Ukrainian, Russian, and Italian poetry and prose. Her own works have been translated into some forty languages, most extensively into Russian, the Scandinavian languages, and German. Belševica has made recordings of her poetry, and many of her poems have been set to music. Her career falls into a youthful period, a mature period interrupted by eight years of enforced silence, and a decade during which she wrote her remembrances of the 1930s and 1940s.

Belševica was born in Riga on 30 May 1931, during Latvia's brief period of independence between the two world wars and in the midst of the worldwide economic crisis, to Jānis Belševics and Ieva Belševica, née Cīrule. The family lived in Grīziņkalns, one of the Latvian capital's poorest sections, where the parents were blue-collar workers. Because at times it was difficult for the family to make ends meet, Belševica spent a considerable part of her childhood with relatives in Ugāle, an enchanting forest-covered region in northern Courland (Kurzeme), a province in the western part of Latvia. The city's shabby proletarian surroundings and the simple, wholesome rural environment of her childhood left indelible impressions on the future writer; she has retained a love of nature, a distaste for urban life, and an indifference to material possessions. Her first poem, written when she was six, is a plea to her parents to move from the "boisterous and ghastly city" to the idyllic peace of the countryside.

The Baltic States were annexed to the Soviet Union when Belševica was nine. The year of Soviet rule, known in Latvia as the Year of Horror, was followed by several years of Nazi occupation. As a seventh-grader Belševica wrote her first love poem; it expresses her infatuation with a fellow pupil, "a fair-skinned, blue-eyed lad." Although she was caught several times composing witty, mocking rhymes about her teachers, she escaped punishment because of her exemplary academic performance. In primary school she was already captivated by literature, especially the works of the Latvian poets Aleksandrs Čaks and Ēriks Ādamsons.

Moscow reestablished its rule in the Baltics at the end of World War II. In 1946 Belševica was scolded at a Komsomol (Young Communist League) meeting for writing poems in free verse, which was officially condemned, and on such trivial subjects as the beauty of nature and blond boys, at a time when writers were expected to assist in the building of a communist society. She made her literary debut with the poem "Zemes atmoda" (Awakening of the Land), published in the 30 April 1947 issue of the Komsomol newspaper *Padomju Jaunatne* (Soviet Youth). Some overzealous critics detected traces of lewdness in the work, associating the poetic image of Belševica's native land's rolling hills with a woman's breasts. Her second published poem, "Vīrs darvo jumtu" (A Man Tarring the Roof), fared better, earning official praise: it was thematically correct, and it used end rhymes, which were stylistically correct.

After graduating from Riga's Poligrāfijas 2. arodskola (Second Trade School for Printers) in 1948 Belševica was assigned· to work for the weekly *Pionieris* (The Pioneer), the publication of the local Pioneer organization for children aged nine to fourteen. She served as a contributing literary editor in 1948–1949 and as editor of the education department in 1952–1953. In 1955, the year Belševica received an external degree from Rīgas Kultūras un izglītības iestāžu darbinieku tehnikums (Riga Technical School for Workers at Cultural and Educational Facilities), her first

book of poems, *Visu ziemu šogad pavasaris* (The Whole Year Nothing but Spring), was published. The slender volume was ideologically acceptable: its tone is conventionally sunny, and it expresses the obligatory pathos over postwar reconstruction along with an anticipation of a happier future. Nonetheless, it bears promise of her more mature work: the syllables of a handful of the poems can almost be tasted on the tongue. The author herself, however, has disavowed the collection, considering it a schoolgirl's concession to the mediocre, standard doggerel of the time. A book of that kind was, however, necessary for acceptance into the Communist Party–guided Writers' Union of the Latvian Soviet Socialist Republic, which was affiliated with the central Writers' Union of the U.S.S.R. and was the essential condition for a recognized literary existence. Belševica's first short story, "Meistars Īlis" (Master Īlis), based on her trade-school experiences, was published in the September 1956 issue of *Karogs* (The Banner), the monthly organ of the Writers' Union and the only Latvian literary journal then in existence.

Belševica became a member of the Writers' Union in 1958. At the time she was enrolled at the Institut mirovoi literatury im. Gor'kogo (Gorky Institute of World Literature) in Moscow, a branch of the Academy of Sciences that gave advanced courses for aspiring writers and critics. In Moscow the young, attractive intellectual from "exotic" Latvia was admired and befriended by such emerging literary figures as the Ukrainian Lina Kostenko, the Abkhazian Fazil Iskander, and the Russians Iurii Kazakov, Bella Akhmadulina, and Andrei Voznesensky.

After the short-lived thaw produced by Soviet Communist Party leader Nikita Khrushchev's denunciation of the late dictator Joseph Stalin at the Twentieth Congress of the Communist Party in 1956, the literary line in the Soviet Union began to harden again in the late 1950s. On 14 November 1959 the weekly organ of the Writers' Union of the U.S.S.R., *Literaturnaia Gazeta* (Literary Gazette), censured several Latvian literary works that were allegedly revisionist, unlawful, and anti-Soviet and charged Belševica and another woman poet, Ārija Elksne, with treating "narrowly intimate themes" in their works. A major attack against the more liberal-minded Latvian writers, critics, and artists followed a few days later at the Ninth Plenum of the Latvian Communist Party Central Committee. The authors considered such treatment a backhanded compliment.

The overanxious Riga censors at first refused to give permission for the publication of Belševica's second book of poems, *Zemes siltums* (Warmth of the Earth). But when Veronika Tushnova's graceful Russian translation of the work, *Teplo zemnoe,* which served as Belševica's thesis at the Gorky Institute, was accepted for publication by the Moscow state publishing house Sovetskii pisatel' (Soviet Writer), the Riga censors, to avoid embarrassment, arranged for its hasty printing in Latvian in 1959 (the Russian edition came out in 1960). The book was not, however, published as submitted by the author. Several poems were found objectionable; for example, "Tālu . . ." (Far-away . . .), which expresses the poet's deep nostalgia for her homeland while she was studying in Moscow, was excluded because some readers might view it as conveying the feelings of Latvians in Siberian labor camps. Another poem, in which the author muses over a dissipating cloud above a lake as observed from an airplane, was omitted because one could read into it criticism of the current Communist Party line. Nevertheless, *Zemes siltums* established Belševica as a talented and innovative poet in her homeland as well as in Moscow. Originality of imagination and an abundance of unexpected associative references characterize her short, clear verses, which convey the notion of a sensitive young woman awakening to life, love, and grief. Other elements that emerge in the book include courage, compassion, a sense of isolation, and mysticism.

Belševica graduated from the Gorky Institute in 1961. Although official restrictions continued to limit the subjects and manner of literature in the 1960s, and litanies of praise for the Communist Party and its leaders still permeated the work of Latvian writers, some authors found it possible to deal with subjects and themes that had been forbidden during the first fifteen postwar years. Censorship was temporarily relaxed in the mid 1960s, bringing about an eruption of talent and vitality. Belševica was one of the most brilliant members of this group of "New Wave Writers."

A stay in the autumn of 1960 in the medieval Baltic fishing town of Salacgrīva in northern Latvia resulted in *Ķikuraga stāsti* (Stories from Ķikurags, 1965), a volume of five highly compressed short stories. Belševica vividly describes the physical appearance of the fishermen and finds the proper psychological and idiomatic rhythm with which to set the mood of each story so as to affect the senses in much the same way as

poetry would. She has a fine ear for the local speech and succeeds in making a confined, unsophisticated world interesting and diverse. Imbued with a jocular spirit, these stories, like her later prose pieces, embody respect and warmth toward what is human, fragile, and imperfect. She changed the village's name to the somewhat comical Ķikurags, she has said,

> because of a rather paradoxical truth, known to every writer, namely, it is impossible to write about immense love—the result will turn out too pathetic, too full of mawkish sentiment. Only two choices remain—either a complete silence or the story must be concealed behind a mask of humor and a touch of irony. I could not remain silent about Salacgrīva, but, because my comical manner at times approaches the grotesque, it would not be appropriate to use the town's real name. Also, had I done it, the reader would immediately try to track down prototypes.

The full range of Belševica's poetic talent made itself evident in 1966 with the release of *Jūra deg* (The Sea Is Burning). This impressive gathering of poems reveals a mastery of a wide range of styles and subjects and demonstrates the poet's complete control of her material. Although it is hard to find a dominant note in the work—the poems range across such themes as love, alienation, childhood, war, art, and the search for wisdom—it is particularly notable for the restrained, elegiac tone of her love poetry, where the power of love and of imagination work in concert to sustain the human heart and spirit in the face of difficult conditions. Her nature poems are also distinctive and always rise above the merely picturesque. Belševica is especially enthralled by the magic of the Baltic Sea and induces the reader to imagine its sights and sounds through a series of poetic images.

A jewel of a poem is "Klusums" (translated as "Silence," 1993). After presenting several examples of silence and serenity in the heart of the poet and in nature, little by little Belševica personifies the sea, engaging in a dialogue with it until, in an unexpected conclusion, the sea is revealed as a tired and sobbing woman hiding her head in the hands of the poet, who tries to console her. Creating a magical, even hypnotizing atmosphere by sound devices that include alliteration and assonance, Belševica masterfully manages the transition from objective observation to metaphorical imagery and, in the end, the transformation of the imagery into reversed reality: the huge sea has metamorphosed into a real woman, and the poet has acquired cosmic dimensions.

Belševica does not convey emotions through invocation or direct expression but through the precisely observed description of an objective correlate, such as a gesture or a locale, and through a rich allusiveness and an intertextuality that hint at greater depths. The dramatic and the lyric are frequently merged in monologues and dialogues; for example, in "Paraksti gleznām" (Painting Signatures) she comments on three world-famous paintings—Sandro Botticelli's *The Birth of Venus*, Francisco Goya's *Saturn Devouring His Children*, and Dante Gabriel Rossetti's *Beatrice and Dante in Paradise*. "Kalna vārdi tam, kas palika ielejā" (The Mountain Speaks to Him Who Has Remained in the Valley) is a dialogue in which the mountain sermonizes to humanity on heroism and cowardice, self-denial, spiritual isolation, and so on. Even Belševica's sermons are dances of syllables.

In *Jūra deg* Belševica is seduced by language, by the imaginative association of words. But a new epic tone also begins to emerge in two poems devoted to social reality. In the first, "Prometeja kliedziens" (The Cry of Prometheus), the myth of the challenger of the tyrant, the defender of people from the doom that threatens them, is applied to the conditions of her day. For Belševica, a loving human being is a carrier of Promethean fire—a spirit admitting no limitations, no arguments other than the power of feeling. The tragedy, as she sees it, is that love is able not only to raise people far above their ordinary selves but also to sear their souls. In the second poem, "Klods Izerlijs" (Claude Eatherly), an American flier is desperately seeking for a way of redeeming his guilt for having been involved in dropping the atomic bomb on Hiroshima:

> Your Mother—Humanity.
> Your Motherland—the Earth.
> Carrying out the order "In Motherland's name!"
> Betray not your Motherland!

Although Belševica condemns the destruction of the Japanese city by the Americans at the end of World War II, the poem also contains veiled criticism of the Soviet Union. "When she was writing about Claude Eatherly," Voznesensky pointed out at a literary conference at Stockholm University on 25 September 1995, "she was clearly referring to our country."

As was the case with most of Belševica's poetry books, *Jūra deg* did not escape alteration by

Belševica in her late twenties (drawing by Rena Ekmanis for the journal Latvija Sodien; *collection of Rolfs Ekmanis)*

the censors. In "Prometeja kliedziens" the line "Prometheuses of all lands, unite!" is repeated several times. Such an obvious paraphrase of the Bolshevik slogan "Proletarians of all lands, unite!" was inadmissible in the view of party officials, and they changed Belševica's line to "Prometheuses locked in chains, unite!" Belševica found the situation comical and did not object. In the non-Russian republics of the Soviet Union the poem was perceived as a battle cry to the intelligentsia to join together to resist Moscow's hegemony. According to official commentators, however, "Prometeja kliedziens" calls for solidarity of the world's working people in their "struggle for human happiness and against the menace of nuclear war."

From the late 1960s onward Belševica was compelled by her frail health to lead a relatively quiet and secluded life in the Latvian capital. But this isolation made her inner life all the more intense. She treated the emotions of her lyrical personae with more depth than any other poet in Latvia and did not feel obliged to involve them in the industrial, agricultural, and political concerns that Communist Party cultural officials decreed should be ingredients in all literature and art. By the time her fourth collection of verse, *Gadu gredzeni* (Annual Rings), was published in 1969, Belševica had achieved prominence not only in her native country but also beyond its borders. Two books of her poetry had been published in Russian—the translation by Tushnova of *Zemes siltums* as *Teplo zemnoe* and selected poems by several translators under the title *Stikhi o solov'inom infarkte* (Verses on a Nightingale's Heart Attack, 1969). Other Russian translations followed over the years, the most notable of which was *Aprel'skii dozhd'* (April Rain, 1978). In 1970 a volume of Belsevica's poems was published in Armenian in a translation by the Armenian poet Vardkes Babaian. Her poems also appeared in literary journals in translations into such languages as Swedish, Norwegian, Danish, German, Polish, Lithuanian, Estonian, Azeri, Moldovan, Ukrainian, Belarussian, and Finnish. It is, however, difficult to translate Latvian poetry adequately because Latvian is a suggestive, sensuous language in which the principal concern is with the sound of words and their rhythmical relations. Belševica's poems, especially, depend on the exactness of their diction, the subtlety of their rhythmic modulations, and the variety of their tones, which range from elegiac to quiet to rebellious and, at times, to the comic and even the grotesque. Belševica has said that if she were forced to live on a deserted island, she would take with her only the most complete dictionary of the Latvian language: *Latviešu valodas vārdnīca,* begun by the renowned linguist Kārlis Mūlenbachs and completed after his death in 1916 by another famous Baltic linguist, Jānis Endzelīns and published in four massive volumes between 1923 and 1932. In this dictionary, Belševica said in *Padomju Jaunatne* (31 May 1981), "the pearls of our folklore, literature, and dialects shine resplendently. This work can bestow upon us everything—love of art, knowledge, inspiration (many of my poems have grown out of this dictionary), ideas. . . . You see, my native language is my life's greatest and most passionate love."

Belševica made other comments concerning the creative process in *Mūsdienu latviešu padomju literatūra 1960–1980* (Contemporary Soviet Latvian Literature 1960–1980, 1985):

> My poems have a difficult birth. Very seldom it happens without pain. The first line of a poem is "a gift from Heaven." The poet gets it from who knows where. If the first line has not fallen from Heaven, the poem, as a rule, will be inferior. If it has, then for a long time I must carry it around like a little baby. I must build up my strength—a laborious and

tormenting process. Consequently I am not a prolific writer. While working on a poem, a torrent of various associations pours over me like a waterfall and the prevalent sensation I have is that within this gushing stream I must hit a certain spot with my finger. The words which it is possible to select with less effort edge out. They force their way to the forefront. I must fight with them in order to find the suitable word. . . . Almost each of my poems has its own melody. At times, even before I have begun writing a poem, I walk around humming musical sounds. The melody determines the poem's mood. Sometimes it shocks me when someone sets the finished poem to music in a different manner than I had envisioned it. . . . When the struggle of creating a poem is over, it has consumed such a voluminous amount of my emotions and energy that a total spiritual and physical fatigue sets in. There are times when I feel downright sick.

In the 1960s Belševica wrote several motion-picture scripts for the Riga Film Studio. The first, co-authored with Janina Markulāne, was for the motion picture *Pieviltie* (The Deceived Ones, 1961). The script for the documentary *Zemes atmiņa* (Earth's Memory, 1961), a meditative essay about life and death, consists largely of Belševica's poems. Belševica complied with the request of the scenarist Viktors Lorencs to write a poem to be included in his script for *Es visu atceros, Ričard* (I Remember Everything, Richard, 1966). The censors, however, demanded that the poem, "Nemieru un gaidu pavasaris" (The Spring Full of Anxiety and Anticipation), be omitted. Eventually, the authorities ordered the entire movie to be shelved, because the World War II years were not depicted according to the official line; only in the late 1980s was it allowed to be screened for the public. In 1968 Belševica also wrote the script for the puppet movie *Dullais Dauka* (The Nutty Dauka), based on a classical Latvian novel by Sudrabu Edžus.

The 1969 collection *Gadu gredzeni,* which was passed intact by negligent censors, is generally acknowledged as Belševica's most original work. Imbued with tragic power and courage, it brought to full flowering what the poet and critic Astride Ivaska called in *World Literature Today* (Spring 1996) "her gift for condensing both emotion and thought to the point—but never beyond—of breaking the poetic form" and a full engagement with the theme of the calling and responsibility of the poet as "witness of his time, a sleepless sentinel with only the word as his weapon." In several poems, especially in "Vārdi par vārdiem" (translated as "Words about Words,"

1984), one finds the thought that the role of the poet in the twentieth century is self-vindicating, that the poet, guiltless on one level but bearing the guilt of others on another, is the creator or the tool of the only thing that can overcome death—the Word: "Birds die, and poets. But not even the axe's edge / can hack out the word that is said before death." This responsibility makes a poet's silence shameful. In this volume Belševica conquers space and time: she understands her contemporaries but also shares the worlds of the Greek myths, the Bible, medieval chronicles, the major nineteenth-century Ukrainian poet Taras Shevchenko, the Latvian poet Jānis Rainis, and the Polish motion-picture director Anjey Vayda. The creative act for Belševica is an act of mediation between animate and inanimate, past and present, and nature and human society.

Belševica's vision of the world is frequently haunted and stricken with horror. The "bonepilers" are in charge, and neither sense, nor tears, nor blood weigh in this world of theirs. In vain her Don Quixotes struggle for justice against lies and subterfuge. The windmills keep grinding out and nourishing the soil with falsehoods, while the heaps of pale bones of innumerable Don Quixotes grow larger and larger all around. But the injustices cannot last forever, because these Don Quixotes never cease to fight; their bones will push out new shoots against the sun, and their deaths will "build a bridge out of their bones, a bridge upon which truth shall stand." The day will come when the blades of these evil windmills will break on hitting the white bone heaps, when "wisdom will be brought into being by insanity."

Belševica frequently employs the word *mēms* (mute) to denote deep feeling. In the often-cited "Latvijas vēstures motīvs: Vecrīga" (Variations on the Theme of Latvian History: Old Riga) she describes how the medieval Old City of Riga keeps silent as the winds howl and beat upon her mute, nude stone women, her mute heraldic beasts, the voiceless key to the city with the conquerors' hands on it, and the invaders' silent blood on the cobblestones. It is pointless to ask whether Riga's quiet strength signifies indifference, obtuseness, or cowardice:

> Ask not. You won't be answered.
> That which passes must shout.
> Must plead. Must prove.
> What is eternal can keep silent.

The howling and raging winds, as well as those who enter by force and try to conquer the city, come and go. They are transitory. But Riga, with her mute inhabitants and her mute roosters on the many mute church steeples, will carry on, in spite of hardships and suffering.

Included in *Gadu gredzeni* is the long poem "Indriķa Latvieša piezīmes uz *Livonijas hronikas* malām" (translated as "The Notations of Henricus de Lettis in the Margins of the *Livonian Chronicle*"), which juxtaposes intense, accusatory poetic commentary with quotations from the pious thirteenth-century chronicle to tell of the pillaging, burning, rape, and murder inflicted on a small nation by a large and powerful one in the name of an ideology—in this case, Christianity. *The Livonian Chronicle*, or *Heinrici Chronicon Livoniae* (Chronicle of Henry of Livonia), is thought to have been written between 1225 and 1227 and describes the German conquest of the region of Livonia, in what is now Latvia and Estonia, between 1180 and 1227. The oldest manuscript of the chronicle is in the fourteenth-century *Codex Zamoiski* in Warsaw. Although the events in the poem occurred some eight hundred years ago, Belševica's poetized "Notations" are conspicuously timely. According to the Latvian poet and critic Gunars Saliņš, among the elements that lend Belševica's story its remarkable contemporaneousness is

> the conspirational urgency with which her Henricus engages the reader. In this, Belševica's conception differs strikingly from the ways in which similar historical material has been treated by most other Latvian poets. Whereas the traditional heroic epic ballade, no matter how splendidly written, tends to present the past as something memorable and yet remote and unredeemable, Belševica's poem renders history with the immediacy of a news broadcast on a current political—and personal—crisis.

"The Notations of Henricus de Lettis" embodies the cri de coeur of an angry, suffering, and disenfranchised people:

> Rome like a jealous wife demands
> That love be sworn to her in public
> At every step . . . With spying eyes she reads
> Between my lines, that she owns not
> This heart, once so naive and yielding.
> I write, and from the words blood does
>   not drip.
> And the barbed bitterness of letters does
>   not gash the page.
> You, Jesus Christ, over my shoulder read
> How Godfearingly for your fame I lie.
> O Christ, your kingdom shall come over us.
> One God and tongue. And nation also one.
> I see the Latvian land with cross nails
>   hammered

To the surface of your holy meekness.
And our destruction—one more sunset
That in unerring concept Rome may
    dawn
Over the earth. . . .

Although Bishop Albert, the overseer of Livonia who died in 1229, was one of the shrewdest German colonizers and diplomats of his time, neither he nor anyone else in that period ever tried to impose a universal tongue in the Baltic. Latin was the official language used in decrees, treaties, and state correspondence, but it was not proposed as a conversational language even for the crusaders themselves, let alone for the native inhabitants. Only some modern "Romes" have tried to force Latvians and the other Baltic peoples to accommodate themselves to the native tongue of the conquerors (under Soviet rule, most official business had to be conducted in Russian).

The poet accuses not only the many invaders who, with "blazing irons," have tortured and tried to "extirpate" her people but also those of her countrymen who carried out the orders of the foreign oppressors, as well as those who did not try to resist. Thus, the Henricus of Belševica's poem curses his own people as a "traitorous," "cur-like," and "servile and slavish nation." Here, as in many of her other poems, Belševica repeatedly uses images of fire and burning in connection with writing: "The strength of poetry lies in burning," she writes. The scribe of the chronicle wishes that his words would burn the paper, and he himself wants to climb up into the sky as a column of flame and shout out the injustices he sees.

These themes were impermissible in official Soviet literary circles. At the June 1969 Communist Party Plenum in Riga several participants claimed to find various political implications in Belševica's poems. One high party official, Roberts Ķīsis, was especially angry at what he considered Belševica's attempt to lead Soviet readers "from socially pure thoughts into the fog of conjectures and remote allusions" by using Aesopian language and double-level symbolism. He branded it an extremely dangerous act, "liable to create utter ideological chaos among politically inexperienced readers." Valija Labrence, a proregime literary critic, recalled that Belševica had been admonished on several earlier occasions for the "lack of social lucidity" in her works and beseeched the poet to treat in her verse the "new Soviet man" who, "imbued with communist morality," advances "along the road toward a new

society." Some of the more-docile Latvian poets, who had built their careers on writing agitprop odes to the leaders in Moscow, felt threatened when printings of Belševica's books sold out in a single day, while their own works moldered on bookstore shelves. Imants Lasmanis, a second-rate poet, reproached Belševica in a poem titled "Nolādējums zaimotājam" (May the Blasphemer Be Damned), and Mirdza Ķempe, a recipient of the designation "People's Poet" and of the 1967 Lenin Prize for her poetry collection *Mirkļu mūžība* (Eternity of Moments), wrote the bombastic poem "Rīga neklusē" (Riga Is Not Mute), condemning Belševica for trying to please the "philistines" and the "petty bourgeois" by planting "double meanings into medieval history."

Although she was never expelled from the Latvian Writers' Union, Belševica spent the next seven years as a "banned person." Her name disappeared from the official media, as well as from the roster of officially recognized Latvian writers in such reference books as Milda Kalve's *Jaunākās latviešu padomju dzejas apcirkņos* (In the Corn Bins of Contemporary Soviet Latvian Poetry, 1975). To Belševica, the inability to publish was a "fate worse than death."

Proscribed writers in the Soviet Union were sometimes permitted to publish children's stories or translations of foreign literature that was unlikely to arouse controversy. Belševica, however, was told that there would be a strict ban on any further publication of her works, including translations. But when the popular poet indicated to the authorities that in such a case she would try to support herself by selling ice cream out of a pushcart either in front of the Latvian Communist Party Central Committee building or at the entrance to Hotel Riga, frequented by foreigners, the state publishing house, Liesma (The Flame), promptly offered her a commission to translate the works of certain foreign authors. She thus had at least semiofficial standing as a translator, making her situation somewhat more bearable. For the next seven years she earned her livelihood and, at the same time, greatly enriched Latvian literature through her many masterful translations, mainly from English.

In Latvia translation has long been recognized as an art in its own right, and it has attracted many distinguished writers. Critics were quick to recognize Belševica's ability as a translator of both poetry and prose. Before the ban she had translated Dante's *La Vita nuova* (1965), William Shakespeare's sonnets and his comedy *Mea-*

sure for Measure (1964), stories by Edgar Allan Poe, Rudyard Kipling, Jerome K. Jerome, and A. A. Milne, poetry collections by the Ukrainians Mikola Vihranovski and Ivan Drach, and prose works by the Russians Aleksandr Grin, Daniil Granin, and Konstantin Paustovskii. Among the works she translated during the ban were Shakespeare's *Macbeth* (1981), poems by T. S. Eliot, Mark Twain's *A Connecticut Yankee in King Arthur's Court* (1976), the Swedish author Axel Mŷnthe's *Story of San Michele* (1971), Ernest Hemingway's novel *Islands in the Stream* (1971), his play *The Fifth Column* (1973), his novella *The Old Man and the Sea* (1973), and P. L. Travers's *Mary Poppins* (1983).

For Belševica, no work was too difficult to translate. The editors at the state publishing house had planned to leave out two chapters of Paustovskii's *Zelta roze* (The Golden Rose, 1958) because, in their view, Latvian equivalents could not be found for many of the Russian expressions in them. Belševica was insulted, both personally and as a Latvian, by the decision, and after strenuous research in old dictionaries and other sources she produced beautiful translations of the "untranslatable" chapters. Before translating *A Connecticut Yankee in King Arthur's Court* she spent an entire year researching old Latvian texts, including periodicals and books of sermons, to find words that corresponded to Twain's nineteenth-century English.

From the late 1950s to the late 1980s Belševica was closely watched by the KGB (Soviet secret police), and her apartment was searched twice. In 1962 the poet, critic, and translator Knuts Skujenieks and several other intellectuals whom the authorities suspected of being connected with a Latvian opposition movement had been sentenced to seven years in the forced-labor camp at Pot'ma for "anti-Soviet activities." Belševica, who knew Skujenieks and his bride, had also come under suspicion, and KGB agents expressed an interest in whether any books or manuscripts in her apartment were prohibited by Soviet law. That search lasted eight hours. In the early 1970s Belševica's apartment was searched by a team of Ukrainian and Latvian KGB agents who suspected that the poet had in her possession the manuscript for the Ukrainian writer Ivan Dzjuba's "dangerously anti-Soviet" book *Internacionalizm chi rusifikacia?* (Internationalization or Russification?). Although the agents discovered the manuscript rather quickly, they continued the search for sixteen hours. Belševica was promised that the official prohibition of her own works would be lifted if she testified against Dzjuba at his trial in the Ukrainian capital, Kiev. Instead, she astonished the court by defending

Belševica at François Rabelais's house in Chinon, France, 1989 (photograph by Rolfs Ekmanis)

Dzjuba and stating that "if it is evident to a writer that his people and his native language are imperiled, then it is his moral obligation to write about it regardless of consequences." The two KGB visits resulted in Belševica's loss of several sacks full of published and unpublished materials, including notes, diaries, and books. Her health problems may have saved her from the imprisonment to which many other persecuted writers and intellectuals in the former Soviet Union were sentenced.

As usually happens, the regime's efforts to transmute the poet into a "nonperson" in the eyes of potential readers backfired. For many, she was the true voice of Latvia. Enthusiasm for her work surged, especially among the younger generation, even though devotees who innocently wrote or called to thank her for her poems and to tell her what she meant to them often found themselves confronted by the security forces. Many of her compatriots regarded her as a symbol of their hopes for liberty and national independence. Belševica's enforced silence served only to heighten her moral authority.

In the mid 1970s several of Belševica's earlier poems were reprinted on the literary pages of periodicals, and in the late 1970s her towering literary reputation and moral steadfastness led to a selective rehabilitation and the lifting of the ban on publication of her original work. *Madarās* (Among the Madder), a subdued but richly evocative collection of poems, appeared in 1976 in an edition of sixteen thousand copies. Several poems that were included in the manuscript, of course, had to be omitted from the published volume. Among them was "Melnais laiks" (translated as "The Black Time," 1998); the title is a Latvian expression for the period in the spring right after the first melting of the snow and before the budding of leaves, but according to the censors, the poem could be read as referring to Latvia's condition under Soviet rule. Belševica watched her rehabilitation by the official literary overseers with ironic detachment.

Madarās is a collection of powerful poems on nature themes and on elemental midlife concerns. Several pieces reflect the poet's determination to awaken concern for the preservation of the environment. In "Pegasiņš" (Pegasus) her "dear little Pegasus" treads lightly with his unshod hooves so as not to harm cranberry shrubs and patches of bear moss. In other poems she writes about the affection of her two sons, the magnificence of the Baltic Sea, the pussy willows in the spring, the fragrance of new-mown grass, the fields basking in the sun or soaking up the rain, the humming of the bees, and the song of the skylark in beautiful similes and metaphors. The primary emphasis in her brief, superbly crafted pieces, however, is on woman's inner life. Several poems are devoted to the arts, notably "Bartoka kvartets" (Bartok Quartet) and "Mākslinieka acis" (The Artist's Eyes), about the legendary Latvian painter Jānis Pauļuks. "Ugunsziedi" (Blossoms of Fire) is dedicated to the poet Jūlijs Dievkociņš, who was executed by the czarist security forces for his involvement in the 1905 revolution. When Belševica wrote of the boots of the Cossack Black Hundreds, many readers saw Soviet tank tracks across the broken Baltic landscape.

Local color that touches on universality characterizes Belševica's second prose collection, *Nelaime mājās* (Misfortune at Home), a group of short stories that many critics consider among the best in post–World War II Latvian literature. It was published in 1979, fourteen years after her first volume of short stories. The six tales, which are humorous but border on the tragic, are peopled by colorful types in grotesquely warped situations. A prominent feature of these "laughter-through-tears" tales is their extraordinary use of language. Belševica plays with the ambiguity of words and meanings, demanding the reader's complete attention and rewarding it with emotional and aesthetic intensity.

Even after Belševica's partial rehabilitation in the late 1970s, the Communist Party continued to try to drive her into obscurity. When the state publishing house Liesma brought out a traditional fiftieth-birthday collection, *Kamola tinēja* (The Clew Winder), in 1981, it was almost impossible to find in Latvian bookstores—even though, at sixteen thousand copies, it had had a large printing for a small country. At the same time, the KGB-affiliated Soviet Latvian propaganda organization for relations with Latvian exiles distributed the book free of charge to Latvians in Western Europe, Australia, and North America to show that the regime was tolerant of opposition writers. In Latvia a rumor—apparently fabricated by the security forces—spread that thieves had stolen nearly all of the copies of Belševica's book from a state warehouse. As late as the mid 1980s obstacles were placed in the path of publishing Belševica's poems in Soviet satellite nations, although they had been provisionally accepted by publishing houses in Prague and Belgrade.

Kamola tinēja was supposed to bring together Belševica's most important poems from all of her previous collections except the first, plus several new poems, including the superb "Nakts atkāpes" (translated as "Night Indentations," 1984). The previously censored poems from *Gadu gredzeni*, such as "Indriķa Latvieša piezīmes uz *Livonijas hronikas* malām," "Vārdi par vārdiem," and "Latvijas vēstures motīvs: Vecrīga," however, were again left out.

In 1982 Belševica was awarded the Andrejs Upīts Literary Prize, named after the Latvian prose writer and critic. In 1986 she received the "Nopelniem bagātā kultūras darbiniece" (Meritorious Cultural Worker), which she regarded as an insult rather than an honor.

Dzeltu laiks (Autumnal Time) was published in 1987, at the outset of Soviet Communist Party first secretary Mikhail Gorbachev's policy of perestroika. It was Belševica's first book to be free of interference from the censors. Almost half of it comprises poems devoted to turning points in Latvian history, from 5 October 1199, when Pope Innocent III proclaimed the Crusade against Livonia, to 1906, when Russian punitive expeditions executed or deported hundreds of Latvian revolutionaries. This part of the book is a blend of poetry and occasional prose passages, of the wild and free with the domestic, of wisdom with childlike wonderment, of irony with intensity, and of realism with romance and dreams.

Belševica's lifelong interest in the verbal creativity of children and in child psychology is reflected in her two books for children. *Ceļreiz ceļš uz pasaciņu* (The Trail to Fairy Tale, 1985) consists of two plays, partly in verse. *Zem zilās debesu bļodas* (Under the Bowl of the Blue Yonder, 1987) is a collection of nineteen animal tales.

On 5 February 1987 Belševica's elder son, twenty-eight-year-old Klāvs Elsbergs, himself a gifted poet and a graceful translator of the works of French poets such as Guillaume Apollinaire, as well as the editor of a newly established avant-garde cultural monthly, died under circumstances that remain unclear. As the result of an argument with several minor Russian literati concerning Moscow's treatment of the non-Russian peoples in the Soviet Union—so the story went—he was beaten and pushed from a ninth-floor window of the Soviet Writers' Union's residential hotel in Dubulti. The local authorities, allegedly on Moscow's orders, refused to investigate the death. There was little doubt—not only in the minds of Belševica and those close to her but also in the minds of many other Latvians—that the incident constituted the same kind of refined punishment of Belševica that had been applied to other inconvenient writers in the Soviet Union: for example, Anna Akhmatova and Marina Tsvetaeva, whose closest family members were killed or imprisoned, and Boris Pasternak, whose mistress was arrested, along with her daughter, when his novel *Doctor Zhivago* (1957) gained worldwide attention and helped him win the 1958 Nobel Prize in literature.

For almost two years after her son's death Belševica was unable to write at all, and she has written no poetry since then. A collection of her previously published poems, *Ievziedu aukstums* (The Coldness of Alder Blossoms), was published in 1988; she dedicated it to her dead son. Also in 1988 a literary prize named after the poet Ojārs Vācietis was awarded to Belševica. She became chairwoman of the Riga chapter of PEN in 1989, holding the office until 1990. In February 1989 she was permitted to visit a Western European country for the first time as a member of a delegation to a conference of women intellectuals in Paris. In 1990 she was elected to honorary membership in the Latvian Academy of Sciences. A selection of her love poems came out in a volume titled *Baltās paslēpes* (Silver-Gray Hide-and-Seek) in 1991.

In late 1988 Belševica had begun working on thinly fictionalized reminiscences of her childhood. The title of the first volume, *Bille,* is the nickname of the narrator-protagonist, Sibilla. Fearing that the work might upset her mother, who was in frail health, if it were published in Latvia, Belševica submitted the manuscript to an exile publisher in Ithaca, New York, who published it in 1992 (with a second printing in 1993). It includes a lengthy interview she gave in Paris in 1989 and the poems that are mentioned in the interview. *Bille* was published in Latvia in 1995. In twenty-seven episodes it takes the reader from Belševica's childhood memories of prewar independent Latvia up to the Soviet takeover of the Baltics in June 1940. The pleasures and disappointments of childhood are convincingly conveyed, and the adults are accurately drawn from a child's perspective. A second volume, *Bille dzīvo tālāk* (Bille Lives On), was published in 1996. It covers, in thirty episodes, the period of the Russian and German occupations from 1940 to the end of 1944. A third volume, *Billes skaistā jaunība* (The Beautiful Youth of Bille, 1999), treats the years of her secondary education at the Trade School for Printers to about 1948. In all three volumes the structure is fragmented, though strict chronology is retained. *Bille* and its sequels were the best-selling books of Latvian fiction of the 1990s, and the first two volumes have been translated into Swedish.

In 1994 Belševica was honored by the president of Latvia, Guntis Ulmanis, with the Order of Three Stars for her contribution to Latvian literature and culture. In 1996 her name was submitted to the Neustadt Prize Committee for literature, and in 1998 she received the Tomas Tranströmer Prize.

Interest in Belševica has been especially high in the Scandinavian countries, thanks to excellent translations into Icelandic, Danish, Norwegian, and Swedish. The four books of her poetry translated by the poet Juris Kronbergs in 1980, 1987, 1992, and 1995 have become an organic part of Swedish literature. None of her books have been translated into English, but individual poems are included in several anthologies.

There is no doubt that Vizma Belševica will be remembered as the foremost Latvian poet of her time, and some critics rank her among the finest poets in the world. At the conference at the University of Stockholm in September 1995 Voznesensky, probably the leading Russian poet of the second half of the twentieth century, called Belševica "the greatest of us all, a genius," and the "Latvian Yeats." The comparison with the Irish poet William Butler Yeats is apt: Belševica and Yeats are characterized by their respect for craftsmanship and for the high calling of literature; both have produced consciously "literary" poetry, as well as poetry that is immersed in and emerges from their personal lives and the political strivings of their homelands; the poems of both writers are hermetic, and their highly condensed, wavering rhythms create an incantatory tone of mystery; and in both there is a strong sense of spiritual unity with the nation.

The Irish poet, essayist, and translator Desmond Egan argued at the Stockholm conference that Belševica "could definitely be Irish" because of her "poetic sense of musicality, terseness, sly humor, and her idea of a strong woman." In nominating Belševica for the Neustadt Prize, Egan said:

> I have only met and heard Belševica on a few occasions . . . her work has proved more than enough to convince me that we have here one of the great poets. . . . Her range is impressive: political poems that transcend mere party politics and become universal in their quest for truth and dignity and for man's duty toward the world and toward his fellow men. In this she is a poet for our time. But Belševica is much more than the voice of conscience, crying in a political wilderness; she is a genius, with the intensity and piercing insight of a great artist. Her love poems are among the finest I have read anywhere; her feeling for nature is, to someone coming from a tradition where this is centrally important, astonishing. She has written long poems and short lyrics; can range from passionate to satirical; from the introspective and personal to the public—so that at times she can speak with authority as the very spirit of her beloved country. Audiences are spellbound by her, and in Latvia she is a legendary figure now, the recipient of every honor which her country can bestow. . . . I know of no finer poet of and for our time.

Interviews:

Jaunākās Grāmatas, 4 (1965): 20;

"Organiskums: Uz literatūras kritiķa Osvalda Kravaļa jautājumiem atbild dzejniece Vizma Belševica," *Karogs,* 4 (1982): 134–142;

Rolfs Ekmanis, "Intervijas: Ar Vizmu Belševicu," in *Latvija Šodien 1989–1990,* edited by Ekmanis (Rockville, Md: PBLA, 1990), pp. 51–71.

References:

Reinis Ādmīdiņš, "Pārsāpētas dzejas dzimšana un atdzimšana," *Karogs,* 5 (1981): 138–141;

Rolfs Ekmanis, "Die kulturellen Probleme in Lettland Ende der sechziger Jahre," in *Acta Baltica,* edited by Andrivs Namsons, volume 9 (Königstein im Taunus: Institutum Balticum, 1970), pp. 229–314;

Ekmanis, "Die Literatur in Lettland in den 60er und 70er Jahren," in *Acta Baltica,* edited by Namsons, volume 18 (Königstein im Taunus: Institutum Balticum, 1979), pp. 208–211;

Ekmanis, "Latvian Literature," in *Discordant Voices: The Non-Russian Soviet Literatures, 1953–1973,* edited by George S. N. Luckyj (Oakville, Ont.: Mosaic Press, 1975), pp. 47–88;

Ekmanis, *Latvian Literature under the Soviets: 1940–1975* (Belmont, Mass.: Nordland, 1978), pp. 254, 298, 303–304, 309, 325–329, 337;

Ekmanis, "Some Notes on Vizma Belševica," *World Literature Today,* 2 (1998): 287–296;

Ekmanis, as Māris Rauda, "Vizma, Belševica: Madarās," *Brīvība,* 6/7 (1978): 12–13;

Viktors Hausmanis, ed., *Mūsdienu latviešu padomju literatūra* (Riga: Zinātne, 1985), pp. 199–209;

Anda Kubuliņa, "Reālisms un Vizma Belševica," *Kritikas gadagrāmata,* 17 (1990): 165–181;

Kubuliņa, *Vizma Belševica* (Riga: Preses nams, 1997);

Kubuliņa, "Vizmas Belševicas iesākumā apgūtais," *Kritikas gadagrāmata,* 18 (1991): 206–228;

Valda Melngaile, "The Sense of History in Recent Soviet Latvian Poetry," *Journal of Baltic Studies,* 2/3 (1975): 130–140;

Melngaile, "Variations on the Theme of Truth: Two Contemporary Latvian Poets," *Books Abroad,* 2 (1971): 242–247;

Valters Nollendorfs, "Riga in the Lyric Poetry of the Postwar Latvian Generation," *Journal of Baltic Studies,* 2 (1974): 100–111;

Gunars Saliņš, "On Allegory: Vizma Belševica's Poem 'The Notations of Henricus de Lettis in the Margins of the *Livonian Chronicle,*'" *Lituanus,* 1 (1970): 22–32;

Juris Silenieks, introduction to *Contemporary Latvian Poetry,* edited by Inara Cedriņš (Iowa City: University of Iowa Press, 1984), pp. 89–102;

Vaira Vīķis-Freibergs, "Echoes of the Dainas and the Search for Identity in Contemporary Latvian Poetry," *Journal of Baltic Studies,* 1 (1975): 17–29.

Miron Białoszewski

(30 July 1922 – 17 June 1983)

Andrzej Busza
University of British Columbia

and

Bogdan Czaykowski
University of British Columbia

BOOKS: *Obroty rzeczy* (Warsaw: Państwowy Instytut Wydawniczy, 1956);

Rachunek zachciankowy (Warsaw: Państwowy Instytut Wydawniczy, 1959);

Mylne wzruszenia (Warsaw: Państwowy Instytut Wydawniczy, 1961);

Było i było (Warsaw: Państwowy Instytut Wydawniczy, 1965);

Pamiętnik z Powstania Warszawskiego (Warsaw: Państwowy Instytut Wydawniczy, 1970); translated and edited by Madeline G. Levine as *A Memoir of the Warsaw Uprising* (Ann Arbor, Mich.: Ardis, 1977);

Teatr Osobny, 1955–1963 (Warsaw: Państwowy Instytut Wydawniczy, 1971);

Donosy rzeczywistości (Warsaw: Państwowy Instytut Wydawniczy, 1973);

Szumy, zlepy, ciągi (Warsaw: Państwowy Instytut Wydawniczy, 1976);

Wiersze (Warsaw: Państwowy Instytut Wydawniczy, 1976);

Zawał (Warsaw: Państwowy Instytut Wydawniczy, 1977);

Odczepić się (Warsaw: Państwowy Instytut Wydawniczy, 1978);

Rozkurz (Warsaw: Państwowy Instytut Wydawniczy, 1980);

Wiersze wybrane i dobrane (Warsaw: Czytelnik, 1980);

Trzydzieści lat wierszy (Warsaw: Państwowy Instytut Wydawniczy, 1982);

Stara proza. Nowe wiersze (Warsaw: Czytelnik, 1984);

Oho (Warsaw: Państwowy Instytut Wydawniczy, 1985);

Obmapywanie Europy, czyli dziennik okrętowy. AAAmeryka. Ostatnie wiersze (Warsaw: Państwowy Instytut Wydawniczy, 1988);

Konstancin (Warsaw: Państwowy Instytut Wydawniczy, 1991).

Collections: *Poezje wybrane* (Warsaw: Ludowa Spółdzielnia Wydawnicza, 1976);

Przepowiadanie sobie: Wybór próz (Warsaw: Państwowy Instytut Wydawniczy, 1981);

Utwory zebrane, 8 volumes (Warsaw: Państwowy Instytut Wydawniczy, 1987–1998);

Moja świadomośćtańczy, edited by Zbigniew Jerzyna (Warsaw: Młodzieżowa Agencja Wydawnicza, 1989).

Editions in English: "And even, even if they take away the stove," "A ballad of going down to the store," "Self-portrait as felt," "Garwolin—a town for ever," and "My Jacobean fatigues," translated by Czesław Miłosz, *Encounter*, 2 (1958): 31–33;

"War Myths" and "Revolutions of Things," translated by Adam Czerniawski, *Times Literary Supplement*, 3 September 1964, p. 822;

"And Even, Even If They Take Away the Stove," "A Ballad of Going Down to the Store," "Garwolin—A Town for Ever," "Self-Portrait as Felt," "My Jacobean Fatigues: My Jacobs of Tiredness," translated by Miłosz, in *Postwar Polish Poetry: An Anthology*, edited by Miłosz (Garden City, N.Y.: Doubleday, 1965), pp. 82–86;

"War Myths" and "How Easy to Lose Faith," translated by Czerniawski; "Secret Freedom," "Suddenly," "Granted, I Could Have Misheard," and "My Jacobs of Exhaustion," translated by Jan Darowski, in *Polish Writing Today*, edited by Celina Wieniewska (Harmondsworth, U.K.: Penguin, 1967), pp. 78–82;

"Secret Freedom," translated by Darowski, in *The Penguin Book of Socialist Verse*, edited by Alan

Miron Białoszewski (from the frontispiece for A Memoir of the Warsaw Uprising, *1977)*

Bold (Harmondsworth, U.K.: Penguin, 1970), p. 403;

The Revolution of Things: Selected Poems of Miron Białoszewski, translated and edited by Andrzej Busza and Bogdan Czaykowski (Washington, D.C.: Charioteer, 1974);

"Of the Revolution of Things," "'Oh! Oh! Should They Take Away My Stove . . .': My Inexhaustible Ode to Joy," "A Ballad of Going Down to the Store," "Green: Hence It Is," "Night Forging of Rails on St. John's of Dukla," "After My Patron Saint," and "How the Question Melted in Me," translated by Busza and Czaykowski, in *Modern Poetry in Translation: Polish Issue,* edited by Czaykowski, 23–24 (1975): 21–22;

"A Fin-de-Siècle Myth" and "I Don't Know How to Write," translated by Busza and Czaykowski, *Durak: An International Magazine of Poetry,* 2 (1979): 12–13;

"Oh! Oh! Should They Take Away My Stove" and "To —," translated by Busza and Czaykowski, in *Introduction to Modern Polish Literature: An Anthology of Fiction and Poetry,* edited by Adam Gillon, Ludwik Krzyżanowski, and Krystyna Olscher (New York: Twayne, 1982), pp. 489–490;

"Autobiography," translated by Busza and Czaykowski, in *Gathering Time: Five Modern Polish Elegies,* edited by Busza and Czaykowski (Mission, British Columbia: Barbarian Press, 1983), pp. 51–63;

"Aniela in the Town of Folino," translated by Stanisław Barańczak and Clare Cavanagh, *Translation: The Journal of Literary Translation,* 21 (Spring 1989): 38–39;

"Study of a Key," translated by Daniel Weissbort and Grzegorz Musiał, *Poetry East,* 29 (1990): 23.

SELECTED PERIODICAL PUBLICATIONS–UNCOLLECTED: "Rozalie: poemat sceniczny (teatr lalki)," *Teksty Drugie,* 1–2 (1998): 259–268;

"Rozalie: 2–5," *Teksty Drugie,* 4 (1998): 221–231;

"Rozalie: 6–12," *Teksty Drugie,* 1–2 (1999): 273–282.

Miron Białoszewski is a singular phenomenon not only in the context of postwar Polish poetry but also of Western poetry in general. After the consolidation of the communist regime, the Party sought to extend control over all aspects of cultural activity, at the levels of both high and popular culture. In the case of literature this control meant the imposition in 1949 of socialist realism, which formally and stylistically derived its models from neoclassicist and nineteenth-century realist poetics, while ideologically it entailed following the Party line. After Joseph Stalin's death, and especially after the mid 1950s, the continuing though somewhat less rigid control over cultural life produced a threefold division among the writers: those who dutifully toed the Party line and acted as its cultural functionaries; those who practiced accommodation but at the same time tried, by employing various stratagems, including Aesopian language, to achieve a measure of authentic expression; and a third group, the so-called dissidents, increasingly prevalent in the seventies, who published abroad and in underground publications. Białoszewski can be identified with none of these groups. In more senses than one, he was a writer apart.

Białoszewski's first volume of poetry, *Obroty rzeczy* (Revolution of Things) appeared in 1956 in Warsaw and created a sensation. This highly successful first volume was followed by several other collections of poetry, as well as a volume of reminiscences of the Warsaw Uprising of 1944 and other narrative prose, mainly autobiographical in character, and travelogues. By the time of his death in 1983, Białoszewski had published more than a dozen books and had established a reputation as one of the most idiosyncratic Polish poets of the second half of the twentieth century; he even became a minor cult figure among some poets in the United States after the appearance in 1974 of *The Revolution of Things: Selected Poems of Miron Białoszewski.*

Białoszewski was born on 30 July 1922 in Warsaw. He came from a lower-middle-class background: his father, Zenon Białoszewski (apparently a womanizer), worked for the post office; his mother, Kazimiera (née Perska), was a seamstress for a time after World War II. He spent the years of German rule during World War II in and around Warsaw, completed his secondary education clandestinely after the Germans closed down Polish schools and universities, and attended underground courses in Polish literature. One of the houses in which he lived with his parents overlooked the Jewish ghetto, and he witnessed its destruction. He also lived through the Warsaw Uprising, sharing the plight of the civilian population and experiencing the death of his city, both as a physical entity (Adolf Hitler had ordered the complete demolition of Warsaw as retribution for the uprising) and as an historically shaped community (its entire population was forcibly expelled by the Germans). Białoszewski and his father were deported to Opole, where they had to work for the Germans, but after a month they managed to escape to Częstochowa, where they engaged in petty trading. After a brief stay in Kraków at the end of the war, they returned to Warsaw.

After the war Białoszewski worked for a year as a letter-sorter and later became a reporter for two Warsaw newspapers. One of his contributions was a photograph of himself on top of the twisted girders of the gutted Prudential high-rise. He says that he cannot remember when he began writing poetry, but at one stage he destroyed his early efforts, dissatisfied with their lack of distinctiveness and connection to the actual living conditions of postwar Warsaw. Białoszewski experienced these conditions firsthand; at one point he shared a single room with three other lodgers, one of whom continuously boiled cabbage on the only stove. During this time Białoszewski developed his eccentric mode of life, sleeping in the daytime and writing and wandering the city streets at night.

Warsaw became not only his city but also, for a time, almost his world. He also became fond of southeastern Poland, of its old towns, quaint churches, icons and polychromes, and folk art, which inspired many of his ballads. He was aided in his exploration of the provincial, rural life and history by a native of the region, painter Leszek Soliński, who later shared Białoszewski's apartment in Warsaw for many years.

Białoszewski managed to publish a few poems before the canons of socialist realism became officially binding. Later, unwilling to adapt his manner and vision to the official requirements, he lived in abject poverty, sporadically earning a little money by contributing to *Świerszczyk* (The Little Grasshopper), a publication for children, and *Świat Młodych* (The World of Youth), a magazine for Scouts. During those difficult years he formed several close friendships that were artistically as well as personally important; of particular significance to his early poetry was a group of painters who were especially interested in Cubist and Surrealist art. When the political stranglehold on culture relaxed somewhat, Białoszewski became involved in the creation of a highly unusual theater, known as the Theatre on Tarczyńska Street. The Theatre grew out of the common interests of a group of bohemian artists, including Swen Czachorowski, a poet; Lech Emfazy Stefański, an admirer of Stanisław Ignacy Witkiewicz's drama; Stanisław Prószyński, a musician; Bogusław Choiński, a playwright; and Białoszewski. The first performance took place in the spring of 1955 and immediately generated a great deal of interest. Unlike all other theatrical activity at the time, which was run by the state, it was a private venture, which made it attractive.

In contrast to the official theater, which had to carry an ideological message and conform to the conventions of narrowly conceived realism, the Theatre on Tarczyńska Street was experimental with a vengeance. The performances took place in a single-room apartment on the fourth floor that could accommodate a maximum of 120 people, although

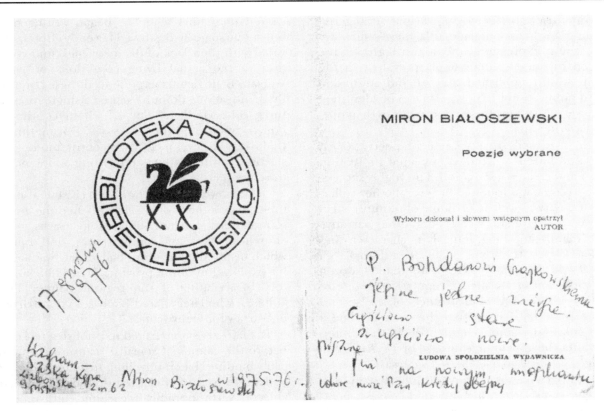

Inside of front cover and title page of copy of a 1976 edition of Białoszewski's selected poems, inscribed by the author. The inscription reads:
"For Bohdan [sic] Czaykowski some more poems. Partly old and partly new, written in 1975 and 76 in my new apartment which perhaps
you may be able to see one day. 17 December 1976. Warsaw Saska Kępa, Lizbońska 2 m 62 9 floor" (Collection of Bogdan Czaykowski).

some had to stand on the stairs. Taking their cue from Jean Cocteau's ideas on modern theater, the members of the troupe were simultaneously actors, scriptwriters, designers, and directors. The sets and props were of the most rudimentary character and served more than one purpose, while the costumes were both simple and highly inventive. During the 1956 season some of the plays that were staged included "The Birth of Aphrodite" by Stefański, "The Grey Mass" and "The Crusades" by Białoszewski, and "The Wall" by Choiński. In Białoszewski's "The Crusades" one actor played the roles of Miss Hybrid, Holy Icon, Nun Templar, Arab Virgin, and Knight Simeon, while Białoszewski played Knight Baldwin. The authorities, who at the time found themselves compelled to make concessions in cultural policy, found the Theatre convenient as a sort of showpiece of their liberalism (one of the performances was allegedly attended by Jean-Paul Sartre and Simone de Beauvoir). Indeed, on one occasion the Theatre received a fairly substantial grant of twenty thousand *złotys* from the Minister of Culture and Art.

The last performances took place in 1958 without Białoszewski's participation; in the meantime he had moved to another apartment in Warsaw, and together with Ludwik Hering (a painter, theoretician of art, and Białoszewski's mentor) and Ludmiła Murawska (a painter and actress) he established Teatr Osobny (Theater Apart), which continued to hold performances until 1963. There has been some controversy about both the precise role of Białoszewski in the Tarczyńska Street venture and the authorship of some of the texts that were included in his publications. Apparently Białoszewski did not initially acknowledge adequately the contributions of his collaborators.

With the exception of his "Kabaret Kici-Koci" (A Kitty-Catty Cabaret), written in the last few years before his death, Białoszewski never returned to the dramatic form after his early experiments with it. The fourteen short plays (some of them no more than a few pages long) collected in the volume *Teatr Osobny, 1955–1963* (1971) can be best described, with one or two exceptions, as performative texts. They were all written in a specific atmosphere of collaborative theatrical experiment, and once that experiment ended, Białoszewski probably had little incentive to write further plays, which he would have had to adapt to the requirements of a more conventional form of theater.

The plays, while embodying basically the same theatrical concept, are quite disparate in character. "Wiwisekcje" (Vivisections) is, strictly speaking, a puppet show, except that instead of puppets, the "actors" are Białoszewski's ten fingers. They discuss abstruse philosophical questions, such as whether existence really exists, in a hieratic manner full of decorum and stylized phrases until the reality of an ordinary comb appearing over them causes them to panic. When the comb is replaced by a salt-cellar, the mood of the fingers becomes initially erotic and then changes into an abortive pursuit of rightness and justice. In the end their discourse is reduced to gibberish, and the fingers exit to the tune of a tango, repeating the absurd: "Gut is fun a haser a hor!" (It's good to pluck a hair off a pig).

"Pieśni na krzesło i głos" (Songs for a Chair and a Voice) is a poetic cabaret, the effectiveness of which depended on the unusual combination of Białoszewski's recitation and Murawska's acting style. In *Teatr Osobny, 1955–1963* Białoszewski described the performance:

> I with a chair draped over my neck to tap the rhythm for myself and Ludmiła as the songs were intoned. And she—Ludmiła—descending and ascending, in a stiff black-and-white costume, with her head as if on a platter, in the words of critics: beautiful, queen-like, hieratic, somnambulistically-ironic.

"Imiesłów" (Participle) is subtitled "gramat," Białoszewski's punning neologism, indicating that the drama in the piece is grammatical in character. "Pani Koch" (Mrs. Koch) is a cruelly effective satire on hospital bureaucracy, done with the utmost economy of means. Perhaps the most accomplished of the plays is "Osmędeusze" (Asmodeans), written with Hering and subtitled "A street-sign oratorio: The greatest scenic epic piece of the closed epoch of suburbia . . . presenting eighteen characters and two choruses." It blends popular rhythms, street language, balladlike "arias," contrived nursery rhymes, and Gothic atmosphere into a lively spectacle of linguistic ingenuity and playful theatricality.

What distinguishes Białoszewski's writing is its oral character. Depending on the region, by the end of the medieval period oral literature in Western and Central Europe had lost its vitality and was supplanted by increasingly conventionalized forms of written discourse. Attempts to return to the oral tradition, especially evident in the Romantic and Neo-Romantic periods, while drawing on folk and dialectal forms, did not revive it. The introduction of elements of spoken language was selective and highly self-conscious, while the use of dialect as a rule amounted to stylization. In either case, the boundary between the literary and spoken languages remained. Białoszewski makes the distinction irrelevant by actually writing the spoken idiom or imitating (and sometimes parodying) its characteristics. In his introduction to the collection *Poezje wybrane* (Selected Poems, 1976) he said, "I try to make the written a transcript of the spoken. So that the written does not swallow up actual speech." After all, he remarked, "It all began with speaking and not with writing."

Many of his texts are close, if not verbatim, reproductions of actual speech: conversations, musings, narrations, descriptions, bits of street wisdom, and apartment-bloc humor, the expressiveness of which derives not only from a well-turned phrase but also from the unintended felicities of colloquial ambiguity and defective grammar. It became common knowledge among Białoszewski's acquaintances that anything one said in his presence might be recorded in his notebook or on slips of paper (he sometimes withdrew to the restroom to write down what he had just heard) and find its way into print. Moreover, Białoszewski's own speech, despite his wide reading of canonical writers, remained consistently demotic and highly individual.

It is a mistake, however, to regard Białoszewski as in any sense a primitive. His treatment of colloquial speech reveals not only a deep understanding of the workings of language, directly or indirectly informed by developments in modern linguistics and linguistic philosophy, but also a surprisingly erudite (though deliberately camouflaged) knowledge of literary traditions and conventions. Moreover, Białoszewski's interests included classical as well as non-European music (he was an avid collector of records), post-impressionist painting, avant-garde theater, and cultural anthropology. He was fascinated by church rituals, icons, folk carvings of saints, architectural styles, fairs and bazaars, and all kinds of objects, both ordinary and quaint. The highly idiosyncratic nature of his haphazard erudition and the range of his associations is well illustrated in his "A Disquisition on Bazaar Rams" from *Obroty rzeczy*:

Oh bizzarerie of left-bank Warsaw
you have Assyrian horns

and one leg
        varnished
               red.
That's the bazaar! Bazaar! Bazaar!
That's the ram! Ramram!
And this — its profile —
       — a bit left-handed —
and that's the beauty of its fleece —
oh! the two profiles of Nefertiti
in gold-specked tete-a-tete. . . .
And over there: rams
In Mechlin lace,
Byzantine rams,
Rams in Aurignac aureoles . . .
. . . .
And all this out of suburban
               caves
an endless folk Menton,
all this
       unbroken dilly-dilly
       diluvium
          of the periphery.

The poem is also a good illustration of the essential playfulness of Białoszewski's writings. Some of his poems and miniplays are, in essence, language games: linguistic structure itself is disrupted; the principle of the segmentation of the flow of speech into words is transgressed, and some passages are written in morphemes; endings float on their own or cross paradigm boundaries; and curious combinations of letters confront each other as in mathematical symbolism. In short, language in all its aspects becomes an object of analytical or playful deconstruction.

At times this playing with language acquires the character of quasi-philosophical argument which is simultaneously parodistic and oddly serious, as in "Wywód jestem'u" (The Syllogization of I-am-ness) from *Mylne wzruszenia* (Misleading Emotions, 1961):

    well I am
    and I am stupid
    so what am I to do
    what indeed
     except to know
     but what do I know
     what I am
    I know I am
    as I am
    maybe not so stupid
    but perhaps only because I know
    that everyone means most to himself
    for even if you don't accept yourself
     you still are what you are

It has been suggested that this poem can be construed as a grotesque microgloss on Sartre's *L'Etre et le néant* (1943; translated as *Being and Nothingness*, 1956).

Białoszewski's use of genres and forms of discourse is as innovative as his approach to language. His work incorporates a great variety of genres, literary as well as oral (what Mikhail Bakhtin calls genres of utterance). In fact, the distinction between the literary and the oral becomes blurred, and such well established forms as the ode, ballad, or epigram, while retaining their essential characteristics, are given distinctly oral features and moved to a lower stylistic register. At the same time he takes actual speech situations and, by isolating them as separate "poems," reveals their form.

Białoszewski emerged as a mature and accomplished poet with *Obroty rzeczy*, which arguably remains his best, while being the least representative of the oral style that prevails in the rest of his work. All the poems in the volume have a formal finish, which he deliberately eschews later; and the volume as a whole is carefully composed. The selection of the poems as well as their arrangement was at least to some degree the work of prominent critic Artur Sandauer, who can be credited with recognizing the singularity of Białoszewski's writing, while at the same time giving it a somewhat one-sided interpretation.

In essence, the volume includes three categories of poems: ballads, quasi-odes, and conceptual lyrics. Białoszewski's ballads are sui generis; although they do not tell a story in the traditional way, they are still narratives of sorts. At one level they present several mininarratives embodied in the iconology of sacred and secular art objects, both high and popular, such as tapestries, statues, various interiors, townscapes, carousels, and bazaars; on another level, these elements are recombined into personal visionary and lyrical narrations, enacting the aesthetic and emotional experience of the poet. In effect, the earlier ballads are highly accomplished stylizations.

His quasi-odes are celebrations of ordinary objects. Białoszewski's "return to things," although it is not without parallels in modern poetry, has interesting features of its own. It is radically anti-ideological; Białoszewski responds to the pressure of ideological abstraction by fabricating a mythology of things. In a deeper sense, Białoszewski's "return to things" also has ethical and even religious dimensions. The nonhuman world can serve as a refuge from inhumanity, and being alone with things has its consolations: solitude, memories, and the fact that one can be a poet. Like St. Francis of Assisi, who talked to animals, Białoszewski talks to things, as in "O mojej pustelni z nawoływaniem" (Of My Hermitage with Calling) from *Obroty rzeczy:*

> Wall, I am not worthy
> that you should fill me with constant wonder,
> and you too, fork . . .
> and you, dusts . . . .

The mere existence of ordinary things is cause for celebration, particularly to someone who has lived in a city destroyed by war. At the same time, regressing to the level of things gives one self-sufficiency, which is a prerequisite of independence and integrity. Moreover, in the contemporary literary context his odes had an ironic edge, since publishable poets were writing odes to such grandiose abstractions as revolution, progress, and the Five-Year Plan in regular meters and elevated diction.

Just as his ballads and his "return to things" manifest Białoszewski's immersion in the plastic arts, so his conceptual lyrics reveal a mind given to philosophy. An example of this mode is "Self-portrait as Felt" from *Obroty rzeczy:*

> They look at me,
> So presumably I have a face.
>
> Of all familiar faces
> I least remember my own.
> Often my hands live apart from me.
> Should I then count them as mine?
>
> Where are my limits?
>
> I am overgrown
> with movement or semi-life.
>
> But full or not
> what crawls in me
> is still existence.
> I carry around
> my own sort of place.
>
> When I lose it,
> it will mean I am no more.
>
> I am no more,
> therefore I do not doubt.

His next three volumes, *Rachunek zachciankowy* (Calculus of Whims, 1959), *Mylne wzruszenia,* and *Było i było* (There Was and Was, 1965), were less favorably received by the critics than *Obroty rzeczy.* Julian Przyboś, the communist archpriest of the Polish poetic avant-garde, who had initially responded enthusiastically to Białoszewski's poetry, called *Było i*

Cover for Białoszewski's collection of short autobiographical prose pieces, published in 1976

było "trash" and said that "if these clumsy sketches had been written not by Białoszewski but someone less well known, hardly anyone would disagree that they are worthless as literature." However, Przyboś and other critics failed to realize that by extending his range to include human situations Białoszewski had become a poet of social themes, in his own peculiar and often humorous way. His early "anthropological" interests had become "behavioral." Moreover, these critics did not recognize the degree of sophistication and reflexivity that went into Białoszewski's seeming abandonment of style and form for the sake of rendering actual situational speech behavior. This mode of writing characterizes almost the entire remaining output of Białoszewski's poetic work after *Było i było,* which includes two substantial volumes, *Rozkurz* (Flour Dust, 1980) and the posthumously published *Oho* (1985).

Białoszewski manages to achieve variety despite the inherent inchoateness of most oral discourse. He does not merely reproduce the stream of speech; he selects, segments, juxtaposes, and distills or foregrounds inner structures. His "poems" range from two-line gnomic or dialogic snippets to stream-of-consciousness renditions of human encounters, anecdotes, arguments, philosophical reflections, lyrical outbursts, and micro-epics. The variety he achieves is partly because of the traces of traditional forms and genres of utterance, in addition to the mixture of the terseness and aptness of oral expression as well as its wordiness, lameness, and sloppiness. Another factor is the wide range of diction and register that characterizes the dynamism of spoken language. Finally, the variety derives from the heterogeneity of his subject matter; his poems deal with anything and everything, from a blocked toilet to martial law and metaphysical questions.

This kind of poetry is not easily distinguishable from prose. What distinguishes it most obviously is length: Białoszewski's poems, with one or two exceptions, are relatively short; the prose pieces include much larger texts in a primarily narrative mode and with a loose structure frequently consisting of serially arranged anecdotal material. His prose masterpiece is *Pamiętnik z Powstania Warszawskiego* (1970; translated as *A Memoir of the Warsaw Uprising,* 1977). It offers a distinctive perspective on human behavior in circumstances of extreme horror; moreover, it is primarily an account not of military action and fighting but of the impact of war on civilians.

Białoszewski characterizes the nature of the work thus:

> All this is after all like a hallucination. Which is not a very original way of putting it. But it's the only way I can put it. It matches what I felt then. But you didn't even have to be a poet to see treble. If I write very little about my impressions. And everything in ordinary language, as if things were as normal. Or if I hardly get into myself, that is as if I was only on the outside. That is because it can't be done any other way. After all, that's the way you felt. And, in general, it's the only way, not something contrived, but the natural way. To convey all of this. For twenty years I couldn't write about it. Although I wanted to so much. And talked a lot. About the uprising. To so many people. All sorts of people. So many times. And all along I kept thinking that I must describe the uprising in writing, somehow or other *write* about it. And I didn't even know that those twenty years of talking (I have been talking about it for twenty years, because it is the most important experience of my life—and it is closed), that precisely that talking, is the only proper way to describe the uprising.

Białoszewski's words convey clearly the extent to which his memoir differs from most, if not all, writing of this kind. Its power is in its authenticity. There is no attempt to make literature out of the experience; while a formal analysis of the work would identify a variety of what could be called devices, they are never foregrounded, and their hallmark is Białoszewski's stubborn striving for fidelity to the way things really happened. The only available English translation, however, fails to provide an adequate equivalent to Białoszewski's oral style.

Several years later Białoszewski wrote *Zawał* (1977, Heart Attack), an account of a purely individual trauma: a heart attack that he had in the street. He was hospitalized and then sent to a sanatorium for a considerable amount of time before returning home. The book is a highly detailed, even overparticular and almost detached narrative that concentrates not so much on the author's subjective experience as on everything that happened to him and around him. Pain, anxiety, and the fear of death are not ignored, but receive no more attention than the reactions of passersby, medical procedures, the building and the working of the hospital, behavior and conversations of personnel and fellow patients, physiological mishaps, and visitors. Overall, *Zawał* is a documentary of an extreme experience rendered ordinary, with considerable insight into the leveling effect of the human predicament and frailty.

Of greater interest, if only because of the sheer diversity of the thematic material, are two other prose works, *Donosy rzeczywistości* (Reports of Reality, 1973) and *Szumy, zlepy, ciągi* (Hums, Lumps, Strings, 1976). Both volumes are miscellanies, but again of a special kind. The first, at least superficially, has the character of a journal; the various segments are dated, often vaguely, and cover the period from 1963 to 1973. At the center is the apartment Białoszewski shared with his partner, Soliński, that served as the meeting place for their circles of friends and acquaintances. Admittance to the apartment was strictly controlled by means of an elaborate system of knocks on the door (one signal was the opening beats of Ludwig van Beethoven's Fifth Symphony). Some of the stories are accounts of visits: on one occasion Białoszewski, who often entertained visitors while lying in bed (where he also ate, read, wrote, and meditated), was visited by an American beatnik; on another, by a group of Polish hippies; and once by a pair of Polish Jehovah's Witnesses with whom Białoszewski and Soliński engaged in a quasi-theological discussion. There are aphoristic snippets, which at times are quite inane, reminiscences, narrations of journeys, stories of marital and extramarital relations among Białoszewski's circle of friends and acquaintances, conversations, and bizarre and humorous anecdotes, the point of which is not always clear. Some of the pieces could have become short stories had the author wanted to reshape the material; however, Białoszewski did not do so because he was primarily interested in how reality came to him through language rather than in the events, people, and issues themselves.

Szumy, zlepy, ciągi, which also has an autobiographical character and consists of a series of short texts, is a more reader-friendly book. There is less insistence on unmediated spoken language; the style and composition of the segments is more conventional; the anecdotes are better developed and of greater intrinsic interest; and the humor is subtler, depending less on the situations themselves than on their treatment. There is also more "poetry" in the book, and what "hums" in it is not just the external world and its resonance but the inner life of the poet. Among the more memorable pieces is an account of the author's visit to a desolate old Jewish cemetery in Warsaw ("Kirkut") with Hering, and several dream sequences. Whereas the earlier work has a kaleidoscopic character, in this volume one can discern certain thematic threads or "strings." These include religion, art, aging, death, the opposition of nature and culture, and the ironies of human relations.

Białoszewski did not travel much beyond Warsaw and the surrounding region until almost the end of his life. His longest trips were to southern Poland and, in 1959, to Paris (which he described briefly in *Szumy, zlepy, ciągi*); however, in the last years of his life he traveled to Egypt, took a cruise around Europe on the Polish ship *Stefan Batory,* and briefly toured several port cities, including London, Valencia, Athens, and Istanbul. In 1982 he flew to New York to receive the Jurzykowski Prize awarded to him that year. These journeys are reflected in several poems and in prose travelogues, *Obmapywanie Europy, czyli dziennik okrętowy* (Mapping out Europe, or a Ship Journal) and *AAAmeryka* (AAAmerica), both published in a single volume in 1988 together with many of his last poems (some of them on American themes).

The travelogues are typical mature Białoszewski: they are a mixture of meticulous observations, reportage of happenings and behavior, personal reflections, philosophizing, and humorous realism. In the descriptions of both journeys the author is interested less in high culture and the exotic than in identifying the underlying sameness of the human condition irrespective of geographical location. The descriptions of New York, which reminds Białoszewski of a medieval city, and of New Yorkers, are espe-

Cover for Białoszewski's 1977 account
of a heart attack he suffered

cially memorable as the author brings down to earth the East European myth of America. One peculiarity of Białoszewski's traveling interests, already evident in his description of a brief trip to Copenhagen, is his fascination with sexual subjects. In the American piece porn shows and sex shops constitute a major motif of Białoszewski's discovery of the great city.

Since Białoszewski's death, interest in his work has increased considerably. To some he is an uncompromising individualist and secular saint, even a mystic of sorts; others find in him a model of the withdrawn, personal, contemplative life. He has also attracted a great deal of critical attention, especially on the part of more theoretically oriented critics associated with the Instytut Badań Literackich (Institute of Literary Research) in Warsaw, partly as a result of close personal links that developed in the last years of Białoszewski's life between him and some scholars of that milieu—particularly with Maria Janion, Maria Żmigrodzka, and Małgorzata Baranowska, the three Eumenides of Białoszewski's "Listy do Eumenid" (Letters to Eumenides, 1991)—but more importantly because of the nature of his work, which is perceived as one of the most original and important experiments of twentieth-century Polish literature. The critical examinations of his life and work have already brought up aspects that the more ideological stance of pre-1989 critical reception failed to reveal; but there is still much that remains to be explored.

Letters:
"Listy do Eumenid," *Teksty Drugie,* 6 (1991): 83–136.

Interviews:
"Szacunek dla każdego drobiazgu. Z Mironem Białoszewskim rozmawia Z. Taranienko," *Argumenty,* 36 (1971);

"Warszawa była mi stale pod ręką. Rozmowa Józefa Barana z Mironem Białoszewskim," *Wieści,* 42 (1978): 5;

Anna Trznadel-Szczepanek, "To w czym się jest—rozmowa z Mironem Białoszewskim," *Twórczość* 9 (1983): 29–38.

Biographies:
Hanna Kirchner, ed., *Wspomnienia o poecie* (Warsaw: Tenten, 1996);

Leszek Soliński, "Karuzela z Rozaliami," *Teksty Drugie,* 1–2 (1998): 269–275;

Soliński, "Kwadrat mowy o Mironie," *Teksty Drugie,* 1–2 (1999): 267–272.

References:
Stanisław Barańczak, *Język poetycki Mirona Białoszewskiego* (Wrocław: Ossolineum, 1974);

Zbigniew Bauer, "Powrót czy ucieczka (W stronę prozy)," *Poezja,* 2 (1976): 46–57;

Stanisław Burkot, *Miron Białoszewski* (Warsaw: Wydawnictwa Szkolne i Pedagogiczne, 1992);

Bogdan Czaykowski, "Postwar Polish Poets," in *The Tradition of Polish Ideals,* edited by Władysław J. Stankiewicz (London: Orbis Books, 1981), pp. 226–284;

Jan Darowski, "'Rachunek zachciankowy': Wstępna rata," *Kontynenty,* 27–28 (1961): 23–26;

Michał Głowiński, "Małe narracje Mirona Białoszewskiego," *Teksty,* 6 (1972): 9–28;

Głowiński and Zdzisław Łapiński, eds., *Pisanie Białoszewskiego: Szkice* (Warsaw: Instytut Badań Literackich, 1993);

Maria Janion, "Polska proza cywilna," *Teksty,* 2 (1975): 13–38;

Hanna Konicka, "Kulturowy sens gatunkowych decyzji Mirona Białoszewskiego," *Teksty Drugie,* 1–2 (1997): 63–80;

Jacek Kopciński, *Gramatyka i mistyka: Wprowadzenie w teatralną osobność Mirona Białoszewskiego* (Warsaw: Instytut Badań Literackich, 1997);

Jerzy Kwiatkowski, "Abulia i liturgia," in his *Klucze do wyobraźni* (Warsaw, 1964), pp. 127–173;

Jacek Łukasiewicz, "Apokalipsa i iluzjoniści," in his *Szmaciarze i bohaterowie* (Kraków: Społeczny Instytut Wydawniczy "Znak," 1963), pp. 28–52;

Łukasiewicz, "Białoszewski," in his *Rytm, czyli powinność* (Wrocław: Towarzystwo Przyjaciół Polonistyki Wrocławskiej, 1993), pp. 88–97;

Poezja, special Białoszewski Issue, 2 (1976);

Julian Przyboś, "Nowy poeta," in his *Linia i gwar: Szkice,* (Kraków: Wydawnictwo Literackie, 1959), volume 2, pp. 171–178;

Krzysztof Rutkowski, *Przeciw literaturze. Esej o "poezji czynnej" Mirona Białoszewskiego i Edwarda Stachury* (Bydgoszcz: Pomorze, 1987);

Artur Sandauer, *Białoszewski,* translated by Adam Czerniawski (Warsaw: Authors Agency/Czytelnik, 1979);

Dorota Siwicka and Marta Zielińska, "Jak fotografowałyśmy 'Kirkut' Mirona Białoszewskiego," *Teksty Drugie,* 3 (1993): 143–148;

Janusz Sławiński, "Miron Białoszewski: 'Ballada od rymu'," in *Liryka polska: Interpretacje,* edited by Jan Prokop and Sławiński (Kraków: Wydawnictwo Literackie, 1971), pp. 498–511;

Sławiński, "Miron Białoszewski: 'Leżenia'," in *Czytamy utwory współczesne: Analizy,* edited by Teresa Kostkiewiczowa, Aleksandra Okopień-Sławińska, and Sławiński (Warsaw: Państwowe Zakłady Wydawnictw Szkolnych, 1967), pp. 156–168;

Anna Sobolewska, "Ja—to ktoś znajomy. O późnej twórczości Mirona Białoszewskiego," in her *Mistyka dnia powszedniego* (Warsaw: Open, 1992), pp. 44–74;

Sobolewska, *Maksymalnie udana egzystencja: Szkice o życiu i twórczości Mirona Białoszewskiego* (Warsaw: Instytut Badań Literackich, 1997);

Zofia Stefanowska, "Białoszewskiego *Pamiętnik z powstania warszawskiego,*" *Teksty,* 4 (1973): 128–138;

Teatr, special Białoszewski issue, 3 (1993);

Kazimierz Wyka, "Na odpust poezji," in his *Rzecz wyobraźni* (Warsaw: Państwowy Instytut Wydawniczy, 1959), pp. 173–194;

Andrzej Zieniewicz, *Małe iluminacje. Formy prozatorskie Mirona Białoszewskiego* (Warsaw: Państwowy Instytut Wydawniczy, 1989).

Papers:
Some of Miron Białoszewski's papers are in the possession of Leszek Soliński, his longtime friend and partner.

Ana Blandiana

(25 March 1942 –   )

Rodica Mihaila
University of Bucharest

This entry originally appeared in Concise Dictionary of World Literary Biography:
South Slavic and Eastern European Writers.

BOOKS: *Persoana întîia plural* (Bucharest: Editura
  pentru literatură, 1964);
Călcîiul vulnerabil (Bucharest: Editura pentru
  literatură, 1966);
A treia taină (Bucharest: Editura tineretului, 1969);
Calitatea de martor: Euseuri (Bucharest: Cartea
  Românească, 1970);
Cincizeci de poeme (Bucharest: Editura Eminescu,
  1970);
Convorbiri subiective, by Blandiana and Romulus
  Rusan (Bucharest: "Albatros," 1971);
Octombrie, Noiembrie, Decembrie (Bucharest: Cartea
  Românească, 1972);
Eu scriu, tu scrii, el, ea scrie: Eseuri (Bucharest: Cartea
  Românească, 1976);
O discuţie la masa tăcerii, by Blandiana and Rusan
  (Bucharest: "Albatros," 1976);
Somnul din somn (Bucharest: Cartea Românească,
  1977);
Cele patru anotimpuri (Bucharest: "Albatros," 1977);
Cea mai frumoasă dintre lumile posibile (Bucharest:
  Cartea Românească, 1978);
Intîmplări din grădina mea (Bucharest: Editura Ion
  Creanga, 1980);
Ochiul de greier (Bucharest: "Albatros," 1981);
Proiecte de trecut (Bucharest: Cartea Românească,
  1982);
Alte intîmplări din grădina mea (Bucharest: Editura
  Ion Creanga, 1983);
Coridoare de oglinzi: Eseuri (Bucharest: Cartea
  Românească, 1984);
Stea de pradă (Bucharest: Cartea Românească, 1985);
Autoportret cu palimpsest: Eseuri (Bucharest: Editura
  Eminescu, 1986);
Oraşe de silabe (Bucharest: Editura Sport-Turism,
  1987);

Ana Blandiana

Intîmplări de pe stradă mea (Bucharest: Editura Ion
  Creanga, 1988);
Arhitectura valurilor: Versuri (Bucharest: Cartea
  Românească, 1990);
Sertarul cu aplauze: Roman (Bucharest: Editura Tine-
  rama, 1992);
Cartea albă a lui Arpagic (Bucharest: Editura Du
  Style, 1998).
Editions and Collections: *Poezii* (Bucharest: Cartea
  Românească, 1974);

Poeme: Colectia "Cele mai frumoase poezii" (Bucharest: "Albatros," 1978);

Ora de nisip (Bucharest: Editura Eminescu, 1983);

Intîmplări din grădina mea si Alte intîmplări din grădina mea (Bucharest: Editura Ion Creanga, 1986);

100 de poeme (Bucharest: Editura Tinerama, 1991);

Imitaţie de coşmar, afterword by Doina Uricariu (Bucharest: Editura Du Style, 1995);

In dimineaţa de după moarte (Bucharest: Editura Du Style, 1996);

Balanţa cu un singur talger. Die Waage mit einer einzigen schale. La balance à un seul plateau. The Balance Scale with a Single Pan (Bucharest: Editura Du Style, 1997).

Editions in English: "From That Moment," translated and edited by Roy MacGregor-Hastie, in *Anthology of Contemporary Romanian Poetry* (Chester Springs, Pa.: Dufour, 1969), p. 162;

Poeme–Poems, bilingual edition, English translations by Dan Duţescu, preface by Dumitru Micu (Bucharest: Editura Eminescu, 1982);

"In the Soul of the Land" and "I Need Only Fall Asleep," in *100 de Ani de Poezie Românească/100 Years of Romanian Poetry*, translated and edited by Ioana Deligiorgis (Jassy: Junimea, 1982), pp. 368–372;

"From a Village," "Song," and "Dance in the Rain," translated by Irina Livezeanu; "Links," translated by Michael Impey, in *Contemporary East European Poetry: An Anthology*, edited by Emery George (New York & Oxford: Oxford University Press, 1983), pp. 344–348;

Don't Be Afraid of Me: Collected Poems, edited by George Alexe (Detroit: "Romanian Communion" Spiritual Poetry Collection, 1985);

"Incantation for Rains," "Parents," "Morning Elegy," and "Psalm," translated by Andreí Bantaş; "Night in the Hay," translated by Duţescu; "When Trees Used to Have Eyes," translated by Bantaş, in *Like Diamonds in Coal Sleep: Selections from 20th Century Romanian Poetry*, edited by Bantaş (Bucharest: Minerva, 1985), pp. 358–363;

"The Couple," "Do You Remember the Beach?" "It's Snowing," "In Falling," "Armour," "Conditions," "Loneliness," "Parents' Land," "Portrait with Cherries for Earrings," "So Simple," "Sometimes I Dream of My Body," "Have I the Right?" and "Pietà," in *Silent Voices: An Anthology of Contemporary Romanian Women Poets*, translated by Andrea Deletant and Brenda Walker, introduction by Fleur Adcock (London & Boston: Forest Books, 1986), pp. 22–36;

Poeme–Poems, translated by Crisula Ştefănescu and Inta Moruss-Wiest (Paris: Revue des Etudes Roumaines, 1989);

The Hour of Sand: Selected Poems 1969–1989, translated by Peter Jay and Anca Cristofovici (London: Anvil Press Poetry, 1990);

"In the Soul of the Land," translated by Stavros Deligioris; "Amber" and "Children's Crusade," translated by Marguerite Dorian, in *Shifting Borders: East European Poetries of the Eighties*, edited by Walter Cummins (Rutherford, N.J.: Fairleigh Dickinson University Press, 1993), pp. 347–348;

"The Gift" and "Purity, I Know," translated by Adam Sorkin and Ioana Ieronim; "We Should," translated by Sorkin; "Bitter Body," translated by Sorkin and Ieronium; "Star Blown in the Wind," translated by Sorkin; "Architecture in Movement," translated by Sorkin and Maria-Ana Tupan; "Calcium Molecules," translated by Sorkin; "A Straight Line," translated by Sorkin and Tupan; "Obsession," translated by Sorkin and Ieronim; "Ballad," translated by Sorkin, in *An Anthology of Romanian Women Poets*, edited by Sorkin and Kurt W. Treptow (New York: Columbia University Press, 1994), pp. 73–86;

"Do You Remember the Beach," "The Country We Come From," "Sometimes I Dream," "Maybe There's Somebody Dreaming Me," "It's Snowing Hostility," "The Morning After I Die," "Inhabited By a Song," "Loneliness," "Hunt," and "As If," translated by Seamus Heaney, in *When the Tunnels Meet: Contemporary Romanian Poetry*, edited by John Fairleigh (Newcastle upon Tyne: Bloodaxe Books, 1996), pp. 25–32;

Balanţa cu un singur talger. Die Waage mit einer einzigen schale. La balance à un seul plateau. The Balance Scale with a Single Pan (Bucharest: Editura Du Style, 1997).

OTHER: Michel de Ghelderode, *Povestiri crepusculare*, translated by Blandiana (Bucharest: Univers, 1973).

Ana Blandiana is one of the most widely acclaimed Romanian writers working today, both at home and abroad. Her books have been published in translation in sixteen countries, and she has received many Romanian and international literary prizes and awards. An outstanding representative of a prodigious generation of young poets who saved Romanian poetry from becoming an instrument of Communist propaganda, she has added to her reputation as a poet that of a prose fiction writer and essayist. Blandiana's dedication to her art has been sustained by an unflinching commitment to spiritual values and moral ideals, despite being banned several times from publishing in her own country.

Blandiana was born Otilia-Valeria Coman on 25 March 1942 in Timişoara, the only child of Gheorghe Coman and Otilia Coman, née Diacu. She was reared in the Transylvanian city of Oradea, where her father was a highly respected Orthodox priest and high-school teacher. She started to write verse when she was eight, rooting her poetry in the religious spirit and Transylvanian milieu of her upbringing. Significantly, that milieu did not include the cities in which she actually lived; instead, her poems are set in the serene beauty of the countryside and in the idyllic Transylvanian village, the repository of old Romanian traditions and moral values, with its soothing slow rhythms of life, its innocence and purity, and its serious and sturdy people.

In 1959, the year of her high-school graduation, Coman made her poetic debut in *Tribuna* (The Tribune), a cultural magazine in Cluj, using for the first time the pseudonym Ana Blandiana, taken from the name of the Transylvanian village where her maternal grandparents lived. In the same year, however, her father was sent to prison for "plotting against the state," and Blandiana was banned from publication for being "the daughter of a people's enemy."

In 1960 Blandiana married the writer and film critic Romulus Rusan. She has described the marriage as "a true symbiosis of writers"; among the many products of this symbiosis are two books of interviews, *Convorbiri subiective* (Subjective Conversations, 1971) and *O discuţie la masa tăcerii* (A Talk at the Table of Silence, 1976), in which they attempt to re-create the Golden Age of Romanian culture, the period between the world wars. After their marriage the couple moved to Cluj. In 1962 Blandiana enrolled in the Faculty of Philology of the University of Cluj.

Blandiana's first book of poems, *Persoana întîia plural* (First Person Plural), came out in 1964, a year during which a degree of political liberalization occurred as a result of Romania's claim to independent development from the Soviet Union. Her father was released from prison in an amnesty that year, only to die shortly afterward in a fire. The book placed Blandiana in a bright constellation of poets, including Nichita Stanescu, Marin Sorescu, Ileana Mălăncioiu, Ioan Alexandru, Constanţa Buzea, and Adrian Păunescu, that emerged in the 1960s, the

"miracle period" of Romanian poetry that flowered with the end of the postwar Stalinist insistence on proletarian realism in literature. The compelling voices of these poets expressed moral intransigence, suspicion of any form of official discourse, mistrust of words, a youthful will to reinstall the poetic self at the center of the universe, and a new poetic sensibility fully responsive to the rediscovery of the best native and Western cultural and spiritual traditions. Blandiana has written that her "generation differed from the generations before it not so much by what we did, as by what we were no longer willing to do. What united us, above all, was an aesthetic refusal."

Blandiana's first volume fits this description well. The exuberance of the young poet is aggressively romantic. The youthful body is in love with the elements, with the rain and the wind, in "Dans în ploaie" (translated as "Dance in the Rain," 1983); the soul is intoxicated with poetry, "the song," the craved realm of purity. The poems mingle sensuousness, grace, a child's capacity for wonder, delight, and playfulness. The poet's solitary oneness with nature and deliberate avoidance of the human presence, the impersonality of the lyrical effusions, and the absence of the love lyric point obliquely to her fear of being morally tainted by living in history, her desperate striving for purity, and her hope of finding in poetry a refuge from the real world.

The poet as tragic figure appears in Blandiana's second volume, *Călcîiul vulnerabil* (The Vulnerable Heel, 1966), which inaugurates her almost obsessive preoccupation with the condition of the poet and the truth of poetry. The book grows out of the irreconcilable oppositions that mark the poet's tragic condition—above all, the opposition between the ideals of purity, moral perfection, and truth, on the one hand, and the brutal, fear-generating evidence of the real world, on the other hand. Perfect poetry, the poetry of truth, is governed by "the law of whiteness," as illustrated in "Elegie de dimineaţă" (translated as "Morning Elegy," 1985), while in "Ştiu puritatea" (translated as "Purity, I Know," 1994) the real world is regulated by "the great principle of stain / Paid tribute in order to be," and the poet is constantly forced to choose between "silence and sin," between "the drama of dying all in white / Or conquering but nonetheless dying." Blandiana dramatizes this conflict in "Torquato Tasso," an imaginary dialogue and final identification with the victim of the Inquisition whose best poetry remained "unwritten through fear" and who paid with his sanity for "the absence of truth" in his poems.

Ana Blandiana

DON'T BE AFRAID OF ME

Collected Poems

**"Romanian Communion"
Spiritual Poetry Collection
Editor-Publisher
George Alexe
Detroit, Michigan
1985**

Frontispiece and title page for the English translation of one of Blandiana's early collections of verse

Fear of telling the truth is associated with the fear of words in Blandiana's recurrent theme of the poet's struggle with language that has too long been abused by misuse. The poet's gift of turning everything she touches into words becomes tragic in "Darul" (translated as "The Gift," 1994), where, as in the legend of King Midas, the gift turns against her: ". . . I am condemned / to wear laurels of guilt"—the words blur the truth of the world. Silence becomes more resonant than speech in "Psalm" (translated, 1985).

In 1967 Blandiana graduated from the University of Cluj, and she and her husband moved to Bucharest. There she embarked on a career as an editor and columnist that revealed her gifts as an essayist and won her tremendous popularity. For six years she was an editor for the student cultural magazine *Amfiteatru* (Amphitheater), for which she wrote monthly essays about poets who had died young. She also wrote columns titled "Anti-Jurnal" (Anti-Journal) and "Corespondente" (Correspon-

dence) for the prestigious cultural weekly *Contemporanul;* she collected these essays in her first volume of prose, *Calitatea de martor* (The Quality of Witness, 1970). From 1974 to 1988 she wrote the "Atlas" column in the leading literary weekly *România Literară*.

In May 1968 Blandiana was invited to give a poetry reading in Paris, where she witnessed the student uprising. She spent the following two months in Prague; the Czechoslovakian government had invited Rusan there to write a book about the political liberalization that became known as the "Prague Spring." Blandiana was working on a new collection of poems, *A treia taină* (The Third Sacrament, 1969), that distills her experiences in Paris and Prague into subversive reflections on the ability of the human will to choose, to act, and to effect change.

One of the two books Blandiana considers her best, *A treia taină* won the Writers' Union Prize for Poetry. In one of the poems, "Hotar" (Border), Blandiana defines her poetry as a poetry on and of the border, "the line separating good from evil," light from darkness, and life from death—a poetry that identifies borders and dwells on them, asking questions about what lies on either side.

The "third sacrament" is the Eucharist, the symbol of deliverance from sin through Christ's atonement. Like Lucien Blaga, a Transylvanian poet and philosopher whose impact on her work becomes profound in this volume, Blandiana expresses her religious feelings by celebrating the miracle of the universe and the mysteries of creation. Religion is assimilated to tradition, mingling in her memory with the past—particularly with the Christlike figure of her father, "the tragic Gheorghe" in the poem "Requiem." The meditations on the limits of knowledge and self-knowledge and the inquiry into the tragic human condition epitomized in the memory of the father can be read as allusions to the oppressiveness of life in Communist Romania.

In many pieces—including the last poem, "Pietà" (translated, 1982), in which a tired, all-too-human Christ wishes he could postpone the moment of resurrection—the book conveys a sense of weariness. The feeling is produced by the futility of action—the loss of the will to act and of the freedom to choose—in "Nealegere" (translated as "Non-choice," 1990) and "Nehotărîre" (Indecision). Tiredness takes cosmic proportions, contaminating all three realms of existence: the living, the dead, and the angels, from "the fogged people" in "Nordul" (translated as "The North," 1990)—an early version of "the vegetal people" in "Eu cred" (I Believe, 1984)—to the "obedient" and tired dead in "Oboseala" (Tiredness) and the angels who fell from heaven ". . . not because of sin, / But of tiredness," in "Cădere" (translated as "Fall," 1982).

The metaphysical dimension of Blandiana's poetry becomes more pronounced in *Cincizeci de poeme* (Fifty Poems, 1970). Most of the poems are elegies written in the solemn language of the Psalms. The abundance of negative words formed with prefixes, such as "nemoarte" (undeath) or "nealegere" (nonchoice), have a mysterious biblical ring, a ritualistic majesty; the metaphysical questions have a touching simplicity, as in "Sufletul" (translated as "The Soul," 1990): "Does the soul shelter within us / From God?"

In 1972 Blandiana and Rusan spent six months at the International Writing Program at the University of Iowa, during which she read and explained her poetry in a twenty-five-minute motion picture commissioned by the Library of Congress. What impressed Blandiana most about the United

States was "the experience of freedom," which, she says, made a tremendous impact on her writing. That year she published the poetry collection *Octombrie, Noiembrie, Decembrie* (October, November, December), the second of the two books that she considers her best. The volume reflects the sense of peace and harmony she felt after her first trip to Italy in 1969. It preserves the meditative tone of great simplicity and candor and the unadorned language, almost totally cleansed of metaphors, of her earlier work, but it also includes, for the first time, the theme of love between man and woman. The real and the ideal coexist in Blandiana's love poems: love is "desperate elation," purged of sexual desire; the ecstasy of love can best be experienced in sleep, and the dream of perfect eternal love comes true only in death, as in "Dacă ne-am ucide unul pe altul" (translated as "If We Killed One Another," 1985).

The theme of ideal love intermingles with those of artistic creation and the craving for sleep. Sleep and its associated silence shelter the lover from the aggressiveness and the corrupting effects of a world governed by sheer blind power in "Visez uneori trupul meu" (translated as "I Sometimes Dream of My Body," 1982); and in "Din apă ieşeau trupuri albe de plopi" (translated as "White Bodies of Poplars Coming Out of the Water," 1990). The poems provide a new setting for this new range of emotions: in the recurrent water images the rain of Blandiana's earlier verse is replaced by calm expanses of water or by the sea and the beach; the purity of love is symbolized by the moonlight reflected on the water. In "Din apă ieşeau trupuri albe de plopi" the lovers are sanctified by the sacredness of love: like Jesus, they can walk on the water.

There are, however, few serene love poems in Blandiana's books. In most cases the lover is a dream projection; love becomes real only in the moment of separation or exists only in memory; and the lovers walk along deserted surreal beaches that play, as in the poetry of Walt Whitman, the role of boundary between life and death, real and ideal. In "Iti aduci aminte plaja" (translated as "Do You Remember the Beach?" 1986) the lover disappears in the waters of the ideal; in "Visez uneori trupul meu" the lover is identified with an oppressive patriarchal order—with God, with the father, and with the fisherman who caught her body in a "trawl-net of wrinkles," pulling it "like a dead weight through snow." Death, the return to the sea, eternalizes not the moment of perfect love but that of the woman's perfect freedom and the escape from the corrupting forces of history. She would prefer to be a poet than a lover.

Starting with this volume, the annihilation of the body preconditions the creation of poetry in such poems as "In cadere" (translated as "In Falling," 1986), "Trup amar" (translated as "Bitter Flesh," 1985), and "Armura" (translated as "The Armour," 1982). In "Singuratate" (translated as "Loneliness," 1986) the poet, "Inhabited by a song," would prefer to inhabit loneliness, "a happy town" located "On the border / Between suffering and death." Poetry grows out of the silences of sleep.

The related themes of sleep, dream, and death, so far only vaguely explored, became the dominant concern of Blandiana's last two volumes of poetry published in the 1970s: *Poezii* (Poems, 1974) and *Somnul din somn* (The Sleep within Sleep, 1977). They also reverberate in the collection *Ochiul de greier* (The Cricket's Eye, 1981). Approaching these themes, Blandiana found inspiration in the work of Blaga and of Mihai Eminescu. In Eminescu's high Romantic vision sleep, dream, and death are means of returning the soul to its cosmic origins, while in Blaga's philosophy they are confirmations of the self's alienation from itself and from the cosmic oneness.

Significantly, in her treatment of these themes Blandiana aims not so much to transcend the real as to view it more clearly; nowhere is her subversive intent expressed with more subtlety than in her dramatization of the dilemmas of her poetic and moral options, her to-and-fro journeys between time and eternity. Sleep kills the will to act, as in "Eu cred." In "Ţara de unde venim" (translated as "About the Country We Come From," 1990) "the only thing missing is death . . . "; in "Poezie" (translated as "Poem," 1990) she coins the word *încănemoarte* (stillundeath) to describe the state of the few "sleepwalking heroes" left in Romania. Imagination can no longer reconcile the real and the ideal, even though the poet's head "rots with dreams" in "Mi-e somn" (translated as "Sleepy I Am," 1982).

The dream is no longer a flight into another reality but a fall; one can no longer dream but "is dreamed," as in "Genealogie" (Genealogy) and "Poate că mă viseazǎ cineva" (translated as "Maybe Someone Is Dreaming of Me," 1982). The Romantic notion of the poet as a dreamer and redeemer, illustrated in "In Dimineaţa de dupǎ moarte" (translated as "The Morning After Death," 1982), is qualified by the transformation of dreams into nightmares, as in "Intre lumi" (translated as "Between Worlds," 1990). The poet who tried to locate the exact border between good and evil discovers now, in dream, the

shifting boundaries of a tragic, transient world devoured by ceaseless conflict. The ideal is totally corrupted by the real. The "snow fall of love" and purity of her earlier poems turns into a snowfall of "ferocity," hatred, and "venom" in "Ninge cu duşmănie" (translated as "It Snows with a Vengeance," 1982).

The solutions the poet suggests are borrowed from Blaga and cherished by most Transylvanian poets: a return to a pastoral ideal of purity centered on the village as a preserver of traditional values, and the recovery by literature of Romanian spirituality and of the mythical past kept alive in the collective memory and represented in the geography of the country by the gentle contours of the hills, as in "Dealuri" (translated as "Hills," 1982). Nostalgia for the purity of the origins and the oneness of being is seen in Blandiana's attempt to invent her own mythology in "Oul" (translated as "The Egg," 1982); in her immersion in the natural world and her fascination with the village as opposed to the city in "Satul întreg" (The Whole Village), "Sat" (Village), "In satul în care mă-ntorc" (The Village to Which I Return), and "Oraş Oriental" (translated as "Oriental Town," 1990); and in her love for her "parents' land," her praise of its history and her pity for the suffering of its people in "Ţara" (Country), "O ţară e făcutǎ şi din pǎsǎri" (A Country Is Also Made of Birds), and "Ţara pǎrinţilor" (translated as "Parents' Land," 1982).

In 1975 Blandiana took a position as a librarian at the Bucharest Institute of Arts. The job gave her the time and opportunity to study art history. In a short essay on Michelangelo included in her *Eu scriu, tu scrii, el, ea scrie* (I Write, You Write, He, She Writes, 1976), a collection of essays, notes, aphorisms, and reflections on poetry, poets, and artists, she admits that "As a writer I have always learned more from music and the arts than from literature."

Blandiana and Rusan were among the few survivors when their apartment building collapsed in an earthquake on 4 March 1977. They decided to establish a second home in a Danube Plain village, where they now spend much of their time. For more than a year after the earthquake Blandiana was unable to write poetry. With her first volume of fantastic stories, *Cele patru anotimpuri* (The Four Seasons, 1977), she found a new approach to her favorite theme: the corruption of the ideal by the real and the action of the "law of maculation" on human values and on the integrity of the self. Exploring the subversive potentialities of the fantastic, she was, like other Eastern European writers during the period, inspired by Edgar Allan Poe,

Blandiana at the time of her 1990 collection The Hour of
Sand: Selected Poems 1969–1989
(photograph by Lori Sauer)

Franz Kafka, Mikhail Bulgakov, and Gabriel García Márquez and by the rich tradition of the fantastic in Romanian literature, particularly in the works of Vasile Voiculescu and Mircea Eliade. The four stories, told in the first person, correspond to the four seasons and to four stages in the life of the narrator/author. The fantastic explores the dichotomy of real and ideal to illuminate the epistemological experience of the self raising moral and ethical questions. "Amintiri din copilarie. (Toamna)" (Memories of Childhood. [Autumn]), the most powerful autobiographical story, is built around a unique introspection into the Communist terror, when, as a child, Blandiana saw her father being forced to burn the most cherished books in his library. The fantastic is not opposed to the real but contained in the abnormal character of the latter.

Blandiana's next book was a collection of travel essays, *Cea mai frumoasă dintre lumile posibile* (The Most Beautiful of All Possible Worlds, 1978), in which she gives her impressions of the United States and Europe. Her first children's book, *Intîmplări din grădina mea* (Events in My Garden, 1980), was awarded the Writers' Union Prize for Children's Literature.

Blandiana's next book of fantastic stories, *Proiecte de trecut* (Projects for the Past, 1982), deals with the nightmarish aspects of life in Romania in the 1950s: political prisoners, deportations, depri-

vations, and the reign of fear. In this volume the Romantic dichotomy of the ideal and the real is transformed into the opposition between the rational and the absurd, that is, between the self's craving for meaning and wholeness and the irrationality of existence under totalitarianism. Far from serving as an escape from reality, the fantastic relates the conscience and its inner time to Romania's postwar history. For Blandiana, "to imagine is to remember." Her flights from the real bring new insights into a reality rendered discontinuous by a highly selective memory triggered by moral questions.

Initially banned from publication for its "antisocial tendencies," *Proiecte de trecut* came out only under international pressure after the poet received the prestigious Gottfried von Herder International Prize in Vienna in 1982. In the same year a bilingual edition of her collected poems, *Poeme–Poems,* was published, with English translations by Dan Duțescu.

With the prize money Blandiana and Rusan went on a tour of the lands around the Mediterranean Sea, including Egypt, Israel, Turkey, Greece, and Italy. The experience found its way into all three of Blandiana's prose books of the 1980s. *Coridoare de oglinzi* (Passage of Mirrors, 1984) and *Autoportret cu palimpsest* (Self-Portrait with Palimpsest, 1986) are collages of short essays, diary entries, notes, and meditations on moral issues that have confronted her as a Romanian intellectual and writer. *Orașe de silabe* (Cities of Syllables, 1987) consists mainly of travel impressions.

Blandiana's transformation into a symbol of the political resistance through literature gathered momentum after 1984, when, following the publication in *Amfiteatru* of four poems that openly denounced Nicolae Ceaușescu's Communist regime, she was not allowed to publish for several months. Blandiana resorted to children's books as another form of resistance. *Alte intîmplări din grădina mea* (More Events in My Garden, 1983) was followed by *Intîmplări de pe strada mea* (Events in My Street, 1988), a subversive work equally addressed to adults that depicted Romania's Communist dictator under the transparent guise of an arrogant, autocratic tomcat. This work brought on her the third, and most severe, interdiction: her books were withdrawn from bookstores and libraries, and her name could not be mentioned in print.

The process of Blandiana's radicalization is visible in the volumes of poetry she wrote in the 1980s, from *Ochiul de greier* to *Ora de nisip* (The Hour of Sand, 1983), *Stea de pradă* (Star of Prey, 1985), and *Arhitectura valurilor* (Architecture of Waves), which was ready for publication in 1987 but, for reasons of censorship, was not published until 1990. They constitute a poetry of witness in which the violence of the language points to the annihilation of the human being by the totalitarian state, as in "Gemeni" (translated as "Twins," 1990): "Twins in the uterus of fear, / Inhabitants of the same cell, / blind and dumb . . . Without right of appeal / Sentenced to birth." Nature itself has been violently deprived of its purity in "Tîrziu" (translated as "Late," 1990): "The sunset is rancid / And the sunrise faked. / A star of prey lies in wait." The apocalyptic image of Romania under the Communist dictatorship is dominated by a "new Apollo," "A rodent god / Ravenous from the years / With haloes / Of trash . . . ," in "Scena" (translated as "Scene," 1990).

As a poet Blandiana has struggled with words that "have lost their word-souls," as she says in "Vinatoare" (translated as "Hunt," 1996), just as she has struggled to maintain her quality of witness. But the need for more action, the wish to become "the exterminating angel," as in "Armura," the feeling of guilt for being only a witness refusing the world "purification by fire," as in "Retorica" (Rhetoric), pervade the poems written in the 1980s. As she writes in the foreword of *Arhitectura valurilor*, the poems reflect mixed feelings of "exasperation and humiliation, anger and despair, shame and revolt." She dedicated them to the martyrs who died in the 1989 revolution. Her commitment to her art and her people is expressed in the last poem in the volume, "Baladă" (translated as "Ballad," 1990). Here the poet identifies herself with Ana, the martyred wife of a master builder in a Romanian legend, whose sacrifice made possible the building of a monastery. The poet willingly walls herself in to prevent a monastery from crumbling by "the mad caprice" of a "somnambulist bulldozer"—a transparent allusion to the demolition of churches and villages by the Communist regime in the 1980s.

In January 1990 Blandiana was appointed a member of the provisional National Salvation Front government. She resigned after a few weeks to protest what she called "the confiscation of the Romanian Revolution by the anti-democratic forces." She went on to become a founding member and president of the "Civic Academy" Foundation; president of the Civic Alliance, a democratic organization with broad popular support; and president of the Romanian PEN Club. With Rusan she founded, on the site of an old Stalinist prison at Sighet, The Memorial of the Victims of Communism and the International Center for the Study of Communism.

She has also been extremely active beyond the Romanian borders, giving lectures and poetry readings, publishing articles in influential newspapers, and attending international conferences, meetings, and festivals. In Guadalajara in 1996 she was the only candidate nominated for the presidency of International PEN, but she withdrew her candidacy to protest the attempts of certain pressure groups to take control of the organization.

Her many commitments have not led Blandiana to neglect her art. The publication of her previously banned and uncollected poems in *Arhitectura valurilor* and *100 de Poeme* (100 Poems, 1991) was followed by *Imitație de coșmar* (Copy of A Nightmare, 1995), a one-volume collection of her two volumes of fantastic stories, and *In dimineața de după moarte* (The Morning after Death, 1996), a selection from all of her poetry collections and from her prose volumes of 1976 and 1984.

Finally, at a time of bewildering changes, when few books were being written in Romania, Blandiana surprised her readers with yet another debut—this time as a novelist. *Sertarul cu aplauze* (The Drawer with Applause, 1992), which she had begun soon after the publication of *Proiecte de trecut*, continues to explore the same vein of the fantastic as that volume, blurring the boundaries between sanity and madness and between absurdity and reality in Communist Romania. Written between 1983 and 1989, *Sertarul cu aplauze* is one of the few extant "drawer" writings, as Romanians call the unpublished subversive texts produced before December 1989 and kept hidden from the secret police. Writing the work allegedly helped Blandiana survive the nightmare of her last interdiction.

The protagonist of the novel, Alexandru Serban, a writer, is placed in a psychiatric clinic where the patients are politically suspect and the doctors are agents of the secret police. Later he is taken to a reeducation center, where success is determined by how readily the prisoners applaud when ordered to do so. The last chapter, written after the 1989 revolution, is a corrupted version of the biblical Flood in which the survivors are the same old oppressors, who easily adapt to the new circumstances. The experimental character of the novel is compounded by a fiction-within-the-fiction structure, for Alexander is writing this work in which he is the main character. Despite the presence of an entire chapter in which the author explains the artifice of her enterprise, *Sertarul cu aplauze* is not a postmodern metafiction but a fantastic, poetic novel held together by the unique lyric voice of the narrator.

At the peak of her career, Blandiana is one of the most compelling and provocative Eastern European voices. She is a member of the European Academy of Poetry and of the Mallarmé Academy of Poetry. The Eminescu Great Prize for Poetry that she received in January 1997 was one more recognition of her achievement. A prolific and versatile writer, publishing at a rate of more than one volume a year, she has received constant critical attention at home and abroad. She has a large audience because of the quality and diversity of her writing; the authenticity, simplicity, and firmness of her voice; the purity of her vision; and the courage with which she has upheld her convictions. Although she has become a symbol of the Romanian democratic society, she remains devoted to her art and resists the temptations of power. As she writes in "Locuită de-un cîntec" (translated as "Inhabited by a Song," 1996): "Inhabited by a song, / Forsaken by a song, / Maybe even a widow of a song / . . . / I am not one for your laurels— / Except insofar as I've been / Its servant, humble and faithful / Right to the end."

Interviews:

George Arion, "Ana Blandiana," *Flacăra*, 45 (10 November 1977): 24;

Boris Buzila, "Ana Blandiana," *România liberă*, 3 December 1980, p. 2;

Nicolae Băciuţ, "Dialog cu Ana Blandiana," *Vatra*, 15 (20 October 1985): 8;

Ursula Ruston, "Ana Blandiana: Total censur frifjorde kreativiteten," *Författaren*, 2 (1991): 8–10;

Dorin Popa, " Ana Blandiana," *Convorbiri literare*, 14 (April 1991): 8–9;

Solvej Balle, "Lidelsens Alfabet—interview med Ana Blandiana," *Blå Port*, 34 (1995): 18–32;

Vitalie Ciobanu, "Interviu cu Ana Blandiana," *România liberă*, 9 January 1997, p. 21;

Ioana Ieronim, "De ce am refuzat preşedenţia International PEN," 22 (January 1997): 17;

Angelika Overath, "'Engel können nicht verbrennen'—Die Rumänien Ana Blandiana zwischen Poesie und Politik," *Neue Bürcher Zeitung*, 18 April 2000, p. 65.

References:

Fleur Adcock, "Independent Europe: Romania: Nina and Ana," *Poetry Review*, 80 (Summer 1990): 22–23;

Florin Bican, "Ana Blandiana: Art of Survival," *Index on Censorship*, 21, no. 9 (1992): 50;

Leons Briedis, "Vakara vingrošana: Ana Blandiana," *Kentaurs XXI*, 5 (October 1993): 62–69;

Hristu Candroveanu, "Ana Blandiana," in his *Literatura română pentru copii* (Bucharest: Albatros, 1988), pp. 239–241;

Nicolae Ciobanu, "'Suava disperare' a feminităţii," in his *Critică în prima instanţă* (Bucharest: Editura Eminescu, 1974), pp. 117–123;

Dan Cristea, "Locuită de-un cintec," *Luceafărul*, 42 (20 October 1984): 3;

Cristea, "Somnul din somn; 'Cele patru anotimpuri,'" in his *Faptul de a scrie* (Bucharest: Cartea Românească, 1980), pp. 116–123;

Valeriu Cristea, "Cu viziera zîmbetului," in his *Modestie şi orgoliu* (Bucharest: Eminescu, 1984), pp. 58–61;

Andreea Deciu, "Intre catharsis şi roman experimental," *România literară*, 34 (28 October – 3 November 1992): 8;

Dennis Deletant, "Crimes against the Spirit," *Index on Censorship*, 18 (September 1989): 25–26, 28;

Victor Felea, "Ana Blandiana: *Poezii*," in his *Aspecte ale poeziei de azi* (Cluj Napoca: Dacia, 1977), pp. 41–47;

Dinu Flamind: "Simţirea în mişcare," *Viaţa românească*, 5 (May 1988): 75–77;

Gheorghe Grigurcu, "Ana Blandiana," in his *Poeţi români de azi* (Bucharest: Cartea Românească, 1979), pp. 372–380;

Grigurcu, "Ana Blandiana in 'Coridoare de oglinzi' si in afara lor," *Viaţa românească*, 81 (March–April 1986): 153–158;

Grigurcu, "Recitind poezia Anei Blandiana," *România literară*, 15 (16–22 April 1997): 5;

Christina Hesselholdt, "Om Ana Blandiana," *Blå Port*, 34 (1995): 5–8;

Adriana Iliescu, "Natură moartă cu două cartuşe," *România literară*, 16 (18 April 1991): 5;

Mircea Iorgulescu, "Ana Blandiana," in his *Scriitori tineri contemporani* (Bucharest: Eminescu, 1978), pp. 285–289;

Mircea Ivanescu, "O stare poetică intensă," *Transilvania*, 11 (November 1977): 35–36;

Kevin Jackson, "Underground Notes," *Independent*, (London), February 1989, p. 30;

Marie-Luise Knott, "Von der Sinnlosigkeit des Bösen," *Tagesspiegel*, 5 October 1993, p. vii;

Karel Kyncl and Peter Jay, "The Most Famous Tomcat in Town," *Index on Censorship*, 18 (September 1989): 34–35;

Turid Larsen, "Poeten Som Fikk Skriveforbud," *Arbeiderbladet*, 26 September 1990, p. 17;

Nicolae Manolescu, "Poezie de dragoste," *România literară*, 44 (31 October 1974): 9;

Manolescu, "Privelişti morale," *România literară*, 3 (14 January 1988); 9;

Mircea Martin, "Călcîiul vulnerabil," in his *Generaţie şi creaţie* (Bucharest: Editura Pentru Literatura, 1969), pp. 94–102;

Dumitru Micu, "*Lirism eutanasic,*" in his *Limbaje moderne în poezia românească de azi* (Bucharest: Minerva, 1986), pp. 253–269;

Marian Papahagi, "Starea de insomnie," *Tribuna*, 44 (31 October 1985): 4;

Mihail Petroveanu, "Ana Blandiana," in his *Traiectorii lirice* (Bucharest: Cartea Românească, 1974), pp. 324–327;

Alexandru Piru, "Ana Blandiana," in his *Poezia românească contemporană*, volume 2 (Bucharest: Eminescu, 1975), pp. 369–381;

Petru Poanta, "Forme abstracte ale liricii," in his *Modalităţi lirice contemporane* (Cluj: Dacia, 1973), pp. 194–197;

Ion Pop, "Ana Blandiana," in his *Poezia unei generaţii* (Cluj: Dacia, 1973), pp. 245–262;

Pop, "Ritmul naturii," in his *Lecturi fragmentare* (Bucharest: Eminescu, 1983), pp. 85–90;

Dumitru Radu Popa, "Realul, dar în formă semnificativă," *România literară*, 23 (9 April 1983): 5;

Lucian Raicu, "Ana Blandiana–Spiritual şi terestru, 'Calitatea de martor,'" in his *Critica, formă de viaţă* (Bucharest: Cartea Românească, 1976), pp. 297–305;

Raicu, "Cunoaştere de sine," in his *Fragmente de timp* (Bucharest: Cartea Românească, 1984), pp. 247–254;

Raicu, "Somnul din somn," in his *Printre contemporani* (Bucharest: Cartea Românească, 1980), pp. 122–126;

Cornel Regman, "Retrospectivă Ana Blandiana," *Viaţa Românească*, 5 (May 1984): 44–52;

Gabriel Rusu, "A existat pur şi simplu," *Luceafărul*, 291 (October 1996): 5;

Eugen Simion, "Ana Blandiana," in his *Scriitori români de azi, IV* (Bucharest: Cartea Românească, 1989), pp. 151–171;

Simion, "O elegie a fiinţei," *România literară*, 14 (31 March 1988): 5;

Adam Sorkin, "Ana Blandiana," *Romanian Civilization*, 2 (Spring 1993): 141–144;

Ognyan Stamboliev, "Four Romanian Poets," *Concerning Poetry*, 2 (Fall 1984): 55–60;

Alex. Ştefănescu, "Ana Blandiana–Contemporanul nostru," *România literară*, 10 (26 March – 1 April 1992): 5;

Crisula Ştefănescu, "De o suta de ori Ana Blandiana," *Romania Literara*, 42 (17 October 1991): 9;

Laurenţiu Ulici, "Lacrima gânditoare," in his *Confort Procust* (Bucharest: Eminescu, 1983), pp. 141–147.

Mircea Cărtărescu

(1 June 1956 –)

Monica Spiridon
University of Bucharest

BOOKS: *Faruri, vitríne, fotográfii* (Bucharest: Cartea Românească, 1980);

Aer cu diamante, by Cărtărescu, Traian T. Cosovei, Florin Iaru, and Ion Stratan (Bucharest: Editura Litera, 1982);

Poéme dé amór (Bucharest: Cartea Românească, 1983);

Totul (Bucharest: Cartea Românească, 1985);

Visul (Bucharest: Cartea Românească, 1989); revised and republished as *Nostalgia* (Bucharest: Humanitas, 1993);

Levantul (Bucharest: Cartea Românească, 1990);

Visul chimeric (Bucharest: Cartea Românească, 1992);

Lulu (Paris: Climats, 1993); original Romanian version revised and published as *Travestí* (Bucharest: Humanitas, 1994);

Drăgostea (Bucharest: Humanitas, 1994);

Orbitor. Aripa stîngă (Bucharest: Humanitas, 1996);

Dublu CD. Antologie de poezie (Bucharest: Humanitas, 1998);

Postmodernismul românesc (Bucharest: Humanitas, 1999).

Edition in English: "To an Artiste," "Slightly in Mourning," "Three Brothers Vodka," "I'm Smiling," "When Love's What You Need," "Adriana," "The Blonde Beast," "Do You Know a Countryside Where the Lemon Trees Are in Bloom?," "A Day-and-a-Half for the Banana-Fish," and "My Everyday Dream," translated by Medbh McGuckian, in *When the Tunnel Meets: Contemporary Romanian Poetry,* edited by John Fairleigh (Newcastle upon Tyne: Bloodaxe Books, 1996), pp. 33–46.

OTHER: "Paianjenul de pămînt," in *Desant 83,* edited by Ovid S. Crohmălniceanu (Bucharest: Cartea Românească, 1983), pp. 350–361.

Mircea Cărtărescu distinguished himself in Romanian literature as the leader of a group of writ-

Mircea Cărtărescu

ers who, during the most oppressive period of the communist regime, refused to accept the limitations imposed by social and cultural isolation and sought instead to create a literature of contemporary relevance and enduring importance. Admonished and rejected by the traditional literary establishment, the generation of the 1980s—referred to in the press in various capacities as "textualists," "the paratroopers," and derogatorily as the "blue jeans generation"—enjoyed an underground following and intellectual prestige that allowed them to challenge the official canons of poetry and prose. As a result, Cărtărescu and other emerging writers—such as Liviu Ioan Stoiciu, Ion Stratan,

Florin Iaru, Mariana Marin, and Bogdan Ghiu—forged a new artistic purposefulness and direction. Known in literary circles first as a poet and then as a prose writer, Cărtărescu is now recognized as an author of international stature. His work has been translated and reviewed in the most important European languages.

Cărtărescu was born on 1 June 1956 in Bucharest, the only child of Constantin, an engineer, and Maria (née Baldovin) Cărtărescu. The product of an urban childhood, Cărtărescu was influenced by the stark contrast between the modern city streets and the quiet lanes of the old town, which later served as an obsessive system of landmarks in his literature. From 1963 to 1975 Cărtărescu attended the Dimitrie Cantemir high school, one of the most prestigious in Bucharest, and he was subsequently admitted to the University of Bucharest.

The period of university studies represents a decisive factor in the development of Cărtărescu's literary career. During this time, he met the prominent critics Nicolae Manolescu and Ovid S. Crohmălniceanu, both of whom influenced his early development as a writer. In 1977 Manolescu, the official columnist of the magazine *România literară* (Romanian Literature) and the most important postwar Romanian literary critic, created the Monday Circle, which served as a literary forum that brought together many of the young poets who emerged in the early 1980s to revitalize contemporary Romanian literature. Those who attended still remember the intellectual exuberance of those Monday evenings as well as the nonconformity, the relaxed atmosphere, and the cosmopolitan, receptive, and stimulating spirit fostered by the circle's mentor. Cărtărescu faithfully attended the circle from the beginning until its end in 1983, making his literary debut with poems published in *România literară* in 1978. Simultaneously, Cărtărescu was affiliated with the prestigious Junimea prose circle, directed by Crohmălniceanu, a professor at the Faculty of Letters in Bucharest. Active in the Junimea circle until 1990, Cărtărescu collaborated on the circle's collective anthology of short fiction, *Desant 83* (Paratroopers 83, 1983), edited by Crohmălniceanu.

After graduation, Cărtărescu secured a teaching position in Romanian literature at a district school in Bucharest. Most of his colleagues, all highly educated and cultivated university graduates, found little opportunity for employment and were forced instead into a precarious and often marginal existence prior to the collapse in 1989 of the communist dictatorship. In 1980 Cărtărescu published his first volume of poetry, *Faruri, vitrine, fotografii* (Headlights, Shop-Windows, Photographs), for which he was awarded the Writers' Union prize for debut work. Although the volume received a mixed critical reception from the official press, the eclectic structure and thematic complexity of the work established Cărtărescu as a poet of talent and creative vision. From the poet's particular perspective, the world is identified with the urban universe of Bucharest. However, although Cărtărescu's early poetry often dealt with daily existence and the mundane affairs of ordinary life, in this book sentimentality is discarded in favor of juvenile irony and emphatically displayed erudite allusions. One of the cycles of verse within this first volume, "Georgicele" (The Georgics), comprises twelve texts that rewrite Romanian rural and pastoral poetry, injecting these traditional rural verses with elements of modern technical civilization and even of industrial kitsch.

In 1982 Cărtărescu participated in the publication of *Aer cu diamante* (Air and Diamonds), a collective volume of the Monday Circle, which also included poems by Traian T. Cosovei, Iaru, and Stratan. This effort was followed in the next year by the publication of Cărtărescu's most controversial book: *Poéme dé amór* (Love Poems). More systematically and stylistically coherent than his first volume, *Poéme dé amór* confirms his reputation as an innovative poetic voice. Since Cărtărescu had been publicly admonished by the cultural review *Săptămîna*, one of the official magazines of the communist regime, as a means to discredit the "poetry in blue-jeans" (a derogatory term coined by the magazine), several printing houses in Bucharest refused to publish *Poéme dé amór* because it was seen as allegedly indecent and irreverent to tradition. However, when the book was finally brought out by a provincial printing house, the attention and publicity that surrounded Cărtărescu only added to the success of the volume. In effect, *Poéme dé amór* does not compromise eroticism, as was alleged; rather, this book questions love as a poetic theme. The poet exists between the two universes that define him. One is poetry itself, from the goliards and the troubadours to Ezra Pound, Wallace Stevens, and Allen Ginsberg (all of whom are frequently quoted in the texts). The other is, once more, the familiar city universe of Bucharest, the landmarks of which include the university, the Dimitrie Cantemir high school, and the streets around it, lined with bus stops, cinemas, and coffee shops.

In the world created by Cărtărescu a lyrical ego evolves for which the image of woman simply provides an opportunity for the creation of poetry. His ultimate goal was to invent a new rhetoric of love, as different as possible from the common language. The author's linguistic fantasy is infinite: the vocabulary of nature coexists with that of mechanics, while jargon and slang are juxtaposed with scientific and pedantic technical terms. Cărtărescu openly seeks a comical effect, but the final result is a total inversion, a turning upside down of the meanings existent within cultural memory.

The publication in 1985 of Cărtărescu's third volume of poetry, *Totul* (Everything), was acknowledged by critics as the best and most homogenous book of poetry the author had produced so far. The volume appears to be a continuation and at the same time a conclusion of Cărtărescu's poetry up to that point. The ostentatious and rebellious rhetoric of the youthful poet is gone. Instead, the turbulent and unconfined lyrics have settled in a wide and generous pattern, and the poet's dominant themes emerge much more clearly. With *Totul* a new character emerges within Cărtărescu's poetry: the writer himself sits by his typewriter and, as if on a theater stage, directly addresses his reader like an accomplice, in a familiar manner. Preeminent in this volume is the wide perspective of the poet, who surpasses all the limits of traditional poetry: he knows and can say everything. Indeed, Cărtărescu declared in a 1990 interview with Monica Spiridon, "No, I don't want to become a great writer. I want to become everything."

With the publication of *Totul*, Cărtărescu was characterized as the first Romanian postmodern poet. He earned this title by juxtaposing the language of elitist and erudite poetry with that of folkish, colloquial, and idiomatic verse. Cărtărescu also transgressed the boundaries of established literary conventions by incorporating his own attitude toward cultural memory into his work. Indeed, the mocking steadfastness of his previous works is replaced by the superior and slightly moved curiosity of a cultivated artist who rediscovers, sometimes with mild amusement, the charm of obsolete literary models.

With the publication in 1989 of his first collection of short stories, *Visul* (The Dream), Cărtărescu established himself as a significant contemporary prose writer. Cărtărescu later claimed that he had been writing novels ever since he was in the third grade and that he had been keeping a diary since he was a teenager. However, his vocation as a prose writer was somewhat precarious. Ostensibly trained by the Junimea prose circle, Cărtărescu was highly indebted to the mentorship of Crohmălniceanu,

Cover for Cărtărescu's epic poem, published in 1990, about a revolt against a despotic nineteenth-century Romanian prince

who had a decisive role in the publication of *Visul*. The book was perceived as "Cosmopolitan" and "decadent" according to communist standards, however, and was violently rejected by the censors. *Visul* was allowed to appear only in an abridged form, without the story titled "Jucătorul de ruletă" (The Roulette Player).

The narrator of all the stories returns to the miraculous universe of his childhood, trying to retrieve its playful spirit, its imaginative force, and its infinite capacity for amalgamating the tenses, candidly admitting the existence of contradictory perspectives, surpassing the constraining limits of civilization, and changing swiftly from one mood to another. In Cărtărescu's short stories the minute realism and local color of Bucharest coexist with poetic symbolism, dream, fantasy, and briefly, with the purest form of science fiction. A vast network of intertextual links underlies the surface of the text, leading not only to the fantastic stories of Mihai Eminescu, Romania's national poet, but also to German Romanticism, South American magical realism, surrealist poems in prose, pop art, even to astrology, magnetism, and theories of parallel worlds. In prose as well as in poetry, Cărtărescu's goal was to encompass the infinite interconnectedness and wholeness of the universe. After the fall of the communist regime, the Romanian Academy awarded the book their 1989 prize for prose.

After 1989 Cărtărescu's career direction changed drastically. He left his teaching position and worked for a short time as a clerk for the Writers' Union and as an editor for the magazine *Caiete critice* (Critical Exercises). In 1990 he became a lecturer in the department of Romanian language and literature at the Faculty of Letters in Bucharest, while beginning work on his dissertation on Romanian postmodern literature. Cărtărescu defended his dissertation in March, 1999, and it was published the same year as *Postmodernismul românesc*. In 1990 he published *Levantul* (The Levant), an epic poem in twelve books, which had been written earlier and partially read in the Junimea circle. At the time, Cărtărescu considered the volume too controversial for publication and preferred not to submit it to the communist censors. With the more relaxed critical environment of the early 1990s, however, he decided to seize the opportunity and release the volume. The critical reception was truly exceptional, and the volume won the prize for poetry from the Writers' Union in 1990. But the critics could not agree on whether to consider the text a heroic fantasy, an epopee, an epic poem, a heroic-comical poem, or simply a book-length poem. Once more, Cărtărescu's literature defied the literary rules while still frequently alluding to them.

At a surface level, *Levantul* is the history of a nineteenth-century conspiracy against tyranny, the goal of which is to unseat one of the despotic princes of the Romanian principalities. As a transparent antitotalitarian parable, the book could not possibly have been published under the communist regime. The protagonist is the young Wallachian poet Manoil. The twelve books tell the tale of his fabulous journey by boat, in a balloon, and through his dreams and imagination. From the Greek Islands, where he recruits plotters and supporters among pirates and all kinds of bizarre individuals, he travels to the Danube and from there to Bucharest, where he dethrones the prince. Meanwhile,

the author and the narrator appear to have joined the fraternity as well.

At a certain point during his journey, Manoil is initiated in the Mechanism of Poetry by a princess called Hyacinta, and seven statues of the great traditional Romanian poets are required to answer Manoil's question: "What is poetry?" The author takes this opportunity to rewrite and to thematically and stylistically review the most important moments of canonical Romanian poetry. Using pastiche, parody, ironic deviation, paraphrase, quotation, and allusion, Cărtărescu creates a genuine comedy of literature in which the main character is himself, the Author, always in the forefront of his poem, commenting on his own text and laughing with his readers at his fictional creatures.

In 1990 Cărtărescu was named a fellow of the International Writers Program at the University of Iowa. His poems were also translated into French and included in the anthology *Quinze Poĉtes Roumains* (Fifteen Romanian Poets). The following summer, he went to Paris with a cultural scholarship and took part in a debate on postmodernism, organized by the Stuttgart Seminar in Cultural Studies. In 1992 he published *Visul chimeric* (The Chimerical Dream), an essay on Eminescu's poetry, written some twelve years earlier. Fragments of this essay had appeared in several literary magazines. Cărtărescu's interpretation of Eminescu's poetic universe is an archetypal analysis. It ultimately charts the topography of Eminescu's work by correlating it to the structure of its creator's unconscious. The book is much more important for the commentators of Cărtărescu's poetry than it is for those of Eminescu, for the way it projects the critic's own formative obsessions on the work of the interpreted poet.

Also in 1992 *Visul* appeared in French translation as *Le Rĕve*. Favorably reviewed in significant periodicals, *Visul* was nominated in France for the Médicis Award and the Prize of the Latin Union. In the following year, the book was published in Spanish as *El Sueño*, and the laudatory reviews from several important critics mention Nikolai Gogol, Franz Kafka, Isidore Lucien Ducasse (Comte de Lautréamont), Novalis, E. T. A. Hoffmann, Gerard de Nerval, Jorge Luis Borges, and Julio Cortázar as Cărtărescu's models. In 1993 Cărtărescu also initiated a fruitful collaboration with the Humanitas publishing house in Bucharest, the manager of which was the philosopher Gabriel Liiceanu. The complete version of *Visul* was published by Humanitas under the title *Nostalgia*.

In 1994 Humanitas published *Drăgostea* (Love), a volume of poetry written before 1989 and forming, in the author's conception, a kind of trilogy with *Poéme dé amór* and *Totul*. In this book the poet bids farewell to the generation of the 1980s before actually distancing himself from the group. The volume shows a different face of erotic poetry, which the author had long hesitated to make public. At its deepest levels, it is reminiscent of the biblical models, particularly in the cycle of "Psalmi" (Psalms): there are allusions to metaphysical love, the love for God, and the anxious search for divinity in all the illusory aspects of life, as well as the love for fellow beings. The latter embraces a particular form—family life, the miracle of being happy, the peacefulness of married life, and the glorification of paternal feelings, especially in the cycle "Dragă Cri" (Dear Cri). In January 1997 Cărtăresca married Christina Ilinca. A daughter, Ioana, was born to the couple in 1998.

After settling accounts with the past, Cărtărescu made a radical renewal with his debut as a novelist in 1994 when he published *Travestí* (Travesty), an earlier version of which was translated into French and published as *Lulu* in the previous year. *Travestí* won the Writers' Union prize for prose and the award of the Association of Romanian Professional Writers (ASPRO) for the best book of the year. In its center is a literary archetype—the Androgyne. In the seclusion of a mountain lodge, Victor, the protagonist and narrator, a famous novelist from Bucharest now in his years of maturity, anxiously searches—by means of memories and writing—for the identity of the teenager he had once been. The turning point of his destiny proves to be his meeting with Lulu, an androgynous high-school pupil, at a summer camp. During a carnival, dressed as a woman, Lulu tries to seduce Victor. As revealing as it is shocking, the scene brings Victor back in his memory to the deeply feminine ego that continuously haunts his dreams: the child he once was, dressed like a girl until the age of four by his mother.

As always in Cărtărescu's fiction, this "plot" is only a frame filled with symbolic events. The book has at least two levels of meaning. One is a meditation on the splendor and abjection of adolescence. The other has to do with the metaphysical anxiety and the cosmic fascination of the ego that gradually and painfully experiences the world. Both themes recur in Cărtărescu's prose as well as in his poetry. Out of their tense dialogue emerges The Book, the text that Victor lives and writes at the same time. The critics were unanimous in identifying the chain

Cover for Cărtărescu's 1996 novel–a mixture of memories, fantasies, scenes from the time of the Romanian dictatorship, descriptions of the cityscape of Bucharest, literary reflections, and philosophical meditations–that constitutes the first volume in a projected trilogy

of literary references to which the writer deliberately links himself: Nerval, Rainier Maria Rilke, J. D. Salinger, Georg Trakl, Kafka, Vladimir Nabokov, Borges, and most notably Frank Wedekind, creator of another famous Lulu. Everything has as a background the illusory and yet real Bucharest of Cărtărescu's childhood.

Between 1994 and 1996 Cărtărescu taught Romanian language and literature in three monthly sessions as a visiting professor at the University of Amsterdam. During this period, his novel was translated into Dutch as *Travestie* (1996) and was laudably reviewed in the literary magazines. The writer used his stays in Holland to work on a trilogy of novels under the collective title of *Orbitor* (Dazzling Light). The first volume, published in Bucharest in the last days of 1996, is titled *Orbitor. Aripa stîngă* (Dazzling Light: The Left Wing); the last two novels that will complete the cycle are "Aripa dreaptă" (The Right Wing) and "Córpul" (The Body). Developing one of the main directions of Cărtărescu's previous work, *Orbitor. Aripa stîngă* begins with a quest for the past. It is a book of the rereading and rewriting of the past of a fictitious character with a double identity: both autobiographic and symbolic. As in Cărtărescu's previous work, the center of this novel is a talking ego that produces the text like a spider in its web. The writing is a mixture of memories, fantasies, chimeras, historical scenes from the time of the dictatorship, descriptions of social environments and of the cityscape of Bucharest, literary reflections, and philosophical meditations. Though still incomplete, Cărtărescu's project may be one of the fundamental experiments of modern Romanian literature.

Emerging as the most prominent and industrious writer of his generation, Cărtărescu has nonetheless moved to distance himself from identification with any particular literary group, preferring instead to forge an independent reputation. Exploring in both his poetry and prose the unbounded capabilities of his creative imagination, Cărtărescu is now recognized as a distinctive voice in Romanian as well as contemporary European literature.

Interview:

Monica Spiridon, "O Generaţiê pusă la index," *Journalul literar*, 1 (1990): 3.

References:

Adriana Babeti, "Ambitextul," *Orizont*, 12 (1994);

Florin Berindeanu, "Manualul de postmodernism," *Contrapunct*, 18 (1991): 3;

Iulian Boldea, "Cunoaçtere luciferică, ori paradizi-acă?" *Echinox*, 5 (1986): 9;

Ovid S. Crohmălniceanu, "On Rem," *Caiete critice*, 1 (1990): 16–18;

Crohmălniceanu, "Euphorion redivivus," *Viata Românească*, 5 (1986);

Radu Ćurcanu, "Plăcerea transformării," *Euphorion*, 3 (1993): 6;

Paul Georgescu, "Supersonic şi înamorat," *România literară*, 37 (1985): 4;

Gheorghe Grigurcu, "Poéme dé amór," *Steaua*, 8 (1983): 12–13;

Nicolae Manolescu, "Camedia literaturii," *România literatară*, 47 (1990): 4;

Manolescu, "Exegi monumentum, I–III," *Luceafărul*, 44–46 (1990): 6; 618;

Manolescu, "Ochiul ciclopului," *România literară*, 52 (1985): 3;

Manolescu, "Paradigma întregului," *Luceafărul*, 2 (1990): 6;

Pierre Mertens, "Reve ou realite?" *Le Soir*, 29 (1992);

Mircea Mihăieç, "Alchimia visului," *Orizont*, 43 (1989): 2;

Ion Mircea, "Faruri, vitríne, fotográfii," *Transilvania*, 2 (1981): 8–9;

Romul Munteanu, "Un poet în blugi," *Flacăra*, 7 (1986): 4;

Mircea Muthu, "Pest metereze şi bazaruri," *Transilvania*, 7 (1986): 10–11;

Tudor Olteanu, "Mircea Cărtărescu in het Nederlands," *Roemenie Bulletin*, 2 (1996);

Pierre Pachet, "L'Apre parfum de la fiction," *La Quinzaine litteraire*, 604 (1992): 5–6;

Ioana Pârvulescu, "Cu cartea în sînge," *Contrapunct*, 18 (1991): 8–9;

Pârvulescu, "Secretul lui Mircea Cărtărescu," *România literară*, 37 (1994): 6;

Gheorghe Perian, "Mircea Cărtărescu," in his *Scriitori români postmoderni* (Bucharest: Editura Didactică şi Pedagogică, 1996): pp. 185–195;

Edgar Reichmann, "L'androgyne et la chimere," *Le Monde*, 14 (1995);

Eugen Simion, "Mircea Cărtărescu," in his *Scriitori români de azi*, volume 4, pp. 345–350 (Bucharest: Cartea Românească, 1989);

Lucian Vasiliu, "Fauru, vitríne, fotográfii," *Convorbiri literare*, 4 (1981): 3;

Juan Carlos Vidal, "Las catacumbas de la razon," *El Pais*, 10 (1993).

Sándor Csoóri

(3 February 1930 –   )

András Görömbei
Kossuth University, Debrecen

This entry originally appeared in Concise Dictionary of World Literary Biography:
South Slavic and Eastern European Writers.

BOOKS: *Felröppen a madár: Versek* (Budapest: Szépirodalmi, 1954);

Ördögpille: Versek (Budapest: Magvető, 1957);

Menekülés a magányból: Versek (Budapest: Magvető, 1962);

Tudósítás a toronyból: Szociográfia (Budapest: Magvető, 1963);

Kubai napló: Útirajz, esszé (Budapest: Magvető, 1965);

A költő és a majompofa: Karcolatok (Budapest: Magvető, 1966);

Második születésem: Versek (Budapest: Magvető, 1967);

Faltól falig: Esszék (Budapest: Magvető, 1969);

Lekvárcirkusz bohócai: Gyermekversek (Budapest: Móra, 1969);

Forradás–Ítélet–Nincs idő: Irodalmi forgatókönyvek, Kósa Ferenccel közösen (Budapest: Magvető, 1972);

Párbeszéd, sötétben: Versek (Budapest: Magvető, 1973);

Biztató (Lyndhurst, N.J.: Kaláka, 1973);

Utazás félálomban: Novellák, esszék, karcolatok (Budapest: Magvető, 1974);

Sose harmadnapon: Versek (Békéscsaba, 1976);

A látogató emlékei: Versek (Budapest: Magvető, 1977);

Jóslás a te idődről: Versek (Budapest: Magvető-Szépirodalmi, 1979);

Nomád napló: Novellák, esszék, karcolatok (Budapest: Magvető, 1979);

80 huszár: Irodalmi forgatókönyv, Sára Sándorral közösen (Budapest: Magvető, 1980);

A tizedik este: Versek (Budapest: Magvető, 1980);

Iszapeső: Kisregény (Budapest: Magvető, 1981);

Készülődés a számadásra: Esszé (New York: Püski-Corvin, 1981);

A magyar apokalipszis: Töprengés a második magyar hadsereg összeomlásáról: Esszé (New York: Püski-Corvin, 1981);

A félig bevallott élet: Esszék (Budapest: Magvető, 1982);

Tenger és diólevél: (Egykor elindula tizenkét kőmives.) Esszék (Bucharest: Kritérion, 1982);

Tenger és diólevél: Esszé, előadás, versek (New York: Püski-Corvin, 1982);

Elmaradt lázálom: Versek (Budapest: Magvető, 1982);

Várakozás a tavaszban: Válogatott versek (Budapest: Magvető, 1983);

Kezemben zöld ág: Versek (Budapest: Magvető, 1985);

Készülődés a számadásra: Esszék (Budapest: Magvető, 1987);

Lábon járó verőfény: Gyermekversek (Budapest: Móra, 1987);

Csoóri Sándor breviárium (Budapest: Eötvös, 1988);

A világ emlékművei: Versek (Budapest: Magvető, 1989);

Virágvasárnap (Budapest: Magyar Bibliofil Társaság, 1990);

Nappali hold: Esszék (Budapest: Püski, 1991);

Senkid, barátod: Válogatott versek (Budapest: Örökségünk, 1993);

Tenger és diólevél: Összegyűjtött esszék, naplók, beszédek, 1961–1994, 2 volumes (Budapest: Püski, 1994);

Hattyúkkal ágyútűzben: Versek (Budapest: Kortárs, 1994);

Ha volna életem: Versek (Budapest: Kortárs, 1996);

Szálla alá poklora Esszék (Miskolc: Felsőmagyarország, 1997);

Csoóri Sándor válogatott versei (Budapest: Unikornis, 1997);

A jövő szökevénye: Összegyűjtött versek (Debrecen: Kossuth Egyetemi Kiadó, 2000).

Editions in English: *Wings of Knives and Nails: Selected Poems,* translated by I. L. Halasz de Beky (Toronto: Vox Humana, 1981);

"A Stranger" and "Maybe Elegies," translated by Jascha Kessler, and "The Door Creaked Three Times," "The Tenant Who Lives in Fire," "A Bullet," and "The Bachelor," translated by Nicholas

Kolumban, in *Contemporary East European Poetry,* edited by Emery George (Ann Arbor, Mich.: Ardis, 1983), pp. 266–269;

Memory of Snow, translated by Kolumban (Great Barrington, Mass.: Penmaen Press, 1983);

Barbarian Prayer: Selected Poems of Sándor Csoóri, edited by Mátyás Domokos, translated by Tony Connor and others (Budapest: Corvina, 1989);

Selected Poems of Sándor Csoóri, translated by Len Roberts (Port Townsend, Wash.: Copper Canyon Press, 1992);

"A Drop of Blood on the Ground," translated by Roberts, and "Postponed Nightmare" and "Questions, to Carriers of the Dead," translated by Roberts and László Vértes, in *Shifting Borders: East European Poetries of the Eighties,* compiled and edited by Walter Cummins (Rutherford, N.J.: Fairleigh Dickinson University Press, 1993), pp. 240–242.

PRODUCED SCRIPTS: *Tizezer nap,* motion picture, Magyar Filmgyártó Vállalat, 1967;

Földobott kő, motion picture, Magyar Filmgyártó Vállalat, 1969;

Ítélet, motion picture, Magyar Filmgyártó Vállalat, 1970;

Nincs idő, motion picture, Magyar Filmgyártó Vállalat, 1972;

Hószakadás, motion picture, Magyar Filmgyártó Vállalat, 1974;

80 huszár, motion picture, Magyar Filmgyártó Vállalat, 1978;

Pergőtűz, motion picture, Magyar Filmgyártó Vállalat, 1982;

Tüske a köröm alatt, motion picture, Magyar Filmgyártó Vállalat, 1987.

A member of the post–World War II generation of modernist writers, Sándor Csoóri is one of the most imposing figures in Hungarian literature of the second half of the twentieth century. A poet of international stature and an essayist of distinguished reputation, Csoóri played a significant role in shaping the social and political consciousness of Hungarian society during the decades of Communist rule and in the years following its overthrow. A salient feature of Csoóri's life and work is his dissatisfaction and restlessness both as a creative artist and as an individual within a cultural milieu that idealizes the impersonal. Throughout his career he has been an exemplary dissenter, resisting any restrictions on personal or artistic freedom. His poetry has undergone a transformation from a simple and graphic realism to a verse that unites elegiac

Sándor Csoóri as shown on the cover for the 1992 translation of his selected verse

and rhapsodic tones and provides a sensual metaphor of the world. His essays, too, have undergone a shift from personal ruminations to a universality comparable in scope and quality to the music of the Hungarian composer Béla Bartók.

Csoóri was born into a peasant family on 3 February 1930 in the village of Zámoly in western Hungary; he was the son of Sándor Csoóri and Julianna Csóri. Zámoly was almost totally destroyed during World War II, and many of Csoóri's recurring motifs date back to the surrealistic nightmares he lived through during the war. He went to grade school in Zámoly, and in 1942, with the help of the Országos Falusi Tehetségkutató Intézet (National Institute for Talent Scouting in Villages), he began high school in Pápa, a small town in the Trans-Danubian region. He then attended the Protestant College in Pápa. Graduating in 1950, he joined the staff of the *Pápai Néplap* (Pápa People's Newspaper) and then that of the *Veszprém megyei Népújság* (People's Newspaper of Veszprém County). Soon, however, he left for Budapest, where he studied Russian, history, and literary translation in 1951–1952 at the Egyetemi Orosz Intézet (University Institute of Russian Studies). He had to abandon his studies after nine months because he contracted tuberculosis, and he spent the next six months in a sanatorium. In 1953–1954 he worked for the *Irodalmi Újság* (Literary Gazette).

Whereas most of his peers had begun to publish immediately after World War II, Csoóri, because of his illness, began to publish his poems regularly only in 1953. By this time László Nagy, Ferenc Juhász, and many others of his generation had become disillusioned with the Communist regime and pessimistic about the state of literature under the postwar Soviet-imposed doctrine of socialist realism. Csoóri, however, was still an enthusiastic supporter of socialist ideals. Highly regarded by the official literary establishment, he was awarded the prestigious Attila József Prize in 1954. That year, as a member of a delegation of writers, he traveled to Transylvania, the region of Romania that had belonged to Hungary until 1920.

In his early poems Csoóri wrote about the harsh realities of peasant life with a deep and impassioned sincerity based on his personal experience. The poems attracted the attention of Gyula Illyés, the best-known and most respected Hungarian poet of the time. Csoóri's first collection of poetry, *Felröppen a madár* (The Bird Soars High), was published in 1954.

In 1955–1956 Csoóri edited the poetry column of the important literary journal *Új hang* (New Voice). Increasingly drawn to the emerging reform movement, Csoóri was profoundly affected by the violent Soviet suppression of the 1956 Hungarian revolution. The experience radically altered both his political perspective and his poetic vision. From that time until the end of the 1960s his poetry is characterized by shifts of tone as he restlessly searches for his own identity. In his second collection, *Ördögpille* (Devilmoth, 1957), his political disappointment is hidden within a myriad of images. A peculiarly noticeable feature in his poetry at this time is his concern for the poor, as illustrated in the widely anthologized "Anyám fekete rózsa" (My Mother Is a Black Rose). His interest in public affairs remained strong, but it was expressed in prose; he reserved his lyrical poetry for the exploration of his emotions, moods, and inner experiences.

In the late 1950 Csoóri broadened his interests to include a diverse range of literary influences, from classical and contemporary Hungarian poets to Federico García Lorca, Paul Éluard, Guillaume Apollinaire, and the American Beat poets. In 1959 the folklorist Zoltán Kallós suggested that he write a play for provincial actors based on Hungarian folk ballads. As a result, Csoóri began studying Hungarian folk poetry and the music of Bartók and Zoltán Kodály, which united folk and modern materials. He traveled with Kallós to Transylvania, where Hungarian folk music had been preserved in its traditional form. These experiences were crucial in shaping Csoóri's worldview and led him to initiate the folklore renaissance that influenced Hungarian literature for the next two decades.

In the late 1950s and early 1960s Csoóri regularly met with such leading Hungarian intellectuals as Miklós Jancsó, Mihály Sükösd, Gyula Hernádi, László Vekerdi, József Tornai, and László Gyurkó at the Belvárosi kávéház (Downtown Café) in Budapest, where, despite the Communist dictatorship, free exchanges of ideas about politics and art were conducted. Csoóri also became a leading figure in the debates and discussions of the Írószövetség (Writers' Union), which provided a forum for opposition politics. In 1962 he published his third poetry collection, *Menekülés a magányból* (An Escape from Loneliness); about this volume Ferenc Kiss says: "The most conspicuous feature is that the new poems by Csoóri, just like the examples taken from folk poetry, have gotten detached from the concreteness of the experience. What they have retained from that experience is intertwined with the things of nature and of the cosmos: with the trees, flowers, rivers, the wind, the rain, the moon, and the sun." Dissatisfied with the work, Csoóri decided that he could not completely express himself in poetry and began to experiment with ethnography, travel writing, essays, and motion pictures.

At the beginning of the 1960s the government forced the Hungarian peasantry into agricultural cooperatives. In response, in 1963 Csoóri published *Tudósítás a toronyból* (Report from the Tower), an ethnographical work based on his experiences in the rural village of his youth and influenced by Illyés's *Puszták népe* (1936; translated as *The People of Puszta*, 1967). The book, which shows the dramatic change in the life of peasantry and the deterioration of traditional values caused by the collectivization, reshaped this genre of Hungarian literature that had developed between the two world wars.

During the winter of 1962–1963 Csoóri spent three weeks in Cuba as a member of a writers' delegation. The trip resulted in *Kubai napló* (Cuban Diary, 1965). That same year Csoóri wrote a short novel, *Iszapeső* (Rain of Mud), about the suicide of a peasant girl, but the work was denied publication by the authorities (it finally appeared in 1981). Csoóri was banned from publishing and public appearances for a year; his government stipend was withdrawn; his contract to write a movie script was voided; and his project for a book was rejected by the authorities.

According to most critics, the publication in 1967 of *Második születésem* (My Second Birth), his fourth volume of poetry, marks the full development of Csoóri's talent. With this collection his poetic personality becomes significantly more complex. The central theme in the volume is a longing for entirety, a desire to live life to its fullest. Around this time Csoóri became a dramaturge for Magyar Filmgyártó Vállalat (Hungarian Film Producing Company), and over the next two decades he endeavored, along with director Ferenc Kósa and cinematographer Sándor Sára, to create motion pictures of emotional depth and complexity. Csoóri and his colleagues wanted to produce movies about issues confronting contemporary Hungarian society, but they were forced by the authorities to restrict themselves to historical themes and to comment only indirectly on current problems.

Awarded the Grand Prix at the Cannes Film Festival, Csoóri, Kósa, and Sára's first collaboration, *Tizezer nap* (Ten Thousand Days, 1967), is a condensed presentation of three decades of peasant life in which documentary realism is mixed with poetic elements. The young protagonist of their next movie, *Földobott kő* (A Tossed Stone, 1969), is an intellectual whose fate is intertwined with the multiple tragedies of his people. *Ítélet* (Verdict, 1970) is about the last days of György Dózsa, the leader of the 1514 Hungarian Peasant Revolt; scenes of the revolt and of the ensuing punishment of the revolutionaries are shown side by side. *Nincs idő* (No Time Left, 1972) is about an imprisoned rebel and asks whether one can remain a revolutionary if the possibility of revolution no longer exists. In *Hószakadás* (Snow Burst, 1974) the fate of the protagonist is a metaphor for the history of the Hungarian nation during World War II: he is consumed by the war despite his intention to stay out of it. Set during the 1848–1849 Hungarian War of Independence, *80 huszár* (80 Hussars, 1978) shows how the goals of the people were lost in the violence and chaos of the struggle—a situation that has occurred many times in Hungarian history.

During this period Csoóri embarked on a deeper exploration of his poetic voice that further established him as the leading poet of his generation in Hungary. His philosophical and passionate motivations give the poems in collections such as

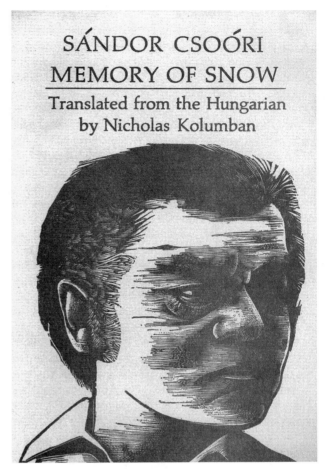

Cover for the 1983 English translation of Csoóri's poem *"Hó emléke"*

Párbeszéd, sötétben (Conversation in Darkness, 1973) and *A látogató emlékei* (Memories of the Visitor, 1977) an unprecedented richness. For Csoóri, a poem is a defense of communal activism. His poetic persona shoulders the responsibilities and concerns of the country: "tódul újra a hideg / a befagyasztott földrészek kamráiból, / a semmire se készülők húsából / estétől reggelig" (cold pours again / from chambers of frozen continents, / from the flesh of those preparing for nothing / night and day). "Anyám szavai" (My Mother's Words) is an extension of the earlier simple and beautiful "Anyám fekete rózsa" and projects greater psychological and philosophical depth. "Másnaposan" (Hangover) expresses the disgust the poet feels at the sight of decay. Csoóri does not resolve the conflicts among his emotions but juxtaposes the collision points, directing attention to the dramatic aspects and absurdities of a given situation. In "Hó emléke" (translated as *Memory of Snow*, 1983) the sight of falling snow prompts the speaker to look back on his life "mintha nem történt volna meg" (as if it did not happen), "és minden, ami politika volt, szerelem, harangzúgás, / óceáni távlatban újra várna" (and everything that was politics, love or peal of bells / would be waiting for me in oceanic distances). "Che Guevara búcsúztatója" (Farewell to Che Guevara) weeps for "a század partizánját" (the partisan of the century); "Levél Gregory Corso amerikai költőhöz" (A Letter to Gregory Corso, the American poet) is addressed to "huszadik század vagányának" (the hipster of the twentieth century). Csoóri's increasingly judgmental and castigating attitude peaks in "Berzsenyi elégiája" (Berzsenyi's Elegy), in which he speaks in the name of his poet predecessor, Dániel Berzsenyi, who died in 1836.

In 1973 Csoóri visited the United States for the first time; he returned on several occasions to lecture on such issues as the oppression of ethnic Hungarian minorities and the appreciation of émigré literature. He became increasingly outspoken in his political dissent and in 1977 jeopardized his career by signing the Czech opposition's "Charta '77" (Charter '77), which advocated social and political reform in Czechoslovakia. He was shaken by the death in January 1978 of his closest literary friend, Nagy, followed shortly by the death of his lover, Éva Kelemen, whose memory he recalled in the passionate poems collected in *A tizedik este* (The Tenth Night, 1980) and *Elmaradt lázálom* (Postponed Nightmare, 1982).

Csoóri enhanced his reputation with the publication of *Kezemben zöld ág* (Green Twig in My Hand, 1985) and *A világ emlékművei* (The Monuments of the World, 1989). He also remained active as a scriptwriter and dramaturge for the Magyar Filmgyártó Vállalat. Most important, however, during this period Csoóri solidified his position as an essayist comparable to such distinguished predecessors as Nagy and Endre Ady. In his essay "Szántottam gyöpöt" (I Have Plowed a Lawn) in the volume *A költő és a majompofa* (The Poet and the Monkeyface, 1966), he proves that the commonly accepted notion of the simple and realistic nature of folk poetry is wrong by showing that all European trends have their roots in folk poetry. In "Egykor elindula tizenkét kőműves" (Once Twelve Bricklayers Went on Their Way, 1982) he explores the tradition of dramatic literature in folk ballads.

Tenger és diólevél (Sea and Walnut Leaf, 1982) is an autobiographical work in which Csoóri's every experience—from skyscrapers to a village cemetery, from Beat poetry to folk ballads, from the poetry of Attila József to that of Allen Ginsberg, and from the chestnut leaf to the sea—plays an important and intricate role.

In other essays, such as "Utazás félálomban" (Traveling Half Asleep, 1974), "Kapaszkodás megmaradásért" (Hanging on for Survival), "Erkölcsi revíziót!" (Moral Revision!), and "Eltemetetlen gondok a Duna-tájon" (Unburied Problems in the Danube Region), Csoóri examines the social and political issues confronting contemporary Hungary as well as all of Central and Eastern Europe. In *A magyar apokalipszis* (Hungarian Apocalypse, 1981) he presents the catastrophe of the Second Hungarian Regiment at the river Don in World War II as a visionary tableau.

In 1981 Csoóri played a significant role in the achievement of the first free democratic election in the Writers' Union; that same year he was awarded Austria's prestigious Herder Prize. In 1987 Csoóri was one of the founders of the Hungarian Democratic Forum, and the next year he was named president of the editorial committee of the newly launched social and literary periodical of the opposition, *Hitel* (Credit). Following the collapse of communism in 1989 Csoóri was actively involved in the political arena at the expense of his writing. When the formerly unified opposition became divided into factions, however, he withdrew from politics. He received the highest Hungarian literary award, the Kossuth Prize, in 1990, having been denied it previously because of his activity in the political opposition. In 1991 he became president of the World Federation of Hungarians, and the following year he was named editor in chief of *Hitel*.

Disillusioned by the political transition, Csoóri turned again to poetry. Volumes such as *Hattyúkkal ágyútűzben* (With Swans under Cannonade, 1994) and *Ha volna életem* (If I Had a Life, 1996) reflect his disappointment and bitterness at the failure of the transition from communism to produce fundamental changes in Hungarian society. Nonetheless, Csoóri has played a leading role in the spiritual revival of the nation's populist tradition and has distinguished himself as one of the leading contemporary poets in modern Hungarian literature.

Interviews:

Bulcsu Bertha, "Csoóri Sándor," in his *Bulcsu: Délutáni Beszélgetések* (Budapest: Szépirodalmi, 1978), pp. 62–105;

Mátyás Domokos, "Csoóri Sándor: Hó emléke," in *Versekről, költőkkel*, by Domokos and László Lator (Budapest: Szépirodalmi, 1982), pp. 485–511.

Bibliography:

Sándor Agócs, *Csoóri Sándor bibliográfiája* (Budapest: Hitel Kft. 1990).

References:

Laszlo Ablonczy, "Apprehensive Patriotism," *New Hungarian Quarterly*, 30 (Summer 1989): 128–133;

Jenő Alföldy, "Bevezetésféle Csoóri Sándor költészetébe," *Tiszatéj*, 11 (1980): 34–39; republished in his *Élménybeszámoló* (Budapest: Szépirodalmi, 1983), pp. 137–148;

Zoltán Bíró, "Egy nemzedék naplója," *Tiszatáj*, 9 (1982): 58–67; republished in his *Vállalások és kételyek* (Budapest: Szépirodalmi, 1987), pp. 225–248;

Ervin C. Brody, "Literature and Politics in Today's Hungary: Sándor Csoóri in the Populist Debate," *Literary Review*, 38 (Spring 1995): 426–428;

Mihály Czine, "Hű lovasok útján," *Jelenkor*, 2 (1980): 147–152; republished in his *Nép és irodalom* (Budapest: Szépirodalmi, 1981), pp. 527–535;

András Görömbei, "Költő a hetvenes években," *Tiszatáj*, 2 (1980): 49–53; republished in his *Ki viszi át . . . ?* (Budapest: Szépirodalmi, 1986), pp. 198–209;

Görömbei, "Tenger és diólevél," in his *A szavak értelme* (Budapest: Püski, 1996), pp. 448–459;

Görömbei, ed., *Tanvlmányok Csoóri Sándorról* (Debrecen: Kossuth Egyetemi Kiadó, 2000);

Ferenc Kiss, *Csoóri Sándor* (Budapest: Magvető, 1990);

Ernő Kulcsár Szabó, "Rapszódia térben és időben," *Kortárs*, 24 (1980): 803–811; republished in his *Műalkotás–szöveg–hatás* (Budapest: Magvető, 1987), pp. 382–401;

Balazs Lengyel, "The Voice Is the Poet," *New Hungarian Quarterly*, 26 (Winter 1985): 197–200;

Béla Márkus, "Az elveszett világ fojtó érzékisége," *Kortárs*, 2 (1995): 92–98;

Márkus, "Megbéklyózva és megigazulva: A filmíró Csoóri Sándorról," *Tiszatáj*, 2 (1980): 66–71;

Géza Pörös, "Őrizd az embert. (A filmekről)," *Forrás*, 12 (1976): 57–71;

Mihály Sükösd, "Csoóri Sándor," in his *Seregszemle* (Budapest: Szépirodalmi, 1986), pp. 377–394;

Lajos Marton Varga, "The Writer and His New Freedom," *New Hungarian Quarterly*, 31 (Spring 1990): 101–102;

Géza Vasy, "A nemzet rebellise," in Csoóri's *Csoóri Sándor Breviárium* (Budapest: Eötvös, 1988), pp. 224–244.

Adam Czerniawski

(20 December 1934 –)

Iain Higgins
University of British Columbia

BOOKS: *Polowanie na jednorożca* (London: Oficyna
   Poetów i Malarzy, 1956);
Topografia wnętrza (Paris: Instytut Literacki, 1962);
Części mniejszej całości: Opowiadania, preface by
   Witold Gombrowicz (London: Oficyna
   Poetów i Malarzy, 1964);
Sen cytadela gaj (Paris: Instytut Literacki, 1966);
Liryka i druk: Szkice i eseje (London: Oficyna Poetów
   i Malarzy, 1972);
Widok Delft: Wiersze z lat 1966–1969 (Kraków:
   Wydawnictwo Literackie, 1973);
*Akt: Opracował Józef Zenon Tynicki zgodnie z para-
   grafami małego kodeksu karnego i cenzury
   wewnętrznej* (London: Oficyna Poetów i
   Malarzy, 1975);
Wiersz współczesny (London: Oficyna Poetów i
   Malarzy, 1977);
Wiek złoty 1969–1981 (Paris: Instytut Literacki,
   1982);
Władza najwyższa: Wybór wierszy z lat 1953–1978
   (Kraków: Wydawnictwo Literackie, 1982);
Jesień (Kraków: Wydawnictwo Literackie, 1989);
Koncert życzeń (Warsaw: Staromiejski Dom Kultury,
   1991);
Scenes from a Disturbed Childhood (London: Serpent's
   Tail, 1991); revised and published in Polish
   as *Fragmenty niespokojnego dzieciństwa* (Lon-
   don: Aneks, 1995);
Poezje zebrane 1952–1991 (Łódź: Wydawnictwo Bib-
   lioteka, 1993);
Muzy i sowa Minerwy (Wrocław: Wydawnictwo Dol-
   nośląskie, 1994);
Krótkopis, 1986–1995 (Katowice: Wydawnictwo
   Gnome, 1998);
Inne wiersze i historia ludzkości (Katowice:
   Wydawnictwo Gnome, 1999).
Editions in English: *Knowledge by Description,* trans-
   lated by Iain Higgins (Hull, U.K.: Carnivo-
   rous Arpeggio Press, 1992);
Selected Poems, translated by Higgins (Amsterdam:
   Harwood Academic, 2000).

*Adam Czerniawski (drawing by Feliks Topolsk, from the cover for
Czerniawski's* Scenes from a Disturbed Childhood, *1991)*

RECORDING: *The Writers at Warwick Archive: Tadeusz
   Różewicz Celebrated,* with Czerniawski, Barbara
   Howard, and Tony Howard (Coventry: Univer-
   sity of Warwick, 1999).

OTHER: *Ryby na piasku: Antologia wierszy poetów
   "Londyńskich,"* edited by Czerniawski (London:
   B. Świderski, 1965);
The Mature Laurel: Essays on Modern Polish Poetry,
   edited by Czerniawski (Bridgend, Wales:
   Seren Books / Chester Springs, Pa.: Dufour,
   1991);
"A Poetical Political History," in *New Perspectives on
   Twentieth-Century Polish Literature,* edited by

Stanisław Eile and Ursula Phillips (London: Macmillan, 1992), pp. 6–27;

Ewa Lipska, *Poet? Criminal? Madman?* translated by Barbara Plebanik and Tony Howard, foreword by Czerniawski (London & Boston: Forest Books, 1991); republished as *White Strawberries* (Kraków: Wydawnictwo Literackie, 2000).

TRANSLATIONS: Tadeusz Różewicz, *The Card Index and Other Plays* (London: Calder & Boyars, 1969; New York: Grove, 1969);

Różewicz, *Faces of Anxiety* (London: Rapp & Whiting, 1969; Chicago: Swallow Press, 1969);

Władysław Tatarkiewicz, *Ancient Aesthetics*, volume 1 of *History of Aesthetics*, translated by Czerniawski and Ann Czerniawska (The Hague: Mouton / Warsaw: PWN-Polish Scientific Publishers, 1970);

Różewicz, *The Witnesses and Other Plays* (London: Calder & Boyars, 1970);

Różewicz, *Selected Poems* (Harmondsworth, U.K. & Baltimore: Penguin, 1976);

Artur Sandauer and Alicja Bałakier, *Białoszewski* (Warsaw: Authors Agency & Czytelnik, 1979);

Leon Stroiński, *Window: Collected Prose Poems* (London: Oasis Books, 1979);

Różewicz, *Conversation with the Prince and Other Poems* (London: Anvil Press Poetry, 1982); enlarged as *They Came to See a Poet: Selected Poems* (London: Anvil Press Poetry, 1991);

Różewicz, *Mariage Blanc* and *The Hunger Artist Departs* (London: Boyars, 1983);

Leopold Staff, *An Empty Room* (Newcastle upon Tyne: Bloodaxe Books, 1983);

Różewicz, *The Trap* (New York: Institute for Contemporary Eastern European Drama and Theatre, 1984; Amsterdam: Harwood Academic, 1997);

Roman Ingarden, *The Work of Music and the Problem of Its Identity*, edited by Jean G. Harrell (Berkeley: University of California Press, 1986);

Cyprian Kamil Norwid, *Poezje/Poems* (Kraków: Wydawnictwo Literackie, 1986);

The Burning Forest: Modern Polish Poetry, translated and edited by Czerniawski (Newcastle upon Tyne: Bloodaxe Books / Chester Springs, Pa.: Dufour, 1988);

Leszek Kołakowski, *The Presence of Myth* (Chicago: University of Chicago Press, 1989);

Wisława Szymborska, *People on a Bridge: Poems* (London & Boston: Forest Books, 1990);

Różewicz, *Poezje wybrane 1952–1991 / Selected Poems* (Kraków: Wydawnictwo Literackie, 1991; enlarged, 2000);

Heraclitus of Ephesus, *Zdania* (Łódź: Wydawnictwo Biblioteka, 1992);

Norwid, *To a Deceased . . . : Finis* (Hull, U.K.: Carnivorous Arpeggio Press, 1992);

Zbigniew Herbert, *Reconstruction of a Poet*, in *Frontiers*, edited by Christopher MacLehose, Leopard, no. 3 (London: Harvill, 1994), pp. 319–331;

Jan Kochanowski, *Treny*, edited and annotated by Piotr Wilczek (Katowice: Wydawnictwo Uniwersytetu Śląskiego, 1996);

Krzysztof Michalski, *Logic and Time: An Essay on Husserl's Theory of Meaning*, translation revised by James Dodd (Dordrecht: Kluwer Academic, 1997);

Różewicz, *Reading the Apocalypse in Bed: Selected Plays and Short Pieces*, translated by Czerniawski, Barbara Plebanek, and Tony Howard (New York: Boyars, 1998).

SELECTED PERIODICAL PUBLICATIONS—UNCOLLECTED: "The Polish Poet as Custodian of the Nation's Conscience," *Polish Review*, 4 (1979): 3–25;

"The Power of Taste in a Beleaguered City: On the Poetry of Zbigniew Herbert," *Poetry Wales*, 2 (1984): 53–71;

"Are Poets Necessary?" *Poetry Review*, 77 (Autumn 1987): 7–10;

"Poetry as Celebration," *Irish Review*, 5 (1988): 92–95;

"'Writing and Translating during the Cold War in a Country of which I Know Something': Exiled in England," *Comparative Criticism*, 16 (1994): 7–18;

"De Amicitia," *Thumbscrew*, 3 (Autumn–Winter 1995): 47–52;

"Polish Poetry in the West, or the Canon that Fired Late," *Thumbscrew*, 8 (Summer 1997): 86–99;

"The Melancholy Pursuit of Imperfection," *Metre*, 5 (1998): 62–72;

"Absurdity and Poetry," *PN Review*, 1 (1999): 49–55;

"Translation of Poetry: Theory and Practice," *Modern Poetry in Translation*, 15 (1999): 260–276.

Adam Czerniawski is a noted poet, critic, and translator who has also published several collections of short fiction and a fine memoir of his "disturbed" childhood. He has published many English translations of contemporary Polish poetry, drama, and philosophy, as well as his essays in English on poetry. His writings are part of the notable body of work produced by the writers known as the *Kontynenty* (Continents) group, who, as a consequence of World War

II, left Poland early in life (Czerniawski at age seven), came to maturity mainly in Britain, and declined to return to their homeland but still chose to write in their native tongue. Deeply influenced by their disparate international, multicultural, and bilingual experiences, Czerniawski and these other writers have brought to their work an unusually profound concern with problems of language, consciousness, experience, identity, and culture, as well as considerable knowledge of other European literary traditions. The crucial question that they have had constantly to answer is: What does it mean to be a Polish writer living in isolation from one's own language, culture, and readers? One of Czerniawski's main answers to this question has been his work against the fragmentation of Polish literary culture; since the 1970s, especially, he has been prominent among the few who have attempted to transcend the barriers that have separated the émigré and home literary communities from one another.

Czerniawski was born on 20 December 1934, the second of two children, into a well-to-do and socially active family in central Warsaw. His father, Emil Jerzy Czerniawski, who had been a member of Marshal Józef Piłsudski's legions during World War I, was deputy director of the Polish Tobacco Monopoly; his mother, Maria (née Tynicka), whose family was related to the Renaissance poet Jan Kochanowski, was born and reared in Ukraine, where she had met her future husband after Piłsudski's abortive military offensive in the spring of 1920.

On 1 September 1939 Germany invaded Poland from the west; on 17 September the Soviet Union, then allied with Germany, invaded from the east. Under the orders of the Polish Ministry of War Czerniawski's father was called up as a reservist at the rank of captain to fight on the eastern front against the Russians. When the front collapsed, Emil Czerniawski was ordered—along with thousands of army personnel and government officials—to escape to Romania. Czerniawski, his sister, and their mother lived mostly in Nazi-occupied Warsaw until the family was reunited in Istanbul in July 1941. They lived in Turkey, Palestine, and Lebanon before settling in London in 1947. For the first five years of this period Czerniawski attended Polish, French, American, and English schools, and for a time was fluent in Arabic and Hebrew; he spent the last year as a cadet in the Polish army. In England he finished his secondary schooling and went on to study English literature at London University. After graduating with a B.A. in 1955 he went to Munich, where he worked as a broadcaster and scriptwriter in the youth program of the Voice of America. He published his first volume

of poems, *Polowanie na jednorożca* (Hunting the Unicorn), in 1956. In July 1957, disillusioned with his post as a minor Cold Warrior, he returned to England. He spent three months without a job before finding a position with an insurance company in London (the parallel with T. S. Eliot's early career could hardly have been lost on Czerniawski, who admired Eliot's work). His second volume of poetry, *Topografia wnętrza* (Interior Topography), appeared in 1962. In 1963 he made a brief visit to Poland, the first of many efforts to overcome the barriers raised by the Cold War against an international Polish literary culture to which writers and intellectuals on both sides of the Iron Curtain could contribute.

Czerniawski remained with the insurance company until 1965: "I deliberately chose the bureaucratic environment so that as a writer I would be free from cold-war pressures," he says in the essay "'Writing and Translating during the Cold War in a Country of which I Know Something': Exiled in England" (1994). In that same essay Czerniawski explains how his literary career began in a way that included the kinds of cultural mediation and border crossing in which he has always engaged:

> In 1952 I enrolled as a student at London University. I became editor of the King's College literary review *Lucifer* and published in it my translations of Cyprian Norwid . . . and a review of Miłosz's *The Captive Mind*. At the same time my first poems and literary essays were beginning to appear in various Polish *émigré* periodicals in London and Paris. I joined the editorial board of a Polish students' magazine which was outgrowing student concerns and was transforming itself into a periodical of young radical intelligentsia: under my editorship the magazine finally broke with the Polish students' union at a stormy meeting in 1958. The chief reason for the implacable disagreement lay in attitudes to the cold war: the students were intransigent in their refusal to have anything to do with communist Poland, we were convinced that it was essential to forge such contacts—not of course with the regime's apparatchiks but with writers and intellectuals. . . .

> The successive changes in our periodical's name from *Życie Akademickie* (Student Life, 1950–1955) to . . . *Kontynenty* (1958–1966) indicate the gradually evolving and broadening outlook of the publication which over the years could boast of publishing works by the majority of the older *émigrés* including . . . Miłosz . . . and Witold Gombrowicz and by new writers in Poland, as well as of course by members of its editorial committee. . . .

As an émigré writer whose life and work were radically affected by World War II and its prolonged aftermath, Czerniawski had to make his literary way under different circumstances from those faced by such well-known Polish exiles as Gombrowicz, Czesław Miłosz, Aleksander Wat, and Stanisław Barańczak, all of whom were established writers when they left Poland.

One of Czerniawski's important early labors on behalf of émigré writing was *Ryby na piasku: Antologia wierszy poetów "Londyńskich"* (Fish on the Strand, 1965), an anthology by thirteen young poets at the rebellious center of Polish postwar literary life in London, which included works by Bogdan Czaykowski, Jan Darowski, Jerzy Sito, and himself. The title of the collection was taken from Czaykowski's 1956 poem "Argument," which defines the cultural placelessness of writers as unavoidably characterized by "two underrealities": in exile, they are beached fish; in their native land, they would be caged "in the horn of plenty." The anthology was the *Kontynenty* group's posthumous swan song, since by the mid 1960s the poets had gone their separate ways; but the independent attitudes and budding poetic careers that the collection revealed were culturally significant enough to be the final work Miłosz discusses in the first edition of his *History of Polish Literature* (1969).

Czerniawski's third volume of poetry, *Sen cytadela gaj* (A Dream a Citadel a Grove), appeared in 1966. After leaving the business world, he studied philosophy, taking another B.A. from London University in 1967, an M.A. from Sussex University in 1968, and a Ph.B from the University of Oxford in 1970. His British education not only influenced his practice as a poet and critic but also gave him the means and the impetus—a reaction against British cultural parochialism—to become a major translator of Polish literature and philosophy. As the 1960s came to a close, Czerniawski published the first four of his more than twenty translated volumes of Polish poetry, drama, and philosophy: Tadeusz Różewicz's *The Card Index and Other Plays* (1969), *Faces of Anxiety* (1969), and *The Witnesses and Other Plays* (1970) and—with his wife, Ann—the first volume of Władysław Tatarkiewicz's three-volume *History of Aesthetics* (1970), a joint undertaking by a Polish and a Western publisher. Czerniawski has acknowledged his wife's help with his translations of poetry. He and his wife (née Daker) were married in 1957. The couple has two children, Irena and Stefan.

Czerniawski taught philosophy and literature at Medway College of Design in Rochester, Kent, from 1970 to 1974 and was a lecturer in philosophy at the Thames Polytechnic in London (now the University of Greenwich), from 1974 to 1986. He published only one book of his own poems, *Widok Delft: Wiersze z lat 1966–1969* (A View of Delft, 1973), between his third volume in 1966 and his fifth and sixth collections, *Wiek złoty 1969–1981* (Golden Age 1969–1981) and *Władza najwyższa: Wybór wierszy z lat 1953–1978* (Supreme Authority: Selected Poems 1953–1978), in 1982. In 1975 he accepted an *Ordre du mérite culturel* from the Polish government and in 1977 a translator's award from the Polish Writers' Union—distinctions that other émigré writers thought it more appropriate to refuse.

In 1986 Czerniawski left academia to become a freelance writer and translator, circumstances that, along with the changed political situation in Poland, allowed him to heighten his literary profile in his native country. His seventh volume of poetry, *Jesień* (Autumn), was published in 1989. In the 1990s Czerniawski took several positions that recognized his longstanding role as cultural mediator: translator in residence (1991) and assistant director (1992 to 1994) at the British Center for Literary Translation at the University of East Anglia in Norwich, and administrator (1996 to 1999) of the International Retreat for Writers at Hawthornden Castle, Scotland.

While Czerniawski does not shun historical or political subjects, he has never wavered in his desire for artistic freedom from the burdens of history and politics. This desire is clearly signaled in the titles of his first poetic collections—the second of which takes as its epigraph a passage from Wallace Stevens's "The Idea of Order at Key West" on "the maker's rage to order words"—and reaffirmed in his later volumes. One of Czerniawski's most telling declarations of poetic independence occurs in the sonnetlike 1954 piece "dulce et decorum" (its ironically Horatian title echoes the English poet Wilfred Owen's harrowing portrait of a soldier's fate in World War I), which mocks the sentimental-religious-patriotic-military Polish cult of the fallen dead; but one can hear it even in unexpected places such as the ironic opening lines of "Złoty wiek" (Golden Age): "How could I have known that in my youth / I would experience the golden age: since as usual / there were wars, invasions, draconian reforms. . . ."

The poems by Różewicz that Czerniawski chose to translate in *Faces of Anxiety* offer suggestive contrasts, as well as some points of contact, with Czerniawski's own maturing work. Both poets reveal a preference for unpunctuated free verse and "unpoetic," even "antipoetic" subjects, sentiments, and forms, as well as a deliberate—one might say rebellious—plainness and discursiveness in their poetic styles. All of these features link them more closely to the experimental practices of the Polish avant-gardes than to the more traditionalist procedures of the "Skamander" poets, a group of Parnassian poets in the 1920s committed to poetic renewal and perfection without breaking with traditional metrics. Their name comes from a poetry magazine with which they were associated in Warsaw called *Skamander* (after the river near Troy in Homer's Iliad). In Czerniawski's case, however, poems of this anti-traditionalist sort initially stand alongside more "literary" compositions in which learned allusions to classical mythology and nineteenth-century French poetry and culture perhaps reveal the influence of Eliot and Ezra Pound, as well as a desire to write a cultured, Pan-European, rather than a narrowly "Polish" poetry—a desire that Czerniawski later found his own ways to satisfy. Still, Eliot, Pound, and especially Cyprian Kamil Norwid, played a part in the development of Czerniawski's often elliptical and "objectively" impersonal style—a poetic mode that stands somewhat apart from Różewicz's "naked" tone.

For instance, one might contrast Różewicz's 1948 poem "Pigtail" with Czerniawski's "Bavaria 1956," in *Topografia wnętrza* (1962). The former matter-of-factly records how at Auschwitz the Nazis shaved the heads of the women who were to be murdered in the gas chambers and then had the hair collected; after the war the hair went on display in the Auschwitz Museum. The poem, in Czerniawski's translation in *Faces of Anxiety*, ends: "In huge chests / clouds of dry hair / of those suffocated / and a faded plait / a pigtail with a ribbon pulled at school / by naughty boys." The force of the poem lies in the juxtaposition of its opening description of banal, adult evil in the camp with the closing image of common schoolroom naughtiness, an image that reminds one of the ordinary individual lives behind the grotesque material record of mass death. Czerniawski's poem, which resembles Różewicz's in being focused through an unmentioned but informed observer, differs from it in Czerniawski's crucial juxtaposition of the almost cloying cosiness of Bavaria's historical and natural landscape with the memory of the crematoria recently housed there. The poem ends:

and again this sweet
and maudlin landscape
lakes drowsing
in the mountains rain
drizzling in the valleys
and the sun

but all around pedantic streams
of smoke still obstinately bleed

(despite those sculptures
of mannered baroque,
the gilded paintings)

The force of this poem lies partly in its obliquely implied moral commentary—defining the smoke created by the burning bodies as "pedantic" and "obstinately bleeding," when one would expect such terms to be attributed to the observer who insists on recalling historical horrors in the presence of "picturesque" natural beauty—and partly in its reversal of the question to which Różewicz has devoted poem after poem: how to write poetry at all after the unprecedented horrors and brutalities symbolized by Auschwitz (such composition, according to Theodore Adorno, would be a barbarous act). The question implied by Czerniawski's poem is, in contrast, how to understand the historical relationship between the radically different kinds of activity—creative and destructive—that have occurred in the Bavarian landscape. Thus, whereas Różewicz's poem stands physically and visually close to its subject, attempting to create and communicate an experience of inhuman horror, Czerniawski's remains, like many of his poems, at a distance, implicitly raising a problem of understanding.

This sort of philosophical concern, which is at once aesthetic, cognitive, and moral, is typical of Czerniawski's poetry, and his manner of presenting it reveals his debt not only to Eliot's "objective correlative" but also to Norwid's elliptically "intellectual" poetry. Czerniawski defended Norwid's poetry in a 1959 essay, "Nieporozumienia" (Misunderstandings), which was republished with other literary and philosophical pieces in *Muzy i sowa Minerwy* (The Muses and the Owl of Minerva, 1994). He argues that such poetry need not be devoid of emotional content, and his own poems are rarely deficient in feeling. A still more powerful influence on this central element of Czerniawski's poetry than Eliot or Norwid has been those European thinkers who do not radically separate poetry from philosophy, especially Edmund Husserl, Martin Heidegger, and Ludwig Wittgenstein, all of whom devoted their attention to the problem of language and consciousness—even though Czerniawski affirms, with Wittgenstein, the independence of poetic language from issues of truth or falsity and appears to share with Anglo-American analytic philosophy a skepticism toward the capacity of language adequately to represent the world.

Occasionally, the philosophical influences on Czerniawski's poetry are direct, even obvious. "Miasto wczoraj i dzisiaj" (The City Yesterday and

Czerniawski as a child

guage or in other media, especially painting. Declining to argue, even in the parabolic manner of, say, Zbigniew Herbert's work, these poems typically proceed by what might be called musical modes of composition (Czerniawski is quite knowledgeable about music): themes are announced, and striking variations are played on them—sometimes the latter accumulate to the point that the poems are best described as fascinating catalogues of poetic examples; conceptual, imagistic, or tonal harmonies and dissonances are created; scherzo passages suddenly break into serious lines of development, and so on. The results of these musico-philosophical poetics are highly distinctive, offering readers the pleasure of watching a highly cultured European mind at work and play.

The pithiest expression of Czerniawski's persistent intellectual concerns occurs in two pieces from *Widok Delft: Wiersze z lat 1966–1969*–"Science Fiction," which briefly and with quiet irony imagines the natural and human world as a wonder of the science-fiction imagination, and the five-poem sequence that was titled "Pentagram" when it was republished in his *Poezje zebrane 1952–1991* (Collected Poems: 1952–1991, 1993). In "trojkąt" (triangle), for example, the third poem in the sequence, Czerniawski sets the geometric flexibility—the realness—of the triangle against the rigid perfection of the circle and the square, concluding with morally resonant irony that "we should be grateful / for a human version of the fierce harmony / of circles and squares." Czerniawski's philosophical-poetic modes in such texts can be contrasted with those of Miłosz, whose intellectualizing poems are distinguished by their author's highly personal grappling with the historical and lived consequences of Continental philosophical and religious ideas.

The personal and the historical have always had a place in Czerniawski's poetry, though sometimes not in his more overtly philosophical poems; and such elements are usually "objectively" distanced, as in "Bavaria 1956" or in "Saint Sebastian," a stylized portrait of the martyred saint that is quietly anachronistic and dedicated to the memory of Czerniawski's older cousin Jacek Świtalski, who died in Warsaw in 1944 while fighting against the Germans with the underground Armia Krajowa (Home Army). In his "Komentarze," however, and in poems such as the long and moving "Lustra i refleksje" (Mirrors and Reflections) in *Jesień* or the new poems in *Poezje zebrane, 1952–1991*, Czerniawski has, in his own distinctive musically inspired way (mixing genres, memories, invention, narration, and reflection), moved closer to Miłosz's mode, gaining in the process an

Today) in *Jesień,* for example, imagines an old city in "an era of functional building" as embodying various outdated poetics in its very architecture, a conceit that presumably takes off from Wittgenstein's image in the *Philosophical Investigations* (1953) of language as an ancient city constantly added to. Similarly, in "Śmierć" (Death), one of the engaging prose-poetic essays in his cycle "Komentarze" (Commentaries)—the first of which were published in *Władza najwyższa: Wybór wierszy z lat 1953–1978* and *Wiek złoty 1969–1981* in 1982—Czerniawski explicitly quotes "M. H." (Heidegger) on the difference between human and animal death.

Generally, though, the intellectualizing impulse in Czerniawski's poetry—which reveals itself in successful poetic form as early as the title poem of his first published volume—requires no support from major philosophers. Rather, it takes its own shape in poem after poem that debates, enacts, or meditates obliquely on puzzles and questions of perception (the root meaning of the term *aesthetic*), consciousness, memory, and representation, whether in lan-

appealing clarity and range. The same is true of the few poems that explicitly quote or "revise" earlier ones: "Pętla" (Loop) in *Jesień*, for example, which returns to the scene of "Bavaria 1956" but more personally and at much greater length. A fortunate result of the clarity and added richness of Czerniawski's more recent poems is that they give his earlier works a greater resonance, unexpectedly bringing out the latent energies of the latter.

Because of the practical and political barriers, Czerniawski's poetry received little published notice in Poland until the 1980s. Since then it has been reviewed and commented on, in general favorably, with increasing frequency and insight. Readers in Poland have appreciated not only the searching cognitive dimensions of his work but also the tonal and perspectival variations the poems embody as a consequence of Czerniawski's lifelong immersion in the English language and English culture: "his poems, very strongly rooted in the Polish language, seem to possess a somewhat different tone, a different 'resonance,'" wrote Leszek Żuliński in *Tygodnik Kulturalny* (Cultural Weekly) in 1982–a view echoed by Tomasz Lebioda in *Metafora* (Winter–Spring 1995): "Sounds heard from afar startle and appear shorn of everyday ordinariness."

As a poet Czerniawski is little known to English-speaking readers even in England, where he has lived for more than half a century, although the edition of his selected poems in English translation published in 2000 may help to remedy that situation. He is, however, well known as an English translator (apart from versions of a handful of English and American poems, his only published translation into Polish is a 1992 volume of the fragments of the pre-Socratic philosopher Heraclitus). In addition to learned treatises by such prominent Polish philosophers as Tatarkiewicz, Roman Ingarden (1986), and Leszek Kołakowski (1989), whose readership is primarily academic, Czerniawski has produced a substantial body of literary translations. Like Miłosz and Barańczak, whose labors in this domain were preceded by his own, Czerniawski has devoted much energy to making the best work of his poetic contemporaries available to an English-speaking readership through translations and critical prose. The bulk of this work offers representative selections of major Polish poets since Norwid, particularly of those whose writings are distinguished not only by intellectual strength but also by clarity of language and thought and by the new modes they have found for poetry. Some of this important mediatory work has been broadcast in talks and readings on BBC Radio.

Since 1969 Czerniawski has published six collections of poetry and four of plays by Różewicz, as well as single volumes of verse by Leon Stroiński (1979), Leopold Staff (1983), Norwid (1986, 1992), Wisława Szymborska (1990), and Kochanowski (1996); a play by Herbert (1994); and, in 1988, *The Burning Forest: Modern Polish Poetry*, his own anthology of modern Polish poetry. For most of the seventeen poets included, from Norwid and Staff to Barańczak and Bronisław Maj, the anthology quotes informative comments by Polish poets and critics, and many of the other volumes have useful brief introductions by Czerniawski himself. Supplementing this material are Czerniawski's English essays—especially "Writing and Translating during the Cold War"—which since the late 1980s have appeared with increasing frequency in various forums, and *The Mature Laurel* (1991), his edition of essays by prominent English and Polish critics on Polish poetry since Norwid. Two of the English contributors to *The Mature Laurel* place Czerniawski's Różewicz translations on a par with George Chapman's famous renderings of Homer in the late sixteenth and early seventeenth centuries. While Herbert and Miłosz seem so far to have been more influential in the English-speaking world, Czerniawski's Różewicz translations have made a sizeable body of important poems and plays accessible to a wide readership, and they also constitute some of his best work as a translator.

Czerniawski's other translations vary in quality, as one might expect when a single translator takes on such a range of poets and poetic styles, but they almost always hold their own against other English translations of the same poems, where such are available, and they are a valuable source both for readers and for potential future translators. *The Burning Forest: Modern Polish Poetry*, in particular, because it can be read along with the third edition of Miłosz's *Postwar Polish Poetry* (1983) and Barańczak and Clare Cavanagh's *Polish Poetry of the Last Two Decades of Communist Rule: Spoiling Cannibals' Fun* (1991), offers English-speaking readers a chance to get acquainted with some of the most important Polish poetry since Norwid. Czerniawski's translations of Szymborska's poems in *People on a Bridge: Poems* (1990) can also be profitably read in conjunction with those of others, whose choices from Szymborska's oeuvre differ somewhat from Czerniawski's: *Sounds, Feelings, Thoughts* (1981), by Magnus J. Krynski and Robert A. Maguire, and *View with a Grain of Sand* (1995), by Barańczak and Cavanagh. Czerniawski's translations are less literal than Krynski and Maguire's but take fewer liberties than the Barańczak and Cavanagh versions; thus, they usually offer readable and accurate renderings.

Perhaps of greater importance are Czerniawski's translations of Norwid's poems and of Kochanowski's *Treny* (Laments, 1580). Norwid is formally and stylistically a world away from Czerniawski's favorite, Różewicz, and Czerniawski's renderings sometimes sacrifice the semantic richness of the poems to clarity and formal fidelity; but they constitute the largest and best selection of Norwid's work available in English, and they make it clear why non-Polish readers should take the nineteenth-century poet seriously. The Kochanowski translation, which is accompanied by a useful close reading of the elegiac sequence, also represents a major achievement. Czerniawski's translation of the sequence lacks some of the more obviously poetical qualities of *Laments* (1995), the translation by Barańczak and Seamus Heaney, which makes Kochanowski sound quite Heaney-like; but it has the important virtue of rendering more accurately the emotional clarity and directness of the images and arguments in the poems without sacrificing their historical novelty and cultural strangeness.

Since the mid 1950s Czerniawski's labors of mediation and advocacy have also included many Polish essays on poetry, the bulk of them collected in three volumes: *Liryka i druk: Szkice i eseje* (Poetry and Print, 1972); *Wiersz współczesny* (The Contemporary Poem, 1977), first published serially from 1967 to 1971 in the Polish weekly *Wiadomości* (News); and *Muzy i sowa Minerwy* (1994). About a third of the essays in *Muzy i sowa Minerwy* are concerned with literary-theoretical and philosophical issues, as is the entire slim volume on contemporary poems; the latter differs from the other two collections, however, in being a connected sequence of meditations, and its brief "chapters" differ from the more abstract essays in *Muzy i sowa Minerwy* in being centered on discussions of poetics illustrated by poems from writers as diverse as Pound, Miłosz, W. H. Auden, Gottfried Benn, John Donne, Stanisław Grochowiak, Adam Mickiewicz, Edwin Muir, and Virgil.

In contrast, the essays in *Liryka i druk: Szkice i eseje*, which were written in the 1950s and 1960s, and more than half of those in *Muzy i sowa Minerwy*, which date from the 1950s to the 1990s, focus on the work of individual poets. Norwid, Miłosz, Różewicz, and Herbert are especially prominent subjects, but Czerniawski also devotes essays to the best of his émigré colleagues—including Darowski, Andrzej Busza, and Czaykowski—and to Anglo-American poets, particularly Pound and Eliot. Influenced by an independent and high-minded tradition of Anglo-American criticism that runs from Matthew Arnold through Eliot, I. A. Richards, and F. R. Leavis, these are a poet's essays. Typically insightful, partial, and generous with quotations and examples, they attend carefully to each poet's poetics, examining its strengths, weaknesses, and implications; they seldom enter into current academic debates. Since clarification, evaluation, and appreciation are his main aims, Czerniawski's essays are rarely as daring or original as his poetry or his prose fiction, though they do not shy away from pointed judgment.

In the 1980s and 1990s Czerniawski has published, in scattered Polish periodicals, a much more adventurous sort of critical prose in the form of aphorisms, *pensées*, jottings, mini-essays, sketches of an intellectual autobiography, and so on. These writings have appeared in book form under the title *Krótkopis, 1986–1995* (1998), Czerniawski's witty neologism from *długopis* (ballpoint pen) and *krótki* (short); an analogous English title might be "Penpoints."

The least known element of Czerniawski's oeuvre is his prose fiction, which has appeared in three slim collections: *Części mniejszej całości: Opowiadania* (Parts of a Lesser Whole, 1964), *Akt* (1975; the title can mean "deed" or "act" in both common English senses of the terms, an act in a stage play, or a nude, 1975); and *Koncert życzeń* (Your Concert Choice, 1991). Difficult to characterize as a whole, since the individual stories differ considerably among themselves, Czerniawski's fiction offers no space to such commonplace devices as rounded characters, gripping narrative, and plot; rather, it stakes out its own distinctive territory in the metafictional tradition of such writers as Gombrowicz, Sławomir Mrożek, Franz Kafka, Samuel Beckett, Jorge Luis Borges, and Vladimir Nabokov—most of whose work, however, is conceptually or thematically more focused than Czerniawski's. In many respects his fiction is continuous with his musico-philosophical poetry, the formal boundaries between the two being most obviously blurred in the poetic "Komentarze"—although the latter also draw on the familiar essay, as well as on Ernest Hemingway's elliptical short stories in dialogue. Consisting mostly of short sketches that are highly playful, even absurdist, and often have a strong parodic or satirical edge, Czerniawski's fiction creates verbal worlds that variously cut across the real one or stand apart from or parallel to it. The sketches freely mix genres and universes of discourse, quote foreign languages, and allow fictional characters to share the stage with historical figures, violating the limits of time and space at every opportunity. The piece titled "Akt," for instance, which features two characters named "Ja" (I) and "On" (He), resembles an official interrogation, an intelligent conversation, and a formal philosophical dialogue on the linguistic and ontological differences between being and existence. Barely has the exchange begun when the characters slip into Dutch for a few resonant moments, including one that sets up World War II as one of the story's concerns: "ON: Mag ik Uw telefonnummer hebben? JA: 19-39-19-45" (HE: May I Have Your Telephone Number? I: 19-39-19-45)." About halfway through, the exchange is interrupted by Stanisław Wokulski (the hero of a major Polish novel by Bolesław Prus [Aleksander Głowacki], *Lalka* [1890; translated as *The Doll*, 1972]), Hamlet, Tertullian, and Ophelia—after which the initial conversation simply resumes as before. On and Ja briefly argue about the existence of an afterlife, while Tertullian stutters out a short Latin speech composed of famous theological aphorisms, and Ophelia worries in William Shakespeare's English about Hamlet's state of mind.

Koncert życzeń includes an amusing scene in a confessional, where a character learns that reading the poetry of Czerniawski, "an enemy of People's Poland and the Catholic Church, an unctuous formalist and provocateur," is a mortal sin. Despite its deliberate sins against the state and the Church, however, Czerniawski's poetry, as well as his critical essays, were at least partly available to Polish readers before the collapse of communism; his fiction was not available in Poland at all. A forthcoming collected edition will allow Polish readers to see an important element of his oeuvre, one that will aid the informed reading of his poetry no less than the poems will help illuminate the fiction.

The story of Czerniawski's unusual childhood and youth—the more common fates of Polish survivors of World War II were existence under Nazi occupation, escape to the West, or deportation to the Soviet Union—is the subject of his well-received memoir, published in English as *Scenes from a Disturbed Childhood* (1991) and in Polish as *Fragmenty niespokojnego dzieciństwa* (Fragments of a Turbulent Childhood, 1995). According to the introduction to the English version, Czerniawski was uncertain whether to write the work in English or Polish; a commission from the BBC Radio for some talks about his childhood decided the matter, and the English version came first. Because of the different audiences to which they are addressed, the Polish version varies from the English in several respects other than language: it lacks the introduction and conclusion that frame the English version, replacing the former with a foreword by the writer Ryszard Kapuściński; in addition, it changes the arrangement and number-

ing of the chapters, curtails some of the material about Czerniawski's experiences in England, elaborates on the Polish ones, includes six of his own poems, offers more and lengthier quotations from family correspondence, and includes more family and documentary photographs.

Both versions of this deceptively simple and sometimes hauntingly serene memoir, however, reveal the same subtle, often drily ironic sensibility. In a passage unique to the English text but not unrepresentative of the Polish version, for example, Czerniawski deals wittily with the question of national nostalgia: asked after a poetry reading in a school in Poland, "'Don't you feel nostalgic for the old country?'" he says, "I had to reply, 'As I have recently moved from Gloucestershire in the west of England to Kent in the east, I currently feel nostalgic for the Gloucestershire countryside.'" Rather than attempt to weave a seamless narrative of his early experiences, Czerniawski is content to recall what he can, supplementing and correcting it with material largely supplied by his mother and sister but sometimes taken from historical records. The result is memorable, as well as paradoxical: the often disconnected scenes from Czerniawski's early life produce a satisfyingly coherent portrait of the future poet and translator as a maturing sensibility, while the counterpointed family and historical materials, as Kapuściński notes, give the memoir distinctly untraditional polyphonic and cubist qualities. For instance, the chapter "War (My View and Some Other Views)" / "Wojna (w moich oczach, w oczach innych)" neatly and sometimes mordantly juxtaposes brief personal and family memories of the first weeks of World War II with equally brief extracts from various diplomatic and government sources. In this case the Polish version represents an improvement on the English in that the polyphonic weave of intimate and official voices is made subtler through changes in their placement relative to one another. The memoir concludes in 1952 with Czerniawski about to enter London University, where his bicultural and bilingual literary career began in earnest.

While the place Czerniawski will come to occupy in the rich field of twentieth-century Polish literature remains to be determined by readers and critics in Poland who finally have access to his work in its entirety, his status as a major English translator of Polish literature is already established. Against long odds and in the face of difficult personal and historical circumstances, Czerniawski has not only made himself into a Polish writer but also has produced a significant body of critical and creative work, the latter characterized by its highly distinctive poetics. His literary essays are informative and range widely across contemporary Anglo-American and Polish poetry, refusing to separate émigré writers from those in Poland, while his poetry and fiction reveal a probing, seriously playful, and highly cultured European mind puzzling over the central poetic and philosophical questions of his turbulent century. Few contemporary writers of poems and fiction offer their readers the sort of artistic consciousness and cultural reach that define his work, let alone its musical and tonal complexity or its range of genres from the poignantly lyrical to the enigmatically philosophical.

Interviews:

Magadalena Czajkowska, "Rozmowa z Adamem Czerniawskim," *Kultura*, 11 (1965): 102–111;

Piotr Wilczek, "Jestem człowiekiem schyłku XX wieku," *Przegląd Powszechny*, 3 (1989): 367–373;

Marian Kisiel, "'Slowem jak perła' z Adamem Czerniawskim rozmawia," *Odra*, 12 (1989): 61–65;

Iwona Smolka, "Osadzony w języku . . . Z Adamem Czerniawskim rozmawia," in *London—Toronto—Vancouver: Rozmowy z pisarzami emigracyjnymi*, edited by Andrzej Niewiadomski (Lublin: Stowarzyszenie Literackie Kresy, 1993), pp. 105–111;

Krzysztof Karwat, "'Niepolski' pragmatyzm: Z Adamem Czerniawskim, poetą, tlumaczem i eseistą rozmawia," *Tygodnik Powszechny* ([Universal] *Catholic Weekly*), 11 June 1995, p. 7;

Beata Tarnowska, "Rozmowa z Adamem Czerniawskim," *Kultura*, 10 (1998): 63–78;

Rafał Witek, "Po złotym wieku zimnej wojny, z Adamem Czerniawskim rozmawia," *Odra*, 11 (1999): 50–54.

References:

Andrzej Busza and Bogdan Czaykowski, "Dwugłos o Adamie Czerniawskim," *Puls*, 20 (1983–1984): 102–105;

Czaykowski, "Glosy do poezji Adama Czerniawskiego," *Archipelag*, 6 (1983): 18–24;

Mariusz Kalandyk, "Słowo o metodzie krytycznej i poezji Adama Czerniawskiego," in *Poetycki krąg "Kontynentów": Artykuły i szkice*, edited by Zbigniew Andres and Jan Wolski (Rzeszów: Wydawnictwo Wyższej Szkoły Pedagogicznej, 1997), pp. 85–97;

Marian Kisiel, *U podstaw twórczości Adama Czerniawskiego* (Gliwice: Instytut Literatury i Kultury Polskiej Uniwersytetu Śląskiego, 1991);

Kisiel, "Poetyka wielogłosowości," "Głosów zbieranie" and "'Poezja jest metafora'" in his *Od Różewicza, małe szkice o poezji* (Katowice: Wydawnictwo Forum Sztuki, 1999), pp. 73–95;

Dariusz Tomasz Lebioda, "Nagi w zaroślach ciemności: O wyobraźni poetyckiej Adama Czerniawskiego," in his *Pragnienie śmierci, Stachura Czerniawski, Herbert, Miłosz* (Bydgoszcz: Instytut Wydawniczy "Świadectwo," 1996), pp. 112–123;

Alicja Lisiecka, *Kto jest "Księciem Poetów"? Czyli Rzecz o Adamie Czerniawskim i innych* (London: Oficyna Poetów i Malarzy, 1979);

Jacek Łukasiewicz, "*Jesień* według Czerniawskiego" and "Jeszcze o Czerniawskim," in his *Rytm i powinność: Szkice o książkach i ludziach po roku 1980* (Wrocław: Towarzystwo Przyjaciół Polonistyki Wrocławskiej, 1993), pp. 180–189;

Kazimierz Maciąg, "O *Częściach mniejszej całości* Adama Czerniawskiego," in *Poetycki krąg "Kontynentów,"* pp. 99–105;

Janusz Maciejewski, "Moje spotkania z Adamem Czerniawskim," *Świat Literacki*, 2 (1991): 76–78;

Magdalena Rabizo-Birek, "Język filozofią moją: O eseistyce literackiej Adama Czerniawskiego," in *Poetycki krąg "Kontynentów,"* pp. 107–131;

Beata Tarnowska, "'Stoję wobec świata': Glosy do poetyckiej epistemologii Adama Czerniawskiego," *Zeszyty Naukowe Wyższej Szkoły Filologicznej w Olsztynie*, 1 (1995): 201–211;

Tarnowska, "Wyobraźnia i forma," *Fraza*, 1, 23 (1999): 247–250;

Alois Woldan, "Adam Czerniawski: Ein Dichter zwischen zwei Nationen?" *Protokolle*, 1 (1996): 111–114.

Mircea Dinescu

(11 November 1950 –   )

Marcel Cornis-Pope
Virginia Commonwealth University

BOOKS: *Invocaţie nimănui* (Bucharest: Cartea Românească, 1971);

Elegii de cînd eram mai tînăr (Bucharest: Cartea Românească, 1973);

Proprietarul de poduri (Stampe europene) (Bucharest: Cartea Românească, 1976);

La dispoziţia dumneavoastră: Poeme (Bucharest: Cartea Românească, 1979);

Teroarea bunului simţ (Bucharest: Cartea Românească, 1980);

Democraţia naturii (Bucharest: Cartea Românească, 1981);

Exil pe o boabă de piper (Bucharest: Cartea Românească, 1983); translated by Andrea Deletant and Brenda Walker as *Exile on a Peppercorn: The Poetry of Mircea Dinescu* (London & Boston: Forest Books, 1985);

Rimbaud negustorul (Bucharest: Cartea Românească, 1985);

Moartea citeşte ziarul (Amsterdam: Rodopi, 1989; enlarged edition, Bucharest: Cartea Românească, 1990);

Proprietarul de poduri: Antologie 1968–1985 (Bucharest: Seara, 1990);

O beţie cu Marx (Bucharest: Editura Seara, 1996);

Pamflete vesele şi triste 1990–1996: Cu o postfata de "un grup de patrioţi din Slobozia" (Bucharest: Seara, 1996).

Editions in English: "Titanic Waltz," "The Short-Sighted Painter," "A Speech against Revolt," "Walls," "Strolling Theatre," "Discovering the Work," and "Seven Drawers," translated by Liliana Ursu, in *Fifteen Young Romanian Poets: An Anthology of Verse*, edited by Ursu (Bucharest: Eminescu, 1982), pp. 23–29;

"Metamorphosis" and "Goat of the Times," translated by Ioana Deligiorgis, in her *100 de ani de poezie românească / 100 Years of Romanian Poetry: Bilingual Series* (Jassy: Junimea, 1982), pp. 434–437;

Mircea Dinescu (photograph by Heiner Wessel)

"Contemporary Goat," "The War of the Emperor with Himself," "Put Off," "Agreed," "Inventory in the Fourth World," translated by Marcel Cornis-Pope and Robert J. Ward, *Micromegas*, 9, no. 2 (1984): 36–38;

"Discovering the Work" and "Scanty Biography," translated by Andrei Bantaş, in *Like Diamonds in Coal Asleep: Selections from 20th Century Romanian Poetry*, edited by Bantaş (Bucharest: Minerva, 1985), pp. 372–373;

"Traveling Salesman," translated by Cornis-Pope, *European Studies Journal*, 3, no. 1 (1986): 25;

"Mammoth and Literature," translated by Fiona Tupper-Carey, *Granta*, 30 (Winter 1990): 171–174;

"Haplea," translated by Alexandru Nemoianu, *ARA Journal*, 15 (1991): 305;

"Metamorphosis" and "Goat of Our Times," translated by Stavros Deligiorgis, and "So?!" and "Not Today," translated by Adam Sorkin and Sergiu Celac, in *Shifting Borders: East European Poetry of the Eighties*, edited by Walter Cummins (Rutherford, N.J.: Fairleigh Dickinson University Press, 1993; London & Cranbury, N.J.: Associated University Presses, 1993), pp. 358–359;

"The Hens," "Manuscript Found Inside a Lamp Globe," "Discovering the Works," "Ridiculous Chess," "The Cows," "Epistle on Accepting the Reality with a Slightly Metaphysical Postscript," "Speech against Revolt," "Avalanche," and "Factory Touching Factory," translated by Brendan Kennelly, in *When the Tunnels Meet: Contemporary Romanian Poetry*, edited by John Fairleigh (Newcastle upon Tyne: Bloodaxe Books, 1996), pp. 65–72.

Mircea Dinescu is the most important representative of the first postmodern generation of Romanian writers, which emerged in the 1970s. Described by the critic Romul Munteanu as the "enfant terrible" of contemporary Romanian poetry, whose "state of grace" is his "condition of permanent revolt," and by Dennis Deletant in his introduction to Dinescu's *Exile on a Peppercorn: The Poetry of Mircea Dinescu* (1985) as the "moralist of the modern age," Dinescu has combined candid lyrical confession with political satire, questioning relentlessly not only totalitarian modes of thinking but also the Enlightenment heritage of technocratic development and overrationalization. An outspoken critic of Nicolae Ceauşescu's dictatorial communist regime in the 1980s and a rallying figure in the early days of the 1989 revolution, Dinescu helped redeem the nation's trust in its intellectual and creative elite. Since 1989 he has continued to act as the country's critical consciousness through his political editorials and the publication of his previously censored poems.

One of three children of Ştefan Dinescu, an industrial worker, and Aurelia (née Badea) Dinescu, a saleswoman, Dinescu was born in Slobozia, a small rural town in the Danube plain east of Bucharest, on 11 November 1950. He attended secondary school in Slobozia. Failing the entrance examination to the Theater Institute in Bucharest,

he moved to Bucharest and held a series of menial jobs, including that of janitor. Later, after he became known as a poet, he took courses in literature at the University of Bucharest. His sparse education weighed in the early evaluations of his poetry: some critics contended that he sought to conceal a dearth of ideas behind extravagant metaphors and a flamboyant style, while others argued that the lack of academic training benefited Dinescu's poetry by allowing it to preserve its spontaneity and candor.

Dinescu published his first poems in 1967 in *Luceafărul* (The Morning Star), a magazine devoted to young writers. The editor, the novelist Ştefan Bănulescu, gave him a part-time job at *Luceafărul* and also helped him obtain a modest position on the staff of the Romanian Writers' Union.

Dinescu's first book, *Invocaţie nimănui* (Invocation to No One, 1971), caught the attention of critics and readers with its intense but stark lyricism, devoid of sentimentality. The poems focus on moments of sensual exuberance, describing raw perceptions rather than reflections. Stylistically they alternate between carefully crafted cadences and violent imagistic outbursts. Awarded the Romanian Writers' Prize for a first book of poetry, *Invocaţie nimănui* made Dinescu famous at the age of twenty-one. His poems were welcomed as a significant break not only with academic poetry but also with the late modernism of such poets as Nichita Stănescu, Ana Blandiana, Marin Sorescu, Ioan Alexandru, and Virgil Mazilescu, all of whom had become established in the 1960s and whose poetry had entered a manneristic phase. Dinescu's plebeian, antipoetic style contrasted sharply with the cultivated sophistication of his older colleagues. The break, however, was not complete: Dinescu's style included an irreverent transformation of techniques used by Stănescu's generation that, in turn, had roots in the interwar Romanian avant-garde. Overuse of the first person, heretical declarations, melancholic vagaries, burlesque vocabulary, and self-parody were features the Stănescu group borrowed from the irreverent poetry of the "lost generation"—Radu Stanca, Constant Tonegaru, Geo Dumitrescu, and Mircea Popovici—of the late 1940s. Dinescu reinvented these techniques, making them contemporary and fresh.

The title of the book suggests a defiant poetic posture that refuses to pay homage to traditional authority figures, preferring to draw on the poet's own resources. An unashamed narcissism characterizes poems, such as "Sînt tînăr, Doamnă" (I'm Young, My Lady), that celebrate the poet's special destiny—"promised to poetry / with blue blood in confusion"—and his jubilant youth:

> I'm young, my lady, and have settled down long
>   enough
> to understand the fall from dream to need,
> but were I to gorge on clods of light
> I would no longer fit my tiger skin.
>
> I'm young, my lady, with a handsome figure,
> suckled on the milk of comets,
> until a sky grows in my soul and stars in my bones . . .
> I'm young, my lady, and my wings still hold me up.

The narcissism is, however, counterbalanced by self-ironic references to the adolescent pose constructed by "a master of words and king of nothing" and by the anticipation of a darker season in which "the archers of evening / rush their boding arrows toward me." Some poems—"Teamă cu ospăţ" (Fear with Feasting), "Ultimul pahar" (The Last Glass), "Nuferii lacrimei" (Lilies of Tear), and "Balanţă cu dragoste" (Balance with Love)—emphasize dualities, describing states of joy, beauty, and plenitude intersected by fear, loss, and entrapment. Dinescu's startling metaphors enhance this antinomic vision, associating love with disruptive passion and redemption, blood with life and death, and poetry with prophecy and forgetting. At a stylistic level, critics noted the sharp contrast between the idiomatic flow of the poetry, on the one hand, and the formal prosody and imagistic artifice, on the other. Eugen Negrici quotes Ov. S. Crohmălniceanu as saying that Dinescu's poetry thrived on "dissonant, shocking metaphor, mixing poetic suavity with prosaic crudeness."

Dinescu's second collection, *Elegii de cînd eram mai tînăr* (Elegies from My Younger Years, 1973), is filled with remarkable sensual imagery—beautiful women "look through my blood like through a window," "flesh tastes like honey," and the world is a "storm of bees" and a body with "whistling pores"—and again suggests that love and death, tenderness and violence are interconnected. A melancholic, circumspect vision replaces the adolescent exuberance of the earlier poems: "Finally, I had to descend / I was tired of being young. . . ." ("Lentilă"). The poet is now aware that the aesthetic oasis he tried to create for himself has proven illusory, because, as he says in "Lentilă" (translated as "Lens," 1985), "from a mirror death mimics" him. In "De-aceea cînt" (That's Why I Sing) the golden boy is forever estranged from the "mother's womb." In "Hidalgo" the speaker enters maturity with anger at the dream

that has failed him and at his own "blindness in the word." In spite of their self-absorption, these poems make an effort to connect to the larger world, violating conventions and tearing away masks. According to Negrici, the poet manifests "intolerance toward weakness, failure, God, everything"—including himself.

Dinescu's next volume, *Proprietarul de poduri (Stampe europene)* (Owner of Bridges, [European Engravings], 1976), received two major awards: the Romanian Writers' Prize for poetry and the Mihai Eminescu Award of the Romanian Academy. It shows considerable progress toward mature social reflection. The youthful candor praised in the earlier books is regarded here as a handicap that increases the vulnerability of the individual. Dinescu frequently uses angels as metaphors of tragic loss: the angel appears as "a young heretic who devours his stake" or as a victim in the "ambulant church" of commercialism; the "owner of angels . . . is consumed by the owner of an oil well." Love develops precariously in the margins of an oppressive technological society in "Elegie la trenuri reci" (Elegy for Cold Trains):

> If you were to fall asleep on the tracks, my love
> flustered trains would circle around you
> big bales of cotton would fall from the sky . . .
> sequoia trees would grow in railway stations
> and soap bubbles would be distributed in squares,
>
> and your hair would conquer cold Siberias.

"Capra contemporană" (translated as "Contemporary Goat," 1984) invents a surrealistic Eastern European version of resistance to totalitarian technocracy:

> this goat eats the roses in the park
> chews streetcars like raw bark
> on mornings doesn't go to work
> doesn't read the evening news
> strips telegraph poles like mulberry trees
> shamelessly ignores traffic lights
> doesn't lust after limousines or parties
> hasn't yet patented artificial grass
> though she still knows a thing or two about forests;
> they've changed the statue in the public square
> the city is rocking in a swing of smoke
> only this one stubborn goat
> keeps giving milk without asking how.

The poet is like this "stubborn goat," obstinately refusing the smokescreens of contemporary ideology, trying in "Potopul" (The Flood) to "don reality like a shirt / until the plaster statues start sweating in the square / and the doting baby liberty / will

Cover for the 1985 English translation of Dinescu's poetry volume
Exil pe o boabă de piper *(1983), which included thinly veiled
attacks on the regime of Romanian dictator Nicolae Ceauşescu*

no longer suckle on pasteurized milk." The poet imagines himself as an owner of bridges, hoping to replace the passage back and forth of ideological stereotypes with a commerce of genuine ideas and metaphors. At the same time, in "Laşitatea de-a scrie versuri" (translated as "The Cowardice of Writing Verse," 1985) he acknowledges the limitations of his poetic enterprise: "I do not know whether / . . . my revolt in words is not the coward shadow of true action." Similarly, in "Viaţă de artist" (translated as "The Artist's Life," 1985) he says: "I almost feel ashamed that I write poetry / and could I but pack my life in cases / I'd abandon them at the edge of the town / as happy as a young cyclist." Dinescu by this time was seeking a more engaged role for poetry.

In 1979 Dinescu married Maria (Masha) Kovacs, an editor at *Secolul XX* (The Twentieth Cen-

tury), Romania's premier magazine of comparative literature; she is the daughter of the translator Albert Kovacs and the literary historian Elena Loghinovski. The Dinescus have two children, Irina and Andrei.

In his article "The Resilience of Poetry" (1990) the critic Mircea Iorgulescu says that Dinescu's *La dispoziţia dumneavoastră* (At Your Disposal, 1979) marks a decisive break "through the wall separating literature from life. While remaining a poet, he entered into the immediate reality; a distorted reality, a grotesque nightmare, a disorder caused by decomposition and degradation. His poetry changed in tone: a grating irony, a strained, nervous, sarcastic and suffering expression, strong, tortured images reminiscent of Bosch's paintings or Goya's 'Los Caprichos.'" "Teroarea bunului simţ" (translated as "In Terror of Good Nature," 1985), the title of which was used for Dinescu's first retrospective collection in 1980, illustrates this radical change in form and attitude:

> in my propensity to regard everything
> from an unfavorable angle
> I begin to believe that the gods pushed forth by the
>   beer tide
> arrive at our table where we decry of course
> their possible impossible existences
> until they disappear with a smile on their deluxe bicy-
>   cles into the inferno.
> An edible reality: I walk down to the beach
> and instead of water I find a poster
> announcing the prohibition of the sea
> and because the wild swarm of wasps
> is chasing a car along the highway
> and because those who have died at the stake now
>   carry faggots
> all that remains for me to do is ask
> how's your family
> how's your cancer thriving,
> how are you treating your freedom. . . .
>   (translated by Dan Duţescu)

Other critics have argued that Dinescu's conversion was mostly a matter of accents. Dinescu has always been a political poet in his rejection of alienating social rituals, his refusal to carry around a "crumpled coffin"—as the poem "Hau, Hau" in *La dispoziţia dumneavoastră* (Dog Barking) quips.

The volume introduced a much blunter, more outspoken political thematics and an impatience with prosodic polish. "Şah absurd" (translated as "Absurd Chess," 1985) denounces the "Madman who moves the villages around," a transparent allusion to Ceauşescu's plan to convert villages into closely controlled urban camps. Another poem reports sarcastically on the nation's institutionalized state of crisis: "I fear even snow will soon be rationed, / yet I continue to accept the glorified lie / . . . And thus, while waiting for the sublime Void to rot / our own cowardice has kept it frozen like a good refrigerator." The poet is well aware of the repercussions his new position might bring: "I've slipped and feel the bite of whip and harness . . . and of a muzzle that smothers every leaf of grass," he says in "Dansul pe jăratec" (Dancing on Hot Coals). Iorgulescu notes in "The Resilience of Poetry" that while the poetry of Stănescu's generation continued to be tolerated and even encouraged by the regime because of its metaphoric indirection, Dinescu's offended the Communist Party censors because it "opened the doors and windows of poetry to life, to reality, to history; to street language; the language of irony, popular language, in which official expressions are comically distorted." Dinescu understood the explosive nature of protest poetry in Romania, but he also knew that poetry alone could not change society: "It is as though someone throwing a lump of sugar / in the tiger's cage / would expect the tiger to quickly reform and start reading Shakespeare," he says in "Şah absurd."

In 1981 Dinescu joined the editorial board of *România literară* (Literary Romania), Romania's premier literary and cultural magazine, published by the Writers' Union. His turn from aesthetics to politics became even clearer in his next two volumes, *Democraţia naturii* (The Democracy of Nature, 1981) and *Exil pe o boabă de piper* (1983; translated as *Exile on a Peppercorn: The Poetry of Mircea Dinescu*). *Democraţia naturii* created a stir among literary critics and party censors with its thinly veiled attacks on Ceauşescu's neo-Stalinist rule. In poems such as "Descoperirea operei" (translated as "Discovering the Work," 1982) Dinescu proposed an activistic definition that would make poetry capable of affecting reality:

> For quite a while I thought that poetry slept under the
>   heron's wing
> or that I would have to rummage the woods to find it
> but like a prophet chased from the desert by the gur-
>   gling oil wells
> now I am ready to enter a pact with reality
> admitting that I was wrong:
> I smash the wall with a pick-axe
> and let you look through.

Particularly obvious in this book is Dinescu's movement away from the carefully crafted musical forms of his earlier poetry. They have been replaced by a nervous, unrhymed line, colloquial diction, and a sarcastic tone. A loss of metaphoric concentration in these poems, which are concerned with historical and political contingencies, is compensated for by witty Brechtian procedures that prevent the act of witnessing from becoming melodramatic. Ironic reportage replaces metaphoric allusion, as in "O fabrică cheamă după ea altă fabrică" (translated as "One Factory Calls For Another," 1985), which describes the destructive effects of Ceauşescu's policy of forced industrialization.

Since this volume broke every political and poetic taboo—except that of mentioning Ceauşescu directly—it is astonishing that it was allowed to appear. Judging from "Indulgenţă de iarna" (translated as "Cold Comfort," 1985), Dinescu had intimations of his coming fate at the hands of the political police:

> Deliver me, Lord, from those who want my good
> of the obliging boys always ready to play the role of joy-
>   ous snitches
> and of the priest with a tape recorder hidden under his
>   frock
> of the blanket under which you cannot sneak without
>   greeting strangers
> of dictators caught in the strings of their harp
> and of those enraged against their own people. . . .

Exil pe o boabă de piper continues the exploration of the condition of Romania under late Stalinism but returns to the more formal prosody of Dinescu's earlier poems. The ironic contrast between the polished surface of the verse and the absurd social realities it describes creates an alienating Brechtian effect, disconnecting form from content and reality from artifice, as in "Comis Voiajori" (translated as "Traveling Salesmen," 1986):

> Even the proletarian chamomile flower
> spends its exile away from the tea land
> for having had the guts to smuggle in pollen.
> From so much care for the welfare of man
> bees are hunted with nets
> through which no child's breath could pass.
> . . . We are counseled to make our meetings scarce
> (through the sterilized gauze
> kisses reach our lips like a reproach).
> . . . All this care for the welfare of man
> will surely banish him to a little mountain town
> where nobody knows anybody
> a perfect laundry for burdensome memories.

Elsewhere, as in "Se amînă" (translated as "Put Off," 1984), the biblical cadences of Dinescu's verse evoke the ominous-ironic theme of a delayed apocalypse:

The rebellion's put off because of rain ahead
the child's put off for reasons of bread
though not only dogs are barking at Mary
though the stars are ripe and the oxen merry
and the Magi are debtors at the Needy Inn
and gossip flourishes under the eaves of sin
the child is put off for reasons of bread
the rebellion's put off because of rain ahead.

Anticipating the postmodernist poetry of the 1980s, Dinescu denounces tired metaphors and ideas. He portrays himself as a "ridiculous individual, carrying around images with my wheelbarrow," out of which he periodically dumps conventional images and looks for alternatives to a culture of clichés. He found one such alternative in the "Balkan" imagination of Ion Barbu's prewar poetry: "Hand me over a provincial journal / and a wooden shed with filthy signboards / and within three days all cities / will smell of vanilla and open harbors," he declares in "De acord?" (Agreed?). Barbu introduced in modern Romanian poetry the theme of "Balkanism" viewed as space of free intellectual and commercial exchanges, a mecca of poetry. The decadent "Balkan" disorder of "Inventar în lumea a patra" (translated as "Inventory in the Fourth World," 1984) did not reassure those who wanted some sense of purpose restored to Romanian society, but it did promise to derail totalitarian control:

A melon rind sailing through the Bosporus of ants
a newspaper with no memory of things
a potato in worn-out socks
an open can rusting in child's tears
a knife excommunicated between an onion and the
    Pope
a bugle grown old in the sewer
a shoe with open sea view
a bottle emptied of its meaning
a hysterical lemon. . . .
Take one more chance, Columbus of the trash pile,
Prophet of beetles,
and bear quiet witness
in the recovery of the world
of things in heaven that are at odds with:
a lemon a bottle a shoe a trumpet
a knife and open can a potato a newspaper
and this melon rind.

Rimbaud negustorul (Rimbaud the Merchant, 1985) announces with brutal candor the coming fate of the rebellious poet: "Get ready you harpooners for the angel is in trouble / in that famous country buried under cold waves of vodka." All of the poems in this volume would merit the title given to one of them, "Epistoloi despre acceptarca realităţŭ çu un postscriptum

uşor metafizie" (translated as "Epistle on Accepting the Reality with a Slightly Metaphysical Postscript," 1996). Here the "metaphysics" is reduced to straightforward questions about the justification of a totalitarian society: "How can one man's bad temper / despoil such vast acreage of farmland, / how can his puny chill spread like ivy over blast furnaces?" (translated by Adam Sorkin and Sergiu Celac). According to Sorin Alexandrescu's preface to Dinescu's next volume, *Moartea citeşte ziarul* (Death Reads the Newspaper, 1989), it was clear by this time that Dinescu had stretched the limits of poetry, both politically and aesthetically, to that "maximum level of admissibility in Romania reached in prose only by [Augustin] Buzura and by Marin Preda's last novel, *The Most Beloved Man on Earth*, published in 1980." *Moartea citeşte ziarul* was refused publication in Romania and could only be circulated clandestinely in an edition published by Alexandrescu in Amsterdam. An explanation for the interdiction of this volume is that it included Dinescu's most sardonic treatments of Ceauşescu— "Doamne fereşte" (God Forbid), which describes the autocrat as a mythic madman who "kills us because he loves us," and "Haplea," which paints a memorable comic-fantastic portrait of Ceauşescu:

It's Haplea. He strikes villages with a spoon
he slurps bells,
he plows churches, he sows panic,
after he harvests it with a mechanical blade,
Wise was the poor Greek when he warned: . . . don't
    buy a house in Wallachia, 'cause in three years it will
    be a wreck;
and that is because the Cumas and the Pechenegs,
and the simpletons and the viceroys plunder there;
and because the leader of the hosts of confusion,
moving his navel and with a ladle in his hand, is our
    Haplea himself.
                (translated by Alexandru Nemoianu)

The final irony of this poem, which identifies Ceauşescu with the greedy ogre of children's fairy tales, is that his destructive campaign against villages tops those of the barbarian pillagers traditionally blamed by Romanians for their underdevelopment. As the supreme "leader of the hosts of confusion," Ceauşescu wrecks havoc on the entire culture.

According to Alexandrescu, another explanation for the banning of *Moartea citeşte ziarul* is that in 1988 Dinescu crossed "the Rubicon, leaving the reservation of the ethical attitude and fiction, entering the domain of the political" as an open dissident. In September of that year, while visiting the U.S.S.R. at the invitation of its Writers' Union, Dinescu made a declaration in support of glasnost—a taboo word for Ceauşescu's regime—on Radio Moscow. That same month he gave a speech titled "Pîinea şi circul" (Bread and Circus) at a literature colloquium sponsored by the West Berlin Academy of Arts. On his return to Bucharest, Dinescu was placed under around-the-clock police surveillance, a move that radicalized his attitude even further. On 14 March 1989 he wrote an open letter to the president of the Writers' Union in which he criticized the organization's passive acceptance of the increased censorship and surveillance exercised over writers by the Ceauşescu regime. As a result, he was fired from the editorial board of *România literară* and from his Writers' Union job and was ordered to discontinue contacts with foreign embassies. After the Paris newspaper *Libération* published a wide-ranging interview with Dinescu on 17 March, he was placed under house arrest and watched over by eighteen police officers. His family was left without a means of support and periodically received anonymous death threats. Friends who tried to contact Dinescu through in-laws who lived on the same street found that house also cordoned off by the police, and the seven Romanian writers who wrote a letter to the president of the Writers' Union on 9 April expressing their solidarity with Dinescu lost their own right to publish. Protests both from within Romania and from abroad culminated in an appeal against the reelection of Ceauşescu signed by some of the same writers who had defended Dinescu earlier. Dinescu's poetry was featured at international festivals and published in neighboring Romanian-speaking Moldova, and in June 1989 he was awarded the International Prize for Poetry in Rotterdam. The jury stated, "Through Mircea Dinescu, we honor all the Romanian writers who, with their work, defend the free spirit of a subjugated nation." Dinescu's anger and frustration during a period that brought the collapse of the Berlin Wall and the "velvet revolution" in Czechoslovakia were poignantly expressed in an anti-Ceauşescu essay, "Mamutul şi Literatura," (translated as "Mammoth and Literature," 1990), that was smuggled to Germany and published in the *Frankfurter allgemeine Zeitung* on 11 November 1989. After likening Stalinist Romania to a mammoth discovered hard-frozen in Siberia, its belly full of corpses, Dinescu asks dramatically:

> Who will intervene in Romania? . . . Where can we go now that the Berlin wall is being preserved brick by brick, and transported to the Romanian border? Who will come to our defense? . . . The situation in our country cannot be compared with anywhere in

the world. When I heard that Vaclav Havel had a television and word processor in his Prague prison, I thought it was a joke. In Romania a writer is not allowed to have a typewriter without permission from the police. A Romanian dissident, a poet, was given the choice between three months in prison, spent in the company of hardened criminals waiting for some young lads to come along, or emigration. The writer chose exile.

And then, suddenly, the mass of what Dinescu in "Mammoth and Literature" called "twenty million protesters in Romania, unpublicized dissidents who live their lives gagged" started to move. On 22 December, after Ceauşescu fled Bucharest in panic, a throng of demonstrators rescued Dinescu from his house arrest and brought him to the Romanian national television station to announce that Ceauşescu's reign had ended and that "God had turned his face toward Romania again." On Christmas Day Ceauşescu and his wife were captured by the armed forces, tried by a military tribunal, and shot by a firing squad. On 28 December, Dinescu was elected president of the Romanian Writers' Union. For the next three years he pursued an aggressive program of restructuring and renewal of membership.

But the triumph did not last long. President Ion Iliescu's "transition" government began to resort to manipulative tactics to salvage part of the old power structure, and Dinescu and other former dissidents resigned from the governing council in 1990, denouncing its "crypto-communist" mentality. In turn, newspapers associated with the chauvinistic elements in Iliescu's coalition attacked Dinescu and other dissidents in an attempt to undermine their moral standing.

An enlarged edition of *Moartea citeşte ziarul*, which includes three of Dinescu's pre-1989 political analyses and interviews, was published by Cartea Românească in 1990. Alexandrescu's preface opens with a suggestive portrait: "I have never met him in person. I only know from photographs his slanted, hard, threatening, and yet tender and fragile glance, the adolescent look . . . in which we like to identify our ideal self-portrait, our ingenuity and rebellion, real or affected. I know very little about his personal life, I admire his public existence, and I search for him in the only space accessible to me, that of his poems and essays." But Dinescu's biography is intimately intertwined with the poems in this book. For example, "Naşterea unei definiţii" (Birth of a Definition) suggests his precarious position as a political poet: "One needs to maintain a certain confusion . . . / otherwise the poor reporter will get

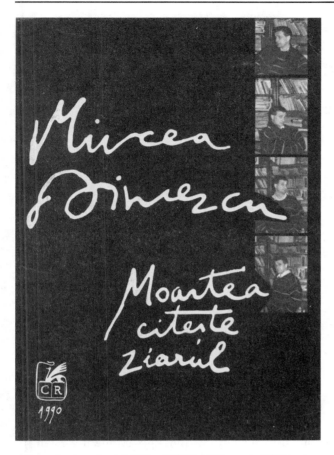

*Cover for the enlarged edition (1990) of Dinescu's 1989 poetry
collection, which continued his attacks on Ceauşescu*

sick from too much reality / and the literary critic
will accuse the fretting sea / of being too manneristic." "Daţi-i şi mesei de bucătărie o şansă" (Give the
Kitchen Table a Chance) reads like a profane prayer
whose object is the daily bread that had become an
exotic staple in Ceauşescu's Romania. Most of the
poems, however, move beyond sarcastic reportage
to become political meditations on the conditions
of totalitarian society, where, as he says in "Scrisoare
către domnul Mihail Bulgakov" (Letter to Mr.
Mikhail Bulgakov), "history is in levitation," "the
city is aborted," and the contemporary Aleksandr
Pushkin "in white pants is about to be deported / in
the Siberia of posthumous texts." In "Doamne
fereşte" (God Help Us) the entire population is
imprisoned unborn in the belly of History at the
mercy of the Madman, who "when we are hungry
paints a fish / when we are cold, arrests the climate." The speaker cries out comically at the end:
"Stop History—I want to get off at the next station /
stop at the God-Help-Us station." But this outcry, he
admits in "Mici exerciţii pentru desfiinţarea timpu-
rilor la verb" (Little Exercises for the Abolishment

of Verbal Tenses), cannot save a generation of "passive accomplices / promoters of white spaces in
political magazines" who "attend to the tired dog of
the vacuum cleaner / and the dirty laundry they do
not fear." The speaker ironically defends this cynical
generation: "who can you complain to / when the
telephone is infested with bugs / anyway, we have
no desire to be arrested / before tea time." Almost
every poem in the book is open to both a cynical
and a hopeful reading, which suggest, respectively,
that history is immovable and that it can be transformed. The more formal prosody and careful
extended metaphors of these poems suggest a stoic,
reconciled attitude on Dinescu's part.

In contrast, the political essays and interviews
collected in the volume are impatient and straightforward. According to Liviu Antonesei, even
though Dinescu is not a political "theorist, he has a
fantastic skill of rendering concepts concrete, of
perceiving the essence of events, and mixing the
tragic with the anecdotal." His pre-1989 essays
denounce, more directly and efficiently than "any
number of books by Hannah Arendt and other ana-
lysts of totalitarianism," the "orthopaedic shoes"—
formal constraints—that Eastern European writers
had to accept to become publishable. At the end of
his Berlin address, "Pîinea şi circul," Dinescu proposes to separate, once and for all, "bread" from
"circus" and honest militant writing from "masks,
costumes, and artificial tears." In the interview with
Libération he argues that the Romanian intellectuals
and their institutions—the Writers' Union, the Film-
makers Association, and the Romanian Academy—
bore the brunt of Ceauşescu's "mini-cultural revolution" by being obstructed and placed under continual surveillance. He denounces the regime's effort
to produce a new human species, "'homo ceausisti-
cus' fattened with ideology and costumed in the vulgar rhetoric of party propaganda," and blames the
passivity of the Romanian intelligentsia on the
repression instituted by Ceauşescu:

> We are Jonah's brothers here, in the belly of com-
> rade Whale, and nobody has a right to judge us. In a
> country where not even the buried dead can be sure
> of their position, being annually shifted around
> and reorganized, you can imagine that the living
> are kept under an even more draconian control. . . .
> There are only two possible solutions to survive—the
> acceptance of a life of privations in the shadow of
> unpublished manuscripts, or emigration. External
> exile is often the last consequence of internal exile.

The interview ends with a surrealistic description of
Romania,

the fabulous domain of social exoticism, of failed suicides who cannot set fire to themselves because of the match crisis and cannot hang themselves because there is no rope or soap; of Bucharest that is on its way to becoming the first nonbelieving city in Europe, where the policemen are more numerous than pigeons . . . an absurd land where the border patrols keep their guns turned inward, where the wheat is reaped only on the TV, not in the fields, where workers are nicknamed proprietors and made to buy what supposedly belonged to them in the first place.

In January 1991 the chauvinistic newspapers publicized accounts of an altercation between Dinescu and another writer, accusing Dinescu of hooliganism. Dinescu pointed out that he had been the victim of aggression by the other writer, a chauvinist and former collaborator with Ceauşescu's secret police. In 1992 he argued that Romanian literature and art deserved to be subsidized because "while Romanian culture can only be produced in Romania, tractors can be produced any where else." He found little support from the government of Iliescu's successor, Theodor Stolojan. After renewed attacks not only from the extremist papers but also from some of his former allies, who accused him of mishandling Writers' Union funds, Dinescu resigned from the presidency of the union on 7 October 1993. With his characteristic barbed wit, he challenged his adversaries to tell him if they had brought even "half a nail to the Writers' Union from their frequent trips to the U.S. and Europe. Let me know where that nail is so that I may hang myself on it, happy that you have also contributed something to our community." While Dinescu's reputation was being tarnished in his own country, however, he was receiving increased recognition abroad. He was awarded a yearlong grant by the German Academy of the Arts in 1993, and his works were translated in France, Germany, Switzerland, England, and Russia.

Dinescu published *O beţie cu Marx* (A Drunken Binge with Marx, 1996) with an obscure press at his own expense and literally peddled copies from town to town, selling them in squares and vegetable markets in order to denounce the paltry position culture holds today in Romania. Written both before and since 1989, these poems have a retrospective flavor, recapitulating not only the poet's biography in "Balada celui plecat" (Ballad of the One Who Left) but also Romania's fate in the last months of Ceauşescu's reign and immediately after. The title poem suggests that Romania is a country where Karl Marx himself would be "quickly shaved and sent to reeducation." With Marx out of the way, "the new

philosophers dizzy themselves with polemical illusions," and the poet tries to dream up "a strange stomach disease / that would allow you to get drunk on a crumb of bread." Death dominates many poems, fraternizing not only with Ceauşescu's moribund communism but also with the shabby postcommunist supermarkets. Like his countrymen who "hide in the bottom of their pocket, / hoping that history / won't start counting its small change," the poet in "Cîntec de buzunar" (Pocket Song) tries to relearn how to write "pocket songs" inspired by "the clinking of small coins."

In 1996 Dinescu published *Pamflete vesele şi triste 1990–1996* (Happy and Unhappy Pamphlets 1990–1996). The volume is a compilation of his satirical editorials in *Academia Caţavencu*, Romania's premier magazine of political humor, which Dinescu edits.

In the afterword to his 1990 retrospective collection, *Proprietarul de poduri: Antologie 1968–1985* (Owner of Bridges: Anthology 1968–1985), Dinescu sums up with good humor the paradoxical evolution of his destiny from persecution to stardom and from stardom to new persecution:

> Punished for my childish folly in crying out that the king was naked, here I am one year later transferred from the cage of the secret police to that of wizard Iosefini and decked like a Christmas tree: [people call me] gypsy from Slobozia, K.G.B. agent, spy for the Dutch, Hungarians and Norwegians, traitor, illiterate, criminal and demented, sold out, bought, destabilizor, grand grandson of Lenin, and Mata Hari's bastard. Born from the crossing of the Vasilii Blajenii Church with the Statue of Liberty, a white gypsy from the slums of Slobozia, I have stumbled over a blunt pencil instead of a violin, a hammer or a mason's trowel, and not knowing what to do with it, I scribbled about eight books of illiterate poems.

With his ironic false modesty, Dinescu defends these "illiterate" poems that have brought him more readers and awards than any poet of his generation; he also stands by his older self-definition as an "owner of bridges," not only because it made him "a capitalist in the days of Communism" but also because it vindicates his conflicting identities as rebel, social pariah, and builder of more imaginative connections between poetry and civil society, between personal and public spaces.

Interviews:
Interview with Gilles Schiller, *Libération*, 17 March 1989, pp. 32–33; republished in Dinescu's *Moartea citeşte ziarul* (Bucharest: Cartea Românească, 1990), pp. 76–88;

"A Romanian Voice," *World Press Review,* 37 (May 1990): 72.

References:

Sorin Alexandrescu, "The Challenge of Power," *TLS: The Times Literary Supplement,* no. 4529 (19–25 January 1990): 55–56;

Alexandrescu, "Poezia refuzului," in Dinescu's *Moartea citeşte ziarul* (Bucharest: Cartea Românească, 1990), pp. 5–14;

Lucian Alexiu, *Idiografii lirice contemporane* (Timişoara: Facla, 1977), pp. 113–115;

Liviu Antonesei, *Jurnal din anii ciumei: 1987–1989* (Iaşi: Polirom, 1995);

Hristu Cândroveanu, "Teroarea bunului simţ," in his *Printre poeţi* (Cluj: Dacia, 1983), pp. 167–173;

Nina Cassian, "Notes on Romanian Poetry," *Parnassus: Poetry in Review,* 18 (1993/1994): 58–80;

V. Fanache, "Mircea Dinescu şi schimbarea la faţă a poeziei," *Steaua,* 36 (April 1985): 26–27;

Gheorghe Grigurcu, *Poeţi români de azi* (Bucharest: Cartea Românească, 1979), pp. 508–522;

Mircea Iorgulescu, "The Resilience of Poetry," *Times Literary Supplement* (19–25 January 1990): 61–62;

Iorgulescu, *Scriitori tineri contemporani* (Bucharest: Eminescu, 1978), pp. 54–56;

Michael March, "Disgust and Revolt in Romania," *TLS: The Times Literary Supplement,* no. 4599 (24 May 1991): 14;

Romul Munteanu, "Mircea Dinescu, l'enfant terrible de la poésie roumaine," in his *La Civilisation des livres: Littérature roumaine, littérature européene* (Bucharest: Univers, 1986), pp. 316–320;

Eugen Negrici, "Mircea Dinescu," in his *Introducere în poezia contemporană* (Bucharest: Cartea Românească, 1985), pp. 77–81;

Al. Protopopescu, "Mircea Dinescu–Îngerul eretic," *Contrapunct,* 4 (21 May – 3 June 1993): 12;

Lucian Raicu, *Practica scrisului şi experienţa lecturii* (Bucharest: Cartea Românească, 1978), pp. 378–382;

Cornel Regman, *Explorări în actualitatea imediată* (Bucharest: Eminescu, 1978), pp. 223–229;

Adam J. Sorkin, "Hard Lines: Romanian Poetry, Truth, and Heroic Irony Under the Ceauşescu Dictatorship," *Literary Review,* 35 (Fall 1991): 26–36;

Domniţa Ştefănescu, *Cinci ani din istoria României: O cronologie a evenimentelor Decembrie 1989–Decembrie 1994* (Bucharest: Editura Maşina de scris, 1995);

Grete Tartler, "Ritmul metaforei, ritmul simbolului," *România literară,* 17 (3 May 1984): 5;

Oliviu Vlădulescu, "Lacrima ca armă," *România literară,* 17 (12 January 1984): 4.

Ştefan Augustin Doinaş

(26 April 1922 –   )

Virgil Nemoianu
Catholic University of America

BOOKS: *Cartea mareelor* (Bucharest: Editura pentru Literatura, 1964);

Omul cu compasul (Bucharest: Editura pentru Literatura, 1966);

Seminţia lui Laokoon (Bucharest: Tineretului, 1967);

Ipostaze (Bucharest: Tineretului, 1968);

Alter Ego (Bucharest: Eminescu, 1970);

Lampa lui Diogene (Bucharest: Eminescu, 1970);

Ce mi s-a-ntîmplat cu două cuvinte (Bucharest: Cartea Românească, 1972);

Poezie şi modă poetică (Bucharest: Eminescu, 1972);

Papirus (Bucharest: Cartea Românească, 1974);

Orfeu şi tentaţia realului (Bucharest: Eminescu, 1974);

Poveşti cum altele nu-s (Bucharest: Creangă, 1974);

Anotimpul discret (Bucharest: Eminescu, 1975);

Povestea celor zece fraţi (Bucharest: Creangă, 1976);

Locuiesc într-o inimă (Bucharest: Militară, 1978);

Hesperia (Bucharest: Cartea Românească, 1979);

Lectura poeziei. Urmată de, Tragic şi demonic (Bucharest: Cartea Românească, 1980);

Vînătoare cu şoim (Bucharest: Cartea Românească, 1985);

Interiorul unui poem (Bucharest: Cartea Românească, 1990);

Măştile adevărului poetic (Bucharest: Cartea Românească, 1992);

Arie si ecou (Cluj: Dacia, 1992);

Lamentaţiile (Bucharest: Albatros, 1993);

Aventurile lui Proteu (Bucharest: Humanitas, 1995);

Psalmi (Bucharest: Albatros, 1997).

Editions and Collections: *Versuri* (Bucharest: Eminescu, 1972);

Alfabet poetic (Bucharest: Minerva-BPT, 1978); translated by Cristina Tătaru as *Poetic Alphabeti* (Sibiu: Editura Universitatii "Lucian Blaga"/Societatea Academica Anglofona, 1996);

Poeme (Bucharest: Cartea Românească, 1983);

Ştefan Augustin Doinaş

Sad. Foamea de unu: Poeme (Bucharest: Eminescu, 1987).

Editions in English: *Alibi and Other Poems*, translated by Peter Jay and Virgil Nemoianu (London: Anvil, 1975);

"Limits" and "Pythia," translated by Ioana Deligiorgis, in *100 de ani de poezie Românească / 100 Years of Romanian Poetry*, edited by Deligiorgis (Jassy: Junimea, 1982), pp. 178–181;

"The Man with Exploded Eyes," "The Ascent," "The Words," and "Moment of Parting," translated by Jay and Nemoianu; "The Woman in the Mirror," translated by Donald Eulert and Stefan Avădanei; and "Pythia," translated by Stavros Deligiorgis, in *Contemporary East European Poetry: An Anthology,*

85

edited by Emery George (Ann Arbor, Mich.: Ardis, 1983), pp. 308–313;

"The Silver-Fanged Boar," "Today We Part," "The Siege," "The Pitcher," and "The Ballad of Parsifal's Question," translated by Andreí Bantaş; "These Two," translated by Dan Duţescu, in *Like Diamonds in Coal Asleep: Selections from 20th Century Romanian Poetry,* compiled by Bantaş (Bucharest: Minerva, 1985), pp. 267–273;

"Pythia," "Limits," "Delphi," and "Mycenae," translated by Stavros Deligiorgis, in *Shifting Borders: East European Poetries of the Eighties,* compiled and edited by Walter Cummins (Rutherford, N.J.: Fairleigh Dickinson University Press, 1993), pp. 333–335.

TRANSLATIONS: Ruben Darío, *Versuri alese* (Bucharest: ELU, 1967);

Pierre Emmanuel, *Poeme* (Bucharest: Univers, 1971);

Friedrich Hölderlin, *Poezii,* translated by Doinaş and Virgil Nemoianu (Bucharest: Albatros, 1971);

Dante, *Opere minore* (Bucharest: Univers, 1971);

Gottfried Benn, *Poeme,* translated by Doinaş and Nemoianu (Bucharest: Univers, 1973);

Johann Wolfgang von Goethe, *Faust: Partea intii si partea a doua a tragediei* (Bucharest: Univers, 1983).

OTHER: *Atlas de Sunete fundamentale,* edited by Doinaş (Bucharest: Univers, 1970).

Ştefan Augustin Doinaş is generally recognized as one of the greatest twentieth-century poets in the Romanian language. He is a man of letters, combining poetry translation, criticism, and theory with social and political activities. Throughout his life he has been steadfast in supporting the values of freedom, tolerance, progress, abundant labor, and openness toward the world—principles he has incorporated in his poetic work.

Doinaş was born Ştefan Augustin Popa on 26 April 1922 in the village of Cporal Alexa in Western Romania. His father, Augustin Popa, and his mother, Floriţa (née Laza), were affluent farmers. He went to the grade school of his native village and thereafter studied at the Moise Nicoară high school in the city of Arad from 1933 to 1941. In college he pursued medical studies from 1941 to 1944 at the University of Cluj–Sibiu, but never graduated; from 1944 to 1948 he studied at the

same university and obtained a degree in literature and philosophy. Between 1948 and 1955 Doinaş taught Romanian literature and language at different provincial schools (in his native village, at Gurahonţ, and Hălmagiu). Between 1955 and 1957 he was a copyeditor for the monthly magazine *Teatru* (Theater) in the capital city of Bucharest, where he and many of his literary friends had relocated.

By this time Doinaş—who adopted his literary pseudonym in 1941 from a rarely used word that appears in a Romanian folk ballad—was a fairly well-known literary figure, although he had published little. He made his debut in 1939 in the prominent *Jurnal literar* (Literary Journal) of Iasi and attached himself to an energetic group of student writers in the early 1940s. This group, Cercul literar de la Sibiu (Sibiu Literary Circle), took an openly antifascist stance and militated for a pro-Western orientation and liberal political values; they also rejected the poetics of rural nostalgia in favor of avant-garde and aesthetic positions. For a few years Doinaş was a member of the (still legal) Liberal Party. In 1945 Doinaş published poems in the *Revista Cercului* (Circle Review) and in 1947 had already obtained a prestigious award for the manuscript volume "Alfabet poetic" (A Poetic Alphabet) when its publication was forbidden by the communist authorities because it failed to repeat the ideological platitudes and sloganeering that the authorities had begun to demand from writers. Doinaş later used this same title for a different collection of poems published in 1978. The manuscript volume groups his youthful poetry, characterized by lush imagery, a spectacular use of language, historical and mythical allusions, and rich Platonizing visions.

Doinaş was on the point of breaking into print again after a long silence when he was arrested in 1957 and spent a year in prison for alleged misdemeanors (he failed to denouce to the totalitarian authorities some oppositional statements made by an interlocutor during a private disccussion). Upon his release he married Irinel Liciu, the first ballerina of the Bucharest Opera. He also held minor editorial positions with the magazines *Lumea* (World) from 1964 to 1967 and later *Secolul XX* (Twentieth Century), beginning in 1968. He rose to assistant editor in chief of the latter publication only to be demoted because of his refusal to become a Communist Party member. His earliest poems after prison release sometimes echo the clichés recommended by the communist cultural authorities, though always on a much higher level of stylistic sophistication.

Meanwhile, Doinaş built a career inside the structures of the Romanian Writers' Union, one of the few areas of public life where a certain amount of free activity was still possible. Thus, in 1968 he was elected a member in the leading council of the Writers' Union and became a member of its executive bureau in 1972. In 1982 he was appointed president of the Union's Literary Fund, and in 1990 he became honorary president of the Union itself. He was much respected for his moderation, integrity, and amiable, cordial behavior. He received the Grand Prize of the Romanian Academy in 1968, won seven awards from the Romanian Writers' Union, gained the "Goethe Medal" of the Munich Goethe Institut in 1982, and received the European Prize for literature from the KOV Institute in Yugoslavia in 1990.

After 1965 Doinaş's poetry changed twice in rather radical ways. The poems collected in *Seminţia lui Laokoon* (Laokoon's Lineage, 1967) and *Alter Ego* (1970) can be described as existentialist and absurdist, dark and pessimistic in tone, always harping on the human lack of epistemological certainty and on doubts about reality and morality, as illustrated in "Asediul" (translated as "The Siege," 1975), written in 1965 and published in *Seminţia lui Laokoon:*

> The walled town on a lance-tip. Unseen army.
> The wells clogged up and low clung the smoke.
> .   .   .   .
> Nothing. Only a star—the body-wound of some god.
> And late, the hour of treason struck. Our draw-
>   bridge
> was lowered by pulleys. Cowards, their foreheads in
>   the dust,
> begging for pardon. No one; only the moon, like the
>   ridge
> of a ship, going by the moat on a wind's crest.
> Then no one again . . . We'll be shedding tears of
>   blood
> until our seventh death; we'll be possessed
> with a sickness of open doors and smashed
> windows. No one's ever about. But we, we have sur-
>   rendered.

Still later in *Papirus* (1974) and *Anotimpul discret* (The Season of Discretion, 1975) Doinaş sought refuge in the creation of vast visions that would (through their very vagueness) catch something of the structure and the texture of the universe as a whole, and reconcile dream with reality, as illus-

trated in the poem "Limite" (translated as "Limits," 1993), published in *Papirus*:

> lion
> standing
> on the way in to the metropolis
> on the way out
> its copy
>
> I wanted to conquer the agora
> the pavement
> was beat
> with chariots and dogma
> I wanted to make love
> in slimy sheets
> I initiated
> moulding gestures
> I wanted to speak
> my truths
> they turned around
> shrugging
>
> in the beginning of every poem
> the name
> at the end
> the pseudonym

Doinaş enthusiastically plunged into translation of great world poetry in Romanian. While several major earlier poets such as Ştefan O. Iosif, Lucian Blaga, and Ion Pillat had done the same, none of them comes close to Doinaş in terms of the range and quality of his poetic translation. He produced exceptional translations of Johann Wolfgang von Goethe's *Faust* (1808, 1832), and of poems by Friedrich Hölderlin, Dante, Stéphane Mallarmé, Ruben Darío, Luis de Góngora y Argote, and Gottfried Benn. He also wrote several volumes of criticism and of theoretical writing, in which he tried to put forward a moderate literary doctrine, based on the significance of language and discourse. His own poems were translated into German, English, Serbian, Slovenian, Macedonian, Hungarian, Bulgarian, Spanish, and Italian.

During the 1980s, despite his personally comfortable social status, Doinaş became more and more outraged by the cruel dictatorship of Nicolae Ceauşescu and more outspoken in his opposition to it. These feelings found a release in his writing style and the subject matter of his poetry. Threats, invectives, anathemas, and images of degradation and disgust became central in his writing.

By 1989 Doinaş seemed ready for open dissidence and was one of the signers of an open letter protesting intellectual persecution. After the revolution of 1989 Doinaş's public recognition increased considerably. He was elected a member of the Romanian Academy, chair of the Paul Valéry Center for French culture in Bucharest, and chair of the Secolul XXI (Twenty-First Century) Foundation. In 1995 he received an honorary doctorate from the University of Sibiu. He also engaged in politics, both as a respected political commentator and as an elected senator on the part of the liberal-democratic Civic Action Party from 1993 to 1996.

Doinaş is emblematic of a type of opposition to totalitarianism, not by violent or open action, but rather by sheer creativity, abundance, and affirmation of the harmony and beauty of the world.

References:

Gheorghe Grigurcu, *Poeţi români de azi* (Bucharest: Cartea Românească, 1979), pp. 51–71;

Ion Mihu, *Stefan Augutin Doinaş* (Bucharest: Recif, 1994);

Ion Negoiţescu, *Lampa lui Aladin* (Bucharest: Eminescu, 1971), pp. 63–108;

Negoiţescu, *Scriitori contemporani* (Cluj: Dacia, 1994), pp. 158–168;

Virgil Nemoianu, *Surîsul anundentei. Cunoaştere lirică şi modele ideologice la Şt. Aug. Doinaş* (Bucharest: Eminescu, 1994);

Cornel Regman, *Cărti, autori, tendine* (Bucharest: Editura pentru Literatura, 1967), pp. 13–19;

Regman, *Cica niste cronicari* (Bucharest: Eminescu, 1970), pp. 82–95;

Regman, *Explorări în actualitatea imediată* (Bucharest: Eminescu, 1978);

Eugen Simon, *Scriitori români de azi*, volume 1 (Bucharest: Cartea Românească, 1978), pp. 141–152.

Péter Esterházy
(14 April 1950 –)

András Kappanyos
MTA Institute of Literary Studies

This entry originally appeared in Concise Dictionary of World Literary Biography:
South Slavic and Eastern European Writers.

BOOKS: *Fancsikó és Pinta: Írások egy darab madzagra fűzve* (Budapest: Magvető, 1976);

Pápai vizeken ne kalózkodj! (Budapest: Magvető, 1977);

Termelési-regény (kisssregény) (Budapest: Magvető, 1979);

Függő: Bevezetés a szépirodalomba (Budapest: Magvető, 1981);

Ki szavatol a lady biztonságáért? (Budapest: Magvető, 1982);

Fuharosok (Budapest: Magvető, 1983); translated by Ferenc Takács as "The Transporters," in *A Hungarian Quartet: Four Contemporary Short Novels,* edited by Maria Korosy (Budapest: Corvina, 1991);

Kis magyar pornográfia (Budapest: Magvető, 1984); translated by Judith Sollosy as *A Little Hungarian Pornography* (Evanston, Ill.: Hydra Books/ Northwestern University Press, 1995; London: Quartet, 1995; Budapest: Corvina, 1995);

Daisy: Opera semiseria egy felvonásban (Budapest: Magvető, 1984);

A szív segédigéi (Budapest: Magvető, 1985); translated by Michael Henry Heim as *Helping Verbs of the Heart* (New York: Grove Weidenfeld, 1991; London: Quartet, 1992; Budapest: Corvina, 1993);

Bevezetés a szépirodalomba (Budapest: Magvető, 1986);

Tizenhét hattyúk, as Csokonai Lili (Budapest: Magvető, 1987);

A kitömött hattyú (Budapest: Magvető, 1988);

Biztos kaland, by Esterházy and Balázs Czeizel (Budapest: Novotrade Rt., 1989);

Hrabal könyve (Budapest: Magvető, 1990); translated by Sollosy as *The Book of Hrabal* (London: Quartet, 1993; Evanston, Ill.: Northwestern University Press, 1994; Budapest: Corvina, 1995);

Péter Esterházy (photograph © by Ulla Montan; from the dust jacket for Harmonia Cælestis*)*

Az elefántcsonttoronyból (Budapest: Magvető, 1991);

A halacska csodálatos élete (Budapest: Pannon, 1991);

Hahn-Hahn grófnő pillantása (Budapest: Magvető, 1991); translated by Richard Aczel as *The Glance of Countess Hahn-Hahn: Down the Danube* (London: Weidenfeld & Nicholson, 1994);

Egy nő, by Esterházy and Ferenc Banga (Budapest: Balassi, 1993); enlarged and republished, without Banga's drawings, as *Egy nő* (Budapest: Magvető, 1995); translated by Sollosy as

She Loves Me (Evanston, Ill.: Northwestern University Press, 1997; London: Quartet, 1997);

A vajszínű árnyalat, by Esterházy and András Szebeni (Budapest: Pelikán, 1993);

Élet és irodalom [by Esterházy] / *Jegyzőkönyv* [by Imre Kertész] (Budapest: Magvető-Századvég, 1993);

Egy kékharisnya följegyzéseiből (Budapest: Magvető, 1994);

Búcsúszimfónia: A gabonakereskedő. Komédia három felvonásban (Budapest: Helikon, 1994);

Egy kék haris (Budapest: Magvető, 1996);

Harmonia Cælestis (Budapest: Magvető, 2000).

Collections: *Könyvek* (Budapest: Magvető, 1993)—comprises *Tizenhét hattyúk, Hrabal könyve,* and *Hahn-Hahn grófnő pillantása;*

Írások (Budapest: Magvető, 1994)—comprises *A kitömött hattyú, Az elefántcsonttoronyból,* and *A halacska csodálatos élete.*

PLAY PRODUCTION: *Búcsúszimfónia,* Budapest, Víg Theater, 12 April 1996.

PRODUCED SCRIPTS: *Idő van,* motion picture, by Esterházy and Péter Gothár, Mafilm, 1986;

Tiszta America, motion picture, by Esterházy and Gothár, Mafilm, 1987.

OTHER: Irene Dische, Hans Magnus Enzensberger, and Michael Sowa, *Esterhazy: Egy házy nyúl csodálatos élete,* translated by Esterházy (Budapest: Magvető, 1996).

One of the most prominent contemporary authors in Hungarian literature, Péter Esterházy is acknowledged as the leader of the so-called middle generation of writers—those born in the decade between World War II and the October 1956 revolution—and is considered by many to be the finest living Hungarian prose writer. Throughout his career Esterházy has generated controversy concerning the quality and interpretation of his work, but there is no doubt of his role in almost single-handedly changing mainstream Hungarian fiction by rejecting the traditional conventions of narrative prose in favor of the linguistic and stylistic techniques of literary postmodernism.

The Esterházy name has been among the most prominent in Hungary since the early seventeenth century, when the family became one of the leading clans of the aristocracy in the Austro-Hungarian Empire. Since then the Esterházys have played a significant though not always favorable role in the turbulent history of Central and Eastern Europe. The family has produced governors, ministers, and prime ministers, as well as rebel leaders and warlords. Esterházy's grandfather, Count Móric Esterházy, was a prime minister for a brief period in 1917 and a member of parliament several times. In 1944 he took part in Governor Miklós Horthy de Nagybánya's unsuccessful attempt to negotiate a peace treaty before the German invasion.

The writer's father, Mátyás Esterházy, was also a count; thus, although he was highly educated and spoke several languages, he was treated by the Communists as a dangerous "déclassé element." He married Lili Mányoky in 1948; soon after the birth of their first son, Péter, on 14 April 1950, the family was relocated to a rural village, where Mátyás and Lili Esterházy were forced to work in the fields. Seeing his parents uphold their aristocratic values amid these ordeals played a significant role in the development of Péter Esterházy's personality and worldview.

After the unsuccessful 1956 revolution the family was allowed to return to Budapest. Esterházy completed elementary school in 1964 and went on to the Piarista Gymnasium, which was among the few remaining secondary schools run by religious orders. The school had remained free of Communist influence and was (and still is) one of the best educational institutions in the country. Throughout his teenage years, apart from reading, Esterházy's main pastime was playing soccer. Even as a well-known writer he continued to play regularly at a local club, and the nuances of the game have an important role in his early writings. (One of his three younger brothers, Márton Esterházy, became a highly successful professional soccer player.)

In 1969 Esterházy entered the Faculty of Mathematics of Eötvös Loránd University in Budapest; one of his idols, Géza Ottlik, author of the novel *Iskola a határon* (1959; translated as *School at the Frontier,* 1966), was also a mathematician. After graduating in 1974, Esterházy was employed as a consultant in systematization in the Ministry of Metallurgy and Machine Industry. The job offered him subject matter for some of his later works. He quit in 1978; since then he has been a freelance writer.

Esterházy married Gitta Reén in 1973. They have two daughters and two sons: Dóra, born in 1975; Marcell, born in 1977; Zsófi, born in 1982; and Miklós, born in 1987. Although his literary interests are many and varied, Esterházy's family gives him his most important themes and is his main source of inspiration. His parents, his brothers, his wife, and his children are all present in his works, generally under their real names. The

Dust jacket for Esterházy's 1987 literary hoax, a novel about a young woman's misfortunes written under a female pseudonym. The photograph on the back of the jacket, purportedly of the author, is actually of Esterházy's wife, Gitta, at age twenty.

most important character, however, is usually Esterházy himself.

Esterházy's first short story appeared in 1974; two years later he published his first book, *Fancsikó és Pinta: Írások egy darab madzagra fűzve* (Fancsikó and Pinta: Writings Filed on a Piece of String), a series of interconnected short stories. The names in the title are those of characters imagined by a young boy, the author as a child. They represent two sides of his own personality, pathetic and ironic, and they accompany him in his little world and comment on his observations. These subtle, exact, and sometimes cruel observations are mainly about his parents. Esterházy does not imitate childish innocence; the book is mostly lyrical, but there is nothing sweet about it. The protagonist and his companions have an adult intelligence, but they have no prejudices and no moral boundaries such as respectfulness or humility. This freedom makes their observations clear and genuine.

Esterházy's second book, *Pápai vizeken ne kalózkodj!* (Do Not Pirate on Papal Waters!, 1977), is another collection of short stories, but this time the works are unrelated to each other. The book is divided into three parts. The first, "Chatter for a Waiter's Voice," follows the method of the previous book in that the narrator is not a real waiter but the author's mind in disguise. The little world of the restaurant becomes a whole universe with its own philosophy. The stories in the second part, "Naughty Text," owe a great deal to James Joyce. When, for example, Esterházy presents three different versions of an ordinary story of marital infidelity, not only Molly Bloom comes to the reader's mind but also her creator's stylistic experiments. The last part of the book, "The Spy's Story," is a short novel. The protagonist is a police informer, presumably in Eastern Europe; Esterházy writes about this way of life as if it were perfectly normal, and this very treatment exposes the contradictions of such a world of suspicion. Esterházy here demonstrates an affinity with Eastern European absurdist writing, such as that of Sławomir Mrożek and István Örkény.

The reaction to Esterházy's initial efforts was muted; few critics understood the significance or magnitude of his thematic and structural innovations. Self-reference, allusive techniques, and metalinguistic "asides" were too difficult for critics whose values were based on nineteenth-century realism to accept or even to recognize. Something bigger was needed to disturb the waters, and Esterházy's next book proved to be big enough.

Termelési-regény (Production Novel, 1979) is a remarkable work, even from the outside. It is almost five-hundred pages long, bound in bright magenta, and has a striking title that refers to the extinct literary genre of the "production novel." In the Stalinist early 1950s production novels and plays were supposed to provide high-quality entertainment, together with ideological education, for the proletariat. Such works were also intended to inspire the proletariat to labor harder and to produce more for the greater glory of the Soviet system and the Communist Party. In the late 1970s such a title was clearly meant to be ironic; and the irony is even stronger because the book really includes a production novel, though quite an unusual one.

Termelési-regény is divided into two parts. The first, which constitutes about a fourth of the book, is the novel itself; the second, much larger part consists of endnotes to the "main" text. The novel takes place in an institute in Hungary, no doubt based on the Ministry of Metallurgy and Machine Industry, in the 1970s. The characters include directors, secretaries, workers, and party activists; the action consists of meetings, debates, victories, and defeats. The story is not particularly exciting, but it is full of brilliant ironic gestures and stylistic tour de forces: a production meeting is described as a violent medieval battle, complete with cut-off limbs and rivers of blood; characters are introduced, and it takes several pages for the reader to realize that they are not humans but hamsters; one chapter includes a report from the Hungarian parliament around the turn of the twentieth century (the era of the eminent novelist Kálmán Mikszáth, with whom Esterházy takes long imaginary walks in the endnotes), and embedded in it is a speech by Mátyás Rákosi, the leader of the Hungarian Communist Party from the mid 1940s to the mid 1950s. There is a peculiar document of the censorship (or self-censorship) of the 1970s: wherever one would expect to read the name of the Russian revolutionary leader Vladimir Ilyich Lenin, one finds, instead, that of the Spanish movie director Luis Buñuel. for example, a picture of Buñuel hangs on the wall in the office of the institute's director. Such passages tell most clearly of the taboos (in this case, against an ironic or frivolous use of Lenin's name) that existed when the book was published.

The last three quarters of the book purport to be the notes of "Peter E."—that is, Johann Peter Eckermann, the secretary and companion of Johann Wolfgang von Goethe, who recorded all of the important and unimportant sayings and doings of the aged German poet and dramatist. Here, however, Peter E.'s master is Péter Esterházy. Peter E. tells stories about Péter Esterházy that are formally comments on passages in the novel in the first part of the book but that, in fact, form a separate novel. Most of this second novel is about a soccer team, of which Esterházy is the captain. Here, just as at the institute, are complicated human relationships, including jealousy, betrayal, and forgiveness. The reader also sees the master with his wife, Gitta, and their baby daughter, Dóra. Even more important, the reader meets the master working on the book the reader is holding—"The novel as it writes itself," says Peter E. The notes include facsimiles of drafts and diagrams for chapters of the novel, and the master is shown checking the proofs of the text that the reader is perusing. Thus, the notes constitute the novel of the production of the "production novel" itself. This amusing system of self-reference is made even tighter because one has to read the two parts in parallel, as the references direct one back and forth between novel and notes. But even this fact is reflected in the book itself: the reader's attention is called to the necessity of using two bookmarks, which were provided with the book.

The book, which is now considered a masterpiece, caused controversy when it was first published. Some critics praised it as a major breakthrough, the beginning of a new era in Hungarian prose—which it was; others condemned it as nonsensical and meaningless. Nevertheless, the book earned Esterházy a reputation as a writer of extraordinary stylistic talent and critical importance.

With his next book, *Függő* (Indirect, 1981), Esterházy began a large-scale project. With the subtitle *Bevezetés a szépirodalomba* (Introduction to Literature), *Függő* was presented as the first part of a longer series, and for the next five years the forthcoming parts of the "introduction" were among the most anticipated and appreciated novelties for Hungarian readers. The other parts were *Ki szavatol a lady biztonságáért?* (Who Does Guarantee the Lady's Security?, 1982), *Fuharosok* (1983; translated as "The Transporters," 1991), *Kis magyar pornográfia* (1984; translated as *A Little Hungarian Pornography,* 1995), and *A szív segédigéi* (1985; translated as *Helping Verbs of the Heart,* 1991). All were published in volumes of identical size, with the same white binding and the same typography. Whereas *Termelési-regény* brought Esterházy the acknowledgment of some critics, with this project he gained popular success.

The first volume in the series, *Függő*, is a full-length novel in one 180-page-long sentence. The main characters are teenagers who try to transform their adolescent relationships into adult loves and friendships. The central figure is called K., like the protagonist of Franz Kafka's *Das Schloß* (1926; translated as *The Castle*, 1930), but here *K.* presumably stands for Dezső Kosztolányi, the poet and novelist who was one of the finest stylists of Hungarian language. The novel is a sophisticated montage of citations, many of them from the works of Kosztolányi. (The title can also mean "Dependent"—presumably, dependent on the prose tradition.) The time shifts repeatedly among the 1960s, the present, and the turn of the century (the time of Kosztolányi's adolescence). These shifts can be spectacular: for example, a simile may continue for several pages and include an embedded story from another time. The work is full of such tricks and stunts and is perhaps Esterházy's most virtuosic novel.

The second part of the series, *Ki szavatol a lady biztonságáért?*, comprises two novels: *Daisy*, a short and somewhat brutal story that takes place in a cheap pub; and *Ágnes*, a much more complicated intellectual "love story." The two novels are interrelated in many ways: situations, relationships, and characters of each text appear in the other. The protagonist of *Ágnes* is nameless throughout most of the work, though at one point someone calls him Péter. He falls in love with Ágnes when he sees her photograph, but there is not much more romance in his world. In essence, the world of the intellectuals proves to be as limited as the one presented in *Daisy*. The only pure soul is a child, Jitka, whose unique status is illustrated by her stylized, anachronistic language—a stylistic experiment that reoccurs in full form in a later book.

If *Függő* is the longest sentence in Hungarian literature, *Fuharosok* is certainly the shortest novel. It was published with large print, wide margins, and thick paper to make a book of reasonable size, but in a normal layout it fills only twelve pages. Time and place are not indicated, but the fact that the narrator, a teenager named Dóra, lives with her mother and sisters with no men around suggests some kind of war situation. The reader does not know who the Transporters (the Hungarian word is much more enigmatic) are, but they are certainly ruthless and merciless. They take everything from the helpless women and rape Dóra. When they leave, the women, rather than bemoaning their fate, choose instead to celebrate their survival.

In 1984 Esterházy published a new version of *Daisy* as an opera libretto. As he does not write

Dust jacket for Esterházy's 1990 novel, in which a writer's wife falls in love with the Czech author Bohumil Hrabal, and God tries to learn to play the saxophone

verse, he borrowed most of his rhymes—mainly from Kosztolányi and from popular songs of the 1970s. But the real continuation of his "Introduction to Literature," published the same year, was *Kis magyar pornográfia*, which became one of his most popular books. It is not a novel but a sort of medley of genres, and its content is much less obscene than the title indicates. The work has four parts. The first is an imitation of a soft-pornographic novel in which women of various social backgrounds tell the "writer" their stories, each in a distinct linguistic style. The second part is a collection of anecdotes from the Stalinist period of the 1950s; some are true, some fictitious, but all are characteristic of the time. The third part is a long text consisting of nothing but interrogative sentences; taken together, the

Péter Esterházy   DLB 232

questions tell a story and also reveal a great deal about the spiritual state of Hungary toward the end of the communist era. The fourth part is a collection of aphorisms and of episodes from everyday life. Apart from its other values, the publication of *Kis magyar pornográfia* is considered an important step toward freedom of expression in Hungary.

The last "little white book" of the "Introduction to Literature" series, *A szív segédigéi*, is a touching account of the illness and death of the author's mother, combined with the construction of a female dream world as an exercise in empathy. Each page is framed with a black border, like a death notice; the narration continues in the upper part, with a comment or citation in the lower part. Some of the comments deal with the process and the struggle of writing and with the moral implications of making literature of life—or, in this case, of death. This book, probably owing to the universality of its subject and its more traditional form, became Esterházy's most popular work outside Hungary; it has been translated into more than ten languages.

In 1986 the true nature of the "Introduction to Literature" came to light with the publication of a vast opus under the title *Bevezetés a szépirodalomba* that included all the previous parts, including both versions of *Daisy*, as well as new material that completes the cycle. The previously published texts are here put into a common context so that the reader can appreciate the repetitions and alterations of motifs, characters, situations, and stories. There are also marginal notes and illustrations, most notably the sources of citations in *Függő*. A list of the cited authors fills several densely printed pages at the end of the book.

Bevezetés a szépirodalomba begins with a new text, "A próza iszkolása" (The Scamper of Prose), a complicated construction with many citations from and references to the other texts. "A próza iszkolása" itself begins with a symbolic date that reappears several times: 16 June. This date is partly a tribute to Joyce's *Ulysses* (1922)—it is Bloomsday, the day on which the action of Joyce's novel occurs. But it is also significant in Hungarian history: 16 June 1958 was the date of the execution of Imre Nagy, the prime minister during the 1956 revolution, mention of which was taboo at the time of the book's publication. It also has a personal meaning: it is the date of the Esterházy family's relocation in 1951. It is, thus, an example of the multiple layers of meaning present in Esterházy's prose.

Between the parts of the book are short related texts, illustrations, and all kinds of amazing, playful experiments, including a movie script, *Idő van* (It's Time), which was later rewritten by Esterházy and the director Péter Gothár and filmed with great success in 1984; a page of scattered mottoes; a cartoon by Ferenc Banga, who had illustrated Esterházy's first two books; a short story by Kosztolányi, retranslated by Esterházy from its German translation; and a facsimile of Ottlik's *Iskola a határon*, copied by hand by Esterházy on a single sheet of paper so that the several "layers" of writing produce a beautiful, though unintelligible, pattern.

At the beginning and end of the book are a pair of parentheses turned outward; thus, the whole world outside the book is placed within parentheses, and the book creates its own universe within its 720 large pages. It is not a work that one should read from beginning to end; it is, rather, like a landscape in which one can take pleasant walks from time to time. The reader can use it as a handbook that includes all the significant facts about belles lettres.

Esterházy received the Aszú Prize in 1982, the Füst Milán Prize in 1983, the Déry Prize in 1984, and the József Attila Prize and the Örley Prize in 1986. In November 1986 a series of highly unusual writings by an unknown author named Lili Csokonai appeared in the literary review *Élet és irodalom*. The name sounded familiar: Mihály Csokonai Vitéz was an outstanding poet at the end of the eighteenth century, and he called the girl he hopelessly loved Lilla or Lili. The pieces in *Élet és irodalom* were about a twenty-two-year-old woman who lost her parents early, was abused in various ways, suffered a great deal, and, after an accident caused by her lover, a married man, became disabled and began writing down the story of her life. It was a detailed, documentary-style, apparently nonfiction work, but it was written in the language of the seventeenth and eighteenth centuries. In 1987 the writings, along with much new material, appeared in book form under the title *Tizenhét hattyúk* (Seventeen Swans). Only a few well-informed people knew that the talented "new" writer was, in fact, Esterházy. He revealed his authorship a few weeks after the book appeared.

In 1988 Esterházy published his first nonfiction work, *A kitömött hattyú* (The Stuffed Swan). Most of the writings collected in the book can be called "essays," though the label does little to indicate the diversity of forms and subjects. There are tributes to masters (most notably Ottlik and Kosztolányi), an appendix to the aphorism chapter of *Kis magyar pornográfia*, an account of the preparation and reception of *Tizenhét hattyúk*, and writings about literature, art, and soccer. Also in 1988 the first book about

Esterházy was published. Edited by the leading critic Péter Balassa, *Diptychon* collects studies of the two most important prose works of the late 1980s in Hungary: *Bevezetés a szépirodalomba,* by Esterházy, and *Emlékiratok könyve* (1986; translated as *A Book of Memoirs,* 1997), by Péter Nádas.

Esterházy joined the progressive magazine *Hitel* (Credit) in 1989. His column, "Az elefántcsonttoronyból" (From the Ivory Tower), forms an outstanding chronicle of the political changes in 1989 and the first free elections in 1990. During this time, however, *Hitel* shifted toward the political right, and when it published an article with anti-Semitic overtones, Esterházy resigned. He always kept his distance from political extremes; when a nationalist author called on writers to think "in terms of people and nation," Esterházy answered that he thought in terms of verb and object.

Also in 1989 Esterházy published an experimental book titled *Biztos kaland* with the typographer and photographer Balázs Czeizel. The work is an essay or enigmatic story made up of found pictures from the 1950s, with some verbal commentary. It begins at the end and includes instructions to turn to certain pages, thereby breaking the traditional linear nature of reading. Esterházy's next novel, *Hrabal könyve* (1990; translated as *The Book of Hrabal,* 1993), is a tribute to the Czech author Bohumil Hrabal, whose novels *Taneční hodiny pro starší a pokročilé* (1964; translated as *Dancing Lesson for the Advanced in Age,* 1995) and *Ostře sledované vlaky* (1965; translated as *Closely Watched Trains,* 1968) are known worldwide; Esterházy visited the old master in Prague before publishing the novel. The narrator, Anna, is the wife of a writer who is working on a book about Hrabal. (One critic, recognizing that the writer is, once again, based on Esterházy, called the novel "The book of Gitta.") She is expecting a child, and God—the other protagonist in the work— sends down two angels to prevent her from having an abortion. Anna writes to and falls in love with Hrabal, while God wants to learn to play the saxophone and summons Charlie Parker to teach him. Anna's son, Miklós, is born, but God remains unable to play the saxophone. A successful motion picture based on the book, *Anna filmje* (The Movie of Anna), was released in 1992.

In 1991 Esterházy collected his columns from *Hitel* as *Az elefántcsonttoronyból.* He also published a new collection of diverse writings, a continuation of *A kitömött hattyú* titled *A halacska csodálatos élete* (The Wonderful Life of the Little Fish), on such diverse topics as politics, language, Eastern Europe, movies, Hrabal, and soccer. Published the same year,

Dust jacket for Esterházy's 1991 book about the Danube, which combines fictional and nonfictional accounts of journeys on the river

the novel *Hahn-Hahn grófnő pillantása* (translated as *The Glance of Countess Hahn-Hahn: Down the Danube,* 1994) has as its protagonist the Danube River; the countess or duchess of the title is not a character but refers to an aphorism of Heinrich Heine's that Esterházy cited previously in *Termelési-regény:* "All woman writers look at a man with one eye and at the paper with the other, except Duchess Hahn-Hahn who is one-eyed." Esterházy combines a nonfiction travel journal, a partly fictional account of a journey he took in his youth with an enigmatic uncle, and telegraph messages from a symbolic journey of a professional traveler (or "hired property") to the latter's unknown employer ("the hirer"). The history of cities and nations along the Danube, as well as the writer's reflections on current political changes, are recorded. Unusual for a novel, the book includes a bibliography and an index of names.

In 1993 Esterházy published three works in collaboration with other artists. *Egy nő* (A Woman) was created with the illustrator Banga. Technically, it is not a book but a scroll, like a small Torah, in a box; the text serves only as an element of the artist's typographic experiment. Three thousand copies of the work were produced; an enlarged edition, without Banga's drawings, was published in 1995 in regular book form (translated as *She Loves Me*, 1997). *A vajszínű árnyalat* (That Shade of Cream), produced with the press photographer András Szebeni, is a photograph album about the previous five years in Hungary: news photographs are combined with artistic portraits and studio settings; Esterházy supplies captions and commentaries. The book is a chronicle of the pathetic, pitiful, and laughable moments of the first years of democracy. The third book has no overall title; it comprises a short story, "Élet és irodalom," by Esterházy, and another, "Jegyzőkönyv" (the title can mean either "Notebook" or "Criminal Record") by Imre Kertész. Kertész describes an awkward episode with a customs officer; Esterházy is writing about a similar situation when the story by Kertész comes to his mind and serves as a pattern for his own observations. Both stories are about the fear and shame that are incurably present in everyone who was brought up in an autocracy. The following year Esterházy published a new collection of nonfiction writings, *Egy kékharisnya följegyzéseiből* (A Bluestocking's Notes), which includes interviews, radio plays, glosses, and journals; the most important pieces are the articles that appeared under the title of the book in *Élet és irodalom* and that he also read on a weekly radio program.

With the first freely elected government in the early 1990s, a struggle erupted between political factions in Hungary for the control of the mass media. Esterházy exposed and ridiculed attempts to restrict free speech; sometimes he did so simply by publishing the bare facts, such as threatening letters to his friends or antidemocratic articles from small right-wing magazines. In 1994 his first play, the three-act *Búcsúszimfónia* (Farewell Symphony), was published. The title refers to a work by Joseph Haydn, who was court musician for an Esterházy prince. The play was written for the drama competition of the Víg Theater in Budapest, where it opened in the spring of 1996. The main characters are a seventy-year-old man, based on Esterházy's father; his four sons, who make up a choir; his daughter-in-law; and a fool. The play is a birthday greeting in dialogue form, during which the four sons recall the important events of their father's life.

In 1995 Esterházy published an enlarged version, without the drawings, of *Egy nő* (translated as *She Loves Me*, 1997). It consists of short, sometimes philosophic but mostly erotic prose pieces about women, love, and hatred. All begin with the same sentence: "There's a woman." This work was followed the next year by a new collection of nonfiction, *Egy kék haris* (the title is a play on *Egy kékharisnaya följegyzéseiből;* literally it means "A Blue Corncrake" and has nothing to do with the contents of the book), which is a continuation of *Egy kékharisnya följegyzéseiből*. His first translation also appeared in 1996. The title of the original German book is *Esterhazy* (1993; translated into English as *Esterhazy, the Rabbit Prince*, 1994); its hero is an Easter bunny (in German, *Oster Hase*). Esterházy takes the pun on his family name as a challenge, and in translating the tale he alters it in as many ways as possible—most notably, in revenge, he makes puns on the names of the original authors, Irene Dische, Hans Magnus Enzensberger, and Michael Sowa.

Esterházy continued to be recognized for his literary accomplishments. Among his many awards are the Vilenica Prize (1988), the Krúdy Gyula Prize (1990), the Soros Oeuvre Prize (1992), the Premio Opera di Poesiea (1993), the Free Press Prize (1994), the Ordre des Arts et des Lettres (1994), the Prize of the Soros Foundation (1995), and the Prize of the Foundation for Hungarian Arts (1995). He was elected a member of Széchenyi Academy in 1994. In 1996 he was awarded the highest Hungarian decoration for living artists, the Kossuth Prize, and he also received the Szép Ernő Prize for his play, *Búcsúszimfónia*. In 1996–1997 he was a fellow at the Wissenschaftskolleg zu Berlin (Berlin Institute for Advanced Studies) and in 1999 he received the Österreichische Staatspreis für europäische Literatur (Austrian State Prize for European Literature).

In 2000 Esterházy published a major new work that is probably his most important volume since *Bevezetés a szépirodalomba*. More than seven hundred pages in length, *Harmonia Cælestis* (Latin for "Heavenly Harmony") owes its title to a baroque musical composition of one of his ancestors, and it resembles a complex suitelike composition of many parts. The book consists of two distinct parts. The first, *Numbered Sentences from the Life of the Esterházy Family*, is built up of 371 fragments of various sizes and genres. They do not form a continuous linear narrative, though many of them are connected by a rich web of intertextual references. The protagonist of all the fragments is called "my father." Sometimes he is the real father of the author, but these fathers are mostly forefathers from earlier historical peri-

Dust jacket for the massive novel, published in 2000, in which Esterházy traces the history of his family over several centuries

ods. As the Esterházy dynasty is deeply rooted in Hungarian history of the last four or five centuries, the book is also a brilliant account of the country's troubled times from the point of view of the sometimes corrupt and intriguing, sometimes brave or even heroic aristocracy. Time lapses and what might be called "person-lapses" are frequent, illustrating the nonlinear quality of historical remembrance. At one point, for example, the reader finds a detailed inventory of the treasury of a seventeenth-century Esterházy count; among the items of extremely sophisticated jewelry, carpets, and other valuables, however, are a greasy old briefcase, a cheap wristwatch, and a pair of eyeglasses—personal items of the author's real father from the 1950s or 1960s. This touching juxtaposition does not mean that Esterházy has nostalgic feelings about the aristocratic way of life of his ancestors; he is interested in the moral consequences of the sudden decline of a social class. But this theme is only one of several. The "my father" characters are not only aristocrats: virtually any man can be "my father," including a blind homeless person and two armed robbers.

If the first part of the novel is the destruction of the "my father" character, or of the notion of a fixed personal identity, the second part, *Confessions of an Esterházy Family*, builds up the "real" father. This part is seamless, traditional storytelling, without stylistic stunts, virtuoso allusions, or avant-garde formalisms. Each of the nine chapters, which are organized in a linear sequence, presents a certain phase in the life of Esterházy's family. It begins around the time of his father's birth and ends in the time of his own adolescence. Thus, the time span includes the most eventful four decades of Hungarian history, from the short-lived communist revolution in 1919 to the 1956 uprising. But the focus is really on the inner life of the family, on the socialization of two generations of Esterházys who are holding on to their moral values in an enemy world. Esterházy quotes long sections from his grandfather's journals, and the narrator is called Péter, so that one might think that one is reading a real memoir, an almost nonfictional documentary account of actual events. Esterházy does not discourage this kind of reading: though a note preceding the text warns of the fictional nature of the characters and events, the note is in quotation marks. Esterházy's estrangement effects are subtle and highly sophisticated. At one point, for example, Béla Kun, the communist leader, fleeing from Budapest in a small airplane after the fall of the 1919 revolution, accidentally drops some of the stolen jewelry he is taking. This scene is not only fiction but the fiction of someone else—namely, Dezső Kosztolányi; it is taken not from reality but from literature. Esterházy thus persuades the reader of the fictional nature of all remembrance, of history itself. The essence, the meaning, or the reason is always supplied by the observer. After the destructive, avant-garde element of the first half of the book, the second half proves to be a postmodernist deconstruction of the notions of historical truth and reality.

Péter Esterházy's major works are considered among the most significant contributions to Hungarian literature in the second half of the twentieth century. He remains one of the most influential literary figures not only in Hungary but throughout Central and Eastern Europe. He is one of the few contemporary Hungarian authors to enjoy an international reputation and one whose ability to surprise and delight has become legendary.

Interviews:

Marianne Birnbaum, *Esterházy-kalauz* (Budapest: Magvető, 1991);

Tibor Keresztúry, "Azt csinálom, amit eddig, nézdegélek," *Félterpeszben* (1991): 7–24;

György Petri, "Nem vagyok egy Berzsenyi," in Esterházy's *Egy kék haris* (Budapest: Magvető, 1996), pp. 159–171.

Bibliography:

András Beck, "Bibliográfia: Esterházy Péter művei és kritikai fogadtatásuk," in *Diptychon*, edited by Péter Balassa (Budapest: Magvető, 1988), pp. 127–134.

References:

Péter Balassa, "Vagyunk," in his *A színeváltozás* (Budapest: Magvető, 1982), pp. 380–410;

Balassa, ed., *Diptychon* (Budapest: Magvető, 1988);

Miklós Béládi, "Az új érzékenység és az elbeszélés személyessége," in his *Válaszutak* (Budapest: Szépirodalmi, 1982), pp. 374–393;

Árpád Bernáth, "Literatur der Postmoderne in Ungarn," *Neohelicon*, 16, no. 1 (1990): 151–170;

Endre Bojtár, *Egy keleteuropéer az irodalomelméletben* (Budapest: Szépirodalmi, 1983), pp. 159–178;

Erzsébet Csányi, "Idézésformák a *Függő*ben," *Új Symposion*, 9 (1981): 297–300;

Miklós Győrffy, "Új magyar prózaszemle," *Jelenkor*, 35 (1992): 185–196;

József Jankovics, "Vezérfonal a műelemzéshez and annotations," in Esterházy's *Függő: Bevezetés a szépirodalomba* (Budapest: Ikon, 1993), pp. 4–8 and *passim;*

Zoltán Kenyeres, "Jelentés egy püspöklila könyvről, avagy kritika püspöklilában," in his *A lélek fényűzése* (Budapest: Szépirodalmi, 1983), pp. 439–468;

Ernő Kulcsár Szabó, *Esterházy Péter* (Pozsony: Kaligram, 1996);

Kulcsár Szabó, "A szöveg tartományai," in his *Műalkotás–szöveg–hatás* (Budapest: Magvető, 1987), pp. 311–331;

Sándor Mészáros, "A kritikus olvasó: Esterházy Péter műveinek recepciója 1986-ig," *Alföld*, 1 (1989): 39–47;

Sándor Radnóti, *Recrudescunt vulnera* (Budapest: Cserépfalvi, 1991), pp. 135–173;

Mihály Szegedy-Maszák, *"Minta a szőnyegen"* (Budapest: Balassi, 1995), pp. 253–265;

Szegedy-Maszák, "Sok, de nem minden," *Jelenkor*, 3 (1992): 277–283;

Szövegmagyarázó műhely [Bojtár Endre, Horváth Iván, Szegedy-Maszák Mihály, Szörényi László, and Veres András], "Ötfokú ének," *Mozgó Világ*, 6 (1979): 114–128;

Beáta Thomka, "Függő világok," in her *Esszéterek, regényterek* (Újvidék: Forum, 1988), pp. 163–169;

Gábor Tolcsvay Nagy, "A nyelv fennköltségének megvonása Esterházy Péter prózájában," *Irodalomtörténet*, 1–2 (1996): 224–239;

Julianna Wernitzer, *Idézetvilág avagy Esterházy Péter a Don Quijote szerzője* (Budapest: Jelenkor-Szépirodalmi, 1994).

Regīna Ezera

(20 December 1930 –   )

Broņislavs Tabūns
University of Latvia

and

Kārlis Račevskis
Ohio State University

BOOKS: *Zem pavasara debesīm: Romāns* (Riga: Latvijas Valsts izdevniecība, 1961);

Un ceļš vēl kūp: Stāsti (Riga: Latvijas Valsts izdevniecība, 1961);

Viņas bija trīs: Romāns (Riga: Latvijas Valsts izdevniecība, 1963);

Daugavas stāsti (Riga: Latvijas Valsts izdevniecība, 1965);

Mežābele: Klāva Mazputniņa atvaļinājums piezīmes: Garstāsts (Riga: Liesma, 1966);

Dzilnas sila balāde: Garstāsts (Riga: Liesma, 1968);

Aiztek Gaujas ūdeņi, aiztek: Stāsti (Riga: Liesma, 1968);

Saules atspulgs: Stāsti ar laimīgām beigām (Riga: Liesma, 1969);

Grieze, trakais putns: Stāsti (Riga: Liesma, 1970);

Nakts bez mēnesnīcas: Mozaīka: Garstāsts (Riga: Liesma, 1971);

Aka: Romāns (Riga: Liesma, 1972);

Pavasara pērkons: Noveles un stāsti (Riga: Liesma, 1973); translated by R. Speirs as *Nostalgia* (Riga: Liesma, 1977);

Vasara bija tikai vienu dienu: Garstāsts (Riga: Liesma, 1974);

Cilvēkam vajag suni: Stāsti un noveles (Riga: Liesma, 1975);

Zemdegas: Romāns Fantasmagorija (Riga: Liesma, 1977);

Baraviku laika dullums: Stāsti (Riga: Liesma, 1978);

Slazds: Noveles un stāsti (Riga: Liesma, 1979);

Izlase: Stāsti (Riga: Zvaigzne, 1979);

Saulespuķes no pērnās vasaras (Riga: Liesma, 1980);

Varmācība: Romāns no cikla "Pati ar savu vēju" (Riga: Liesma, 1982);

Nodevība: Romāns no cikla "Pati ar savu vēju" (Riga: Liesma, 1984);

Dzīvot uz savas zemes (Riga: Liesma, 1984);

Princeses fenomens: Raibi Stāsti (Riga: Liesma, 1985);

Pie klusiem ūdeņiem: Stāsti par nomodu un sapņiem (Riga: Liesma, 1987);

Virtuve bez pavārgrāmatas (Riga: Liesma, 1989);

Visticamāk, ka ne . . . Stundu kalendārs: Stāsti (Riga: Liesma, 1993);

Zvaigžņu lietus: Miniatūras (Riga: Preses nams, 1994);

Pūķa ola: Pilnatnes stāsti (Riga: Preses nams, 1995);

Mazliet patiesības: Nedaudz melu . . .: Ekscentriskas piezīmes (Riga: Liktņstāsti, 1997);

Varbūt tā nebūs vairs nekad: Proza un nedzeja (Riga: Preses nams, 1997).

Collection: *Stāsti un noveles* (Riga: Zvaigzne ABC, 2000)—comprises "Kinozvaigzne Inita," "Skaistākās kājas rajonā," "Nostaļģija," "Cilvēks ar suņa ožu," "Hiēna," "Zilonis," "Princeses fenomens," and "Dvēseļu ceļošana."

Edition in English: *The Swing* (Moscow: Raduga, 1984).

Regīna Ezera belongs to the generation of writers who began their careers after World War II and is one of the most prominent figures in modern Latvian literature. Her more than thirty works of prose bring to life the land—its fields, streams, and forests—and the people of Latvia. Her writing combines realism with late-modernist aesthetics, and her work includes the genres of novel, novella, short story, and essay. Her major themes are frequently psychological, exploring the relationship between humans and nature—the place of humans in the chain of being and of destiny.

Ezera was born Regīna Šamreto on 20 December 1930 to Lūcija and Roberts Šamreto in Riga. Her father was a bookkeeper, and her mother was a nurse. From her father, she believes she inherited her sense of irony and humor, and from her mother, an extreme sensitivity and restlessness. Regīna began her education in Riga's Elementary School No. 28 and soon revealed a precocious predisposition for both literature and mathematics. She also became familiar with farm life and work—subjects that became central components of her writing. During World War II she witnessed the evil and the brutality of the times, subjects that are central to her novella *Dzilnas sila balāde* (The Ballad of the Pinewood Bird, 1968). Remembering those war years, Ezera once noted that, as a writer, she was descended "from that barefoot little girl who, standing under the vast dome of the sky, with her cowherd's switch under her arm, suddenly discovered the connection humans have with Time and Space, understood the brevity of life—as well as the eternity of Life: everything that was to become the permanent and basic theme of the later writer's inspiration."

In the fall of 1944, as the Soviet armies advanced into Latvia, Regīna and her parents were evacuated to Germany. With the arrival of American troops in April 1945, the Šamreto family was transferred to Magdeburg, which eventually was occupied by Soviet forces. As a result, the Šamretos were forced to return to Latvia.

Following the return to Riga in October 1945, Ezera began her high school studies. Demonstrating a particular aptitude for Latvian literature, composition, and dramatic reading, she was especially fascinated by the novel *Zvejnieka dēls* (1947; translated as *The Fisherman's Son*, 1954) by Vilis Lācis. This book inspired her to begin writing, as she explained: "There are many books I have read two or three times. But none as often as *Zvejnieka dēls*. For several days, I walked around as in a daze under its spell; at night, I saw the sea in my dreams, I saw strong people who laughed at danger, I heard the cry of seagulls. A week later, I picked up my pen and tried to write something more than the ordinary school composition. I was sixteen then." Ezera graduated with honors in 1950 and continued her studies in the department of journalism at the University of Latvia—although she admits to having been tempted also by a major in forestry. While at the university, she became an avid reader of the works of Petrarch, Guy de Maupassant, Fyodor Dostoyevsky, Leo Tolstoy, Theodore Dreiser, and William Faulkner, as well the Latvian writers Rūdolfs Blaumanis and Jānis Jaunsudrabiņš. In the summer of 1954, Ezera began working for the magazine *Bērnība* (Childhood) and later that year became a special correspondent for the children's newspaper *Pionieris* (Pioneer), where she continued to work for two years following her graduation from college in 1955.

In 1955 *Bērnība* published her story "Pat īkšķis nelīdzēja" (Even the Thumb Could Not Help), the first publication to appear under her pen name, Regīna Ezera, suggested to her by the editor Vladislavs Kaupužs and her future husband, the journalist Česlavs Kindzulis. Marriage and family responsibilities forced Ezera to give up her job as a reporter. "My third daughter was born when I was twenty-six," she remembers. "I was able to raise all three without any outside help. I managed to do quite a lot, without much sleep, and without taking holidays." Her youngest daughter, Aija, born in 1957, also became a writer, publishing under the name Aija Vālodze.

During these years Ezera matured as a writer and became further acquainted with literature, cultural history, and the natural sciences. She strove above all to fully develop her linguistic capabilities: "I consider Latvian to be a part of my very being and I have learned to approach the matter of language with utmost respect. I have learned it humbly and relentlessly for a full forty years, and I am constantly uncovering its nuances and riches with a joyful wonder. I am still acquiring these riches. And I will continue to do so as long as my tongue speaks and my hand writes."

Ezera became an established and popular writer in the 1960s. She was inducted into the Latvian Writers' Union in 1961. That same year, her first collection of short stories, *Un ceļš vēl kūp:* (And the Mist Still Rises from the Road), and her first novel, *Zem pavasara debesīm* (Under Spring Skies), were published. These works, together with her second novel, *Viņas bija trīs: Romāns* (They Were Three Women: Novel, 1963), represent a period of social realism in her writing style. They have as their main subject the destinies of people caught in the dramatic events of World War II and its aftermath. Social conflicts are at the center of the next collection of short stories, *Daugavas stāsti* (Tales of the River Daugava, 1965), and of the novella *Dzilnas sila balāde,* which evokes the atmosphere of the Latvian countryside during the time of the Nazi occupation. Already prominent in these early works is Ezera's tendency to bring out the psychological dimension of the narrative by emphasizing the subjective side of the characters' experiences. In her article "Par vai pret psiholoģismu?" (For or Against Psychologism?) Ezera singles out this tendency as a fundamental principle of her creative work: "The question of literature's depth is to a large extent precisely the question of its psychological depth," she writes. This attention paid to the individual's psyche implied a clear rejection of the officially sanctioned themes of collective destiny and party allegiance—a seemingly paradoxical departure from party norms at a time when Ezera had decided to join the Communist Party. Nevertheless, while she remained a Party member until 1991, the year the U.S.S.R. recognized the independence of Latvia, she consistently avoided the officially sponsored themes and problems in her writing, adopting instead an explicitly democratic and humanistic outlook.

Ezera's next novella, *Saules atspulgs: Stāsti ar laimīgām beigām* (Reflection of the Sun: A Story with a Happy Ending 1969), is written in the form of a concentrated and laconic interior monologue. The story warns of the dangers of sacrificing life's true values—the love of one's land and its people— in the interests of a career. This stylistic approach characterizes also two other works of this period—the summery and colorfully evocative collection *Aiztek Gaujas ūdeņi, aiztek* (They Flow Away, the Waters of the Gauja, They Flow Away, 1968), and the fragmentary yet deeply meditative

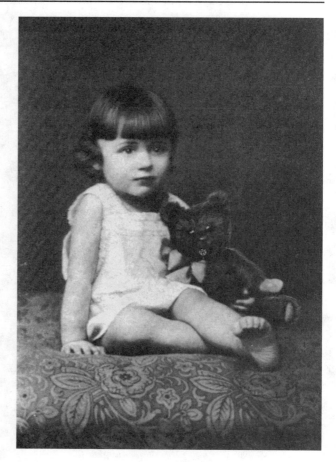

Ezera as a child

narrative, *Nakts bez mēnesnīcas: Mozaīka* (Moonless Night, 1971). The latter volume chronicles the events and colorful characters that make up the story of a night spent at a remote railway station. It is also the story of a people's destiny and a reflection on the fate of Latvia. Ezera's third novel, *Aka* (The Well, 1972), is a dramatic love story that revolves around a couple's quest for happiness and the emotional conflicts that quest raises. The ethical issues at the heart of a woman's destiny are further developed in the novella *Vasara bija tikai vienu dienu* (The Summer Lasted Only One Day, 1974). Ezera's conceptualization of the role of women was highly innovative in the context of postwar Latvian prose literature. Her female characters have neither important positions in society nor dramatic life stories. Their work and occupations are generally de-emphasized in order to bring out the importance of personal experiences and human relations. Yet, these ordinary women who people her fictional world with their simple joys and commonplace suffer-

Ezera with two of her three daughters

house that eventually became her permanent residence. At Brieži she wrote her best-known works, received visitors, colleagues, and admirers, and gave interviews to reporters and literary critics. During her stays she covered thousands of kilometers on her daily walks, and her love of the land and its people grew deep roots. A most important place in her affections was also reserved for the animals and birds of her native land, for all living creatures—and, in particular, for the dog who was her constant companion. Her encounters with animals provided sources of inspiration for her writing. Thus, one of Ezera's more original contributions to Latvian literature is the genre of the zoological novel or story. Many of these stories have creatures of the wild as their principal subject, bringing out the characteristics, strength, and beauty they display in their natural surroundings. Most of Ezera's fictional creations bring in both worlds—the animal as well as the human—and examine them in terms of their contacts, parallels, and contrasts. In these tales, Ezera often combines realism with fantasy and dreams, thus providing her imaginary universe with its special mood. In some of her stories the principal characters are not animals but humans who display animal-like characteristics. Ezera believes strongly in a nature in which the human is inseparable from the animal. She therefore stresses the responsibility humans bear for preserving this nature, which is the all-encompassing environment for all human activities.

One of the more striking creations in Ezera's fiction is the swan Guārs—the elegant white bird with the onomatopoeically evocative name who appears in *Vasara bija tikai vienu dienu*. After the swan has been mortally wounded by a man, its desperate struggle with death becomes a cry of protest against the cruelty and brutality of humans, a reminder of their irresponsibility. A similar plea is sounded in a story about the killing of an elephant, in which the author's dramatic imagery is interspersed with segments of a narrative taken from the journal of an elephant hunter. At the same time, Ezera can also present human beings as the most miraculous of nature's creations: each existence, however brief, is an irreplaceable episode within the eternal pulsating of nature's rhythms.

The dilemmas of human psychology intensify in the context of family and social relations, as Ezera shows in *Varmācība* (Persecution, 1982), the first volume of her still to be completed tetralogy, *Pati ar savu vēju* (Myself, With My Own Wind). Here, a blind and irrational motherly love turns into a pos-

ing have also a special attitude toward life. For a woman, as Ezera shows, to love means to fully assume the responsibilities of wife, mother, homemaker, and provider—roles that are as important as any a woman might hold. The figure of woman as mother and life-giver appears in several variations throughout Ezera's writings.

The novel *Zemdegas: Fantasmagorija* (Underground Fires: Phantasmagoria, 1977) is devoted to a study of the depths of the human psyche and constitutes one of Ezera's most creative works. Using certain writing techniques borrowed from surrealist poets—unusual word associations, subversion of narrative logic and chronology—Ezera effectively blurs the boundaries separating the real from the unreal, wakefulness from dreams, the past from the present, and the actual from the virtual. The effect is to bring out the strangeness of the ordinary, the distinctiveness of the individual's psyche, and the relativity of human potential.

Ezera liked to spend her summers away from Riga, in the county of Ogre on the banks of the Daugava River, staying at "Brieži," the summer

sessive will to dominate others' lives. The second volume, *Nodevība* (Betrayal, 1984), examines the subjects of creativity and the writer's mission. It is one of Ezera's most markedly autobiographical works, combining documentary evidence with fantasy, the lyrical with the dramatic, and the intimately personal with the socially relevant.

Ezera is also well known for indulging in a special kind of narrative genre known as her "dullie stāsti" (wacky stories), tales written with an expressly ironic or humorous purpose in mind. These stories present characters with good intentions but whose thinking is often flawed and whose behavior is highly idiosyncratic. In a more serious vein, Ezera has also written many critiques and review essays over the years—either for publication or for the internal uses of Liesma, who publishes her works. They appear in such anthologies as *Dzīvot uz savas zemes* (To Live in One's Own Land, 1984) and *Virtuve bez pavārgrāmatas* (A Kitchen Without A Cookbook, 1989). These essays reveal not only a remarkable aptitude for literary criticism but speak as well of Ezera's deeply felt convictions about life and literature.

Ezera's literary activities remained intensive in the 1990s, following Latvia's independence. As in her earlier writing, the focus in her later publications is on the contradictions of the human psyche and on the experience of its encounter with the world it discloses around itself. Also notable is the elaboration of an increasingly philosophical thought, as well as the polyphonic quality of writings that effectively combine dramatic, tragic, and comical narrative strands. In 1993 Ezera's work and accomplishments were recognized with the award of Latvia's highest distinction—the "Triju Zvaigžņu Ordenis" (The Order of the Three Stars). Her work has been translated in Russian, Lithuanian, Estonian, German, and other languages.

Interviews:

Vija Jugāne, "Ieklausies sevī un apkārtnē!" *Padomju Jaunatne* (Riga), 4 February 1973, p. 5;

Aivars Kalve, "Rieciens klusumā," *Zvaigzne*, 5 (1973): 3;

Silvija Geikina, "Dzīvot tomēr ir skaisti. Regīna Ezera par sevi un pasauli," *Literatūra un Māksla* (Riga), 17 November 1973, p. 6;

Vija Jugāne, "Ko es atzīstu par labu esam," *Kritikas gadagrāmata*, 3 (1974): 134–154;

Ivars Alksnītis, "Mēs visi esam zem viena Piena Ceļa—kā Mūžības kripatiņas. Saruna ar rakstnieci," *Rīgas Balss*, 22 December 1995, p. 12;

Ina Eglīte, "Regīna Ezera," *Neatkarīgā* (Riga), 28 December 1996, p. 10;

Ieva Miķelsone, "Par viršanas procesiem politikas katlā, kultūru un laimi. Rakstnieces Regīnas Ezeras saruna ar Ministru prezidentu Andri Šķēli," *Neatkarīgā* (Riga), 21 June 1997, p. 3.

References:

Inta M. Ezergailis, "Women in Soviet Latvia: Regina Ezera," in her *Nostalgia and Beyond: Eleven Latvian Women Writers* (Lanham, Md.: University Press of America, 1998), pp. 183–204;

Maija Mezerina, "Some Aspects of Feminism in the Novella 'Satanic Story' by Regina Ezera," in *Feminism and Latvian Literature,* edited by Ausma Cimdiņa (Riga: Latvian Women's Studies and Information Center, 1998), pp. 121–129;

Mārtiņš Poišs, "Noklusētā drāma. Ieskats Regīnas Ezeras daiļradē," *Karogs*, 11 (1973): 137–149; *Karogs*, 12 (1974): 108–122;

Broņislavs Tabūns, *Regīna Ezera. Dzīves un jaunrades apskats: mozaīka* (Riga: Liesma, 1980);

Pēteris Zeile, "Regīnas Ezeras prozas pasaulē," parts 1 and 2, *Karogs*, 2 (1979): 133–139; 3 (1979): 145–149.

Sigitas Geda

(4 February 1943 –   )

Indrė Žekevičiūtė-Žakevičienė
Kaunas Vytautas Magnus University

BOOKS: *Pėdos: Eilėraščiai* (Vilnius: Vaga, 1966);
Strazdas: Poema (Vilnius: Vaga, 1967);
Užmigę žirgeliai (Vilnius: Vaga, 1970);
26 rudens ir vasaros giesmės (Vilnius: Vaga, 1972);
Mėnulio žiedai (Vilnius: Vaga, 1977);
Baltojo Nieko dainelės (Vilnius: Vaga, 1977);
Mėlynas autobusiukas (Vilnius: Vaga, 1980);
Žydinti slyva Snaigyno ežere: Eilėraščiai (Vilnius: Vaga, 1981);
Dainuojantis ir šokantis mergaitės vieversėlis (Vilnius: Vaga, 1981);
Varnėnas po mėnuliu: Eilėraščiai ir poemos (Vilnius: Vaga, 1984);
Vasara su peliuku Miku: Eilėraščiai (Vilnius: Vaga, 1984);
Mamutų tėvynė: Eilėraščiai ir poemos (Vilnius: Vaga, 1985);
Praniukas Pramaniūgas: Trumpi ir ilgi eilėraščiai (Vilnius: Vyturys, 1986);
Žalio gintaro vėriniai: Eilių romanas (Vilnius: Vaga, 1988);
Ežys ir Grigo ratai: Žodžiai apie kitus (Vilnius: Vaga, 1989);
Karalaitė ant svarstyklių: Poemos ir eilėraščiai (Vilnius: Vaga, 1989);
Močiutės dainos: Eilėraščiai (Vilnius: Vyturys, 1991);
Septynių vasarų giesmės: Eilėraščiai (Vilnius: Vaga, 1991);
Babilono atstatymas: Eilėraščiai (Vilnius: Vaga, 1994);
Skrynelė dvasioms pagauti (Vilnius: Vaga, 1996);
Gedimino valstybės fragmentas (Vilnius: Vyturys, 1997);
Jotvingių mišios: Eilėraščiai (Vilnius: Vaga, 1997);
Mangrėžiausias klebonas–Varnėnas Pokalbiai ape poeziją ir apie gyvenimą (Vilnius: Vaga, 1998);
Lubinų žydejimas piliakalnių fone (Vilnius: Seimo leidykla "Valstybės žinios," 1999).

Editions in English: "I Walked Out into Lithuania," "Take Me to Zarasai," "Weaved—Fate, the Skull and the Rose," "Longing for the Lord's Roses," "Repentance: The Devil's Blossom," "God's Family," "The Feast of the Minotaurs," "Sebastian's Lament," "Sweet-flag Blossom," and "Steep Eyes of Wooden Gods," in *Selected Post-War Lithua-*

Sigitas Geda

nian Poetry, edited and translated by Jonas Zdanys (New York: Manyland Books, 1978), pp. 292–315;
Songs of Autumn, translated by Zdanys (Pittsburgh: Slow Loris, 1979);
"I Walked Out into Lithuania," "Repentance: The Devil's Blossom," "God's Family," "Sebastian's Lament, 1943," and "Steep Eyes of Wooden Gods," translated by Zdanys, in *Contemporary East European Poetry: An Anthology,* edited by Emery George (Ann Arbor, Mich.: Ardis, 1983), pp. 93–97;

Four Poets of Lithuania: Vytautas P. Bložė, Sigitas Geda, Nijolė Miliauskaitė, Kornelijus Platelis, selected and translated by Zdanys (Vilnius: Vaga, 1995).

PLAY PRODUCTIONS: *Pasaka apie stebuklingą berniuką*, Vilnius, Lėlė Theater, 1974;
Ak, vija pinavija, Vilnius, Lėlė Theater, 1979.

PRODUCED SCRIPTS: *Velnio nuotaka*, Lithuanian TV, Vilnius, 1974;
Kaip kiškis vilko namus sergėjo, Lithuanian TV, Vilnius, 1979;
Ką senelis padarys, viskas bus gerai, Lithuanian TV, Vilnius, 1980.

OTHER: Jurgis Juozapaitis, *Marių paukštė*, libretto by Geda, Lithuanian Academic Theater of Opera and Ballet, 1979;
Bronius Kutavičius, *Kaulo senis ant geležinio kalno*, libretto by Geda;
Tarybinių lietuvių rašytojų autobiografijos, volume 1, edited by Alfonsas Maldonis and others (Vilnius: Vaga, 1989), pp. 353–360;
Poezijos pavasaris, 1990, edited by Geda and others (Vilnius: Vaga, 1990).

TRANSLATIONS: Kornejus Čiukovskis, *Painiava* (Vilnius: Vaga, 1972);
L. Nadis, *Poezija* (Vilnius: Vaga, 1972);
Johannes Bobrovskis, *Sarmatijos metas*, translated by Geda and Bronys Savukynas (Vilnius: Vaga, 1974);
Dėdės Gorgudo sakmės, translated by Geda and Vagif Minad Arzumanov (Vilnius: Vaga, 1978);
Paulis Celanas, *Aguona ir atmintis*, translated by Geda and Vytautas Karalius (Vilnius: Vaga, 1979);
Giesmių giesmė (Vilnius: Vaga, 1983);
Sergejus Jeseninas, *Ieva: Eilėraščiai* (Vilnius: Vaga, 1983);
Vytautas Liūdėnas, *Šaunūs vyrai tie meldukai: Eilėraščiai* (Vilnius: Vyturys, 1987);
Lekia mano žirgelis: latvių dainos: viduriniam ir vyresniam mokykliniam amžiui (Vilnius: Vyturys, 1989);
Gėlė ir poezija: Jap, hokus (haikus), tankos, ikebanos, translated by Geda and Romualdas Neimantas (Kaunas: Orientas, 1992);
Rainer Maria Rilke, *Poezija: Die Gedichte*, translated by Geda (Vilnius: Lietuvos rašytojų sąjungos kidykla, 1996);
Psalmių knygos, translated by Geda (Vilnius: Vaga, 1997);
Uldis Bērzinš, *Vabzdžių žingsniai: Poezija*, translated by Geda and others (Vilnius: Baltos lankos, 1997);
Dante Alighieri, *Naujas gyvenimas*, translated by Geda and Inga Tuliševskaitė (Vilnius: Vyturys/Vilspa, 1998);
Panditas Bilhanas, *Penkiasdešimt posmų apie slaptąjį meilės džiaugsmą* (Vilnius: Žuvėdra / Kaunas: Aušra, 1998).

Emerging in the early 1960s as a poet of extraordinary breadth and complexity, Sigitas Geda has since established a reputation as one of the leading figures in contemporary Lithuanian literature and as a writer of international importance. Resistant to the dominant literary trends imposed by the postwar cultural establishment, Geda sought to redefine the creative experience by portraying the metamorphosis evolving within the human consciousness as a process of rebirth and discovery. As a poet, translator, essayist, and author of literature for children, Geda has amassed a significant body of work in which he attempts to explore the collective consciousness of the human experience, incorporating mythological and symbolic imagery as a means to juxtapose primordial life with modern existence. As critic and translator Jonas Zdanys notes in a 1998 article in *World Literature Today*, Geda's work reveals "a poetic sensitivity of great emotional intensity that seeks to unite the individual and nature into a single inseparable unit, often within landscapes tending toward the visionary and the fantastic."

As a translator, Geda ranges widely from authors in the Far East to those of Western Europe. The motivation for translating Far Eastern writers came mostly from his interest in Buddhism and in Indian thought in general. Western authors, including Paul Celan and Johannes Bobrowski, attracted him because of their interest in marginal areas of human experience—between sanity and madness, Germanic and Baltic, or, in general, between Eastern and Western cultures. François Villon was to some extent a spiritual model for him—a desperate, highly poetic wanderer between the depths of despair and crime, and the supreme realm of poetry. Geda was fascinated by the inherently deep poetry of biblical texts, particularly the Book of Psalms, which he translated in 1977. Another major poet, Rainer Maria Rilke, also fascinated Geda, and he translated some of Rilke's poems from "Das Stundenbuch." Geda not only engaged in translating his favorite authors, but also responded to them in his own poetry, producing a fine cycle of poems dedicated to Villon in 1997; and another cycle to the Indian epic "Bilhana."

Frontispiece and title page for one of Geda's collections of verse

Geda's verses for children are grounded in the Lithuanian (or general) mythological consciousness so that the simplest verses appeal to a child's curiosity about the world, nature, and some secret bonds between the presence of a pantheistic god in the clouds, trees, rivers, and the young human heart. In essence, he addresses not particularly the children, but the wonder-struck child in all people at the sight of a living universe.

The son of Zigmas Geda and Aleksandra Gavu-tytė-Gedienė, Sigitas Geda was born on 4 February 1943, the fourth of seven children in a farming family in Paterai, an area of Lazdijai in southwestern Lithuania. In an autobiographical sketch published in *Tary-binių lietuvių rašytojų autobiografijos* (Autobiographical Sketches of Soviet Lithuanian Writers, 1989), the poet remembers the intense rural beauty of his childhood: "I observed the hills, forests, and streams of my native

land with my childish eyes wide open; and now I am sure, that everything begins in this observation of one's childhood, in listening and in recollection . . . the sight and sound of bones, earth, meat, horn, stone, hair, clay, eyes, and heart; of spirit, books, ideas, and blood; of sword and iron; of melodies of malice, love, poverty, and pity; of suffering, hope, and patience." For Geda, the recollections of childhood—as well as his inherent belief in the quality and essence of beauty—played an important role in both his development as an individual and in the vision and images of his creative work.

In 1959 Geda began publishing his poetry in a variety of literary periodicals and magazines. Before that, however, his poems circulated in manuscript form, passed from hand to hand, arousing a great deal of interest and discussion because of their originality and inventiveness. In 1966 he left his native village to begin his studies at the University of Vilnius, where he studied Lithuanian philology and literature. During this time, he also became interested in Latvian folklore and in Russian literature, notably the works of such authors as Aleksandr Pushkin, Mikhail Lermontov, A. V. Koltsov, Nikolai Gogol, Velimir Khlebnikov, and Boris Pasternak. In 1966 he began working as an editor at the newspaper *Kalba Vilnius* (Vilnius on Air). Shortly before the publication of his first collection of poetry, Geda was the subject of an article titled "Susipažinkime: Sigito Gedos lyrika" (Make Your Acquaintance: The Lyrics of Sigitas Geda) that appeared in the Communist youth organization newspaper, *Komjaunimo tiesa* (The Truth of Komsomol), earning him widespread literary notoriety. Written by the prominent Lithuanian literary critic Ricardas Pakalniškis, the article acknowledged Geda as a significant writer of major stature and generated debate within the literary community as well as vehement criticism from, among others, Vytautas Petkevičius, secretary of the Lithuanian Writers' Union, who challenged Pakalniškis's appraisal of Geda's talent as premature and unfounded.

In Geda's first two collections of poetry, *Pėdos* (Footprints, 1966) and *Strazdas* (Thrush, 1967), his lyrical verses portray the joys and pleasures of earthly existence while simultaneously reaching infinitely to the heavens and conjoining the material and spiritual planes of existence in spontaneous, quixotic, and imagistic leaps of time and imagination. For Geda, all life forms have concrete attributes but have no concrete environment or history; rather, they evoke sensations of an endless cycle of life and death in its fundamental, unifying essence. The liberated souls of formless creatures are marked by the "white light of the heart," where instead of completion there is movement, progression, and change.

Innovative as well as provocative, the book-length poem *Strazdas* forms around the Catholic priest and poet Antanas Strazdas (1763–1833), who broke his vow of celibacy and had a wife and children. Persecuted by the religious and secular authorities, Strazdas is transformed by Geda into a mythological creature—half man, half bird, in a play on *Thrush*, the literal translation of Strazdas's name—possessed of a spiritual essence unified by the vast contradictions of his personality that represents the synthesis of the disparate characteristics of existence. Thus, Geda creates a metaphor that allows the reader to identify hidden connections between various aspects of the world. Geda's poetry embraces the physical, sensual, even erotic human experiences that reflect pure and unqualified love. In effect, both Geda and Stazdas emerge as poet-priests of organic, natural impulses, not of asceticism. Thus, everything that is condemned by religion

and art now appears to be full of emotional and metaphysical importance. The juxtaposition of heavenly love with earthly love, and the juxtaposition of the stench of alcohol and perspiration with linguistic and mythological elements expresses the depth of Lithuanian consciousness.

Leaving his position at the newspaper in 1967, Geda began working for the magazine *Mūsų gamta* (Our Nature), where he remained until 1976. In 1972 he published his third collection of poems, titled *26 rudens ir vasaros giesmės* (26 Songs of Autumn and Summer), followed in 1977 by *Mėnulio žiedai* (Blossoms of the Moon), both of which demonstrated the influence of ancient Eastern poetry, evident through a set of poems devoted to the Indian poet Bihan, on Geda's worldview. Many of the poems resemble hymns and are somewhat elegiac, full of spiritual purity and unusual inner musicality. In these volumes, Geda's tone becomes calmer, purer, more tender and melodious. There is no element of anger, suffering, or despair; rather, the intonations of the poems suggest tremendous excitement and astonishment with the world. Once again, Geda attempts to portray an eternal metamorphosis, based on mythological images, in which all phenomena constantly turn into something else. The poet achieves this feat through processions of abstract and unbelievable metaphors—"snowy penguins / hold on their beaks the falling sea." Rejecting logic and structure in the presentation of plot and theme, Geda creates a dynamic flow of synergy through a synthesis of images that run as a continuous thread throughout the poems.

In his poetry, Geda places a special importance on love. Geda's childlike imagination breaks through the limitations of language and transcends the logical linguistic rules that adults usually follow. In effect, this childlike imagination is capable of transforming mundane images into metaphysical reflections and small forms into enormous descriptive pictures, giving the reader a sense of the all-encompassing love between a child and his mother.

Geda's childlike outlook allows him to create new myths, in which the whole of humankind exists in simplistic and euphoric harmony. Thus, the mythological figures within his poetry resemble those of childhood fairy tales, insofar as their forms, their mutual relationships, and their correspondence with nature are ruled by a different kind of logic—a logic suggestive of the inner structure of a child's feelings and emotional experiences. For example, in one poem a giant lark, in a deep expression of love, turns into the wind, and a woman becomes one with both a butterfly and the earth. The subject of the poem is capable of comprehending this kind of love quite nat-

Cover for Geda's 1997 volume of poetry

tis to Geda's contemporary Jonas Mekas, in which common, everyday speech is elevated through poetic connections and relationships.

In later collections, such as *Žydinti slyva Snaigyno ežere* (A Blossoming Plum Tree in Snaigynas Lake) and *Mamutų tėvynė* (The Mammoth's Homeland), published in 1981 and 1985 respectively, Geda creates an elaborate network of thematic motifs, wherein each image is surrounded by a system of metaphors that finally converge in the central idea of the poem. Other sentences complete ideas before they end; thus, what would have been the last word if the sentence followed traditional grammatical rules becomes the beginning of a new sentence, which cannot even be separated by a comma. For example, in "Delčia rudenė deivė" (The Wane–Goddess of Autumn) in *26 rudens ir vasaros giesmės*, he writes:

> Ten spindi mano tėvo balana:
> gražiai jis sėdi kiaukuto
> balne . . . Žydryne amžinujų
> marių . . . Užtvindo plotą
> vakaro vanduo . . . Sesuo,
> tave aš lekiančią regiu
> tenai, kur dausos žalios, be krantų,
> kur pilkas skliautas
> staigiai atsidaro . . .
>
> My father's splinter's shining there:
> he looks so beautiful in his shell's saddle
> over there . . . The azure of eternal
> sea . . . And evening waters flood
> the space . . . My sister,
> I can see you running,
> where the skies are green and have no end,
> where greyish dome of heaven
> suddenly flings open . . .

urally turns to such an expression of love himself, merging with everything such that, at the moment of observing the lark's transformation, his "eyes get overgrown with grass." Thus, Geda appears to be creating a mythology of his own as observation and creation become the same action. While doing so, Geda maintains a casual, simple tone that appears to belong more to colloquial language than to either poetry or mythology; however, the tonal and rhythmic flexibility of this language contains deeper echoes of ancient Lithuanian incantations or ritual songs through its trajectory toward the sacred. Thus, Geda's poetry consecrates existence itself, connecting Geda to a lyrical tradition in Lithuanian literature, one that extends from the eighteenth-century poet Kristijonas Donelai-

However, despite differences in his construction of sentences and images, Geda's later work is dominated by the same motifs as in his earlier poetry: the transformative power of nature upon human beings, with a tendency toward mythological and metaphysical reflections. Indeed, his later poetry is characterized by literary critic Rimvydas Šilbajoris in his *Netekties ženklai: Lietuvių literatūra namuose ir svetur* (Signs of Loss: Lithuanian Literature at Home and Abroad, 1992) as an elaboration upon earlier works: "Instead of a simple reed-pipe being played by a herdsboy, we hear the fantastic organ of Geda playing." In Geda's later work, the distant journey to the depth of the human spirit takes on many forms, where sights and symbols of mythological consciousness appear to be manifestations of one great universal love.

Geda's poetry reflects a vision of the connection of humans and nature as an everlasting process that leads to a specific spiritual state. Geda presumes that a certain kind of knowledge exists within nature, and this knowledge continuously enters the human consciousness to be expressed through poetry. This presumption is exemplified in his poem "Mamutų tėvynė."

In his more recent collections of poetry—*Žalio gintaro vėriniai: Eilių romanas* (String of Green Ambers: A Novel in Verse, 1988), *Septynių vasarų giesmės* (The Songs of Seven Summers, 1991), *Babilono atstatymas* (The Rebuilding of Babylon, 1994), and *Jotvingių mišios* (The Jotvingian Mass, 1997)—Geda is less dependent on mythological and symbolic configurations of poetic complexity and turns more to the realities of everyday life in the repressive socialist society of Soviet Lithuania. Geda exchanges his lyrical style for one that often employs confrontation and anger, depoeticizing his verses. The poet attempts to observe the world through a different perspective, as he constantly expands his vocabulary, searching for new forms and stylistic devices with which to express his sentiments.

During the last decade of the twentieth century, Geda further enhanced his literary reputation with the publication in the Lithuanian weekly *Šiaurės Atėnai* (Northern Athens) of a series of expressive, autobiographic, and analytic essays that proved extremely popular with the general reading public. They were collected as *Lubinų žydėjimas piliakalnių fone* (The Flowering of Lupines on the Background of Mounds, 1999). Rich in poetic sensitivity and introspection, the essays enabled Geda to expound on a wide range of subjects from the importance of truth to the inherent quality of the poetic experience. Reflecting on his own life, Geda emphasizes the need to act, to create, and to learn from others while reminiscing of his wanderings, both physical and spiritual, through the huge territory between the Baltic Sea and Gurzuf—the Caucasus, the Urla, Ryga, Karaliaučius, Cracow, Gdansk, Lvov, Odessa, Alupka—in search of inspiration and direction. Geda also uses the format to discuss the influence on his career of both Mykalojus Konstantinas Čiurlionis, the Lithuanian painter and composer of the late nineteenth and early twentieth centuries, and Vincas Krėvė-Mickevičius, the well-known Lithuanian writer who was forced to flee the country at the close of World War II and who died in exile in the United States in 1954.

Taking up residence in the resort town of Druskininkai in southwestern Lithuania near the Byelorus-sian border, Geda lives removed from the literary and intellectual circles of Lithuanian cultural life but maintains an artistic bond with other writers in and around Druskininkai who have made the region a significant part of their creative lives, most notably the poets Vytautas P. Bložė; Bložė's wife, Nijolė Miliauskaitė; and Kornelijus Platelis. Geda's poetry is rooted in a love for his native land and in a love of life that grows and extends outward to embrace the whole of existence. Each of his books reflects this all-pervasive love, with its organic and magical essence. The voice of Geda's lyrics is modern, but at the same time, it delves into the poetic sentiments of ancient mythological symbols; thus, while his poetry displays an experimental outlook, Geda remains a true bard of nature. He appears to feel no need to assimilate modern, mechanical images of urban realities; rather, the teleological trajectory of his poetry leads toward a merging with nature, a turn to the promise of resurrection and the eternal continuation of life.

Bibliographies:

Jonas Lankutis, ed., *Lietuvių literatūros istorija*, volume 2 (Vilnius: Vaga, 1982), pp. 428–430;

Tarybų Lietuvos rašytojai (Vilnius: Vaga, 1984), pp. 85–86;

Vytautas Kubilius, *XX amžiaus literatūra* (Vilnius: Alma Litera, 1996), pp. 550–553.

References:

Živilė Bilaišyte, "Sigitas Geda—gyvybės ir mirties poetas," *Akiračiai*, 2 (1984): 6–8;

Ričardas Pakalniškis, "Poetai veikiasavo buvimu," in his *Poezijos kryžkelės* (Vilnius: Lietuvos rašytojų sąjungos leidykla, 1994), pp. 194–205;

Rimvydas Šilbajoris, "Existential Root Concepts of Lithuania in the Poetry of Sigitas Geda," *Lituanus*, 39 (Winter 1993): 5–12;

Šilbajoris, "The François Villon Cycle of Sigitas Geda," *Journal of Baltic Studies*, 15 (Spring 1984): 3–9;

Šilbajoris, "Sigitas Geda: Iš toliau ir iš arčiau," in his *Netekties ženklai: lietuvių literatūra namuose ir svetur* (Vilnius: Vaga, 1992), pp. 403–424;

Gražina Skabeikytė, "Poezija vaikams ir tautosaka," *Pergalė*, 6 (1984): 147–150;

Bronius Vaškelis, "Pokalbis su Sigitu Geda apie Lietuvos ir išeivijos poeziją," *Metmenys*, 55 (1988): 88–110;

Jonas Zdanys, "The Poets of Druskininkai," *World Literature Today*, 72 (Spring 1998): 241–252.

Václav Havel
(5 October 1936 –   )

Jan Čulík
University of Glasgow

This entry originally appeared in Concise Dictionary of World Literary Biography:
South Slavic and Eastern European Writers.

BOOKS: *Autostop,* by Ivan Vyskočil with contributions by Havel (Prague: Dilia, 1963);
Josef Čapek: Dramatik a jevištní výtvarník, by Havel and Věra Ptáčková (Prague: Divadelní ústav, 1963);
Zahradní slavnost: Hra o 4 dějstvích, afterword by Jan Grossman (Prague: Orbis, 1964); translated and adapted by Vera Blackwell as *The Garden Party* (London: Cape, 1969);
Vyrozumění: Hra o dvanácti obrazech (Prague: Dilia, 1965); translated by Blackwell as *The Memorandum* (London: Cape, 1967; New York: Grove, 1967);
Protokoly: Sborník textů, foreword by Grossman (Prague: Mladá fronta, 1966);
Ztížená možnost soustředění: Hra o 2 dějstvích, afterword by J. Šafařík (Prague: Orbis, 1969); translated by Blackwell as *The Increased Difficulty of Concentration* (London: Cape, 1972; New York: S. French, 1976); Czech version republished (Purley, U.K.: Rozmluvy, 1986);
Spiklenci: hra (Prague [samizdat], 1971); republished as *Spiklenci (1971)* (Prague: Edice Expedice, 1979); translated into German by Franz Peter Künzel as *Die Retter* (Rheinbek bei Hamburg: Rowohlt Theater Verlag, 1972); early Czech version published as *Spiklenci,* in Havel's *Hry 1970–1976: Z doby zakázanosti* (Toronto: Sixty-Eight Publishers, 1977); definitive Czech version published as *Spiklenci,* in *Svět a divadlo,* 3, no. 9–10 (1992): 121–161;
Žebrácká opera: na téma Johna Gaye (1972) (Prague: Edice Petlice [samizdat], 1973); republished as *Žebrácká opera,* "first edition" (Prague: Edice Expedice [samizdat], 1976); translated into German by Künzel as *Die Gauneroper: Nach John Gay* (Rheinbek bei Hamburg: Rowohlt Theater Verlag, 1974); original Czech version pub-

Václav Havel (photograph by The Guardian*)*

lished as *Žebrácká opera,* in *Hry 1970–1976: Z doby zakázanosti,* pp. 105–184;
Audience: jednoaktová hra, published together with *Vernisáž: jednoaktová hra* (Prague: Edice Petlice [samizdat], 1975); translated into German by Gabriel Laub as *Audienz: Einakter* (Rheinbek bei Hamburg: Rowohlt Theater Verlag, 1975); translated by George Theiner as *Conversation: A One Act Play,* in *Index on Censorship,* 5, no. 3 (1976): 41–50; original Czech version pub-

lished as *Audience*, in *Hry 1970–1976: Z doby zakázanosti*, pp. 241–267;

Vernisáž: jednoaktová hra, published together with *Audience: jednoaktová hra* (Prague: Edice Petlice [samizdat], 1975); translated into German by Laub as *Vernissage: Einakter* (Rheinbek bei Hamburg: Rowohlt Theater Verlag, 1976); original Czech version published as *Vernisáž*, in *Hry 1970–1976: Z doby zakázanosti*, pp. 273–296;

Horský hotel: hra o pěti dějstvích (Prague: Edice Petlice [samizdat], 1976); translated into German by Laub as *Das Berghotel: Ein Schauspiel in fünf Akten* (Rheinbek bei Hamburg: Rowohlt Theater Verlag, 1976); original Czech version published as *Horský hotel*, in *Hry 1970–1976: Z doby zakázanosti*, pp. 189–239;

Protest: jednoaktová hra (1978) (Prague: Edice Expedice [samizdat], 1979); translated into German by Laub as *Protest: Einakter* (Rheinbek bei Hamburg: Rowohlt Theater Verlag, 1978); original Czech version published as *Protest*, in Havel's *Soubor her z let 1963–1988* (Prague: Lidové noviny, 1991); translated and adapted by Blackwell as *Protest*, in *Drama Contemporary: Czechoslovakia*, edited by Marketa Goetz-Stankiewicz (New York: Performing Arts Journal Publications, 1985), pp. 69–90;

Moc bezmocných (London: Londýnské ústředí Naardenského hnutí, 1979); translated by Paul Wilson as "The Power of the Powerless," in *The Power of the Powerless: Citizens against the State in Central-Eastern Europe*, edited by John Keane (London: Hutchinson, 1985; Armonk, N.Y.: M. E. Sharpe, 1985), pp. 23–97;

Dopisy Olze: Červen 1979–září 1982 (Prague [samizdat edition], 1983; Toronto: Sixty-Eight Publishers, 1985; Brno: Atlantis, 1990); translated by Wilson as *Letters to Olga: June 1979–September 1982* (New York: Knopf, 1988; London: Faber & Faber, 1988);

Chyba, in *Obsah* (May 1983); translated into German by Joachim Bruss as *Der Fehler* (Rheinbek bei Hamburg: Rowohlt Theater Verlag, 1983); original Czech version published as *Chyba*, in *Svědectví*, 18, no. 69 (1983): 149–153; translated by Theiner as *Mistake*, in *Index on Censorship*, 13 (February 1984): 13–14;

O lidskou identitu: Úvahy, fejetony, protesty, polemiky, prohlášení a rozhovory z let 1969–1979 (London: Rozmluvy, 1984; Prague: Rozmluvy, 1990);

Largo desolato: hra o sedmi obrazech (Prague: Edice Petlice [samizdat], 1984); translated into German by Bruss as *Largo desolato: Schauspiel in sieben Bildern* (Rheinbek bei Hamburg: Rowohlt Theater Verlag, 1984); original Czech version published as *Largo desolato: Hra o 7 obrazech* (Munich: Obrys/Kontur-PmD, 1985); translated by Tom Stoppard as *Largo desolato* (New York: Grove, 1987);

Pokoušení: hra o deseti obrazech (Prague: Edice Petlice [samizdat], 1985; Munich: Obrys/Kontur-PmD, 1986); translated by Theiner as *Temptation* (London & Boston: Faber & Faber, 1988);

Dálkový výslech: rozhovor s Karlem Hvížďalou: Bonn-Praha 1985–1986, by Havel and Karel Hvížďala (Prague: Edice Expedice [samizdat], 1986); republished as *Dálkový výslech: Rozhovor s Karlem Hvížďalou* (Purley, U.K.: Rozmluvy, 1986; Prague: Melantrich, 1989); translated by Wilson as *Disturbing the Peace: A Conversation with Karel Hvížďala* (New York: Knopf, 1990; London: Faber & Faber, 1990);

Politics and Conscience (Stockholm: Charta 77 Foundation, 1986);

Asanace: Hra o pěti jednáních (Prague: Edice Petlice [samizdat], 1987; Munich: Obrys/Kontur-PmD, 1988); translated by James Saunders and Marie Winn as *Redevelopment* or *Slum Clearance* (London: Faber & Faber, 1990);

Do různých stran: Eseje a články z let 1983–1989 (Scheinfeld-Schwarzenberg, Germany: Československé středisko nezávislé literatury, 1989; Prague: Lidové noviny, 1990);

Projevy: Leden-červen 1990 (Prague: Vyšehrad, 1990);

Letní přemítání (Prague: Odeon, 1991); translated by Wilson as *Summer Meditations* (New York: Knopf, 1992);

Hry: Soubor her z let 1963–1988 (Prague: Lidové noviny, 1991);

Vážení občané: Projevy červenec 1990–červenec 1992 (Prague: Lidové noviny, 1992);

Slovo o slovu/A Word about Words (New York: Cooper Union, 1992);

Antikódy: Sbírka typogramů (Prague: Odeon, 1993);

Václav Havel 1992–1993: Projevy (Prague-Litomyšl: Paseka, 1994);

Václav Havel '94: Projevy 1994 (Prague-Litomyšl: Paseka, 1995);

Václav Havel '95: Projevy 1995 (Prague-Litomyšl: Paseka, 1996);

Eduard (Prague: Akademie múzických umění, 1996);

Václav Havel '96: Projevy 1996 (Prague-Litomyšl: Paseka, 1997);

Václav Havel '97: Projevy 1997 (Prague-Litomyšl: Paseka, 1998).

Collection: *Spisy,* 7 volumes (Prague: Torst, 1999)—comprises volume 1, *Básně. Antikódy;* volume 2, *Hry;* volume 3, *Eseje a jiné texty z let 1953–1969;* volume 4, *Eseje a jiné texty z let 1970–1989. Dálkový výslech;* volume 5, *Dopisy Olze;* volume 6, *Projevy z let 1990–1992. Letní přemítání;* volume 7, *Projevy a jiné texty z let 1992–1998.*

Editions in English: *Sorry . . . : Two Plays,* translated and adapted by Vera Blackwell (London: Eyre Methuen/British Broadcasting Corporation, 1978)—comprises *Audience* and *Private View;*

The Anatomy of a Reticence, translated by Erazim Kohák (Stockholm: Charta 77 Foundation, 1985);

The Vaněk Plays: Four Authors, One Character, edited by Marketa Goetz-Stankiewicz (Vancouver: University of Columbia Press, 1987);

Acceptance Speech Written on the Occasion of the Award of the Erasmus Prize 1986 (Amsterdam: Foundation Praemium Erasmianum, 1986);

Cards on the Table (Scheinfeld, Germany: Documentation Center for the Promotion of Independent Czechoslovak Literature, 1988);

Open Letters: Selected Prose 1965–1990, edited by Paul Wilson (London: Faber & Faber, 1991); republished as *Open Letters: Selected Writings 1965–1990* (New York: Knopf, 1991);

Selected Plays 1963–1983 (London: Faber & Faber, 1992); republished as *The Garden Party and Other Plays* (New York: Grove, 1993)—comprises *The Garden Party,* translated by Blackwell; *The Memorandum,* translated by Blackwell; *The Increased Difficulty of Concentration,* translated by Blackwell; *Audience (Conversation),* translated by George Theiner; *Unveiling (Private View),* translated by Jan Novák; *Protest,* translated by Blackwell; and *Mistake,* translated by Theiner;

Selected Plays 1984–1987 (London & Boston: Faber & Faber, 1994)—comprises *Largo desolato,* translated by Tom Stoppard; *Temptation,* translated by Theiner; *Redevelopment (Slum Clearance),* translated by James Saunders;

Tomorrow! translated by Barbara Day, in *Czech Plays,* edited by Day (London: Nick Hern Books, 1994), pp. 1–26;

The Art of the Impossible: Politics as a Morality in Practice. Speeches and Writings, 1990–1996, translated by Wilson and others (New York: Knopf, 1997);

Toward a Civil Society: Selected Speeches and Writings 1900–1994, translated by Wilson and others (Prague: Lidové noviny, n.d.).

PLAY PRODUCTIONS: *Autostop,* by Ivan Vyskočil with contributions by Havel, Prague, Divadlo Na zábradlí, 15 March 1961;

Zahradní slavnost, Prague, Divadlo Na zábradlí, 3 December 1963;

Vyrozumění, Prague, Divadlo Na zábradlí, 25 July 1965;

Ztížená možnost soustředění, Prague, Divadlo Na zábradlí, 11 April 1968;

Die Retter, translated into German by Franz Peter Künzel, Baden-Baden, Theater Baden-Baden, 8 February 1974; original Czech version, *Spiklenci,* Prague, Divadlo na tahu at the Divadlo Na zábradlí, 1 November 1992;

Žebrácká opera, Horní Počernice, U Čelikovských restaurant, 1 November 1975; professional premiere, Prague, Činoherní klub, 14 June 1990;

Audience, underground premiere in a barn at Hrádeček, summer 1976; official premiere, translated into German by Gabriel Laub as *Audienz,* Vienna, Akademietheater, 9 October 1976; professional premiere of Czech version, Prague, Divadlo S. K. Neumanna, 12 December 1989;

Vernissage, translated into German by Laub, Vienna, Akademietheater, 9 October 1976; Czech version, *Vernisáž,* staged informally in an apartment in Brno by the unofficial Brno theatre VáHa, 26 October 1989; official premiere, Brno, Kulturní dům, Kamenná kolonie, 29 December 1989;

Protest, translated into German by Laub, Vienna, Akademietheater, 17 November 1979; sections of the original Czech version were staged in Prague, Městská divadla pražská (Rokoko), 15 December 1989;

Das Berghotel, translated into German by Laub, Vienna, Akademietheater, 23 May 1981; original Czech version, *Horský hotel,* public rehearsal, Hrádeček, 10 August 1991; official premiere, Prague, Divadlo Na zábradlí, 18 October 1991;

Felet, translated into Swedish by Kent Andersson and Eva Lindekrantz, Stockholm, Stadsteater, 28 November 1983; original Czech version, *Chyba,* Prague, Divadlo Rokoko, 25 October 1992;

Largo desolato, translated into German by Joachim Bruss, Vienna, Akademietheatre, 13 April 1985; original Czech version, Divadlo Na zábradlí, 9 April 1990;

Die Versuchung, translated into German by Bruss, Vienna, Akademietheater, 23 May 1986; original Czech version, *Pokoušení,* unofficial premiere, Prague, Vyšehrad battlements, 14 April 1988, secretly disseminated on video-cassettes; professional premiere, Plzeň, Divadlo J. K. Tyla, 27 October 1990;

Sanierung, translated into German by Bruss, Zurich, Schauspielhaus Zurich, 24 September 1989; original Czech version, *Asanace,* Prague, Realistické divadlo Zdeňka Nejedlého, 30 March 1990;

Zítra to spustíme, Brno, joint production of Divadlo na provázku and HA-divadlo, 21 October 1988;

Mlýny, Kostelec, Divadlo Nad Orlicí, 9 March 1991; Prague, Na Dobešce, 14 March 1991;

Rodinný večer, Prague, Divadlo na Vinohradech, 3 February 2000.

PRODUCED SCRIPTS: *Anděl strážný,* radio, Second Program of Czechoslovak Radio, 18 June 1968;

Fledermaus auf der Antenne, radio, Germany, Norddeutscher Rundfunk, 25 February 1975;

Audience and *Private View,* radio, BBC Radio, 3 April 1977; television, BBC, 21 November 1978;

Vernisáž, television, Czech TV Prague, 8 April, 1990;

Žebrácká opera, motion picture, Barrandov, 1990;

Motýl na anténě, television, Second Program of Czechoslovak Television, 28 December 1991;

Zítra to spustíme, television, Czech TV Brno, 28 October 1992;

Horský hotel, television, Czech TV Prague, 27 November 1999.

RECORDING: *Audience,* with Havel as Ferdinand Vaněk, vinyl recording, Uppsala, Sweden, Šafrán, 1978; reissued, Prague, Bonton & Šafrán, 1990; reissued on compact disc, Prague, Bonton & Šafrán, 1998.

OTHER: *Hostina: filozofický sborník,* edited by Havel (Toronto: Sixty-Eight Publishers, 1989);

Karin Thomas, *Tradition und Avantgarde in Prag,* contribution by Havel, translated into German by Susanna Roth (Osnabrück: Galerie Pravis/Cologne: Dumont, 1991).

SELECTED PERIODICAL PUBLICATIONS—UNCOLLECTED: "Politics and the Theater," *Times Literary Supplement,* 28 September 1967, pp. 879–890;

Anděl strážný, in *Studie a úvahy,* 1, no. 3–4 (1968): 117–127;

"On Kafka," translated by Paul Wilson, *New York Review of Books,* 37 (27 September 1990): 19;

"A New European Order?" translated by Wilson, *New York Review of Books,* 42 (2 March 1995): 43–44.

Václav Havel has played a major role in the cultural and political life of Czechoslovakia—and, after the breakup of that country in 1993, of the Czech Republic—throughout the second half of the twentieth century. During the Stalinist oppression of the 1950s Havel and some like-minded colleagues made systematic contact with major figures in Czech literature and the arts who were ostracized by the communist regime. In the 1960s Havel was active in the movement of artists and writers whose efforts culminated in 1968 in the liberal revolution known as the Prague Spring. At that time Havel wrote significant plays in the genre of absurdist drama that shed light on the nature of the communist system. During the Soviet-led invasion of Czechoslovakia in August 1968 he spoke out against the aggression in radio broadcasts. As a result of the cultural and political clampdown after the invasion, Havel and several hundred other Czech writers were turned into nonpersons: their work was banned, they were forbidden to make public appearances, and they were harassed by the secret police. An alternative dissident culture emerged in the 1970s and 1980s, and Havel was one of its main representatives. He was a founder of *Charta* (Charter) 77, a human-rights movement; he was also active in the *Výbor na obranu nespravedlivě stíhaných* (Committee for the Defense of the Unjustly Prosecuted) and was imprisoned for several years by the communist authorities for his work on the committee. Toward the end of the 1980s Havel became a potent international symbol of the efforts of Czechoslovakians to overthrow the totalitarian communist system. During the collapse of the communist regime in November and December 1989 he helped to negotiate the transfer of power to the democratic government. In December 1989 he was elected president of the Czechoslovak Republic—a meteoric rise, indeed, for someone who earlier that year had been languishing in prison.

Havel's absurdist plays of the 1960s primarily analyze the role of language as an instrument of power, enslavement, and dehumanization. His protagonists have a choice: to behave naturally and use normal human speech and be destroyed, or to adopt bureaucratic jargon, adapt themselves to the dehumanized society, and make a successful career at the cost of losing their personal identity. Havel's

Havel with his first wife, Olga Šplíchalová, at the Divadlo Na zábradlí (photograph by ČTK)

plays show brilliantly how ideological language under communism penetrated all spheres of life; banished meaningful, authentic human discourse; and made society mute and incapable of discussing its problems.

The phrase *theater of the absurd* was coined by the critic Martin Esslin in 1961 to characterize plays written in the 1950s by such dramatists as Eugène Ionesco, Samuel Beckett, Arthur Adamov, Jean Genet, and Harold Pinter. The concept of the absurd was derived from the French philosopher Albert Camus's essay *Le Mythe de Sisyphe* (1942; translated as *The Myth of Sisyphus,* 1955), which characterized the human situation as ultimately meaningless. Western theater of the absurd highlights the fundamental bewilderment and confusion that stems from the fact that human beings have no answers to the basic existential questions: why they are alive, why they have to die, why injustice and suffering exist. In Eastern Europe, however, communism proclaimed that it had answers to these questions and that it was capable of eliminating suffering and setting all injustices right. The communist ideology dominated all spheres of life and thereby managed to spread an acute feeling of absurdity to everyone, bringing an experience to whole nations in the East that was a concern for only a small number of sensitive intellectuals in the West.

Although Eastern European absurdist theater was inspired by Western absurdist drama, it was far less abstract and esoteric than its Western European counterpart. While the Western European plays deal with the predicament of an individual or a small group of individuals in a situation stripped to bare and metaphysical essentials, the Eastern European plays generally show an individual trapped within the cogwheels of a social system. The social context of the Western European absurdist plays is usually subdued and theoretical: in the Eastern European plays it is concrete, menacing, and fairly realistic.

Like the Western absurdist plays, Havel's dramas are highly stylized. In the book-length interview *Dálkový výslech: Rozhovor s Karlem Hvížďalou* (1986; translated as *Disturbing the Peace: A Conversation with Karel Hvížďala,* 1990) Havel explained that before writing a play he always drew a diagram of its structure; his plays, consequently, often seem like geometrical constructions. By highly stylizing life under communism, they present it in terms of caricature.

Havel was born on 5 October 1936 into an affluent Prague family. His mother, Božena, née Vavrečková, was the daughter of Hugo Vavrečka, a co-editor of *Lidové noviny* (People's Newspaper), ambassador to Hungary and Austria during the Czechoslovak First Republic, and, in 1938, minister of propaganda. Havel's paternal grandfather, Vácslav Havel, had been an architect and entrepreneur who put up several important buildings in Prague around the turn of the twentieth century, including Lucerna (The Lantern), a large modern entertainment complex that was the first ferroconcrete building erected in the city. Havel's father, Václav M. Havel, also an architect-entrepreneur, built fashionable villas on the hill of Barrandov, overlooking the river Vltava to the west of the Prague city center. An uncle, Miloš Havel, ran the Barrandov Film Studios. Between the world wars the Havels conducted soirees that were attended by the major figures in Prague's intellectual and political circles. They were democrats and republicans and supported the policies of Czechoslovak Republic president Tomáš Garrigue Masaryk.

Havel regarded his privileged background as a disadvantage; it created barriers between him and other children that he found difficult to overcome. He began attending school in the village of Žďárec, near his parents' summer country estate in Moravia, where the family spent most of their time during and immediately after World War II. What may have been his only direct encounter with the war occurred, paradoxically, on 9 May 1945, a day after the war officially ended in Europe: Žďárec was bombed, and Havel saw Russian soldiers shooting at retreating German troops.

Havel was often taught at home by au pairs; the teaching was supervised by his energetic and intellectually demanding mother. Shortly before the communist takeover in February 1948 he was sent to a private boarding school, the King George School in Poděbrady. The aim of this demanding institution was to produce future leaders who would help to heal war-torn Europe. In the spring of 1950, however, Havel was branded a member of the bourgeoisie and expelled. He attended various state schools in Prague but was ostracized because of his class background. Refused admittance to secondary school, he briefly worked as an apprentice carpenter in 1951 before his parents helped him to find a job as an apprentice laboratory assistant at the Institute for Chemical Technology in Prague. He attended night classes and received his secondary school-leaving certificate in 1954. He tried to enroll at Charles University and other universities but was rejected. Finally, he began studying urban transport at the Economics Faculty of Prague's Technical University. He also received private tutoring from the Czech philosopher J. L. Fischer, who had a considerable influence on him.

In 1952, during the Stalinist show trials that led to the execution of several Communist Party leaders and the long imprisonment of tens of thousands of "class enemies," Havel, with the help of his mother, organized a group of his sixteen-year-old friends into a debating and literary circle called the "Thirty-Sixers" after the year of their birth. The circle discussed banned writers such as Franz Kafka, Hermann Hesse, and Anna Akhmatova and writers and artists connected with the culture of the prewar Czech Republic, including the poets Jaroslav Seifert, Vítězslav Nezval, and Vladimír Holan. They also published two samizdat literary magazines, *Stříbrný vítr: Básnická revue 36* (The Silver Wind: A Poetic Review 36) and *Rozhovory 36* (Discussions 36). Perhaps only the youth of the members of the circle prevented them from becoming victims of political persecution.

In November 1956 Havel gave a bold speech during a conference at the Czechoslovak Writers' Union's castle at Dobříš. The conference had been organized by the editors of a new journal for young writers, *Květen* (May), that concentrated on the "poetry of the everyday." Havel had been invited to the conference because he had sent a letter to the editors, taking them to task for ignoring the work of Skupina (Group) 42, whose poetry dealt with modern urban life and its problems. Although the Soviet army was crushing the anticommunist revolution in neighboring Hungary, this period was a time of great uncertainty for the Czechoslovak communist regime: the Soviet leader, Nikita Khrushchev, had recently condemned the late dictator Joseph Stalin's crimes in a secret speech to the Soviet Communist Party, and the poets Seifert and František Hrubín had given courageous anti-Stalinist speeches at the Second Congress of the Czechoslovak Writers' Union; thus, Havel felt that he could speak relatively freely. In his speech he made a plea for openness and pluralism and criticized the organizers of the conference and the editors of *Květen* for ignoring earlier noncommunist Czech writers such as Karel Čapek and the modernist poets Jiří Kolář, Josef Kainar, and Jiřina Hauková. Havel later remembered that in the informal discussions that continued well into the night the writers would "alternately heap ashes on their heads and accuse me of betraying socialism."

In 1957 Havel gave up his laboratory assistant's job and his studies at the Technical University and was drafted into the army for two years of national service. As a "class enemy" he was sent to a regiment of sappers in the Fifteenth Motorized Artillery Division in České Budějovice. Havel got his first practical theatrical experience in the army when he and a friend, Karel Brynda, staged Pavel Kohout's mildly reformist play *Zářijové noci* (September Nights, 1955). Havel played the role of an ambitious soldier too convincingly: the commanding officer thought that Havel was after his position, and Havel was demoted. Later Havel, with the assistance of Brynda, wrote his first play, *Život před sebou* (You Have Your Whole Life Ahead of You; adapted as *Mlýny* and performed in 1991); with tongue in cheek, they entered it in an army theater competition.

In *Život před sebou* a soldier, Pavel Maršík, falls asleep on guard duty. He is awakened by gunfire and sees a wounded civilian lying on the ground. It turns out that the shot was fired by mistake by an officer, Jan Kubeš. Kubeš agrees to cover up Maršík's falling asleep; in return, Maršík pretends that he did the shooting. He is rewarded for his lies by being promoted and, eventually, offered membership in the Communist Party. Maršík finally cannot go through with the duplicity, however. Even this early work of Havel's highlights the predicament of an individual facing an inhuman bureaucratic system. The play was highly successful at the lower levels of the army theater competition; but when there was a likelihood that it would win in the final round, the officers investigated the authors'

Havel (right) and his brother, Ivan, on furlough from the army in 1959

ence at Werich's ABC Theater persuaded him to choose the theater as his life's work.

While working at the theater Havel wrote a few theoretical articles for the periodical *Divadlo* (Theater) and was pleased when he received praise from Werich for one of them. He also wrote *Rodinný večer* (An Evening with the Family), a play in the spirit of Ionesco, and a first version of *Vyrozumění* (1965; translated as *The Memorandum*, 1967). *Rodinný večer* was not performed until 3 February 2000; but on the basis of the manuscript Havel was offered a job in the summer of 1960 at a fringe theater in Prague, Divadlo Na zábradlí (Theater on the Balustrade), which had been founded two years earlier by the director Helena Philipová. The atmosphere at Divadlo Na zábradlí was democratic and anti-ideological. The theater acquired a major political role soon after Havel's arrival, becoming one of the most daring centers of the arts and pushing for freedom in Czechoslovakia in the early 1960s.

The head of the drama section at Divadlo Na zábradlí was the playwright, actor, and director Ivan Vyskočil, who was influenced by the casual, semi-improvised comic theater of Voskovec and Werich; he liked to engage the audience by highlighting urgent problems in what he called "text appeals," a phrase jokingly formed as a parallel to *sex appeal*—readings of short texts, satirical comments, and improvised dialogues interspersed with music. From Vyskočil, Havel learned that plays should be like open-ended dialogues.

In 1961 Havel became repertory adviser at Divadlo Na zábradlí, and in 1963 he was made an assistant director. That year the director Jan Grossman succeeded Vyskočil as head of the drama section and turned Divadlo Na zábradlí into a major center for absurdist drama, staging plays by Ionesco, Samuel Beckett, Alfred Jarry, and Havel.

From 1962 to 1966, while working at Divadlo Na zábradlí, Havel was also an extramural student of dramaturgy in the Theater Faculty of the Academy of Performing Arts. On 9 July 1964 he married Olga Šplíchalová, whom he had met in 1953; she came from the Prague working-class district of Žižkov and was an independent-minded and uncompromising anticommunist. They had no children. Havel completed his studies at the Academy of Performing Arts with a commentary on his play *Eduard*. This play became the basis of *Ztížená možnost soustředění* (performed, 1968; published, 1969; translated as *The Increased Difficulty of Concentration*, 1972). (In 1996, on the occasion of awarding the degree of doctor honoris causa to Havel, the Academy of Performing Arts published the fac-

backgrounds, discovered that they were "class enemies," concluded (rightly, says Havel) that the play was mocking the idea of the competition, and condemned the play as an "anti-army" work. Nevertheless, Havel and his friends had enjoyed a week's leave at the army theater festival in the West Bohemian spa Mariánské Lázně.

Toward the end of his army service Havel applied to study motion pictures at the Academy of Performing Arts but was rejected. Through family connections he was offered a job as a stagehand at the ABC Theater in Prague. He worked there in 1959–1960, the final season during which the theater was managed by Jan Werich, the "comedian-philosopher" who, with his partner, Jiří Voskovec, had created the avant-garde comedy theater Osvobozené divadlo (The Liberated Theater) in the interwar period. Under Werich's influence Havel realized that a theater can become a center of national culture, "a seismograph of the times, an area of freedom, an instrument of human liberation." In *Dálkový výslech* Havel says that his experi-

simile of the original version of *Eduard* in book form.) All of Havel's well-known plays from the 1960s were performed at Divadlo Na zábradlí.

With the production at Divadlo Na zábradlí in December 1963 of *Zahradní slavnost* (published, 1964; translated as *The Garden Party*, 1969) Havel became a leading representative of the East European theater of the absurd. The protagonist of *Zahradní slavnost*, Hugo Pludek, attends a garden party thrown by the Liquidation Office, a powerful bureaucratic institution. Hugo is looking for a highly placed friend of his father's who is to secure his future career. The other attendees are automatonlike creatures, functionaries of the Liquidation Office and the competing Inauguration Office, who control the world about them by means of a special bureaucratic language. This language is deprived of its primary communicative content; it consists of political clichés that are caricatures of the wooden way in which Czechoslovak Communist Party officials actually expressed themselves. To a Western reader the bureaucratic jargon of *Zahradní slavnost* is almost incomprehensible, but in Czechoslovakia people were exposed daily to this type of language. When it was presented on stage at Divadlo Na zábradlí, it elicited howls of laughter from the audience.

The speech of the bureaucrats is a mixture of aggressive geniality and vigilance; its purpose is control. While the language is devoid of content, in form it respects the laws of Marxist dialectics. Each person is constantly watching all the rest to make sure that they do not step out of line. At the same time, since language cannot be used for normal communication, nobody really knows what the current rules are and who the boss is. Thus, everyone is in a constant state of uncertainty. Hugo Pludek quickly learns to use this bureaucratic language, and he becomes so proficient in it that he wins a language duel with the director of the Inauguration Office. In the prevailing atmosphere of secretiveness, the director cannot know who Hugo is; it cannot be ruled out that he might be important. The end of their "debate" shows convincingly that the bureaucratic speech is an instrument for controlling others for the personal benefit of the rulers:

THE DIRECTOR AND HUGO TOGETHER: Caused by the fact that as a result of an unhealthy isolation of the whole office certain positive elements in the work of the Inauguration Office were uncritically overrated, and at the same time certain negative elements in the work of the Liquidation Office were one-sidedly magnified, which finally resulted in the fact that the era— (The DIRECTOR cannot keep pace with HUGO any more)

HUGO: —when the new activization of all the positive forces inside the Liquidation Office placed the Liquidation Office once more in the forefront of our work as a firm and mighty stronghold of our unity, it was unfortunately precisely the Inauguration Service which succumbed—
DIRECTOR: — to the hysterical atmosphere of certain imprudent excesses—
HUGO: —insinuating themselves by means of effective arguments taken from the arsenal of abstract humanistic cant—which however in reality did not span the confines of the generally conventionalized types of work—and these clichés are reflected in their typical form, for example, in—
DIRECTOR: —the hackneyed machinery—
HUGO: —of the pseudo-familiar inaugurational phraseology hiding behind the routine of professional humanism a profound dilution of opinions which finally and necessarily led the Inauguration Service into the position of one who undermines the positive endeavor of the Liquidation Office toward consolidation, and the absolute historical necessity of all this is expressed in the wise act of its liquidation.
DIRECTOR: I couldn't agree more.
HUGO: You keep agreeing, but you do nothing about it! This way we'll never finish the liquidation. Time is money. Bring me a cup of coffee!!

Hugo becomes highly successful as a top bureaucrat, but he loses his identity. When he visits his parents at the end of the play, they no longer recognize him.

Language is also the instrument of a power struggle in Havel's *Vyrozumění*. At the beginning of the play the relatively reasonable and tolerant Josef Gross, director of a bureaucratic institution, learns that "ptydepe," a new "scientific" synthetic language, is being introduced into his office to make it easier for bureaucrats to express themselves precisely. The lifeless, extremely complex, and absurd language, which nobody can learn properly, is a metaphor for Marxist-Leninist ideology: like Marxism-Leninism, it is used by unscrupulous individuals—especially Gross's deputy, Baláš—to enslave others.

The plot of *Vyrozumění* is based on a catch-22 situation: Gross receives an official memorandum written in ptydepe, which Baláš is introducing into the organization; but no one will translate it for him because he does not have the appropriate certificates, and he cannot receive these certificates until he has had the memorandum translated. Gross loses his post as director. Eventually a secretary, Marie, translates the memorandum for him on the side, and it turns out that even though it is written in ptydepe it is a sharp criticism of ptydepe that calls for the language to be withdrawn and for its disseminators to be punished. Gross is reinstated as director, but Baláš saves himself by making a public self-criticism. He decides that henceforth he will wield his influence from a secondary position, which is much more influential and much less dangerous than being the man at the top. Toward the end of the play he begins to introduce another synthetic language, chorukor, again without the director's knowledge.

The secretary, Marie, is typical of the idealistic characters in many of Havel's plays who are destroyed by the whirlwind of manipulation that goes on around them. Marie is fired for making an unauthorized translation of the memorandum for Gross; by then Gross's position in the organization has been weakened, and he does not dare to intercede on her behalf. Like other characters in similar positions in Havel's plays, he is only able to offer her a banal rhetorical exercise, rationalizing why he is incapable of saving her job.

The structure of Havel's *Ztížená možnost soustředění* highlights the fragmentedness of modern life. The three parallel actions of the play are broken up into short episodes that are shuffled together so that the dimension of time is abolished. Even this play, however, has a precise symmetrical structure, with many parallelisms in its dialogues. The main character is a scientist, Dr. Eduard Huml, who divides his time between his wife, Vlasta, and his girlfriend, Renata, and makes detailed reports to both of them about the state of his relationship with the other, assuring each that he is about to leave her rival. Huml is visited by a scholarly team from the Sociological Institute who want to analyze his mind using the "Puzuk" computer in order to "construct a model of human individuality." Paradoxically, the computer is the only "human" individual among the dehumanized and mechanized scholars. Puzuk is moody and spoiled: it must be cooled in a refrigerator, then warmed up in an oven. When it eventually deigns to speak, the questions it hurls out are a mixture of absurdities. Some are typical Havel parodies of well-known sayings: "Which is your favorite tunnel? Do you like musical instruments? How many times per year do you air the square? Where have you buried the dog? When did you lose your claim? What is the crux of the matter? What is it like in our homeland today? Do you urinate in public or sometimes?"

Zahradní slavnost, Vyrozumění, and *Ztížená možnost soustředění* were written at a time when Havel was in direct contact with the audiences at the Divadlo Na zábradlí. The plays were often revised during rehearsals and according to the reactions of audi-

ences, and they include jokes that undoubtedly originated onstage.

In 1965 Havel was invited to become a member of the editorial board of a highbrow anticommunist cultural and political monthly, *Tvář* (The Face), which had come into being in 1964 as the result of a decision by the Third Congress of Czechoslovak Writers in 1963 to create a periodical for young writers. In 1964 and 1965 *Tvář* published a considerable amount of important noncommunist writing by Czech and foreign authors. Even in the relatively liberal atmosphere in the mid 1960s, however, the publisher of the monthly, the Union of Czechoslovak Writers, did not want to enter into conflict with the ruling Communist Party, and it imposed impossible conditions on the magazine. A petition was organized in support of the monthly, and Havel and *Tvář* editor Jan Nedvěd took it to Slovakia. Two Czech writers tried physically to prevent them from boarding a train at a Prague railway station. The petition eventually collected some six hundred signatures. In an attempt to make the support network more permanent the Young Writers's Action Group was founded, and Havel was chosen as its chairman. At a Union of Czechoslovak Writers Conference in June 1965 Havel gave a passionate speech, "O úhybném myšlení" (On Evasive Thinking), in which he attacked the allegedly reformist and liberal leadership of the union for failing to support the publication and give space to top-rank noncommunist Czech writers. Several times during 1965 Havel mediated between the *Tvář* editorial board and the writers' union, but the magazine ceased publication at the end of the year. (It was revived in the autumn of 1968 and appeared until June 1969.)

In June 1967 Havel spoke at the Fourth Congress of the Union of Czechoslovak Writers. He again criticized the evasive and passive tactics of the union, which he saw as a retrograde, bureaucratic organization, and called on it to offer membership to several noncommunist Czech authors. On the orders of the Central Committee of the Czechoslovak Communist Party Kohout, Havel, Ludvík Vaculík, and Ivan Klíma were removed from the ballot for the Central Committee of the writers' union.

In January 1968 Alexander Dubček replaced Antonín Novotný as first secretary of the Czechoslovakian Communist Party. Dubček's liberalizing reforms resulted in the brief period of freedom known as the Prague Spring. Havel did not play a major role in the Prague Spring: reform Communists were in the forefront at the time, and Havel was not a Communist. In April he published an article,

Havel, as Ferdinand Vaněk, and Pavel Landovský, as the Head Maltster, in a performance of Havel's one-act play Audience *in the late 1970s*

"Na téma opozice" (On the Theme of an Opposition), in *Literární listy* (Literary Gazette), in which he advocated the foundation of an opposition party. That same month he became chairman of the Circle of Independent Writers. In May and June he spent six weeks in the United States and Western Europe, witnessing at firsthand the West European student rebellion. In France, he met Pavel Tigrid, the publisher of the most important Czech cultural and political émigré quarterly, *Svědectví* (Testimony), and a major organizer of independent Czech cultural life in the West. In New York he met another Czech émigré, Ferdinand Peroutka, a journalist and writer of the Karel Čapek generation and the first head of the Czechoslovak Service of Radio Free Europe. In *The New York Times* (5 May 1968) Havel called on Czechoslovakia "to remove censorship and guarantee freedom of speech and freedom of assembly." In July, Havel, along with the writers Vaculík and Josef Škvorecký, was invited to meet with top Communist Party officials; Havel tried to persuade Dubček to be even more daring. Havel spent most of the rest of the "glorious summer" before the Warsaw Pact invasion of Czechoslovakia on 21 August 1968 giving large parties at his country estate in the village of Hrádeček, near Trutnov in northern Bohemia, which he had purchased for a modest price in 1967.

After the invasion all of Czechoslovakia embarked on a week of passive resistance and protest guided by the free media, which had acquired unprecedented authority with Czechoslovak citizens in the previous months. Havel, who happened to be in the northern Bohemian town of Liberec at the time of the invasion, barricaded himself in the studios of the Liberec radio station and, along with a well-known actor, Jan Tříska, worked nearly around the clock as a commentator. During the six or seven months after the invasion that certain vestiges of freedom lingered in Czechoslovakia, Havel contributed to the public debate with several important essays. In February 1969 he published in *Tvář* "Český úděl?" (The Czech Destiny?), a response to Milan Kundera's piece, published in *Listy* (as *Literární listy* was renamed after the Warsaw Pact invasion) in December of the previous year. Havel rejected Kundera's messianic notion of the "mission of the small nations which in today's world have been delivered to the tender mercies of the Great Powers," criticized his self-congratulatory stance toward the passive resistance of August 1968, and demanded a rational, unsentimental analysis of the current situation. Havel said that he did not believe in the "Czech predicament," the notion that it was predetermined that the Czechs would always be oppressed by a large power. He maintained that the Czechs were responsible for their situation and that it was in their power to change it. He also rejected the idea that the Prague Spring was an event of earthshaking importance: "If we keep telling ourselves that a country which wished to introduce freedom of speech—a normal thing in most countries of the civilized world—and which wanted to curb arbitrary rule by the secret police has become the center of world history, we will turn ourselves into smug hypocrites, ridiculous as a result of their provincial messianism!"

In June 1969, in a speech to the newly formed Union of Czech Writers (the Union of Czechoslovak Writers had split into separate Czech and Slovak organizations after an attempt was made to turn Czechoslovakia into a federation of two states), Havel demanded that the union safeguard writers' freedoms and protest the closing down of the most popular and influential cultural and political weekly, *Listy*, by the authorities. In a 9 August 1969 letter Havel warned Dubček, who had been deposed as first secretary and premier, not to condemn the 1968 Prague Spring publicly, even though he might be pressured to do so by the pro-Soviet politicians who were then in charge: "If you resist and stick to your own truth . . . you will do a great service from the point of view of the future: you will show clearly that communism is not inextricably associated with lying and with lack of integrity." He also warned Dubček not to disappear quietly from the public scene: "such an embarrassing attempt to hide in a crowd would make people despise you." In fact, however, Dubček did disappear, giving up without a fight after the suppression of the short-lived liberal era.

During the political clampdown following the Warsaw Pact invasion—the so-called period of normalization of the 1970s and 1980s—Czechoslovakia was a virtual colony of the Soviet Union. All of the cultural and political protagonists of the Prague Spring were turned into nonpersons: their work was banned, and they were forbidden to make public appearances. A lively dissident community gradually emerged, but the secret police isolated the dissidents from the rest of the society by erecting a wall of fear around them. Most people pretended to forget about politics and refrained from contacting or even speaking about the dissidents. Havel emerged as the most significant writer, thinker, and organizer among the dissidents. Apart from writing plays, he was an astute political commentator and analyst of the postinvasion regime. In December 1972 he was one of thirty-five Czech writers who signed a petition addressed to the Czechoslovak president demanding an amnesty for political prisoners. In the afterword to his *Hry 1970–1976* (Plays 1970–1976, 1977) Havel wrote of the new era:

> August 1968 was not just one of the usual replacements of a more liberal regime for a more conservative one . . . it was something more: it was the end of an era, a disintegration of a spiritual and social climate, a deep mental watershed. . . . The whole existing world, which we knew so well and in which we could easily operate, the peaceful, slightly comic, rickety and biedermeier world of the 1960s had collapsed. . . . On its debris, a totally different world, ruthless, gloomy and serious, harsh and Asiatic, began ominously to emerge. . . .

In 1970–1971 Havel wrote *Spiklenci* (The Conspirators), which was first published (1972) and performed (1974) in German translation as *Die Retter;* it was first published in Czech in 1977. It was the first play that came into being without Havel's having had direct contact with audiences at the Divadlo Na zábradlí, from which he had resigned in 1968, and the author himself has said that he finds it somewhat dry and theoretical. The play is an attempt to dramatize for a Western audience the corrupting effects of the sort of power struggle that is common in totalitarian systems. Four politicians and a widow are preparing a coup d'etat but cannot agree on who is to be the new ruler after the revolution. The conspirators plot behind each other's backs, forming coalitions of three or four, but they are immediately betrayed to the missing members of the team. Once they learn that the latest conspiracy has been betrayed, everyone changes his or her tune. Constant hypocrisy is the main theme of the play. Nobody can ever be sure who supports whom, because nobody is willing to adhere to a consistent point of view for any length of time. All attitudes are absolutely changeable and relative.

In April 1975 Havel wrote the courageous "Dopis Gustávu Husákovi" (translated as "Letter to Dr. Gustáv Husák, General Secretary of the Czechoslovak Communist Party," 1975), a political essay that brilliantly analyzes the postinvasion regime in Czechoslovakia over which Husák, who had replaced Dubček as general secretary of the Czechoslovak Communist Party, presided. Havel argues that life in Husák's Czechoslovakia is based on empty rituals and hypocrisy and that the primary motivation of everyone's actions is fear. People are afraid of losing their jobs for political reasons, and the country is run by the omnipresent and all-powerful secret police. Selfishness, indifference, and superficial adaptation to the status quo are becoming the salient features of Czech society. Havel warns that the "current castration of Czech culture" will lead to "a profound spiritual and moral impotence of the Czech nation in future." Those who have sacrificed the spiritual future of the

Scene from the premiere of Havel's one-act play Vernissage *at the Akademietheater des Burgtheaters in Vienna, 9 October 1976, with Joachim Bissmeier as Bedřich, Sebastian Fischer as Michal, and Sonja Sutter as Věra (photograph by Elisabeth Hauptmann)*

nation to their yearning for power will bear a burden of historical guilt.

Havel's *Žebrácká opera* (The Beggars' Opera), first published in German in 1974 as *Die Gauneroper* and in Czech in 1977, is a sophisticated and amusing version of John Gay's 1728 English opera burlesque. It deals with Havel's favorite theme: the loss of one's personal identity and integrity as a result of lying, blackmailing, and manipulation. Language is again the instrument of hypocrisy. In Havel's version, as in Gay's original, Peachum and Macheath are the bosses of competing gangs of thieves in London. Peachum is trying to persuade his daughter, Polly, to seduce and perhaps even to marry Macheath so that she can act as Peachum's spy in Macheath's camp. But Polly falls in love with Macheath; so, in cooperation with the chief of police, Lockit, Peachum arranges for Macheath to be arrested. It turns out that Peachum is Lockit's long-term collaborator and has built up his organization of thieves so that the London police can have it under their control. At least, that is what Peachum tells Lockit; on the other hand, he tells the members of his gang that he is only pretending to be collaborating with Lockit. It is impossible to know which is the truth.

Instead of having Macheath executed, Lockit wants to master Macheath's soul. He demands that Macheath merge his gang of thieves with Peachum's organization so that Macheath can report on Peachum to Lockit just as Peachum reports to Lockit on Macheath. Thus, the bosses of both gangs find themselves in a police trap from which they cannot escape.

Just as in other plays by Havel, even here there is a character who is an uncompromising idealist: the "independent pickpocket" Filch, who first wants to join Peachum's organization because he highly esteems the gang leader. Soon, however, he discovers that Peachum's life is full of compromises, and he leaves in disgust. He is arrested but refuses to relinquish his ideals even in prison, so he is executed. In an atmosphere of widespread hypocrisy Filch's obstinate faith in principles seems absurd. *Žebrácká opera* also includes, once again, a critique of language. Its protagonists use a modern, pseudoscientific, seemingly rational jargon that hides a reality that people would not accept if it were described in plain speech. *Žebrácká opera* was originally written for the Prague theater Činoherní klub, and it became the first play by Havel for which the official production was banned. Thus it was first staged unofficially, by the originally amateur theater group Divadlo na tahu, directed by Andrej Krob. This theatrical troupe consisted of Havel's friends and admirers, and it has been staging his plays ever since.

Divadlo na tahu performed *Žebrácká opera* in a public hall in Horní Počernice, on the outskirts of Prague, on 1 November 1975 for a closed gathering of some three hundred guests. When the secret police learned about it later, they staged a hysterical witch-hunt against the organizers, performers, and audience, going so far as to fire an actress from an officially permitted theatrical production because her father had attended the Horní Počernice performance and banning a play for children because a few members of the audience had been present at Horní Počernice.

Three one-act plays from the 1970s—*Audience* (first published in German as *Audienz*, 1975; translated as *Conversation*, 1976; published in Czech, 1977) and *Vernisáž* (first published and performed in German as *Vernissage*, 1976; published in Czech, 1977; translated as *Private View*, 1978), both written in 1975, and *Protest* (first published in German in 1978 and in Czech in 1991; translated as *Protest*, 1985), written in 1978—rank among the most successful of Havel's dramatic pieces, probably because they were based on the author's direct experience of ordinary life in Czechoslovakia at the time; this experience weakened his tendency to create theoretical, almost mathematical models of reality. Havel did not make his usual elaborate plans before writing these plays; he wrote them "quickly and with gusto, originally only to entertain my friends." By the time the communist regime fell in 1989, *Audience* and *Vernisáž* had been staged more than forty times in more than eleven countries, becoming the most often produced of Havel's plays.

Havel's life as a dissident in the 1970s was the inspiration for these plays only in part. *Audience*, for instance, includes scenes based on Havel's experience working in a brewery in Trutnov in northern Bohemia while he was banned from publishing. The plays, however, also have a universal meaning; as a result, they resonate with audiences in many countries.

The protagonist of *Audience* is a banned writer, Ferdinand Vaněk, who rolls casks in a brewery to earn a living. He is invited in the office of his superior, the Head Maltster, for a talk. The Head Maltster speaks to Vaněk informally and in a friendly manner, but the writer is nervous. He has been torn out of his middle-class environment, he finds it difficult to get used to such working-class habits as drinking large amounts of beer, and he cannot be sure that his superior will not come up with some nasty trick sooner or later. The trick, of course, duly appears. It is an extraordinary proposal: the Head Maltster is under pressure from the secret police to write regular reports on the banned writer, but he is incapable of doing so; he therefore proposes that Vaněk write the reports on himself. Vaněk refuses to take part in the conspiracy, eliciting a long accusatory speech from the Head Maltster. He points out that the dissidents, by assuming a heroic, uncompromising moral stance, have isolated themselves from the "morally fragile" majority of society. *Audience* shows the subconscious desire of the "ordinary people" to reabsorb the dissidents into the "normal"—that is, politically compromised—majority community so that the dissidents will cease being a living reprimand to them.

In *Vernisáž* another dissident writer, Bedřich, visits a successful middle-class family. The head of the family, Michal, is able to travel to the West; in the Czechoslovakia of the 1970s, such freedom meant that he was a collaborator with the communist regime. But this issue remains in the background. Michal and his wife, Věra, try to impress Bedřich with their consumerist way of life. They take him on a tour of their newly decorated apartment, which is filled with objets d'art; they treat him to unusual food; they tell him enthusiastically about their way of life; they even offer to show him how they make love. They do not like Bedřich's casual attitude and want to change his ways. When Bedřich refuses to succumb to their efforts, his hosts are affronted, and Věra throws a hysterical tantrum. The audience realizes that the consumerist existence of the middle-class couple is an empty one: Michal and Věra's lives are defined only in relation to that of their dissident friend Bedřich, whose life they are trying to master.

Although they feel realistic, Havel's one-act plays are structurally related to Havel's previous work, written in the genre of absurd theater. Both *Audience* and *Vernisáž* have a circular structure: scraps of conversation are regularly repeated. All of Havel's one-act plays from the 1970s probe the complex relationship of "ordinary people" to the Czech dissident community.

Although *Horský hotel* (The Mountain Hotel; first published in German as *Das Berghotel*, 1976; published in Czech, 1977) was not completed until 1976, thematically it seems to belong to an earlier stage of Havel's dramatic writing than *Audience* and *Vernisáž*. In *Horský hotel* Havel attempted to "complete and close one particular stage of my earlier theatrical experimentation" in an "experimental composition of movement and speech." Thirteen people sit around the garden of a mountain hotel making clichélike statements that are repeated so frequently that they finally no longer attach to particular characters. All of the characters mechanically repeat at random everything that has already been said. Havel was trying to test whether statements that emancipate themselves from the characters who make them can have an independent meaning. The play again deals with the loss of human identity through mechanized and stereotyped living.

In Havel's third one-act play, *Protest*, the dissident author Vaněk from *Audience* is invited to visit the officially recognized establishment writer Staněk. Staněk asks Vaněk to write a petition demanding the release of the imprisoned musician Javůrek. Staněk is acting not out of public-spiritedness but out of personal interest: his daughter is pregnant by Javůrek. It turns out that Vaněk already has such a petition and is collecting signatures for it. He asks Staněk to sign it. Staněk refuses and embarks on a long monologue to explain why it would be detrimental to Javůrek's cause if he signed the petition. Language is, again, the main theme of the play—language as an instrument of alibis and pseudorational argumentation. Other Czech dissident writers—Kohout, Pavel Landovský, and Jiří Dienstbier—used the character of Ferdinand Vaněk in one-act plays depicting life in Husák's Czechoslovakia in the 1970s.

In the second half of the 1970s Havel became a major defender of human rights in Czechoslovakia. In August 1976 he was one of the signatories of a letter to the German writer Heinrich Böll, asking Böll to show solidarity with members of the Czech underground music bands Plastic People of the Universe and DG307, who had been put on trial by the communist authorities. The suppression of these musicians mobilized several Czech independent intellectuals and led to the setting up of the human-rights movement Charter 77.

At the 1975 international summit in Helsinki, Finland, the Soviet-bloc countries, including Czechoslovakia, had signed the International Covenant on Civil and Political Rights and the International Covenant on Economic, Social and Cultural Rights. These rights became part of Czechoslovak law on 23 March 1976, but Czechoslovakia failed to adhere to them. For instance, although the covenants guaranteed the rights to free movement and free speech, it was still practically impossible for most Czechoslovaks to travel abroad, and Western radio broadcasts

in Czech and Slovak were still fiercely jammed. In January 1977 Charter 77 was launched in Prague, with Havel as one of its founders and one of its three elected spokespersons. Charter 77 was careful not to call itself an organization or a political party, which would have made it liable to prosecution under Czechoslovak law; instead, it described itself as a loose grouping of committed citizens who wished to enter into a dialogue with the political authorities. (Havel has always been wary of the role of political parties; even as president of the Czech Republic he has encouraged political activity outside the party system.) The Charter 77 Founding Declaration respectfully pointed out that Czechoslovakia had failed to observe the international covenants and that the regime was based on a rule of fear.

The communist regime was caught by surprise by this initiative, and it reacted ferociously. Neither the Charter 77 founding document nor any subsequent Charter 77 documents were ever published in Czechoslovakia under communist rule. On their way to deliver the petition to the Czechoslovak Federal Assembly on 6 January 1977 Havel and the other spokespersons for the movement were arrested and taken in at gunpoint for questioning. The regime started a fierce propaganda campaign against the movement; it forced practically the entire population to sign documents condemning Charter 77 (without allowing them to read its founding declaration), harassed Charter 77 signatories, and succeeded in isolating the dissidents from the majority of the nation. The Charter 77 Founding Declaration was signed by 243 individuals; in all, only 1,886 Czechoslovak citizens joined Charter 77 before the fall of communism in November 1989. Vaculík, who was one of the signatories, wondered publicly whether Charter 77 did not demand too much: surely people could not be asked to be heroes; they could not be asked to jeopardize their lives. Havel countered that there are values for which it is always worthwhile to stand up.

In October 1978 Havel wrote *Moc bezmocných* (1979; translated as "The Power of the Powerless," 1985), which ranks among the best analytical essays on the nature of the communist regime. In much of his political and philosophical writing Havel was influenced by the Czech phenomenologist philosopher Jan Patočka, another of the spokespersons of Charter 77, who died during interrogation by the secret police on 13 March 1977. In *Moc bezmocných* Havel argues that the subjugated always have within themselves the power to improve their situation and that if they do not do so, they are the cause of their own oppression. Every citizen contributes in a cer-

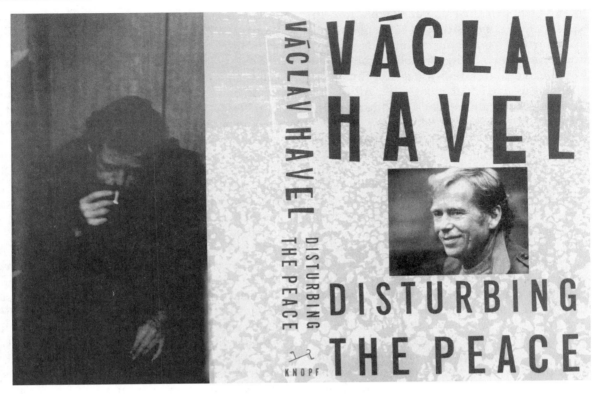

Dust jacket for the U.S. edition (1990) of the English translation of Dálkový výslech
(1986), Havel's book-length interview with Karel Hvížďala

tain measure to the functioning of the totalitarian monolith, but it is possible to start dismantling the system from within by deciding to "live in truth"—to repudiate the institutional lie and create independent, antipolitical, nonviolent, authentic structures such as Charter 77 that run parallel to the state. Havel maintains that the structures of the totalitarian state will gradually dissolve in the emerging non-political structures of the "parallel polis." Havel and Patočka took over the concept of "living in truth" from Kafka; the notion of "nonpolitical politics," used by Havel, was taken over from Tomáš Garrigue Masaryk, the first president of Czechoslovakia. Havel brilliantly explains the role of proregime political slogans displayed in public places under communism:

> The manager of a fruit and vegetable shop places in his window, among the onions and carrots, the slogan: "Workers of the World, Unite!" Why does he do it? What is he trying to communicate to the world? Is he genuinely enthusiastic about the idea of unity among the workers of the world? . . . I think it can safely be assumed that the overwhelming majority of shopkeepers never think about the slogans they put in their windows, nor do they use them to express their real opinions. That poster was delivered

to our greengrocer from the enterprise headquarters along with the onions and carrots. He put them all into the window simply because it has been done that way for years. If he were to refuse, there could be trouble. Obviously, the greengrocer is indifferent to the semantic content of the slogan on the exhibit. This, of course, does not mean that his action has no motive or significance at all, or that the slogan communicates nothing to anyone. The slogan is really a sign, and as such it contains a subliminal but very definite message. Verbally, it might be expressed this way: "I, the greengrocer XY, live here and I know what I must do. I behave in the manner expected of me. I am obedient and therefore I have the right to be left in peace." The message is directed above, to the greengrocer's superior and at the same time it is a shield that protects the greengrocer from potential informers.

> If the greengrocer had been instructed to display the slogan, "I am afraid and therefore unquestioningly obedient," he would not be nearly as indifferent to its semantics, even though the statement would reflect the truth. The greengrocer would be embarrassed and ashamed to put such an unequivocal statement of his own degradation in the shop window. To overcome this complication, his expression of loyalty must take the form of a sign which indicates a level of disinterested conviction. It must allow the greengrocer to say, "What's wrong with the workers of the world uniting?" Thus the sign helps the greengrocer to conceal from himself

the low foundations of his obedience, at the same time concealing the low foundations of power. It hides them behind the facade of something high. And that something is ideology.

Moc bezmocných became a debating point in many Eastern European societies—for instance, some of the leaders of the Solidarity trade union in Poland later used its arguments as the theoretical basis for their actions.

After the launch of *Charter 77* Havel was even more frequently harassed by the police. He was in detention from January to May 1977; in October 1977 he was given a fourteen-month suspended sentence for "damaging the interests of Czechoslovakia abroad"; and in January 1978 he was arrested at a railwaymen's ball in Prague and was held until March.

In April 1978 Havel was a cofounder of *Výbor na obranu nespravedlivě stíhaných,* which gathered and published information about human-rights abuses committed by the Czechoslovak police. Naturally, the members of the committee became prime targets of the wrath of the secret police. In 1978–1979 Havel was held under house arrest for six months. He was arrested again on 29 May 1979 and held in pretrial detention until October. Before his trial he was given permission to emigrate, but he declined. Tried along with the human-rights activists Dienstbier, Petr Uhl, Otka Bednářová, Václav Benda, and Dana Němcová, Havel was sentenced to four and a half years' imprisonment for subversion of the republic. Conditions in communist penitentiaries were incredibly harsh, and Havel fell ill with pneumonia that remained untreated. As a result of international pressure he was released in March 1983, having served three and a half years.

While in prison Havel had written almost 150 weekly letters to his wife. In composing these letters he had had to grapple with strict and absurd rules imposed by the prison governor: he was forbidden to write about life in prison, to make jokes, even to use quotation marks or underlining. In the course of time Havel learned that simple, intelligible letters were almost always intercepted; only convoluted, almost incomprehensible messages had a chance of slipping through. Therefore, he deliberately adopted a convoluted and impenetrable style and discussed such abstruse philosophical topics as the essence of being. The letters were published as *Dopisy Olze,* first in samizdat in Prague in 1983, then commer-

cially in Toronto in 1985; the book was translated as *Letters to Olga: June 1979–September 1982* (1988).

Havel's *Largo desolato* was first published in German in 1984 and in Czech the following year in Munich; it was translated into English in 1987. The play was strongly influenced by his harrowing prison experiences, as well as by a bout of depression he suffered after his release when his marriage almost broke up because of his repeated extramarital relationships. *Largo desolato* was written in four days in July 1984; the rapidity with which it was composed may be accounted for by Havel's fear that the manuscript might be confiscated by the police. John Keane says that *Largo desolato* is a "comic parable about the condition of powerlessness, about what life is like when the individual finally crumbles under the weight of all-consuming power—a chilling tragicomic picture of what happens when the power of the individual to think, speak and act in the world is utterly routed by personal and political failure." In this play Havel examines the relationship between the dissident and the nondissident majority society, which has intolerably high expectations of human-rights activists rather than acting on its own behalf.

The protagonist of *Largo desolato,* the dissident philosopher Leopold Kopřiva (his last name means "nettles") is a nervous wreck after continual secret-police harassment. He does hardly anything but passively sit in his living room, listening for the approach of the police or obsessively preoccupying himself with the state of his health. He almost never goes out, thinking "what if they came and I was not at home?" In spite of his difficult psychological condition, many people place burdensome demands on him. Each of his friends and acquaintances make him conform to their own image and expect him to behave accordingly. Two workmen from a paper mill visit Kopřiva; they see him as a spokesman for ordinary people who has almost superhuman power and expect him to accomplish deeds of which they themselves are not capable. The pompous dissident intellectual Olbram demands that Kopřiva "fulfill his duty" and act in the way that is expected in the dissident ghetto. In the second half of the play two secret policemen visit Kopřiva and make him an offer: if he signs a document in which he renounces his past and his personal identity, denying that he is the author of his own philosophical writings, he will not have to go to prison. Because Kopřiva does not immediately refuse to sign the document but wishes to think about it, he is despised by his partner Zuzana, who is disappointed by his "cowardice." Later the secret police tell Kopřiva that his signature is no longer needed: the authorities have realized that his personal identity has already fully disintegrated.

Havel's periods of imprisonment were traumatic. When he was in detention after the launch of Charter 77 in 1977, he says, he "fell victim to curious, almost psychotic moods." He did not know what was happening in the outside world and only saw the hysterical official media campaign directed against Charter 77 and its signatories. He began to believe that he had acted irresponsibly, that by helping to bring Charter 77 into existence he had endangered others. He mentioned this belief in one of his appeals for release, only to find that the police immediately distorted it by spreading the news that he regretted his role in Charter 77. Later Havel confessed that he felt that he had been "tempted by the devil" during this period.

Perhaps to exorcize this experience, Havel wrote a Faustian play, *Pokoušení* (1986; translated as *Temptation*, 1988), which was published in Munich. It is a mature and eminently watchable piece that is filled with tension as a result of the presence of a rationally unexplained supernatural element. The play is set in an institute set up to fight mystical influences in socialist society. Dr. Foustka, an employee of the institute who privately studies magic, is visited at his home by a man named Fistula, a strange individual who smells of sulphur. Through most of the play it is left uncertain whether Fistula is the devil. Fistula offers to help Foustka with his research into black magic. Foustka accepts the offer; but when his superiors learn about his contacts with Fistula, he claims that he wants to study black magic so as to be able to fight it more efficiently. Foustka thus succumbs to the hypocrisy, verbal relativism, and manipulation of others that Havel criticizes in many of his plays. *Pokoušení* also includes a Havelesque naive idealist: a secretary, Markéta, falls in love with Foustka and tries selflessly to defend him to the head of the institute; she is fired and ends up in a lunatic asylum. Toward the end of the play it becomes evident that Fistula was the institute head's agent provocateur; the head of the institute, who affects everything with his destructive force, is the main "devil" of the piece. Foustka realizes that it is pernicious to lie and to try to serve two masters at the same time, but in the dehumanized environment of the institute he

is destroyed when he decides to defend objective moral values uncompromisingly.

In the late 1980s the Czech dissidents viewed Communist Party First Secretary Mikhail Gorbachev's liberalizing attempts in the Soviet Union with a considerable amount of skepticism. Havel's tragicomedy *Asanace* (1988; translated as *Redevelopment* or *Slum Clearance*, 1990) seems to be an expression of this skepticism and a reflection of the stagnant political situation in Czechoslovakia in the second half of the 1980s. *Asanace* is a parody of the repeated, abortive attempts of communist rulers to bring about liberalization. The play is set in a medieval castle, where a team of architects is preparing plans for the redevelopment of the ancient town nearby. The director of the team is Zdeněk Bergman, but a mysterious Secretary is the real power wielder. Two visitors from the town bring Bergman a petition demanding that the plans be scrapped. Bergman explains that he cannot go against official decision-making, but that for technical reasons the redevelopment of the town is highly unlikely, anyway. When the Secretary learns of the supplicants' presence, he submits them to an interrogation and throws them into the castle prison.

The set for *Asanace* is a spacious hall. In the rear of the stage are several staircases leading to various doors. At key moments the Secretary runs up and down the stairs, entering one door and coming out of another. This comic element indicates a change in the political leadership, as well as a change in the overall political line at the castle. When the first change takes place, the Secretary introduces a new Inspector to the architects. The Inspector is a cruel parody of Khrushchev, Gorbachev, and Dubček. He uses jovial but primitive language. The Inspector tells the architects that he knows that they have been suffering from oppression. But he is bringing the end of oppression: the redevelopment project, the only purpose of which was to enslave the people, will be scrapped. The architects are enthusiastic, but on the following day the Secretary introduces them to the Second Inspector. The Second Inspector reads a speech, explaining that the reforms proposed by the First Inspector were too daring and had caused chaos and anarchy. It will, accordingly, be necessary to return to the old practices but with "a new dynamicism." The redevelopment project will continue, and those who disagree with it will be punished. A bit later the Second Inspector appears again and reads another speech. Apparently it is impossible to realize the redevelopment project because of the "boulder of stagnation." The Second Inspector remarks that "obviously, it is not possible to proceed without freedom." He calls on the architects "freely to seek out new, unconventional methods." But in spite of his talk about freedom, the two supplicants from the beginning of the play remain in the castle prison. The architects continue to be skeptical and devote themselves to their private affairs. At the end of the play the idealist among the architects, Kuzma Plekhanov, commits suicide.

One of the effects of Charter 77 was that the Czech samizdat literary scene developed rapidly in the later 1970s. Several typewritten samizdat series were produced, and many of the titles in the series were reprinted by Czech émigré publishing houses in the West, such as Josef and Zdena Škvorecký's Sixty-Eight Publishers in Toronto. Havel was a prime mover behind many samizdat publishing ventures. In 1987 he became a member of the editorial board of a new samizdat monthly, *Lidové noviny* (The People's Paper), which was produced on a modern copying machine in an attempt to restart the tradition of serious newspapers of the interwar period. After the fall of communism in Czechoslovakia *Lidové noviny* became a daily.

In September 1988 Havel made his first public appearance in nineteen years at a folk music festival in Lipnice nad Sázavou. Antiregime activities were increasing, and Havel came to be regarded as the leader of the movement. He was detained for a few days in October 1988 and again in November 1988.

Zítra to spustíme (Tomorrow Is the Day; translated as *Tomorrow!*, 1994), published anonymously in the paper *Moravské noviny* on 25 October 1990 and republished in a collection of Havel's plays (*Hry*) in 1991, is an "historical meditation in five acts" about the events of 28 October 1918, when the democratic republic of Czechoslovakia was founded on the debris of the Austro-Hungarian Empire. A shortened version of the play was staged on 21 October 1988 by two Brno fringe theaters, Divadlo na provázku (The Theater on a Shoestring) and HA-divadlo (HA-Theater).

On 10 December 1988, Human Rights Day, Havel was allowed to give a public speech to a gathering at Škroupovo náměstí, a small square outside the Prague city center. In January 1989 demonstrations took place in Prague to commemorate the twentieth anniversary of the immolation of Jan Palach, who had killed himself in January

Havel with his second wife, Dagmar Veškrnová, in 1997

1969 to protest the Warsaw Pact invasion and the erosion of freedom in Czechoslovakia. The police reacted brutally, and the demonstrations developed into a weeklong running battle with the authorities. During the disturbances Havel was arrested while attempting to lay flowers at Prague's Wenceslas Square and was sentenced to nine months in prison. As a result of widespread international protests he was conditionally released in May. In June he became one of the main initiators of a petition, "Několik vět" (Just a Few Sentences), demanding political freedoms; it was signed by tens of thousands of Czechoslovakians.

In October 1989 Havel was again detained for a few days. He was not in Prague when the so-called Velvet Revolution began on 17 November with a student demonstration commemorating the fiftieth anniversary of the closing down of Czech universities and the execution of several students by the Nazis. He quickly returned, and on 19 November he met with members of several opposition groups to set up a citizens' umbrella group, Občanské fórum (Civic Forum). Havel quickly became a leading personality in the group, taking part in negotiations with the departing representatives of the communist regime. On 21 November 1989 he addressed the first of several mass demonstrations in Wenceslas Square. On 29 December 1989 he was elected president of Czechoslovakia.

As the leader of the newly free, democratic Czechoslovakia, Havel became the target of immense adulation both at home and abroad. He has received many honorary doctorates and various international awards. Andrew Stroehlein has pointed out that for a time Havel fulfilled the role of a Christlike savior to the Czech nation. The thinking seems to have been: "We may have collaborated with communism under the previous regime, but our president, Václav Havel, who was fiercely persecuted by the communists, is not angry with us. So we are all right, aren't we?" Havel's image as the ideal "president-philosopher" has survived longer in the West than in his own country. Some critics claim that he contributed to the division of Czechoslovakia into the Czech Republic and Slovakia through clumsy handling of relations between the two ethnic groups. He has generally remained above party politics, and he has usually exercised diplomatic caution in his relations with politicians. He has, however, occasionally tried to make political moves, and these attempts have been criticized on a partisan basis. It has been difficult, for example, for Havel to suppress his differences with the right-wing premier, the economist Václav Klaus, whose Civic Democratic Party (ODS) dominated Czech politics between 1992 and 1996. When it turned out that Klaus's economic "reforms" were far from faultless, Havel's reputation seems to have been affected by the general discontent of the Czech citizens.

Havel's image was also harmed by his second marriage. His first wife, Olga, who had devoted herself to charity work after the fall of communism, died of cancer in January 1996; that same year Havel himself was diagnosed with lung cancer. His friend, the actress Dagmar Veškrnová, a woman much younger than he, noticed during a hospital visit that his medical care was highly unsatisfactory. According to some observers, the fuss she created about it saved his life. Havel married her shortly after being released from the hospital in January 1997. His reputation has also been tarnished by several lawsuits (one of which was against the authors of a satirical billboard mocking Havel and his new wife), a controversy over ownership of the Lucerna, and various political disputes—for instance, when Havel was reelected president by a single vote in January 1998, a parliamentary deputy of an extremist nationalist party who would not have voted for Havel was being held in prison. Havel has, however, used his unique international position to try to integrate the Czech Republic into Western political, economic, and military structures. In March 1999 he succeeded almost single-handedly in making the Czech Republic a member of the North Atlantic Treaty Organization (NATO).

Throughout his life Václav Havel has played an important cultural, literary, and political role in his country and has come to be regarded as an extremely important figure on the world scene. It is, however, regrettable that since becoming president of Czechoslovakia he has virtually ceased his literary activities. He has continued to write speeches and essays; internationally, he speaks primarily about globalization and the future of human civilization on earth.

Interviews:

"Breaking the Ice Barrier," *Index on Censorship,* 7 (January–February 1978): 25–28;

Antoine Spire, "I Take the Side of Truth," *Index on Censorship,* 12 (December 1983): 3–7;

Leonid Shinkarev, "Metamorphosis in Prague: The East Is Green for Havel," *World Press Review,* 37 (May 1990): 36–40;

Michel Bongiovanni, "A Clandestine Interview with Václav Havel," *Unesco Courier,* 43 (June 1990): 4–10;

Dana Emingerová and Luboš Beniak, "An Uncertain Strength: An Interview with Václav Havel," translated by Paul Wilson, *New York Review of Books,* 14 (15 August 1991): 6;

Adam Michnik, "A Conversation with President Havel," *World Press Review,* 30 (March 1992): 14–16;

Igor Blazevic, "Out of Unity, Discord," *Index on Censorship,* 23 (July–August 1994): 59–65;

Andrzej Jagodzinski, "A Conversation with Václav Havel," translated by Daniel Borune, *Artful Dodge,* no. 26–27 (1994): 23–29;

Viktor Loshak, "We Must Respect Russia's Interests, but Russia, Too, Must Respect How We Will Decide Our Future," *Moscow News,* 10 June 1994, p. 6;

Maximilian Schell, "Europe at the fin de siècle," *Society*, 32 (September–October 1995): 68–73;

Charles Lambroschini, "A Vote for Nostalgia," *Index on Censorship*, 25 (May–June 1996): 76–77;

Valerie Masterov, "An Apolitical Politician," *Moscow News*, 10 July 1997, p. 1.

Bibliographies:

Vilém Prečan, "Ediční poznámky" in Václav Havel, *O lidskou identitu: Úvahy, fejetony, protesty, polemiky, prohlášení a rozhovory z let 1969–1979* (London: Rozmluvy, 1984; Prague: Rozmluvy, 1990);

Prečan, *Bibliografie díla Václava Havla* and *Chronologický přehled o životě a díle Václava Havla*, in *Do různých stran: Eseje a články z let 1983–1989* (Scheinfeld-Schwarzenberg, Germany: Československé středisko nezávislé literatury, 1989; Prague: Lidové noviny, 1990).

Biographies:

Michael Simmons, *The Reluctant President: The Political Life of Václav Havel* (London: Methuen, 1991);

Eda Kriseová, *Václav Havel–životopis* (Brno: Atlantis, 1991); translated by Caleb Crain as *Václav Havel: The Authorized Biography* (New York: St. Martin's Press, 1993);

John Keane, *Václav Havel: A Political Tragedy in Six Acts* (London: Bloomsbury, 1999).

References:

Veronika Ambros, "Fictional World and Dramatic Text: Václav Havel's Descent and Ascent," *Style*, 2 (Summer 1991): 310–319;

Ambros, "Jevištní řeč v avantgardním divadle, v *Zahradní slavnosti* a v *Largu desolatu*," *Česká literatura*, 40, no. 3 (1992): 286–290;

Ambros, "Tribute to a Very Small Theatre, or, Eulogy for the Balustrade," *Slavic and East European Performance*, 15 (Spring 1995): 27–33;

Timothy Garton Ash, "Intellectuals and Politicians in Prague," *New York Review of Books*, 42 (12 January 1995): 34–40;

Stanisław Barańczak, "All the President's Plays," *New Republic*, 203 (23 July 1990): 27–32;

Paul Berman, "The Philosopher King Is Mortal," *The New York Times Magazine*, 11 May 1997, pp. 32–59;

Igor Blazevic, "Out of Unity, Discord," *Index on Censorship*, 23 (July–August 1994): 59–65;

M. C. Bradbrook, "Václav Havel's Second Wind," *Modern Drama*, 27 (March 1984): 124–132;

Jarka Burian, "Václav Havel's Notable Encounters in His Early Theatrical Career," *Slavic and East European Performance*, 16 (Spring 1996): 13–29;

Walter H. Capps, "Interpreting Václav Havel," *Cross Currents*, 47 (Fall 1997): 301–316;

Phyllis Carey, "Face to Face: Samuel Beckett and Václav Havel," *Christianity and Literature*, 44 (Autumn 1994): 43–57;

Carey, "Living in Lies: Václav Havel's Drama," *Cross Currents*, 42 (Summer 1992): 200–222;

K. Coob, "Ernst Troeltsch and Václav Havel on the Ethical Promise of Historical Failure," *Journal of Religious Ethics*, 22 (Spring 1994): 53–74;

Jan Čulík, "Václav Havel, John Keane a demokratická revoluce 1989," in . . . *jak Češi jednají*, edited by Čulík (Chomutov: Milenium, 1989), pp. 7–47;

George Gibian, "Havel's Letters from Prison," *Cross Currents: A Yearbook of Central European Culture*, 3 (1984): 87–119;

Marketa Goetz-Stankiewicz, "Shall We Dance? Reflections on Václav Havel's Plays," *Cross Currents*, 10 (1991): 213–222;

Goetz-Stankiewicz, *The Silenced Theatre: Czech Playwrights without a Stage* (Toronto: University of Toronto Press, 1979);

Goetz-Stankiewicz, "Václav Havel: A Writer for Today's Season," *World Literature Today*, 55 (Summer 1981): 389–393;

Goetz-Stankiewicz, "Variations of Temptation—Václav Havel's Politics of Language," *Modern Drama*, 33 (March 1990): 93–105;

Goetz-Stankiewicz and Phyllis Carey, eds., *Critical Essays on Václav Havel* (New York: Hall, 1999);

Josef Herman, "Václav Havel," *Amatérská scéna*, 12 (1992): 10;

Herman, "Václav Havel 2," *Amatérská scéna*, 1 (1993): 10–11;

Jiří Holý, "Die Reflexion der tschechischen Tradition bei Václav Havel," *Zeitschrift für slavische Philologie*, 58, no. 1 (1999): 139–149;

Zdeněk Hořínek, "Člověk systemizovaný," *Divadlo*, 10–11 (1968): 4–11;

Miroslav Kačer, "K významové výstavbě dramatické grotesky," in *Struktura a smysl literárního díla*, edited by Milan Jankovič, Zdeněk Pešat, and Felix Vodička (Prague: Československý spisovatel, 1966), pp. 215–228;

Milan Kundera, "A Life Like a Work of Art," *New Republic*, 202 (29 January 1990): 16–17;

Karen von Kunes, "The National Paradox: Czech Literature and the Gentle Revolution," *World Literature Today*, 65 (Spring 1991): 237–240;

Kunes, "A Reflection on the 'Burden of Being' in Havel's *Largo Desolato*," *Czechoslovak and Central European Journal*, 8 (Summer–Winter 1989): 128–135;

V. V. Kusín, "Václav Havel's First Term," *Report on Eastern Europe*, 1 (20 July 1990): 11–13;

Jan Lopatka, *Předpoklady tvorby* (Prague: Československý spisovatel, 1991);

Peter Majer, "Time, Identity and Being: The World of Václav Havel," in *Twentieth-Century European Drama*, edited by Brian Docherty (New York: St. Martin's Press, 1994), pp. 172–182;

Martin J. Matustik, *Postnational Identity: Critical Theory and Existential Philosophy in Habermas, Kierkegaard, and Havel* (New York: Guilford, 1993);

Jude R. Meche, "Female Victims and the Male Protagonist in Václav Havel's Drama," *Modern Drama*, 40 (Winter 1997): 468–476;

Charles Molesworth, "The End Once Again: Art and Politics at the Close of the Century," *Mosaic*, 29 (March 1996): 123–134;

Jan Obrman, "President Havel's Diminishing Political Influence," *RFE/RL Research Report*, (13 March 1992): 18–23;

Jiří Pehe, "Civil Society at Issue in the Czech Republic," *RFE/RL Research Report*, 3 (19 August 1994): 13–18;

Pehe, "Václav Havel's First Two Months in Office," *Report on Eastern Europe* (16 March 1990): 11–15;

M. Quinn, "*Largo Desolato* by Václav Havel," *Slavic and East European Performance*, 12 (Spring 1992): 8–12;

Steven Saxonberg, "A New Phase in Czech Politics," *Journal of Democracy*, 10 (January 1999): 96–111;

Leonid Shinkarev, "Metamorphosis in Prague: The East Is Green for Havel," *World Press Review*, 37 (May 1990): 36, 38;

Robert Skloot, "Václav Havel: The Once and Future Playwright," *Kenyon Review*, 15 (Spring 1993): 223–231;

Josef Škvorecký, "The President Wrote Absurdist Plays," *World & I* (March 1990): 418–428;

J. P. Stern, "Havel's Castle," *London Review of Books*, 12 (22 February 1990): 5–8;

Andrew Stroehlein, "Svatý Václav," in *. . . jak Češi myslí*, edited by Jan Čulík (Chomutov: Milennium, 1999), pp. 420–422;

Alfred Thomas, "Philosophy and Politics in Václav Havel's *Largo Desolato*," in his *The Labyrinth of the Word: Truth and Representation in Czech Literature* (Munich: Oldenbourg, 1995), pp. 144–157;

Paul I. Trensky, *Czech Drama since World War II* (White Plains, N.Y.: Sharpe, 1978);

Trensky, "Václav Havel and the Language of the Absurd," *Slavic and East European Journal*, 13 (1969): 42–65;

Trensky, "Václav Havel's 'Temptation Cycle,'" *Czechoslovak and Central European Journal*, 10 (Winter 1991): 84–95;

Aviezer Tucker, "Václav Havel's Heideggerianism," *Telos*, 85 (Fall 1990): 63–78;

Jan Vladislav, ed. *Václav Havel, or, Living in Truth* (London: Faber & Faber, 1987);

Paul Wilson, "The End of the Velvet Revolution," *New York Review of Books*, 39 (13 August 1992): 57–64.

Papers:

Václav Havel's papers prior to 1990 remain in his personal possession. His papers since 1990 have been gathered at the Presidential Office of the Czech Republic, the Prague Castle. Samizdat editions of Havel's works are deposited at the Prague library Libri prohibiti, Senovážné nám. 2, Praha 1.

Zbigniew Herbert

(29 November 1924 – 28 July 1998)

Bogdana Carpenter
University of Michigan

This entry originally appeared in Concise Dictionary of World Literary Biography:
South Slavic and Eastern European Writers.

BOOKS: *Struna świata* (Warsaw: Czytelnik, 1956);
Hermes, pies i gwiazda (Warsaw: Czytelnik, 1957);
Studium przedmiotu (Warsaw: Czytelnik, 1961);
Barbarzyńca w ogrodzie (Warsaw: Czytelnik, 1962); translated by Michael March and Jarosław Anders as *Barbarian in the Garden* (Manchester, U.K.: Carcanet Press, 1985; San Diego: Harcourt Brace Jovanovich, 1986);
Napis (Warsaw: Czytelnik, 1969);
Dramaty (Warsaw: Państwowy Instytut Wydawniczy, 1970);
Wiersze zebrane (Warsaw: Czytelnik, 1971);
Poezje wybrane (Warsaw: Ludowa Spółdzielnia Wydawnicza, 1973);
Wybór poezji: Dramaty (Warsaw: Czytelnik, 1973);
Pan Cogito (Warsaw: Czytelnik, 1974); translated by John Carpenter and Bogdana Carpenter as *Mr. Cogito* (Oxford & London: Oxford University Press, 1993; Hopewell, N.J.: Ecco Press, 1993);
Wiersze zebrane (Warsaw: Czytelnik, 1982);
18 Wierszy (Kraków: Oficyna Literacka, 1983); enlarged as *Raport z oblężonego miasta i inne wiersze* (Paris: Instytut Literacki, 1983); translated by Carpenter and Carpenter as *Report from the Besieged City and Other Poems* (New York: Ecco Press, 1985; Oxford & London: Oxford University Press, 1987);
Elegia na odejście (Paris: Instytut Literacki, 1990);
Still Life with a Bridle: Essays and Apocryphas, translated by Carpenter and Carpenter (Hopewell, N.J.: Ecco Press, 1991); original Polish version published as *Martwa natura z wędzidłem* (Wrocław: Wydawnictwo Dolnośląskie, 1993);
Rovigo (Wrocław: Wydawnictwo Dolnośląskie, 1993);
Epilog burzy (Wrocław: Wydawnictwo Dolnośląskie, 1998);

Zbigniew Herbert (photograph by Michal Kapitaniak)

89 wierszy (Kraków: Wydawnictwo a5, 1998);
Poezje (Warsaw: Pańtwowy Instytut Wydawniczy, 1998).

Editions in English: *Selected Poems,* translated by Miłosz and Peter Dale Scott, introduction by A. Alvarez (Harmondsworth, U.K.: Penguin, 1968);

Selected Poems, edited and translated by John Carpenter and Bogdana Carpenter (Oxford & New York: Oxford University Press, 1977);

"Mirror," translated by Carpenter and Carpenter, *Encounter*, 62 (January 1984): 3–7;

"The Gordian Knot," translated by Carpenter and Carpenter, *Kenyon Review*, 6 (Summer 1984): 34–40;

"Kleomedes," translated by Carpenter and Carpenter, *Cross Currents*, 3 (1984): 235–244;

"Atlas," translated by Carpenter and Carpenter, *Parnassus*, 15, no. 2 (1989): 26–30;

"Voice," translated by Carpenter and Carpenter, in *Parnassus: Twenty Years of Poetry in Review*, edited by Herbert Leibowitz (Ann Arbor: University of Michigan Press, 1994), pp. 353–359;

Elegy for the Departure and Other Poems, translated by Carpenter and Carpenter (Hopewell, N.J.: Ecco Press, 1999);

The King of the Ants: Mythological Essays, translated by Carpenter and Carpenter (Hopewell, N.J.: Ecco Press, 1999).

In many ways Zbigniew Herbert is a paradigmatic twentieth-century Eastern European poet. His life and poetry, like the fate of his native country and the history of the region, were indelibly marked by the experiences of World War II and of communism. Herbert responded to the nihilism and destructiveness of twentieth-century history and politics with moral intransigence. His respect for concrete, sensory reality made him suspicious of all philosophical systems based on transcendence and of all ideologies that serve as a screen for seizing power and for oppression. His system of values, deeply rooted in European tradition, was based on honor, loyalty, dignity, stoicism, and compassion. To convey his moral message with full force, he strove for a severe and unambiguous style stripped of embellishments; but his aesthetic sensibility counterbalanced his stern moralism, and the result is a poetry that is stylistically rich and sophisticated. Herbert's work has been translated into almost every European language, and among the honors he received are the prize of the Polish Institute for Arts and Sciences in America, the Lenau Prize, the G. Herder Award, the Petrarch Prize, the Prize of the Welsh Arts Council, the Jerusalem Prize, and the T. S. Eliot Prize. Along with Czesław Miłosz, Herbert exerted the most significant influence on Polish poetry of the last forty years of the twentieth century.

Herbert was born on 29 November 1924 in Lwów (Lviv) to Bolesław Herbert and Maria Herbert, née Kaniak. His father was the director of a bank and a professor of economics; in a poem Herbert describes him as a liberal. When World War II broke out in September 1939, Herbert was three months short of his fifteenth birthday; when it ended in Europe in May 1945 he was twenty. The war thus coincided with his adolescence and was an important formative factor. A particularly momentous event for him was the seizure of Lwów in September 1939 by the Soviet army in accordance with the Stalin-Hitler Pact; in a 1984 interview with John and Bogdana Carpenter, Herbert traced his rejection of communism to this early experience: "I have known this since 20 September 1939. When I came into contact with the Soviets in Lwów, as a boy. . . . I had my revelation *ad oculos*. And not through Marx or Lenin. The city was changed within a few days into a concentration camp. This system attacks a European through smells and tastes; while I am a partisan of goodness and beauty." The same argument can be found in Herbert's well-known poem "Potęga smaku" (translated as "The Power of Taste") in *Raport z oblężonego miasta i inne wiersze* (1983; translated as *Report from the Besieged City and Other Poems*, 1985), where resistance to communism is justified on aesthetic rather than on moral grounds:

> It didn't require great character at all
> our refusal disagreement and resistance
> we had a shred of necessary courage
> but fundamentally it was a matter of taste
>   Yes taste
> in which there are fibers of soul and the cartilage of
>   conscience

In the five years after the Soviet invasion Lwów changed masters twice more: invaded by the Germans in 1941, it was recaptured by the Soviets in 1944 and annexed, along with the rest of Poland east of the Curzon Line, to the Soviet Union. During the war Herbert graduated from a clandestine high school and studied literature at an underground university. He also organized an anti-Soviet resistance group, "White Eagle," and participated in the activities of the underground Home Army. In 1944 he moved to Kraków to study painting and economics. In 1948–1949 he studied law and philosophy at the Nicolaus Copernicus University in Toruń, receiving his law degree in 1949. In 1950 he moved to Warsaw, where he studied philosophy at Warsaw University. In Toruń his professor and mentor was Henryk Elzenberg, an anti-Marxist philosopher and ethicist who had a considerable influence on him. Herbert earned a master's degree in economics from Kraków's Academy of Commerce in 1947.

Between 1946 and 1950 Herbert published some critical reviews in periodicals, but with the advent of Stalinism (which in Poland is usually associated with the 1949 Congress of Writers in Szczecin, when socialist realism became obligatory in literture and the arts) he retired from any form of public life and stopped publishing. In 1951 he withdrew from the Writers' Union. During this period he held a variety of jobs: in the peat industry, in the department for retired pensioners of the Teachers' Cooperative, in a bank, in a store, and in the legal department of the Composers' Association.

Herbert's first collection of poems, *Struna świała* (Chord of Light), was published in 1956, during the period of liberalization in Poland under Władysław Gomułka; it comprises poems written during the previous fifteen years. These early poems are dominated by Herbert's experience of war, which made him aware of the vulnerability of art, the failure of traditional philosophical systems, and the inadequacy of language to deal with contemporary reality; their tone is tragic, often elegiac, and betrays a deep emotional involvement. Many of the themes are common to other Polish writers of the World War II generation, such as Tadeusz Borowski, Tadeusz Różewicz, and Miron Białoszewski, but Herbert's attitude is unique in that the experience of war leads him not to a negation but to a reaffirmation of values.

The poem "Dwie krople" (translated as "Two Drops," 1968), which opens the volume, describes lovers in a bomb shelter who ignore fear and whisper "shameless words" of love:

> To the end they were brave
> To the end they were faithful
> To the end they were similar
> like two drops
> stuck at the edge of a face

Despite his realization that the barbarism of his time has no equivalent in history, Herbert does not reject tradition but tries to build on it. In "Do Marka Aurelego" (translated as "To Marcus Aurelius," 1968) he extends his hand "across the dark" to the Roman emperor and Stoic philosopher. The poems in *Struna świała* foreshadow the major tenets of Herbert's ethical system: the value of courage, loyalty, and faithfulness; the duty to remember and to give testimony; and the priority of concrete reality over abstract philosophical systems, of the senses over imagination, and of experience over literature.

Herbert's second volume, *Hermes, pies i gwiazda* (Hermes, Dog, and Star, 1957), brings a

Herbert in the early 1960s

resolution to many of the questions posed in the earlier volume: the decision to write despite the destructiveness of war, to defend beauty despite ugliness and evil, and to defend values despite their vulnerability. In "Pięciu" (translated as "Five Men," 1968), a poem describing the execution of five men by a platoon of German soldiers, Herbert poses a question asked by many other contemporary writers and poets:

> I did not learn this today
> I knew it before yesterday
> so why have I been writing
> unimportant poems on flowers

The answer is not imposed from without by an arbitrary decision but arises, paradoxically, from the situation itself: the night before the execution the condemned men talked about dreams, cards, vodka, and girls—about life, not death. Herbert, therefore, answers his question in the affirmative:

> thus one can use in poetry
> names of Greek shepherds
> one can attempt to catch the color of morning sky

write of love
and also
once again
in dead earnest
offer to the betrayed world
a rose

The experience of World War II is now put into a larger and more universal context; its victims join all other victims of history. In "U wrót doliny" (translated as "At the Gates of the Valley," 1968) a procession of the dead at the last judgment bears a striking resemblance to the process of selection in a Nazi concentration camp.

In his second volume Herbert's political attitudes are sharper, his moral stance more definite, his tone harsher and often ironical. The appearance of irony is related to a change in subject matter: although the experience of war is still present in this volume, it is no longer central, and it does not determine the overall tone; other experiences and concerns—political, artistic, and philosophical—come to the fore. Although these experiences and concerns also command intense emotional involvement, Herbert can write about them from a greater distance, either in a critical, detached manner or with irony. Irony as a method of distancing is a salient feature of Herbert's mature poetry.

Beginning with his second volume Herbert adopts the attitude of a moralist, an attitude that determines the nature of his poetics. Using biblical words and imagery (from Matt. 5:37), Herbert describes this poetics in "Kołatka" (translated as "A Knocker," 1968):

my imagination
is a piece of board
my sole instrument
is a wooden stick

I strike the board
it answers me
yes—yes
no—no

In 1958 Herbert traveled in England, France, Greece, and Italy. His third volume of poetry, *Studium przedmiotu* (Study of the Object), was published in 1961, the year he was named "Prince of Poets" at the student festival in Gdańsk. In *Studium przedmiotu* Herbert's moral intransigence achieves an unexpected effect and leads at times to attitudes that seem to be its negation. The title poem praises "the object that does not exist" and perfection outside of human society. At the same time, the volume includes one of Herbert's strongest indictments of perfection, the famous "Apollo i Marsjasz" (translated as "Apollo and Marsyas," 1968). The suffering of Marsyas, whose howls of pain turn the "hair" of the tree to which he is fastened white, is opposed to the indifference and cruelty of the symbol of perfection: Apollo, "the god with nerves of artificial fiber."

Herbert's travels in Western Europe in 1958 resulted in 1962 in a volume of essays on Western art, *Barbarzyńca w ogrodzie* (translated as *Barbarian in the Garden,* 1985). In these essays Herbert is simultaneously a scholar of art, an historian, and an anthropologist; but above all, he is a poet who is interested in concrete detail rather than erudite abstractions. His goal is to penetrate beyond the aesthetic dimension of the art and architecture that he describes to find the living human elements that formed the original matrix of the works.

Herbert spent the years 1965 to 1971 abroad. While serving as poet in residence at the Free University in West Berlin he traveled to many countries, among them Austria, Greece, and France. During the academic year 1970–1971 he taught at Los Angeles City College.

Herbert's fourth volume of poems, *Napis* (Inscription, 1969), includes the important "Dlaczego klasycy" (translated as "Why the Classics," 1968). In his poetry Herbert frequently refers to ancient history and makes use of mythological figures, a practice that led some critics to accuse him of "classicism." "Dlaczego klasycy" is a reply to such critics, and it is also a declaration of a poetic stance. The poem praises the Greek historian Thucydides, who described his unsuccessful expedition in the Peloponnesian War by reporting only facts: "that he had seven ships / it was winter / and he sailed quickly." Herbert contrasts Thucydides' objectivity, modesty, and restraint with the arrogance, self-pity, and garrulousness of modern generals and poets. The poem is an excellent illustration of Herbert's approach to history: the past is not a value in itself but a means by which to describe and critique the present. In 1970 a volume of Herbert's plays, several of which were written for the radio, was published.

Herbert's fifth volume of poems, *Pan Cogito* (1974; translated as *Mr. Cogito,* 1993), marks a pivotal point in his oeuvre. In his earlier poetry personal references and self-analysis are conspicuously absent; here he attempts for the first time to analyze himself and to define his sense of identity. In previous volumes he tried out a variety of personae from history; here, in his most extended use of a single persona, he writes about himself in a way that he never did before.

Dust jacket for the U.S. edition (1985) of the English translation of Herbert's 1983 collection Raport z oblężonego miasta i inne wiersze, *in which he treats Polish history as a cyclical process*

The volume bears a marked imprint of Herbert's stay in the United States that is discernible not only in the themes of poems such as "Sekwoja" (translated as "Sequoia"), "Ci którzy przegrali" (translated as "Those Who Lost," about American Indians), "Pan Cogito o magii" (translated as "Mr. Cogito on Magic"), and "Pan Cogito a pop" (translated as "Mr. Cogito and Pop") but also in a new historical perspective. To an extent he adopts American ahistoricity and becomes like "the Tacitus-geometrician" of "Sekwoja," who records only birth, death, and suffering. In "Historia Minotaura" (translated as "The History of the Minotaur") he criticizes conventional history and advocates in its place a "real" history that, he claims, was written in a language called Linear A that has not yet been deciphered. This history is based on hard experience; wisdom begins with the death of theory, which is symbolized in this poem by the death of the Minotaur, ordained by its own father, Minos.

One of the most important philosophical themes of *Pan Cogito* is the critique of transcendence. In earlier poems such as "Raj teologów" (1957; translated as "The Paradise of the Theologians," 1968) and "Żeby tylko nie anioł" (1961; translated as "Anything Rather Than the Angel," 1968) Herbert attacked bloodless abstraction, favoring the creaking of the floor over shrilly transparent perfection. This attitude is carried a step further here as he attacks transcendence in its philosophical form in the ideas of Baruch Spinoza ("Pan Cogito opowiada o kuszeniu Spinozy," translated as "Mr. Cogito Tells about the Temptation of Spinoza") and in its poetic form in the ideas of Georg Heym ("Georg Heym—przygoda prawie metafizyczna," translated as "Georg Heym—the Almost Metaphysical Adventure"). The critique is carried out with great skill and intensity of feeling. Nontranscendence or imperfection itself threatens to become a transcendent goal in the place of transcendence,

*Dust jacket for an English translation of Herbert's poems,
published in 1998, the year of his death*

but Herbert avoids this result through playfulness, irony, humor, lack of traditional form and punctuation, and avoidance of high-flown rhetoric. Finally, the device of the Mr. Cogito persona underlines the impurity of the poems.

Mr. Cogito has elicited many critical discussions. He is clearly a "little man." His concerns are ordinary and practical; he enjoys reading sensational newspaper articles, he fails at Transcendental Meditation, he needs advice, and so on. Herbert uses Mr. Cogito to show how the ordinary person in the modern world can achieve the heroism of a Hector, a Roland, or a Gilgamesh. In the final analysis, Herbert seems to say, one must act against human nature: suffering does not release one from certain duties. In "Przesłanie Pana Cogito" (translated as "The Envoy of Mr. Cogito"), the moral manifesto of the volume, the final word is the imperative: "Be faithful Go."

Pan Cogito marks a return to Herbert's earlier attitude, but it is a return enriched by experience and a new self-awareness. It is a return to heroism, but a heroism quite different from the spontaneous heroism of "Dwie krople." This heroism is one "with open eyes"; it is difficult because it realizes its limitations, ridicules itself, and ultimately fails. "Przesłanie Pana Cogito" became a manifesto for the generation of poets, writers, and intellectuals who later became active in the Solidarity movement. Adam Michnik called the poem "a prayer of people who are free," and Stanisław Barańczak said that Herbert was "a great exemplar." Mr. Cogito has also gained popularity among some American poets; a poetry magazine under this title has been published in Portland, Oregon, since 1975.

Herbert moved to West Berlin in 1973; he returned to Poland in January 1981, a few months after the emergence of Solidarity. His *Raport z oblężonego miasta i inne wiersze* was published in 1983 by an émigré publishing house in Paris. Many of its poems evoke Poland's martial law, fulfilling the task expressed with such force in "Przesłanie Pana Cogito":

> you were saved not in order to live
> you have little time you must give testimony

The poet, "too old to carry arms," adopts the role of a chronicler. In some respects the volume can be regarded as an example of a trend in Polish literature in the late 1970s and 1980s: literature as the recording of events. At the same time, the breadth of Herbert's vision of history, the originality of his interpretations, and his polemical attitude toward history as a discipline make *Raport z oblężonego miasta* more philosophically and artistically complex and more accomplished than other works of the time.

Herbert sees Polish history as cyclical, constantly repeating itself. It is like a hall of mirrors in which the past and the present send each other familiar images: the events of 1981 and 1982 reflect the events of 1956, 1939, 1863, 1795, and so on. In his vision, historical moments not only echo each other but also combine to form a single image of Poland as the treasure-house of all misfortunes. Polish history follows a pattern of which the most characteristic features are heroic but hopeless struggle, isolation, and defeat. The reflections occur not only along a temporal but also along a geographical axis: Herbert establishes analogies between Polish history and the histories of other oppressed nations, the defenders of the Dalai Lama, the Kurds, and the Afghan rebels. Herbert's language is symbolic; that is, it is specific and general at the same time. Sentences, as well as entire poems, operate simultaneously on three levels: they refer to the present, they allude to analogous situations in Polish history, and they make statements about experiences that are universal, transcending the specifically Polish context.

Herbert's sober view of history as a process has its counterpart in his jaundiced opinion of history as a discipline. He distrusts historical accounts because they tend to be records of politicians and political events, bypassing what is most important in any given historical situation—its human content.

Between 1984 and 1990 Herbert lived in Paris, where he suffered bouts of depression and a debilitating illness. The volume *Elegia na odejście* (Elegy for the Departure), published in Paris in 1990, bears the imprint of his condition. A sense of his vulnerability determines the tenor of the volume. Abandoning politics, the poet turns to philosophical and ethical questions such as the problem of evil, the nature of heroism, the persistence of memory, and the need for compassion. Rebelling against the simplistic cogwheels of history, he expresses his desire to return to the innocence of childhood and his resolve to immerse himself in the beauty of the physical world in "Podróż" (translated as "A Journey"):

learn the world anew like an Ionian philosopher

taste water and fire air and earth

because they will remain when everything passes away

In 1991 a volume of Herbert's essays on Dutch seventeenth-century painting appeared in English translation as *Still Life with a Bridle: Essays and Apocryphas;* the Polish version, *Martwa natura z wędzidłem,* followed in 1993. The book substantiates Miłosz's claim that Herbert was always an art historian as well as a poet. One of the most striking features of the essays is the sensitivity to color, light, and texture Herbert displays in them—a notable departure from his usual poetic practice, based on his self-imposed role as moralist, of restraint and sparseness.

Herbert's penultimate volume of poems, *Rovigo,* was published in 1993, after his return to Poland. It has a strong personal bias: of the twenty-six poems, fifteen are either addressed to specific individuals or dedicated to friends. They are dialogical, and at times polemical, in character. Herbert's last volume of poems, *Epilog burzy* (Epilogue to the Storm), appeared just before his death from complications of emphysema on 28 July 1998.

The title refers both to a well-known painting by Giorgione and to Herbert's own life.

Herbert's poetry was shaped in equal measure by ethics and politics: the ethical values form the core of the poetry, politics the context. Politics provided a negative stimulus, a reality against which he reacted and took a moral stand. Although the evolution of Herbert's poetry was closely tied to the changes in Poland's political situation, its greatness lies in the universality of its message. The values it defends—faithfulness, courage, and compassion—transcend national frontiers and are valid for all times and places.

Interviews:

Krystyna Nastulanka, "Jeśli masz dwie drogi . . . Rozmowa ze Zbigniewem Herbertem," in her *Sami o sobie: Rozmowy z pisarzami i uczonymi* (Warsaw: Czytelnik, 1975), pp. 278–287;

Adam Michnik, "Płynie się zawsze do źródeł pod prąd, z prądem płyną śmiecie: Rozmowa ze Zbigniewem Herbertem," *Krytyka,* 8 (1981): 48–64;

Marek Oramus, "An Interview with Zbigniew Herbert," translated by Maria Szmidt, *PN Review,* 26 (1982): 8–12;

John Carpenter and Bogdana Carpenter, "Interview with Zbigniew Herbert," *Manhattan Review,* 3 (Winter 1984–1985): 4–8;

"Conversation on Writing Poetry," translated, with a note, by Carpenter and Carpenter, *Manhattan Review,* 3 (Winter 1984–1985): 9–17;

Jacek Trznadel, "Wypluć z siebie wszystko: Rozmowa ze Zbigniewem Herbertem," in his *Hańba domowa: Rozmowy z pisarzami* (Paris: Instytut Literacki, 1986), pp. 181–223.

References:

Marek Adamiec, *Wiersze Zbigniewa Herberta* (Gdańsk: Wydawnictwo Marek Rożak, 1994);

A. Alvarez, "Noble Poet," *New York Review of Books,* 32 (18 July 1985): 6–9;

Edward Balcerzan, "Poeta wśród ideologii artystycznych współczesności (Zbigniew Herbert)," in his *Poezja polska w latach 1939–1965. Cz. II: Ideologie artystyczne* (Warsaw: Wydawnictwa Szkolne i Pedagogiczne, 1988), pp. 220–254;

Stanisław Barańczak, *Uciekinier z utopii: O poezji Zbigniewa Herberta* (London: Polonia Book Fund, 1984); translated by Barańczak as *A Fugitive from Utopia: The Poetry of Zbigniew Herbert* (Cambridge, Mass.: Harvard University Press, 1987);

Jan Błoński, "Tradycja, ironia i głębsze znaczenie," in his *Romans z tekstem* (Kraków: Wydawnictwo Literackie, 1981), pp. 57–87;

Bogdana Carpenter, "The Barbarian and the Garden," *World Literature Today*, 1, no. 3 (1983): 388–393;

Carpenter, "The Lesson of Art: Zbigniew Herbert's Essays," *Cross Currents*, 11 (1992): 127–138;

Carpenter, "The Prose Poetry of Zbigniew Herbert: Forging a New Genre," *Slavic and East European Journal*, 1 (1984): 76–88;

Carpenter, "Zbigniew Herbert: The Poet as Witness," *Polish Review*, 1 (1987): 5–14;

Carpenter and John Carpenter, "The Recent Poetry of Zbigniew Herbert," *World Literature Today*, 2 (Spring 1977): 210–214;

Carpenter and Carpenter, "Zbigniew Herbert and the Imperfect Poem," *Malahat Review*, 54 (1980): 110–122;

Carpenter and Carpenter, "Zbigniew Herbert: The Poet as Conscience," *Slavic and East European Journal*, 1 (1980): 37–51;

Paul Coates, "Gardens of Stone: The Poetry of Zbigniew Herbert and Tadeusz Różewicz," in *The Mature Laurel: Essays on Modern Polish Poetry*, edited by Adam Czerniawski (Bridgend, Wales: Seren Books / Chester Springs, Pa.: Dufour, 1991), pp. 175–188;

Przemysław Czapliński, Piotr Śliwiński, and Ewa Wiegandt, eds., *Czytanie Herberta* (Poznań: Wydawnictwo Wis, 1995);

Bogdan Czaykowski, "Postwar Polish Poets," in *The Tradition of Polish Ideals: Essays in History and Literature*, edited by Władysław J. Stankiewicz (London: Orbis, 1981), pp. 226–284;

Adam Czerniawski, *Muzy i sowa Minerwy* (Wrocław: Wydawnictwo Dolnośląskie, 1994), pp. 102–133;

Karl Dedecius, "Anbau der Philosophie: Zbigniew Herbert auf der Suche nach Selbstgewissheit," in his *Polnische Profile* (Frankfurt am Main: Suhrkamp, 1975); translated into Polish by Elżbieta Feliksiak as "Uprawa filozofii: Zbigniew Herbert w poszukiwaniu tożsamości," *Pamiętnik Literacki*, 3 (1981): 217–252;

Andrzej Franaszek, *Ciemne źródło* (London: Puls, 1998);

Franaszek, ed., *Poznawanie Herberta* (Kraków: Wydawnictwo Literackie, 1998);

Franaszek, ed., *Poznawanie Herberta 2* (Kraków: Wydawnictwo Literackie, 2000);

Seamus Heaney, "Atlas of Civilization," in *Parnassus: Twenty Years of Poetry in Review*, edited by Herbert Leibowitz (Ann Arbor: University of Michigan Press, 1994), pp. 403–418;

Andrzej Kaliszewski, *Gry Pana Cogito* (Kraków: Wydawnictwo Literackie, 1982);

Julian Kornhauser and Adam Zagajewski, *Świat nie przedstawiony* (Kraków: Wydawnictwo Literackie, 1974);

Jerzy Kwiatkowski, "Zbigniew Herbert," in his *Magia poezji* (Kraków: Wydawnictwo Literackie, 1995), pp. 304–326;

Jacek Łukasiewicz, *Poezja Zbigniewa Herberta* (Warsaw: Wydawnictwa Szkolne i Pedagogiczne, 1995);

Włodzimierz Maciąg, *O poezji Zbigniewa Herberta* (Wrocław: Zakład Narodowy Imienia Ossolińskich, 1986);

Adam Michnik, "Potęga smaku," *Z dziejów honoru w Polsce* (Paris: Instytut Literacki, 1985), pp. 199–280;

Tom Paulin, "Zbigniew Herbert: 'Elegy of Fortinbras,'" in *The Mature Laurel: Essays on Modern Polish Poetry*, pp. 124–130;

John Pilling, "Zbigniew Herbert: 'Mr. Cogito and the Imagination," in *The Mature Laurel: Essays on Modern Polish Poetry*, pp. 119–123;

Krystyna Poklewska, ed., *Dlaczego Herbert: Wiersze i komentarze* (Łódź: Łódzkie Towarzystwo Naukowe, 1993);

Artur Sandauer, "Głos dzielony na czworo," in his *Poeci czterech pokoleń* (Kraków: Wydawnictwo Literackie, 1977), pp. 313–341;

Jacek Trznadel, "Herberta apokryf ironiczny; Kamienowanie mądrości," in his *Płomień obdarzony rozumem* (Warsaw: Czytelnik, 1978), pp. 124–142;

W. L. Webb, "Exemplary Poet in a Traumatic World," *Guardian* (London), 2 August 1981;

Kazimierz Wyka, "Składniki świetlnej struny," in his *Rzecz wyobraźni* (Warsaw: Polski Instytut Wydawniczy, 1977), pp. 177–185.

Miroslav Holub
(13 September 1923 – 14 July 1998)

Jiří Holý
Charles University, Prague

and

Jan Čulík
University of Glasgow

This entry originally appeared in Concise Dictionary of World Literary Biography:
South Slavic and Eastern European Writers.

BOOKS: *Denní služba* (Prague: Československý spiso-
vatel, 1958);
Achilles a želva (Prague: Mladá fronta, 1960);
Slabikář (Prague: Československý spisovatel, 1961);
republished as *Sla bi kář* (Prague: Českoslo-
venský spisovatel, 1961);
Jdi a otevři dveře (Prague: Mladá fronta, 1961);
Kam teče krev (Prague: Československý spisovatel,
1963);
Tak zvané srdce (Prague: Mladá fronta, 1963);
Zcela nesoustavná zoologie (Prague: Mladá fronta,
1963);
Anděl na kolečkách: Poloreportáž z USA (Prague: Česko-
slovenský spisovatel, 1963; revised, 1964);
Anamnéza: Výbor z poezie, 1958–1963 (Prague: Mladá
fronta, 1964);
Tři kroky po zemi: Příběhy a myšlenky kolem vědy (Prague:
Naše vojsko, 1965);
New York, by Holub, Eva Fuková, Marie Sechtlová,
and Miloň Novotný (Prague: Mladá fronta,
1966);
Ačkoli (Prague: Československý spisovatel, 1969);
Žít v New Yorku (Prague: Melantrich, 1969);
Beton: Verše z New Yorku a z Prahy (Prague: Mladá
fronta, 1970);
Události (Prague: Umprum, 1971);
Struktura imunitního systému (Prague: Academia,
1979);
Interferon, or, On Theater, translated by David Young
and Dana Hábová (Oberlin, Ohio: Oberlin
College, 1982); original Czech version pub-

Miroslav Holub (photograph by Barney Taxel; from the cover of
Interferon, or, On Theater, *1982)*

lished as *Interferon čili O divadle* (Prague: Mladá
fronta, 1986);
Naopak (Prague: Mladá fronta, 1982); translated by
Ewald Osers as *On the Contrary and Other Poems*
(Newcastle upon Tyne: Bloodaxe Books,
1984);
*K principu rolničky: Poznámky a námitky na 43 řádek
doprovozené myšlenkami druhých o vědě, kultuře a
jiných nesnázích* (Prague: Melantrich, 1987);
translated by James Naughton as *The Jingle Bell*

Principle (Newcastle upon Tyne: Bloodaxe Books, 1992);

Sagitální řez (Prague: Odeon, 1988); translated by Stuart Friebert and Hábová as *Sagittal Section: Poems, New and Selected* (Oberlin, Ohio: Oberlin College, 1980);

Maxwellův démon, čili O tvořivosti (Prague: Československý spisovatel, 1988);

Immunology of Nude Mice (Boca Raton, Fla.: CRC Press, 1989);

Nepatrně ne: Zcela malá knížka nadávek, zákazů, odkazů apod (Prague: Československý spisovatel, 1989);

Skrytá zášt' věků (Prague: Avicenum, 1990);

Syndrom mizející plíce (Prague: Mladá fronta, 1990); translated by Young and Hábová as *Vanishing Lung Syndrome* (London: Faber & Faber, 1990; Oberlin, Ohio: Oberlin College Press, 1990);

O příčinách porušení a zkázy těl lidských (Prague: Pražská imaginace, 1992);

Ono se letělo: Suita z rodného města (Plzeň: NAVA, 1994);

Aladinova lampa: Poloreportáže ze zemí na východ od ráje (Prague: Baronet, 1996);

Narození Sisyfovo: Básně 1989–1997 (Prague: Mladá fronta, 1998).

Editions in English: *Selected Poems*, translated by Ian Milner and George Theiner (Harmondsworth, U.K.: Penguin, 1967; Baltimore: Penguin, 1967);

"'Heat with a Little Warmth,'" "The Fly," and "Polonius," translated by Milner and Theiner, in *New Writing of East Europe*, edited by George Gömöri and Charles Newman (Chicago: Quadrangle Books, 1968), pp. 222–223;

"The Annunciation," "The Invention of Fire," "The Corporal Who Stabbed Archimedes," and "The Anatomy of Silence," translated by Theiner, in *New Writing in Czechoslovakia*, edited by Theiner (Baltimore: Penguin, 1969), pp. 140–142;

Although, edited and translated by Ian and Jarmila Milner (London: Cape, 1971);

"Rockefeller Center," translated by Holub, in *White Stones and Fir Trees: An Anthology of Contemporary Slavic Literature*, edited by Vasa D. Mihailovich (Lewisburg, Pa.: Bucknell University Press, 1977), pp. 487–488;

Notes of a Clay Pigeon, translated by Ian and Jarmila Milner (London: Secker & Warburg, 1977);

"Experimental Animals," "The Franklin Bridge in Philadelphia," "The Gila Desert in Arizona," and "A One-Way Conversation about Radio City Music Hall," translated by Daniel Simko, and "Brief Reflection on Charlemagne," "Cro-

cheting," and "The Garden of Old People," translated by Stuart Friebert and Dana Hábová, in *Contemporary East European Poetry: An Anthology*, edited by Emery George (Ann Arbor, Mich.: Ardis, 1983), pp. 219–223;

The Fly and Other Poems, translated by Ewald Osers and others (Newcastle upon Tyne: Bloodaxe Books, 1987);

"Heart Transplant," "The Clock," "Fish," "Glass," and "The Fall from the Green Frog," *Field*, 42 (Spring 1990): 5–11;

Poems Before and After, translated by Ian and Jarmila Milner, Osers, and Theiner (Newcastle upon Tyne: Bloodaxe Books, 1990);

The Dimension of the Present Moment and Other Essays, edited by David Young (London & Boston: Faber & Faber, 1990);

"Duties of a Train Conductor," translated by Hábová and Young, *Grand Street*, 10, no. 4 (1991): 191–192;

"The Wall in the Corner by the Stairs" and "The End of the Week," translated by Hábová and Young, *Field*, 45 (Fall 1991): 41–43;

"In Search of the Enemy," translated by Young, *Common Knowledge*, 1 (Spring 1991 [i.e., 1992]): 19–27;

"Spinal Cord" and "My Mother Learns Spanish," translated by Hábová and Young, *Field*, 47 (Fall 1992): 75–77;

"The Ten Commandments" and "The British Museum," translated by Hábová and Young, *Common Knowledge*, 1 (Fall 1992): 22–24;

"Nature, Green in Tooth and Claw," *Harper's*, 286 (May 1993): 26–27;

"The Journey," translated by Young, and "The Autumn Orchard," translated by Hábová and Young, *Partisan Review*, 60 (Summer 1993): 418–419;

"The Day of the Pollyanna," "Whale Songs," and "Metaphysics," translated by Hábová and Young, *Grand Street*, 13 (Spring 1995): 58–60;

Supposed to Fly: A Sequence from Pilsen, Czechoslovakia, translated by Osers (Newcastle upon Tyne: Bloodaxe Books, 1996);

Intensive Care: New and Selected Poems (Oberlin, Ohio: Oberlin College Press, 1996);

The Rampage, translated by Holub, Young, Hábová, and Rebekah Bloyd (London: Faber & Faber, 1997);

Shedding Life: Disease, Politics, and Other Human Conditions, translated by Young, Bloyd, and others (Minneapolis: Milkweed, 1997);

"The Afterlife," translated by Young, *Harper's*, 296 (January 1998): 28–30.

OTHER: *Mechanisms of Antibody Formation: Proceedings of a Symposium Held in Prague, May 27–31, 1959,* edited by Holub and L. Jarošková (New York: Academic Press / Prague: Publishing House of the Czechoslovak Academy of Sciences, 1960);

Edgar Allan Poe, *Poe čili Údolí neklidu,* edited anonymously by Holub (Prague: Československý spisovatel, 1972).

TRANSLATIONS: Zbygniew Herbert, *Studium předmětu,* translated by Holub and Vlasta Dvořáčková (Prague: Odeon, 1965);

Ritchie R. Ward, *Živé hodiny* (Prague: Mladá fronta, 1980);

Lewis Thomas, *Buňka, medúza a já* (Prague: Mladá fronta, 1981);

Umění ve století vědy, translated by Holub and J. Vaněk (Prague: Mladá fronta, 1988);

Thomas, *Myšlenky pozdě v noci* (Prague: Mladá fronta, 1989);

Charles Olson, *Profese poezie* (Prague: Československý spisovatel, 1990).

One of the foremost Czech poets of the second half of the twentieth century, Miroslav Holub was also a scientist whose work in the field of immunology was respected both in the former Czechoslovakia and abroad. In addition, he was an accomplished essayist and translator.

Holub was born on 13 September 1923 in Plzeň in western Bohemia to Josef and Františka (née Dvořáková) Holub. His father was a lawyer who worked at the headquarters of the state railway; his mother was a secondary-school teacher of French and German descent. When the Czech universities were closed down during the Nazi occupation in World War II, Holub worked as a laborer at a warehouse and at a railway station. After the war he entered the Faculty of Natural Sciences at Charles University in Prague, switching to the Faculty of Medicine in 1946. He pursued research in immunology as a member of an association of the university natural scientists and at the Institute for Philosophy and the History of Natural Sciences. On 30 November 1948 he married Věra Koktová, an actress; the marriage ended in divorce in 1952. After receiving his M.D. from Charles University in 1953, he worked as a pathologist in a Prague hospital. In 1954 he joined the Institute of Biology (later Microbiology) at the Czechoslovak Academy of Sciences, and from 1951 to 1965 he was the executive editor of the popular scientific journal *Vesmír* (The Universe).

Holub had begun writing poetry at the end of the war under the influence of Vítězslav Nezval and the Czech avant-garde. His early poems appeared in the daily *Svobodné slovo* (Free Word); in the journal *Kytice* (Garland), edited by Jaroslav Seifert; and in the anthology *Ohnice* (Charlock, 1947). Holub stopped publishing after the communist coup in February 1948, resuming at the time of the cultural "thaw" in the late 1950s. Along with several other poets, including Jiří Šotola, Miroslav Florian, and Karel Šiktanc, as well as the novelist, dramatist, and poet Milan Kundera, he was part of a literary circle that formed around the journal *Květen* (May), which was published from 1955 to 1959. Inspired by the work of Jacques Prévert and by Italian cinematic neorealism, Holub rejected the abstract ideological proclamations of the poetry of the Stalinist period and wrote about everyday life. As Holub said in his article "Náš všední den je pevnina" (Our Ordinary Day Is Firm Land), published in *Květen* in September 1956, "Only by capturing life around us we may be able to express its dynamicism, the immense developments, rolling on around us and within us." The goal of capturing real life meant giving up rhymed and melodious poetry and adopting irregular and free verse, as Holub did in his first two collections, *Denní služba* (Day Duty, 1958) and *Achilles a želva* (Achilles and the Tortoise, 1960).

In addition to his innovations in form and technique, Holub brought to Czech poetry the new themes, based on his professional experience, of work in research laboratories and operating theaters. The doctors, researchers, and other main characters of these poems are unheroic and mostly anonymous "pawns of history" who are instrumental in moving humankind forward. These themes are expressed in free verse that is often closer to prose than poetry; the poems are effective because they are laconic and semantically exact. Holub deliberately avoids traditional poetic lyricism. As he explained in *Večerní Praha* (The Evening Prague) on 5 July 1963: "I prefer to write for people untouched by poetry. . . . I would like them to read poems in such a matter-of-fact manner as they read the newspaper or go to football matches. I would like people not to regard poetry as something more difficult, more effeminate or more praiseworthy." Although Holub's poetry is highly intellectual and seems to be under the author's strict rational control, there are elements of surrealism and humor, as in "Dveře" (The Door) in *Jdi a otevři dveře* (Go and Open the Door, 1961):

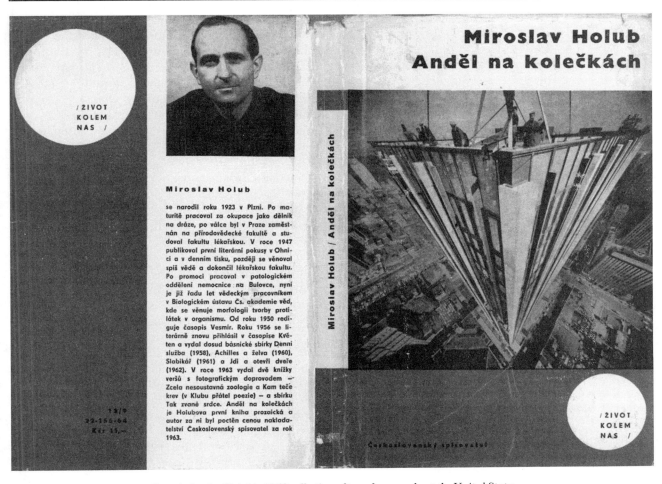

Dust jacket for Holub's 1963 collection of travel essays about the United States

Go and open the door.
Maybe a dog's rummaging.
Maybe you'll see a face,
or an eye
or the picture
          of a picture. . . .

Go and open the door.
Even if there's only
the darkness ticking
even if there's only
the hollow wind
even if
          nothing
                    is there
go and open the door.

At least
there'll be
a draft.

Even these early collections included poems in which Holub seemed to be commenting implicitly on the constraints of the totalitarian system and,

on another level, on the unsatisfactoriness of the human condition in general. These proto-political poems were part of the effort of Czech artists and intellectuals to liberalize the communist system from within. The liberalizing movement had begun in the second half of the 1950s and had suffered many setbacks. In the early 1960s the drive for freedom gained increased momentum, culminating in the Prague Spring of 1968, which was brutally suppressed by the Warsaw Pact invasion in August of that year. In the poem "Popelka" (Cinderella) in *Denní služba* Holub presents his own "modern" version of the traditional fairy tale. Unrewarded, the heroine of his poem dutifully fulfills her assigned task; she is resigned to her lot. Life is elsewhere:

Cinderella is sorting the peas:
bad ones those, good ones these,
yes and no, no and yes. No cheating. No untruthful-
          ness.

. . . .

No blood is flowing. Just red birds
from distant parts are clearly heard
as, plumage ruffled, they alight.

. . . .

No little nuts, no prince that charms
and we all long for mother's arms
yet there is but one hope:

Cinderella is sorting her peas:
softly as one fits joints together
with fingers gentle as a feather,
or as one kneads the dough for bread.

And though it may be light as air,
merely a song in someone's head
a gossamer of truth is there.

Cinderella is sorting her peas:
bad ones, those, good ones these,
yes and no, no and yes,
no cheating in this bout.

She knows that she is on her own.
No helpful pigeons: she's alone.
And yet the peas, they *will* be sorted out.

"Napoleon" in *Achilles a želva* can be seen as an homage to personal experience, which always eventually prevails over theory, ideology, or interpretations of history. "Children, when was Napoleon Bonaparte born?" asks the teacher. No one knows, and after several unsuccessful attempts at answers the poem concludes:

Our butcher had a dog
called Napoleon,
says František.
The butcher used to beat him and the dog died
of hunger
a year ago.

And all the children are now sorry
for Napoleon.

Since he was not a member of the Communist Party, Holub was not allowed to travel abroad for research or to attend scientific conferences until the early 1960s, when he was able to visit such countries as the United Kingdom, Germany, Ireland, China, India, Australia, and Mexico. On 31 January 1963 he married Marta Svikruhová. He traveled to the United States in 1962 and 1963 and worked at the Public Health Research Institute in New York City from 1965 to 1967; from the end of the 1970s he traveled to the United States every third year. His American trips inspired two vol-umes of lyrical travel essays in prose, *Anděl na kolečkách: Poloreportáž z USA* (An Angel on Wheels: A Semireport from the USA, 1963) and *Žít v New Yorku* (To Live in New York, 1969), and a collection of poems, *Beton: Verše z New Yorku a z Prahy* (Concrete: Poems from New York and from Prague, 1970). Holub is enchanted as well as perplexed by the United States, which he sees as a land of sharp contrasts, a paradoxical mixture of the profane and the sacred; this impression is expressed by the image of the "angel on wheels," a statue of a Baroque angel on casters that he saw at a New York airport. In his travel essays Holub includes quotes from newspapers and graffiti (for instance, "God is not dead, he just can't find a parking space") from the New York subway and from building walls.

Influenced by his exposure to the West and disappointed by political developments in Czechoslovakia after the August 1968 invasion put an end to the liberalizing reform movement, Holub began to concern himself with metaphysical questions. His faith in progress disappeared, as is illustrated most effectively in his collection *Ačkoli* (Although, 1969), which includes not only poems but also lyrical micro-essays and aphorisms. In one poem he says:

Although a poem arises when there's nothing else to
     be done,
although a poem is a last attempt at order when one
     can't stand disorder any longer,
although poets are most needed when freedom, vita-
     min C, communications, laws and hypertension
     therapy are also most needed
although to be an artist is to fail and art is fidelity to
     failure, as Samuel Beckett says,
a poem is not one of the last but one of the first things
     of man.

The poem "Tramvaj v půl šesté večer" (A Tram at Half Past Six in the Evening), a polemical counterbalance to the optimistic "Tramvaj v půl šesté ráno" (A Tram at Half Past Six in the Morning) in Holub's first collection, is typical: in dark, disconsolate images it depicts a world that is losing substance and meaning.

Holub had taken an active part in the reform movement in Czechoslovakia in the 1960s, publishing essays in the liberal cultural and literary periodicals *Literární noviny* (The Literary Gazette), *Plamen* (The Flame), and *Orientace* (Orientation). As a result, he was dismissed from the Institute of Microbiology in 1970. He was divorced from his second wife in 1971; on 5 July of that year he married Jitka Langrová. Also in

O PŘÍČINÁCH PORUŠENÍ A ZKÁZY TĚL LIDSKÝCH

MIROSLAV HOLUB

PRAHA
1992

Title page for one of Holub's collections of essays and aphorisms. The title means "On the Causes of the Degeneration and Destruction of Human Bodies."

(Bavarian Academy of Fine Arts) and of the New York Academy of Science and received an honorary doctorate from Oberlin College in Ohio.

After the fall of communism in 1989 Holub was not fully accepted into the literary mainstream in Czechoslovakia, or in the Czech Republic after Czechoslovakia broke apart in 1993. Some of his compatriots felt betrayed by his self-criticism in 1973, and some could not forget that he had never come out openly against communism in the 1970s and 1980s. Furthermore, since he had been able to travel to the West in the 1980s while other Czech authors were languishing as nonpersons in the dissident ghetto, there were allegations that he had cooperated with the secret police. From a literary standpoint, many writers and critics could not accept Holub's rational, terse poetic style. This style is, however, extremely well suited to English translation and has helped to make Holub an internationally known author.

Holub's work of the 1980s and the 1990s consists mainly of essays and aphorisms that examine technological civilization and the place of poetry in the modern world; such pieces are collected in *K principu rolničky: Poznámky a námitky na 43 řádek doprovozené myšlenkami druhých o vědě, kultuře a jiných nesnázích* (1987; translated as *The Jingle Bell Principle*, 1992), *Maxwellův démon, čili O tvořivosti* (Maxwell's Demon; or, On Creativity, 1988), and *O příčinách porušení a zkázy těl lidských* (On the Causes of the Degeneration and Destruction of Human Bodies, 1992). His poetry of the period, influenced by Samuel Beckett, T. S. Eliot, and the Czech poet Vladimír Holan, continued along the line of development that had begun at the end of the 1960s. Reality is seen as opaque, irrational, and full of paradoxes. The meanings of these poems are sometimes hidden and ambiguous. Holub's poetic style remains close to prose, avoiding traditional ornamental lyricism and subjective impressions; his language is terse and matter-of-fact. His poems are characterized by allusions to the Bible, mythology, and contemporary culture; an effective division into lines; and provocative innuendo and playfulness, as in "Krátká úvaha o smrti" (Brief Reflection on Death) in the collection *Naopak* (1982; translated as *On the Contrary and Other Poems*, 1984):

Many people act
as if they hadn't been born yet. Meanwhile, however,
William Burroughs, asked by a student,
if he believed in life after death,

1971 he, along with many other Czech writers, was forbidden to publish, travel abroad, or make public appearances, and his books were removed from libraries. The printing plates for a new collection of his poems, "Stručné úvahy" (Brief Contemplations), were destroyed; a book of selections from the work of Edgar Allan Poe that he had compiled, *Poe čili Údolí neklidu* (Poe; or, The Valley of Restlessness), was published anonymously in 1972. After making a degrading public statement of self-criticism in 1973 Holub was able to find employment in a junior position at the Institute for Clinical and Experimental Medicine. His literary work, however, could not be published in Czechoslovakia until 1982.

Although Holub was ostracized in his native country, his literary and scientific work became well known abroad. Much of his writing was translated into English, German, and more than thirty other languages. In 1985 he was made a member of the Bayerische Akademie der schönen Künste

replied:

—And how do you know you haven't died yet?

In his final collection of poetry, *Syndrom mizející plíce* (1990; translated as *Vanishing Lung Syndrome*, 1990), which was published after the fall of the communist regime, Holub returns to the concern with social problems that characterized his early poems. The narrator of the poems, however, retains the persona developed in Holub's later works, that of the intellectual who questions everything that is normally regarded as self-evident. In "Krajina s básníky" (translated as "Landscape with Poets") he develops the image of the singing of a modern-day Orpheus who

> underground will sound
> the upper harmonic registers
>
> and the words will float like clouds,
> across the information threshold,
> up to the shallow sky . . .
>
> and there will be
> either a new form of life
> or, possibly,
> nothing.

In 1995 Holub returned to the Institute of Microbiology. He died on 14 July 1998, leaving behind a unique combination of literary experimentation and scientific humanism. Holub was a cerebral, analytical writer whose intellectual curiosity about the evolution of human existence was satisfied in his ability to merge art and science into a single, creative endeavor of universal importance.

Interview:

"Death Has No Adjectives," *Economist*, 315 (2 June 1990): 97–98.

Bibliography:

MUDr. Miroslav Holub, CSc. Publikované práce 1956–1983, edited by A. Nováková (Prague: Institut klinické a experimentální medicíny, 1983).

References:

Jiří Brabec, "O autorovi," in Holub's *Anamnéza: Výbor z poezie, 1958–1963* (Prague: Mladá fronta, 1964), pp. 137–145;

Miroslav Červenka, "Holub a Brukner," in his *Obléhání zevnitř* (Prague: Torst, 1996), pp. 250–260;

Herbert Eagle, "Syntagmatic Structure in the Free Verse of Miroslav Holub," *Rackham Literary Studies*, 3 (1972): 29–49;

Seamus Heaney, "The Fully Exposed Poem," *Parnassus*, 11 (Spring–Summer 1983): 4–16;

Jiří Holý, "Achilles a želva," in *Česká literatura 1945–1970*, edited by Jiřina Táborská and Milan Zeman (Prague: SPN, 1992), pp. 216–222;

Vladimír Karfík, "Z mladší poezie," in *Jak číst poezii*, edited by Jiří Opelík, enlarged edition (Prague: Československý spisovatel, 1969), pp. 236–242;

Dennis O'Driscoll, "Miroslav Holub," *Poetry Review*, 75 (October 1985): 12–14;

Jiří Opelík, "Denní služba," in his *Nenáviděné řemeslo* (Prague: Československý spisovatel, 1969), pp. 29–31;

Ewald Osers, "Death Darkens a Prague Summer," *New Statesman*, 127 (7 August 1998): 49;

Josef Peterka, "Poezie výzkumu—výzkum poezie," in Holub's *Naopak* (Prague: Mladá fronta, 1982), pp. 109–116;

Bohumil Svozil, *Vůle k intelektuální poezii* (Prague: Československý spisovatel, 1971);

Svozil, ed., *Časopis Květen a jeho doba* (Prague-Opava: Ústav pro českou literaturu- Slezská univerzita, 1994);

Rueul Wilson, "Three Contemporary Slavic Poets: A View from the Other Side," *New Quarterly Cave*, 1, no. 4 (1976): 46–58.

Papers:

As of 2000, Miroslav Holub's papers were in private hands. Negotiations were underway for their transfer to the Literary Archives of the Memorial to Czech Literature in Prague.

Bohumil Hrabal

(28 March 1914 – 3 February 1997)

Václav Kadlec

BOOKS: *Hovory lidí* (Prague, 1956);

Perlička na dně (Prague: Československý spisovatel, 1963);

Pábitelé (Prague: Mladá fronta, 1964);

Taneční hodiny pro starší a pokročilé (Prague: Československý spisovatel, 1964); translated by Michael Henry Heim as *Dancing Lessons for the Advanced in Age* (New York: Harcourt Brace, 1995);

Ostře sledované vlaky (Prague: Československý spisovatel, 1965); translated by Edith Pargeter as *A Close Watch on the Trains* (London: Cape, 1968); republished as *Closely Watched Trains* (New York: Grove, 1968);

Inzerát na dům, ve kterém už nechci bydlet (Prague: Mladá fronta, 1965);

Automat svět (Prague: Mladá fronta, 1966); translated by Heim as *The Death of Mr. Baltisberger* (Garden City, N.Y.: Doubleday, 1975);

Morytáty a legendy (Prague: Československý spisovatel, 1968);

Poupata (Prague: Mladá fronta, 1970; Cologne: Index, 1982; Prague: Mladá fronta, 1992);

Obsluhoval jsem anglického krále (Prague: Edice Petlice [samizdat], 1971); republished as *Jak jsem obsluhoval jsem anglického krále* (Cologne: Index, 1980); published semi-clandestinely as *Obsluhoval jsem anglického krále,* Jazzpetit Series no. 9 (Prague: Jazzová sekce, 1982); translated by Paul Wilson as *I Served the King of England* (London: Chatto & Windus, 1989; San Diego: Harcourt Brace Jovanovich, 1989);

Postřižiny (Prague: Edice Petlice [samizdat], 1974; Prague: Československý spisovatel, 1976);

Městečko, kde se zastavil čas (Prague: Edice Petlice [samizdat], 1974; Prague: Odeon, 1991); republished as *Městečko, ve kterém se zastavil čas* (Innsbruck: Comenius, 1978);

Krasosmutnění (Prague: Československý spisovatel, 1979);

Bohumil Hrabal (from the dust jacket for The Little Town Where Time Stood Still, *1993)*

Něžný barbar (Prague: Edice Petlice [samizdat], 1974; Cologne: Index, 1981; Prague: Odeon, 1990);

Příliš hlučná samota (Prague: Edice Expedice [samizdat], 1977; Cologne: Index, 1980; Prague: Odeon, 1989); translated by Heim as *Too Loud a Solitude* (San Diego: Harcourt Brace Jovanovich, 1990);

Slavnosti sněženek (Prague: Československý spisovatel, 1978);

Každý den zázrak (Prague: Československý spisovatel, 1979);

Harlekýnovy miliony (Prague: Československý spisovatel, 1981);

Kluby poezie (Prague: Mladá fronta, 1981);

Domácí úkoly z pilnosti (Prague: Československý spisovatel, 1982);

Městečko u vody (Prague: Československý spisovatel, 1982);

Život bez smokingu (Prague: Československý spisovatel, 1986);

Svatby v domě (Prague: Pražská imaginace [samizdat], 1986; Toronto: Sixty-Eight Publishers, 1987; Prague: Československý spisovatel, 1991);

Vita nuova (Prague: Pražská imaginace [samizdat], 1986; Toronto: Sixty-Eight Publishers, 1987; Prague: Československý spisovatel, 1991);

Proluky (Prague: Edice Petlice [samizdat], 1986; Toronto: Sixty-Eight Publishers, 1986 Prague: Československý spisovatel, 1991);

Kličky na kapesníku (Prague: Pražská imaginace [samizdat], 1987);

Můj svět (Prague: Československý spisovatel, 1988);

Chcete vidět zlatou Prahu? (Prague: Mladá fronta, 1989);

Kdo jsem (Prague: Pražská imaginace, 1989);

Kouzelná flétna (Prague: Československý spisovatel, 1990);

Bambino di Praga; Barvotisky; Krásná Poldi (Prague: Československý spisovatel, 1990);

Listopadový uragán (Prague: Tvorba, 1990);

Schizofrenické evangelium: 1949–1952 (Prague: Melantrich, 1990);

Totální strachy (Prague: Pražská imaginace, 1990);

Ponorné říčky (Prague: Pražská imaginace, 1991);

Atomová mašina značky Perkeo: Texty z let 1949–1989, edited by Václav Kadlec (Prague: Práce, 1991);

Slavná Vantochova legenda (Prague: Nejmenší nezávislé nakladatelství, 1991);

Ztracená ulička (Prague: Melantrich, 1991);

Růžový kavalír (Prague: Pražská imaginace, 1991);

Aurora na mělčině (Prague: Pražská imaginace, 1992);

Křik: Naivní fuga, by Hrabal and František Kořínek (Prague: Nejmenší nezávislé nakladatelství, 1992);

Večerníčky pro Cassia (Prague: Pražská imaginace, 1993);

Já si vzpomínám jen a jen na slunečné dny (Nymburk : S. Klos, 1998).

Edition: *Sebrané spisy Bohumila Hrabala,* edited by Václav Kadlec and others (Prague: Pražská imaginace, 1991–1997)—comprises volume 1, *Básnění;* volume 2, *Židovský svícen;* volume 3, *Jarmilka;* volume 4, *Pábení;* volume 5, *Kafkárna;* volume 6, *Obrazy v hlubině času;* volume 7, *Obsluhoval jsem anglického krále;* volume 8, *Rukověť pábitelského učně;* volume 9, *Hlučná samota;* volume 10, *Nymfy v důchodu;* volume 11, *Svatby v domě;* volume 12, *Kdo jsem;* volume 13, *Dopisy Dubence;* volume 14, *Pojízdná zpovědnice;* vol-

ume 15, *Domácí úkoly;* volume 16, *Naivní fuga;* volume 17, *Kličky na kapesníku;* volume 18, *Ze zápisníku zapisovatele;* volume 19, *Dodatky, rejstříky, bibliografie.*

Editions in English: "A Breath of Fresh Air," translated by Marian Wilbraham, in *White Stones and Fir Trees: An Anthology of Contemporary Slavic Literature,* edited by Vasa D. Mihailovich (Rutherford, N.J.: Fairleigh Dickinson University Press, 1977), pp. 558–567;

"The Magic Flute," translated by Lesley and Jan Čulík, *Scottish Slavonic Review* (Spring 1991): 7–17;

The Little Town Where Time Stood Still; and, Cutting It Short, translated by James Naughton (London: Abacus, 1993; New York: Pantheon, 1993);

Total Fears: Letters to Dubenka, translated by Naughton (Prague: Twisted Spoon, 1998).

PLAY PRODUCTION: *Hlučná samota,* by Hrabal and Evald Schorm, Prague, Divadlo Na zábradlí, March 1984.

PRODUCED SCRIPTS: *Fádní odpoledne,* by Hrabal and Ivan Passer, motion picture, Filmové studio Barrandov, June 1965;

Sběrné surovosti, by Hrabal and Juraj Herz, motion picture, Filmové studio Barrandov, September 1965;

Perličky na dně–comprises *Smrt pana Baltazara,* by Hrabal and Jiří Menzel; *Podvodníci,* by Hrabal and Jan Němec; *Dům radosti,* by Hrabal and Evald Schorm; *Automat Svět,* by Hrabal and Věra Chytilová; and *Romance,* by Hrabal and Jaromil Jireš, motion picture, Filmové studio Barrandov, January 1966;

Ostře sledované vlaky, by Hrabal and Menzel, motion picture, Filmové studio Barrandov, November 1966;

Skřivánci na niti, by Hrabal and Menzel, motion picture, Filmové studio Barrandov, completed in 1969, premiered in January 1990;

Postřižiny, by Hrabal and Menzel, motion picture, Filmové studio Barrandov, February 1981;

Slavnosti sněženek, script by Hrabal and Menzel, motion picture, Filmové studio Barrandov, January 1984.

OTHER: *Bohumil Hrabal uvádí . . . ,* edited by Hrabal (Prague: Mladá fronta, 1967);

Bohumil Hrabal uvádí pražské pavlačové anekdoty, edited by Hrabal (Prague: Pražská imaginace, 1994).

Dust jacket for the U.S. edition (1995) of the English translation of Hrabal's 1964 novella, a monologue in which an old man gives advice to a young woman

Bohumil Hrabal's work has had a profound influence on the development of twentieth-century Czech prose both in style and subject matter. He has also been a significant influence on movies and the theater. His prose works are his main contribution to Czech literature; mostly short and colloquial in style, they introduce common Czech language and show the ordinary man as the unheroic hero. Irony, humor, a trenchant style, and acutely observed details create a milieu the reader can relate to, one in which the author freely alternates between pub talk, philosophical aphorisms, folk wisdom, and the precepts of historians. As a rule the resultant texts have no substantial plot, but they fascinate the reader with separate dramatic incidents connected by a continuous flow of speech. Hrabal also had a mostly unintentional but considerable influence on politics. At the time of the post-1968 "normalization" in the 1970s and the 1980s, when Czechoslovakia suffered a neo-Stalinist backlash and much first-class Czech literature was driven underground or abroad, Hrabal's work

served (without the author's intention for it to do so) as an integrating force between the officially permitted and the unofficial Czech literature.

Hrabal was born on 28 March 1914 in Brno-Židenice. His mother was Marie Kiliánová (called Maryška in his memoirs); his father's name was not on the birth certificate. At first the boy was brought up mostly by his maternal grandmother, Kateřina. In 1916 Marie married František (Francin) Hrabal, and the family moved to Polná, where František was a bookkeeper in a brewery. František Hrabal accepted Bohumil as his own son and cared just as much for him as for his brother, Slávek, who was born in 1917. In the summer of 1919 František Hrabal took the job of manager in a brewery in Nymburk, where Bohumil went to primary and secondary school. Having to go to school was a trial for him; he did not like schoolwork and was not good at it. He preferred roaming about, observing what people did and listening to them talking. The colorful life of the small brewery enchanted him, especially after František's brother Josef came to the Nymburk brewery for a short visit and stayed for the rest of his life. This lively uncle, called Pepin, completely won over the ten-year-old Bohumil, who became more attached to him than to his parents. The endless stories Pepin told provided the first great source of material for the future writer. Pepin also became one of the great characters that Hrabal contributed to literature.

After he passed his graduation examinations with difficulty, literature became Hrabal's absorbing passion. Karel Marysko, a musician and poet who was a year younger than Hrabal, and the artist and poet Antonín Frýdl were chiefly responsible for introducing Hrabal to modern literature. They borrowed books, had discussions, went to football matches and cheap restaurants together, and read their first poetic efforts. The small town had everything the young poets needed, and the local bookshop always had the latest in literature; there the friends discovered Surrealism, Dadaism, and poetism. Hrabal continued his intensive exploration of modern art in Prague. After a year of private lessons in Latin, on 7 August 1935 he enrolled as a full-time student in the Faculty of Law at Charles University. His first efforts at poetry date from that time. Like thousands of others, he attempted to give expression to his thoughts, emotions, and moods. He published some of these little, unexceptional early poems in the local Nymburk papers, *Občanské listy* (The Civic Newspaper) and in *Nymburské listy* (The Nymburk Newspaper).

Hrabal's student record book, dated 30 August 1939, includes a list of all the lectures he attended in eight terms between 1935 and 1939. He had passed the state examination in ancient law but had not yet taken the rest of the examinations. The funeral of Jan Opletal, a Czech student who was killed during student demonstrations in Prague in the autumn of 1939 against the Nazi occupation of Czechoslovakia, and the subsequent closing of the Czech universities meant that Hrabal did not finish his studies until six years later. From 1 December 1939 until 31 August 1940 Hrabal worked in the office of Josef Možuta, a notary, in Nymburk. From 4 August 1940 until 31 January 1941 he attended Eckert's private business school in Prague and received a first-class certificate with distinction. From 10 September 1940 until 15 August 1941, at the same time he was engaged in these studies, he was employed in the office of the Railway Consumers' and Manufacturers' Cooperative in Nymburk. Then he worked in the railway station Kostomlaty, near Nymburk. Hrabal's various jobs as a maltster, a railway worker, a linesman, and (after taking a course in Hradec Králové) a guard, gave him a wealth of material for his writing. At this time he was still primarily interested in poetry, composing his lyrical verses on a typewriter in the brewery office. But he was storing up incidents and stories in his remarkable memory.

After the war Hrabal, at the age of thirty-one, took the opportunity to finish his degree at the university. On 22 March 1946 he graduated as a doctor of laws; however, he still had to complete his deferred military service. This service did not last long—from 1 April to 31 August 1946. On 16 September Hrabal took up the post of director of the Tradesmen's Health Insurance and Pension Fund. In the legends and myths that he invented about himself Hrabal maintained that he worked as an insurance agent to overcome his innate shyness. However, he was more likely struggling with a larger dilemma. He was a university graduate, in the prime of life, unmarried, without encumbrances, who could not decide whether to hold a steady job, find a family, and live quietly in a small town—something his friends, Marysko in particular, were emphatically against—or to devote his whole life to and sacrifice everything for art, as those same friends strongly challenged him to do. For the moment the dilemma remained unresolved. Meanwhile, he continued to write poetry and to store up bizarre stories in his memory. It soon became obvious that, no doubt because of his job, Hrabal's poetic work was already moving away from whimsical lyrics and poetism to reality.

On 9 September 1947 the young Hrabal, who did not wish to practice law, took a job as a commercial traveler for the wholesalers H. K. Klofanda, selling brushes and supplies for chemist shops. He continued to type out dozens of lyrical poems reflecting on his life and times. Volume one of his *Sebrané spisy* (Collected Works, 1991–1997) includes Hrabal's literary output between the years 1937 and 1948.

From his poems he put together an anthology, *Ztracená ulička* (The Lost Street, 1991), and tried to have it published at his own expense at the Nymburk printer Hrádek in 1948. But the February coup of 1948—through which the Communist Party came to power and Czechoslovakia became a part of the Soviet bloc for the next forty-one years—shattered the basis on which the rising standard of living of the postwar era was built. The Hrádek printer was finished, and with it Hrabal's hope of publishing his first work; in fact, it was not published until forty-three years later. The firm H. K. Klofanda also closed down. Hrabal joined the nationalized firm Obchodní domy (The Department Stores) and in June 1949 volunteered for the labor brigade SONP Kladno (The National United Steelworks, Kladno). It was the end of an era and the end of a poet.

Hrabal lived in a single-men's hostel in Kladno. Later he lived in Prague in the working-class quarter of Libeň at 24 Na Hrázi (On the Dyke—he called it "On the Dyke of Eternity"). Kladno and Libeň became vast sources of inspiration for him. In Kladno he met the artist Vladimír Boudník, who moved to Libeň in December 1950. At one time Marysko also lived there. The philosopher and poet Egon Bondy and the writers Vladimír and Stanislav Vávra were frequent visitors. They read each other's work and went for beers. Hrabal wrote prolifically about Kladno and recorded many of Uncle Pepin's sayings. In the autumn of 1950 he had two long poems ready—"Bambino di Praga" (The Baby Jesus of Prague) and "Krásná Poldi" (The Beautiful Poldi)—but they were not published until 1990.

On 10 July 1952 Hrabal was seriously injured on the job at Kladno, and for a long time after he left the hospital he was not able to work. He spent a month recuperating in a sanatorium in Vráž near Písek. On 7 March 1953 he was deemed fit for light work. Because he could no longer do heavy work, he left Kladno, and in October 1954 he began working for Sběrné suroviny (Collectible materials), a firm that collected wastepaper and other material for recycling. In the wastepaper recycling center in

Spálená Street in Prague (now closed) Hrabal met his second great character—the former weight lifter, pole-vaulter, and rugby player Jindřich Peukert, known as Haňťa. He made increasing use of this character in his later work.

Hrabal's typewritten texts were gradually circulated and were discovered by the poet, graphic artist, and critic Jiří Kolář and other literary figures. Kolář and Josef Hiršal published a typewritten almanac, *Život je všude* (Life Is Everywhere), in 1956. Five of Hrabal's stories were included, and two of these appeared that same year in *Příloha Zpráv spolku českých bibliofilů* (The Supplement to the Bulletin Issued by the League of Czech Bibliophiles), which came out in a print run of two hundred and fifty copies as *Hovory lidí* (People Talking). The texts from that period comprise volumes two and three of Hrabal's *Sebrané spisy*.

Through the efforts of his friends, Hrabal was awarded a six months' grant from the Czech Literary Fund to finish a collection of short stories. Because he had the grant, he was dismissed from the wastepaper recycling center. As a result, in mid February he began to work as a scene-shifter in the S. K. Neumann Theater in Libeň. He completed the collection, "Skřivánek na niti" (Lark on a String); the book was typeset and the proofreading was completed, but in the end its publication was banned because his style was too idiosyncratic and unconventional, and the publisher was afraid of political trouble. So Hrabal worked in the theater, and he and his wife, Eliška, whom he married in 1956, lived around the corner from the theater and close to at least five of his favorite pubs. During this time he did not write much. Things were not getting better politically, and he had little hope of being published. Once again Kolář intervened, urging him on, and from 1 January 1962 Hrabal became a freelance writer. His short stories appeared in magazines, and at the end of January 1963 his first book, *Perlička na dně* (The Pearl in the Deep), was published. His second book, *Pábitelé* (Palaverers), followed the next year.

These two collections of short stories were developed from the rejected "Skřivánek na niti," which had been made up from revised texts written during the 1950s. Many further revisions and adaptations at the demand of the publishing-house editors removed much of the original rawness of the texts. The editors changed colloquial speech into standard Czech, giving the stories a more formal style. In spite of that, the stories created a sensation at the time and won immediate acclaim. A group of young directors—Juraj Herz,

Věra Chytilová, Jaromil Jireš, Jiří Menzel, Jan Němec, Ivan Passer, and Evald Schorm—made them into motion pictures that ushered in the "new wave" of Czech cinema.

The stories are set in the places familiar to Hrabal: a small town, the outskirts of Prague, the Kladno ironworks, and the wastepaper-recycling center. The characters were also based on living models, and Hrabal reproduced their language skillfully. They are altogether ordinary people with everyday concerns. The stories have a fairly restricted background, and they are made up of a series of unrelated anecdotes without a strong story line. If there is any suggestion of a plot, it is retroactive, arising out of references to previous self-contained stories. For example, "Bambino di Praga" (1947) is a prose text artificially collated from several stories.

Hrabal's texts do not have substantial punch lines. First and foremost they are concerned with the rich, earthy speech of ordinary people—as illustrated in the symbolic title of the 1956 special edition of two of the stories, *Hovory lidí*. Hrabal's titles and subtitles always indicate the essence of the work. His heroes are free souls like the lark out of sight above the ploughed field, but their flight is restricted by fate, by the ties of laws and social conventions. They are simple, ordinary people, but at the bottom of the soul of each shines an unsuspected pearl, making him or her exceptional. These people are simply *pábitelé* (palaverers, tellers of tall stories, originals), a word that Hrabal introduced into the Czech language and keeps using in connection with his characters.

In his next book, *Taneční hodiny pro starší a pokročilé* (1964; translated as *Dancing Lessons for the Advanced in Age*, 1995), Hrabal carried the principle of continuous talk to the extreme. The novella is a revised version of the story "Utrpení starého Werthera" (Old Werther's Sufferings, 1949). The story consists of a single sentence, uttered by an old man (Uncle Pepin) for the consolation and guidance of Miss Kamila. This monologue—spoken by a man who equally admires the European Renaissance, the Czech nineteenth-century democratic journalist Karel Havlíček Borovský, young Wolfgang Amadeus Mozart, and "Mr. Batista's Manual of Sex Education"—is introduced by a quotation from the philosopher Ladislav Klíma: "Victory consists of nothing else but being beaten into a pulp." In this sense the speaker is victorious over and over in any situation. The novella displays all the characteristics fundamental to the author's work. Comparison with the original extant manuscripts, housed at the Memorial of National Literature in Prague, shows in detail Hrabal's uses of cutting, collating, surprising shifts of meaning, and novel associations in his textual development. Hrabal makes full use of a whole range of subjects—pub talk, man's basic instincts, sex, the contrast between outward (noble) and inner (selfish) motives—that brought him fame but at the same time made him the target of a great deal of critical abuse. History, philosophy, and politics are interpreted from the point of view of those at the bottom of the social scale. There are quotations from the most varied sources, including conversations overheard and set down into provocative contexts. Once again there is no basic plot, no punchline.

With the novel *Ostře sledované vlaky* (1965; translated as *A Close Watch on the Trains*, 1968; republished as *Closely Watched Trains*, 1968), Hrabal tried out a different, more traditional form. He used part of his existentialist story "Kain" (Cain, 1949), took the famous stamp scene from his short story "Fádní stanice" (The Deadly Dull Station, included in *Poupata*), and revised and reshaped everything into compact classical form. The young hero, Miloš Hrma, is a trainee guard in a small railway station near the end of World War II, as history is reaching a crucial point. Miloš has a personal problem with ejaculatio praecox. He tries to commit suicide, then returns to the station office and gets some advice from the experienced guard Hubička, who is due to be officially reprimanded for his scandalous behavior on duty toward the telegraphist, Zdenička Svatá (he had stamped her buttocks with the official railway rubber stamps). A committee of inquiry, headed by senior railways official Zedníček, takes away the stationmaster's hope of being promoted to railway inspector. At night a messenger from the resistance movement, Viktoria Freie, arrives, bringing explosives to blow up a closely watched military transport train. At the same time she solves Miloš's problem for him. The next day Miloš takes the charge up to the signal post and throws it down onto the ammunition train; in the course of the diversion, he is killed. Hrabal seems to be warning his Czech audiences: as long as you remain in a childlike state, you may survive; the moment you reach maturity and adulthood, you die.

This traditional story seems to retain all the attributes of Hrabal's style, including humor, cleverly juxtaposed scenes, and a large amount of sex. The great days of the end of the war are seen through the eyes of small, insignificant people. In fact, only certain surrealistic details indicate the wartime background. War fever is contrasted with

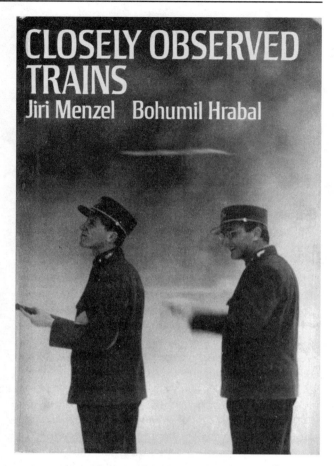

Cover for the English version (1971) of the script for the 1966 movie based on Hrabal's 1965 novel about a railroad-station guard whose sexual difficulties are cured shortly before he is killed in an act of anti-Nazi sabotage

the outlook of the unheroic heroes; the destinies of insignificant people are the little wheels on which history moves forward. Contemporary critics mostly welcomed Hrabal's movement toward a more traditional form. Some critics, however, chiefly Jan Lopatka, immediately saw the pitfalls. In any case the author must have been aware of them himself, and none of his later work has such a conventional form. *Ostře sledované vlaky* is much like a movie script, and it was made into a motion picture in 1966. The movie was extraordinarily successful, winning many awards—the Grand Prix of the city of Mannheim in 1966, an Academy Award in 1967, and the Klement Gottwald State Prize in 1968.

Hrabal's greatest achievement in the period when his work was first published was the collection *Inzerát na dům, ve kterém už nechci bydlet* (Advertisement for a House I Don't Want to Live in Anymore, 1965). Each of the seven stories in this book is a rigorous adaptation of an older text. Long epics and shorter lyric poems were reworked into prose form, and the whole is held together by an autobiographical figure with the symbolic name Kafka. Hrabal shifted his position to one of political confrontation while retaining all the fundamental stylistic elements of previous books. The oppressive climate of the 1950s had eased somewhat by the exposing of the cult of Joseph Stalin; but in spite of that, to write the truth about such contentious questions as the placing of the enormous statue of Stalin overlooking Prague and its almost immediate demolition, or the work of the "class enemies" in the "voluntary" labor brigade in heavy industries, required personal courage on the part of the author and the publishers. *Inzerát na dům, ve kterém už nechci bydlet* was one of the decisive steps toward the political liberalization of the Prague Spring of 1968.

Every title of Hrabal's published at that time was an event. His books sold out rapidly, and new editions were brought out. In 1966 the popular series Máj, published by Mladá fronta, brought out the wide-ranging selection *Automat svět* (The World Cafeteria; translated as *The Death of Mr. Baltisberger*, 1975) in a huge edition of 102,000 copies. It had an important afterword by Emanuel Frynta and was illustrated by Kolář. A year later the book *Bohumil Hrabal uvádí . . .* (Bohumil Hrabal Presents . . .) came out, a kind of anthology of his favorite authors. Another book, a collage of texts with photographs by Miroslav Peterka, *Toto město je ve společné péči obyvatel* (This Town Is in the Care of Its Inhabitants), inaugurated the HU+SA (Humor a satira, Humor and Satire) series from Československý spisovatel, the publishing house of the Czechoslovak writers.

Of course there was another side to the enormous popularity and fame that Hrabal had gained so rapidly. There was no time for writing, and nothing new appeared. In the end the author delved into his store of older writings and produced the book *Morytáty a legendy* (Legends and Broadside Ballads of Murder, 1968). In this collection the cuts and revisions are somewhat perfunctory, and the work lacks any unifying element. Besides collages from letters, conversations, and literary extracts, there are unrevised texts and also other stories that have undergone many changes (for example, "Legenda o krásné Julince," The Legend of Beautiful Julinka). The whole book appears scrappy and does not manage to conceal the fact that it was composed from leftovers. Hrabal's work from the 1960s is included in volumes four and five of his *Sebrané spisy*.

On 21 August 1968 Czechoslovakia was invaded by the Warsaw Pact armies. For a year thereafter everyone still hoped that at least some of the freedom of the 1968 Prague Spring might be retained. It soon became obvious that all these hopes were unfounded. Hrabal had delivered two books, *Poupata* (Buds, 1970, 1982) and "Domácí úkoly" (Homework), to the publisher Mladá fronta. In 1970 both were printed, bound, parceled up, and ultimately sent to the wastepaper recycling center—the very place where he had made up bales of old paper ten years previously, and the place where his wife was working, filling out documents for the removal of banned books. (The consignment of *Poupata* was broken into by literary enthusiasts, however, and several hundred copies of the doomed edition survived.) Hrabal was suddenly persona non grata, having become too closely associated in the popular mind with the liberal 1960s, a period that was then being ferociously condemned. He withdrew from public life and lived in the village of Kersko, outside Prague. During this period he wrote some of his best works.

From the late 1960s Hrabal had been talking about writing his memoirs, in which he would return to the Nymburk of his childhood and youth, to the brewery and his Uncle Pepin. The first of these texts was *Postřižiny* (A Ceremonial Haircut, 1974), in which the author looks at the small town as it once was through the eyes of his mother, the wife of the manager of the brewery. The language of the narrator is less terse, more metaphorical and fluid. The plot is not fundamental to the story; the pictures, characters, and situations are what matters. Uncle Pepin became the most impressive figure in all Hrabal's work. Even the liberal, samizdat editors (those who circulated banned works in small numbers of privately typed and bound copies) did not begin to understand the extravagant, unrestrained language of this novel, however, and they made a great many corrections, changing the style and the order of words. In fact, Hrabal had invented a style full of deliberate repetitions, often using synonyms and recurring themes. He used many coordinating conjunctions and kept reusing the same favorite words and idioms. His writing became increasingly like impressionist painting or symphonic music from the turn of the century. The key to his technique was his prodigious memory, where he stored up details, stories, anecdotes, subjects, and even words he had heard. In some indescribable way all this material in his head reacted, combined, and arranged itself; then he would type it out in bursts at the rate of 2,500 words an hour. These first drafts were submitted to scissors and paste, and the result sent to the editors. Beginning with *Postřižiny,* Hrabal gave up repeatedly revising and "improving" his texts. He became more inclined to leave them in their original form.

The novel *Obsluhoval jsem anglického krále* (1971; translated as *I Served the King of England,* 1989) is reputed to have been written in three weeks in the summer in Kersko and left in its original state. Five chapters are introduced by the words "Pay attention to what I'm going to tell you," and they all finish in the same way: "Have you had enough? I'm finishing here for today." Hrabal thus indicates he is telling readers a story—or, more accurately, he is having a chat with them. That is what the otherwise apparently confusing subtitle *Povídky* (Stories) refers to: the expression *Povídky* is derived from the word *povídat,* meaning "to talk." Hrabal has returned to the original meaning of the word. *Obsluhoval jsem anglického krále* is undoubtedly a novel; the subtitle merely stresses the fact that there is only one narrator telling the reader everything. This narrator is first an apprentice waiter, later a waiter, then owner of a hotel, and ultimately a road mender. His appearance and personal qualities are not described, and even his name is withheld. In the first three chapters neither the narrator's first name nor a surname is mentioned. With the arrival of the Nazis and their racial inquiries, readers learn that the narrator's grandfather was called Johann Ditie. Later from the context it becomes clear that his surname was Dítě (Child). The symbolism of this surname is just as obvious as the fact that in the last chapter the narrator's name is once again consistently not mentioned.

The novel is set in Bohemia about the time of World War II, and social and political events form one of the main backgrounds to the story even though they are not central to the narrator's tale. This novel is one of the most convincing portrayals of Czech-German relations in Czech literature. It follows the narrator's life more or less continuously and chronologically from his apprenticeship in the Zlatá Praha (Golden Prague) Hotel, through his years as a waiter in the hotels Tichota and Paříž, as far as the fourth, "German" chapter, in which the young waiter feels important for the first time because people have stopped calling him "son" or "boy" and address him as Herr Ditie. The last chapter is the longest. After the war the narrator serves six months for some slight "infringement" of the law but afterward builds a hotel in the outskirts of Prague. His dreams come true, and he becomes a millionaire. Then, when a tax is imposed on millionaires, he begins to worry that nobody is demanding that tax of him and that he is not a real millionaire. However, the moment he manages to have his millionaire status recognized, a communist coup takes place, and he is interned with the other millionaires; but even then he is not fully recognized as one of them. Throughout his life, the hero of *Obsluhoval jsem anglického krále* attempts to become part of the establishment, but the historical situation changes so quickly that he finds it impossible to keep up with developments. In the end, when he has to choose between prison and working in the forest with the labor brigade, he leaves the community and settles in the border region of Czechoslovakia, where he finishes up as a roadman repairing in solitude the same road over and over again, year after year.

Obsluhoval jsem anglického krále represents a further step forward in Hrabal's creative development. It has all the merits of his previous works, and in addition it clearly has a plot and a well-thought-out system of symbols, metaphors, and parables. From the reader's point of view it is the most rewarding of Hrabal's works.

Městečko, kde se zastavil čas (1974; translated as *The Little Town Where Time Stood Still,* 1993) continued the nostalgic strain of *Postřižiny.* Again it is about Nymburk, before and after the war, this time seen through the eyes of the author as a boy. Mother, Francin, and Pepin are again the main characters of individual chapters, although the novel has many other distinctive characters. The end of the war and the nationalization of the brewery are portrayed evocatively; this type of subject, of course, could not be published in the politically oppressive 1970s and 1980s.

Broadly speaking, in his work Hrabal kept to the facts regarding the smallest details. Perhaps he considered these details provided the truest basis for his work. However, if it was in the interest of the story, he would change anything and everything as long as it resulted in a better metaphor or hyperbole. For example, at the end of *Městečko, kde se zastavil čas* Francin, with the gesture of a Cyrano de Bergerac, throws the famous sailor's cap belonging to the dying Uncle Pepin into the Elbe and returns home and reacts to the news of Pepin's death with the words "Yes, I know"; in real life, at that time Francin had been dead for nearly a year.

At the same time that he was writing *Městečko, kde se zastavil čas,* Hrabal was working on a collection titled *Něžný barbar* (The Gentle Barbarian, 1974). The book was dedicated to his friend Boudník on

Dust jacket for the U.S. edition of the English translation of Hrabal's autobiographical 1974 novel about the town where he spent much of his youth

the fifth anniversary of his premature death. Once again it is a book of memoirs, this time chiefly about Libeň of the 1950s. Anyone with a pedantic interest in facts would again find some departures from the truth; however, the volume was intended primarily to portray Boudník, which it did with total success. Boudník not only continues to be recognized as an innovator in graphic technique but also is one of the most important figures in Hrabal's work. Memoirs from the first half of the 1970s form volume six of Hrabal's *Sebrané spisy*.

In the early years of the 1970s Hrabal also wrote short stories that he collected as *Slavnosti sněženek* (A Celebration of Snowdrops, 1978). The stories are dedicated to the village of Kersko and the people living there. The collection as Hrabal originally planned it also included important texts from this time, for example "Variace na téma jedné slečny" (Variations on the Theme of One Young Lady), "Družička" (The Bridesmaid), and "Rukověť pábitelského učně" (Handbook for

an Eccentric Apprentice). However, in the official edition of 1978 these pieces, influenced by existentialism and hence frowned upon by the offical establishment, were left out. The original version of *Slavnosti sněženek* was published in volume eight of the *Sebrané spisy*.

The culmination of Hrabal's work is the novel *Příliš hlučná samota* (1977; translated as *Too Loud a Solitude*, 1990). The author finished it in July 1976 but had been working on it since at least 1974. There are many preparatory sketches and three final versions—the first written in Guillaume Apollinaire–style verse, the second in common Czech, and the third in the literary language. Although all three versions were later published in his collected works, at the time only the version in literary Czech, the one Hrabal considered the best, was published. The hero of the novel is Hanťa, a worker in the wastepaper recycling center who has been operating the ancient press for thirty-five years. From piles of old paper he saves rare books and keeps them in his little room. By reading them he becomes educated "in spite of himself." The entire novel is really an inner monologue by Hanťa, written in sonata form with several recurrent motifs. The reader meets Hanťa's first love, Mančinka, and the gypsy girl Ilonka, who disappeared in a concentration camp. Hanťa describes the daily struggle with mountains of paper and endless tankards of beer, quotes philosophy, and speaks of his dreams of retirement, when he means to take the outdated mechanical press with him. Work is a ritual for Hanťa; bales of paper are works of art, in the entrails of which are found treasures of the spirit. The modern recycling unit that Hanťa visits horrifies him. It is so impersonal and sterile that he cannot imagine working there; so when he is moved to a center for collecting clean paper, where he cannot admire beautiful books, he becomes suicidal from despair.

In Hrabal's later work a theme of power and subjugation appears. His texts can be seen as treatises on how to deal with power from the point of view of the oppressed. Hanťa does obediently what is required as his job, thus contributing to the destruction of scores of rare libraries. Nevertheless, he is horrified by what he is forced to take part in—his only consolation is that the process of destruction in which he participates is not too efficient. Only when he is introduced to the modern technology, the epitome of total, absolute obliteration, does he finally despair. Hanťa is just a cipher, but in his inner being he represents Hrabal, and *Příliš hlučná samota* is the author's supreme statement of his beliefs. All three versions of this novel are included in volume nine of the *Sebrané spisy*.

In January 1975 the official communist cultural weekly *Tvorba* (Creative Work) carried a half-page interview in which Hrabal basically said he would vote for the National Front candidates (in communist Czechoslovakia, the National Front was an umbrella organization of smaller political parties and various associations whose task it was to support the ruling communists). The interview was supposed to have been an act of submission, which should have made it possible for Hrabal to get back into officially permitted Czech literature. All things considered, this interview was no help to him at all. Certainly he could have his books openly published again in Czechoslovakia, but not as he wrote them. *Městečko, kde se zastavil čas* was revised and republished as *Krasosmutnění* (Aesthetic Mourning, 1979) and there are other extracts from it in *Harlekýnovy miliony* (Harlequin's Millions, 1981). These two texts are in volume ten of the *Sebrané spisy*. A completely altered version of *Příliš hlučná samota* came

out as a kind of collage with extracts from *Něžný barbar* under the title *Kluby poezie* (The Poetry Clubs, 1981). In 1982 *Domácí úkoly z pilnosti* (Extra Homework by a Diligent Pupil) was published—with deletions and corrections. *Život bez smokingu* (Life without a Dinner Suit, 1986) included several new texts, which were altered again. The author approved of this publication chiefly because in it the novella *Autíčko* (A Little Car) was left in its complete form. In a 1990 interview after the fall of communism Hrabal admitted that he often did the rewriting of his texts himself, in order to make them acceptable for the communist publishers. More anthologies, mostly of old texts, continued to be published, and readers soon realized the author was not writing anything new.

In his fifties Hrabal went back to writing memoirs. He surveyed his life through the eyes of his wife and made ironic comments about it. This long text was divided into three volumes. *Svatby v domě* (Weddings in the House, 1986) tells of his meeting with Eliška and their lives up until their marriage. *Vita nuova* (A New Life, 1986) is made up of pictures of life at Na Hrázi věčnosti (At the Dyke of Eternity). These are sketches once again portraying Boudník. The last book, *Proluky* (Vacant Lots, 1986), is like a kaleidoscope of miniatures projected onto a roughly plastered wall. It covers the years from 1963 to 1969, and its political subtext meant that it was much copied in samizdat and published abroad earlier than the first two works.

Perhaps the most important theme of all three parts of Hrabal's autobiography is the relations between the Czechs and the Germans: German fanaticism and barbarity during World War II, and the cruel Czech retribution after the war. In Hrabal's view, the Germans brought Russian despotism into Central and Eastern Europe: by attacking the Soviet Union they unintentionally extended the Soviet sphere of influence to the river Elbe. Hrabal rejects the idea of revolution, which liberates the basest human instincts and ends in a whirlwind of violence. He abhors man's barbarism and inhumanity; throughout his writings there are recurring motifs of brutality perpetrated against people as well as animals. Hrabal's autobiography forms volume eleven of the *Sebrané spisy*, and those parts left over from the original papers and other work from the 1980s are in volume twelve.

The political climate at the end of the 1980s was somewhat unusual. People kept waiting for something to happen, and nothing did. It was like living in a museum directed by the government; day by day life became more monotonous. Hrabal did not write much at this time until the repressive police actions against student demonstrators in January 1989 marking the twentieth anniversary of the death of student Jan Palach, who had immolated himself in January 1969 in protest against the Warsaw Pact invasion. These actions led him to write the short story "Kouzelná flétna" (translated as "The Magic Flute," 1991). After that there followed a more or less continuous series of short texts, journalistic in nature. These texts were published as individual books: *Listopadový uragán* (The November Hurricane, 1990), *Ponorné říčky* (Subterranean Streams, 1991), *Aurora na mělčině* (The Aurora Is Grounded, 1992), and *Večerníčky pro Cassia* (Bedtime Stories for Cassius, 1993). These "Dopisy Dubence" (Letters to the Girl Named April; that is, Czech scholar April Gifford, with whom Hrabal had fallen in love), as it has become customary to call them, go beyond the bounds of personal confession. The author, completely uninhibited, left everything in its original, unrevised form, so the confession, inconsistent as it is, nevertheless produces a picture that lends itself to various interpretations. Hrabal's description of November 1989, the time when the communist regime collapsed in Czechoslovakia, and the months that followed offers a sense of the naiveté and enthusiasm of these days. Although readers and critics alike have given these texts a lukewarm reception, they are important in the context of contemporary Czech prose. They are perhaps the only ones reflecting the authentic atmosphere of the time. Texts from 1989 to 1995 are included in volumes thirteen and fourteen of the *Sebrané spisy*.

Throughout his career Hrabal published his work occasionally in newspapers and magazines. In addition, he gave interviews, opened exhibitions, and wrote introductions to the work of other authors. All this material is included in volumes fifteen to eighteen of the *Sebrané spisy*. Volume nineteen has a selected index with a bibliography and biographical information.

On 3 February 1997 Hrabal either jumped or fell from the fifth floor of the orthopaedic clinic of the Prague Bulovka hospital. He had mentioned in some of his texts that he was likely to commit suicide by jumping from a fifth-floor window.

Critical reaction to Hrabal's work has always depended on contemporary circumstances. Published in 1996, Milan Jankovič's monograph offered the first comprehensive look at Hrabal's work. The first definitive, most detailed study on Hrabal is Susanna Roth's monograph, published in 1993, which offers critical analysis of Hrabal's

canon extending from the 1970s. A writer with a deep, intrinsic vision, Hrabal is now recognized as an instrumental and imposing figure in the emergence of Czech literature in the second half of the twentieth century.

Letters:

Dílo Karla Maryska, volume 11, edited by Václav Kadlec and Maxi Marysko (Prague: Pražská imaginace, 1996);

Buďte tak hodná, vytáhněte rolety! Výbor z milostné korespondence (Prague: Triton, 1999).

Interview:

Jan Čulík, "Hrabal o Hrabalovi ve Skotsku," *Tvorba*, no. 32 (1990): 12–13.

References:

Václav Černý, *Za hádankami Bohumila Hrabala, pokus interpretační: Eseje o české a slovenské próze* (Prague: Torst, 1994);

Jan Čulík, "Bohumil Hrabal—Looking Back," *Scottish Slavonic Review*, 10 (Spring 1988): 285–288;

Květoslav Chvatík, *Melancholie a vzdor: Eseje o moderní české literatuře* (Prague: Československý spisovatel, 1992);

Chvatík, *Pohledy na českou literaturu z ptačí perspektivy* (Prague: Pražská imaginace, 1991);

Emanuel Frynta, "Pábitel Bohumil Hrabal," afterword to Hrabal's *Pábitelé*, third edition (Prague: Československý spisovatel 1969), pp. 239–244;

George Gibian, "Forward Movement through Backward Glances: Soviet Russian and Czech Fiction (Hrabal, Syomin, Granin)," in *Fiction and Drama in Eastern and Southeastern Europe*, edited by Henrik Birnbaum and Thomas Eekman (Columbus, Ohio: Slavica, 1980), pp. 161–175;

Gibian, "*The Haircutting* and *I Waited on the King of England*: Two Recent Works by Bohumil Hrabal," in *Czech Literature Since 1956: A Symposium*, edited by William Edward Harkins and Paul Trensky (New York: Bohemica, 1980), pp. 74–90;

Václav Havel, "Nad prózami Bohumila Hrabala," *Haňťa Press*, no. 11 (1991): 3–10;

Michael Heim, "Hrabal's Aesthetic of the Powerful Experience," in *Fiction and Drama in Eastern and Southeastern Europe*, edited by Birnbaum and Eekman (Columbus, Ohio: Slavica, 1980), pp. 201–206;

Hrabaliana, edited by Josef Zumr and Milan Jankovič (Prague: Prostor, 1990);

Milan Jankovič, "Hrabalova poetika 'zapisovatele,'" *Česká literatura*, 44, no. 2 (1996): 115–145;

Jankovič, "Jarmark života a řeči (Od pábení k morytátům)," *Haňťa Press*, 18 (1995): 34–47;

Jankovič, *Kapitoly z poetiky Bohumila Hrabala* (Prague: Torst, 1996);

Jankovič, "Nad 'vnitřním hovorem' pozdního Hrabala (Pozorování a přisvojování textů)," *Česká literatura*, 43, no. 3 (1995): 237–268;

Jankovič, *Nesamozřejmost smyslu* (Prague: Československý spisovatel, 1991);

Jankovič, "Pozdní Hrabal," *Kritický sborník*, 14, no. 4 (1994): 55–59;

Jankovič, "Proud vyprávění, proud hovoru, psaní proudem," *Česká literatura*, 42, no. 1 (1994): 23–42;

Jaroslav Kladiva, *Bohumil Hrabal (Život a dílo)* (Frankfurt am Main: Dialog Publishers, 1984);

Kladiva, *Literatura Bohumila Hrabala (Struktura a metoda Hrabalových děl)* (Prague: Pražská imaginace, 1994);

Helena Kosková, "Magnus parens současné české prózy—Bohumil Hrabal," in her *Hledání ztracené generace* (Toronto: Sixty-Eight Publishers, 1987; expanded edition, Jinočany: H+H, 1996);

Jan Lopatka, "Nebývalé problémy textologické," in his *Podoby II* (Prague: Československý spisovatel, 1969), pp. 144–151;

Karel Marysko, "Krátká úvaha na téma Hašek-Hrabal," in *Dílo Karla Maryska*, volume 9 (Prague: Pražská imaginace, 1995), pp. 141–152;

Jiří Pechar, "Hrabalova hořká krása," in his *Nad knihami a rukopisy* (Prague: Edice Petlice-samizdat, 1980), pp. 8–43;

Radko Pytlík, *Bohumil Hrabal* (Prague: Československý spisovatel, 1990);

Pytlík, "Hrabalovo pábení," afterword to *Hovory lidí* by Hrabal (Prague: Československý spisovatel, 1984), pp. 429–434;

Pytlík,"Poznámky k poetice Bohumila Hrabala," *Tvorba*, 12 (1988): supplement;

Sylvie Richterová, "Totožnost člověka ve světě znaků," in her *Slova a ticho* (Munich: Arkýř, 1986), pp. 67–78;

Susanna Roth, *Hlučná samota a hořké štěstí Bohumila Hrabala* (Prague: Pražská imaginace, 1993);

Roth, *Laute Einsamkeit und bitteres Glück: zur poetischen Welt von Bohumil Hrabals Prosa* (Bern & New York: Lang, 1986);

Roth, "The Reception of Bohumil Hrabal in Czechoslovakia and in the West," *Czechoslovak and Central European Journal*, 11 (Summer 1992): 66–72;

Josef Škvorecký, "American Motifs in the Work of Bohumil Hrabal," *Cross Currents: A Yearbook of Central European Culture*, 1 (1982): 207–218;

Miloslava Slavíčková, "Hrabalovy literární montáže," *Slavica Lundensia*, 5 (1977): 135–167;

Slavíčková, "Některá pozorování o technice literární koláže u Hrabala," *Slavica Lundensia*, 8 (1980): 65–112.

Papers:
An archive of Bohumil Hrabal's papers has been deposited at the Memorial of National Literature, Prague. Other documents are in private collections and housed in the archives of the Pražská imaginace Publishing House.

Astrīde Ivaska

(7 August 1926 -   )

Inta Ezergailis
Cornell University

BOOKS: *Ezera kristības: Dzejoļi, 1957–1965* (Shippenville, Pa.: Upeskalns, 1966);

Ziemas tiesa: Dzejoļi, 1965–1967 (Shippenville, Pa.: Upeskalns, 1968);

Solis silos: Dzejoļi, 1968–1971 (Stockholm: Daugava, 1973);

Līcu loki: Ainas un ainavas (Stockholm: Daugava, 1981);

Gaisma ievainoja: Dzejoļi, 1971–1981 (Stockholm: Daugava, 1982);

Pārsteigumi un atklājumi (Ann Arbor, Mich.: Ceļinieks, 1984);

Vārdojums: Dzejoļu izlase, 1951–1987 (Boston: LaRa, 1987);

Oklahoma Poems (Norman, Okla.: Poetry Around, 1990);

Ceļi un atceļi: Atmiņas, dzejoļi, esejas, by Ivaska and Melānija Vanaga (Tukums: Atauga, 1991);

. . . jo rudens ir mans atgriešanā laiks (Riga: Preses nams, 1998).

Collection: *Vārdojums; Līcu loki: Dzejproza* (Rīga: Liesma, 1993).

Editions in English: *At the Fallow's Edge: A Selection of Poems,* edited and translated by Inara Cedriņš (Santa Barbara: Mudborn Press, 1981);

"For My Godmother," "Autumn in the Cascade Mountains," "K. H.," "To the Memory of a Poet," "That Which Has Remained Unlived," translated by Cedriņš, in *Contemporary East European Poetry: An Anthology,* edited by Emery George (Ann Arbor, Mich.: Ardis, 1983), pp. 45–48;

"Table after Supper," translated by Ivar Ivask; "In Vienna's Forests," "Swans," translated by Cedriņš; "Zinnias and Smoked Fish," "On the Island of Paros," "September in Scotland," translated by Ivask; "K. H.," "I Awaken," "Frailty," from "Seawords," translated by Cedriņš; "Returning to Ross, California" and "Spring, Oklahoma," originally written in English; and "The Rain and I," "Ancestors,"

Astrīde Ivaska

"News from the Sea," and "Tide," translated by Cedriņš, in *Contemporary Latvian Poetry,* edited by Cedriņš (Iowa City: University of Iowa Press, 1984), pp. 18–30;

"Moon Poem," translated by Ivaska, and "Lady in the Mirror," translated by Cedriņš, in *Shifting Borders: East European Poetries of the Eighties,* edited by Walter Cummins (Rutherford, N.J.: Fairleigh Dickinson University Press, 1993; London & Cranbury, N.J.: Associated University Presses, 1993), pp. 89–92.

OTHER: "Par sevi," in *Pašportreti: Autori stāsta par sevi,* edited by Teodors Zeltiņš (New York: Grāmatu Draugs, 1965), pp. 134–135;

"Latvian Literature," in *Encyclopedia of World Literature in the 20th Century*, volume 2, edited by Wolfgang Bernard Fleischmann (New York: Ungar, 1969), pp. 250–254; revised version, by Ivaska and Rolfs Ekmanis, in *Encyclopedia of World Literature in the 20th Century*, volume 3, edited by Leonard Klein (New York: Ungar, 1983), pp. 15–19.

Astrīde Ivaska has long been an important literary voice in the Latvian émigré community; since the fall of communism in her homeland, that voice is being heard there, as well. She has published a strong body of poetry as well as some excellent poetic prose. Exile is an enduring theme in her texts, but Ivaska's working through of the exile problem is original and goes well beyond mere nostalgia. Her poetry is subtle, sophisticated in form, and richly varied thematically. While deeply involved in the history and tradition of Latvia, she is a cosmopolitan writer, fluent in several languages, and acquainted with poetry and poets from all over the world.

Astrīde Helēna Hartmane was born in Riga on 7 August 1926 to Mārtiņš Hartmanis and Irma Liepiņa Hartmane. Her father, a general in the Latvian army, was arrested by the Soviet occupiers early in World War II and never returned. Only with the opening of files after the collapse of the Soviet Union did Ivaska find out that he had been shot in Moscow on 27 July 1941.

Ivaska's father is an important figure in her poetry. She dedicates several poems to him, and he permeates her memories of her childhood. In her entry in *Pašportreti: Autori stāsta par sevi* (Self Portraits: Authors Talk about Themselves, 1965), a collection of autobiographical sketches by writers, she says that her father "was the only human being in whom I could see myself as in a mirror. Life with him would have been the kind of life that gods do not grant to mortals. . . . He loved to fish, to meditate, to walk the fields and visit bookstores, to wear his uniform, to talk little and to watch the sun set."

Like many other Latvians, Astrīde Hartmane, with her mother and younger brother, Furis Hartmanis, left Latvia in 1944, just before the Soviets retook the country from the German occupation forces. For the next five years she lived in Germany, where she studied Romance, Slavic, and Germanic philology at the University of Marburg. In her autobiographical sketch she says: "In Marburg-on-the-Laan European intellectual life was opened for me. In three years at the university, I worked with seven foreign languages, some living,

some dead long ago, and I married into the area of Finno-Ugric culture." Her husband, Ivar Ivask, whom she married on 26 February 1949, became a prominent Estonian poet and, in 1967, editor of *World Literature Today*.

In 1949 the couple immigrated to the United States, where Ivaska taught Russian and German at St. Olaf College in Minnesota. The first collection of her poetry, *Ezera kristības: Dzejoļi, 1957–1965* (The Lake's Baptism: Poems, 1957–1965), was published in 1966. In 1967 the couple moved to Norman, Oklahoma, where Ivaska took a part-time position teaching Russian, German, and French at the University of Oklahoma. Her second poetry volume, *Ziemas tiesa: Dzejoļi, 1965–1967* (Judgment of Winter: Poems, 1965–1967), appeared in 1968 and received the Zinaída Lazda Biennial Poetry Prize. *Solis silos: Dzejoļi, 1968–1971* (A Step in the Woods: Poems, 1968–1971, 1973) brought the author the Latvian Culture Foundation Prize for Literature in 1974. The palindromic title, in conjunction with the image of the step, suggests Ivaska's resistance to rigid positions: one should be able to step in various directions at the same time.

A volume of poetic travel sketches, *Līču loki: Ainas un ainavas* (Curving Bays: Views and Landscapes, 1981), received the Jānis Jaunsudrabiņš Prose Prize. The book reveals Ivaska's sense of being at home in many places, cultures, and traditions as it ranges from Finland and Iceland to Ireland, Spain, Northern Italy, Vienna, Hungary, Colorado, and Greece. The essay "Par sevi" (About Myself) appears at the beginning of the volume; the next-to-last poem, "Jonijas jūrā: Itaka" (In the Ionian Sea: Ithaca), is dedicated to her mother, who died in Ithaca, New York, and is a meditation on homecoming and death. Ivar Ivask's artistic photographs form an integral part of the volume instead of merely accompanying or illustrating the lyrical prose. Another volume of poems, *Gaisma ievainoja: Dzejoļi, 1971–1981* (The Light Wounded: Poems, 1971–1981) came out in 1982.

The collection *Vārdojums: Dzejoļu izlase, 1951–1987* (Wordings: Collected Poems, 1951–1987) was published in 1987. Rather than being organized chronologically, the volume is divided into twelve sections according to theme: section titles include "Senči" (Ancestors), "Tapio, silu valdnieks" (Tapio, Master of the Woods), "Saules pakāpes" (The Phases of the Sun), "Mēmais laiks" (Time of Silence), "Mans gadalaiks" (My Season), and "Vārdi, mani mīlie veļi" (Words, My Dear Spirits). In his review of *Vārdojums* in *World Literature Today*

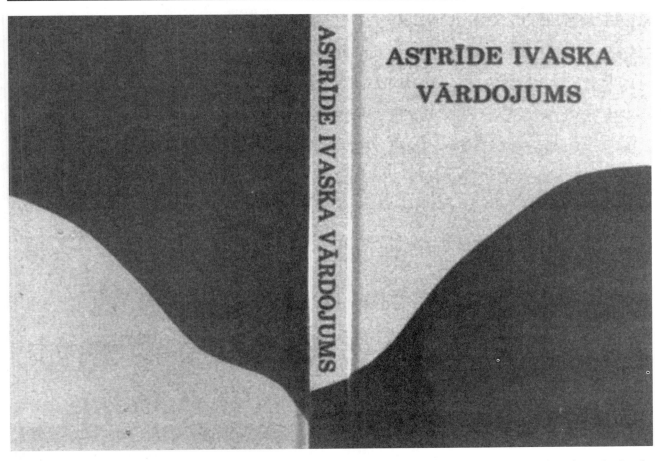

Dust jacket for Ivaska's collection of poems written from 1951 to 1987. The book is unusual among such retrospective volumes in that the poems are arranged according to theme rather than order of composition.

(Autumn 1988) Juris Silenieks approved of Ivaska's decision to avoid a chronological presentation: "Such ordering would not be very relevant, since it would not reveal any discernible path from apprenticeship to mastery." None of the poems are apprentice works; all reveal a poet who has achieved mastery of her craft. Silenieks also noted Ivaska's use of "a panoply of forms, ranging from intimations of ancient folkloric rhythms to a kind of free verse, neither canonical nor ostentatiously avant-gardist."

A recurrent concern in the volume, as for many émigré writers, is the attempt to make sense of the experience of exile. A key difference from much émigré writing, however, is Ivaska's refusal to acquiesce in a simple dualism of Latvia as a childhood paradise and the fallen state of the present. Her cosmopolitan life, her contacts with writers of many nations, and her extensive travels result in a richer, subtler, and more differentiated treatment of the exile experience in which past and present are not sharply divided from each other but are brought together in a single vision. This "seeing-together" of present and past is exemplified in "Rīgas aizkari" (Riga Curtains):

In the new house, we put up
the Riga curtains, long unused.
Eating breakfast and supper,
we look at the elm on the lawn,
at the flowerpots and the street
through the curtains mother made:
winged   hunters   deer
lions   quick   fauns
peacocks   little dogs   songbirds
much   tinier   dogs
all of it woven into the net, fished
from some ancient windstill depth.
We ponder this catch,
and every morning we look
into the face of the world
through Riga curtains.

This artifact made by her mother helps the poet and her husband filter the exile experience through a personal, ethnic, and even mythical background. Like the palindrome *Solis silos,* the pattern in the curtain can be read from left to right, or right to left; it can also be read downward or upward. As she does so often, the poet forces the reader to remain open to various possibilities.

Language is another recurrent theme in the volume; Ivaska is at home in many languages and is familiar with the literatures written in them and the traditions and cultures from which the literatures come. "Valoda, tu esi koks" (Language, you are a tree) shows her sense of the relatedness of all languages:

> Language, you are a tree,—we the leaves,
> torn in the wind. Wherever each has wafted,
> we have no strength to return.
> Words remain, gates remain,
> a linden alley, a hedge of fir,
> crabapple tree, crooked birch.
> Roads remain, tracks remain,
> trod before us in the clay,
> the tracks of words in memory.
> Language, you are a many-branched tree,—
> we the birds. And when night comes
> we all tumble into your branches.

Ivaska has also written with great success for children, contributing to the émigré childrens' journal *Mazputniņš* (Little Bird) and publishing a volume of poems and stories for children, *Pārsteigumi un atklājumi* (Surprises and Discoveries, 1984), which was awarded the Goppers Prize. She has worked on the editorial boards of several émigré journals, notably *Jaunā Gaita* (New Way) and *Ceļa Zīmes* (Road Marks). Her translations of poetry from English into Latvian, which include work by Robert Lowell, Elizabeth Bishop, John Ashbery, and Gary Snyder, have appeared in various publications, most frequently in *Jaunā Gaita.* She has also translated poetry from Estonian, Finnish, Lithuanian, Russian, and Spanish into Latvian. Her translations of German and Baltic-language poetry into English have appeared in *Dimension, Lituanus, The Literary Review,* and *Teutonic Literature.* Ivaska has written on Latvian literature in the *Encyclopedia of World Literature in the Twentieth Century* and has been a frequent reviewer for *World Literature Today.* Her poetry is often anthologized and has appeared in translation in Estonian, Finnish, French, German, Icelandic, Irish, Italian, Lithuanian, Romanian, Spanish, and Swedish.

The collection *Oklahoma Poems* (1990), a sampler of Ivaska's poetry written in English, deals with the Oklahoma landscape and weather and her neighbors in Norman. Longing for her childhood in Latvia surfaces in a poem dedicated to "Irene, Lightning Girl, descendant of White Turtle." Other poems about Native Americans reveal a sense of kinship based on the shared experience of being robbed of one's language and culture and being colonized. In "For Louis Little Coon Oliver" Ivaska fears for the survival of the Indian poet's language: "I went away wondering whether your words / would ever emerge and be heard again, / your Creek words, or whether / they would go home with you forever." In "Talking with Linda Hogan" Ivaska identifies strongly with the "Chickasaw poet, Oklahoma poet" as she writes: "Linda, let us go together / to find the resting places / of our fathers, to gather / their scattered bones. / Yours lost on trails of tears, / mine on treks of death." Other poems mourn friends lost to death and celebrate the time spent with them. In "Sun in Leo" she finds an almost haiku-like formulation for the state of mind of a poet who refuses, on the one hand, to be frozen into nostalgia and, on the other, to embrace an easy forgetfulness: "We should not forget, / nor must we remember. / The poem alights / somewhere in between."

Ivaska and her husband moved to Ireland in 1991. Ivar Ivask died on 23 September 1992, soon after they had moved into their home, "Baltica," in the County Cork countryside. Much of Ivaska's time since then has been devoted to managing her husband's literary estate, but she continues to write. Among her projects is a memoir of her childhood, especially the idyllic summers spent at the family estate, Lestene, in Courland. She has taken an active interest in Irish history, poetry, and art and is a member of the Irish Writers' Union.

Interview:

Anita Rožkalne, "Mes no sakta gala esam jau tas . . . ," *Karogs,* 8 (August 1996): 118–142.

References:

Jānis Andrups, "Aizvalodas Dzeja," *Ceļa Zīmes,* 44 (1970): 62–67;

Andrups, "Intensīvais Dzejas Vārds," *Ceļa Zīmes,* 53 (1973): 317–319;

Andrups, "Līču Loki," *Ceļa Zīmes,* 62 (1982): 76–77;

Indra Avena, "Valodas un stila īpatnības Astrīdes Ivaskas 'Līču lokos,'" in *Zari,* edited by Velta Ruke-Dravina (Stockholm: Riksby Tryck, 1983), pp. 32–49;

Alfrēds Gāters, "Dzīvot pretī mūžībai," *Latvija,* 12 December 1981, p. 2;

Elza Jaunzeme, "Mūslaiku modernā dzeja un Astrīdes Ivaskas dzejas māksla," *Akadēmiskā Dzīve,* 31 (1989): 51–55;

Mirdza Krastiņa, "Balto īrisu gaismā," *Latvija,* 17 January 1983, p. 2;

Anda Kubuliņa, "Astrīde Ivaska," *Grāmata,* 11 (November 1990): 65–67;

Mārtiņš Lasmanis, "Apdraudētais līdzsvars," *Laiks,* 9 July 1988, p. 2;

Gundars Pļavkalns, "Astrīde Ivaska un Istenības poēzija," *Laras Lapa,* 28 (1982): 18–21;

Pļvavkalns, "Iedaba un māksla," *Jaunā Gaita,* 172 (April 1989): 56–59;

Jānis Rudzītis, "Atgriešanās pie Dabas un Īstenības" and "Ziemas Tiesa," in his *Raksti* (Copenhagen: Ziemedblāzma, 1997), pp. 711–712, 713–714;

Sniedze Ruņģe, "Slepenā skaņu mijiedarbe," *Grāmata,* 11 (1990): 67–72;

Gunars Saliņš, "'Pirtī runāsi somiski,'" *Laras Lapa,* 28 (1982): 15–18;

Rimvydas Šilbajoris, "Tēvzeme, zeme un mīlestība: Janinas Degutytes un Astrīdes Ivaskas poezijā," *Latvijas Zinātņu Akademijas Vēstis,* 537 (1992): 36–39;

Juris Silenieks, "Astrīde Ivaska, *Vārdojums: Dzejoļu izlase, 1951–1987,*" *World Literature Today,* 62 (Autumn 1988): 699–700;

Nora Valtere, "Astrīde Ivaska–Gaisma ievainoja," *Laiks,* 1 December 1963, pp. 3–7;

Valtere, "Astrīde Ivaska–Līču Loki," *Laiks,* 16 December 1981, p. 2;

Valtere, "Atmatas malā," *Laiks,* 6 June 1981, p. 2;

Valtere, "Īstenības tvērums," *Ceļa Zīmes,* 49 (1972): 403–436;

Valtere, "Ziemas Tiesa–Astrīde Ivaska," *DV Mēnešraksts,* 4 (1969): 60–61;

Pēteris Zirnītis, "Uguns kā liktens deg," *Karogs,* 7 (1989): 141–143.

Jaan Kaplinski
(22 January 1941 –   )

Ele Süvalep
University of Tartu

BOOKS: *Jäljed allikal* (Tallinn: Eesti Raamat, 1965);
Kalad punuvad pesi (Tallinn: Eesti NSV Riiklik Kunstiinstituut, 1966);
Tolmust ja värvidest (Tallinn: Perioodika, 1967);
Valge joon Võrumaa kohale: 54 luuletust 1967–1968 (Tallinn: Eesti Raamat, 1972);
Kuhu need värvid jäävad, by Kaplinski and Tiia Toomet (Tallinn: Eesti Raamat, 1975);
Ma vaatasin päikese aknasse: Luulet (Tallinn: Eesti Raamat, 1976);
Uute kivide kasvamine (Tallinn: Eesti Raamat, 1977);
Kes mida sööb, kes keda sööb (Tallinn: Eesti Raamat, 1977);
Udujutt (Tallinn: Eesti Raamat, 1977);
Jänes (Tallinn: Perioodika, 1980);
Karusellharen: En tecknad filmsaga (Tallinn: Perioodika, 1982);
Raske on kergeks saada (Tallinn: Eesti Raamat, 1982);
Olemisen avara hiljaisuus: Esseitä ihmisestä, luonnosta, runoudesta (Helsinki: Otava, 1982);
Tule tagasi helmemänd (Tallinn: Eesti Raamat, 1984);
Õhtu toob tagasi kõik (Tallinn: Eesti Raamat, 1985);
Jalgrataste talveuni (Tallinn: Eesti Raamat, 1987);
Kust tuli öö: Proosat (Tallinn: Eesti Raamat, 1990);
Vieläkö Tartossa laulaa satakieli: Kirjeenvaihto, by Kaplinski and Johannes Salminen (Helsinki: Tammi, 1990);
Hinge tagasitulek: Poeem (Tallinn: Eesti Raamat, 1990);
Tükk elatud elu: Tekste 1986–1989 (Tartu: Eesti Kostabi Selts, 1991); translated by Hildi Hawkins as *Through the Forest: Poems* (London: Harvill, 1996);
I Am the Spring in Tartu and Other Poems Written in English, edited, with an introduction, by Laurence P. A. Kitching (Vancouver, B.C.: Laurel Press, 1991);
Poliitika ja antipoliitika (Tallinn: Olion, 1992);
Teekond Ayia Triadasse (Tartu: Greif, 1993);
Jää ja Titanic (Tallinn: Perioodika, 1995);

Jaan Kaplinski (photograph by Arno Saar Foto)

Mitu suve ja kevadet: Luulet ja märkmeid, as Kai Pu Lin, with calligraphy by Peng Lin (Tallinn: Vagabund, 1995);
See ja teine (Tartu: Tartu Ülikooli Kirjastus, 1996);
Võimaluste võimalikkus (Tallinn: Vagabund, 1997);
Öölinnud, öömõtted=Yölintuja, yöajatuksiä=Night Birds, Night Thoughts: Luuletusi 1995–1997, edited by Riina Tamm, Fiona Sampson, and Anja Salokannel (Tallinn: Vagabund, 1998);

Usk on uskmatus (Tallinn: Vagabund, 1998);
Silm; Hektor (Tallinn: Tänapäev, 2000);
Kevad kahel rannikul ehk Tundeline teekond Ameerikasse (Tallinn: Vagabund, 2000).
Collection: *Käoraamat: Luulet 1956–1980* (Tallinn: Eesti Raamat, 1986).
Editions in English: *The New Heaven and Earth of Jaan Kaplinski: Poems,* translated by Ants Eert, edited by Lars Nordstrom (Portland, Ore.: Portland State University Poetry Committee, 1981);
The Same Sea in Us All: Poems, translated by Kaplinski and Sam Hamill (Mission, B.C.: Barbarian Press, 1985; Portland, Ore.: Breitenbush Books, 1985; London: Collins-Harvill, 1990);
The Wandering Border: Poems, translated by Kaplinski, Hamill, and Riina Tamm (Port Townsend, Wash.: Copper Canyon Press, 1987; London: Harvill, 1992);
A Language I Do Not Know: Poems, translated by Kaplinski, illustrated by Edda Renouf (Edinburgh: Morning Star Publications, 1994).

PLAY PRODUCTIONS: *Põgenik,* Tallinn, Noorsooteater, 30 May 1976;
Neljakuningapäev, Tallinn, Draamateater, 25 February 1977;
Liblikas ja peegel, Viljandi, Ugala Theater, 7 March 1982;
Neljän kuninkaan päivä, Pori (Finland), Porin Teatteri, 19 September 1991.

OTHER: "Jutt kolmest astjast" and "Jutt ubaõiest ja tainakausist," in *13 autorit* (Tallinn: Ajalehtede-Ajakirjade Kirjastus, 1964), pp. 41–54;
Malek Haddad, *Viimne lehekülg,* translated by Nora Kaplinski, afterword by Jaan Kaplinski (Tallinn: Eesti Raamat, 1968);
"Laulude sünnimailt," in *Teose sünd,* edited by Endel Priidel (Tallinn: Eesti Raamat, 1976), pp. 108–117;
Kaljo Põllu, *Kodalased: 13 reproduktsiooni,* text by Kaplinski, preface by Ene Asu-Õunas and Ago Künnap (Tallinn: Kunst, 1978);
Torupill, haldjad ja hiiglased: iiri ja šoti rahvajutte, translated by Tiia Rinne, afterword by Kaplinski (Tallinn: Eesti Raamat, 1978);
Põllu, *Kalivägi: 25 reproduktsiooni: Metsotinto,* text by Kaplinski, preface by Asu-Õunas (Tallinn: Kunst, 1988);
Ex oriente: Tõlkekogumik, edited, with an introduction, by Kaplinski (Tallinn: Perioodika, 1989);
Viivi Luik, *Le septieme printemps de la paix: Roman,* translated by Antoine Chalvin, afterword by

Kaplinski (Paris: Christian Bourgois Éditeur, 1992);
Anne Nahkur, *Kirjandus: Õpik-lugemik 7: klassile,* edited by Tiiu Haljamaa, foreword by Kaplinski (Tallinn: Koolbri, 1996);
Selection of Estonian Radio Plays: Estonian Radio, Radio Drama Department, Estonian Radio Drama Cycle, introduction by Kaplinski and Mari Tuulik (Tallinn: Estonian Radio, 1996).

TRANSLATIONS: Eerik Teder, ed., *Vabaduskoidiku rütmid: Aafrika poeesiat,* translated by Kaplinski and others (Tallinn: Eesti Riiklik Kirjastus, 1964);
Andrzej Szczypiorski, *Minevik* (Tallinn: Perioodika, 1965);
Teder, ed., *Antillide luulet,* translated by Kaplinski and others (Tallinn: Eesti Raamat, 1966);
Miguel Otero Silva, *Surnud majad: Romaan* (Tallinn: Eesti Raamat, 1966);
Stanislaw Lem, *Ijon Tichy mälestused,* translated, with an afterword, by Kaplinski (Tallinn: Perioodika, 1967);
André Gide, *Halvasti aheldatud Prometheus* (Tallinn: Perioodika, 1969);
Nelly Sachs, *Eeli: Müsteerium Iisraeli kannatustest* (Tallinn: Perioodika, 1971);
T. S. Eliot, *Valik esseid,* translated by Kaplinski and Jaak Rähesoo (Tallinn: Perioodika, 1973);
Octavio Paz, *Alati on olevik,* translated by Kaplinski, Ain Kaalep, Asta Põldmäe, and Jüri Talvet (Tallinn: Perioodika, 1984);
Täiskuutaeva all: Valimik hiina ja jaapani luulet, translated by Kaplinski and Rein Raud (Tallinn: Perioodika, 1985);
Suve tagasitoomine: Põhja-Ameerika indiaanlaste muinasjutte (Tallinn: Kunst, 1986);
Thomas Tranströmer, *Luulet* (Tallinn: Eesti Raamat, 1989);
Kai Laitenen, Satu Apo, and Gun Herranen, *Soome kirjanduse ajalugu: Kai Laitenen; Soome rahvaluule: Satu Apo; Soome rootsikeelne rahvaluule: Gun Herranen,* translated by Kaplinski, Piret Saluri, Ruth Mirov, and Joel Sang (Tallinn: Vagabund, 1994);
Hans Hattenhauer, *Euroopa õiguse ajalugu: 1. raamat,* edited by Peeter Järvelaid, translated by Kaplinski, Marju Luts, and Jaan Sootak (Tartu: Fontes Iuris, 1995);
Alain Fournier, *Minu sõber suur Meaulnes,* translated by Kaplinski and Nora Kaplinski (Tallinn: Perioodika, 1996);

Georg Henrik von Wright, *Minerva öökull*, translated by Kaplinski and others (Tallinn: Vagabund, 1996);

Knuts Skujenieks and Guntars Godiņš, eds., *Läti uuema luule valimik*, translated by Kaplinski and others (Tallinn: Eesti Raamat, 1997).

SELECTED PERIODICAL PUBLICATIONS–
UNCOLLECTED: "Kalad punuvad pesi," *Mana 33* (1968): 14–17;

"Kirjanduse tähendusest," *Looming* (March 1968): 432–441;

"Eelarvamused ja eetika," *Looming* (December 1968): 1861–1865;

"Parallelismist lingvisti pilguga," *Keel ja Kirjandus* (February 1972): 132–145;

"Mõtisklusi inimkultuurist ja ökosüsteemidest," *Eesti Loodus* (July 1973): 433–437; (August 1973): 502–508; (September 1973): 569–574;

"Põgenik," *Looming* (March 1974): 434–450;

"Mis on luule?" *Looming* (December 1975): 2069–2079;

"Interpretatsioone ja impressioone viimase veerandsajandi luuleilmast," *Keel ja Kirjandus* (May 1983): 232–240;

"Jää ja kanarbik. Migrandi märkmeid," *Looming* (November 1989): 1443–1457.

Jaan Kaplinski is one of the leading poets and essayists in contemporary Estonian literature; his works have gained recognition abroad and have been translated into several languages. Kaplinski belongs to the generation that entered the literary scene in the 1960s, a period of political liberalization in the Soviet Union, which had annexed Estonia in 1940. The 1960s were also a period of radical renewal in Estonian poetry, brought about by a young, better educated, and more sophisticated generation of authors. Kaplinski has been a significant innovator of poetic form and language and has enriched Estonian poetry and widened its range primarily as a result of his knowledge of Far Eastern cultures. As a versatile author, he has also written fiction and drama. Since the end of the 1980s, when the Soviet Union began disintegrating, and especially since 1991, when Estonia regained its independence, Kaplinski's essays have played an important role in Estonian society and politics.

Jaan Kaplinski was born on 22 January 1941 in Tartu, the old university town of southern Estonia. He was the only child of Jerzy and Nora Kaplinski. His Polish father taught his native language and literature at the University of Tartu, while his Estonian mother was a dancer who had lived in Paris and who became a translator and teacher of French after World War II. The time of Kaplinski's birth and childhood was a tragic period in Estonian history. In June 1940 the Soviet Union occupied the country, and within twelve months killed, deported, or forcibly conscripted into the Red Army close to sixty thousand individuals. Kaplinski's father was arrested in June 1941 by the NKVD (the Soviet secret police), accused of anti-Soviet activity, and deported to a labor camp in the Soviet Union. His subsequent fate, including the time and circumstances of his death, is unknown. In August 1941 the German army invaded Estonia, annexing the country into the Third Reich. In the autumn of 1944, with the collapse of the Third Reich, Estonia returned to the iron grip of Stalinist Russia.

Kaplinski spent the first years of his life at his grandfather's house near Tartu. In 1943 the house was requisitioned for the use of the German military, and the family moved to Tartu, only to experience frequent bombing raids from the Soviet air force. The apartment, with all the books, art works, and furniture, was destroyed by bombs, and Kaplinski had to adjust to life in war-torn Tartu. He was a lonely and sensitive boy and was often ill. His most beautiful childhood memories are of the summers spent with relatives in the southern Estonian district of Võrumaa, where he enjoyed the peace of rural life. In addition to books, which Kaplinski discovered early, contact with nature was important for his development.

From 1947 to 1958 Kaplinski attended Tartu's Secondary School No. 1, formerly the historical Treffner Gymnasium, where many Estonian writers had studied. It had been Sovietized, but the faculty included several prewar teachers who tried to uphold old standards. While under their tutelage, Kaplinski began to write poems at age thirteen. He took for his models two Romantic poets, the Russian Mikhail Lermontov and the Englishman Percy Bysshe Shelley, whose works he tried to read in the original languages. Kaplinski has also acknowledged the influence of French symbolists (such as Charles Baudelaire and Arthur Rimbaud) and the Anglo-American poet T. S. Eliot. Of Estonian poets, Juhan Liiv and the 1930s group known as the *Arbujad* (Logomancers)—Betti Alver, Heiti Talvik, August Sang—have left their imprint on his work.

In the fall of 1958 Kaplinski enrolled at the University of Tartu. He studied French philology and structural and mathematical linguistics, continued to learn new languages, and was interested in philosophy, religion, and history. At the same time, he became personally acquainted with erudite

Kaplinski with his mother, Nora, in the garden of his grandfather's house near Tartu in the summer of 1943

humanists of the older generation, the most important of whom was the theologian and poet Uku Masing. Masing's original and liberal approach to Christianity and its relationship to other, especially Eastern, religions deeply influenced young Kaplinski and led him to study Asian cultures. Buddhism and the literatures and philosophies of China, India, and other Asian countries have played a decisive role in the formation of Kaplinski's views on life and in shaping his poetry.

Kaplinski's first poems were written in the 1950s. These works are mostly romantic outpourings, dealing with sadness, loneliness, and the poet's longing for something more beautiful and free than everyday dullness. The best of these poems were published in the 1960s. Kaplinski's outstanding book of this period is *Tolmust ja värvidest* (1967). His first published poem, "Tervitus tulevikku" (Greeting the Future), dated 1959, appeared in the university newspaper *Tartu Riiklik Ülikool* (Tartu State University) and showed a belief in social progress. Thus, the optimism of the period of

Soviet premier Nikita Khruschev's political "thaw" had also influenced him.

Kaplinski graduated from the University of Tartu in 1964. That same year he married Küllike Kolk, and his first child, a handicapped daughter, Maarja, was born. (In 1969 the marriage ended in divorce.) In 1964 Kaplinski also published two short stories in a collection of work by young writers, *13 autorit* (13 Authors). From 1964 to 1968 he worked at the university computer center while continuing to write. Despite personal problems, this period proved to be a fruitful one for him. As his lyric gifts grew, he gradually won acceptance as a poet to be reckoned with. He also translated from French, Spanish, and other languages, and at the end of the 1960s he began to publish critical essays about literature and culture.

Kaplinski's first collection of poems, *Jäljed allikal* (Tracks at the Spring), appeared in 1965 as part of a boxed set of slim volumes by fledgling authors. Such a slip-case method of publishing the first books of young writers, mostly poets, was repeatedly used in Estonia in the 1960s. Many talented newcomers, among them Paul-Eerik Rummo, Viivi Luik, Hando Runnel, and others, made their literary debuts in this way. Kaplinski's first volume of verse reveals social concerns characteristic of the period as well as typically lyric qualities. He writes about the richness of the life around him and uses free verse, as in the poem "Maast, veest ja mitmest muust asjast" (About Earth, Water, and Many Other Things). His vision of all-embracing nature and its continuous cycle points toward a theme to which Kaplinski has returned many times. *Jäljed allikal* received a mixed critical reception, no doubt colored by political and ideological attitudes prevalent at the time. Some reviewers objected specifically to his superior, even contemptuous attitude toward mankind. In fact, the poet expresses man's sense of guilt. In his opinion, being human is not always something to be proud of, especially when considering man's relationship with nature in general and animals in particular.

A second collection of Kaplinski's poems, *Kalad punuvad pesi* (Fish Weave Nests), was published in 1966. It had original drawings by a young artist, Enno Otsing, and was printed in only fifteen copies, thus becoming immediately a bibliophilic rarity. The volume includes some remarkable poems that have not appeared in Kaplinski's other collections, but these have been reprinted in the Estonian exile cultural journal *Mana* in North America. In such untitled poems (that begin with capitalized words) as "KÕIK MAGAVAD" (All Sleep) or "KULTUUR ON" (Culture Is) the poet returns to the expression of guilt, now in the form of an accusation against the "great men" of history whose greedy or colonialist-expansionist actions have destroyed a host of small nations and innumerable old cultures. These verses form a link with the poems published in Kaplinski's next collection, *Tolmust ja värvidest* (Of Dust And Color), which appeared in 1967 and is the most widely known of his works. The volume includes exceptionally powerful imagery that communicates two basic areas of concern: nature and civilization.

Tolmust ja värvidest reveals a Whitmanesque respect for nature. Kaplinski observes in *The Same Sea in Us All: Poems* (1985) that nature can produce events of cosmic proportions, as, for example, the Creation: the boundless night gives birth to "something utterly new." But there are also small "blades of grass"—the flowers, insects, and jellyfish that are as important as the more majestic aspects of nature. In *Tolmust ja värvidest* the cosmos and the grain of sand are both a part of the same whole, or,

as Kaplinski phrases it, "IN EVERY EYE / of every globe-flower / last year's sun rises / and silently watches / with its own eyes. . . ." The eternal cycle of nature, of deaths and rebirths, constitutes the essence of that world: "NEW BUTTERFLIES ARE MADE of dust and color, but we / are planted in the ground like broken bones to replace ourselves." The "we" of these lines, though belonging to nature, as do the butterflies, clearly refers to humanity, but human beings as a rule are not satisfied with just being themselves. Instead, they endeavor to dominate nature as well as other humans. In Kaplinski's opinion, the bloody and tragic history of mankind is by and large the result of such striving, of being "civilized." The poet's critical attitude toward the human world is best summed up by the verses that begin with "VERCINGETORIX SAID: Caesar, you can take / the land where we live away from us, / but you cannot take the land from us where we have died." The poet laments here, as he does elsewhere, not only the fate of the Gauls who were conquered by Caesar but also that of the American Indians, the ancient Livonians and Estonians, and every other small culture that has been swallowed up by more powerful civilizations. But even in this context the answer may lie with nature, which has the power to redeem man and his bloody history. As Kaplinski puts it in the concluding line of "WHITE CLOVER ASKS NOTHING": "crimson was the question green is the answer."

Though Kaplinski speaks about the unity of everything that exists, he sees and depicts two different universes. Influenced by Eastern thought and the folklore of American Indians, he projects an ideal world of natural harmony, which is opposed by materialistic and militaristic values. This sharp conflict makes his poetry ecologically fashionable today. However, at the time of publication, his verses were seen as an allegory of the relationship of peaceful, rural Estonia—represented by Gaul—with the imperialistic new Rome, that is, the U.S.S.R. This reading accounts, perhaps, for the remarkably lively critical reception of *Tolmust ja värvidest*, making its author one of the best-known Estonian poets. But there were aesthetic reasons as well, for Kaplinski had succeeded in renewing the form and language of Soviet Estonian poetry. He boldly uses free verse, but the collection also includes metrically controlled ballads and songs. His images are obviously based on free association, but there is usually an underlying ideational structure. He does not as a rule use punctuation marks or titles, and the first lines of poems are marked by capital letters (though in later collections he reverts to a more traditional approach).

The "dust and color verses" of *Tolmust ja värvidest* were awarded the Juhan Liiv prize for the best Estonian poem published in 1967. In 1968, Kaplinski was admitted to the Estonian Writers' Union. In the same year his first two comprehensive essays, "Kirjanduse tähendusest" (On the Meaning of Literature) and "Eelarvamused ja eetika" (Prejudices and Ethics) were published in the literary magazine *Looming* (Creation). The first of these essays attempts to answer age-old questions: what is literature? why do people need it? what will its future be like? The second investigates the relationship between man and nature. Kaplinski supports and explicates Albert Schweitzer's views, finding that man's relationship with other creatures should be based on the same principles as relationships between people. This essay marks as well the starting point of ecological awareness in Estonia.

In 1969 Kaplinski married Tiia Toomet, a poet and writer of children's books as well as director of the Tartu Toy Museum. They have four children of their own—sons Ott-Siim, Lauris, and Lemmit, and daughter Elo-Mall—and Kaplinski's daughter from his first marriage has also grown up in their family. In 1970 he bought an old farmhouse in southern Estonia, and this house is where Kaplinski prefers to spend his time, for his hobbies are mostly connected with nature: he has planted about a hundred different species of trees and shrubs on his land. However, Kaplinski has had to spend a great deal of time in town. From 1968 to 1972 he did postgraduate work at or was employed by the University of Tartu, dealing with problems of language, and writing about linguistics, literature, and culture. In 1972 the publication of a collection of his essays was blocked by the Soviet authorities, but he had better luck with his verse; that year a new volume of poetry, *Valge joon Võrumaa kohale: 54 luuletust 1967–1968* (A White Line Over Võrumaa: 54 Poems 1967–1968), was published. It includes poems written immediately after the publication of his previous collection. However, the dominant tone of the new poems is quite different from those in the previous book— they are more intimate, restrained, and melancholy. The poet is moving in more-restrictive surroundings, in the middle of everyday life and its tensions. The vision of the possibilities of harmony expressed in *Tolmust ja värvidest* is now overshadowed by feelings of grief and doubt. Still, the redeeming power of nature has not totally disappeared. In *Valge joon Võrumaa kohale: 54 luuletust 1967–1968*, Kaplinski writes, "All that is worth to be believed in is found

somewhere." The collection is remarkably unified, the diction simple and concise, the poems without titles and punctuation (but the capital letters have disappeared), forming a harmonious whole.

Kaplinski worked as a freelance writer and translator in Tartu until 1974, at which time he moved to Tallinn and worked there until 1980 as a researcher at the Botanical Gardens. He continued to write articles and essays, though some of these works remained unpublished until 1996. In the mid 1970s he returned to belletristic prose. Some autobiographical short stories, written in 1973, appeared in *Kust tuli öö: Proosat* (Whence the Night: Prose, 1990). A story of another kind, "Põgenik" (Fugitive), published in *Looming* (1974), is an inner monologue of a young man escaping both from his pursuers and his bad conscience at the time of serfhood, when peasant women were subjected to extreme forms of manorial sexual harassment. Defending his girl, the youth had reason enough to attack the bailiff of the estate, but he is now wondering if it is right to kill another human being. A surprise ending reveals that the man may be mad. The monologue was performed at the Noorsooteater (Youth Theater) of Tallinn in 1976.

The following year the Draamateater (Drama Theater) in Tallinn staged Kaplinski's first original play, *Neljakuningapäev* (The Day of the Four Kings), in which the past is even more important than in the earlier work. *Neljakuningapäev* is a play within a play about one of the most tragic events of medieval Estonian history. In 1343, during the St. George's Night Rebellion, four Estonian rebel leaders, or "kings," as they are called in the chronicles, were treacherously killed while negotiating with the occupying Germans. In *Neljakuningapäer* a group of wandering actors arrives in the town where the kings were murdered and enacts the story. The fate of the four kings is not only emblematic of the fate of the Estonian nation, but also suggests the defeat of life's positive values, which Kaplinski had been proclaiming in his poetry. The kings want to live a peaceful, nonaggressive life in accordance with nature, only to exist, to be what they are. It becomes evident, however, that such dreams are in collision not only with historical wars of conquest but also with modern materialism and greed. *Neljakuningapäev*, which has had revivals in Estonia, has also been staged in Finland.

In addition to prose fiction and drama, Kaplinski wrote several books for children and published two collections of verse in the 1970s. *Ma vaatasin päikese aknasse: Luulet* (I Looked into the Sun's Window: Poetry, 1976) includes previously unpublished poems from the 1960s. *Uute kivide kasvamine* (New Stones Growing, 1977) is composed of many new and remarkable poems, especially in the cycle titled "Seesama meri meis kõigis" (The Same Sea in Us All). The poet has now become an observer of "the little / flowing / world" of everyday life and speaks plainly about his perceptions, sometimes like a child looking for the exact word. The poems have extremely short lines, usually consisting of one or two words, suggesting the slow process that leads to recognition, to an epiphany, as in: "THE SAME / SEA / in us all / red / dark / warm / / throbbing / winds from / every quarter / in the sails / of the heart. . . ."

From 1980 to 1982 Kaplinski worked as a literary adviser at the Ugala Theater in Viljandi, where his play *Liblikas ja peegel* (The Butterfly and the Mirror) was staged in 1982. This work deals with a marriage triangle as well as with some of the problems of the contemporary urban world. However, it ends on a note of resolution, which can be found also in his next collection of poetry, *Raske on kergeks saada* (It Is Hard to Become Light, 1982). Undoubtedly influenced by Buddhist beliefs, the poet is now saying that it is possible to find the gift of happiness almost anywhere. Love, family, and home assume a central place in this volume, and the child sleeping in the poet's lap is more important than the abstractions of destiny, nation, or culture. However, this inner peace and balance has not come easily, as the title of the collection suggests, and the new poems seem to be less polished than in his previous collections.

From 1983 to 1988 Kaplinski worked again at the University of Tartu, teaching courses on translation. During this period he published three books of verse: *Tule tagasi helmemänd* (Come Back, Amber-Pine, 1984), *Õhtu toob tagasi kõik* (Evening Brings Everything Back, 1985) and *Käoraamat: Luulet 1956–1980* (The Cuckoo's Book: Poems 1956–1980, 1986). This last book—the title of which can be read as meaning either "Cuckoo's Book" or indicating a species of orchid—is a collection of poems from earlier volumes. Kaplinski's changed attitude and mood of expression are evident in the second collection, *Õhtu toob tagasi kõik*. The poet's peace of mind has deepened, and his acceptance of the world has grown. Because of that, he can see "the openness of things" as he concentrates on the minutiae of everyday existence, on the changing seasons, on family life, though, as Kaplinski writes in *Õhtu toob tagasi kõik*, the "laundry never gets done" and the "books never get read." The poet's keener understanding of the mundane world finds expres-

Dust jacket for Kaplinski's 1976 collection of verse

sion in simple declarative sentences that begin to sound like ordinary prose.

The other new collection, *Tule tagasi helmemänd*, can be said to be, at least in part, a return to Kaplinski's earlier themes. The amber-pine of the title of the book (and of the first cycle of poems) is an extinct species of conifer. Kaplinski is here yearning for the lost state of edenic beauty and freedom. Some of the poems, however, express his acceptance of everyday life, persons, and things, as does, for example, the one that begins "My son can eat his porridge all by himself," but Kaplinski keeps returning to his longing for the mystery and majesty of primeval nature. The formal aspects of his verse have also reverted to earlier patterns of Estonian poetry, the traditional quatrains of (mostly) trochaic trimeter or tetrameter. The last part of the collection is a long prose poem, "Luuletamise kunstist" (On the Art of Poetry), an example of the Chinese *fu* genre of rhetorical prose poems.

There have been translations of Kaplinski's poems since the 1960s, but these were usually of single poems and were printed in periodicals or anthologies. In the 1980s collections of his poems began to appear in the United States. *The Same Sea in Us All: Poems* (1985) and *The Wandering Border: Poems* (1987) have received the most attention. Collections of Kaplinski's poetry have also appeared in Swedish, Czech, Finnish, Russian, Norwegian, Polish, and Japanese translations. Kaplinski's first collection of essays, *Olemise avara hiljaisuus: Esseitä ihmisestä, luonnosta, runoudesta* (Spacious Silence of Being: Essays on Man, Nature, Poetry), appeared in Finland in 1982, years before he was allowed to publish anything similar in Estonia.

The late 1980s were a period of radical political change in Estonia. When Mikhail Gorbachev came to power in 1985, liberalization began in the U.S.S.R. Its full impact reached Estonia in 1987–1988 and led to a struggle for total freedom. Kaplinski had published political commentary in newspapers and journals since 1987, and in 1992, one year after Estonia regained independence, he collected these articles into *Poliitika ja antipoliitika* (Politics and Anti-Politics). Kaplinski's cultural essays from such journals as *Vikerkaar* (Rainbow) and *Akadeemia* (Academy) are often occasioned by current political problems, but their treatment embraces larger, mostly aesthetic and philosophical, domains. Most of these were collected in *See ja teine* (This and That, 1996). Kaplinski's political activity was not limited to his writings, however. In 1992 he was elected a member of the Riigikogu, the Parliament of the Republic of Estonia, where he served until 1995.

The political situation in the second half of the 1980s enabled Kaplinski, like so many others, to travel abroad. Since then he has been often to Scandinavia, Western Europe, and North America, and he has also visited the sites of several ancient cultures, particularly those in Greece and China. There are many comments about his trips scattered throughout his writings, but his most extensive travel book is *Teekond Ayia Triadasse* (Journey to Ayia Triada, 1993), describing his visit to Crete. It is not a traditional travelogue, however, as much of it deals with myths and various cultural phenomena as well as with his private thoughts. Kaplinski's later works are a peculiar synthesis of fiction and nonfiction. A relatively straightforward volume is *Kust tuli öö*, which includes autobiographical short stories about his childhood and an approach to the psychology of artistic creation. A year later his "Jää ja kanarbik" (Ice and Heather), a semiscientific evocation of the world before the last ice age, appeared in *Looming*. In 1995 he published *Jää ja Titanic* (Ice and the Titanic), probably the most representative example

of this kind of writing. Its documentary leitmotif is the well-known sinking of the *Titanic*, which leads the writer to reflect on nature and civilization. The book has been translated into Finnish and Swedish.

Although prose makes up the greater part of Kaplinski's more recent work, he published several collections of poetry in the 1990s. *Hinge tagasitulek: Poeem* (Soul's Return: Long Poem, 1990), written in the 1970s, is a shaman's song calling back a soul, possibly that of his nation. *Tükk elatud elu: Tekste 1986–1989* (A Piece of Lived Life, 1991) was written in the 1980s. It comprises pictures of everyday life as well as meditations. At one point the author focuses on the relationship of poetry and life, considering questions such as: does writing "poems" necessarily create poetry? can a way of life become poetic? does genuine poetry need the application of "poetic techniques"? Kaplinski's views, influenced by Zen Buddhism, give interesting and original answers to these and other such questions. In 1996 this volume was translated into English by Hildi Hawkins and published in London as *Through the Forest: Poems*. A collection of English-language poetry, *I Am the Spring in Tartu and Other Poems Written in English*, was published in Canada in 1991. It deals with the timeless problems of man, nature, history, and society. *Mitu suve ja kevadet: Luulet ja märkmeid* (Several Summers and Springs: Poetry and Notes, 1995) includes both original poems by Kaplinski, who uses the pseudonym Kai Pu Lin, and those of the Chinese poet Su Dong Po in Kaplinski's translation. Several of Kaplinski's poems are rendered in Chinese calligraphy by Peng Lin. Kaplinski's contribution is formally restrained, mingling concrete social issues and subjective visions. The poems are dated as pages in a diary and untitled, full of references to political events and everyday situations, but above all they are the self-expressions of the poet, who stresses the inseparableness of man and the cosmos in laconic but searing images: "The center of the world is right here. / I am carrying it with me / as we all do. The center of the world / is thrust through me / like a pin through the body of an insect. / It hurts again and again. / The center of the world is painful; / it is the pain."

Kaplinski continues to receive recognition for his achievements. Since 1993 he has been a member of the Universal Academy of Cultures, and in 1997 he was awarded the Baltic Assembly Prize for literature. He will return to the University of Tarta for the 2000–2001 academic year as an "invited professor of liberal arts."

One of the few Estonians who have been nominated as candidates for the Nobel Prize in litera-

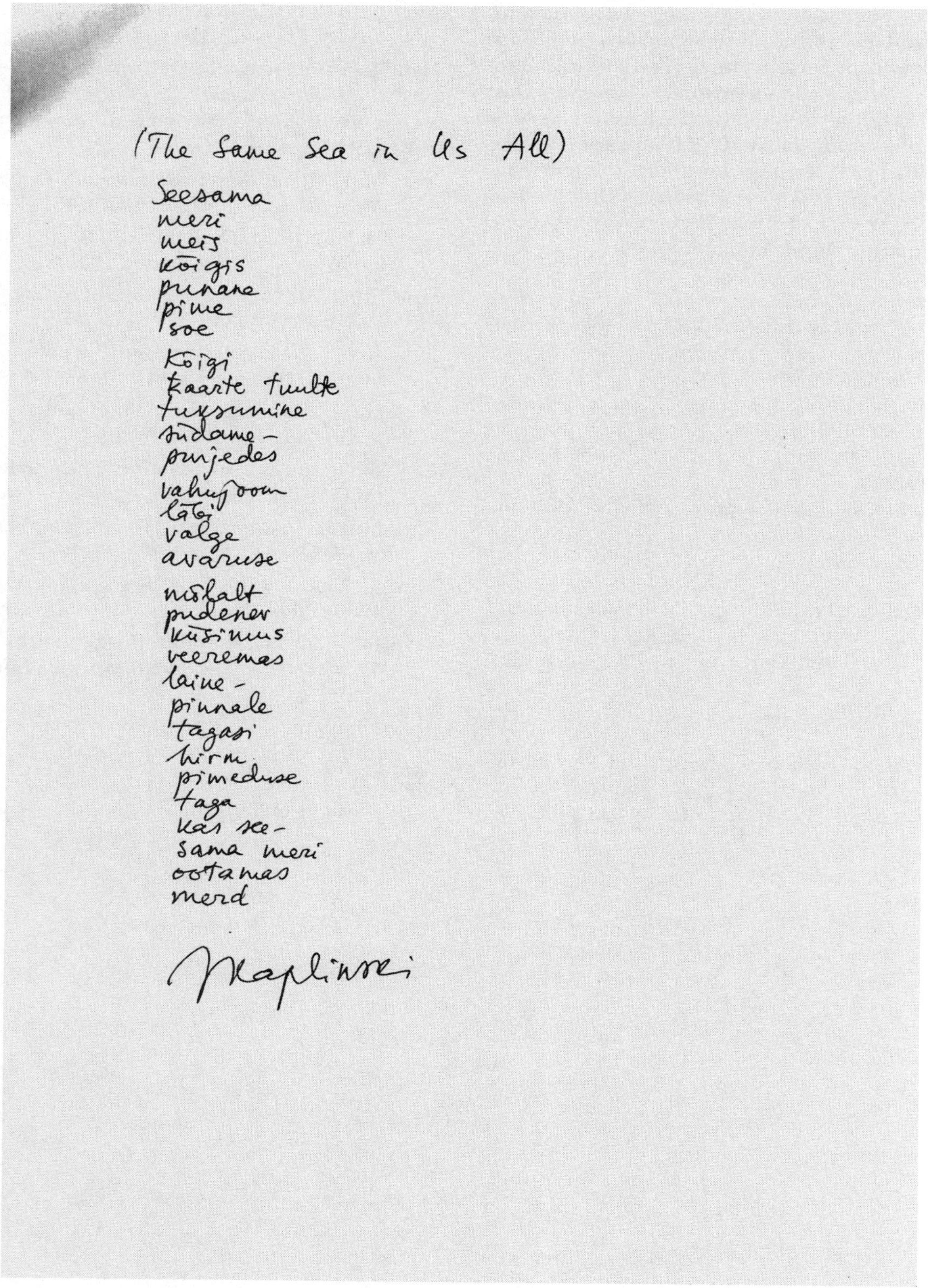

(The Same Sea in Us All)

Seesama
meri
meis
kõigis
punane
pime
soe

kõigi
kaarte tuulte
tuysumine
südame —
purjedes
vahujoom
lõtei
valge
avaruse

mõõalt
pudenev
küsimus
veeremas
laine —
pinnale
tagasi
hirm
pimeduse
taga
kas see —
sama meri
ootamas
merd

Kaplinski

Fair copy of the manuscript for Kaplinski's poem "The Same Sea in Us All" (Collection of Jaan Kaplinski)

ture, Jaan Kaplinski has written poetry, fiction, drama, and essays that form a unified whole in which dominant ideas, images, and attitudes are repeated, varied, and intertwined. However, this body of work is not a closed system. Kaplinski is constantly transcending all kinds of boundaries, for he is a mediator of world culture and the spirit of ancient Estonia. He is an erudite writer and thinker, but his poetry fascinates readers because of its intuitive wisdom and simple humanity.

Interviews:

"*Keele ja Kirjanduse* ringküsitlus kirjanikele: Jaan Kaplinski," *Keel ja Kirjandus* (November 1973): 684–686;

Märt Väljataga, "Kõigest eimidagi," *Keel ja Kirjandus* (January 1991): 39–41.

Bibliography:

Oskar Kruus, ed., *Eesti kirjarahva leksikon* (Tallinn: Eesti Raamat, 1995), pp. 182–183.

Biography:

Silvia Nagelmaa, "Jaan Kaplinski," in *Eesti kirjanduse ajalugu,* volume 5, book 2, edited by Maie Kalda (Tallinn: Eesti Raamat, 1991), pp. 499–506, 541.

References:

Hellar Grabbi, "For a New Heaven and New Earth: Comments on the Poetry of Jaan Kaplinski," *Books Abroad,* 47 (Autumn 1973): 658–663;

Ivar Grünthal, "Sähvatavad pinnad," *Mana 33* (1968): 123–125;

Henn-Kaarel Hellat, "Kõigel on kõigega seos," in *Kirjanduse jaosmaa '85,* edited by Endel Mallene (Tallinn: Eesti Raamat, 1987), pp. 123–129;

Ivar Ivask, "Jaan Kaplinski. *Tolmust ja värvidest,*" *Books Abroad,* 42 (Winter 1968): 159–160;

Ain Kaalep, "Kust eksib lapse naeratus kuningakotta," *Looming* (December 1967): 1912–1915;

Sirje Kiin, "All you need is love," *Looming* (August 1985): 1138–1141;

Hasso Krull, "Jaan Kaplinski teine ja pööratav aeg," *Vikerkaar* (February 1991): 81–83;

Mart Mäger, "Luule ja maailm ühes luuletuses," *Keel ja Kirjandus* (April 1985): 201–208;

Ene Mihkelson, "Vastandamine," *Keel ja Kirjandus* (May 1973): 304–305;

Karl Muru, "Ääremärkusi 'Käoraamatu' juurde," *Sirp ja Vasar,* 27 March 1987, p. 5;

Muru, "Jaan Kaplinski igatsused," *Looming* (May 1985): 700–702;

Sean O'Brien, "Vicissitudes of a Genial Estonian," *TLS: The Times Literary Supplement,* 5 June 1992, p. 22;

Terje Trubon, "Ida peegeldusi Jaan Kaplinski luules," *Keel ja Kirjandus* (May 1991): 272–282;

Mardi Valgemäe, "Tolmu ja värvide Kaplinski," *Mana 55* (1986): 30–38.

Ivan Klíma
(14 September 1931 –   )

Jiří Holý
Charles University, Prague

and

Jan Čulík
University of Glasgow

This entry originally appeared in Concise Dictionary of World Literary Biography:
South Slavic and Eastern European Writers.

BOOKS: *Bezvadný den* (Prague: Mladá fronta, 1960);
Mezi třemi hranicemi (Prague: Československý spisovatel, 1960);
Karel Čapek (Prague: Československý spisovatel, 1962; revised, 1965);
Hodina ticha (Prague: Československý spisovatel, 1963);
Milenci na jednu noc (Prague: Československý spisovatel, 1964);
Zámek (Prague: Orbis, 1964);
Kokrhací hodiny a jiné příběhy (Prague: Albatros, 1965);
Návštěva u nesmrtelné tetky: Polské zápisky (Prague: Mladá fronta, 1965);
Mistr (Prague: Orbis, 1967);
Porota (Prague: Dilia, 1968);
Klára a dva páni–Cukrárna Myriam (Prague: Dilia, 1968);
Loď jménem Naděje (Prague: Československý spisovatel, 1969);
Milenci na jeden den (Prague: Československý spisovatel, 1970; Purley, U.K.: Rozmluvy, 1985); translated by Gerald Turner as *Lovers for a Day* (New York: Grove, 1999);
Malomocní (Prague: Edice Petlice [samizdat edition], 1972);
Milostné léto (Prague: Edice Petlice [samizdat edition], 1972); translated into German by Alexandra and Gerhard Baumrucker as *Ein Liebessommer: Roman* (Lucerne: Bucher, 1973); original version republished (Toronto: Sixty-Eight Publishers, 1979);

Ivan Klíma (photograph by Nancy Crampton)

translated by Ewald Osers as *A Summer Affair* (London: Chatto & Windus, 1987);
Pokoj pro dva a jiné hry (Pokoj pro dva, Hromobití, Ministr a anděl) (Prague [samizdat edition], 1973); *Hromobití* translated into German by the Baumruckers as *Blitz und Donner* (Kassel-Wilhelmshöhe: Bärenreiter, 1973); excerpt from Czech version published as *Ministr a anděl* (Prague: Dilia, 1990);

Hry (Prague [samizdat edition], 1973); translated into German by the Baumruckers as *Spiele* (Kassel-Wilhelmshöhe: Bärenreiter, 1974);

Machtspiele, translated into German by the Baumruckers (Lucerne: Reich, 1977);

Amerika, by Klíma and Pavel Kohout, translated into German by the Baumruckers (Kassel-Wilhelmshöhe: Bärenreiter-Verlag, 1978); original Czech version published as *Amerika* (Prague: Dilia, 1991);

Kristinka und die Pferde, translated into German by Erika Homolka (Recklinghausen: Bitter, 1978; Vienna: Herold-Verlag, 1978);

Má veselá jitra (Prague: Edice Petlice [samizdat edition], 1978; Toronto: Sixty-Eight Publishers, 1979); translated by George Theiner as *My Merry Mornings: Stories from Prague* (London & New York: Readers International, 1985);

Der Gnadenrichter, translated into German by the Baumruckers, Christine Auras, and Helena Kolárová (Hamburg: Hoffmann & Campe / Lucerne: Reich, 1979); original Czech version published as *Soudce z milosti* (Purley, U.K.: Rozmluvy, 1986); translated by A. G. Brain [Alice and Gerald Turner] as *Judge on Trial* (London: Chatto & Windus, 1990; New York: Knopf, 1993);

Moje první lásky (Prague: Edice Petlice [samizdat edition], 1981; Toronto: Sixty-Eight Publishers, 1985); translated by Ewald Osers as *My First Loves* (London: Chatto & Windus, 1986; New York: Harper & Row, 1988);

Čekání na tmu, čekání na světlo (Prague: Edice Petlice [samizdat edition], 1982; revised edition, Prague: Český spisovatel, 1993); translated by Paul Wilson as *Waiting for the Dark, Waiting for the Light* (London: Granta in association with Penguin, 1994; New York: Grove, 1995);

Franz a Felice: Už se blíží meče (Prague: Edice Petlice [samizdat edition], 1984); translated by Jan Drábek as "Kafka and Felice," *Cross Currents*, 5 (1986): 337–382; revised as *Už se blíží meče: Eseje, fejetony, rozhovory* (Prague: Novinář, 1990);

Láska a smetí (Prague [samizdat edition], 1987; Purley, U.K.: Rozmluvy, 1988; Prague: Československý spisovatel, 1990); translated by Osers as *Love and Garbage* (London: Chatto & Windus, 1990; New York: Knopf, 1991);

Markétin zvěřinec (Prague: Albatros, 1990);

Moje zlatá řemesla (Brno: Atlantis, 1990); translated by Wilson as *My Golden Trades* (London: Granta in association with Penguin, 1992; New York: Scribner/Maxwell Macmillan International, 1994);

Rozhovor v Praze (Prague: Evropský literární klub, 1990);

Ostrov mrtvých králů (Prague: Rozmluvy, 1992);

Prague, text by Klíma and Erna Lackner, photographs by Alfred Seiland (Zurich: Edition Stemmle, 1994; London: Thames & Hudson, 1994);

Jak daleko je slunce (Prague: Hynek, 1995);

Milostné rozhovory (Prague: Hynek, 1995);

Poslední stupeň důvěrnosti (Prague: Hynek, 1996); translated by Brain as *The Ultimate Intimacy* (London: Granta, 1997; New York: Grove, 1997);

Kruh nepřátel ceského jazyka: Fejetony (Prague: Hynek, 1998);

O chlapci, který se nestal číslem (Prague: Židovské museum, 1998);

Ani svatí, ani andělé (Prague: Hynek, 1999).

Collection: *Spisy Ivana Klímy*, 5 volumes to date (Prague: Hynek, 1995–).

Editions in English: "Journey to a Dead Man," edited and translated by Jeanne W. Němcová in her *Czech and Slovak Short Stories* (London & New York: Oxford University Press, 1967), pp. 239–257;

A Ship Named Hope: Two Novels, translated by Edith Pargeter (London: Gollancz, 1970)—comprises "The Jury" and "A Ship Named Hope";

"A Christmas Conspiracy," translated by Peter Kussi, in *The Writing on the Wall: An Anthology of Contemporary Czech Literature*, edited by Kussi and Antonín Liehm (Princeton: Karz-Cohl, 1983), pp. 87–105;

The Spirit of Prague and Other Essays, translated by Paul Wilson (London: Granta in association with Penguin, 1994; New York: Granta Books, 1995);

Between Security and Insecurity, translated by Gerald Turner (New York: Thames & Hudson, 1999).

PLAY PRODUCTIONS: *Zámek*, Prague, Divadlo Na Vinohradech, 1964;

Porota, Prague, Komorní divadlo, 17 April 1969;

Cukrárna Myriam, Vienna, Kleines Theater in der Josefstadt, 1969;

Klára a dva páni, Vienna, Akademietheater des Burgtheatres, 1971;

Hry, Vienna, Kleines Theater in der Josefstadt, 1975;

Amerika, by Klíma and Pavel Kohout, Krefeled, Germany, 1978;
Ženich pro Markétu, Vienna, Kleines Theater in der Josefstadt, 1979.

PRODUCED SCRIPTS: *Veverčí chvost,* Czech TV, 1962;
Pokoj pro dva, Czech TV, 1990;
Franz a Felice, Czech TV, 1991;
Prezident a anděl, Czech TV, 1993.

OTHER: *Karel Čapek, Ukradený spis 139/VII odd. C,* edited by Klíma (Prague: Československý spisovatel, 1960);
"Jak hluboké je moře," in *Die Zauberwurzel: Märchen von tschechischen Dichtern,* translated by Alexandra Baumrucker, edited by Klíma (Munich: Blanvalet, 1978), pp. 127–139; volume published in Czech as *Uzel pohádek* (Prague: Lidové noviny, 1991);
Jakémusi Alexandru K., edited by Klíma (Prague [samizdat edition], 1979);
Sborník nad procesem, edited by Klíma (Prague [samizdat edition], 1980);
"Living in Fiction and History," in *Fictions and Histories,* by Klíma, Michael Heim, Czesław Miłosz, and Martina Moravcová (Berkeley, Cal.: Doreen B. Townsend Center for the Humanities, 1998), pp. 1–15;
Karel Čapek, *War with the Newts,* introduction by Klíma, Penguin Twentieth-Century Classics (London: Penguin, 1998).

Ivan Klíma belongs to the generation of Czech writers who lived through two totalitarian regimes—Nazism and communism. In his creative work Klíma includes a great deal of autobiographical material and many keenly observed realistic details. Most frequently he returns to his experiences of these regimes and the moral questions they pose for humanity. Outspoken in his criticism of the communist regime, Klíma was expelled from the Communist Party, and his works were banned from publication, following the suppression in 1968 of the Prague Spring reform movement. As a result many of his works first appeared in typewritten volumes with homemade bindings—the so-called samizdat editions—or in German translation before being published in Czech either abroad by émigré publishing houses or, after the fall of communism and the breakup of Czechoslovakia, by publishers in the Czech Republic.

Klíma was born in Prague on 14 September 1931 to Ing Vilém Klíma, an electronics engineer,

Klíma with his wife, the sociologist Helena Malá, whom he married in 1958

and Marta Klíma, née Synková. Since he was part Jewish, he was sent to the Theresienstadt concentration camp in Bohemia in December 1941 and spent three and a half years there. After World War II he went to secondary school in Prague and then studied Czech language and literature at Charles University. He submitted his thesis on Karel Čapek in 1956; it was revised and published in book form in 1962. Klíma worked as an editor from 1956 to 1963. On 24 September 1958 he married Helena Malá, a sociologist, with whom he had two children.

As a young man, Klíma, like many of his contemporaries, believed that communism was the fairest political and economic system, but his father's arrest and other experiences after the communists came to power in February 1948 led him to abandon the ideology. His literary debut in the young writers' journal *Květen* (May) and his first books, the story collections *Bezvadný den* (A Perfect Day, 1960) and *Mezi třemi hranicemi* (Within Three Frontiers, 1960), bear witness to this change

Dust jacket for the English translation of Klíma's Milenci na jeden den *(1970), a collection of stories
in which the characters use sex to escape the monotony of life in communist Czechoslovakia*

of heart. Instead of the oversimplified, idealized picture of the world current in Czech literature in the 1950s, in these works the characters are not merely representatives of an ideology or a social group but individuals with vivid inner lives.

Klíma's first novel, *Hodina ticha* (The Hour of Silence, 1963), is narrated from various points of view: after each character tells his or her story, there is an intermezzo in which the author delves deeply into the inner life of the main hero. The plot does not proceed smoothly; Klíma deliberately unfolds it bit by bit in fragments, thereby shattering the idea, prevalent in the writing of the previous decade, of a monolithic, "objectively existing world." *Hodina ticha* includes scenes resembling the propagandistic political novels of the 1950s—Martin Petr, a civil engineer, comes to a backward region to build a great modern dam—but the structure of the propagandistic novel is subverted. As the novel proceeds, more and more questions arise. Martin asks himself, "What was the point of it all?" The narrator notes, "Great ideas

and projects that had seemed so important to him and had driven him to come to this place were now slowly fading away into silence."

Klíma worked as deputy editor of the weekly *Literární noviny* (The Literary Newspaper) from 1963 until it was suppressed in 1967; he continued in the same position on its successors *Literární listy* (The Literary Gazette) from March to August 1968 and *Listy* (The Gazette) from autumn 1968 until spring 1969. Far from being purely literary journals, these cultural and political papers were in the forefront of the efforts of Czech writers, artists, and intellectuals to liberalize the communist regime; they were also quite popular—their circulation never fell below a hundred thousand in a nation of ten million. Thus, they were the chief platform for the political and cultural reform movement that led to the Prague Spring.

Existentialist, absurd, and satirical motifs appear in Klíma's fiction at this time. In the trio of stories collected as *Milenci na jednu noc* (Lovers for a Single Night, 1964) he criticizes modern life as stereotyped and routine. The stories are primarily monologues by young people who are trying to escape the monotony of their lives by searching for an intense emotional bond to a partner of the opposite sex. Klíma added to his critique of life in contemporary society in *Milenci na jeden den* (1970; translated as *Lovers for a Day*, 1999). In these texts, for the first time in Czech literature, eroticism and sex emerge as the individual's way of achieving self-realization, counterbalancing a rigidly conventional and outwardly circumscribed life. The story "Klára a dva páni" (translated as "Klara and the Two Gentlemen") in *Milenci na jeden den* is strongly influenced by absurdist drama: it includes circular, almost meaningless dialogues and horrifying props and effects such as cages and barbed wire in a wardrobe and a telephone that rings at night but is silent when answered—a terrifying occurrence in a police state. The drama *Zámek* (The Castle, 1964) aroused interest as an indirect reference to the castle at Dobříš, where the state-sponsored Czechoslovak writers lived in luxury, and as a parable of relentless power, especially during the Stalinist years.

In 1969–1970 Klíma was a guest lecturer at the University of Michigan in Ann Arbor. When he returned to Czechoslovakia, he found himself one of some four hundred writers who could neither publish their work nor appear in the media. His earlier works had been removed from the libraries, and his new books were distributed illegally in samizdat editions; they were also published abroad by Czech exiles and in translations, mainly in German. This situation lasted until the fall of communism at the end of 1989, although in the final months of the communist regime, negotiations were underway to allow Klíma's *Má veselá jitra* (translated as *My Merry Mornings*, 1985), which had appeared in samizdat in 1978 and had been published in Canada in 1979, to be published officially in Czechoslovakia. During the 1970s and 1980s Klíma held jobs as a hospital porter, postman, seasonal seller of carp (a Czech Christmas dish), and assistant surveyor.

In the early 1970s Klíma wrote a series of plays that were staged only abroad. These works, which show the influence of Franz Kafka (whose work Klíma analyzed in his essays) and of absurdist drama, continued in the same vein as his plays of the 1960s such as *Zámek. Klára a dva páni* (1968), adapted from his short story, and *Pokoj pro dva* (A Room for Two, 1973) clearly reflect the depressing situation in Czechoslovakia, which is further illustrated in the novel *Milostné léto* (translated as *A Summer Affair*, 1987), circulated in samizdat in 1972 and published the following year in German translation by a Swiss firm. David, a research biologist, falls madly in love with a bohemian student, Iva. He leaves his wife and children and gives up his work and his lifelong dream of becoming a research fellow in Britain—only to discover how empty his affair has been when his student lover, having destroyed his existence, commits suicide. The novel may be taken as a critique of the "scientific" approach to life, but manic infatuation is a recurrent theme in Klíma's novels.

Klíma pursued the topic of disillusionment in the long novel *Soudce z milosti* (1986; translated as *Judge on Trial*, 1990), which has been translated into six languages and on which Klíma worked for thirteen years. He had previously dealt with the themes of a corrupt judiciary and manipulation of power in a play that he reworked into the novel *Porota* (1968; translated as "The Jury," 1970).

Soudce z milosti is set in Prague at the beginning of the 1970s, but the reminiscences of the hero take the reader back to the German occupation during World War II and to the Stalinist 1950s. Judge Adam Kindl is faced with the dilemma of whether to join the powers that be or to adhere to his moral principles. There are clearly autobiographical elements in the character, including his confinement in a concentration camp, his joining the Communist Party, his disillusionment with communism, and his work in the reform movement of 1968. In the end Kindl decides not to cooperate with the political establishment, refusing to send an innocent man to the gallows as demanded by his superior, and gives up his post. In so doing, in spite of his subsequent difficulty in earning a living, he becomes a free man. *Soudce z milosti*, like novels by such authors as Alexander Kliment, Ludvík Vaculík, and Karel Pecka, describes the lot of Czech intellectuals who refused to submit during the neo-Stalinism of the 1970s and 1980s. Unlike these other novels, however, *Soudce z milosti* has a strong spiritual dimension: it includes mystical moments of grace in which people feel themselves to be integral parts of the natural world. Previously Klíma's style had often tended toward lyricism, but in this work it becomes realistic. The novel is a gripping read, as was demonstrated when it was serialized by the Czechoslovak Service of Radio Free Europe in the late 1980s (although the impact of the programs may have been enhanced by the listeners trying to hear the text through the noise of the communist jamming transmitters).

Dust jacket for the U.S. edition of the English translation of Klíma's novel Soudce z milosti *(1986), about a judge who defies the communist authorities by refusing to condemn an innocent man to be hanged*

Three volumes of Klíma's highly autobiographical short stories—*Má veselá jitra, Moje první lásky* (samizdat, 1981; published, 1985; translated as *My First Loves*, 1986), and *Moje zlatá řemesla* (1990; translated as *My Golden Trades*, 1992)—are also written in relatively realistic style. In *Moje první lásky* Klíma describes in gently nostalgic prose the first erotic experiences of his childhood and youth. In most of these texts the political background of the times acts as an important counterbalance to the development of the often tentative personal relationship. Thus, love, a genuine and natural human feeling, has a precarious existence when manifestations of the natural world are curtailed by political oppression. For instance, the title character of "Myriam" is a girl who gives out milk to the prisoners in the Theresienstadt concentration camp. For several days, without saying a word, she shows affection to the protagonist, a young boy, by giving him a double portion. The boy falls deeply in love with the girl but is too shy to speak to her. The

girl is disappointed, and the boy plunges into despair. The poignancy of the story is enhanced by the fact that it is set in a concentration camp and, thus, potentially at the threshold of death.

In the other two collections Klíma deals unsentimentally with various grotesque situations in which the narrators find themselves when they have to work at a variety of jobs far removed from literature. *Má veselá jitra* consists of seven clearly autobiographical texts, each of which is set on the morning of an ordinary day in the subjugated Czechoslovakia of the 1970s, after the August 1968 Warsaw Pact invasion ended the Prague Spring. The stories are a testimony to the lives of ordinary people in Czechoslovakia's "really existing socialism." The communist regime took all moral and religious values from the people and gave them nothing to replace those values. Without leading personalities with a genuine moral standing, without the humanizing role of free literature and art, Czechoslovak society had become a headless body whose demoralized and corrupt members staggered aimlessly through their existence; degenerate consumerism reigned supreme. In *Má veselá jitra* the narrator stands helpless before social demoralization. The volume is an homage to those individuals who maintained the "eccentric" ethical values that were no longer regarded as relevant. In the final story of the collection, "V neděli ráno" (translated as "On Sunday Morning") various country "eccentrics" appear; there is more rationality in their oddness than in the mindless accumulation of property by "normal" people.

Láska a smetí (samizdat, 1987; published, 1988; translated as *Love and Garbage*, 1987) falls into the same category as *Má veselá jitra* and is Klíma's most successful book to date, having been translated into as many as thirteen languages. In a mosaic of encounters, memories, and events the narrator describes his work as a street sweeper in Prague and his affair with the sculptress Darja. Surrealist motifs include the image of garbage piling up and flooding the streets of Prague. This image symbolizes the key themes of Klíma's later work: death, destruction, and the threat of the collapse of modern civilization. Like Milan Kundera, Klíma reexamines his motifs and images over and over again from various angles, transforming them and firmly integrating them into the structure of his work. *Láska a smetí* is like a tapestry in which all motifs are interrelated by means of secondary ties and associations. As Klíma puts it in *Má veselá jitra*, the individual's only choice is "between two kinds of suffering, two forms of vanity, two varieties of despair." He or she is, however, free to decide which of them he or she "would find more bearable or even more attractive, while being left with the semblance of heroism or at least satisfaction."

Klíma's works could not be published by Czech publishing houses until after the fall of communism in 1989, and only then was he again able to take part in public life and to travel abroad. In December 1989 he became one of the founders of Obec spisovatelů (The Association of Writers), and from 1990 to 1993 he was chairman of the Czech PEN club. He also began writing on current affairs for Prague newspapers, especially for *Lidové noviny*. Since 1991 he has been writing a regular column, "Letters from Prague," for *New York Newsday* and the Swedish *Svenska Dagbladet*. He also writes articles for the German daily *Frankfurter Rundschau*.

Klíma's novels *Ostrov mrtvých králů* (Island of Dead Kings, 1992) and *Poslední stupeň důvěrnosti* (1996; translated as *The Ultimate Intimacy*, 1997) deal with the time just after the democratic revolution of 1989 and again examine the life, temptations, and failures of an intellectual, this time a Protestant minister. In these novels there are more reflective passages about humanity's place in the modern world. Klíma's outlook is more somber than before, and he has become more skeptical. In addition to his fiction for adults, since the 1960s Klíma has been successful with his books for children and young people, notably *Kokrhací hodiny* (Cockcrow, 1965), *Markétin zvěřinec* (Margaret's Menagerie, 1990), and *Jak daleko je slunce* (How Far Is It to the Sun, 1995). Accomplished in several genres, Klíma is one of the preeminent Czech writers of the second half of the twentieth century.

Interviews:
Philip Roth, "A Conversation in Prague," *New York Review of Books*, 37 (12 April 1990): 14–22;

Miloš Čermák, *Lásky a řemesla* (Prague: Academia, 1995).

Biographies:
Antonín J. Liehm, "Ivan Klíma," in his *Generace* (Prague: Československý spisovatel, 1990), pp. 284–299;

Jiří Lederer, "Mým tématem je vždycky znovu polemika s fanatismem," in his *České rozhovory*, second edition (Prague: Československý spisovatel, 1991), pp. 105–125.

References:
Marketa Goetz-Stankiewicz, *The Silenced Theatre* (Toronto, Buffalo, N.Y. & London: University of Toronto Press, 1979), pp. 116–145;

Igor Hájek, "Profile: Ivan Klíma," *Index on Censorship*, 12 (April 1983): 39–41;

Pete Hausler, "A Strange Kind of Exile: Hope and Despair in Ivan Klíma," *Agni*, 48 (1998): 246–251;

Helena Kosková, "Perspektiva mravní odpovědnosti," in her *Hledání ztracené generace*, second edition (Prague: H+H, 1996), pp. 165–173;

Marie Mravcová, "Ivan Klíma: *Má veselá jitra*," in *Český Parnas*, edited by Jiří Holý and J. Táborská (Prague: Galaxie, 1993), pp. 178–194;

Jiří Pechar, "Krize racionalistického idealismu v díle Ivana Klímy," in his *Nad knihami a rukopisy* (Prague: Torst, 1996), pp. 47–64;

Milan Suchomel, "Alternativy historické všednosti," in his *Literatura z času krize* (Brno: Atlantis, 1992), pp. 38–57;

Suchomel, "Hodina ticha" and "Hledání tvaru," in *Co zbylo z recenzenta*, edited by J. Bednářová (Brno: Vetus Via, 1995), pp. 62–66, 112–113;

Ian Ward, "Ivan Klíma's *Judge on Trial*: A Study of Law and Literature," *Scottish Slavonic Review*, 20 (Spring 1993): 23–44.

György Konrád

(2 April 1933 –   )

András Veres
Institute of Literary Studies, Hungarian Academy of Sciences

This entry was updated by Professor Veres from his entry in Concise Dictionary of World Literary Biography:
South Slavic and Eastern European Writers.

BOOKS: *A látogató* (Budapest: Magvető, 1969); translated by Paul Aston as *The Case Worker* (New York: Harcourt Brace Jovanovich, 1974; London: Hutchinson, 1975);

Az új lakótelepek szociológiai problémái, by Konrád and Iván Szelényi (Budapest: Akadémiai, 1969);

Der Stadtgrunder: Roman, translated into German by Mario Szenessy (Munich: List, 1975); translated into French by Veronique Charaire as *Les fondateurs: Roman* (Paris: Editions du Seuil, 1976); censored Hungarian version published as *A városalapító* (Budapest: Magvető, 1977); translated by Ivan Sanders as *The City Builder* (New York: Harcourt Brace Jovanovich, 1977; London: Sidgwick & Jackson, 1977 [i.e., 1980]); unexpurgated version published as *A városalapító* (Budapest: Pesti Szalon, 1992);

Az értelmiség útja az osztályhatalomhoz: Esszé, by Konrád and Szelényi (Bern & Paris: Európai Protestáns Magyar Szabadegyetem, 1978; Budapest: Gondolat, 1989); translated by Andrew Arato and Richard E. Allen as *The Intellectuals on the Road to Class Power* (Brighton, U.K.: Harvester Press, 1979; New York: Harcourt Brace Jovanovich, 1979);

Az autonómia kísértése: Kelet-nyugati utigondolatok 1977–1979 (Paris: Magyar Füzetek könyvei 2, 1980);

Der Komplize, translated into German by Hans-Henning Paetzke (Frankfurt am Main: Suhrkamp, 1985); translated by Sanders as *The Loser* (San Diego: Harcourt Brace Jovanovich, 1982; London: Allen Lane, 1983); original Hungarian version published as *A cinkos* (New York: Püski, 1986; Budapest: Magvető, 1989);

Antipolitics: An Essay, translated by Allen (San Diego: Harcourt Brace Jovanovich, 1984; London: Quartet, 1985); original Hungarian version

György Konrád (photograph by Layle Silbert; from the dust jacket for A Feast in the Garden, *1992)*

published as "Antipolitika," in *Az autonómia kísértése–Antipolitika* (Budapest: Codex RT, 1989);

Ölni vagy nem ölni (Budapest: ABC Független [samizdat edition], 1985);

Kerti mulatság (Budapest: ABC Független [samizdat edition], 1987); translated by Imre Goldstein as *A Feast in the Garden* (New York: Harcourt Brace Jovanovich, 1992; London: Faber &

Faber, 1992); Hungarian version revised as *Agenda I: Kerti mulatság. Regény és munkanapló* (Budapest: Magvető, 1989);

Hangulatjelentés: "Hat esszé" (Cologne & Budapest: Irodalmi Levelek, 1989);

Európa köldökén: Esszék 1979–1989 (Budapest: Magvető, 1990);

Az újjászületés melankóliája (Budapest: Pátria, 1991); translated by Michael Henry Heym as *The Melancholy of Rebirth: Essays from Post-Communist Central Europe, 1989–1994* (New York: Harcourt Brace, 1995);

91–93: Napló és esszék (Budapest: Pesti Szalon, 1993);

Kőóra: Agenda II (Budapest: Pesti Szalon, 1994); translated by Sanders as *Stonedial* (New York: Harcourt Brace, 2000);

Várakozás: Esszék, cikkek, naplórészletek (Budapest: Pesti Szalon, 1995);

Áramló leltár (Budapest: Pesti Szalon, 1996);

A láthatatlan hang: Zsidó tárgyú elmélkedések (Budapest: Palatinus, 1997); translated by Peter Reich as *Invisible Voice: Meditations on Jewish Themes* (San Diego: Harcourt Brace, 2000);

Hagyaték (Budapest: Palatinus, 1998);

Útrakészen: Egy berlini müteremben (Budapest: Palatinus, 1999);

Mit tud a levelibéke? Válogatott essék, naplórészletek (1993–1996) (Budapest: Palatinus, 2000).

SELECTED PERIODICAL PUBLICATIONS–
UNCOLLECTED: "Örkény István: Hóviharban," *Új Hang*, 4 (1955): 103–111;

"A lemondás irodalma: A francia 'absztrakt' regényről," *Nagyvilág*, 5 (1960): 416–423;

"A klasszikus regény a huszadik században. Roger Martin du Gard: A Thibault család," *Jelenkor*, 3 (1960): 57–68;

"Gogol: A Miklós-kori Oroszország," *Jelenkor*, 4 (1961): 687–698;

"Emlékezés az Oblomov írójára," *Nagyvilág*, 7 (1962): 1368–1373;

"Széljegyzetek a 'huligán'-arcképhez," *Jelenkor*, 6 (1963): 255–262, 340–345;

"A korszerű háború korszerűtlensége," *Valóság*, 6, no. 6 (1963): 16–30; 7, no. 1 (1964): 2–13;

"A célja vesztett háború," *Kortárs*, 8 (1964): 924–933;

"A késleltetett városfejlesztés társadalmi konfliktusai," by Konrád and Iván Szelényi, *Valóság*, 14 (1971): 19–35;

"Mondatok egy képzeit regényről," *Valóság*, 25, no. 2 (1982): 69.

OTHER: Nikolai Gogol, *Művei*, edited by Konrád (Budapest: Magyar Helikon, 1962);

Ivan Turgenev, *Elbeszélések*, edited by Konrád (Budapest: Magyar Helikon, 1963);

Fyodor Dostoyevsky, *A játékos: Válogatott elbeszélések*, edited by Konrád (Budapest: Magyar Helikon, 1963);

Leo Tolstoy, *Lev Tolsztoj művei*, 10 volumes, edited by Konrád (Budapest: Magyar Helikon, 1964–1967);

A francia "új regény," 2 volumes, edited by Konrád (Budapest: Európa, 1967).

The publication of György Konrád's first novel, *A látogató* (1969; translated as *The Case Worker*, 1974), placed him at the forefront of Hungarian literature. At the beginning of the 1970s he turned against the Communist regime; as a result, he was not allowed to publish in Hungary. His novels and essays were published in translations into several other languages, however, making him the best-known contemporary Hungarian writer. His "Antipolitika" (1989), first published in English translation as *Antipolitics* (1984), provoked great interest in Western European and American public opinion. This book, along with the Czech author Milan Kundera's famous 1984 essay "The Tragedy of Central Europe," published in *The New York Review of Books*, pointed out the untenability of the situation created by the Yalta Conference and the imperative need to aid an abandoned Central and Eastern Europe. As a participant in the illegal Hungarian democratic opposition movement and then, after the fall of communism in 1989, as an influential member of the Szabad Demokraták Szövetsége (Alliance of Free Democrats), Konrád has been one of the most active figures shaping Hungarian political life despite the fact that he has never accepted any significant leadership position within the party. An indication of his international reputation was his being elected chairman of the international writers' organization PEN from 1990 to 1993.

Konrád was born on 2 April 1933 in Debrecen to Róza Klein and József Konrád. His father was a well-to-do hardware-store owner in Berettyóújfalu, which had a Jewish community of some one thousand people. Konrád's only sibling is his elder sister, Éva, a biologist who has lived in New York City since 1956. The immediate family survived World War II and the Holocaust: the parents returned from the Austrian camp where they had been taken, while Konrád, his sister, and two of their cousins spent the period between June 1944 and February 1945 in one of the houses in Budapest protected by the safe pass of Carl Lutz, a representative of the Swiss government. (The other two hundred children of Berettyóújfalu were sent to Auschwitz; six returned home.)

Konrád started his education at the celebrated Reformed College in Debrecen and continued his studies at the Madách Gimnázium in Budapest. There he was expelled from the student union because he refused to disavow his admiration of the literary and aesthetic writings of György Lukács, who was stigmatized by the Communist Party as a deviationist. Konrád applied to major in Hungarian and French in the Faculty of Arts of the University of Budapest, but, as a "class-alien" of bourgeois origin, he was turned down. He was, however, accepted by the Russian Institute of the university, where teachers of Russian were trained, because of a shortage of applicants. In 1953 he was able to continue his studies as a second-year Hungarian major thanks to the easing political climate generated by the appointment of Imre Nagy as prime minister. A supporter of the 1953 reforms, Konrád wrote his first reviews for the journal *Új Hang* (New Voice) in 1954–1955. The language and approach of these writings show the influence of Lukács, whose seminars on the aesthetics of the novel Konrád attended in 1954.

In August 1955 Konrád married Vera Varsa, a Russian-English major at the university. That year Mátyás Rákosi returned to power in Hungary and attempted to reverse the reform process, and Konrád and many of his colleagues were expelled as "excessive" reformists. But with the help of some of his professors—especially István Sőtér, who had been appointed deputy minister of culture—he was able to continue his studies. He wrote his diploma thesis on Károly Pap, the novelist who had placed the Jews' search for identity at the center of his works and who died in the Buchenwald concentration camp. Konrád graduated in the summer of 1956 and became an editor of a newly established journal, *Életképek* (Conversation Pieces), where he was in charge of sociological articles and criticism. The proofs of the first issue were ready on 23 October 1956, when the Hungarian Revolution broke out. The journal ceased to exist in March 1957 without a single issue having been published.

During the revolution Konrád acted as a bodyguard for Ferenc Mérei, the renowned psychologist who became head of the University Students' Revolutionary Committee at the Faculty of Arts, then served as one of the guardsmen who protected the members of the Intellectuals' Revolutionary Committee at the Faculty of Law. Unwilling to give up his independence, he rejected invitations to join the

editorial boards of new journals and tried to make his living as a freelance writer. The Magvető Press commissioned Konrád, who had a good command of French and Russian (he later learned German and English, as well), to translate works by Jean-Paul Sartre and Simone de Beauvoir; the books ultimately could not be published, however, because Hungarian cultural officials considered existentialism ideologically dangerous.

In 1959 Konrád became a social services caseworker and was assigned to supervise young people in one of the slum districts of Budapest. In 1960 he took a part-time job as a proofreader and series editor at Magyar Helikon Press. During the day he visited the poor people in his district; in the evenings he exchanged views with writers such as Gyula Hernádi and Sándor Csoóri, who met regularly at the downtown café Belvárosi Kávéház.

Konrád matured as an essayist at the end of the 1950s and the beginning of the 1960s. Although he wrote relatively few essays, and not all of them have been published (for example, his essays on László Nagy, Miklós Szentkuthy, and Albert Camus), in literary circles he was considered perhaps the most profound essayist of his generation. Modeling himself on Camus, he "decided to become a novelist and a philosopher: a kind of essayist philosopher who equates thinking and poetry."

Konrád's favorite essay subjects were French and Russian writers and literary movements. He published an extensive essay on Roger Martin du Gard's novel cycle *Les Thibault* (1922–1940) in 1960 and planned a monograph on Nikolay Gogol but finished only a few chapters. In 1960 he was the first in Hungary to give a survey of the most outstanding representatives of the French *nouveau roman* (or, as he termed it, the "abstract novel"), from which he received the main inspiration for his own writing technique. He contended that the representatives of the *nouveau roman* experienced meaninglessness, one of the two basic qualities of existentialism, but that they completely ignored the other: freedom. The influence of the masters of nineteenth-century Russian fiction—especially Gogol's sense of absurdity, Fyodor Dostoyevsky's feeling of abandonment, Leo Tolstoy's religion of love, and the problem of the title character in Ivan Goncharov's novel *Oblomov* (1859) of freedom growing into nothingness—has also been significant. Among Hungarian authors, Konrád most admired Gyula Krúdy and Miklós Szentkuthy. His first novel, *A látogató*, drew as much from these literary sources as it did from his personal experiences as a caseworker.

Although Konrád's early career was dominated by the literary essay, there were exceptions. In 1963 he wrote an extensive study, the first two chapters of which were serialized in 1963–1964 under the title "A korszerű háború korszerűtlensége" (The Obsoleteness of Modern War) in *Valóság* (Truth); the final chapter, "A célja vesztett háború" (The War with No Purpose), appeared in *Kortárs* (Contemporary). In this work he examines the threats and advantages of the contemporary world, primarily the nuclear balance of power. The technical military data—which, according to the author, were clipped from Western newspapers—that he cited as evidence drew the attention of the Hungarian security service. One department of the Ministry of Defense invited him to be an adviser; at the same time, a colonel in another department wrote an article sharply criticizing him. Konrád also showed the first signs of his interest in sociology during this period. A sociological essay, "Széljegyzetek a 'huligán'-arcképhez" (Marginal Notes on the Image of "Hooligans"), published in *Jelenkor* (Modern Age) in 1963, offers an objective description of the juvenile-delinquent subculture, as opposed to the moralizing approach to the topic that was usual at the time. A study of poverty that he wrote in 1965 could not be published; the existence of poverty did not fit Communist propaganda, and even the use of the word was prohibited. He later included the essence of the essay in *A látogató*.

At the beginning of 1963 Konrád divorced his first wife, and in July he married Júlia Lángh, a Hungarian-French major who became a teacher and then worked for the Hungarian Radio. They have two children: Anna, born in 1965 and called Dorka in Konrád's works, and Miklós, born in 1967; Anna grew up to become a psychiatrist, Miklós an historian. In 1965 Konrád quit his caseworker job and went to work as a sociologist at the Town Development Scientific and Planning Institute of the Ministry of Housing and Public Construction. He soon became acquainted with the urban sociologist Iván Szelényi, and they began to conduct empirical studies together. At this time Konrád began writing his first novel, which he finished in 1967. The original title, "Menetgyakorlat" (Marching Drill), referring to the protagonist's situation of having continually to march on the peripheries of society, was later replaced by *A látogató*, emphasizing his social position. Konrád found the choice of title so successful that he gave similar titles to his subsequent novels, *A városalapító* (1977; translated as *The City Builder*, 1977) and *A cinkos* (1986; first published in English translation as *The Loser*, 1982).

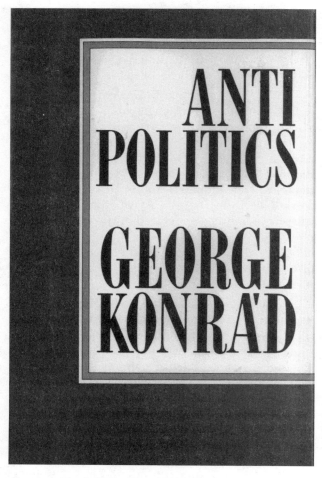

Dust jacket for the U.S. edition (1984) of the English translation of Konrád's essay calling for Western aid to Central and Eastern Europe

A látogató is essentially an enormous monologue: T., the chief official of the child-welfare authority, discusses his work, his clients, the measures he has taken, his failures and successes, his doubts and certitudes, his temptations and compromises. Although the work encompasses only one day, this day seems to represent the official's entire life. The description of the office changes into reflections of grotesque tragedies, as it is gradually revealed that every object, from the main door to the photographs in the filing cabinet, represents a failed human life. The central "case" in the novel—T. has to provide for Ferike, the mentally disturbed son of the Bandulas, who have committed suicide—becomes a depressing parable of the official's incompetence: unable to arrange for the child to be taken immediately into the custody of the state, T. places him in the care of a neighbor, who is a prostitute. T. at first looks at the events he is narrating with an ironic and cynical distance; this attitude gives way to a more sympathetic approach. The changing attitude reflects a radical change in T.'s viewpoint during his relating of the story, which is, at the same time, a process of self-revelation.

The slow-paced narration, consisting of sentences that are several pages long, with no clear direction but with a clear structure, creates the linguistic equivalent of T.'s incompetence as an official and a human being. He calls himself "the agent of indifference and the average" within essentially uncontrollable human relations. He does not particularly believe in the efficacy of interference, nor does he seem to be convinced of the wisdom of the regulations he enforces. He does what he can, choosing the lesser evil in the face of constant doubt, uncomfortable with his role and yet recognizing that "there is nothing better."

A látogató created considerable controversy on its publication not only by informing its readers of the extent of poverty and deviant behavior in the underworld of Budapest but also by questioning whether it was possible for state institutions to provide happiness. A spirit of blame is absent from the novel, setting it against the main trend in Hungarian fiction of the 1960s and making it a forerunner of the prose of the 1970s. Konrád is interested in the limits of human endurance, which are different for each individual and, consequently, cannot be explained by social conditions. *A látogató* suggests that the casting of the roles of client and official is rather relative: the Bandulas were once a well-to-do, middle-class family but have fallen on hard times, and T. started his career as an attorney, then worked as a manual laborer in the storeroom of a slaughterhouse before getting a job at the child-welfare authority. The existence of deviation itself is disturbing, but it becomes even more so if one recognizes its possibility in the course of one's own life.

At the same time, the narrator-protagonist of *A látogató* is a man of greater stature than the official as whom he identifies himself. His language and literary style are strikingly different from what would be expected of such a figure. Konrád does not try to imitate bureaucratic jargon; on the contrary, he puts poetic images, precise physical descriptions, and philosophical statements into the mouth of his protagonist. As a result, T. gains in stature and rises above the world in which he lives. The book closes with the remark: "let everybody who wishes come; one of us will talk, the other will listen, and we will at least be together." If nothing else, one can at least talk about the cares of the world.

Konrád offered his novel to the Szépirodalmi Press, but it was rejected for ideological reasons. It was finally published by Magvető in May 1969 for Book Week, the Hungarian book festival that has been held each year since 1929. The six thousand copies printed were sold in a few hours. This success may have been partly a result of the fact that the Communist Party newspaper, without even waiting for the book to appear, attacked it viciously, calling the style derivative, questioning the sociological authenticity of the work, and rejecting, somewhat contradictorily, both the "pessimistic submissiveness" and "the propagation of Christian charity" in the novel.

Also in 1969 Konrád and Szelényi published *Az új lakótelepek szociológiai problémái* (Sociological Problems in the New Housing Projects). They found that the population of the new high-rise housing projects was younger, better educated, and more active than residents of traditional housing and that neighborly relationships were formed more easily and proved to be more stable than had been thought. These conclusions, of course, reflect the situation of the mid 1960s, when, before the establishment of modern chain stores, those living in the housing projects had to rely on each other to a greater extent than they do today, and the rapid deterioration of the buildings had not yet resulted in migration from the complexes.

While *A látogató* was a popular success, the sociological essay won the admiration of the profession. The authors continued their collaboration, and their study "A késleltetett városfejlesztés társadalmi konfliktusai" (Social Conflicts of Delayed Town Development, 1971) created a stir even beyond professional circles. The essay argues that, contrary to expectations, the socialist housing policy—the distribution of apartments as social benefits—actually increases inequality. Konrád and Szelényi's book "Urbanizáció és területi gazdálkodás" (Urbanization and Regional Economy), written in 1972–1973, could not be published because of the scandal caused by the article.

In May 1973 Konrád was accused of smuggling the manuscript for Miklós Haraszti's sociological essay "Darabbér" (Job Rates) out of the country. His apartment was searched; he was warned by the authorities; he lost his job; and his second novel, *A városalapító*, which he had written between 1969 and 1973, was rejected by Magvető Press. Then the security service found out about an essay on the intelligentsia written by Konrád and Szelényi in great secrecy in an isolated peasant house they had rented in the village of Csobánka. On 23 October 1974, three weeks after finishing the work, they were taken into detention, and their manuscript was confiscated. The charge of subversive activity, however, had to be dropped because the authorities could not prove that anybody had read the essay.

The essay, which was not published until 1978—and then not in Hungary but in Bern and Paris (it was not published in Hungary until 1989, after the fall of the Communist regime)—was *Az értelmiség útja az osztályhatalomhoz* (translated as *The Intellectuals on the Road to Class Power*, 1979). The thesis of the work is that the intellectuals have become an independent class and that they, not the workers, are the real beneficiaries of communism. Konrád and Szelényi modify the classical Marxist analysis to maintain that, just as at the transition from feudalism to capitalism the bourgeoisie had to present its standpoint as that of humankind in general in order to fight against the aristocracy together with the other oppressed layers of society, so today the intelligentsia—not the proletariat, as in Marxist theory—has to do the same vis-à-vis the bourgeoisie. While in the early phase of socialism the intelligentsia constituted a social category that was more or less tolerated, in the second, post-Stalinist phase they are—at first in a concealed, then in a more and more open way—becoming partners with the bureaucracy in wielding political power. In the third stage, by about the end of the millennium, they will become the ruling class, dominating the whole society. The authors contend that the road of the intellectuals to power is not characteristic only of Eastern Europe but is a universal phenomenon: the intelligentsia has always and everywhere been opposed to the market economy.

To escape from police persecution Szelényi and his family emigrated (Szelényi became head of the Department of Sociology at UCLA in 1988), while Konrád, who had just started to write his third novel, chose internal exile. Soon his wife was banned from Hungarian Radio, leaving them with only the royalties from the foreign publications of *A látogató* to support them.

The plot of Konrád's second novel, *A városalapító*, is even simpler than that of *A látogató*. The title character is a nameless architect—he does not even have an initial—who is meditating rather than narrating. His biography is no more than a sketch. Coming from a dynasty of architects, he has denied his bourgeois ancestors and become fully committed to the new socialist world. In the "heroic age," the early period of socialism that was the time of his adolescence, he took part in the building of the new society with the confidence of the committed, and he enjoyed the absolute power he had gained over others—then suffered from the same absolute power when it put him in prison, as well. Now, in the more peaceful stage of socialism, he has settled down as the chief architect of a provincial town, and he takes great care to secure his position and comfort. He shows indulgent patience toward his son, who calls him a technocrat and rebels against him. Not only family ties make him tolerant but also the understanding that "since the ruling intellectuals cannot make a revolution against themselves, they have to do it among themselves."

A városalapító illustrates the main theses of Konrád and Szelényi's essay on the intelligentsia. The protagonist, who takes part in the planning and control of the new order by virtue of his profession, describes his situation: "I used to be a construction engineer in the early stage of socialism, and then I became a bourgeois-turned-intellectual, a pro-regime bureaucrat and agent of an open future rolled into one. My father was a private architect, and I am a state architect; to make decisions about others, he had money, while I have an office." The social position of the intelligentsia is radically different in the new world from what it was in the old. "I plan; therefore, I exist," declares the narrator confidently. He places himself at the center of the universe and regards his activity as dominant in society.

A városalapító was published in German (1975) and in French (1976) before it appeared in Hungarian: after long wrangling, Magvető Press published the novel in 1977, but in a severely censored version that distorts Konrád's meaning. Konrád's political problems created a difficult situation for the reviewers of the book, who generally acknowledged the linguistic innovativeness of the novel—Konrád uses a language that is rich in aphorisms and metaphors, features that had long been neglected in Hungarian literature—but they criticized it as abstract and formless.

In 1976 Konrád's three-year travel prohibition ended, and he went to West Berlin, where he was granted a one-year fellowship at the Deutscher Akademischer Austauschdienst (German Academic Exchange Service). After visiting New York, San Francisco, and Paris he was allowed to return to Hungary in March 1979 on the condition that he give no interviews for three months. He and his wife had divorced in September 1978, and she and their two children had settled in Paris.

Konrád had started to write his third novel, *A cinkos*, in 1975; he completed it in New York in 1978, but the first legal Hungarian edition did not appear until 1989. After losing his job, he had conceived the idea of becoming acquainted with life in a home for the mentally ill—which he was able to do in a provincial hospital—and making it the subject of his next work. Later he modified his plan, and only the action of the first chapter takes place in this environment. Konrád's hero, T., is an intellectual whose life becomes intertwined with Hungarian history from the early 1940s to the mid 1970s. A member of a well-to-do Jewish family, he becomes involved with an illegal political movement as a university student; he is caught, tortured, and forced to watch the torture of his lover. From this point onward prison becomes the recurring "intermission" of his life. During World War II he does forced labor for Germans, escapes to the Russians, fights with Hungarian partisans, and returns home as an officer of the Soviet army. In 1945 he becomes vice president of Hungarian Radio. He witnesses the mistreatment of his colleagues by the omnipotent and feared Állam-védelmi Hatóság (State Security Authority), the Hungarian equivalent of the Soviet KGB, then himself becomes a victim of a show trial and is sent to prison. During the 1956 revolution he is a close associate of Imre Nagy; when the revolution fails, he is imprisoned by the János Kádár regime. After his release, tired of the "algorithm of prison life," he decides to become a social scientist and "tame the slogans of the revolution into reform proposals." In 1973 he is briefly imprisoned, and his apartment is searched: the police are trying to find the manuscript for his theoretical work on the socialist regime. He decides to hide behind the protective walls of a home for the mentally ill, where he can enjoy the sunshine and listen to the strange but amusing stories of the patients. Such is the course of life of "a loser in the upper circles" in east-central Europe.

Konrád's third novel is different from the previous ones in that the protagonist is not his alter ego but a character created from the fates of distinguished left-wing figures of the previous generation, such as Mérei, Ferenc Donáth, György Fazekas, Sándor Haraszti, and Miklós Vásárhelyi. The message of the novel is: we always try, and we always lose. This attitude is a typically east-central European one that Konrád treats with both empathy and criticism in his volume of essays *Az autonómia kísértése* (The Temptation of Autonomy, 1980):

> Our moral itself is regressive. To retreat, hide, wait, withdraw, give up, and feast over the ruins of enterprises with spiteful pleasure turned against our-

selves. This is the meeting point of Western and Eastern cultures. According to Eastern philosophy, it is not even worth starting. According to Western thought, enterprises will be successful. According to Eastern-European philosophy, it must be given a try, but we must be aware that we are going to lose.

Between 1982 and 1984 Konrád again traveled to West Berlin, New York, and Paris. In September 1984 he married Judit Lakner, an historian and author of children's books whom he had known since 1978. They have three children: Áron, born in 1986; József, born in 1987; and Franciska, born in 1995, who appears in Konrád's writings as Zsuzska. In 1987–1988 he lectured on world literature at Colorado College in Colorado Springs. He was virtually excluded from Hungarian cultural life, since for a decade and a half only the censored version of *A városalapító* and an essay, "Mondatok egy képzelt regényről" (Sentences on an Imaginary Novel, 1982), could be published legally. The authorities considered him persona non grata: in 1981 they banned a textbook merely because it included a sentence mentioning the name György Konrád and the title *A látogató.*

Konrád's next work of fiction, *Kerti mulatság* (1987; translated as *A Feast in the Garden,* 1992), written in 1985, does not feature a dominant protagonist-narrator; nevertheless, there is a favored narrator, who speaks more often than the others. Though he is nameless, he is clearly the author himself, who is no less fictitious than the other characters of the novel: "He who is writing these lines is born on this page. . . . I am no more and no less than this text."

Kerti mulatság consists of three layers. The first is the writer's memories of his childhood, the concentration camp, and the moment of liberation; the second comprises his seemingly improvised reflections and associations. The recalling and meditative sections of the novel alternate in an almost regular rhythm. The significance of these two layers is indicated by Konrád's characterization of *Kerti mulatság* as "an autobiographical essay novel about finding one's orientation." They are complemented by the third layer, the stories of the various characters, which is the main fictional element in the work. Konrád was not satisfied with the novel and later radically rewrote it.

In the 1980s Konrád's sociopolitical essays drew more attention than his novels—especially "Antipolitika," in which he holds that the consequences of the Yalta agreement can be eliminated by peaceful means. In his later essays his formerly dominant interest in literary criticism has been almost completely replaced by a concern with political theory and ideology. The later essays are also characterized not by a systematic but by a problem-solving approach: they tend to consist of fragments that retain their independence in spite of belonging to a whole. The third, and perhaps most conspicuous, feature of his later essays is a repetitiveness that seems almost forced, as if he were always talking about the same things: the alternatives of capitalism and socialism, democracy and dictatorship, and liberalism and nationalism; the wretchedness of the small east-central European states; the historical role and mission of the bourgeoisie and the intelligentsia; the intertwining of power and culture that leads either nowhere or to catastrophe; and the real and alleged threats to minorities, especially Jews.

During his stays abroad Konrád made many contacts that were used by the Hungarian democratic opposition that emerged after 1980. He wrote articles for *Beszélő* (Speaker) and *Hírmondó* (Gazetteer) and made his novels and political essays available to Hungarian samizdat publishers. In the autumn of 1982 the social historian Edward P. Thompson, a founder of the Campaign for Nuclear Disarmament, delivered a lecture in Konrád's apartment after it was banned at the Faculty of Arts of the Loránd Eötvös University. Konrád was also present at the illegal meeting in Monor in June 1985 at which forty-five Hungarian opposition intellectuals tried to address the difficult situation of the country and the chances of finding a way out. On 30 January 1988 he called on the delegates to the Democratic Forum to consider themselves an "alternative parliament."

Konrád's homecoming as a writer occurred in 1989, when his works that had been available only in foreign or samizdat editions began to be published in Hungarian. As a result, he emerged not only as a major novelist but also as a noted political scientist, one whose opinion was influential not only in his own party, the Szabad Demokraták Szövetsége, but also for a significant part of the Hungarian general public. In 1991, opposing the attempts of the government of Premier József Antall to restrict the freedom of the media, he initiated the human-rights movement that became known as the Democratic Charter and served as its official spokesman. This movement marked the first joining of forces of liberals and socialists and was the first step toward the liberal government formed after the 1994 elections. Unfortunately, Konrád's collection of his lectures and diarylike notes, *91–93* (1993), records only the

Cover for Konrád's 1996 collection of essays, diary notes, and meditations

final results; the political and psychological context is missing from the volume. In recognition of his political stance and artistic accomplishments Konrád received the Herder Prize in 1983; the Charles Veillon Prize in 1986; the Kossuth Prize, the highest Hungarian award for intellectual achievement, in 1990; the Peace Prize of the German Booksellers in 1991; and the French Legion of Honor in 1996.

In 1989 Konrád had rewritten *Kerti mulatság* as *Agenda I: Kerti mulatság. Regény és munkanapló* (Agenda I: A Feast in the Garden. Novel and Working Diary), the first part of a novel cycle. The second part, *Kőóra: Agenda II* (translated as *Stonedial*, 2000), was published in 1993. The common title, *Agenda*, has the double meaning of a book of rituals and a book in which one records things to do. *Agenda I* is a family saga, while *Kőóra* has elements of the adventure story. The protagonists of the novels, Dávid Kobra and János Dragomán, are the author's alter egos: Kobra is a writer; his father's name is Konrád; the surname of Dragomán's lover, Melinda Kadron, is an anagram of the author's name, as are Kandor, the name of the town where *Kőóra* takes place, and Darnok, the name of the multinational company for which Dragomán works; and Dragomán's name means "interpreter," "mediator," "guide," or "conductor"—all appropriate appellations for a writer—as well as "dragon" and "drug addict."

Although the two protagonists are opposites of each other—Dragomán is a womanizer, a troublemaker, and a restless wanderer, while Kobra is a calm, cheerful, and staid man who tries not to tempt fate—they represent the possibilities of one and the same personality: Kobra is the "daytime" alter ego; Dragomán, the "nighttime" one. While Kobra, Dragomán, and Melinda are all featured in *Agenda I*, in *Kőóra* Dragomán is the only protagonist.

In each novel two time periods are involved: in *Agenda I* the 1980s and the 1940s, in *Kőóra* the early 1990s and the 1950s. The narrators reach down into the depths of their consciousness and choose from their memories as they please. *Agenda I* is a series of monologues, mostly in the form of portraits of the members of the extensive Kobra family, which are interrupted by two longer episodes: the persecution of the Jews in 1944–1945 and Dragomán and Melinda's love affair. *Kőóra* is the story of the return of the globetrotter Dragomán to the town where he spent his adolescent years—the most successful parts of the novel depict the 1956 revolution—and from which he escaped because he had been unable to bear the lack of freedom under communism; he returns to the town because it has become free. He is forced to face the phantoms of the past, and, in spite of his best intentions, he stirs new storms. He learns that in his absence a daughter and even a grandchild have been born; a young man commits suicide by jumping from the balcony of his hotel room; and when he pushes the university rector away during an argument, the man falls, strikes his head, and dies on the spot.

Konrád has said, "I would most willingly write a book whose pages can be taken out and rearranged." The chapters are loosely connected in *Agenda I*, and in *Kőóra* the abandonment of linearity is even more pronounced. There is no sooner or later; episodes are interchangeable. Hungarian critics have been unable to appreciate the highly experimental nature of the two novels, and in the case of *Kőóra*, the distorted picture of the conditions that emerged after the fall of communism met with incomprehension. In the Netherlands, however, *Agenda I* was named Book of the Year in 1990.

The essays, diary notes, and meditations of Konrád's *Várakozás* (Waiting, 1995) and *Áramló leltár* (Flowing Inventory, 1996) are mainly traveler's observations and general reflections. They continue the fragmentary style of the aphoristic essays of the 1980s, but the political interest has been pushed aside by the issues of private life and human existence in general.

Interviews:

Katalin Rangos, "Önarckép-befejezetlen," *Kritika II,* 13, no. 7 (1989): 16–20;

Erzséber Eszéki, "Szeretek normális lenni," in her *Kibeszéljük magunkat: Íróportrék* (Budapest: Múzsák, 1990), pp. 206–211;

Zsuzsa Kartal, "Kérdésekre válaszok," in Konrád's *Európa köldökén: Esszék 1979–1989* (Budapest: Magvető, 1990), pp. 460–469;

György Petri, "Komótos bátorság, szép relativizmus," *Beszélő II,* 3 (19 October 1991): 40–44;

Éva V. Bálint, "A látogató visszatér" and "Az ember kalandjaiban leginkább önmaga," in her *Rendiség a romokon: Vélekedések a rendszerváltás éveiből* (Budapest: Pesti Szalon, 1994), pp. 133–149;

Bálint, "Aki másnak nem árt, az nem bűnös, nem is büntethető," *Magyar Hírlap,* 27 (10 December 1994): 1.

References:

Miklós Almási, "A cinkos; Antipolitika," *Kritika II,* 18 (1989): 26–27;

Timothy Garton Ash, "Létezik-e Közép-Európa?," *Kell-e nekünk Közép-Európa? Századvég,* special issue (1991): 87–103;

Éva Bálint and András Veres, "A sikerképtelenség környezetrajza," *Valóság,* 17 (1974): 58–74;

Ákos Benkő, "Egy elhamarkodott bírálatról," *Forrás,* 2 (1969): 137–138;

Marianna D. Birnbaum, "An Armchair Picaresque: The Texture and Structure of George Konrad's *The Case Worker,*" in *Fiction and Drama in Eastern and Southeastern Europe,* edited by Henrik Birnbaum and Thomas Eekman (Columbus, Ohio: Slavica, 1980), pp. 61–85;

Endre Bojtár, "Az irodalmi mű jelentése. Konrád György: A látogató," in his *Egy kelet-européer az irodalomelméletben* (Budapest: Szépirodalmi, 1983), pp. 129–158;

Francois Bondy, "Elmélkedés a Kelet és a Nyugat közös kultúrájáról," *Világosság,* 30 (1989): 597–600;

Péter Dérczy, "Agenda, 1. Kerti mulatság," *Jelenkor,* 33 (1990): 263–267;

Dérczy, "A városalapító," *Kritika II,* 7 (1978): 25–26;

Ferenc Fehér, "A látogató," *Kortárs,* 14 (1969): 1489–1495;

Fehér, Ágnes Heller, and György Márkus, *Diktatúra a szükségletek felett* (Budapest: Cserépfalvi, 1991), pp. 182–183;

József Fórizs, "A korszerű háború néhány elméleti kérdéséről," *Valóság*, 8 (1965): 19–35;

Gergely Hajdú, "A házigazda: *Agenda, 1: Kerti mulatság*," *Holmi*, 2 (1990): 229–232;

Zoltán Kenyeres, "Egy hivatalnok pokolra száll," *Új Írás*, 9 (1969): 125–127;

János Kis, "Egy prófécia útja a nyilvánossághoz: Az értelmiség útja az osztályhatalomhoz," *Magyar Napló*, 2 (1990): 10;

László Lengyel, "Két író közt," in his *Magyar alakok* (Budapest: 2000-Pénzügykutató, 1994), pp. 154–156;

Vilma B. Mészáros, "A látogató dilemmája," *Kritika*, 7 (1969): 32–37;

András Pályi, "A szabadságfogyatkozás természetrajzához. A látogató," *Kortárs*, 34 (1989): 155–160;

Sándor Radnóti, "Grandezza, kolorit (A cinkos)," *Holmi*, 2 (1990): 226–229;

Ernő Kulcsár Szabó, "A városalapító," *Alföld*, 24 (1978): 81–84;

Imre Szász, "Books in the Street," *New Hungarian Quarterly*, 11 (1969): 152–157;

Sándor Szilágyi, "Az irónia rekordereként, farral a jövőnek: *A cinkos*," in *Beszélő Összkiadás, I. kötet*, edited by Fanny Havas (Budapest: AB-Beszélő, 1992), pp. 148–150;

Ferenc Tallár, "Értékválság és prózaforma," *Medvetánc*, 3 (1983): 33–48;

Tallár, "'Valóság vagy történelem?' Különösség és a mai magyar próza," *Mozgó Világ*, 4 (1978): 47–56;

Beáta Thomka, "Metaforikus folyamatok a regényben," *Híd*, 53 (1979): 1205–1214;

Tamás Turai, "Kié a kert?," *Jelenkor*, 33 (1990): 268–270;

Mihály Vajda, "Az értelmiségi osztály és a társadalmi önmegismerés lehetősége," in his *Marx után szabadon, avagy miért nem vagyok már marxista?* (Budapest: Gondolat, 1990), pp. 97–128;

András Veres, "Fordulat Konrád György írói pályáján: Kerti mulatság," *Literature*, 23 (1996): 74–80;

Veres, "Látogatás egy cinkosnál," *2000*, 1 (August 1989): 60–63;

Veres, "Látogatóban, kerti mulatságon: Konrád György vázlatos pályaképe," *Kritika II*, 24 (1995): 13–16;

Veres, "Value Perception in Hungarian Prose, 1969–1980," *Values, Networks and Cultural Reproduction in Hungary: Research Review*, 3 (1991): 93–106.

Tadeusz Konwicki

(22 June 1926 –   )

Edward Możejko
University of Alberta

BOOKS: *Przy budowie* (Warsaw: Czytelnik, 1950);
Godzina smutku (Warsaw: Czytelnik, 1954);
Żelazna kurtyna, by Konwicki and Kazimierz Sumierski (Warsaw: Filmowa Agencja Wydawnicza, 1954);
Władza (Warsaw: Czytelnik, 1954);
Klucz (Warsaw: Nasza Księgarnia, 1955);
Rojsty (Warsaw: Czytelnik, 1956);
Z oblężonego miasta (Warsaw: Iskry, 1956);
Dziura w niebie (Warsaw: Iskry, 1959);
Sennik współczesny (Warsaw: Iskry, 1963); translated by David Welsh as *A Dreambook for Our Time* (Cambridge, Mass.: M. I. T. Press, 1969); republished, with an introduction by Leszek Kołakowski (Harmondsworth, U.K. & New York: Penguin, 1976);
Ostatni dzień lata: Scenariusze filmowe (Warsaw: Iskry, 1966)—includes *Zimowy zmierzch, Ostatni dzień lata, Zaduszki, Salto, Matura,* and *Jak daleko stąd, jak blisko;*
Wniebowstąpienie (Warsaw: Iskry, 1967);
Zwierzoczłekoupiór, illustrated by Danuta Konwicka (Warsaw: Czytelnik, 1969); translated by George Korwin-Rodziszewski and Audrey Korwin-Rodziszewski as *The Anthropos-Spectre-Beast* (New York: Phillips, 1977; Oxford & New York: Oxford University Press, 1977);
Nic albo nic (Warsaw: Czytelnik, 1971);
Kronika wypadków miłosnych (Warsaw: Czytelnik, 1974);
Dlaczego kot jest kotem? illustrated by Danuta Konwicka (Warsaw: Krajowa agencja wydawnicza, 1976);
Kalendarz i klepsydra (Warsaw: Czytelnik, 1976);
Kompleks polski: Powieść, Zapis, no. 3 (London: Index on Censorship, 1977 [i.e. 1978]; Warsaw: Wydawnictwa Alfa, 1989); translated by Richard Lourie as *The Polish Complex* (New York: Farrar, Straus & Giroux, 1982); republished, with an introduction by Joanna Rostropowicz Clark (Harmondsworth, U.K.: Penguin, 1984);

Tadeusz Konwicki (photograph © 1990 by Jerry Bauer; from the dust jacket for New World Avenue and Vicinity*)*

Mała apokalipsa, Zapis, no. 10 (London: Index on Censorship, 1979; Warsaw: Niezależna Oficyna Wydawnicza, 1979); translated by Lourie as *A Minor Apocalypse* (New York: Farrar, Straus & Giroux, 1983; London: Faber & Faber, 1983);
Wschody i zachody księżyca, Zapis, no. 21 (London: Index on Censorship, 1982; Warsaw: Krąg, 1982); translated by Lourie as *Moonrise, Moonset* (New York: Farrar, Straus & Giroux, 1987; London: Faber & Faber, 1988);
Rzeka podziemna (Warsaw: Krąg, 1984); republished as *Rzeka podziemna, podziemne ptaki* (London: Aneks, 1985; Warsaw: Wydawnictwa Alfa, 1989);

Nowy Świat i okolice, illustrated by Konwicki (Warsaw: Czytelnik, 1986); translated by Walter Arndt as *New World Avenue and Vicinity* (New York: Farrar, Straus & Giroux, 1991);

Bohiń (Warsaw: Czytelnik, 1987); translated by Lourie as *Bohin Manor* (New York: Farrar, Straus & Giroux, 1990; London: Faber & Faber, 1992);

Zorze wieczorne (Warsaw: Wydawnictwa Alfa, 1991);

Czytadło (Warsaw: Niezależna Oficyna Wydawnicza, 1992);

Pamflet na siebie (Warsaw: Niezależna Oficyna Wydawnicza, 1995).

PRODUCED SCRIPTS: *Żelazna kurtyna,* motion picture, by Konwicki and Kazimierz Sumierski, released as *Kariera,* WFF Łódź, 1955;

Zimowy zmierzch, motion picture, Rytm/WFF Wrocław, 1957;

Ostatni dzień lata, motion picture, by Konwicki and Jan Laskowski, ZAF Kadr, 1958;

Matka Joanna od Aniołów, motion picture, by Konwicki and Jerzy Kawalerowicz, based on Jarosław Iwaszkiewicz's short story, Film Polski Film Agency/ZAF Kadr, 1961; released in the United States as *Joan of the Angels,* Telepix, 1962;

Zaduszki, motion picture, ZAF Kadr, 1961;

Faraon, motion picture, by Konwicki and Kawalerowicz, based on Bolesław Prus's novel, Film Polski Film Agency/WFF Łódź/ZAF Kadr, 1965; released in the United States as *Pharaoh,* Horizon Films, 1977;

Salto, motion picture, ZAF Kadr, 1965;

Matura, motion picture, ZAF Kadr, 1966;

Jowita, motion picture, based on Stanisław Dygat's novel *Disneyland,* Film Polski Film Agency/ WFF Łódź/ ZRF Syrena, 1967; released in the United States as *Jovita,* Audio Brondon Films, 1976;

Jak daleko stąd, jak blisko, motion picture, Plan, 1972;

Dolina Issy, motion picture, based on Czesław Miłosz's novel, Zespół Filmowy Perspektywa, 1982; released in the United States as *The Issa Valley,* Contal International, 1988;

Austeria, motion picture, by Konwicki, Kawalerowicz, and Julian Stryjkowski, based on Stryjkowski's novel, Zespół Filmowy Kadr, 1983;

Kronika wypadków miłosnych, by Konwicki and Andrzej Wajda, based on Konwicki's novel, Filmowy Perspektywa/Zespoły Filmowe, 1986;

Lawa: Opowieść o "Dziadach" Adama Mickiewicza, motion picture, based on Adam Mickiewicz's play *Dziady* (1989).

OTHER: "Podróż w lata sześćdziesiąte naszego wieku," by Konwicki and Tadeusz Papier, in *Nad Wisłą i Pilicą* (Warsaw: Książka i Wiedza, 1953).

Tadeusz Konwicki belongs to that group of prominent contemporary Polish writers who since the early 1970s have gained unprecedented popularity abroad. With his works widely read in both Europe and America, Konwicki's success is mainly owing to his prose published in the late 1960s, 1970s, and 1980s, though the beginnings of his literary career go back to the late 1940s. Throughout this long period of time marked by exceptionally prolific literary output, Konwicki also showed a keen interest in motion pictures. He directed several movies that placed him in the forefront of what has been called the "Polish film school" and brought him international recognition. He became well known for screenplays that he wrote either by himself or in cooperation with other moviemakers and writers.

The only child of Michał Konwicki, a technical school instructor, and Jadwiga Konwicki (née Kieżun), a homemaker, Tadeusz Konwicki was born on 22 June 1926 in Nowa Wilejka, a small suburb of Wilno, known today as Vilnius—the capital of Lithuania. At the end of World War II this part of prewar Poland was annexed by the Soviet Union and incorporated into Soviet Lithuania, and this region, which had become to Konwicki a foreign country, is the setting of several of his novels. The sense of the loss of his beloved native land, the Lithuania of his youth, has undoubtedly been responsible for Konwicki's obsessive concern for and interest in the region, feelings that were probably intensified by the fact that his mother refused to resettle in the territory of postwar Poland. His father had died of tuberculosis when Konwicki was three, and his mother, who had to go to work, preferred to stay with her sister in the small town of Szczecinek. Because of her poor health, Konwicki spent most of his childhood under the care of his maternal grandparents.

He graduated from high school by attending clandestine classes in Wilno and, shortly before the retreat of German troops from the city in 1944, Konwicki joined the underground resistance movement, *Armia krajowa* (Home Army), which remained under the control of the Polish government-in-exile in London. The activity of this guerrilla force was directed in the second half of 1944 and the early months of 1945 against the advancing Soviet army, which was considered by the majority of patriotic Poles to be another occupying force whose "libera-

Dust jacket for the U.S. edition (1987) of the English translation of Konwicki's novel Wschody i zachody księżyca *(1982), an open attack on the failures of communism in Poland*

tion" of Polish territory had to be opposed by military means. It soon became obvious, however, that their patriotic impulse could not match the might of the Soviet war machine. After the defeat, thousands of Home Army soldiers were captured and imprisoned, executed, or sent to perish in the concentration camps of Siberia. Konwicki's participation in the war against the Red Army was short-lived but left an indelible mark on his personality and made a lasting impression on his writing. Such issues as the conflict between allegiance to patriotic ideals and their betrayal, between unreserved loyalty to Polish ideals of freedom and conformity in relation to victorious communists, and between duty and pragmatism haunt many of Konwicki's protagonists. He described some of these painful dilemmas his generation had to face in an autobiographical novel, *Rojsty* (Marshes, 1956).

Konwicki managed to work his way to Poland, thus avoiding the fate of many of his peers. For a

short while he settled in Kraków, where he enrolled in architecture at the Polytechnical University but quickly switched (as he admits, he was horrified by mathematics) to an entirely different specialization: he entered the Jagiellonian University to study Polish literature. His sojourn in Kraków did not last long. As a student, he began to write for the literary weekly *Odrodzenie* (Renaissance). In 1947 *Odrodzenie* moved to Warsaw and, as a member of its editorial board, Konwicki followed suit. Two years later, in 1949, he married Danuta Lenica, the sister of a well-known printmaker and cinema operator, Jan Lenica (their father, the late Alfred Lenica, was also a painter). Danuta Konwicka is an artist in her own right, known for illustrations of children's books. Since their marriage, the capital of Poland has remained their permanent place of residence. They have two daughters: Maria, born in 1952, and Ewa Anna, born in 1959.

During the late 1940s Konwicki came into contact with some prominent Polish intellectuals and writers, notably Zbigniew Bieńkowski, Karol Kuryluk, Wilhelm Mach, and Tadeusz Borowski, and published his first literary essays, short stories, and fragments of two unfinished novels in *Odrodzenie* and other periodicals. Few readers realize that at this early stage of his career Konwicki wrote some poetry and even drew cartoons for newspapers.

Konwicki's first novel, *Przy budowie* (At the Building Site), appeared in book form in 1950. The writer sensed the political and ideological demands of the time. A year earlier, at the conference of Polish Writers Union in Szczecin, the doctrine of "socialist realism" was introduced and imposed as the only valid method by which new postwar literature and art ought to be created. *Przy budowie* was a typical product of this doctrine. Its action takes place at a construction site where a railway track is being laid, and in completing this track the workers encounter some serious difficulties. Typically, the characters are presented in accordance with the premises of socialist realism: they are divided into so-called positive and negative bearers of political and ideological values. This simplification of their behavior and thoughts is maintained throughout the entire novel and illustrates well the rise of what became known as schematism; that is, a particularly stereotyped disposition of narrative parts that had to include the motif of class struggle, the figure of a "positive hero" who would personify the ideological virtues of new socialist men, and an optimistic outcome of the plot (in the latter case, the implied triumphant victory of socialist, Marxist ideals over the "forces of backwardness and reaction").

Konwicki's next major novel, *Władza* (Power, 1954), was also based on these principles. As in *Przy budowie*, the narrator preserves an authoritarian, omniscient perspective, suggesting to the reader all the "right" answers and the way in which the unfolding intrigues of the plot are to be understood. Its action takes place between June of 1947 and October 1948, an important period in the political stabilization of the Polish People's Republic, a puppet state established under Soviet pressure and coercion. The novel, indeed, depicts the struggle for power between those who want to preserve the "old" capitalist order and the "new" forces who proclaim the necessity of building a "new socialist country of justice and peace." The conflicts here are drawn more sharply than in *Przy budowie*: there exists clandestine, armed opposition groups fought by the Urząd Bezpieczeństwa (U.B.; the state security or secret police), and there are those who hesitate to take a stand and try (unsuccessfully) to remain neutral. *Władza*, however, is not limited just to these issues: it seems to express an ambition to give a broader gamut of the political spectrum in Poland during this dramatic time of transition. It reflects the activity of the Communist Party (known at that time as the Polish Workers' Party) and its ideological adversary, the Polish Peasant Party led by Stanisław Mikołajczyk. It also presents the reader with a more particular picture of the existing divisions within the party, alluding to the struggle between the hardliners who would not accept anything less than a blind imitation of the "Soviet experience" (such as Mikołaj Gałecki) and the moderates advocating a more cautious approach to the construction of socialism in Poland (such as Ignacy Korejwa). This particular controversy ended in the condemnation of the alleged "right-wing, nationalistic deviation" within the party represented by Władysław Gomułka, who was deposed as the Secretary General of the party in 1948 and then imprisoned.

Władza is a typical "illustrative" novel, depicting the significance of historical events in accordance with the directives of the Communist Party, but one may also detect in it some personal anxieties of the author. After the atrocities and sufferings of the war, after the crisis of moral values and of faith in humanity, Konwicki began a search for new positive ideals. It seems that he had believed, or at least remained for a while under the illusion, that they could be identified with the new political regime based on Marxist philosophy; in 1951, as if

to confirm his allegiance to its basic tenets, he joined the Communist Party. He left it in 1966.

In 1956 Konwicki brought out two important novels: *Rojsty* and *Z oblężonego miasta* (From the Besieged Town). Placed within their historical context, they reflect a certain liberalization in the cultural policy of the party, known as "the thaw." *Rojsty*, for example, was written around 1948 but could not be published until eight years later, when censorship was somewhat relaxed. More importantly, *Rojsty* also demonstrates Konwicki's ability to think for himself. In fact, the novel occupies a peculiar, ambiguous place in Konwicki's writing and became the subject of considerable controversy.

The ambiguity of *Rojsty* ensues from the author's critical approach to its subject matter. If in socialist-realist novels the writer generally strikes a positive and optimistic tone of acceptance, in *Rojsty* Konwicki surprises the reader with a somber and negative assessment of his own youth as a guerrilla fighter. Autobiographical threads have always made up a major part of Konwicki's writing, and, in this respect, *Rojsty* is a particularly good example of how Konwicki incorporates personal elements in his works: what he aims to achieve is to settle accounts with his own past. While defending his generation for its commitment to the cause of national independence, the writer gives a critical description of a guerrilla detachment in which he served, illustrating its moral degeneration and a gradual slide into ordinary criminality. Torn between the noble ideal of its duty to fight the enemy and the realization of its hopeless situation in the face of Soviet power, the platoon disintegrates into a group of pitiful losers, even criminals. In the eyes of those who cherished the image of the heroic struggle of the Home Army against foreign powers, Konwicki was a traitor, but for those representing the new order, he did not go far enough in his criticism. Whatever the merits of the book, the controversy over it made Konwicki an author considered worthy of close critical attention.

Konwicki's next novel, *Z oblężonego miasta*, confirmed this perception. It raised similar issues as in *Rojsty* but presented them in a more sympathetic light by emphasizing the question of faithfulness to the patriotic principles defended by the generation of the Home Army soldiers. If in *Rojsty* Konwicki took a critical view of what happened to the young soldiers of the Home Army, demonstrating with bitterness the final and tragic outcome of their struggle, in *Z oblężonego miasta* he distanced himself from the official propaganda that tried to discredit and condemn the activities of the Home Army. This change marked, as some critics noticed, the begin-

Dust jacket for the U.S. edition (1990) of the English translation of Konwicki's novel Bohiń *(1987), which is based on his imagining of his paternal grandmother*

ning of a process of recanting some of the ideas expressed or formulated in earlier published works, similar to the poetic genre known as a palinode. This process of recantation was generated by the thaw and affected many writers. In Konwicki's case it meant a departure from the style and ideological disposition that he developed mainly in *Przy budowie* and *Władza*. The first, cautious step in this direction was *Z oblężonego miasta*. Three novels written in the late 1950s and the 1960s, namely *Dziura w niebie* (A Hole in the Sky, 1959), *Sennik współczesny* (1963; translated as *A Dreambook for Our Time*, 1969) and *Wniebowstąpienie* (Ascension,1967) testify to Konwicki's artistic and ideological transformation.

Although Konwicki began writing screenplays in the early 1950s, in 1958 he arrived in the international community of moviemakers. Unexpectedly, his directorial debut, *Ostatni dzień lata* (The Last Day of Summer) took top prizes at the 1958 International Short Film Festival in Venice. The movie fea-

tured some obsessions related to the horrors of the war and the universal angst brought about by the dangers of the nuclear age. One of the main assets of *Ostatni dzień lata* was its universal appeal to contemporary human anxiety, free of the specificity of Polish historical experience or national mythology. This screenplay and others were published in *Ostatni dzień lata: Scenariusze filmowe* (The Last Day of Summer: Movie Scenarios, 1966).

With the publication of new prose and the broadening of his creative range with his move into cinema, Konwicki entered the 1960s with increased confidence and a reputation as a writer on the rise. For his novel *Dziura w niebie* he received the literary award of the weekly *Nowa Kultura* (New Culture). Throughout the 1950s and 1960s he traveled as a member of official delegations of the Polish Writers Union, visiting the Soviet Union in 1952 and China in 1956. In the 1960s he visited France, the Federal Republic of Germany, Italy, and revisited the Soviet Union. Later trips in the 1970s and 1980s took him to the United States (where his daughter Maria established permanent domicile), and to other parts of the world.

As for his novels, *Dziura w niebie* turned out to be one of the first in a series devoted to the days of his childhood and early youth in Wilno. It also meant a definite end to the novice period of his writing and represented the beginning of a search for a new artistic identity. In this novel Konwicki made use of different generic strategies by using conventions of the novel of initiation, the social novel, and Gothic romance. In the end the entire narrative structure of *Dziura w niebie* is bound together by a parable, telling the story of a childish belief in an idea that proves to be a hoax. The novel is free of the ideological controversies of the time, except that "the childish belief in an idea" may have been a veiled allusion to the Communist Party faithful who suddenly realized after Nikita Khrushchev's revelations about the excesses of Stalinism at the Twentieth Congress of the Communist Party of the Soviet Union in 1956 that "the Emperor has no clothes." Polek Krywko, the protagonist of the novel, believes that "something great will happen," and when all who surround him renounce this kind of thinking, he still adheres to his illusions. Thus, Konwicki notes in his 1986 conversations with Stanisław Nowicki that, in fact, *Dziura w niebie* constitutes a defense of a Stalinist.

Two other novels of this cycle, *Zwierzoczłekoupiór* (1969; translated as *The Anthropos-Spectre-Beast*, 1977) and *Kronika wypadków miłosnych* (Chronicle of Erotic Events, 1974) show similar characteristics: the protagonists are children, recollections of the war are absent, and the narrative texture constitutes a blend of various novelistic techniques. Childhood is described as a stage in human development in which the individual attempts to find some sense in life—the same teleological certainty that adults are often missing.

Three other novels, generically akin to *Dziura w niebie*, namely *Sennik współczesny*, *Nic albo nic* (Nothing or Nothing, 1971), and *Wniebowstąpienie* bring out yet another characteristic feature in Konwicki's writing—a search for one's own identity and truth through the recollection and contemplation of the painful, even tragic past. In this respect *Sennik współczesny* is particularly typical. Its protagonist, Paweł, lives in two worlds: the world of the emotionally and even physically oppressive present and the world of the horrible past. His fate is strangely intertwined with that of a character called Car (pronounced "tsar"). As Paweł arrives in a town and learns about Car, he gradually realizes that Car is his former colleague from the resistance movement, who betrayed its cause. For his betrayal Car was sentenced to death, and Paweł agreed to carry out the sentence. Indeed, he had shot at Car, but without a firm intention to kill him; Car was wounded but survived. Now their paths cross again. *Sennik współczesny* constitutes a clear break with Konwicki's style in the early 1950s, when his novels exhibited a distinctive rectilinear progression of the plot. With his 1963 novel Konwicki began to disrupt the sequential unity of his prose by disregarding both its temporal and spatial logical order. The novel leaves the impression of being chaotic, with many loose ends left hanging, and the reader is left to unravel the mysteries of the story for himself. This sense of disorder is reinforced by intimations of the impending disaster that is about to befall the town where Paweł arrives; it is to be flooded for the purpose of building a dam. He is surrounded by unhappy people, outsiders who cannot find their place in life and are doomed to defeat. These apocalyptic motifs occur again in *Nic albo nic* and find their culmination in *Mała apokalipsa* (1979; translated as *A Minor Apocalypse*, 1983). Novels from both of the two cycles have one thing in common: they express doubt about the ability of human beings to create a world of trust in which they can find solutions to their frequently irrational lives. Their protagonists experience the pains of total isolation and disappointment, and they reach existential blind alleys. While not openly critical of the reigning system of totalitarian oppression, these novels definitely break with the optimistic vision prescribed by the communist authorities.

Konwicki took one step further in this direction in 1976 by publishing *Kalendarz i klepsydra* (The Calendar and the Hourglass); some critics go as far as to consider this novel, together with *Kompleks polski: Powieść* (1977; translated as *The Polish Complex*, 1982), to be the writer's second debut. These two novels mark a new beginning in Konwicki's writing in two ways: thematically they can be defined as the prose of protest and rejection, and formally they constitute an opening to metafictional narratives that clearly link them to the postmodernist tendencies which dominate Konwicki's writing throughout the 1980s and 1990s. *Kalendarz i klepsydra*, written in the form of a diary, strikes one with the directness of its descriptions, in which the denotative function of language comes clearly to the fore. One of its features is the presentation of portraits of writers and artists, mainly from the Warsaw creative milieu; thus, the reader learns about creative types such as Antoni Słonimski, Stanisław Dygat, Marek Hłasko, Andrzej Łapicki, Roman Bratny, Jan Himilsbach. Some of these depictions are unflattering, some full of praise, yet all are interspersed with gossip and anecdotes that can be neither confirmed nor denied. This lack of verifiability is probably why in his self-referential comments the author calls the book a "pseudo-diary," "a simulated diary," or even "a false diary" and deplores the fact that it is not always possible to reveal the truth. The only principal character of this narrative is Konwicki himself, and the book delights with its manifold observations about either his life or the broader framework of his artistic, political, and social milieu. Here is a literary collage with a succession of themes, subjects, and images that occur with kaleidoscopic speed. The book includes some threads that Konwicki later developed into full-scale stories—for example, reminiscences about his paternal grandmother formed the basis of the novel *Bohiń* (1987; (translated as *Bohin Manor*, 1990)—as well as comments about his previous works (both as moviemaker and writer), confessions about friendships, negative opinions about Polish television and the Union of Writers, and frustrations expressed about inconveniences and nonsense in everyday life. But, above all, Konwicki carries out a sort of squaring up with his own past. He candidly admits that in his early years as a writer he embraced Stalinism, or at least its cultural policy, not out of fear but out of conviction. He became angry, he claims, with the messianic ideas of Polish romanticists, particularly Adam Mickiewicz, who projected Poland as a "chosen nation" that would

Cover for Konwicki's 1992 novel, a postmodernist mixture of
romance and detective fiction in which the author
acknowledges that literature is ultimately
unsatisfying to both the reader
and the writer

show other nations a new vision of life—a mythology that led to the catastrophe of 1939.

Consequently, he tried to embark on the new program of national renewal proposed by the Communists. He now confesses that he made the wrong choice but cannot blame anyone but himself for his mistakes. At the same time, he warns that though Stalinism may be dead, the people who implemented its policy in the past still occupy powerful positions in society—an unmistakable reference to the political establishment of the time, to his generation as a whole, and even to his friends. In this book Konwicki came as close as possible to testing the patience and vigilance of the censor. Beyond this point lay the imminent ban on publishing. He crossed this line in his next novel, *Kompleks polski.*

In *Kompleks polski* three thematic threads run parallel: Communist Poland in the 1970s, reevaluation of the troubling past, and the writer's quasi diary about his personal mishaps, which are happening while he stands in line in a jewelry store to buy Soviet gold. Seemingly unrelated, the threads merge into one image of the country haunted by its historical adversity, that is, the loss of independence and the January Insurrection, the abortive and costly uprising against Russian rule in 1863. This historical situation has its bearing on and corresponds with the situation of the 1970s: Poland still remained under Russian domination imposed by the Soviet totalitarian system, but now Soviet Russia was presenting itself as a "friend." Several narrative voices refer to this disguised hostility, but the most revealing and accusatory one is expressed in a letter by a Pole who emigrated to another country. Konwicki uses the device of misattribution: the sender, now living in a faraway country on another continent, bitterly complains about his adopted homeland's being invaded by the "omnipotent neighbor to the north" and forced to accept its political system. Combining these historical and political injustices with the misery of standing in a queue, the principal narrator of *Kompleks polski* (who represents the writer's alter ego) unfolds before the reader a portrayal of total social depravation and moral decay. Written in a typical postmodernist style with many intertextual and metatextual indicators, a variety of subtexts, and ever-changing narrative perspectives, *Kompleks polski* became one of the most vivid examples of criticism directed against the existing political regime in Poland. First published in 1977 by the clandestine quarterly *Zapis* (The Record), it was the writer's first book to appear in the underground press. Although this book appeared in Polish as a publication of the London-based human rights group Index on Censorship, it was not published in complete book form in Poland until 1989.

Konwicki preserves the same critical attitude in two other important books that were also first published clandestinely: *Mała apokalipsa* and *Wschody i zachody księżyca* (1982; translated as *Moonrise, Moonset,* 1987). The former is a dystopian Orwellian fiction about a society subjected to the tight control of the state; irony and the grotesque interplay throughout the entire novel. "We have built socialism" proclaims a neon sign, and the authorities organize massive demonstrations in the capital in support of close friendship with a mighty neighboring power that is soon to subsume the smaller country. A small group of dissidents is plotting to prevent their country from being taken over, but they are hopelessly divided, phony, and inefficient. An air of absurdity and a catastrophic mood reign over the actions of the characters and of the events of the novel. Catastrophism is a persistent component of Konwicki's writings, but in *Mała apokalipsa* it has reached its culmination.

Wschody i zachody księżyca, written during the period of Solidarity and the subsequent imposition of martial law, has many critical and political overtones similar to those in *Mała apokalipsa* but lacks the figurative dimension of the earlier novel. It is an open attack on the failures of Communism, presented in the form of a diary recording the events of the memorable year of 1981. It may be argued that a critical assessment of the Polish crisis of that year reached its pinnacle in these two books: Konwicki is critical not only of the Communists who crushed the people's aspirations for freedom but also of the nation as a whole. Even the dissidents are not exempt from his criticism. In displaying a certain evenhandedness in his judgment, the author preserves an attitude typical of postmodernist writing: while leaving no doubt on which side of the conflict his sympathies lie, at times he discerns positive features in those individuals who act on behalf of the authorities.

Two works in this period of Konwicki's writing deserve special attention, although for different reasons: *Rzeka podziemna, podziemne ptaki* (Underground River, Underground Birds, 1985) and *Bohiń.* In the former the author touches upon certain leitmotifs akin to those in *Kompleks polski* and *Mała apokalipsa,* which reveal some painful constants of Polish history and, at the same time, represent Konwicki's own preoccupations with the destiny of Poland as a nation. Taken together, these two novels and *Rzeka podziemna, podziemne ptaki* constitute a triptych: they draw a parallel between historical events and the contemporary struggle for liberation. The theme is conveyed through three different narrative forms. In *Kompleks polski* Konwicki uses a personalized account, the diary or a notebook that records the narrator's reflections and provides evidence of various events. *Mała apokalipsa* is a hyperbolic example of dystopian science fiction, and *Rzeka podziemna, podziemne ptaki* is written in a realistic style about the events surrounding the imposition of martial law in 1981. Its action starts on 13 December 1981—the day martial law was imposed by the regime of General Wojciech Jaruzelski. There is a clear division into those who represent the regime ("they") and those who are fighting against it ("we"). The political situation is described as analogous to the historical

past: it is yet another failed uprising against the oppressor, except that the oppressor, now in Polish uniform, speaks the same language. Polish criticism qualified *Rzeka podziemna, podziemne ptaki* as a novel belonging to the so-called antisocialist literature of the 1970s and 1980s that laid the blame for the national anguish on the Communist system and its demoralizing and divisive policies; tendentious in its essence, this literature ascribes moral rightness to those who oppose Communism.

Published in 1987, the novel *Bohiń* is an evocation of the writer's past in his attempt to recover his roots and can be read as an attempt at mythologizing Lithuania. According to Konwicki, the novel is a mystification of his family's past: the plot of the novel is based on an assumed love affair between the author's paternal grandmother, Helena Konwicka, and a young Jew named Elias Szyra. Konwicki has admitted that he does not know anything about his real grandmother's life; yet, the invented story allows him to create a marvelous romance with a deeper meaning, revealing the breakdown of traditional racial prejudices and class divisions: the love of a woman of the Polish nobility for a poor Jew and her preferring him to a nobleman throws an unusual light on the contradictions of the patriarchal way of life in the seemingly pastoral nineteenth-century Lithuanian province. Judged from a strictly literary point of view, *Bohiń* is Konwicki's most obvious and interesting affirmation of his postmodernist mode of writing, woven of many metafictional digressions, autotelic reflections, and changes in the narrative perspective.

In two of the books published in the first half of the 1990s, *Czytadło* (A Read, 1992) and *Pamflet na siebie* (Self-Lampoon, 1995), Konwicki continued developing this postmodernist tendency, with his writing marked by a palimpsestic use of his own texts, constant alternation between the perspectives of a fictitious narrator and that of the author himself, documentary or autobiographical insertions, the blurring of the boundary between reality and fiction, fragmentation, hybridization of genres, and so on. *Czytadło* is a mixture of romance and detective fiction in which the writer takes a break from his prevalent concern with the social and political issues of his country and its history. Rather, he settles his personal account with literature as the field of his activity: he seems to acknowledge that it can neither satisfy the ever-changing tastes or demands of readers nor rescue the writer from loneliness and alienation. In *Pamflet na siebie,* subordinated entirely to the tenet of narrative fragmentation, Konwicki enters a new realm of creative experience—he examines the workings of human consciousness and conscience. *Pamflet na siebie* is a book of observations and reflections on a variety of topics, events, facts, and encounters with people. It is a subtle blend of self-irony and irony aimed at everything that surrounds one.

Throughout his long literary career, Konwicki has experienced many artistic changes and ideological upheavals and shifts. Three developmental stages can be distinguished in his writing: the earliest stage is associated with the doctrine of socialist realism; the second signifies a departure from the principles of socialist realism, combined with a growing scepticism regarding the surrounding world; and the third stage constitutes a clear rejection of socialist realism. Konwicki will go down in the history of Polish literature as the writer who tried to overcome the romantic tradition so deeply entrenched in Polish culture and, through the "ordinariness" of his prose to challenge, as he said to Nowicki, "our terrible chase after elitism and fear of commonness." In pursuing this goal he brought about a reevaluation of many Polish national myths and came to represent an attitude that resembles that of another great Polish writer—Witold Gombrowicz, who mocked so-called "Polishness," the conservative tradition, backwardness, and pomposity that hindered open-minded appreciation of other cultures. Tadeusz Konwicki has modernized Polish perceptions about art and literature and linked them through his postmodernist stance to their Western counterparts. This modernization constitutes his originality and most valuable contribution to the Polish cultural scene.

Interviews:

Konrad Eberhardt, "Pisarz przy kamerze," *Film*, 51 (1960);

"Trzy głosy o problemach adaptacji filmowej. Wypowiedź Tadeusza Konwickiego," *Kwartalnik Filmowy*, 4 (1960);

Ewa Bon (Ewa Boniecka), "Rozmawiamy z autorem książki stycznia—Tadeuszem Konwickim," *Kurier Polski*, 33 (1964);

Krystyna Nastulanka, "O pogodzie, kompleksach i zabobonach," *Polityka*, 47 (1964);

Barbara Mruklik, "Tadeusz Konwicki o swym najnowszym filmie, o polskim XX-leciu, o supergigantach," *Ekran*, 47 (1964);

Beata Sowińska, "'Nigdy nie zaglądam do swoich książek' mówi *Życiu* Tadeusz Konwicki," *Życie Warszawy*, 3 (1965);

Andrzej Drawicz, "Piętnastolatek Tadeusz Konwicki," *Sztandar Młodych*, 103 (1965);

Alfred Zejman, "Rozmowa z Tadeuszem Konwickim," *Panorama*, 32 (1965);

Jacek Fuksiewicz, "'Producent żąda rozrywki.' Wywiad z Tadeuszem Konwickim," *Film*, 3 (1966);

Zbigniew Taranienko, "'Współautorstwo czytelnika.' Z Tadeuszem Konwickim rozmawia Zbigniew Taranienko," *Argumenty*, 44 (1971): 8–9;

L. J., "'Literatura będzie miała mniej białych plam.' Rozmowa z Tadeuszem Konwickim," *Kurier Polski*, 239 (1971);

Urszula Biełous, "'Film bez literatury?' Rozmowa z Tadeuszem Konwickim," *Literatura*, 1 (1972);

Konrad Eberhardt, "'Powinienem zadebiutować na nowo.' Rozmowa z Tadeuszem Konwickim," *Kino*, 4 (1972);

Michał Komar, "Tadeusz Konwicki: Sen pocieszający," *Studio*, 11, no. 12 (1972);

Wanda Wartenstein, "'Nie miałem pojęcia o robieniu filmów'—mówi Tadeusz Konwicki," *Film*, 14 (1974);

Alojzy Michalski, "T. Konwicki o: Filmowym warsztacie, nie zrealizowanych pomysłach," *Nadodrze*, 15 (1974);

Stanisław Nowicki, *Pół wieku czyśćca: Rozmowy z Tadeuszem Konwickim* (Warsaw: Przedświt, 1986; London: Aneks, 1986);

Witold Szaniawski, "Chciałbym znaleźć klucz do polskości," *Przegląd Katolicki*, 35 (1987): 4–5;

Elżbieta Sawicka, "Nasi bracia w grzechach i świętości," *Odra*, 12 (1987): 16;

Sawicka, "W szponach romantyzmu," *Odra*, 1 (1988): 22–31;

Andrzej Werner, "Wróżby z dnia dzisiejszego. Rozmowa z Tadeuszem Konwickim," *Kino*, 1 (1991): 2–7;

Monika Kuc, "Prawo do Buntu. Rozmowa z Tadeuszem Konwickim," (supplement to *Życie Warszawy*), *Kultura i Życie*, 12 (1991): 1–2;

"Łupież na mózgu. Z Tadeuszem Konwickim rozmawiała Elżbieta Sawicka," *Przegląd Polski*, 1, no. 8 (1991): 6–7;

Wiesław Kot, "Fundamentaliści atakują. Rozmowa z Tadeuszem Konwickim, pisarzem," *Wprost*, 5 (1991): 11–12;

Adam Michnik, "Na świecie jestem przejazdem," *Gazeta wyborcza* (7 December 1991);

Przemysław Czapliński i Maciej Mazurek, (supplement to *Gazeta Wielkopolska*), *Format*, 1 (1992);

Tadeusz Sobolewski, "O magiczności i zmiennych koniunkturach mówi Tadeusz Konwicki," *Kino*, 9 (1992): 6–9;

Elżbieta Chęcińska, "Kronika wypadków rodzinnych. Z Tadeuszem Konwickim i jego córkami

Marią Konwicką i Anną Wesołowską rozmawia Elżbieta Chęcińska," *Twój Styl,* 7–8 (1993);

Teresa Zaniewska, "Moje oczy pełne Białorusi," *Gazeta wyborcza,* 173 (27 July 1993): 10–11;

Danuta Sosnowska, "Kresy mogą być zarzewiem Karabachu," *Kresy,* 13 (1993);

Małgorzata Terlecka-Reksnis, "Nasze histerie i nasze nadzieje," *Gazeta wyborcza,* 1 (1994);

Dorota Sobieska, "'Everything comes from what I said at the beginning, from this territory': An Interview with Tadeusz Konwicki," *Review of Contemporary Fiction,* 3 (1994): 112–123.

Bibliographies:

Słownik współczesnych pisarzy polskich, volume 2 (Warsaw: Państwowe Wydawnictwo Naukowe, 1964), pp. 162–163;

Polscy pisarze współcześni. Informator 1944–1970 (Warsaw: Agencja Autorska, 1972), p. 138;

Literatura polska. Przewodnik encyklopedyczny , volume 1 (Warsaw: Państwowe Wydawnictwo Naukowe, 1984), pp. 471–472;

Edward Czerwiński, ed., *Dictionary of Polish Literature* (Westport, Conn. & London: Greenwood, 1994), pp. 192–196.

Biographies:

Jacek Fuksiewicz, *Tadeusz Konwicki* (Warsaw: WaiF, 1967);

Waldemar Wilk, *Tadeusz Konwicki* (Wrocław: DKF Politechnika, 1986);

Przemysław Czapliński, *Tadeusz Konwicki* (Poznań: Dom Wydawniczy Rebis, 1994).

References:

Judith Arlt, *Tadeusz Konwickis Prosawerk von Rojsty bis Bohiń: Zur Entwicklung von Motivebestand und Erzählstruktur* (Bern & New York: Peter Lang, 1997);

Stanisław Bereś, *"Bohiń Manor:* Romance with Nothingness," *Review of Contemporary Fiction,* 14, no. 3 (1994): 189–196;

Adisson Bross, "Tadeusz Konwicki's *A Dreambook for Our Time:* A Polish Classic," *Review of Contemporary Fiction ,* 14, no. 3 (1994): 172–179;

Stanisław Eile, *"Bohiń* de Tadeusz Konwicki et le postmodernism," *Revue des études slaves,* 63, no. 2 (1991): 529–545;

Aleksander Fiut, "Histeria? (O Tadeuszu Konwickim)," in his *Pytanie o tożsamość* (Kraków: Universitas, 1995), pp. 77–92;

Maria Janion, "Where the Marshes Are: Romantic Mediumism in the Novels of Tadeusz Konwicki," *Review of Contemporary Fiction,* 14, no. 3 (1994): 156–171;

Piotr Lis, "A jednak się kręci. Konwicki," *Gazeta,* 42 (Toronto, 1991): 17;

Tadeusz Lubelski, *Poetyka powieści i filmów Tadeusza Konwickiego* (Wrocław: Wydawnictwo Uniwersytetu Wrocławskiego, 1984);

Maria Malatyńska, "Guślarz Konwicki," *Tygodnik Powszechny,* 27 (1996): 14–15;

Thomas Mayers, "Training the Memory: Dystopian History in Konwicki's *Minor Apocalypse,*" *Review of Contemporary Fiction,* 14, no. 3 (1994): 180–187;

Edward Możejko, "Beyond Ideology: The Prose of Tadeusz Konwicki," *Review of Contemporary Fiction,* 14, no. 3 (1994): 139–155;

A. N., "Bogini," *Kultura niezależna,* 3 (1988): 110–115;

Maciej Prus, "Koniec świata Konwickiego," *Kontakt,* 1 (1982): 71–72;

Prus, "Lęki Konwickiego," *Kontakt,* 3 (1986): 35–39;

Dorota Sobieska, "Tadeusz Konwicki: An Introduction," *Review of Contemporary Fiction,* 14, no. 3 (1994): 96–111;

Edyta Święcianowicz, "Powrót syna marnotrawnego," *Kultura niezależna,* 43 (1988): 116–123;

Carl Tighe, "Tadeusz Konwicki's *A Minor Apocalypse,*" *MLR: The Modern Language Review,* 91 (January 1996): 159–174;

Jan Walc, "Nieepickie powieści Tadeusza Konwickiego," *Pamiętnik Literacki,* 1 (1975);

Marek Zaleski, "Literatura i wyobcowanie: casus Tadeusza Konwickiego" in *Literatura i wyobcowanie. Studia,* edited by Jerzy Święch (Lublin: Lubelskie Wydawnictwo Naukowe, 1990), volume 27, pp. 265–274.

Jaan Kross

(19 February 1920 –   )

Maire Liivamets
The National Library of Estonia

BOOKS: *Söerikastaja* (Tallinn: Eesti Riiklik Kirjastus, 1958);

Tuule-Juku: Poeem (Tallinn: Ajalehtede-Ajakirjade Kirjastus, 1963);

Kivist viiulid (Tallinn: Eesti Riiklik Kirjastus, 1964);

Lauljad laevavööridel (Tallinn: Eesti Raamat, 1966);

Muld ja marmor: Möödasõitnu meenutusi, by Kross and Ellen Niit (Tallinn: Eesti Raamat, 1968);

Vahelugemised, 6 volumes (volumes 1–5, Tallinn: Eesti Raamat, 1968–1990; volume 6, Tallinn: Bibliotheca Baltica, 1995);

Vihm teeb toredaid asju (Tallinn: Eesti Raamat, 1969);

Kolme katku vahel: Balthasar Russowi romaan, 4 volumes (Tallinn: Eesti Raamat, 1970–1980);

Neli monoloogi Püha Jüri asjus (Tallinn: Eesti Raamat, 1970);

Michelsoni immatrikuleerimine (Tallinn: Perioodika, 1971);

Voog ja kolmpii: Luuletusi 1938–1968 (Tallinn: Eesti Raamat, 1971);

Klio silma all (Tallinn: Eesti Raamat, 1972);

Mardileib (Tallinn: Eesti Raamat, 1973);

Kolmandad mäed (Tallinn: Kunst, 1975);

Taevakivi (Tallinn: Eesti Raamat, 1975);

Keisri hull (Tallinn: Eesti Raamat, 1978); translated by Anselm Hollo, from the Finnish translation by Ivo Iliste, as *The Czar's Madman* (London: Harvill, 1992; New York: Pantheon, 1993);

Kajalood (Tallinn: Perioodika, 1980);

Ülesõidukohad (Tallinn: Perioodika, 1981);

Rakvere romaan (Tallinn: Eesti Raamat, 1982);

Professor Martensi ärasõit (Tallinn: Eesti Raamat, 1984); translated by Hollo as *Professor Martens' Departure* (New York: New Press, 1994; London: Harvill, 1994);

Vastutuulelaev (Tallinn: Eesti Raamat, 1987);

Silmade avamise päev (Tallinn: Eesti Raamat, 1988); translated by Eric Dickens, with the addition of "The Ashtray," as *The Conspiracy and Other Stories* (London: Harvill, 1995)—comprises "The

Jaan Kross

Wound," "Lead Piping," "The Stahl Grammar," "The Conspiracy," "The Ashtray," and "The Day His Eyes Were Opened";

Wikmani poisid (Tallinn: Eesti Raamat, 1988);

Väljakaevamised (Tallinn: Eesti Raamat, 1990);

Tabamatus (Tallinn: Kupar, 1993);

Järelehüüd (Tallinn: Perioodika, 1994);

Mesmeri ring: Romaniseeritud memuaarid nagu kõik memuaarid ja peaaegu iga romaan (Tallinn: Kupar, 1995);
Paigallend (Tallinn: Virgela, 1998).
Editions and Collections: *Teosed*, 6 volumes (Tallinn: Eesti Raamat, 1987–1989);
Kogutud teosed: 1. Kolme katku vahel, 2 volumes (Tallinn: Virgela, 1997, 1998).
Editions in English: *The Rock from the Sky*, translated anonymously (Moscow: Raduga, 1983)—comprises "Four Monologues on the Subject of Saint George," "The Elevation of Michelson," "The Story of Two Lost Notes," "An Hour on a Revolving Chair," and "The Rock from the Sky";
"The Tightrope Walker," translated by Tiina Kirss, *Cross Currents*, 6 (1987): 405–418;
"Estonian Character," translated by Eric Dickens, *Index on Censorship*, 21 (November 1992): 5–14;
"Hallelujah" and "The Day His Eyes Are Opened," translated by Ritva Poom, in *Estonian Short Stories*, edited by Kajar Pruul and Darlene Reddaway (Evanston, Ill.: Northwestern University Press, 1996), pp. 92–140.

PLAY PRODUCTIONS: *Pöördtoolitund*, Tallinn, Draamateater, 30 December 1979;
Keisri hull, adapted by Kross from his novel, Tallinn, Draamateater, 25 March 1984;
Tohtori Karellin vaikea jö, translated into Finnish by Raili Kilpi, Helsinki, Suomen Kansallisteatteri, 15 November 1991;
Doktor Karelli raske öö, Tallinn, Draamateater, 22 December 1994.

PRODUCED SCRIPT: *Kolme katku vahel*, television, "Tallinnfilm," June 1970.

OTHER: Juhan Sütiste, *Luuletused*, compiled by Kross (Tallinn: Eesti Raamat, 1964);
Az eszt irodalom kistükre, edited by Kross (Budapest: Europa Könyvkiado, 1969).

TRANSLATIONS: Pierre-Jean de Béranger, *Laulud* (Tallinn: Eesti Riiklik Kirjastus, 1963);
Bertolt Brecht, *Kolmekrossiooper* (Tallinn: Ajalehtede ja Ajakirjade Kirjastus, 1963);
Alexander Gribojedov, *Häda mõistuse pärast* (Tallinn: Eesti Riiklik Kirjastus, 1964);
Romain Rolland, *14. juuli: Revolutsioonidraama* (Tallinn: Eest Raamat, 1964);
William Shakespeare, *Othello*, in *Kogutud teosed 5*, edited by Georg Meri (Tallinn: Eesti Raamat, 1966), pp. 403–502;

Edmond Rostand, *Cyrano de Bergerac* (Tallinn: Eesti Riiklik Kirjastus, 1967);
Shakespeare, *Macbeth*, in *Kogutud teosed 6*, edited by Meri (Tallinn: Eesti Raamat, 1968), pp. 137–213;
Paul Eluard, *Veel enne kostma peab* (Tallinn: Eesti Raamat, 1969);
Imre Madach, *Inimese tragöödia* (Tallinn: Eesti Raamat, 1970);
Lewis Carroll, *Alice imedemaal* (Tallinn: Eesti Raamat, 1971);
Stefan Zweig, *Kolm meistrit* (Tallinn: Eesti Raamat, 1985);
Karl Ristikivi, *Hurmakägu on surma nägu* (Tallinn: Kupar, 1992);
Zweig, *Tervenemine vaimu läbi* (Tallinn: Kuldsulg, 1998);
Zweig, *Eurooplase mälestused* (Tallinn: Eesti Raamat, 1998).

Jaan Kross entered Estonian literature as a poet in the mid 1950s; in the 1970s, however, he became famous for his historical fiction. The lives and times of notable Estonians from the past have remained his favorite subject. Kross has said that he finds it fascinating to familiarize himself with a past world that was once as real as the one that exists now, and in most of his novels he succeeds in creating an illusion of such a world. In a few—especially *Kolme katku vahel: Balthasar Russowi romaan* (Between Three Plagues: Balthasar Russow's Novel, 1970–1980) and *Keisri hull* (1978; translated as *The Czar's Madman*, 1992)—the past comes alive with unusual clarity.

Kross was born in Tallinn on 19 February 1920. His father was a machine-manufacturing plant foreman whose modest home library contained books in several languages. Kross studied at the elite Westholm Gymnasium in Tallinn from 1928 to 1938; during this time his early literary attempts found their way into such periodicals as *Eesti Noorte Punane Rist* (The Estonian Youth Red Cross, 1935), *Tuleviku Rajad* (Future Paths), *Tänapäev* (Today), and *Eesti Noorus* (Estonian Youth). In 1938 he entered the University of Tartu to study law but continued to write. In June 1940, after the Soviet Union annexed Estonia, he found a job in the cultural section of the newspaper *Noorte Hääl* (Voice of Youth). In the same year he married Helga Pedusaar, a student of philology who became a teacher and translator of German. Kross's own knowledge of languages is remarkable: he is fluent in German, French, English, Russian, and Finnish and can translate from Swedish.

During the German occupation of Estonia, Kross worked from 1941 to 1943 as a secretary at the

Cover for Kross's first book, a volume of poetry published in 1958

Tallinn City Bank and in 1943 as an interpreter at a military installation. For the last five months of the occupation he was incarcerated in the Tallinn Central Prison. After his release he went back to Tartu, graduated from the university, and stayed on to teach the theory of law and international justice and to work for an advanced degree. He was unable to complete his dissertation, "The Concept of the International Contract," however, because the Soviets, who had reoccupied Estonia, arrested him and deported him to Siberia in 1946. From 1948 to 1951 he was in the Komi Autonomous Soviet Socialist Republic in northeastern Russia and from 1951 to 1954 in the Krasnoyarsk district of Siberia.

Kross returned to Estonia in 1954 and married Helga Roos, a librarian and translator, with whom he had a daughter. In 1958 he joined the Estonian Writers' Union; married his third wife, Ellen Niit, a poet and writer of children's books, with whom he has three children; and published his first book of verse, *Söerikastaja* (The Coal Enricher).

Kross's use of free verse led to heated discussions in Estonia in the 1950s. His poetry reflects his extensive reading, with allusions to the Bible, ancient cultures, mythology, and history; he lists Marie Under, Betti Alver, and Aleksandr Pushkin as his major influences. Several poems in *Söerikastaja* resemble the intellectual lyrics of the poets of the 1930s Estonian literary group *Arbujad* (Logomancers).

The pieces in *Söerikastaja*, which were written between 1955 and 1958, amount to a hidden condemnation of the socialist way of thinking: the figure of the coal enricher symbolizes a society that should purify itself of the Stalinist cult of personality, hypocrisy, bureaucracy, and low-grade sham. The long poem *Tuule-Juku* (Weathercock, 1963) continues in this vein, heaping sarcasm and irony on the easily manipulated *homo sovieticus*.

The collection *Kivist viiulid* (Stone Violins, 1964), on the other hand, expresses the optimism and hope that prevailed in Estonia in the 1960s, an era of liberalization and greater access to information. The world was expanding; life was becoming less monotonous; and yet the widening of horizons in Soviet Estonia failed to measure up to expectations. In his next book of verse, *Lauljad laevavööridel* (Singers on Ship Prows, 1966), Kross looks at the world in a more realistic manner. He senses new dangers threatening humanity, reverts to sarcasm, and refocuses on the negative aspects of the life he sees around himself. A more intimate and sensitive approach characterizes the collection *Vihm teeb toredaid asju* (The Rain Does Wonderful Things, 1969). Touches of autobiography are embedded in the work, and a new theme—history—begins to emerge. His final collection of poetry, *Voog ja kolmpii* (The Wave and the Trident, 1971), includes poems written from 1938 to 1968, some of them published here for the first time. Kross also revised some previously published poems to clarify obscurities and, occasionally, to soften the tone.

Though an accomplished poet, Kross is better known as a writer of historical fiction. In this capacity he is primarily concerned with the social and ethical issues facing his characters, noted personalities who are in one way or another connected with Estonia and are firmly rooted in their historical eras. Strong characters who can reach beyond the limitations set by their origins are his favorites, though the theme of striving upward, of escaping from the mass of faceless peasants, has sometimes been disapproved of, particularly by Soviet critics. Another characteristic of Kross's historical figures is their willingness to compromise. Natural talent, willpower, and an ability to survive enable the extraordinary people he depicts to achieve their goals, but such individuals usually pay a price. These overachievers often feel insecure, are ostracized by those who consider them upstarts, and feel guilty for betraying their origins.

Kross is a master of realistic presentation. He brilliantly evokes the feel of long periods of time, even of several centuries in duration. Kross's protagonists, all of whom are ethnic Estonians, leave their mark, more often than not, as Germans or Russians. By stretching the time frame or moving his players to slightly different locations than those in which they actually existed, he creates intriguing connections between individuals who never, in fact, encountered one another. His characters, though historically based, are artistic creations: the details of their lives are mostly invented. Kross often uses monologues to capture a character's inner world, which is where the most profound struggles in his works usually take place. At other times he sets up ideological arguments between his main characters, creating some of the best debates in recent Estonian literature.

Kross's epic novel *Kolme katku vahel* appeared in four volumes in 1970, 1972, 1977, and 1980. It covers roughly the period of the Livonian Wars, 1558 to 1583, when Russia, Sweden, Poland, and the Livonian Order, a branch of the Teutonic Knights, were fighting over Estonia. As the minister of a Tallinn church during this time, Balthasar Russow (1536?–1600) is serving the conquerors of his homeland; he has also become alienated from his people because of his German education and his marriages to non-Estonians. Russow struggles with the question "Who am I?" and tries to salve his conscience by helping Estonians during the peasants' revolt of 1560, but his ultimate goal is to write an honest chronicle of the time in which he lives: the *Chronica der Prouintz Lyfflandt* (Chronicle of the Province of Livonia, 1578). Kross's rich vocabulary is at times almost Joycean, and his archaic syntax is often quite complex. As is his custom, he makes frequent use of interior monologues.

In *Neli monoloogi Püha Jüri asjus* (1970; translated as "Four Monologues on the Subject of Saint George," 1983) the artist Michel Sittow (1469–1525), who has made his name in Western Europe and represents the liberating spirit of the Renaissance, faces a dilemma in the city of his birth: to be allowed to make a present of one of his artworks to the people of Tallinn, Sittow has to serve for a year as an apprentice to the hopelessly medieval local guild; otherwise, he will have to leave his hometown and the girl he loves. The wily artist decides to stay and to portray himself in the painting as a victorious St. George who has slain the dragon.

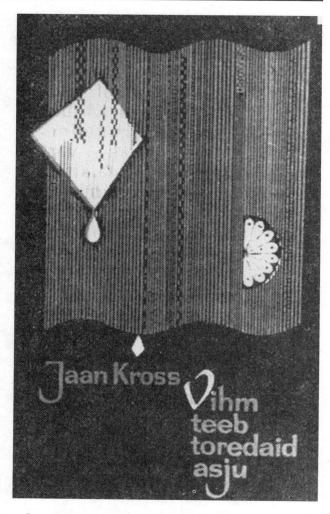

Cover for Kross's 1969 collection of poetry, in which historical themes begin to emerge in his work

Michelsoni immatrikuleerimine (1971; translated as "The Elevation of Michelson," 1983) grapples with the issue of social rank. General Johann Michelson (1735 or 1740–1807) puts down the Pugachev revolt in Russia and becomes a favorite of Catherine the Great. When he is raised to the peerage, he invites his parents, who are Estonian peasants, to the reception. Observing the reaction of the nobility to his parents' simple clothes and shoes without heels forces him to reassess his social position and, indeed, his whole life.

Kross collected *Neli monoloogi Püha Jüri asjus* and *Michelsoni immatrikuleerimine* with two shorter pieces as *Klio silma all* (Under Klio's Eyes, 1972). "Kahe kaotsiläinud paberi lugu" (translated as "The Story of Two Lost Notes," 1983), which had originally appeared in the journal *Looming* (Creation) in 1966, is based on the historical fact that Otto Reinhold Holtz (1757–1828), a German clergyman, taught lan-

Cover for Kross's 1972 collection of fiction, which includes Neli monoloogi Püha Jüri asjus *and* Michelsoni immatrikuleerimine *along with two shorter works*

guages to the physician and writer Friedrich Reinhold Kreutzwald (1803–1882), the compiler of the national epic *Kalevipoeg* (Son of Kalev, 1857–1861). The plot of the story involves their disagreement over Kreutzwald's choice of profession: Holtz wants Kreutzwald to become a man of the cloth, but the latter prefers to heal bodies rather than souls. Kross raises the possibility that Kreutzwald might have begun gathering materials for the *Kalevipoeg* in his youth; but, as the title of the story indicates, the papers were lost. Kross brings into the action other people of the period, including a doctor who pioneered the therapeutic use of mud baths.

The novella "Pöördtoolitund" (translated as "An Hour on a Revolving Chair," 1983) had appeared in *Looming* in 1971. Johann Voldemar Jannsen (1819–1890), the founder of Estonian journalism

and revered by Estonians as one of the leaders of the National Awakening, is accused of having betrayed his people by taking money from Baltic Germans in exchange for disseminating their political ideology in his popular newspaper. In an inner monologue Jannsen's son struggles with the question of why his father did it. Kross also casts light on other unpleasant matters involving the Jannsen family, including alcoholism and kleptomania.

In the short novel *Taevakivi* (1975; translated as "The Rock from the Sky," 1983) Otto Wilhelm Masing (1763–1832), a linguist, pastor, writer, and believer in the ideas of the Enlightenment, and Kristian Jaak Peterson (1801–1822), a poet and philologist, meet at the Äksi manse in southern Estonia. (There is no historical evidence that such a meeting ever took place.) They represent different generations, as well as diametrically opposite ideas: age versus youth and the cool light of reason versus romantic passion. Masing, whose father, like Peterson's, was Estonian, identifies with the Germans in the hope of making a better career for himself, while the poet emphasizes the importance of being Estonian. Masing's young Italian wife, Cara, adds a touch of eroticism to the plot; although she appears to be the sensible wife of a clergyman, she is not above developing an emotional relationship with Peterson.

In *Kolmandad mäed* (The Third Mountain Range, 1975) Johann Köler (1826–1899), art instructor to the czar's family, paints an altarpiece for a Tallinn church in 1879. When it is revealed that his model for Christ was Handsome Willy, a sadistic peasant, Köler is accused of fomenting a satanic plot.

Kross's most widely translated novel, *Keisri hull* has occasioned more commentary than any of his other books. Baron Timotheus von Bock (1787–1836), who is married to an Estonian peasant girl, tries to convince his friend Czar Alexander that Russia needs constitutional reforms. Von Bock's honesty and courage earn him nine years in solitary confinement as a lunatic, and he dies under mysterious circumstances. The novel can be interpreted as an allegory of the Soviet practice of incarcerating political prisoners in insane asylums. The work is presented in the form of a found diary interlaced with letters and documents.

Rakvere romaan (The Novel of Rakvere, 1982) is set in the small northern Estonian town of the title in the second half of the eighteenth century. The autonomy of the townspeople of Rakvere under the liberal Lübeck charter has been eroded after the Great Northern War by the Tiesenhausens, lords of the local manor. To right these wrongs the townspeople rely on Count von Sievers, a former peasant who lived on the Rakvere manor. The narrator, the Estonian Berend Falck, who works as a tutor and secretary for the Tiesenhausens, must choose sides. Falck's romance with the shoemaker's daughter brings lighter moments into the novel, but Falck and the townspeople eventually lose their struggle.

Professor Martensi ärasõit (1984; translated as *Professor Martens' Departure*, 1994) takes place on one day, 7 June 1909, toward the end of which Professor Friedrich von Martens (1845–1909), a counselor in the Russian Foreign Ministry, dies in a provincial railroad station on his way to St. Petersburg; the novel, which takes the form of a monologue by Martens, ends in midsentence with his death. The son of a poor Estonian parish clerk, Martens rose in the world because of his abilities and hard work, but his humble origins have come to haunt him. Kross adds to the plot an extramarital romantic entanglement, introduces other contemporary figures of note such as the Estonian-Finnish writer Hella Wuolijoki, and manages to convey superbly the backdrop of the social and political atmosphere four years after the 1905 Revolution in czarist Russia.

Vastutuulelaev (Sailing into the Wind, 1987) is a biographical novel about Bernhard Schmidt (1879–1935), the inventor of the Schmidt telescope. Born on a small island near Tallinn, Schmidt lost his right hand in an explosion of a homemade rocket but developed the ability to grind and polish fine lenses with his left hand. He "sails into the wind" metaphorically by overcoming his handicap and literally, for one of his other inventions was a sailboat that could do just that. But he begins to lose his grip on reality while working in pre–World War II Germany, and his hallucinations become deeply symbolic. Among many such images, perhaps the most obvious are the gigantic brown cockroaches that represent the brown-shirted Nazis. Though Schmidt succumbs to mental illness, he is at least spared having to witness the social madness that soon engulfs Adolf Hitler's Germany.

The novel *Tabamatus* (Elusiveness, 1993) speculates about the fate of Jüri Vilms (1889–1918?), a politician and journalist who vanished at the time of the creation of the first Estonian republic. According to the novel, Vilms was killed in Finland by Germans. The narrator, a communist lawyer who tries to piece together the events of Vilms's last years, himself suffers imprisonment and will suffer death at the hands of the German occupiers during World War II.

In addition to poetry and historical fiction, a third category of Kross's oeuvre consists of autobiographical stories and novels. Kross has collected most such stories into the volumes *Kajalood* (Echo Sounder,

Kross at the University of Helsinki to receive an honorary doctorate in 1990 (Eesti Kirjandusmuuseum)

1980), *Ülesõidukohad* (Crossings, 1981), and *Silmade avamise päev* (The Day His Eyes Are Opened, 1988). All of them feature the character Peeter Mirk, who is clearly the author's alter ego. The five stories in *Silmade avamise päev* and a sixth, previously uncollected, have appeared in English as *The Conspiracy and Other Stories* (1995).

The novel *Wikmani poisid* (The Wikman Boys, 1988) describes Kross's school years at the Westholm Gymnasium (here changed to Wikman) and the catastrophic events of 1939 and the early 1940s. While the student body as a whole could be termed the protagonist of the novel, Jaak Sirkel—rather than Peeter Mirk—stands out as the author's double. Most of the situations are predictable: socially conscious youths in a conservative school, their crushes on girls, and the peculiarities and idiosyncrasies of the teachers. But history intervenes: Jaak is sent to a German prison; some of his schoolmates are deported to Siberia; others flee to the West. What began as a traditional bildungsroman takes on a more somber hue as the idealism instilled in the students by the faculty turns out to be meaningless.

In *Väljakaevamised* (Excavations, 1990) Peeter Mirk returns from Siberia in 1954 to face want, hostility, suspicion, and informers. He finds temporary work excavating medieval ruins in the Old Town of Tallinn. The diggings yield a thirteenth-century manuscript that has the potential of being turned into anti-Soviet propaganda. The novel includes portraits of well-known contemporary Estonians, who are given more or less transparent pseudonyms. The main thrust of *Väljakaevamised*, however, as with much of Kross's fiction, is the suffering of the Estonian people, whether in the thirteenth or the twentieth century.

Mesmeri ring: Romaniseeritud memuaarid nagu kõik memuaarid ja peaaegu iga romaan (Mesmer's Circle: Fictionalized Memoirs, as Are All Memoirs and Almost All Novels, 1995) reintroduces Jaak Sirkel as Kross's double. While Jaak is studying law at Tartu University, one of his friends is deported to Siberia and tortured to death.

Kross's travel book, *Muld ja marmor* (Earth and Marble, 1968), written with his wife, allowed Estonian readers to learn about life in foreign countries at a time when travel abroad was highly restricted. His essays, criticism, speeches, and lectures are collected in *Vahelugemised* (Interleavings), published in six volumes from 1968 to 1995. His novels *Keisri hull, Rakvere romaan, Taevakivi, Kolmandad mäed,* and *Michelsoni immatrikuleerimine,* as well as the novella "Pöördtoolitund," have all been dramatized and staged in Estonia, and *Taevakivi* has also been produced in Hungary; and a television movie was made of *Wikmani poisid* in 1995. The first volume of *Kolme katku vahel* was originally written as a teleplay and was broadcast in 1970. An original drama, *Doktor Karelli raske öö* (Doctor Karell's Difficult Night), produced in Finnish translation in Helsinki in 1991, deals with an Estonian who served as the personal physician of Czar Alexander II. Kross is also the author of opera libretti, and several of his poems have been set to music. Kross's remarkable linguistic abilities are confirmed by his translations of works by such authors as William Shakespeare, Bertolt Brecht, Lewis Carroll, Romain Rolland, and Stefan Zweig.

Kross was secretary of the board of the Writers' Union from 1971 to 1977 and deputy chairman from 1981 to 1989. In 1971 he was accorded the title Merited Writer, and in 1985 that of Peoples' Writer of the Estonian Soviet Socialist Republic. He received honorary doctorates from Tartu University in 1989 and

Helsinki University in 1990. In 1992 he was elected to the Estonian parliament but returned to full-time writing after only one year. He was decorated by the governments of Germany in 1995 and of Estonia in 1996. In addition to many literary prizes in his native country, in 1988 he was the recipient of the Finnish Eeva Joenpelto Prize, in 1990 of Amnesty International's Golden Flame Award, and in 1997 of the German Herder Prize, and he has been nominated more than once for the Nobel Prize in literature. In 1995 an international conference was held in honor of his seventy-fifth birthday. He is one of the most-translated Estonian authors, with works published in English, German, Russian, French, Spanish, Finnish, Swedish, Norwegian, Polish, Czech, Slovakian, Hungarian, Latvian, Lithuanian, Ukrainian, Bulgarian, Georgian, Dutch, Portuguese, Danish, Italian, and Japanese.

Interviews:

Maire Liivamets, "Mõni sõna Martensite asjus: Vestlus Maire Liivametsaga romaanist 'Professor Martensi ärasõit,'" *Sirp ja Vasar,* 2 March 1984, p. 7;

Toomas Haug, "Kirjanikuna päikeseriigis: Intervjuu," *Looming* (February 1995): 231–241.

Bibliographies:

Vaime Kabur, *Jaan Kross: Personaalnimestik* (Tallinn: Eesti NSV Kultuuriministeerium, Fr. R. Kreutzwaldi nim. Riiklik Raamatukogu, 1982);

Kabur and Gerli Palk, *Jaan Kross: Bibliograafia* (Tallinn: Bibliotheca Baltica, 1997).

Biographies:

Endel Nirk, *Estonian Literature* (Tallinn: Eesti Raamat, 1970), pp. 345–347;

Nirk, *Eesti kirjandus* (Tallinn: Perioodika, 1983), pp. 239–242;

Mart Mäger, *Eesti kirjanduse ajalugu,* volume 5, part 2 (Tallinn: Eesti Raamat, 1991), pp. 316–355;

Oskar Kruus, *Eesti kirjarahva leksikon* (Tallinn: Eesti Raamat, 1995), pp. 228–230.

References:

Nigol Andresen, "Faktide ja fantaasiaga loodud ajastupilt," *Keel ja Kirjandus* (June 1975): 371–373;

Andresen, "Jaan Kross," in his *Inimesi ja raamatuid* (Tallinn: Eesti Raamat, 1973), pp. 36–40;

Andresen, "Lüürika ja satiir," *Keel ja Kirjandus* (February 1959): 112–115;

Eve Annuk, "Cara mia, eks ole: Seksuaalsest koodist Jaan Krossi 'Taevakivis,'" *Vikerkaar* (February 1995): 61–64;

R[iho] G[rünthal], "Jaan Kross in the Waves of the 20th Century," *Estonia*, no. 2 (1988): 82–83;

Toomas Haug, "Jaan Krossi 'Kajaloodi' puhul," *Looming* (January 1981): 135–136;

Lindsey Hughes, "A Sense of Honour," *TLS: The Times Literary Supplement* (11 December 1992): 21;

Ea Jansen, "Klio ja kompromissid," *Looming* (November 1972): 1921–1924;

Jaak Jõerüüt, "Kakssada aastat hiljem," *Looming* (May 1983): 710–711;

Mall Jõgi, "Jaan Kross Maarjamaa kroonikuna," *Keel ja Kirjandus* (February 1980): 65–73;

Olev Jõgi, "Laterna magica kahe Martensiga," in his *Hetki ja viipeid* (Tallinn: Eesti Raamat, 1988), pp. 233–238;

Maie Kalda, "'Vahelugemised' autorist ja ise," *Keel ja Kirjandus* (May 1977): 306–308;

Jaan Kaplinski, "Jaan Krossi teine tulemine," in *Kirjandus kriitiku pilguga*, edited by Kalju Kääri (Tallinn: Eesti Raamat, 1977), pp. 43–53;

Tiina Kirss, "History and Narrative: An Introduction to the Fiction of Jaan Kross," *Cross Currents*, 6 (1987): 397–404;

Kirss, "Optika Jaan Krossi ajaloolistes romaanides," *Looming* (January 1991): 113–120;

Pärt Lias, "Balthasar Russow' köietrikk," *Keel ja Kirjandus* (April 1971): 238–241;

Lias, "Jakob Mättiku päevaraamat," in *Kirjanduse jaosmaa '79*, edited by Endel Mallene (Tallinn: Eesti Raamat, 1981), pp. 111–115;

Lias, "Kontekst ja kiri," *Keel ja Kirjandus* (March 1989): 182–183;

Lias, "Romaan 70-ndail aastail," in his *Eesti nõukogude romaan* (Tallinn: Eesti Raamat, 1985), pp. 124–129;

Maire Liivamets, "Ajaloo köiel, ajaloo pöördlaval," in *Karl Ristikivi 75. sünniaastapäevale pühendatud konverertsi materjalid, 2*, edited by Jaan Undusk (Tallinn: Eesti NSV Kirjanike Liit, 1988), pp. 49–59;

Liivamets, "Palju siin lisada enam polegi . . . ," *Keel ja Kirjandus* (February 1995): 129–130;

Liivamets, "Tallinn Jaan Krossi ajaloolises proosas," *Looming* (January 1978): 147–162;

Mart Mäger, "Kivist viiulid kui probleem ja luuletuskogu," in his *Luule ja lugeja* (Tallinn: Eesti Raamat, 1979), pp. 188–193;

Mäger, "Lehitsetud leheküljed," *Looming* (October 1970): 1589–1591;

Mäger, "Tegelaste, probleemide ja kujutusvõtete vahekordi Jaan Krossi proosas," *Keel ja Kirjandus* (June 1978): 321–328;

Lembit Remmelgas, "Monoloog Jaan Krossi asjus," *Looming* (February 1980): 263–268;

Paul-Eerik Rummo, "Lustlikust Tuule-Jukust inspireeritud tõsimeelseid targutusi," in *Kirjandus kriitiku pilguga: Arvustusi ja aastaülevaateid 1962–1972*, edited by Kääri (Tallinn: Eesti Raamat, 1975), pp. 122–125;

Malle Salupere, "Raamatukangelane ja tegelik Timotheus Bock," *Kultuurileht*, 30 June 1995, p. 7;

Leenu Siimisker, "Ühest debüüdist, pealegi topeltkolumbuslikust," in *Kirjandus kriitiku pilguga: Arvustusi ja aastaülevaateid 1962–1972*, pp. 486–493;

Karl Martin Sinijärv, "Mesmeri kera," *Vikerkaar* (October 1996): 109–111;

Leo Soonpää, "Kolmandate mägede jalamil," in *Kirjandus kritiku pilguga: Artikleid, arvustusi ja aastaülevaateid 1975–1976*, edited by Kääri (Tallinn: Eesti Raamat, 1978), pp. 149–151;

Ülo Tonts, "J. Krossi kolmas kogu," *Keel ja Kirjandus* (April 1967): 240–241;

Tonts, "Romaan ja memuaar," *Keel ja Kirjandus* (June 1996): 413–415;

Udo Uibo, "Armastus geomeetria vastu," *Looming* (March 1982): 422–424;

Mardi Valgemäe, "The Antic Disposition of a Finno-Ugric Novelist," *Journal of Baltic Studies*, 24 (Winter 1993): 389–394;

Valgemäe, "'Keisri hull' ja 'Hamlet,'" *Vikerkaar* (July 1993): 33, 36–37, 40;

Seppo Zetterberg, "Jaan Krossiga Jüri Vilmsi mõjuväljas," translated by Livia Viitol, *Keel ja Kirjandus* (February 1995): 73–76.

Milan Kundera
(1 April 1929 –   )

Jan Čulík
University of Glasgow

This entry originally appeared in Concise Dictionary of World Literary Biography:
South Slavic and Eastern European Writers.

BOOKS: *Člověk, zahrada širá: Verše* (Prague: Československý spisovatel, 1953);

Poslední máj (Prague: Československý spisovatel, 1955);

Monology: Kniha o lásce (Prague: Československý spisovatel, 1957; revised and enlarged, 1964; revised and enlarged, 1965);

Umění románu: Cesta Vladislava Vančury za velkou epikou (Prague: Československý spisovatel, 1960);

Majitelé klíčů: Hra o jednom dějství s čtyřmi vizemi (Prague: Orbis, 1962; enlarged, 1964);

Směšné lásky: Tři melancholické anekdoty (Prague: Československý spisovatel, 1963); translated by Suzanne Rappaport as *Laughable Loves* (New York: Knopf, 1974; London: Murray, 1978); definitive edition published as *Směšné lásky* (Toronto: Sixty-Eight Publishers, 1981; Brno: Atlantis, 1991);

Druhý sešit směšných lásek (Prague: Československý spisovatel, 1965);

Žert (Prague: Československý spisovatel, 1967); abridged version translated by David Hamblyn and Oliver Stallybrass as *The Joke* (London: Macdonald, 1969; New York: Coward-McCann, 1969); complete version translated by Michael Henry Heim as *The Joke* (New York: Harper & Row, 1982; London: Faber & Faber, 1983);

Třetí sešit směšných lásek (Prague: Československý spisovatel, 1968);

Dvě uši, dvě svatby: Divadelní hra (Prague: Dilia, 1968); revised as *Ptákovina, Divadlo,* 1 (1969): 84–100;

La vie est ailleurs, translated into French by Françoise Kérel (Paris: Gallimard, 1973); translated by Peter Kussi as *Life Is Elsewhere* (New York:

*Milan Kundera (photograph copyright © 1998
by Fridrik Rafusson)*

Knopf, 1974; London: Faber & Faber, 1986); original Czech version published as *Život je jinde* (Toronto: Sixty-Eight Publishers, 1979);

The Farewell Party, translated by Kussi (New York: Knopf, 1976; London: Murray, 1977); original Czech version published as *Valčík na rozloučenou* (Toronto: Sixty-Eight Publishers, 1979);

Le livre du rire et de l'oubli, translated by Kérel (Paris: Gallimard, 1979); translated by Heim as *The Book of Laughter and Forgetting* (New York: Knopf, 1980; Harmondsworth, U.K.: Penguin, 1981); original Czech version published as *Kniha smíchu a zapomnění* (Toronto: Sixty-Eight Publishers, 1981);

Jacques et son maître: Hommage à Denis Diderot en trois actes (Paris: Gallimard, 1981); translated by Heim as *Jacques and His Master: An Homage to Diderot in Three Acts* (New York: Harper & Row, 1985; London: Faber & Faber, 1986); original Czech version published as *Jakub a jeho pán* (Brno: Atlantis, 1992);

The Unbearable Lightness of Being, translated by Heim (New York: Harper & Row, 1984; London & Boston: Faber & Faber, 1984); original Czech version published as *Nesnesitelná lehkost bytí* (Toronto: Sixty-Eight Publishers, 1985);

L'art du roman: Essai (Paris: Gallimard, 1986); translated by Linda Asher as *The Art of the Novel* (New York: Grove, 1988; London: Faber & Faber, 1988);

L'immortalité, translated by Eva Bloch (Paris: Gallimard, 1990); translated by Kussi as *Immortality* (London & Boston: Faber & Faber, 1991; New York: Grove Weidenfeld, 1991); original Czech version published as *Nesmrtelnost: Román* (Toronto: Sixty-Eight Publishers, 1993; Brno: Atlantis, 1993);

Les testaments trahis (Paris: Gallimard, 1993); translated by Asher as *Testaments Betrayed: An Essay in Nine Parts* (New York: HarperCollins, 1995);

La lenteur (Paris: Gallimard, 1995); translated by Asher as *Slowness* (New York: HarperCollins, 1996);

L'identité (Paris: Gallimard, 1997); translated by Asher as *Identity* (New York: HarperFlamingo, 1998; Bath, U.K.: Chivers Press / Thorndike, Me.: Thorndike Press, 1999);

La ignorancia, translated from French by Beatriz de Moura (Barcelona: Tusquets, 2000).

Editions in English: "A Game of Make-Believe," translated by George Theiner, in *New Writing in Czechoslovakia,* edited by Theiner (Baltimore: Penguin, 1969), pp. 184–201;

Jacques and His Master, translated by Simon Callow (Boston: Faber & Faber, 1986);

The Book of Laughter and Forgetting, translated by Aaron Asher (New York: HarperPerennial, 1996).

PLAY PRODUCTIONS: *Majitelé klíčů,* Prague, National Theater, 29 April 1962;

Ptákovina, Liberec, F. X. Šaldy Theater, 18 January 1969;

Jakub fatalista, Ústí nad Labem, Činoherní Studio Theater, 17 December 1975; English translation, Cambridge, Mass., American Repertory Theater, January 1985.

PRODUCED SCRIPTS: "Sestřičko mých sestřiček," Czechoslovak Television, 1963;

"Já, truchlivý Bůh," Czechoslovak Television, Brno, 1967;

Já, truchlivý Bůh, motion picture, by Kundera and Antonín Kachlík, 1969;

Žert, motion picture, by Kundera and Jaromil Jireš, Barrandov, 1969.

OTHER: František Gellner, *Básně,* edited by Kundera (Prague: Československý spisovatel, 1957);

Guillaume Apollinaire, *Pásmo, a jiné verše,* edited by Kundera and Adolf Kroupa (Prague: Státní nakladatelství krásné literatury, hudby a umění, 1958);

Vladislav Vančura, *Rozmarné novely,* edited by Kundera (Prague: Státní nakladatelství krásné literatury, hudby a umění, 1959);

Básnický almanach 1959, edited by Kundera (Prague: Státní nakladatelství krásné literatury, hudby a umění, 1960);

Vítězslav Nezval, *Podivuhodný kouzelník,* edited by Kundera (Prague: Československý spisovatel, 1963);

Apollinaire, *Alkoholy života,* edited by Kundera (Prague: Československý spisovatel, 1965);

Kundera's speech at the June 1967 Congress of Czechoslovak Writers, see *Čtvrtý sjezd Svazu československých spisovatelů, Prague 27.–29. června 1967. Protokol* (Prague: Československý spisovatel, 1968), pp. 22–28; translated by D. Orpington in *Writers against Rulers,* edited by Dušan Hamšík (London: Hutchinson, 1971), pp. 167–177.

SELECTED PERIODICAL PUBLICATIONS—UNCOLLECTED: "O sporech dědických," *Nový život* (1955): 1290–1306;

"Český úděl," *Listy,* 1 (19 December 1968): 1, 5;

"Radikalismus a exhibicionismus," *Host do domu,* 15 (1969): 24–29;

"The Making of a Writer," *New York Times Book Review,* 24 October 1982, p. 37;

"The Tragedy of Central Europe," *New York Review of Books,* 31 (26 April 1984): 33–38;

"Totalitarian Kitsch," translated by Michael Henry Heim, *Harper's*, 268 (June 1984): 30–31;

"The Novel and Europe," translated by David Bellos, *New York Review of Books*, 31 (19 July 1984): 15–19;

"A Little History Lesson," translated by Linda Asher, *New York Review of Books*, 31 (22 November 1984): 9;

"Somewhere Beyond," translated by Bellos, *Cross Currents: A Yearbook of Central European Culture*, 3 (1984): 61–70;

"'Man Thinks, God Laughs,'" translated by Asher, *New York Review of Books*, 32 (13 June 1985): 11–12;

"An Introduction to a Variation," translated by Heim, *Cross Currents: A Yearbook of Central European Culture*, 5 (1986): 469–476;

"Esch Is Luther," translated by David Rieff, *Review of Contemporary Fiction*, 8 (Summer 1988): 266–272;

"On Criticism, Aesthetics, and Europe," translated by Lois Oppenheim, *Review of Contemporary Fiction*, 9 (Summer 1989): 13–16;

"A Life Like a Work of Art: Homage to Václav Havel," translated by Asher, *New Republic*, 202 (29 January 1990): 16–17;

"The Face," translated by Kussi, *New Yorker*, 65 (15 April 1991): 34–54;

"In Saint Garta's Shadow," translated by Barbara Wright, *TLS: The Times Literary Supplement*, 24 May 1991, pp. 3–5;

"The Umbrella, the Night World, and the Lonely Moon," translated by Bellos, *New York Review of Books*, 38 (19 December 1991): 46–50;

"Three Contexts of Art: From Nation to World," *Cross Currents: A Yearbook of Central European Culture*, 12 (1993): 5–14;

"You're Not in Your Own House Here, My Dear Fellow," translated by Asher, *New York Review of Books*, 42 (21 September 1995): 21–24;

"Such Was Their Wager," translated by Asher, *New Yorker*, 75 (10 May 1999): 94–96.

Milan Kundera is one of the few Czech writers who have achieved wide international recognition. In his native Czechoslovakia, Kundera has been regarded as an important author and intellectual since his early twenties. Each of his creative works and contributions to the public political and cultural discourse has provoked a lively debate in the context of its time. In the first part of his creative career Kundera was a Communist, although from the beginning his fellow believers considered him an unorthodox thinker. His story is that of

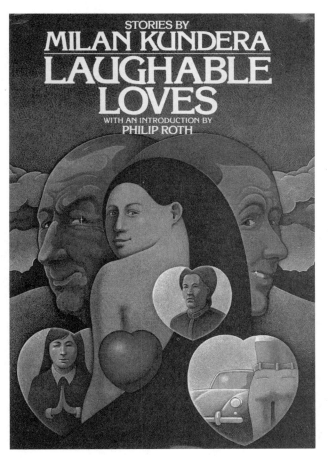

Dust jacket for the U.S. edition (1974) of the English translation of a collection of Kundera's short stories, originally published in the 1960s, about people whose jokes and tricks have unanticipated consequences

many Czech intellectuals of his generation: it is the story of freeing oneself of Marxist dogma and of gaining and communicating important insights based on the traumatic experience of life under totalitarianism in Eastern and Central Europe.

Kundera is an extremely private person who considers the details of his personal life "nobody's business." This attitude is consistent with the teachings of Czech structuralism, which argues that literary texts should be considered as self-contained structures of signs, without regard to extraliterary reality. In a 1984 interview with the British writer Ian McEwan, Kundera said: "We constantly rewrite our own biographies and continually give matters new meanings. To rewrite history in this sense—indeed, in an Orwellian sense—is not at all inhuman. On the contrary, it is very human." He strictly controls public information about his life; in the latest French editions of his works, his "official biography" consists of one sentence:

"Milan Kundera was born in Czechoslovakia in 1929 and since 1975 has been living in France."

Kundera also asserts his right as an author to exclude from his oeuvre "immature" and "unsuccessful" works, as composers do, and he now rejects and suppresses most of his literary output of the 1950s and the 1960s. In his mature fiction he creates a self-contained world that he constantly analyzes and questions, opening up multitudinous ways of interpreting the incidents he depicts. As Květoslav Chvatík points out, Kundera treats the novel as an ambiguous structure of signs; playing with these signs enables him to show human existence as open to countless possibilities, thus freeing human beings from the limitedness of a single unrepeatable life.

Kundera was born on 1 April 1929 in Brno to Ludvík Kundera, a prominent musicologist and pianist who had been a pupil of the composer Leoš Janáček, and Milada Kunderová, née Jánošíková. Kundera's father taught him to play the piano; later, he studied musicology, and musical influences can be found throughout his work. In 1945 he published translations of work by the Russian poet Vladimir Mayakovsky in the journal *Gong;* in 1946 a surrealist poem by Kundera, written under the influence of his cousin Ludvík Kundera, a well-known Czech writer and poet, was printed in the journal *Mladé archy* (The Young Notebooks).

Kundera completed his secondary-school studies in Brno in 1948 and began to study literature and aesthetics in the Faculty of Arts at Charles University; that year he also joined the Communist Party. After two terms he transferred to the Film Academy, where he attended lectures in movie direction and scriptwriting. In 1950 he and another Czech writer, Jan Trefulka, were expelled from the Communist Party for "anti-party activities." Trefulka described the incident in his novella *Pršelo jim štěstí* (Happiness Rained on Them, 1962), and Kundera used it as the main theme of his novel *Žert* (1967; translated as *The Joke*, abridged edition, 1969; complete edition, 1982). After graduating in 1952, Kundera was appointed lecturer in world literature at the Film Academy.

Kundera's first book, a collection of lyrical poems titled *Člověk, zahrada širá* (Man, a Wide Garden, 1953), came out five years after the Communist takeover of Czechoslovakia, during the period of rampant Stalinism. Attempting to bring about the rehabilitation of the pre-war Czechoslovak avant-garde, the work was an unorthodox departure from the poetics of socialist realism imposed by Communist cultural authorities, which pre-

scribed that poems and novels were to deal with the "mass proletarian movement," the "class struggle," and the "successful progression of society toward communism." In his collection Kundera assumes a critical attitude toward this kind of "literature," but he does so from a strictly Marxist point of view as he tries to illustrate and enliven the official dogma by introducing personal experience. Thus, the poet feels encouraged when he hears a young boy, playing near a railroad track in Brno, singing the hymn of the left-wing movement, the *Internationale*. Kundera uses the familiar Czech surroundings as a symbol of comfort and peace, and the Communist regime is shown as the guarantor of all the values associated with home. In another poem an old woman does not understand the political jargon of the new era, but at the end she is happy when her grandson, a Communist Young Pioneer with his red scarf around his neck, embraces her and takes her by the hand. Misogyny surfaces in a poem in which a party activist complains that his wife is not interested in listening to his account of his daily political "struggle"; she is concerned only with preparing supper. The hero of another poem criticizes himself for being too detached from his party companions; he realizes that it is treason to be alone and promises his comrades that he will never again act on his own. This poem clearly foreshadows one of the main themes of Kundera's perhaps most profound novel, *Žert*.

In 1955 Kundera published a blatant piece of Communist propaganda. The long poem *Poslední máj* (The Last May) is an homage to Julius Fučík, the hero of Communist resistance to the Nazi occupation of Czechoslovakia. Full of bathos, the work conforms to the tenets of socialist realism and to the official Communist version of history. Some commentators have speculated that Kundera was commissioned by the party to write the piece; others have said that Kundera wrote this work as an act of cool calculation—to enable him to become a member of the Communist Party again. In a parallel to Christ's temptation by the devil, Commissar Boehm, Fučík's interrogator in a Nazi prison in Prague, takes the Communist activist for an evening out in a restaurant in a hillside park overlooking the city. The Nazi policeman hopes that the magic of Prague on a June evening, symbolizing the beauty of life, will make Fučík try to save himself from death by collaborating with his interrogator. One typical Kunderaesque theme, used later in a quite different context, appears here: ethnicity is used as a reaffirmation of the authenticity and value of national life as three young men in the restaurant boisterously sing Moravian folk songs; this performance gives Fučík the strength to resist Boehm.

Kundera was readmitted into the Communist Party in 1956. In 1957 he published *Monology* (Monologues), a collection of love poems. Many of the poems are based on paradoxes ("I cannot live with you, you are too beautiful"); some highlight the irrationality of love, which often conquers those who would be guided by the intellect alone. These themes are also typical of Kundera's later work. In some of the poems the speaker is physically repulsed by women, while at the same time being attracted to them. Erotic passion can be a burden; the sexual impulse is disconcerting. Love-making serves as an escape from unpleasant realities. The theme of the pettiness of everyday female concerns, which makes women unaware of what is really going on in life, reappears in this collection. Women are shown as obedient, while men are depicted as warriors who are trying to understand the meaning of existence; in the attempt they invariably break their heads against impenetrable walls. Some of the poems deal with infidelity; others are preoccupied with fear of aging and death. The 1965 edition of *Monology* includes a poem in which a man is unjustly accused and condemned by his party colleagues at a political meeting; a woman's love is offered as a healing instrument for all the ills that the man has experienced.

Kundera was a celebrity in Communist Czechoslovakia from the mid 1950s. He wrote for several literary magazines, and his articles were followed with considerable interest. His 1955 article "O sporech dědických" ("Arguing about Our Inheritance") stood up for Czech and European avant-garde poetry, which had been condemned as decadent by official Communist literary scholars. Kundera defends avant-garde poetry, however, from a strictly communist point of view. He argues that even his politically orthodox poem about Fučík could not have been written without the legacy of Czech and international avant-garde poets. The art of the "decadent," "receding" capitalist era may be pernicious, but a poet, composer, or artist can avoid the unacceptable content and use the formal innovations even of "idealist" avant-garde poetry to produce authentic socialist art. Those poets who cut themselves off from the glorious tradition of the Czech interwar poetic avant-garde produce worthless doggerel instead of poetry. To give credence to his arguments, Kundera quotes Vladimir Ilyich Lenin, who said that only vulgar

materialists rejected philosophical idealism. "O sporech dědických" even speaks rather boldly of those poets who have been "buried alive in the cells of incomprehensible abstraction"—maybe a reference to the many writers who were languishing in communist prisons.

Equally well received was *Umění románu: Cesta Vladislava Vančury za velkou epikou* (The Art of the Novel: Vladislav Vančura's Journey to the Great Epic, 1960), which analyzes the writings of an outstanding Czech interwar avant-garde prose writer who was also a member of the Communist Party. A strictly Marxist defense of experimentation in narrative fiction, the work was significantly influenced by the Hungarian Marxist theoretician György Lukács's concept of the development of the epic—but writers were not allowed to quote Lukács in Czechoslovakia at that time, so his name is not mentioned. According to Kundera, Vančura was trying to create convincing and yet topical fiction in an era of "stagnant, alienated, dehumanizing, and decomposing capitalism, a time when dramatic conflict between proud, independently acting individuals was no longer possible." Kundera shows the stylistic and thematic devices Vančura used to try to overcome this problem and how he learned from the history of the European novel as he was doing so. His study of Vančura's fiction influenced Kundera's own writing by showing him the importance of an ever-present, subjective narrator, a philosopher who comments on the story as it develops. He rid himself of lyricism, descriptiveness, and psychological analysis and became aware that good fiction must be based on dramatic conflict. In these respects he drew close to the poetics of the eighteenth-century novel of enlightenment.

Umění románu was regarded as an important landmark in Czechoslovak Marxist literary scholarship; it was given a special award "to mark the fifteenth anniversary of the birth of Popular Democratic Czechoslovakia," as well as the 1961 annual prize of the Československý spisovatel (Czechoslovak Writer) publishing house. Kundera disowns the work today; he has tried to negate its existence by publishing a new volume of literary essays, which first appeared in French as *L'art du roman* (1986; translated as *The Art of the Novel*, 1988).

During this period Kundera wrote plays in addition to poetry and literary analysis. In *Majitelé klíčů* (The Owners of the Keys, 1962), which was successfully staged in April 1962 at the National Theater in Prague by the experimental director Otomar Krejča, Kundera again attempts gently to

 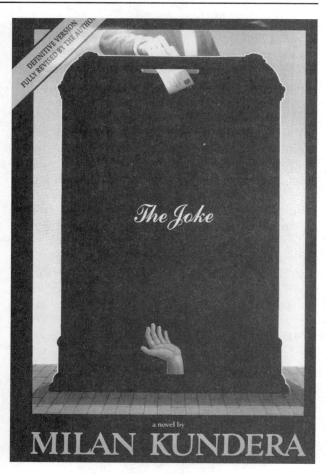

*Dust jackets for the U.S. editions of the first (1969) and unabridged (1982) English translation of Kundera's
1967 novel Žert, about personal and political betrayal in Czechoslovakia in the 1950s*

humanize totalitarian communism from within the framework of its own referential system. The ideology of the play is orthodox, but Kundera gives it a mildly reformist slant. In a small Moravian town during the Nazi occupation Jiří Nečas and his wife, Alena, live in one room of a small apartment; Alena's parents live in another room. Věra, a woman Jiří met when he was involved with the Communist resistance movement, turns up at the apartment; she is on the run from the Gestapo and needs Jiří's help. When she raises the suspicions of a Nazi concierge, Jiří is forced to kill the man and hide his body in the apartment. Jiří cannot tell his naive wife and her narrow-minded parents what has happened: they would create a scene, attract the attention of the Gestapo, and get everyone killed. Jiří tries to lure Alena away from the apartment, but she refuses to leave. Finally, Jiří and Věra escape, abandoning Alena and her parents to certain death.

Majitelé klíčů is still written from a Communist point of view; the members of the Communist resistance are given the expected heroic qualities. The play, however, includes lyrical interludes—"visions"—in which Jiří emotionally probes his situation; Kundera later came to reject such lyricism. His afterword to the 1964 edition of *Majitelé klíčů* shows that his propensity to explain and interpret his work to the reader dates back to this early stage of his career.

Kundera's works of the 1950s and early 1960s, while avowedly Marxist, were slightly in advance of their time; they provoked much debate and made an important contribution to the gradual freeing of Czech literature from the yoke of Stalinism. In *Majitelé klíčů* Kundera for the first time openly voiced his revulsion for "the desire for order, which equals the desire for death." Alena's father's view that it is necessary to "line-up, to adapt one's life to the momentarily prevailing conditions and not to waste time by futile philosophizing" is an open reference to the beginning of a conflict between the relatively independent Czech intellectuals who were trying to moderate the excesses of Stalinism and the authoritarian Communist Party leadership.

Czech writers clashed openly with the Communist leadership for the first time at the Fourth Congress of Czechoslovak Writers in June 1967. Kundera gave a speech at the congress that is regarded a landmark in the history of independent, self-critical Czech thought. In the speech Kundera looked back to the legacy of the nineteenth-century Czech National Revival, at the inception of which a handful of Czech intellectuals resurrected the Czech language as an instrument of educated discourse and brought the Czech nation back from the threshold of extinction. In 1886 the journalist Hubert Gordon Schauer asked whether the effort of re-creating modern Czech national culture had been worthwhile. Would it not have been simpler and wiser for the Czechs to merge with the larger and more sophisticated German community, rather than having to start from scratch in all the fields of human activity in their own language? Applying Schauer's question to the contemporary situation, Kundera replied that there is no point in preserving a separate Czech identity if this community is incapable of making its own innovative and unique contribution in the arts. To do so, Czech literature and culture must develop in conditions of total freedom. Truth can only be reached in a dialogue conducted by individuals who are equal and free. Having experienced democracy, Nazi subjugation, Stalinism, and socialism, the Czechs are favorably placed to produce a unique testimony about the human predicament. The question remains, concluded Kundera, whether the Czech national community is aware of this opportunity and whether it will use it.

Kundera has claimed that his mature period started in 1958 or 1959 (he has given both years), when he "found himself as a writer" while working on his first short story, "Já, truchlivý Bůh" (translated as "I, the Mournful God," 1974), which was included in the first of the three slim volumes of *Směšné lásky* (published in 1963, 1965, and 1968; translated as *Laughable Loves*, 1974) but was left out of the definitive edition of the book in 1981 because it was superfluous to the seven-part structure that Kundera imposed on the collection. Kundera wrote "Já, truchlivý Bůh" as relaxation during his work on the play *Majitelé klíčů*. Like most of the texts in *Směšné lásky*, it is a brilliant miniature drama of intimate human relationships.

The odd-numbered stories in *Směšné lásky* are based on strong dramatic conflicts; the even-numbered stories tend to be light and playful variations on the theme of sexual pursuit, most of which take the form of witty dialogue filled with paradoxes. The even-numbered stories form a background for the odd-numbered ones, which evolve from what always seems to the hero at the inception as an innocent joke. These jokes, however, have catastrophic consequences both for their perpetrators and for their victims. Thus, the arrogance of the perpetrator of the joke, who believes that he can control history and manipulate people, is exposed as a fallacy.

In "Já, truchlivý Bůh" a young man fails to win a beautiful girl who is a student at the Brno conservatory. In revenge, he decides to make fun of her snobbery and introduces her to his friend, an illiterate Greek immigrant laborer whom he represents as the director of the Athens Opera on a brief visit to Prague. The Greek and the girl make love, and the Greek supposedly returns to Athens. Nine months later the girl gives birth to a beautiful boy. She proudly shows off her son; but where there was one unhappy young man spurned by the girl at the beginning of the story, now there are two: the Greek laborer has hopelessly fallen in love with the Czech girl, but she does not recognize him in his workman's clothes.

In the highly dramatic "Falešný autostop" (translated as "The Hitchhiking Game") a boy and girl are driving in his car at the beginning of their summer vacation. They start to play a manipulative game in which they pretend that they do not know each other and have just met for the first time. The boy pretends to be a womanizer; the girl plays at being a hitchhiker who is looking for a sexual encounter. The game destroys their relationship.

In "Eduard a Bůh" (translated as "Eduard and God") a young teacher in a Stalinist society, where religion is frowned on, tries to win the favors of a religious-minded girl by pretending that he is extremely devout. This charade gets him into trouble with the school authorities, who set about reeducating him in the spirit of Marxist atheism. The young man is unable to tell them that he was only pretending to be religious to get a girl into bed; such behavior would not be regarded as serious. When you try to explain what you mean to idiots, does not this mean that you are also becoming an idiot? asks Kundera through one of his characters. Another character in *Směšné lásky* argues:

"When you believe in something literally, you will turn it into an absurdity through your faith. Genuine adherents of a political philosophy never take its arguments seriously, but only its practical aims, which are concealed beneath these arguments. Political arguments do not exist, after all, for people to believe in them, rather they serve as a common, agreed-upon excuse. Foolish people who take them in earnest sooner or later discover inconsistencies in them, begin to protest and finish finally and infamously as heretics."

Truth is usually left by the wayside in these stories of mutual sexual manipulation: once Kundera's characters start perpetrating a joke, they are invariably forced by circumstances to stick to it as though they had always meant it seriously. As Chvatík points out, this situation highlights the crisis of language: a linguistic message—a sign—emancipates itself from reality, then imposes its meaning on reality. This theme reappears in *Žert* and all of Kundera's other mature novels.

In *Směšné lásky* Kundera for the first time uses a large number of witticisms based on paradoxes to show how facts imperceptibly change into their opposites. By concentrating on human sexual games he produces a modern version of the Don Juan myth, which he debunks at the same time. Several of the stories are set in the Czech society of late Stalinism and provide authentic testimony about the atmosphere of that era. Kundera regards *Směšné lásky* as his first truly mature work, and he likes it the best of all his work because it "reflects the happiest time of my life," the liberal 1960s. He completed the last story of the collection three days before the Warsaw Pact invasion of Czechoslovakia on 21 August 1968.

The Soviet-led invasion ended the period of liberalization in Czechoslovakia, which had culminated in several months of total media freedom in the spring and summer of 1968—the period known as the "Prague Spring"—and threw the country into a harsh, neo-Stalinist freeze. This rigid regime continued practically unchanged until the disintegration of communism in Czechoslovakia in November 1989. Four months after the invasion, in the essay "Český úděl" (The Czech Destiny), published in the journal *Listy*, Kundera expresses his belief "in the great mission of the small nations which in today's world have been delivered to the tender mercies of the Great Powers. . . . By their incessant search for their own identity and by their fight for survival, the small nations resist the terrifying push toward uniformity on this earth, making it glitter with a wealth of traditions and customs, so that human individualism, marvel, and originality can find a home in this world." Nevertheless, Kundera says that he still sees himself as a "person belonging to the world of socialism (i.e., communism)" and criticizes the writer Václav Havel for using the arguments of a person who has never accepted communist ideals.

Kundera wrote his play *Jakub a jeho pán* (first published in French translation as *Jacques et son maître*, 1981; translated as *Jacques and His Master*, 1985; published in the original Czech, 1992) in 1971, after he, along with some four hundred other writers, had become a nonperson in his native country. As he explains in the 1981 French preface to the piece, the work was the product of a yearning for Western rationality, a spirit of doubt and playfulness, and an awareness of the relativity of human matters. It was a reaction to the imposition on Czechoslovakia of Russian "emotionality, regarded as a value, as a criterion on truth." In 1975 it was staged in the Czech city of Ústí nad Labem under the direction of Ivan Rajmont, but Kundera's authorship was kept secret because he was a banned and exiled writer. Denis Diderot was given as the author of the play, which was said to have been dramatized by Evald Schorm. Between 1975 and the fall of communism in 1989 the play had a successful run of 226 performances.

Jakub a jeho pán is an homage to the French Enlightenment writer Diderot and is a set of variations on his novel *Jacques le fataliste et son maître* (Jacques the Fatalist and His Master, 1796). Inspired by Diderot and by the English writer Laurence Sterne, whose masterpiece *Tristram Shandy* (1759–1767) is made up of playful digressions, the play consists of three amorous stories that are intertwined in a continuous dialogue of the protagonists, whose speeches are constantly interrupted by the other characters. Kundera gives up unity of action in favor of the techniques of polyphony and variation: the three amorous stories are variations on the same theme. In the preface to the published version of the play Kundera attacks the notion of "seriousness." In one of his typical challenging but apodictic remarks, which should not be accepted at face value, he states that "to take the world seriously means to believe what the world wants us to believe."

Kundera's mature work is littered with such declarations. They are paradoxes, true and untrue at the same time. By making them Kundera encourages the reader to think independently and draw his or her own conclusions. At first *Jakub a jeho pán* certainly seems to be a playful, unserious, amusing piece dealing with matters of love. As it goes along, however, one sees that it can be construed as a protest against the bleakness of the world and the human predicament. The playful conversation about lovemaking and the art of spinning a yarn becomes a shield that is supposed to protect the characters from inhospitable reality. Jakub says:

> Don't be afraid, sir. I don't like unnecessary truths. An unnecessary truth is the stupidest thing I know. For instance that we will die. Or that this world is rotten. As though we did not know all this. Do you know them, those men who heroically enter the stage to exclaim: This world is rotten! The public applauds but Jakub is not interested. Jakub knew this two hundred, four hundred, eight hundred years before them, so while they are exclaiming that the world is rotten he is trying to invent for his master a few women with very large bottoms, the way his master likes it. . . .

Life is repetition. Everything has been here before: "The one above who has written all this repeated himself an awful lot, and since he has done so, he has probably been making fun of us."

That life is a giant joke perpetrated on the human race is the message of *Žert,* in which Kundera develops in great depth his most important theme: that it is impossible to understand and control reality. *Žert* is a challenge to the optimistic proposition, advanced by the communists in Czechoslovakia in the 1950s, that reality can be mastered by the intellect and that human beings can create their own destiny. With typically Kunderaesque irony, the author points out that the Communists' belief in an all-powerful human intellect, the culmination of the rationalist optimism of the Enlightenment, produced nothing but destruction. *Žert* masterfully conveys the bleak atmosphere of Czechoslovakian Stalinism, whose propaganda was based on officially manipulated lyricism. Kundera is warning against the destructiveness of emotions elevated to the status of truth.

Most Western critics understood *Žert* as a protest against Stalinist totalitarianism. Kundera, however, objected to such a simplified interpretation. He pointed out that the 1950s in Czechoslovakia attracted him as a scene for the novel "because this was a time when History made as yet unheard of experiments with Man. Thus it deepened my doubts and enriched my understanding of man and his predicament." Czech critics of the 1960s correctly understood *Žert* as a work that probes the deepest essence of human existence.

Daniel Day-Lewis as Tomáš and Juliette Binoche as Tereza in a still from the movie version (1988) of Kundera's novel The Unbearable Lightness of Being *(1984)*

To win a girl, Ludvík Jahn, a communist student, plays an innocent joke. The girl is attending a political training course at a summer camp. Frustrated by her absence, Ludvík sends her a provocative postcard. The postcard gives rise to a witch-hunt, and Ludvík is expelled from the party and the university and is placed in a penal army unit that works in the mines. Many years later, in the 1960s, Ludvík sees that an opportunity has arisen to revenge himself on Pavel Zemánek, the former fellow student who was the main perpetrator of his downfall. He seduces Zemánek's wife, Helena, hoping to destroy their marriage. But Zemánek no longer lives with his wife, and by seducing her, Ludvík actually helps him. Moreover, the chameleon-like Zemánek is now a liberal reformer fighting against communist authoritarianism and is extremely popular with the students at the university where he teaches. Thus, Ludvík realizes that one is never in control; there is no point in trying to revenge oneself: "Everything will be forgotten. There will never be any redress for anything."

Ludvík's most traumatic experience is the realization that his closest friends did not hesitate to vote for his expulsion from the party when they were commanded to do so. In a similar incident the soldiers in the penal unit in which Ludvík served ruthlessly subjected an innocent individual to undeserved torment. Whenever Ludvík finds himself in a group, he wonders how many of the others would be willing to send their fellow mortals to their death if the collective demanded it.

The structure of *Žert* is derived from the principles of musical composition. It is pluralist, polyphonic, and strictly mathematical. Four main characters tell their stories, often recounting the same events from different points of view. By confronting their accounts, the reader comes to the conclusion that each of the characters is the victim of his or her own fallacious interpretation of reality. Ludvík Jahn is proud of his intellectual analytical abilities, but he fools himself by believing that he is in full, rational control of his life. His actions are as much based on impulse as are those of a "lyrical," emotional character such as Helena, who behaves in an embarrassing and destructive way. The characters in *Žert* make many brief philosophical statements and paradoxical wisecracks about the events transpiring around them; as is always the case with Kundera, these comments are only partially true.

The motif of the native land, always dear to Kundera, appears at the end of the novel. When everything is collapsing around him, Ludvík turns, somewhat unconvincingly, to his heritage, but even it can give him only a partial consolation, since his homeland has been despoiled by the arrogance of rampant official rationalism turned into lyricism.

The theme of lovemaking as an instrument of subjugation reappears in Kundera's play *Dvě uši, dvě svatby* (Two Ears, Two Weddings), printed in a mimeographed edition in 1968 and published the following year in a revised version in the journal *Divadlo* (Theater) under the original title, *Ptákovina* (Nonsense). One of the works that Kundera now excludes from the canon of his writing as an immature piece, *Ptákovina* is first and foremost a political satire in the tradition of Eastern European absurdist drama. In this respect, it is closely related to the early absurdist plays of Havel.

The play is set in a school, which serves as a symbol of a society under totalitarian subjugation. Under totalitarianism, truth becomes meaningless; people dissimulate and put on a multiplicity of masks. The headmaster of the school, who terrorizes his teaching staff, draws the female sexual organ on the blackboard in one of the classrooms, labeling the picture, in a child's handwriting, "headmaster." A commission is set up to investigate the matter. An innocent pupil is accused, and he confesses in the hope that his punishment will be less severe. Instead, his ears are cut off. Furthermore, the local Communist Party chairman decrees that the culprit's teacher, Eva, should be punished by whipping, and the chairman carries out the punishment himself as a sexual treat. But Eva is the headmaster's lover, and he is livid with jealousy. Since the headmaster has a reputation as a great womanizer—he has slept with four hundred women—the chairman invites him to test the fidelity of his fiancée, Růžena. Růžena succumbs to the headmaster, but he reports to the chairman that she has remained faithful. Encouraged by Eva, the headmaster continues to sleep with Růžena in revenge for the chairman's whipping of Eva. But Růžena, who has recorded the headmaster's abusive comments about the chairman, blackmails him into becoming her sexual slave. She particularly relishes the fact that although the headmaster hates her, he must repeatedly make love to her. The Kunderaesque theme of women who are at the same time attractive and repulsive thus appears in this play, as does the theme of lovemaking as punishment or as an instrument of enslavement.

Kundera started writing *Život je jinde* (first published in French as *La vie est ailleurs*, 1973; translated as *Life Is Elsewhere*, 1974; published in the original Czech, 1979) during the Prague Spring of 1968 and completed it in 1970, during the first wave of the postinvasion clampdown. In this novel Kundera confronts his past and frees himself from it, viciously stripping away all remnants of his youthful lyrical personality as well as of Communist ideology. The novel is a scathing, rational analysis of an immature, narcissistic lyrical attitude that is destructive in its impotence.

In *Jakub a jeho pán* Kundera's and Diderot's characters created amusing stories because they wanted to shield themselves from an inhospitable human predicament. *Život je jinde* is a variation on this theme. In Kundera's view, "lyrical" characters cannot cope with reality and therefore create an independent reality, poetry, in which they take shelter. An artificial sign takes over the role of reality. In lyrical poems, words turn into things. Reasoning is not required in lyrical poetry: any statement becomes the truth. The lyrical poet might say, "Life is as futile as crying" or "Life is as cheerful as laughter," and both statements will be "true" because they are beautiful.

Lyricism is often associated with a desire for revolution: lyrical poets always try to find a better world in their poetry than the one in which they actually live. The title of Kundera's novel is a quotation from the French poet Arthur Rimbaud that was used by André Breton as the last sentence of his first surrealist manifesto in 1924; it was also used as a slogan by French students during their demonstrations in Paris in May 1968. Lyricists yearn for a different world and are convinced that a radical revolution can bring it about.

Život je jinde is a scathingly analytical account of the life of a fictitious poet, Jaromil, who is of Kundera's generation. His adventures are compared and contrasted with episodes in the lives of the major European lyrical poets Rimbaud, Percy Bysshe Shelley, John Keats, Mikhail Lermontov, Vladimir Mayakovsky, and Jiří Wolker. Kundera condemns the immaturity and destructiveness of the European lyrical avant-garde, as well as their political views, which are based on emotion. In Kundera's view, lyrical poets are controlled by women: Jaromil is subjugated by his neurotic middle-class mother, who systematically reinterprets facts and events so that they fit into an emotional account of reality that is favorable to her.

Like his mother, Jaromil cannot cope with reality; but he escapes into the world of poetry. Yearning to become part of a community of active individuals, he is easily used by the Stalinist regime that comes to power in Czechoslovakia in 1948 as he strives for fame and adapts his poetry to the official demands of the day. Self-centeredness turns Jaromil into a monster: he reports his girlfriend to the police, and she is unjustly condemned to prison for several years. After an altercation at a party Jaromil, acting like a spoiled child, stays out on a balcony in freezing weather, contracts pneumonia, and dies a banal death. By killing Jaromil in this grotesque way, Kundera symbolically does away with the fallacies of his own youth.

In *L'art du roman* Kundera notes that the number seven is an important element in the mathematical structures of his novels. *Život je jinde* is similar to a seven-part sonata, with the parts of the novel composed in varying tempos. Jaromil's story is told dispassionately by a critical third-person observer. Toward the end of the novel the angle of vision suddenly changes: Jaromil disappears from the center of attention and becomes an insignificant and irrelevant character. *Život je jinde* was the first novel Kundera completed as a banned writer; in it and his subsequent novels he radically simplified his language, knowing that he was writing for translation because his work could no longer be published in his native country.

Kundera had been dismissed from his teaching post at the Prague Film Academy; his books had been withdrawn from bookshops and libraries; along with hundreds of other writers, he was to be erased from Czech cultural history. Paradoxically, however, after he had become a nonperson, he experienced a feeling of total freedom: for the first time in his life, he could write freely. He knew that his works would "never be published in Bohemia and that no censor would be reading them." The first product of this attitude was *Valčík na rozloučenou* (translated as *The Farewell Party*, 1976; published in Czech, 1979). Completed in Prague in 1972, it was supposed to be Kundera's last novel; its original title was "Epilog" (The Epilogue).

Formally, *Valčík na rozloučenou* is a farce, but Kundera has filled the comic French form with a serious, ironic content. The result is an overwhelming feeling of the grotesque. The novel deals with misunderstandings in the relationships of five couples. The main character, Klíma, is a trumpet player who is deeply in love with his beautiful wife, Kamila. He demonstrates his love for her by sleeping with other women and always "returning to Kamila." He has had a brief sexual encounter with a nurse in a West Bohemian spa; the nurse has become pregnant, possibly by another man, but she ascribes the pregnancy to the famous musician Klíma, hoping thus to wield control over him. Much of the novel is devoted to Klíma's efforts to persuade the nurse to have an abortion. A series of misunderstandings culminates in the killing of the pregnant nurse; the perpetrator is never discovered. The novel shows all human "dramas" to be futile, insubstantial, and irrelevant. The atmosphere of the work is influenced by the barren climate in Czechoslovakia after the Soviet-led 1968 invasion. The protagonists are calculating and selfish: they aim to gain advantage at the expense of others. Their own pleasure is the primary motivation of their behavior.

The oppressive atmosphere of the outside world intrudes only occasionally: in the grotesque scene of old-age pensioners chasing and catching stray dogs, in the proceedings of the abortion commission, and in the tendency of the characters to create little hidden cells of nepotism, secret brotherhoods of friends who exchange special favors, ignoring ordinary people and shielding themselves from the inhospitable reality on the outside. From a modern Western point of view, the depiction of women is decidedly "politically incorrect": women exist primarily to be manipulated into bed. Again, male characters are often simultaneously both attracted to and repulsed by women. Men are "chased" into marriage. They are almost pathologically afraid of the "trap of pregnancy" and are horrified by the notion that their sexual adventures could produce "brats." Older women are regarded with hardly concealed disgust.

Dust jacket for the English translation (1996) of Kundera's novel
La lenteur (1995), about absurd behavior at a meeting of
entomologists in a French château

continued to look at his native country with an attitude of affectionate melancholy. During his first years in the West, Kundera maintained that he had said all that he had to say in fiction and would write no more novels.

Kniha smíchu a zapomnění (first published in French as *Le livre du rire et de l'oubli,* 1979; translated as *The Book of Laughter and Forgetting,* 1980; published in the original Czech, 1981), completed in 1978, heralded a new stage in Kundera's career; at the same time, it is a continuation of his onslaught on the left-wing myths of his youth. *Kniha smíchu a zapomnění* highlights some of the themes in *Žert* and *Život je jinde,* but this time from a Western vantage point.

Finding that the early Western translations of *Žert* were inaccurate, Kundera resorts in this work to an extremely rational, intellectual style of expression. But he does not give up the notion of writing as a game. While his language is precise, the meaning of his statements remains ambiguous. An ironic detachment is, again, a pervading characteristic of the novel. The structure of *Kniha smíchu a zapomnění* is looser than that of his earlier works; it is divided into seven chapters, which consist of stories, memories, anecdotes, and philosophical essays. The chapters are bound together by the musical principles of polyphony and variation: various aspects of the same facts are highlighted, one at a time. The novel is not supposed to impose particular truths on the reader; it examines and asks questions.

Kniha smíchu a zapomnění includes several story lines; the characters in any one story line never meet those in the others. The narratives are related to one another only as variations of the same set of concepts. One of the main themes of the work is forgetting. On the one hand, at the beginning of the novel Mirek is looking for letters he wrote to a lover when he was a young man so that he can destroy them and change—forget—the past. He believes that he is entitled to rewrite his own life. On the other hand, Tamina, a Czech émigré stranded in France, is trying desperately to reclaim letters she had written to her now-dead husband while they were still living in Prague. She wants to be able to re-create the memories of her life with him, which are fading fast. In the East forgetting is forced on people by the authorities; in the West people embrace forgetting on their own initiative. Tamina's story is also a story of misunderstanding: as in other prose works by Kundera, there is never a meeting of minds; everybody interprets what is going on in his or her own way; and

Another Kunderaesque theme that reappears in *Valčík na rozloučenou* is that of violence perpetrated on innocent individuals with the active approval of other members of society. Like Ludvík Jahn in *Život je jinde,* Jakub, a skeptical dissident intellectual who is about to leave his native country forever, bitterly comes to the conclusion that anyone in Czechoslovakia would send innocent people to death without hesitation. Paradoxically, Jakub is guilty of the arbitrary killing of the nurse, thus confirming that in spite of his lifelong support of human rights he belongs among his countrymen.

In 1975 Kundera and his wife—he had married Věra Hrabánková on 30 September 1967—left Czechoslovakia for France, where Kundera had been invited to teach at the University of Rennes. In interviews he has said that although the departure from the oppressive atmosphere of occupied Czechoslovakia brought him profound relief, he

the same action changes its meaning depending on circumstances and on the observer's angle of vision. Eventually, Tamina is taken from her isolation in France to an island inhabited by a community of children who play constantly but are, at the same time, subjected to rigid discipline. This image is an obvious parallel to life in a communist state but also to the mindless, consumerist society of the West. In trying to escape from the island, Tamina drowns.

The other main theme of the novel is laughter. Angelic, optimistic, collective laughter, expressing simple joy in being alive, is a sign of the mindless destruction of individuality. Devilish, subversive laughter, on the other hand, blasphemes against the ideal of divine perfection. It pricks pomposity and seriousness, whether of group sex or of attempts to create an ideal communist society. In a soul-searching manner, Kundera again reexamines the communism of his youth. He sees the communist revolution as a "deed which has got out of hand, it has escaped from under the control of its creators." He contrasts the enthusiasm of the early youthful Czech communist revolutionaries with the arid regime of post-1968 Czechoslovakia. For the rest of their lives, he concludes, the young revolutionaries were unsuccessfully trying to recapture their original deed, which had emancipated itself from them.

Mirek, the intellectual from the first chapter who wishes to reclaim and rewrite his past, is being followed by the secret police and is eventually sentenced to a long prison term. Another chapter deals with two American students in Paris and their equally simpleminded teacher, who think that they have understood Eugène Ionesco's absurd humor. The chapter "Lítost" (Pity) is a study of an emotion that Kundera defines as "a state of torment which arises when we look at our own wretchedness." The final chapter, "Frontier," gives examples of how easy it is to overstep the borderline beyond which things lose their meaning.

In 1978 the Kunderas moved to Paris, where Kundera had accepted a position at the Ecole des Hautes Etudes. In 1982 he completed the novel *Nesnesitelná lehkost bytí* (translated as *The Unbearable Lightness of Being*, 1984; published in Czech, 1985), his most popular work with Western readers and critics. This novel made Kundera an internationally known author, especially after it was filmed by director Philip Kaufman in 1988. Kundera, however, was unhappy with the movie. Neither it nor Jaromil Jireš's movie version of *Žert*, made in Czechoslovakia in 1969, in any way do justice to the complex, polyphonic structure of the novels. (Kundera, however, likes the Jireš movie. Some Czech critics think that the best motion picture ever made of a work by Kundera is *Já, truchlivý Bůh*, a 1969 Czech adaptation of the short story from *Směšné lásky* directed by Antonín Kachlík.)

Nesnesitelná lehkost bytí returns to a more traditional narrative story line—although even here the narrator continually interrupts, explaining to the reader what he means and examining events from various angles. While many of the narrator's witticisms are insightful, some of them do not ring true. This situation may be intentional on Kundera's part: Alfred Thomas has pointed out that the narrative voice in Kundera's novels must be regarded as one of many in the polyphony of views competing for the reader's attention. The events of the novel often transcend the narrow interpretations offered by the narrator. While the novel was hailed in the West as a masterpiece, it became the subject of fierce controversy among critics in Czechoslovakia: perhaps not realizing that the narrator's emphatic pronouncements are to be taken as only one of many polyphonic voices and as an invitation to critical thinking, Czech commentators contended that the author's vision of reality was too black and white to be convincing.

Kundera's theme in the novel is that life is unrepeatable; hence, one cannot go back and correct one's mistakes. This realization leads to a feeling of vertiginous lightness, a total lack of responsibility. The idea of lightness, which Kundera takes from the Greek philosopher Parmenides, and which originally meant playfulness, here turns into lack of seriousness, into meaningless emptiness. Kundera also takes over the concept of kitsch from the German writer Hermann Broch: kitsch is a beautiful lie that hides all the negative aspects of life and deliberately ignores the existence of death. The hero of the novel, the neurosurgeon Tomáš, is, like Klíma in *Valčík na rozloučenou*, a passionate womanizer who loves his wife, Tereza, a beautiful photographer. He is at the same time attracted to and repelled by women. Tereza's mother, a typical "lyrical" character, is an aggressive proponent of the notions of collectivism, optimism, and lack of privacy; Tereza, however, is shy and yearns for privacy. Destructive lyricism is again associated with left-wing political ideology. Tomáš and Tereza defect to Switzerland after the Soviet invasion of 1968, but Tereza cannot abide Tomáš's infidelities and returns to Czechoslovakia. Tomáš follows her, giving up his medical career and becoming a window cleaner. (Czech

Dust jacket for the U.S. edition (1998) of the English translation of Kundera's novel L'identité (1997), about lovers whose game-playing almost destroys their relationship

critics complained that this element does not ring true: although many professionals were forced to abandon their work and support themselves in menial jobs in the post-1968 clampdown, doctors were not persecuted in this way.) To escape the attention of the secret police, the couple move to the Czech countryside, where they live in happiness and humility for a few years before dying in a traffic accident.

A parallel plot, concerning the relationship of the Czech émigré painter Sabina and the Swiss lecturer Franz, is based on the misunderstandings that follow from their different backgrounds. (The novel includes a "Vocabulary of misunderstood expressions" that are used quite differently by Franz and Sabina.) Franz is the victim of several naive myths and dies a nonsensical death in Thailand during a protest march against the genocide in Cambodia.

Kundera always expressed a strong affection for his native country and its culture. After moving to the West he broadened the concept of the culture to which he belonged to one of Central Europeanness. In many writings and interviews he has argued that Eastern and Central Europe gave birth to a unique civilization with great figures such as Janáček, Broch, Sigmund Freud, Albert Einstein, Gustav Mahler, Franz Kafka, and Robert Musil. In Kundera's view this culture was destroyed by Russian subjugation. Kundera caused an international controversy with his 1980 interview with Philip Roth in *The New York Times Book Review* and his 1984 essay "The Tragedy of Central Europe" in *The New York Review of Books* by directly accusing the "unEuropean, alien" Russians of destroying Eastern and Central European culture and threatening European culture as a whole. The Russian was not "one of us," he contended: "Nothing could be more foreign to Central Europe and its passion for variety than Russia: uniform, standardizing, centralizing . . . determined to transform every nation of its empire into a single Russian people."

Kundera appears to have no use for Russian culture; even Fyodor Dostoyevsky is, for him, a symbol of Russian intolerance and brutality. In his preface to the U.S. edition of *Jacques and His Master* Kundera says: "What irritated me about Dostoyevsky was the climate of his novels: a universe where feelings are promoted to the rank of value and truth." For Kundera, Dostoyevsky is a non-European who lacks the Western balance between rationality and sentiment. Many people agreed with Kundera; others—especially, of course, the Russians, including the poet Joseph Brodsky—disputed his views. Even a Czech dissident writer, Milan Šimečka, pointed out that Eastern and Central European culture was destroyed not by Joseph Stalin's Russia but by Adolf Hitler's Germany. Other Czech writers criticized Kundera for styling himself a dissident writer, as though he had never been a communist. In the interview with Roth, Kundera says:

Then they expelled me from University. I lived among workmen. At that time, I played the trumpet in a jazz band in small-town cabarets. I played the piano and the trumpet. Then I wrote poetry. I painted. It was all nonsense. My first work which is worth while mentioning is a short story, written when I was thirty, the first story in the book *Laughable Loves*. This is when my life of a writer began. I had spent half of my life as a relatively unknown Czech intellectual.

The leading Czech literary critic Milan Jungmann reacted to these statements: "Those who used to know Milan Kundera in the 1950s and the 1960s, can hardly recognize him in this account. The self-portrait has been retouched in such a way that Kundera's real appearance has vanished. Everything essential that formed Kundera's image as a leading intellectual of the past few decades of Czech history has been suppressed." In the 1950s and the 1960s Kundera was a major liberalizing force in Czech literature. *Směšné lásky* and *Žert* are seen by many as heralding the openly antitotalitarian stage in Kundera's writing.

Since the fall of communism, the political culture of the Eastern and Central European countries has often displayed characteristics that seem to be closer to the Soviet Russian or the old Austrian imperial models than to the Western European model. Possibly for this reason, Kundera has cut almost all of his ties with his native land, visiting it rarely. Three of his major novels—*Život je jinde, Kniha smíchu a zapomnění*, and *Nesnesitelná lehkost bytí*–have so far not been published in the Czech Republic.

The novel *Nesmrtelnost* (published in French as *L'immortalité*, 1990; translated as *Immortality*, 1991; published in the original Czech, 1993) still reflects Kundera's Eastern and Central European experience, but indirectly; it is the most French of his longer novels. None of the protagonists are Czech; all are French. The work is a criticism of Western civilization near the end of the twentieth century, based on Kundera's experiences in France and elucidated through comparisons with relevant events from European cultural history. Thus, *Nesmrtelnost* is a European novel with French overtones. The work is a "novel as a debate" in which the characters are personifications of ideas and in which the narrator freely interrupts the story and reflects on it for the benefit of the reader. Discursive passages are more frequent in *Nesmrtelnost* than in Kundera's earlier work; yet, the book retains the character of a polyphonic fictional narrative.

One of the major grievances that Kundera holds against the contemporary world is its tendency to reduce everything to a superficial, easily digestible simplification. For this reason he deliberately writes his novels in such a way that they cannot easily be summarized. He produces a complicated mosaic in which motifs from various parts of the novel are interrelated in an intricate, precarious balance. As in his earlier novels, themes are analyzed from many different angles. The themes in this work are drawn mainly from Kundera's traumatic experiences in Eastern Europe and his adjustment to life in the West.

In *Nesmrtelnost* a Frenchwoman, Agnes, is born in the mind of the narrator, a writer, when he sees an attractive, flirtatious, feminine gesture made by an old lady to a young swimming teacher at a public bath. The writer interprets the gesture as indicating a desire to enter history, to become famous and thus gain "immortality." Kundera explores this theme by digressing to the story of Bettine von Arnim and her relationship to the great classical German poet Johann Wolfgang von Goethe. Bettine was attracted to famous men and wanted to enter history with them, and in 1835 she published the love letters she had allegedly exchanged with Goethe. Not until the twentieth century was it discovered that she had considerably rewritten the letters to create an image highly flattering to herself.

The creation of fake images is a major theme in *Nesmrtelnost*. Ideologies such as communism and Nazism no longer present a threat; the danger now comes from "imagology," that is, from the media and advertising. The "imagologists" create systems of ideals and anti-ideals that people are supposed to follow unthinkingly; thus, reality is destroyed. Agnes unsuccessfully fights these pressures. A character who defies the modern world is the narrator's grotesque friend, Professor Avenarius, who punctures the tires of parked cars during his forays into the night streets of Paris as a gesture of his hatred of the destructiveness of modern civilization. The theme of accidental, unintentional outcomes of events, familiar from *Žert*, recurs here: Avenarius punctures the tires of the car owned by Agnes's husband, Paul, so that he is delayed in traveling to a country hospital where Agnes has been taken after a car accident. Paul arrives at the hospital fifteen minutes after Agnes's death.

Another topic to which Kundera returns in *Nesmrtelnost* is the conflict between the maturity of classicism and the immaturity of Romanticism; one section of the novel is an extended critique of sentimental lyrical poets and their attitudes. Romantic love is always an unconsummated, precoital emotion. Ecological themes are also important in *Nesmrtelnost*, contributing forcefully to the overall impression of a superficial, mechanized, dehumanized, and alienated modern world. *Nesmrtelnost* poses the question of whether contemporary human beings can escape from the crisis of emptiness and absurdity of existence in a world without God. Kundera's heroes live in an enclosed world of closed systems, which reproduce themselves and have nothing in common with reality.

La lenteur (1995; translated as *Slowness*, 1996) is the first work of fiction that Kundera has written in French. An accomplished short novel, it is a playful and amusing counterbalance to the seriousness of *Nesmrtelnost*. It displays all the well-tried and tested characteristics, methods, and approaches of Kundera's mature writing: it is a bravura performance, a mathematical, musiclike structure built up from a collection of abstract basic themes. It includes essayistic, contemplative interludes that interrupt several narrative lines, most of them from the present and one from the past. In the spirit of playfulness, Kundera includes fictional versions of himself and his wife.

The starting point of the novel is a debate about the meaning of hedonism. Pleasure is defined, in the manner of the Greek philosopher Epicurus, as the absence of suffering. In the past the notion of sensuality was associated with slowness. The more slowly one acts, the more intense is one's memory of acting. The present-day obsession with speed is, for Kundera, the epitome of superficiality and emptiness. Kundera here intensifies his criticism of contemporary Western civilization as manipulative, empty, lacking in knowledge and wisdom. His protagonists are spoiled, vainglorious, and pretentious. By contrasting their attitudes and perceptions of reality, he creates a grotesque image of the contemporary world.

The novel is set in a French castle where Kundera and his wife, Věra, spend a midsummer night. The castle becomes a microcosm, a stage where Kundera can closely observe the preposterous behavior of his characters and compare it to an amorous encounter that took place in the same castle two hundred years before and was recorded in a novella published in 1777. The manipulation carried out by the members of the nobility in the eighteenth century was more sophisticated than the clumsy, illiterate, and grotesque behavior of people today. All human encounters in the novel are based on misunderstandings that are so absurd that they become comic.

A congress of entomologists is being held in the castle. One of the scientists is a former dissident, now in the Czech government, who was forced to support himself as a manual worker for twenty years in Czechoslovakia. This background fills him with self-centered pride. When he is called on to give his paper, he is so moved by the occasion that he makes an emotional extemporaneous speech about his past persecution and then leaves the platform, totally forgetting to give his lecture. He becomes a laughingstock among the French scientists, who misspell and mispronounce his name, do not know where his country is, confuse it with other countries, and are uninterested in anything but themselves. Two men and two women pair off, but their relationships are unsuccessful because of misunderstandings that culminate in simulated copulation beside the swimming pool and a histrionic jump into the pool by a woman in an evening dress. These actions are witnessed by the Czech entomologist, who, in total incomprehension, strips to his swimming trunks to display his muscles. Kundera concludes that the contemporary world is crazy.

L'identité (1997; translated as *Identity*, 1998), another short novel written in French, is a love story; it can perhaps be seen as a sophisticated variation on the stories in *Směšné lásky*, in particular "Falešný autostop." Here, too, a relationship between two lovers—this time a middle-aged pair— is put to the test by what at the beginning seems to be an innocent, although manipulative, game. The woman, Chantal, complains that "men do not look at me any more," so her lover, Jean-Marc, begins sending her anonymous love letters. The game, which is interpreted differently by the man and the woman, leads to a misunderstanding that almost breaks up their relationship. Toward the end of the playful though serious work, however, the narrator insists that at some imperceptible point the story has become a dream. Thus, instead of a tragedy, the work remains on the level of a warning: love is the only value that protects one from the outside world, even though its basis may be uncertain because one's perception of the world is unreliable.

La ignorancia (Ignorance, 2000) is a novel in which a major theme is a return to one's native land after many years of exile, when that homeland is no longer recognizable. Kundera wanted the novel to be published first in Spanish translation, because of its particular relevance to the many émigrés from Spain during Francisco Franco's era as well as to his own relationship to Czech culture.

When Kundera was young, he, like many of his compatriots, fell into the trap of a destructive ideology. It took him almost twenty years to free himself from its constraints. The trauma he suffered taught him to assume a skeptically critical attitude toward reality. It showed him the importance of pluralism. It made him realize that humanity is infinitely fallible and does not understand its environment. Once Kundera left Czechoslovakia for the West, he was able to use the critical faculties he gained from his encounter with communism to compare and contrast the Western and the Eastern and Central European experience to elucidate important aspects of contemporary human existence. Kundera has highlighted the modern crisis of language, which is a crisis of meaning and a crisis of communication. His novels are about various forms of delusion. In many of his works a text, a sign, or an image comes to life and begins to act in the real world with an unstoppable destructive force.

Interviews:

Antonín J. Liehm, "Milan Kundera," translated by Peter Kussi, in his *The Politics of Culture* (New York: Grove, 1972), pp. 131–150;

"An Interview with Philip Roth," *New York Times Book Review,* 30 November 1980, pp. 7, 78, 80;

Alain Finkielkraut, "A Milan Kundera Interview," translated by Susan Huston, *Cross Currents: A Yearbook of Central European Culture,* 1 (1982): 15–29;

"In Defense of Intimacy," *Sunday Times Magazine* (London), 20 May 1984, pp. 49–51;

Ian McEwan, "An Interview with Milan Kundera," *Granta,* 11 (1984): 34–35;

Jason Weiss, "An Interview with Milan Kundera," *New England Review and Bread Loaf Quarterly,* 8 (Spring 1986): 405–410;

George Plimpton, ed., *Writers at Work: The "Paris Review" Interviews, Sixth Series* (New York: Viking Penguin, 1986), pp. 207–223;

Christian Salmon, "Conversation with Milan Kundera on the Art of the Novel," translated by Linda Asher, *Salmagundi,* 73 (Winter 1987): 119–135;

Lois Oppenheim, "Clarifications, Elucidations: An Interview with Milan Kundera," *Review of Contemporary Fiction,* 9 (Summer 1989): 7–11;

Jan Šabata, "Není to můj film: Milan Kundera o Nesnesitelné lehkosti bytí," *Lidové noviny,* 3 (5 July 1990): 8.

Bibliographies:

Andreas W. Mytze, "Beiträge zur einer Kundera-Bibliographie," *Europäische Ideen,* 20 (1976);

Darina K. Vašková, "Paradoxní žertování," *Proměny,* 16, no. 3 (1979): 75–86;

Glen Brand, *Milan Kundera: An Annotated Bibliography* (New York & London: Garland, 1988);

Brand, "Selective Annotated Bibliography of Kundera Criticism," *Review of Contemporary Fiction,* 9 (Summer 1989): 97–106.

References:

Aron Aji, ed., *Milan Kundera and the Art of Fiction: Critical Essays* (New York & London: Garland, 1992);

Timothy Garton Ash, "Reform or Revolution?" *New York Review of Books,* 35 (27 October 1988): 47–56;

Calvin Bedient, "On Milan Kundera," *Salmagundi,* 73 (Winter 1987): 93–108; republished in *The New Salmagundi Reader,* edited by Robert and Peggy Boyers (Syracuse, N.Y: Syracuse University Press, 1996), pp. 232–248;

Miroslav Bednář, "Milan Kundera's Fiction and the Czech Critics: The Seventies and the Eighties," *Czechoslovak and Central European Journal,* 10 (Winter 1991): 104–117;

Milan Blahynka, "Milan Kundera prozaik," *Plamen,* 1 (1967): 44–45;

Robert Boyers, "Between East and West: A Letter to Milan Kundera," in his *Atrocity and Amnesia: The Political Novel Since 1945* (New York: Oxford, 1985), pp. 212–233;

Joseph Brodsky, "Why Milan Kundera Is Wrong About Dostoyevsky," *New York Times Book Review,* 17 February 1985, pp. 31, 33–34; republished in *Cross Currents: A Yearbook of Central European Culture,* 5 (1986): 477–483;

Václav Černý, *Tvorba a osobnost,* volume 1 (Prague: Odeon, 1992), pp. 836–848;

Květoslav Chvatík, *Die Fallen der Welt: Der Romancier Milan Kundera* (Munich & Vienna: Hanser, 1994); republished in Czech as *Svět románů Milana Kundery* (Brno: Atlantis, 1994);

Chvatík, Josef Škvorecký, Petr Král, and Ivo Bock, "Ještě o románech Milana Kundery," *Svědectví,* 79 (1986): 614–633;

Michael Cooke, "Milan Kundera, Cultural Arrogance and Sexual Tyranny," *Critical Survey,* 4, no. 1 (1992): 79–84;

Dialog, special Kundera issue, 6 (1986);

Lubomír Doležel, "'Narrative Symposium' in Milan Kundera's *The Joke,*" in his *Narrative Modes in Czech Literature* (Toronto: University of Toronto Press, 1973), pp. 112–125;

A. M. Drozd, "Polyphony in Kundera's *The Joke,*" *Czechoslovak and Central European Journal,* 11 (Winter 1993): 81–90;

Herbert Eagle, "Genre and Paradigm in Milan Kundera's *The Book of Laughter and Forgetting,*" in *Language and Literary Theory: In Honor of*

Ladislav Matejka, edited by Benjamin A. Stolz, I. R. Titunik, and Lubomir Dolezel (Ann Arbor: University of Michigan Press, 1984), pp. 251–284;

Europäische Ideen, special Kundera issue, 20 (1976);

Alfred French, *Czech Writers and Politics: 1945–1969* (Boulder, Colo.: East European Monographs, 1982), pp. 100–101, 119–120, 161–164, 202, 236–239, 282–283;

Carlos Fuentes, "The Other K.," *TriQuarterly*, 51 (Spring 1981): 256–275; republished in his *Myself with Others* (New York: Farrar, Straus & Giroux, 1988), pp. 160–179;

Richard T. Gaughan, "'Man Thinks; God Laughs': Kundera's 'Nobody Will Laugh,'" *Studies in Short Fiction*, 29 (Winter 1992): 1–10;

Marketa Goetz-Stankiewicz, *DramaContemporary: Czechoslovakia* (New York: Performing Arts Journal Publications, 1985);

Goetz-Stankiewicz, *The Silenced Theatre: Czech Playwrights without a Stage* (Toronto: University of Toronto Press, 1979), pp. 206–209, 226–228, 236–238;

James S. Hans, "Kundera's Laws of Beauty," *Essays in Literature*, 19 (Spring 1992): 144–158;

Hermes, special Kundera issue (March 1995);

Daniela Hodrová, "Kunderovo Umění románu-zpověď romanopisce, nebo teorie románu?" *Česká literatura*, 38, no. 5 (1990): 470–473;

Jiří Holý, "Mitteleuropa in der Auffassung von Milan Kundera und Václav Havel," *Wiener Slavistisches Jahrbuch*, 37 (1991): 27–36;

Jerzy Illg, ed., *Kundera–Materialy z sympozjum zorganizowanego v Katowicach v dniach 25.–26. kwietnia 1986 r.* (London: Polonia, 1988);

L'Infini, special Kundera issue, 5 (1984);

L'Infini, special Kundera issue, 44 (1993);

Manfred Jahnichen, "The Destruction of a Myth: The Novel as a Possibility for the Exploration of Human Existence," *Czechoslovak and Central European Journal*, 10 (Winter 1991): 96–103;

Milan Jungmann, "Kunderovské paradoxy," *Svědectví*, 77 (1986): 135–162; republished in his *Cesty a rozcestí: Kritické stati z let 1982–1987* (London: Rozmluvy, 1988), pp. 214–254;

Jungmann, "Otvírání pasti na kritika (ještě ke kritikám románů Milana Kundery)," *Svědectví*, 83–84 (1988): 721–733;

Christine Kiebuzinska, "Jacques and His Master: Kundera's Dialogue with Diderot," *Comparative Literature Studies*, 29 (Winter 1992): 54–76;

Helena Kosková, "Memento mori v próze Milana Kundery," in her *Hledání ztracené generace* (Toronto: Sixty-Eight Publishers, 1987), pp. 153–189;

Kosková, *Milan Kundera* (Prague: H & H, 1998);

Zdeněk Kožmín, "Fenomén X v Kunderově próze," in his *Studie a kritiky* (Prague: Torst, 1995), pp. 348–355;

Jiří Kratochvil, *Příběhy příběhů* (Brno: Atlantis, 1995), pp. 163–184;

Peter Kussi, "Kundera's Novel and the Search for Fatherhood," in *Czech Literature since 1956: A Symposium*, edited by William E. Harkins and Paul I. Trensky (New York: Bohemica, 1980), pp. 56–61;

Kussi, "Milan Kundera: Dialogues with Fiction," *World Literature Today*, 57 (Spring 1983): 206–209;

Eva Le Grand, *Kundera ou La mémoire du désir* (Montreal: XYZ éditeur, 1995); published in Czech as *Kundera aneb Paměť touhy* (Olomouc: Votobia, 1998);

Liberté, special Kundera issue, 121 (1979);

Liberté, special Kundera issue, 5 (1984);

Antonín J. Liehm, "Milan Kundera: Czech Writer," in *Czech Literature since 1956: A Symposium*, pp. 40–55;

Colette Lindroth, "Mirrors of the Mind: Kaufman Conquers Kundera," *Literature/Film Quarterly*, 19, no. 4 (1991): 229–234;

David Lodge, "Milan Kundera and the Idea of the Author in Modern Criticism," *Critical Quarterly*, 26, no. 1–2 (1984): 105–121; republished in his *After Bakhtin: Essays on Fiction and Criticism* (London & New York: Routledge, 1990), pp. 154–167;

Sigrid Löffler, "Anmerkungen zu Milan Kundera," *Literatur und Kritik*, 199–200 (November–December 1985): 473–478;

Ladislav Matějka, "Milan Kundera's Central Europe," *Cross Currents: A Yearbook of Central European Culture*, 9 (1990): 127–134;

Fred Misurella, *Understanding Milan Kundera: Public Events, Private Affairs* (Columbia: University of South Carolina Press, 1993);

Susan Moore, "Kundera: The Massacre of Culture," *Quadrant*, 31 (April 1987): 63–66;

E. Narrett, "Surviving History: Milan Kundera's Quarrel with Modernism," *Modern Language Studies*, 22 (Fall 1992): 4–24;

Maria Němcová-Banerjee, *Terminal Paradox: The Novels of Milan Kundera* (New York: Grove Weidenfeld, 1990);

John O'Brien, *Dangerous Intersection: Milan Kundera and Feminism* (New York: St. Martin's Press, 1995);

225

O'Brien, "Milan Kundera: Meaning, Play, and the Role of the Author," *Critique*, 34 (Fall 1992): 3–18;

Jiří Opelík, "Kunderovo 'hoře z rozumu'," in *Nenáviděné řemeslo: Výbor z kritik 1957–1968* (Prague: Československý spisovatel, 1969);

Peter Petro, ed., *Critical Essays on Milan Kundera* (New York: G. K. Hall, 1999);

Hana Píchová, "The Narrator in Milan Kundera's *The Unbearable Lightness of Being*," *Slavic and East European Journal*, 36 (Summer 1992): 217–226;

Ellen Pifer, "*The Book of Laughter and Forgetting*: Kundera's Narration against Narration," *Journal of Narrative Technique*, 22 (Spring 1992): 84–96;

Norman Podhoretz, "The Open Letter to Milan Kundera," *Commentary*, 78 (October 1984): 34–39; republished in his *The Bloody Crossroads: Where Literature and Politics Meet* (New York: Simon & Schuster, 1986), pp. 167–183;

Miloš Pohorský, "Žert na začátku jedné epiky," in his *Zlomky analýzy: K poválečné české literatuře* (Prague: Československý spisovatel, 1990), pp. 270–280;

Robert C. Porter, *Milan Kundera: A Voice from Central Europe* (Aarhus, Denmark: Arkona, 1981);

Proměny, special Kundera issue, 28, no. 1 (1991);

Francis L. Restuccia, "Homo Homini Lupus: Milan Kundera's *The Joke*," *Contemporary Literature*, 31 (Fall 1990): 281–299;

Review of Contemporary Fiction, special Kundera section, 9 (Summer 1989): 7–107;

Sylvie Richterová, "Otázka Boha ve světě bez Boha," in her *Ticho a smích* (Praha: Mladá fronta, 1997), pp. 132–150;

Richterová, "I romanzi di Kundera e i problemi della communicazione," *Strumenti critici*, 45 (June 1981): 308–334;

Richterová, "Tři romány Milana Kundery," in her *Slova a ticho* (Munich: Arkýř, 1986), pp. 33–67;

Richard Rorty, "Heidegger, Kundera and Dickens," in his *Essays on Heidegger and Others* (Cambridge & New York: Cambridge University Press, 1991), pp. 66–82;

Philip Roth, introduction to Kundera's *Laughable Loves* (New York: Knopf, 1974); republished in his *Reading Myself and Others* (New York: Farrar, Straus & Giroux, 1975), pp. 200–209;

Ján Rozner, afterword to Kundera's *Majitelé klíčů: Hra o jednom dějství s čtyřmi vizemi*, second edition (Prague: Orbis, 1964), pp. 93–123;

Salmagundi, special Kundera issue, 73 (Winter 1987);

Milan Suchomel, "Čas románu," in his *Literatura z času krize. Šest pohledů na českou prózu 1958–1967* (Brno: Atlantis, 1992), pp. 66–68, 122–131;

Svědectví, special Kundera section, 74 (1985): 333–368;

Alfred Thomas, "Fiction and Non-Fiction in Milan Kundera's *Kniha smíchu a zapomnění*," in his *The Labyrinth of the Word: Truth and Representation in Czech Literature* (Munich: Oldenbourg, 1995), pp. 132–143;

Paul I. Trensky, *Czech Drama since World War II* (White Plains, N.Y.: M. E. Sharpe, 1978);

John Updike, "Czech Angels," in his *Hugging the Shore: Essays and Criticism* (New York: Knopf, 1984), pp. 509–514;

Igor Webb, "Milan Kundera and the Limits of Scepticism," *Massachusetts Review*, 31 (Autumn 1990): 357–368.

Kalju Lepik

(7 October 1920 – 30 May 1999)

Õnne Kepp
Under and Tuglas Literature Center

BOOKS: *Nägu koduaknas* (Stockholm: Eesti Raamat, 1946);

Mängumees (Stockholm: Eesti Raamat, 1948);

Kerjused treppidel (Vadstena: Orto, 1949);

Tõrvapõletaja poja õpetussõnad (Stockholm: "Tuulisui," 1950);

Merepõhi (Stockholm: "Tuulisui," 1951);

Martin Musta saladus, by Lepik, Raimond Kolk, Arvo Mägi, Karl Ristikivi, and Ilmar Talve (Stockholm: Sõna, 1954);

Muinasjutt Tügrimaast (Lund: Eesti Kirjanike Kooperatiiv, 1955);

Kivimurd (Lund: Eesti Kirjanike Kooperatiiv, 1958);

Vilemees (Stockholm: Autori kirjastus, 1958);

Kollased nõmmed (Lund: Eesti Kirjanike Kooperatiiv, 1965);

Tuuleveski: Nelikümmend ja üks koltunud kirja lisadega, by Lepik and Mägi, as Rein Kaljumägi (Lund: Eesti Kirjanike Kooperatiiv, 1967);

Mälestus on pihlakas (Stockholm: "Bibliophila," 1967);

Marmorpagulane (Lund: Eesti Kirjanike Kooperatiiv, 1968);

Verepõld (Lund: Eesti Kirjanike Kooperatiiv, 1973);

Klaasist mehed (Lund: Eesti Kirjanike Kooperatiiv, 1978);

Kadunud külad (Lund: Eesti Kirjanike Kooperatiiv, 1985);

Öötüdruk (Tallinn: Eesti Raamat, 1992).

Editions and Collections: *Ronk on laululind: Valitud luuletused* (Lund: Eesti Kirjanike Kooperatiiv, 1961);

Sina oled kuusik ja mina lepik: Luuletused (Tallinn: "Kodumaa" lisa, 1965);

Surmal on lapse silmad/Death Has a Child's Eyes (Rome: Maarjamaa, 1976);

Kogutud luuletused, 1938–1979 (Lund: Eesti Kirjanike Kooperatiiv, 1980);

Rukkilille murdmise laul: Valitud luuletused, compiled by Paul-Eerik Rummo (Tallinn: Eesti Raamat, 1990);

Kalju Lepik (photograph by R. Tippo)

Pihlakamarja rist: Kolmeteistkümnes kogu luuletusi (Tartu: Ilmamaa, 1997).

Editions in English: "By the Waters of Toonela" and "Wooden Crosses," translated by W. K. Matthews, in *Anthology of Modern Estonian Poetry,* edited by Matthews (Gainesville: University of Florida Press, 1953), pp. 144–145;

"The Sea," "Let Me Hold Your Hand," "Curse," and "Nobody Talks Earth's Language," translated by Ivar Ivask, in *Contemporary East European Poetry*, edited by Emery George (Ann Arbor, Mich.: Ardis, 1983), pp. 19–21.

OTHER: *Homse nimel*, edited by Lepik and Imant Rebana (Stolkholm: Bloms, 1945);
Gustav Suits, *Kogutud luuletused*, compiled by Lepik (Uppsala: Eesti Kirjanike Kooperatiiv, 1963);
Esto 80: Ülemaailmsed Eesti Päevad/Estonian World Festival, edited by Lepik (Stockholm: ESTO 80 Peakomitee, 1981).

Though born and educated in Estonia, Kalju Lepik became one of the best-known poets of the younger generation while in exile. A member of the émigré community that developed in Sweden in the 1940s as a result of World War II (that included established writer Marie Under), Lepik became an active public figure in cultural and literary circles, renowned both for his own verse and for his fierce commitment to the preservation of Estonian literature that languished under Soviet domination. Lepik's poetry is valued for his startling modernist imagery and sophisticated treatment of folkloric elements.

Kalju Lepik was born on 7 October 1920 in Koeru, Estonia, to Hilda and Bernhard Lepik. Shortly after his birth, Lepik's parents divorced. In 1926 his mother remarried, and Lepik grew up with three stepsisters. From 1928 to 1934 he attended the Koeru primary school, and in 1939 he graduated from the Tartu Commercial Secondary School, having meanwhile won a poetry prize. Then the Soviet Union annexed Estonia, and in 1941 Germany invaded the country. From 1939 to 1941 Lepik studied at the Tartu Commercial Gymnasium. In the fall of 1940 he was one of the founders of a literary group called *Tuulisui* (a neologism suggesting something like "free as the wind"). In 1942 he entered the University of Tartu, majoring in history and archaeology. The following year, Lepik was drafted into the German army, but in the autumn of 1944, when the Soviets reoccupied Estonia, he escaped to Sweden. While still in Estonia, Lepik had assembled a collection of poems, but the manuscript was destroyed during his escape.

From the mid 1940s to the end of the decade, Lepik held several part-time jobs in and around Stockholm, contributed to and edited several Estonian publications, briefly studied archaeology and ethnography at the University of Stockholm, and wrote verses that reflected the views of a war refugee. In 1949 he married Asta Priuhka. A son was born to them in 1952, and a daughter in 1961. Lepik settled with his wife and family in Stockholm, a city that provided inspiration for many of his poems.

Many other members of *Tuulisui* had escaped to Sweden, particularly to Stockholm. Thus, the activities of the literary group *Tuulisui* began to bear fruit in exile, notably with the publication in 1945 of an anthology, *Homse nimel* (In the Name of Tomorrow), which included a selection of poems by Lepik. In addition, the group was instrumental in launching several cultural journals, including *Sõna* (Word), the most substantial émigré publication in the second half of the 1940s. *Tuulisui* held discussions and presented musical and literary evenings, thus helping the Estonian refugees in Sweden to form a viable émigré community. Lepik's active participation in such organizations as the Estonian Writers' Union in Exile and his work as a newspaper columnist, tackling cultural issues and writing literary criticism, likewise helped his fellow Estonians to preserve their ethnic identity. Lepik's political views were also formed at this time. He contributed to such journals as *Radikaaldemokraat* (Radical Democrat) and *Eesti Raamat* (Estonian Book), later called *Vaba Eesti* (Free Estonia), and was one of the founders of an émigré publishing house.

In these early years of exile, the publication of Lepik's first book of poems, *Nägu koduaknas* (A Face in My Window, 1946), was an encouraging sign. Childhood memories and the author's experiences as a soldier and as a refugee find pithy expression in this volume. The cycle "Korstnad öös" (Chimneys in the Night) uses free verse to depict the destructive aspects—physical as well as moral—of war. The verses grouped in "Maapagu" (Exile) comprise the most deeply felt part of the collection and include several forceful poems directly inspired by the aftermath of World War II. Among these are "Kisendad, kodumaa!" (You Scream, My Country), written in response to the Swedish government's capitulation to the Soviet Union to forcibly repatriate former Baltic soldiers, and "Meie laulame" (We Sing), a poem of righteous wrath and defiance. Elegiac recollections of a peaceful, bucolic existence become mixed with the pathos of the passing of time in the cycle "Õhtu põldudel" (Evening in the Fields). There are also love poems, though some of these tend toward ironic bitterness. In spite of occasional sarcasm, Lepik's first volume was exactly what an émigré, still sitting on his or her suitcases, needed most of all: familiar pictures of the lost homeland; oracular, almost prophetic anger at the evil deeds of the despised enemy; and an iron steadfastness not to lose one's resolve even in exile.

The bravura mode did not, however, stay long in Lepik's repertoire. In his second collection, *Män-*

gumees (The Fiddler, 1948), the poet wears the mask of a jester. His rhythms are playful, the rhymes often humorous, the diction occasionally coarse, the tone anti-aesthetic, and the subject matter, for the most part, what was then called "decadent." A quick perusal of this volume may create the impression that Lepik is grinning at the reader from a distorted fun-house mirror in the guise of a François Villon or a Charles Baudelaire, especially in poems such as "Topsisõbra matus" (Death of a Drunkard) or "Timuka unenägu" (Hangman's Dream). Such confrontational verse that destroyed the conventions of Estonian poetry shocked readers and irritated conservative émigré critics. Other poems suggest that drinking and womanizing may be a not so unusual by-product of war, as in "Relvavennad" (Comrades-in-Arms), or simply the result of a sudden awareness of the entropy of life, as in "Lõõtspillilood" (Accordion Pieces). There is often a sense of something's being slightly askew in almost any volume by Lepik, something that subtly anticipates later innovations by the poet. In this collection the lyric "Ahel ja tuul" (Chain and Wind), for example, foreshadows Lepik's subsequent formal experiments, for the poem includes surrealistic elements.

The first two collections of Lepik's poetry suggest a possible approach to his later work. At the beginning of his new life in Sweden, this standard-bearer of young émigré poets became a singer of patriotic Estonian verses by evolving two strategies that made possible his innovative restructuring of such lyrics. On the one hand, there is his tacit acceptance of patriotic values; on the other, he commits himself to an exploration of, indeed an immersion in, the metaphysics of the Manichean duality of good and evil.

In the period from 1949 to 1955 Lepik moved from the absolute patriotic values typical of Estonian poetry to a more relativistic, existential approach. Trips to Germany, Spain, France, and England no doubt contributed to the broadening of his intellectual horizons. In the collections *Kerjused treppidel* (Beggars on the Stairs, 1949), *Merepõhi* (The Bottom of the Sea, 1951), and *Muinasjutt Tiigrimaast* (A Fairy Tale of Tigerland, 1955), he also discards traditional poetic realism. In *Kerjused treppidel* Lepik mixes allusions to some of the oldest religions, including Christianity, with depictions of the materialism and absence of belief that characterize the modern world. A ghoulish intermezzo introduces literary characters as well as historical personages, including Agatha Christie. An early poem in this volume hints that the world will end not with a whimper but with a nuclear bang. Another depicts the Creator searching for humankind but finding only wolves.

Lepik in 1939, the year he graduated from the Tartu Commercial Secondary School and entered the Tartu Commercial Gymnasium

In *Merepõhi* Lepik attacks blind patriotism, hidebound émigrés, and the critics of his verses, for the cycle "Ma armastan neegritari" (I Love a Negress) had been controversial even before publication. The volume originally had this title, but "Ma armastan neegritari" was considered inappropriate by the publishing house, and the manuscript was turned down. Another drawback in the eyes of the publishers had been the author's inexact diction and semantic obscurity. In actuality, the forty-nine poems in this collection offer examples of negation presented in a playful and teasing manner and show firm resistance to any kind of societal restrictions. Lepik's form is irritating on purpose, playing with rhymes that occasionally lean toward the vulgar. He mocks chauvinism, as well as some biblical characters, in *Merepõhi;* however, Lepik is searching for meaning, even if he has to look for it at the ends of the earth: "The bottom of the sea," he declares, "is death." From these depths the poet's insights rise in the form of air bubbles that discover "in the pain of resurrection / the truth of time / and space."

Muinasjutt Tiigrimaast, favoring strange colors and exotic flora and fauna, was inspired by Lepik's reading of Rudyard Kipling's works about India. The imagery in the first part of this volume is often surrealistic and playfully musical, as in "Kantaat vilele ja inglikoorile" (Cantata for Fife and a Choir of Angels). The second half of the book is more down-to-earth and, in places, delightfully satiric. Lepik's targets are the materialism and philistinism of his fellow émigrés. The teasing ballad "Lili Marlen" occupies a special place in this collection. Based on a well-known song of World War II, sung originally by German soldiers and later by allied servicemen as well, Lepik's version presents a series of associations involving contemporary life and violent (war) imagery as well as spiritual allusions–all filtered, however, through the alembic of a disturbed mind. Lepik had experimented with such serial poems earlier, such as "Umbsed tõed" (Stale Truths) and "Kuus kurbust" (Six Sorrows) in *Kerjused treppidel.* Although these lack a "plot," the writer's aim was to create a mini-epic by lyrical means. Even the title *Muinasjutt Tiigrimaast* is an allusion to the epic tradition. "Lili Marlen" is the poet's first successful attempt in this field, which he developed later into highly visual poems named after various colors and for which he coined the term *poheem.*

Lepik spent the summer of 1958 in Finland. He met with writers and critics, participated in cultural events, and made arrangements for the translation, publication, and popularization of Estonian exile literature in a country practically next door to Soviet Estonia. Soon, however, this activity was terminated, as Finland had to be extremely careful not to irritate the Soviet Union. Nevertheless, Lepik's sixth collection of poetry, *Kivimurd* (Stone Quarry, 1958), reaped an emotional benefit from his having spent time with the nearest linguistic relatives of the Estonians and from being in close physical proximity to his homeland. The most emotional cycles of this collection are "Rukkilille murdmise laul" (The Song of Breaking a Cornflower) and "Velkari-laulud" (Songs of Velkari), dealing with recollections of the poet's childhood and with nature, mostly in carefree summertime. The noteworthy achievement in this volume involves Lepik's use of ancient Estonian folk songs in a modernist idiom. Examples of such restructured lyrics that allude to the fate of his native land include "Tule mulle, kitsekene!" (Come to Me, Little Goat), a clever fusion of well-known folkloric ditties with imagery suggestive of Nazi atrocities, and "Kellele ma kaeban kurja?" (To Whom Should I Complain about Evil?), an indictment of the Soviets' deportations of so many Estonians to Siberia. Equally "metaphysical" (as Samuel Johnson has defined the yoking together of heter-

ogeneous ideas in seventeenth-century English poetry) are several other lyrics. The best include "Mõru mõte" (A Bitter Thought) and "Ma lendan mesipuu poole" (Winging toward the Beehive). The first introduces contemporary violence into a brief paraphrase from the national epic *Kalevipoeg* (Son of Kalev), while the second concludes with a totally unexpected and therefore doubly startling image from the best-known poem published during the aftermath of the National Awakening–"Ta lendab mesipuu poole" (Winging toward the Beehive, 1905), by Juhan Liiv.

In the 1960s and 1970s Lepik extensively used his method of reinventing patriotic lyrics. Old-fashioned declarative statements and sentimental images disappear, incidentally, from patriotic poetry written at the same time in Estonian, as well. A more subtle and discreet approach replaces the former reliance on pathos. In the process, allusions to contemporary European history enrich and universalize these poems. Lepik's method thus counters the official lies and falsifications of history actively cultivated in Soviet Estonia. In the West, where Lepik's books were readily available, the younger generation of Estonian exiles was beginning to lose their native language and, hence, their ability to grasp the nuances of such metaphysical intertextuality. In Soviet Estonia, on the other hand, where Lepik's openly anticommunist works were banned, his poems (and those by other exiles) were copied and circulated by hand.

In 1961 Lepik collected some occasional verses, especially those in memory of his son (who was killed in an accident at the age of six), and about a hundred previously published lyrics into a volume of selected poems, *Ronk on laululind* (The Raven is a Songbird). The book attracted attention even in Soviet Estonia, where the weekly newspaper *Kodumaa* (Homeland), a propaganda sheet aimed at the exile community, acknowledged for the first time that Lepik was one of a handful of exile authors who might actually have talent. Though other commentators pointed out his anti-Soviet stance, the beginning of the Nikita Khrushchev–era "thaw" made it possible to publish a small selection of Lepik's poetry in the Estonian SSR in 1964. The title of that volume—*Sina oled kuusik ja mina lepik* (You're a Spruce Forest And I'm an Alder Grove)—puns on Lepik's name, which translates as "alder grove." Lepik was also becoming known to non-Estonian speakers. His poems have been translated into Dutch, English, Finnish, French, German, Hungarian, Italian, Karelian, Latvian, Lithuanian, Russian, and Swedish. In 1976 the publishing house Maarjamaa in Rome published a selection of his poems in nine languages under the title *Surmal on lapse silmad/Death Has a Child's Eyes.* In 1966 Lepik became the head of the Baltic Archive, an important repository of émigré culture. During this decade he also lectured abroad—in Canada, England, Finland, Italy, and the United States—and published two new volumes of his poetry.

Kollased nõmmed (Yellow Heaths, 1965), sets up a contrast between dictators, nuclear scientists, and space exploration, on the one hand, and two lovers, as well as elegiac nature, on the other. There are also metaphysical verses linking patriotic or politically resonant images with innocuous lines and a surprisingly eloquent concrete poem, "Kangelaskalmistu" (Military Cemetery), which consists of eight lines of crosses that conjure up endless rows of identical grave markers. Marmorpagulane (The Marble Refugee, 1968) grapples with the fossilization of the exile community. By the 1960s, the former refugees had become citizens. They faced an identity crisis—or, rather, denied vehemently that there was a crisis—while many of their children had more or less assimilated into the culture of the host country. This process was inevitable and natural. Lepik does not condone the limited vision of the émigrés who cling to the old ways; yet, he does not as a rule condemn them either. Instead, he hints at the real problem, namely the fate of Estonians in a world that quickly forgets its minorities.

The core of Marmorpagulane, the cycle "Pää kohal surnud linnud" (Dead Birds Overhead) clarifies a further refinement of Lepik's already subtle form of patriotic verse. The homeland is now a girl with whom the speaker was enamored in his youth, but she is all but forgotten now, nothing more than a poignant erotic memory. Soviet Estonian critics praised Marmorpagulane, no doubt because of the satire aimed at the exiles. Notwithstanding such political readings, commentators on both sides of the Baltic Sea noted that Lepik's diction had abandoned stereotypes and abstractions and that he spoke forcefully through concise visual images. The volume also includes several witty concrete poems. Marmorpagulane attempts an experimental structural technique as well. The collection begins and ends with "prologues," some of which are occasional poems alluding to contemporary events.

The framework of occasional poems as "prologues" also characterizes Lepik's next two volumes, Verepõld (Field of Blood, 1973) and Klaasist mehed (Men of Glass, 1978). In addition, both works make extensive use of allusions to Estonian folklore and the Bible. The title of the first volume, Verepõld, has a double meaning. It refers to both Judas Iscariot's field of blood (Acts 1:18–19) and to the Estonian killing fields of the abortive anticzarist revolution of 1905. Klaasist mehed connects the image of the biblical Israelites' flee-

Lepik's wife, Asta, and their daughter, Aino, in 1968

ing through the Red Sea to that of the Estonians' crossing the Baltic Sea in small boats to escape the Red Army in the fall of 1944. The Reds are also the obvious targets of a short but powerful shamanistic incantation, titled simply "Needmine" (The Curse). The characteristic structure of Lepik's poetry is based on the sacred number 3: theme, countertheme, and a variation on the theme, as exemplified by such triads as Estonia, its history, and exile, or (on a more universal level) the ideal, the real, and the human. Lepik's patriotic verses helped to preserve the collective national memory of Estonians, and his innovative use of metaphysical imagery undoubtedly influenced some of the writers in Soviet Estonia in the 1960s, for obscure allusions and hidden references were needed to evade the censors. The same tactics were used at the time of the "singing revolution" or the new national awakening in the late 1980s, which led to the regaining of Estonian independence in 1991.

In 1982 Lepik became the chairman of the Estonian Writers' Union in Exile. In 1990 he visited his homeland for the first time after nearly fifty years of exile and received the Juhan Liiv literary prize. That same year his seventieth birthday was celebrated both at home and abroad, and the first respectable selection of his poems to appear in Estonia, Rukkilille murdmise laul (The Song of Breaking a Cornflower), was published to mark that event.

Lepik's last two collections, *Kadunud külad* (Lost Villages, 1985) and *Öötüdruk* (Night Girl, 1992), repeat in concentrated form his earlier themes, counterthemes, and variations, but a deep resignation prevails in these verses. The poet views his homeland in pessimistic tones, and a personal premonition of death grows into intimations of a general apocalypse, for some of the poems create an ominous undertone that emerges at times as a vision of a postnuclear world. In the first line of the untitled first poem in *Kadunud külad* the speaker asks, "Where have all the villages gone?" Neither cellular phones nor denuded angels with plucked feathers are able to offer redemption. Lepik reached this state of despair just a few years before the re-achieving of Estonian independence. *Öötüdruk* is rich in Christian and medieval imagery. The cycles "Öökotkad põlevate lippudega" (Night Eagles with Burning Flags) and "Tulejuuksed maatüdruku põskedel" (Tresses of Fire Framing the Face of a Country Girl) conjure up such modern evils as pollution and the possible destruction of Planet Earth. In searching for a solution, the poet no longer distinguishes between his homeland (the Night Girl) and the world at large (the Country Girl). Only one beloved remains to be shared by all—"the earth above the burned moonscape." Lepik died in Tallinn, Estonia, on 30 May 1999.

Kalju Lepik's poetry has the characteristics of a sacred vow, redeeming prayer, and biblical curse. The exiled poet worshiped occupied Estonia as a lost Eden and quickly became a singer of innovative melodies, owing to which the modern Estonian patriotic lyric was born. It preserved within its specific structure the memory and identity that nourished the émigrés scattered throughout the world, as well as those who lived in their ancestral homeland but under an alien yoke. Exile and the political/cultural resistance in Estonia have become history. Lepik as a small nation's major poet surely belongs there as well.

Interviews:

"Kirjutada inimese ja ta vabaduse nimel. Intervjuu Kalju Lepikuga," *Mana 3* (1965): 54–56;

Sirje Ruutsoo, "Mälestus olen ma ise möödunus," *Looming* (October 1989): 1407–1415.

Bibliographies:

Bernard Kangro, *Eesti kirjakuulutaja eksiilis* (Lund: Eesti Kirjanike Kooperatiiv, 1989), pp. 25–26, 72;

Anne Valmas, *Kalju Lepik: Personaalnimestik* (Tallinn: Eesti Rahvusraamatukogu, 1990);

Oskar Kruus, *Eesti kirjarahva leksikon* (Tallinn: Eesti Raamat, 1995), pp. 282–283.

Biography:

Arvo Mägi, *Kalju Lepik* (Lund: Eesti Kirjanike Kooperatiiv, 1970; enlarged edition, Tallinn: Faatum, 1993).

References:

Alexander Aspel, "Ice, Stars, Stones, Birds, Trees: Three Major Postwar Estonian Poets Abroad," *Books Abroad*, 47 (Autumn 1973): 642–652;

Maie Kalda, "Kalju Lepiku proosatekstide luulelikkus," in *Väliseesti kirjanduse konverents. Ettekanded 22. ja 23. oktoobril 1990*, edited by Õnne Kepp and Piret Kruuspere (Tallinn: Eesti Teaduste Akadeemia Underi ja Tuglase Kirjanduskeskus, 1991), pp. 31–38;

Õnne Kepp, "*Digitus Dei est hic*: Se neützist Annast Öötüdrukuni. Kalju Lepik," in *Eesti Pagulaskirjandus. Luule*, edited by Kepp and Arne Merilai (Tallinn: Eesti Teaduste Akadeemia Underi ja Tuglase Kirjanduskeskus, 1994), pp. 93–112;

Kepp, "Painaja ja kiituselaul," in *Väliseesti kirjanduse konverents. Ettekanded 22. ja 23. oktoobril 1990* (Tallinn: Eesti Teaduste Akadeemia Underi ja Tuglase Kirjanduskeskus, 1991), pp. 20–24;

George Kurman, "Kalju Lepik. *Marmorpagulane*," *Books Abroad*, 43 (Winter 1969): 141;

Ilse Lehiste, "Estonian Writers and the Experience of Exile," *Lituanus*, 18 (Spring 1972): 15–31;

Toomas Liiv, "Kaliu Lepik luuletajana," *Looming* (October 1989): 1415–1423;

Aivo Lõhmus, "Kalju Lepik ja eesti rahvusluse käekäik," *Looming* (March 1993): 415–417;

Arvo Mägi, "Kolmas kiri Kalju Lepikule: Satiiri asjus," *Tulimuld*, no. 2 (1991): 78–83;

Anneli Mihkelev, "Sul ärgu olgu teisi jumalaid mu kõrval. (2. Mo 20:3). Allusioonid Piiblile Kalju Lepiku luules," in *Kirjandusteadus. Mõte ja ulm, rakendus ja uurimus*, edited by Luule Epner and Arne Merilai (Tartu: Tartu Ülikooli, 1996), pp. 49–57;

Arno Oja, "Kalju Lepiku 'Tõde ja õigus,'" in *Väliseesti kirjanduse konverents. Ettekanded 22. ja 23. oktoobril 1990* (Tallinn: Eesti Teaduste Akadeemia Underi ja Tuglase Kirjanduskeskus, 1991), pp. 13–19;

Sirje Olesk, "Kivisilla vari. Tartu Kalju Lepiku luules," in *Välismaise eesti kirjanduse konverents*, volume 2 (Tallinn: Eesti Kultuurifond, 1989), pp. 13–19;

Karl Ristikivi, "Noor Kalju Lepik," *Tulimuld*, no. 3 (1970): 111–119;

Paul-Eerik Rummo, "Kalju Lepiku luule," in *Välismaise eesti kirjanduse konverents*, volume 2, (Tallinn: Eesti Kultuurifond, 1989), pp. 5–12.

Arnošt Lustig

(21 December 1926 –   )

Aleš Haman
South Bohemia University, České Budějovice

BOOKS: *Noc a naděje* (Prague: Naše vojsko, 1958); translated by George Theiner as *Night and Hope* (New York: Dutton, 1962; London: Hutchinson, 1962); Czech version revised (Prague: Československý spisovatel, 1992);

Démanty noci (Prague: Mladá fronta, 1958); translated by Iris Urwin-Levit as *Diamonds in the Night* (Prague: Artia, 1962);

Ulice ztracených bratří (Prague: Naše vojsko, 1959); revised and republished as *Ulice ztracených* (Cologne: Index, 1973; Prague: Hynek, 1996); translated by Jeanne W. Němcová as *Street of Lost Brothers*, foreword by Jonathan Brent (Evanston, Ill.: Northwestern University Press, 1990);

Můj známý Vili Feld (Prague: Mladá fronta, 1961);

První stanice štěstí: Reportáže (Prague: Mladá fronta, 1961);

Dita Saxová (Prague: Československý spisovatel, 1962); translated by Theiner as *Dita Sax* (London: Hutchinson, 1966); translated by Němcová as *Dita Saxova* (New York: Harper & Row, 1979);

Nikoho neponížíš (Prague: Naše vojsko, 1963);

Modlitba pro Kateřinu Horovitzovou (Prague: Československý spisovatel, 1964); translated by Němcová as *A Prayer for Katerina Horovitzova* (New York: Harper & Row, 1973; London: Quartet, 1990);

Vlny v řece (Prague: Československý spisovatel, 1964);

Bílé břízy na podzim (Prague: Československý spisovatel, 1966; revised, with reinstated censorship deletions, Brno: Atlantis, 1995);

Hořká vůně mandlí (Prague: Mladá fronta, 1968);

Miláček (Prague: Československý spisovatel, 1969; Toronto: Sixty-Eight Publishers, 1973);

Film and the Holocaust, by Lustig and Josef Lustig (Chicago: Spertus College of Judaica, 1978);

Z deníku sedmnáctileté Perly Sch. (Toronto: Sixty-Eight Publishers, 1979); republished as *Nemilovaná. Z deníku sedmnáctileté Perly Sch.* (Prague:

Arnošt Lustig in 1950

Odeon, 1991); translated as *The Unloved: From the Diary of Perla S.* (New York: Arbor House, 1985; London: Macmillan, 1986);

Porgess, in *Velká trojka* (Prague: Galaxie, 1991);

Tma nemá stín (Prague: Československý spisovatel, 1991);

Colette, dívka z Antverp (Prague: Kvarta, 1992);

Tanga, dívka z Hamburku (Prague: Kvarta, 1992);

Dům vrácené ozvěny (Prague: Mladá fronta, 1994); translated by Josef Lustig as *The House of Returned*

Echoes (Evanston, Ill.: Northwestern University Press, forthcoming 2001);

Kamarádi (Prague: Victoria Publishing, 1995);

Neslušné sny (Prague: Hynek, 1995);

Propast (Prague: Hynek, 1996);

Oheň na vodě: Povídky (Prague: Melantrich, 1998);

Krásné zelené oči (Prague: Peron, 2000); translated by Ewald Osers as *Lovely Green Eyes* (London: Harvill, forthcoming 2001);

Lea z Leeuwardenu (Prague: Eminent, 2000).

Editions and Collections: *Noc a den* (Prague: Československý spisovatel, 1962)—comprises *Noc a naděje*, *Démanty noci*, and *Můj známý Vili Feld*;

Spisy Arnošta Lustiga, edited by Jiří Navrátil (Prague: Hynek, 1995–)—comprises volume 1, *Neslušné sny* (1995); volume 2, *Ulice ztracených bratří* (1996); volume 3, *Dita Saxová* (1997); volume 4, *Modlitba pro Kateřinu Horovitzovou* (1998); volume 5, *Démanty noci* (1998); volume 6, *Propast* (1998); volume 7, *Noc a naděje* (1999).

Editions in English: "The White One," translated by Iris Urwin-Levit, in *The Linden Tree: An Anthology of Czech and Slovak Literature 1890–1960*, edited by Mojmír Otruba and Zdeněk Pešat (Prague: Artia, 1962), pp. 286–293;

"The Black Lion," translated by Urwin-Levit, in *Stories from Jewish Authors*, edited by Kenji Inoue and Haijime Kijima (Tokyo: Eihosha, 1966), pp. 101–116;

"The White One," translated by Jeanne W. Němcová, in *Czech and Slovak Short Stories*, edited by Němcová (London & New York: Oxford University Press, 1967), pp. 212–226;

"The Children," translated by George Theiner, in *New Writing in Czechoslovakia*, edited by Theiner (Baltimore: Penguin, 1969; Harmondsworth, U.K.: Penguin, 1969), pp. 36–52;

"The Beginning and the End," translated by Urwin-Levit, in *More Tales of Unease*, edited by John F. Burke (London: Pan Books, 1969), pp. 64–77;

Children of the Holocaust: The Collected Works of Arnošt Lustig, 3 volumes (Washington, D.C.: Inscape, 1976–1977)—comprises volume 1, *Night and Hope*, translated by Theiner; volume 2, *Darkness Casts No Shadow*, translated by Němcová; and volume 3, *Diamonds of the Night*, translated by Němcová;

"The River Running into the Milky Way," translated by Lesley and Jan Čulík, *Fiction* (April–May 1987): 23–31;

Indecent Dreams, translated by Urwin-Levit, Vera Borkovec, and Paul Wilson (Evanston, Ill.: Northwestern University Press, 1988);

"Night," translated by Lesley and Jan Čulík, *Argo*, 8, no. 1(1988): 26–40;

"Tanga," translated by Káča Poláčková, *Formations* (1988);

"Return to Czechoslovakia: Snapshots of a Revolution," translated by Josef Lustig, *Kenyon Review*, 12 (Fall 1990): 1–15;

"Colette," translated by Tim Whipple, *Kenyon Review*, 13 (Spring 1991): 6–67;

"The House of Echo Returns: The Echo," translated by Josef Lustig, *New England Review*, 15 (Summer 1993): 99–142;

"The Lemon," translated by Němcová, in *Truth and Lamentation: Stories and Poems on the Holocaust*, edited by Milton Teichman and Sharon Leder (Urbana: University of Illinois Press, 1994), pp. 90–106.

PRODUCED SCRIPTS: *Transport z ráje*, by Lustig and Zbyněk Brynych, motion picture, Barrandov Films, 1962;

Démanty noci, by Lustig and Jan Němec, motion picture, Barrandov Films, 1964;

Theresienstadt, by Lustig and E. E. Pendrell, television, ABC, 1965;

Modlitba pro Kateřinu Horowitzovou, Prague, Czechoslovak television, 1965;

Stolen Childhood, television, RAI, Rome, 1965;

Pražské křižovatky, Prague, Czechoslovak Radio, 1966;

Člověk ve velikosti poštovní známky, Prague, Czechoslovak Radio, 1968;

Dita Saxová, by Lustig and Antonín Moskalyk, motion picture, Barrandov Films, 1968;

Precious Legacy, television, PBS, 1984;

Fighter, motion picture, Next Wave Films, 2000.

RECORDING: *Noc a naděje*, text by Lustig for a symphonic poem by Otmar Mácha, Prague, Supraphon, 1963.

OTHER: "Memory: Negligible Part?" introduction to *Seeing through "Paradise": Artists and the Terezin Concentration Camp* (Boston: Massachusetts College of Art, 1991).

SELECTED PERIODICAL PUBLICATIONS—UNCOLLECTED: "Ota Pavel: The Short Life of a Czech Writer," *World Literature Today*, 55 (Summer 1981): 412–416;

"Continuing the Revolution," *World & I* (March 1990): 50–57;

"Magic from Prague," *World & I* (July 1990): 438–445;

"Artistic Life under a Playwright President," *World & I* (December 1990): 194–199;

"Transition and Political Morality," *Problems of Communism*, 41 (January–April 1992): 81–82.

Arnošt Lustig is one of several writers who based their work on the suffering of the Jews in Nazi concentration camps. He personally witnessed these horrors as an adolescent and made up his mind to use his experiences in fictional form to warn against the dehumanization of people in totalitarian regimes. His first works from the end of the 1950s shed a new light on the theme of war and the Holocaust. Lustig's approach to the subject was new because he did not write about conventional heroics but concentrated on nonheroic types such as old people and children. In his works the moral values recognized by the human conscience are represented as "diamonds" in the "night" of inhuman suffering. These moral values come to the surface in extreme situations when a man's life hangs in the balance and when, in spite of everything, he is able to overcome the instinct of self-preservation. Lustig's short stories use the motion-picture technique of fast, intercutting sequences that highlight conflicts in tense situations between individual conscience and external events.

Lustig was born in Prague to Emil and Terezie Lustig on 21 December 1926. They were a middle-class family who lived in modest but not deprived circumstances in the district of Libeň, on the outskirts of Prague. Lustig's novel *Dům vrácené ozvěny* (1994; translated as *The House of Returned Echoes*, forthcoming 2001) gives a faithful picture of the environment in which he grew up. In one interview the author said of his childhood, "I grew up in a district of very poor and unemployed people whom I got to know well. These people fully relied on luck, they constantly dodged problems and responsibilities and even committed petty offences in order to get money and survive. When I arrived in the concentration camp I saw that my life there had become a distillation of the lives of these people. I was better equipped to survive knowing how they had lived. However it was a lot harder there."

Lustig attended a *měšťanská škola* (junior technical school) but was expelled after the occupation of Czechoslovakia by the Nazis in 1939 and the introduction of the Nuremberg race laws into the so-called Protectorate of Bohemia and Moravia. He got a job in a tailor's workshop and later in a leather-goods factory. He used experiences from this period of his life in the original short-story version of *Dům vrácené ozvěny*, which appeared in the

Dust jacket for Lustig's first book (1958), a collection of stories about courage shown by Jewish children and elderly people under the Nazis

1968 collection *Hořká vůně mandlí* (The Bitter Smell of Almonds). As a sixteen-year-old he was deported with his family to Theresienstadt in central Bohemia. In the days of Austria-Hungary it had been a fortified military town; during the Nazi occupation it became a reception center—more exactly a ghetto—for the Jewish population of Bohemia and Moravia. There, in the monstrous system devised by the Nazis for the ultimate "solution" of the Jewish question, Lustig suffered the most dreadful experiences of his life.

From Theresienstadt the Lustig family—parents, an uncle, Lustig, and his sister—were transported to Auschwitz, one of the most brutal concentration camps. His father died there, and his mother and sister were removed to the women's section. Lustig remembers seeing his mother, barefoot and wearing a flimsy shirt, stumble along a street in the camp with a group of other women, in foggy twilight. The adolescent boy was left dependent on himself and his friends. A strong constitution, a cheerful disposition, and the ability to get along with other people made it possible for the future writer to endure the harsh conditions, though his life was always in danger. Several of his experiences from this time provided him with ready-made dramatic stories. All they needed was to be written down and cast in a literary form. In a 1990 interview for the American magazine *World & I* Lustig described one of these experiences: "'The Second Round' is a story . . . about a friend of mine who also appears in 'Tma nemá stín' (Darkness Casts No Shadow). He saved my life in the most incredible fashion." Lustig had been attempting to steal some bread for fellow prisoners on the transport train when he was stopped by a German soldier:

> He said if I didn't give him the bread before he counted three he would shoot me. I repeated I hadn't any bread, hoping that that would save me. He aimed his pistol at me and began counting. I kept my eyes on the man's pistol and on his thick finger on the trigger. He said "two" and cocked the pistol. I knew that at three it would be all over. At that moment my best friend leapt out in front of me shielding me from the pistol. The German said "Shit!" but with a note of admiration. He couldn't believe the courage of the boy who had run between me and the gun.

Lustig has spoken rarely about the transports of Jews from Theresienstadt; he has done so primarily in his interviews for various American magazines. He did mention that a few weeks after he and his family had been sent to Theresienstadt, five thousand people were moved from there to the extermination camps. In another interview Lustig recalled learning of his father's death: "I asked a friend where my father was. He said, 'You see, your father didn't take off his glasses.' In Auschwitz, anyone who wore glasses or had grey hair, or seemed old or ill, went to the gas chamber. Because I had worked as a blacksmith and a bricklayer I was strong physically, so they put me among those who were to live. My father wore glasses. They sent him to the gas chamber."

Lustig and his uncle were transported from Auschwitz to the concentration camp at Buchenwald to work in a munitions factory; his uncle died there. Lustig's mother and sister were sent from Auschwitz to the camp in Freiburg, where they worked in an aircraft factory. Later they were transferred to Mauthausen, and they survived the war. Out of fifteen thousand Jewish children, Lustig and his sister were among only a few to return from a concentration camp.

The fictional escape in the short story "Tma nemá stín" (later extended into a novella and translated in 1977 as *Darkness Casts No Shadow*) was based on Lustig's own dramatic escape from the transport taking prisoners to the concentration camp at Dachau. In the spring of 1945 a train carrying hundreds of prisoners, including Lustig, was attacked by an American dive-bomber. In the ensuing pandemonium Lustig and his friend managed to jump from the train and escape the fire of the guards. Then they set off on the hazardous journey to Bohemia. Several times they were caught by German peasants, but they finally managed to reach Prague. There Lustig hid until May, when he took an active part in the May rising of the people of Prague. His experiences of this time surface again in the story "Chlapec u okna" ("Boy at the Window") from his collection *Démanty noci* (1958; translated as *Diamonds in the Night*, 1962). During the revolt the central character has to cross a street under fire from the Nazis in order to get food for a hospital full of wounded fighters.

When the country was free again, several career possibilities were open to the twenty-year-old Lustig. He decided on journalism and began working for Czechoslovak radio. He wrote articles for several journals, particularly for *Židovský věstník* (The Jewish Gazette). In 1948 and 1949 he was a war correspondent in Israel, which was at that time engaged in fighting for recognition as an independent state. The Czechoslovak government then supported the Israeli fight for independence (its position changed only to be in line with the position of the Soviet bloc, which came to support the Arab world). In 1949 in Israel, Lustig married Věra Weislitz, the daughter of a furniture maker from Ostrava and herself the author of a collection of poems. The couple has two children—a son, Josef, and a daughter, Eva.

From 1951 to 1954 Lustig studied at the School of Political and Social Sciences in Prague. He also became interested in the work of the Czech-German journalist Egon Erwin Kisch. As a radio reporter Lustig frequently traveled out of the country. In 1958, after the success of his first book, *Noc a naděje* (1958; translated as *Night and Hope*, 1962), he joined the staff of the weekly magazine *Mladý svět* (Young World) for two years. From 1960 he was a scriptwriter in the Barrandov motion-picture studios in Prague.

Lustig felt that movies offered him greater creative freedom than journalism. Talking of journal-

Krystyna Mikolajewska as Dita and Bohuš Záhorský as Professor Munk in a still from the 1968 movie version of Lustig's 1962 novel, Dita Saxová

ism and movie work and of his experiences as a reporter, he said in an interview, "Journalism teaches you economy of expression, discipline, humor and humility. . . . You can't wait for inspiration. You have to set out to do and finish whatever your boss tells you to. It teaches you to write with the reader in mind, to use the simplest and most precise expressions to suit the subject matter and the reader. Then after a time it all becomes routine and you stop enjoying it." Although he spoke appreciatively about the work of a scriptwriter, especially about the financial rewards, he was nevertheless clearly aware of the difference between the work of an author and that of a scriptwriter: "Writing is for contemplation, for inner vision. A film is something to be looked at." Scriptwriting was certainly profitable, but a writer's career was what really mattered to Lustig. As he said, "Everything—including films— stems from books."

Noc a naděje was favorably received by the critics. Readers were impressed chiefly by the unpretentious way Lustig portrayed the passions and lives of weak, defenseless people crushed by an inhuman system. The characters were primarily old people and children, victims of violence, unlike the heroes who had been the norm in postwar Czech literature until then. Lustig discovered in these people flashes of moral courage that came to the surface from the depths of their souls when their lives were in greatest danger. The moments when people showed they were capable of acting independently according to their own consciences, in situations where abnormal, crazy behavior replaced reason, were what most interested the author.

Lustig's debut was successful undoubtedly because of the fact that the stories looked at the wartime past from a new point of view. At the same time they drew attention to the previously neglected predicament of the Jews, making them a symbol, focusing attention on individuals as members of a group discriminated against by society and by the state system. Lustig's books about the suffering of the Jews in concentration camps started a series of Czech literary works with Jewish subjects that appeared in the early 1960s, by such authors as Josef Škvorecký, Ladislav Fuks, and Hana Bělohradská.

At the end of the 1950s and the beginning of the 1960s Lustig's literary output was prolific. By 1959 he had published his third book of short stories, *Ulice ztracených bratří* (translated as *Street of Lost Brothers*, 1990). Contemporary critics found that not all the stories in this collection were of the same high standard. In some of them Lustig tried to relate his themes of wartime suffering to the present; but where he yielded to contemporary convention, their impact was considerably weakened. One story, "Můj známý Vili Feld" (My Friend Vili Feld), suggested that the author's work might find a new direction. It is the story of a man, once a prisoner in a concentration camp, who had emigrated but had found no sense of security either at home under communist rule or abroad in the West and who longs in vain to go back. The story is told from the point of view of a young reporter who carelessly breaks a promise to the lonely émigré and is indirectly responsible for his attempt to commit suicide. Lustig, as was his habit, reworked this story into a novel in 1961.

At that time in Czechoslovakia, art and literature were expected to be basically educational. From that point of view Lustig was criticized for concentrating on a "peripheral phenomenon" of minor importance. However, Lustig continued focusing on the theme of total human deprivation. He reworked it again in an independent short novel, *Dita Saxová* (1962; translated as *Dita Sax*, 1966), the story of a Jewish girl seeking her place in the postwar world after dreadful experiences as a child in a concentration camp. When she returns from the camp, she lives in a hostel with people of her own age, but she cannot find a common language with them. Neither her surroundings nor the ideas of an old Marxist intellectual can reach her through the dark curtain of her past. Nor does she find contentment in the West when she eventually emigrates; on the contrary, she is so distressed by the prevailing attitudes in the West that she commits suicide. Dita Saxová had her own concept of the good life, which she could not live either in a world prohibiting pain and imposing joy on people, or in a world offering comfort and luxury at the cost of losing one's integrity and self-esteem. The influence of communist ideology, depicting the West as a jungle, is still evident in this work. Lustig later spoke of these prejudices in an interview for an American magazine when he was describing his feelings after he arrived in the United States.

Modlitba pro Kateřinu Horovitzovou (1964; translated as *A Prayer for Katerina Horovitzova*, 1973) is one of Lustig's most successful novels. It was also made into a motion picture. Lustig based his novel on a one-sentence legend he had heard about a girl who shot an SS guard in the anteroom of the gas chambers. The central character is a beautiful Jewish girl, whom a rich American of Jewish origin saves from death. He is one of a group of American Jews captured in Italy who try to use their money to secure their release from the Nazis and certain extermination. The devilish game played by the German officer on these gullible victims gives the story its effect. By promising them freedom he inveigles the wealthy prisoners into parting with more and more money. But he is merciless, and, when they have nothing left, he sends them to the gas chamber. The girl, Kateřina, who has seen through this deception, turns on her torturer at the last moment and, with the gun belonging to the officer preparing the prisoners for the gas chamber, shoots him—only to die herself in the murderous fire cutting down the condemned men.

With its dramatic climax, influenced by the fashion of the times, this work shows that the author had learned from his experience in movies how to build up a situation and construct a plot. The theme of this story is one that runs all through Lustig's work: rebellion and revenge. The author mentioned in an interview that long after the story had been written he found some new facts about the legend in Abraham Shulman's *The Case of Hotel Polski: An Account of One of the Most Enigmatic Episodes of World War II* (1982) that radically changed the character of the heroine. The truth was that she had been promised her release in return for collaborating with the Nazis.

In the mid 1960s Lustig was one of the favored artists and intellectuals who enjoyed advantages and opportunities denied the ordinary citizen. Lustig gave an example of this privilege when he answered a question about this period of his life in an interview: "As an author and scriptwriter I lived well. When I wanted to visit Honolulu . . . they sent me there twice. When I wanted to visit San Francisco and . . . look for Jack London's house and grave, they made it possible for me." Of course the author was intelligent enough to know that the opportunities offered him by the communist authorities were at the expense of people who were being persecuted and whose freedom was restricted because they would not submit to political pressure. In the mid 1960s he was invited by high-ranking communist officials to a private showing of Leni Riefenstahl's propaganda movie about Adolf Hitler and Nazi Germany. Afterward one of the officials suggested that kind of movie might serve as an example for contemporary moviemakers. Lustig was deeply offended by such praise for Nazi propaganda, and that was one of the reasons he began to look critically at contemporary life.

In 1966 *Bílé břízy na podzim* (The White Birches in Autumn) was published. Although not overtly stated, the theme of the work was provocative. It is the story of an unsophisticated love affair set in the so-called punitive units of the Czechoslovak army, to which criminals and politically unreliable intellectuals were sent. The author conveyed perfectly this dehumanizing environment by the use of his own special language, by slangy nicknames, and by characters that are merely embodiments of the functions they carry out. There is a contrast between the environment and the growing love of a young man, one of these social outcasts, for an unsophisticated village girl prostituting herself with members of the labor brigade. In this way Lustig allied himself with those authors who drew attention to the degradation people might suffer even in a so-called socialist society. For the first time, novels by writers with experience of communist concentration camps and prisons (such as Jan Beneš, Karel Pecka, and Jiří Mucha) were frankly exposing the inhuman face of the system that Lustig's previous work had merely hinted at.

Lustig's turning to the present day for his subjects was also connected with the change in Czech culture and society in the 1960s, when demand for reform and liberalization of the communist regime began to gain ground. Literature and the arts were the areas where the reforming movement made the greatest impact. Above all, the movement criticized the aesthetic norms of so-called socialist realism and insisted that aesthetic ideas are not absolute and can recognize different principles. This attitude was prevalent in 1968 when Lustig's eleventh book, the collection of stories *Hořká vůně mandlí*, was published. The centerpiece of the collection was "Dům vrácené ozvěny" (The Echoing House), reworked as a novel more than twenty-five years later. The background is autobiographical. It is the story of a Prague Jewish family at the mercy of the evils unleashed by Nazism. Signs of these evils that had a fateful influence on the lives of millions of Europeans were becoming apparent, but only a few people were capable of reading them. The majority, represented by the characters in Lustig's story, had not enough vision to foresee the threatening storm that would sweep them off to a cruel death. The "bitter smell of

Dust jacket for Lustig's 1995 novel about life in a boarding school for Jewish boys during the German occupation of Prague

almonds" was the smell given off by the gas Cyclon B, which the Nazis used in the gas chambers. This story, particularly in its adapted form as a novel, is also a memorial to the author's father, who up to the last moment kept thinking of the family he could not save from a tragic fate. Contemporary critics regarded this book merely as a return to traditional and psychological realism. However, they missed the symbolic, almost mythological imagery—for example, the motif of the gasometer, a building typical of the district of Prague where most of the novel takes place, foreshadowing the deaths of the characters in the gas chambers.

The publication of *Hořká vůně mandlí* marked the beginning of the end of Lustig's successful career at home as a writer. Lustig was preparing to return home from holiday in Italy in 1968 when his country was invaded by Soviet troops. He made the decision not to go back to Czechoslovakia. In 1969, when the party and the state were heading toward what they called "normalization" (a political clampdown following the Warsaw Pact invasion), Lustig's wide-ranging novel *Miláček* (Darling) was published. In it the author returned to his experiences at the end of the 1940s as a young war correspondent in the Israeli-Arab war. The plot is based on the love that two men actively engaged in the fight for Israeli self-determination share for the same woman. The story unfolds through a succession of tense scenes of action alternating, in a fashion typical of Lustig, with more peaceful scenes representing the love of a Czech reporter for a Jewish woman. In trying to present a wide panorama of the time, Lustig introduces additional characters, but the extra material causes the novel to lose cohesion. In some parts, facts about the progress of the war and locations stand in the way of what the author intended as the basic message of the book: that war destroys love through the invisible wounds it inflicts on a man's innermost being. The subject was unacceptable to the communist regime of the day; authorities confiscated the book and destroyed the type, a decision strengthened by Lustig's refusal to return to his occupied country. This act was a blow to the international reputation of the regime, for Lustig's name was by now well known abroad.

Lustig's books were translated into English and other languages and won international acclaim, as did the movies made from them. In spite of that recognition, Lustig did not have an easy time when he left the country for good. He reached the United States in 1970 by way of Italy, Israel (where he lived in the kibbutz Hachotrim), and the former Yugoslavia, where he worked for a time in the Jadran motion-picture studios in Zagreb. Through the offices of the International Writing Program, Lustig obtained a grant to work for a year at the University of Iowa, where he lectured on script- and short-story writing. He was a guest lecturer at Nebraska State University, then went to American University in Washington in 1973. Five years later he became a professor, and he continues to lecture about war in movies and literature and about the relationship of literature, movies, and the work of a writer.

For Lustig, going to the United States meant a radical change in lifestyle and opinions. In several interviews for American magazines he said that when he first arrived he had to overcome certain prejudices and fears about the American way of life. Soon, however, he came to feel that a free society offered many opportunities to people capable of using them. He revised several of his earlier works. The story "Dívka u oleandrového keře" (The Girl Beside the Oleander Tree) ends up in its new form as an indictment of a world in which people are manipulated and prevented from enjoying basic

human relationships, such as that between a man and a woman. There are three versions of this story—the original from 1959 in *Ulice ztracených bratří*, the second from the 1973 Index edition of that work, and the English version of 1990, which was republished in Czech in 1996.

The changes in his life and outlook were not the only reason Lustig adapted his original texts. He explained in various interviews that he never considered the texts of his works as definitive. For that reason he constantly attempted to improve them. Typical additions include factual details to make the world of his characters more real, and deeper probing into their inner beings so that the reader is better able to understand the working of their minds. The original short stories thus take on the dimensions of short or full-length novels, a practice Lustig has used from the beginning of his literary career. He also has continued to bring out his collected works at the Hynek publishing house in Prague. Most of these works have been extended and/or partially rewritten, making them arguably new works, certainly in the case of the novel *Propast* (1996) and *Dům vrácené ozvěny*.

Another work adapted and expanded from a short story is *Tma nemá stín* (1991), a novella about two boys who escape from a transport. Hungry, dirty, and cold, they make their way to the Czech border, evading their German pursuers. The central scene of the short story, in which one of the escapees clashes with a countrywoman in a lonely spot where he is trying to get food, provided most of the material for the novel. The author portrays the conflict in the mind of the boy, who has decided to use force—even murder—to get food. Ultimately, however, his moral conscience is stronger than the powerful instinct of self-preservation and makes it impossible for him to kill. The end of the story is ambiguous. The two escapees are caught by armed villagers and are chased at gunpoint from the village. The author inclined toward a tragic ending, hinting at the deaths of the boys. However, if the story is read as a metaphor for a traditional theme, the road to salvation, then escape cannot be ruled out; this interpretation would be in keeping with the autobiographical background.

The collection of stories *Oheň na vodě* (Fire on Water, 1998) again deals with Nazi concentration camp themes and also includes a story from Italy after World War II. The character of Vili Feld appears in this collection, first introduced by Lustig in the short story "Můj známý Vili Feld."

Lustig also published two stories about Jewish girls struggling to gain self-respect in the degrading circumstances of their lives—*Colette, dívka z Antverp* (translated as "Colette," 1991) and *Tanga, dívka z Hamburku* (translated as "Tanga," 1988). A third story about Kůstka (A Chick), a girl from Prague, appeared in the *Kenyon Review* and the Czech-language version of *Playboy* in 1998. Two novels related to these themes, *Krásné zelené oči* (translated as *Lovely Green Eyes* and *Lea z Leeuwardenu* (Lea of Leeuwarden) appeared in 2000. Other stories about young people include *Porgess* (Porgess, 1991), the story of the son of a Prague businessman, bedridden as a result of wounds received while escaping from a transport, and *Kamarádi* (Friends, 1995), describe life in a Prague boarding school for Jewish boys after the occupation by the Nazis.

In the United States, Lustig is considered one of the most important writers on the Holocaust, and in the Czech context he represents the continuing traditions of Prague Jewish literature. In his work Lustig does not simply make accusations of racial hatred. His scope is much wider. On this subject the author says, "It is important for me to show that my books are universal, that they are for all people. . . . It is important for me to show that the fate of the Jews is the fate of all people of the present age. Even if I weren't a Jew, I would choose Jewish themes to write about."

Lustig's books began to reappear in the Czech Republic after the fall of communism in 1989. The author began to visit the Czech Republic again, where he was publicly acclaimed. In 1996 he was nominated for the Karel Čapek Prize by the Czech PEN Club. In the early 1990s he became editor of the literary section of the Czech version of the magazine *Playboy*. Critics sometimes differ in their opinions about his new books. The younger ones especially reproach him for a certain superficiality of style. His work represents the new realism in Czech postwar writing, however, and cannot be dismissed lightly. In the atmosphere of postmodern relativism and skepticism prevailing as the twentieth century draws to a close, Lustig's work effectively offers the reader hope that there are hidden sources of love, fellowship, and dignity. His best stories will remain a lasting part of Czech and world literature.

Interviews:

Josef Vohryzek, "Arnošt Lustig o sobě," *Květen*, 3, no. 9 (1958): 518–521;

Karel Hvížďala, "Arnošt Lustig," in *České rozhovory ve světě*, edited by Hvížďala (Köln: Index, 1981), pp. 333–348;

Jiří Sýkora, "Jiří Sýkora s Arnoštem Lustigem o kráse a ošklivosti," *Západ*, 11, no. 2 (1989): 12–17;

Jana Bednářová, "Povídání o Katce a jiných . . . ," *Květy*, 1, no. 47 (1990): 10–11;

Josef Hajný, "O talentu a pravdě," *Kmen*, 3, no. 1 (1990): 10–11;

Jiří Lederer, "Arnošt Lustig," in *Tak tedy . . . přijďte!* (Prague: Videopress, VNT, 1990), pp. 184–188;

František Mareš, "Rozhovor se spisovatelem Arnoštem Lustigem . . . ," *Literární revue*, 19, no. 6 (1990): 136–139;

Ota Ornest, "Poutník na prahu domova," *Věstník židovských náboženských obcí v Československu*, 52, no. 2 (1990): 5–6;

Jiří Pittermann, "Vraždily se knížky. Návraty Arnošta Lustiga," *Nové knihy*, 3 (1990): 1, 16;

Harry James Cargass, ". . . aby uměli říct: 'Ne!' Rozhovor se spisovatelem Arnoštem Lustigem," *Listy*, 22, no. 4 (1992): 88–97, no. 5 (1992): 65–71;

Jana Šmídová, "Chamtivost k snídani. Arnošt Lustig: Ti slušní jsou jako slunce, ohřívají všechny," *Lidové noviny*, 5, no. 9 (1992): 1, 13;

Antonín Přidal, "Arnošt Lustig," in his *Z očí do očí* (Prague: Ivo Železný, 1994), pp. 116–125;

Michal Bauer, "Literatura je jediná nesmrtelnost člověka," *Tvar*, 10, no. 14 (1998): 8–9.

Biography:

Aleš Haman, *Arnošt Lustig* (Prague: H + H, 1995).

References:

Mary Jo Binker, "Studenti americké univerzity nadšeně o Lustigovi," *Nové knihy*, supplement, 49 (1990): 6;

Lubomír Doležel, "Slohové problémy A. Lustiga," *Plamen*, 2, no. 8 (1960): 92–95;

Karel Dostál, "Lustigovo hledání a nacházení," *Plamen*, 6, no. 12 (1964): 158–160;

Vladimír Dostál, "Dvou lásek shoda," *Tvorba*, 12 (1969): 10–11;

Aleš Haman, "O tak zvané 'druhé vlně' válečné prózy v naší současné literatuře," *Česká literatura*, 9, no. 4 (1961): 513–520;

Haman, "Proč zemřela Dita Saxová?," *Kulturní tvorba*, 1, no. 5 (1963): 13;

Haman, "Prózy Arnošta Lustiga a dnešní čtenář," *Tvar*, 3, no. 10 (1992): 4–5;

Zdeněk Heřman, "Co je člověk," *Tvar*, 3, no. 23 (1992): 10;

Milan Jungmann, "Knihy Lustigova hledání," *Literární noviny*, 12, no. 6 (1963): 5;

Jungmann, "Proměna jedné povídky," *Literární noviny*, 10, no. 12 (1961): 4;

Jungmann, "*Ulice ztracených bratří* aneb povídky z rozpaků," *Literární noviny*, 9, no. 7 (1960): 4;

Jungmann, "Umělec tragického vidění," *Literární noviny*, 7, no. 42 (1958): 4;

Vítězslav Kocourek, "Povídky a lidé z gheta," *Literární noviny*, 7, no. 9 (1958): 5;

Zdeněk Kožmín, "Čas a moderní próza," *Červený květ*, 10, no. 6 (1965): 187–188;

Arno Linke, "Devátá Lustigova kniha," *Listy*, 2, no. 5 (1969): 11;

Marie Mravcová, "Arnošt Lustig: *Démanty noci* (1958)," *Česká literatura*, 39, no. 2 (1991): 159–166;

Jiří Navrátil, "Síť vzpomínek aneb Podmanivý valčík Arnošta Lustiga," *Tvar*, 5, no. 8 (1994): 17;

Jaroslava Novotná, "Nová kniha—staré problémy. (K tvůrčí problematice Arnošta Lustiga)," *Plamen*, 10, no. 11 (1968): 108–110;

Jiří Opelík, "Chuděrka reportáž," *Kultura*, 5, no. 48 (1961): 4;

Opelík, "Ve špatných službách," *Host do domu*, 10, no. 2 (1963): 81;

Karel Palas, "Textové variace Lustigovy povídky *Můj známý Vili Feld*," *Sborník prací filozofické fakulty brněnské univerzity*, 14, no. 12 (1965): 137–144;

Miroslav Petříček, "Lustig známý i neznámý," *Literární noviny*, 15, no. 30 (1966): 4;

Petříček, "Modernost tradice povídky," *Literární noviny*, 11, no. 24 (1962): 4;

Petříček, "Naděje a noc," *Literární noviny*, 3, no. 20 (1992): 4;

Petříček, "Prohloubení tématu?," *Host do domu*, 15, no. 7 (1968): 60–61;

Petříček, "S povídkou do života," *Nový život*, 8 (1958): 625–630;

Milan Suchomel, "Noc jednou, noc podruhé," *Host do domu*, 6, no. 2 (1959): 85;

Suchomel, "Nový a starý Lustig," *Host do domu*, 11, no. 8 (1964): 59;

Suchomel, "Proudy a zátoky současnosti," *Plamen*, 5, no. 2 (1963): 110–112;

Suchomel, "Rozmezí bez záruk. (Kapitola už historická)," *Host do domu*, 15, no. 13 (1968/1969): 10–18;

Suchomel, "Skutečnost zrozená z přeludů," *Host do domu*, 10, no. 7 (1963): 299–300;

Suchomel, "Zadržitelný sestup Arnošta Lustiga," *Host do domu*, 7, no. 4 (1960): 186;

Ivana Vízdalová, "Deník se žlutou hvězdou," *Almanach autorů*, 1 (1991): 231–233;

Josef Vohryzek, "Modlitba pro Kateřinu Horovitzovou," *Literární noviny*, 13, no. 26 (1964): 5;

Vohryzek, "Próza dnes. Pokračování III," *Květen*, 4, no. 1 (1959): 25–27;

Vohryzek, "Prozaická prvotina," *Květen*, 7 (1958): 389–391.

Ileana Mălăncioiu

(23 January 1940 –   )

Rodica Mihăilă
University of Bucharest

BOOKS: *Pasărea tăiată* (Bucharest: Tineretului, 1967);

Către Ieronim (Bucharest: Albatros, 1970);

Inima reginei (Bucharest: Eminescu, 1971);

Crini pentru domnişoara mireasă (Bucharest: Cartea Românească, 1973);

Ardere de tot (Bucharest: Cartea Românească, 1976);

Vina tragică: Tragicii greci, Shakespeare, Dostoievski, Kafka (Bucharest: Cartea Românească, 1978);

Peste zona interzisă (Bucharest: Cartea Românească, 1979);

Sora mea de dincolo (Bucharest: Cartea Românească, 1980; revised edition, Bucharest: Litera, 1992);

Linia vieţii (Bucharest: Cartea Românească, 1982);

Urcarea muntelui (Bucharest: Albatros, 1985; enlarged edition, Bucharest: Litera, 1992);

Călătorie spre mine însămi (Bucharest: Cartea Românească, 1987);

Crimă şi moralitate: Eseuri politice (Bucharest: Editura Litera, 1993);

Cronica melancoliei (Bucharest: Editura Enciclopedică, 1998).

Editions and Collections: *Poezii* (Bucharest: Cartea Românească, 1973);

Poeme, Cele mai frumoase poezii, no. 180 (Bucharest: Albatros, 1980);

Peste zona interzisă / A travers la zone interdite, traduit du romain par Annie Bentoiu (Bucharest: Eminescu, 1984);

Ardere de tot, Poeţi Contemporani Români series (Bucharest: Eminescu, 1992);

Poezii (Bucharest: Vitruviu, 1996);

Linia vietii (Jassy: Polirom, 1999).

Editions in English: "Bear's Blood" and "Now There Is So Much Earth, Alas, Between Us," in *100 de ani de poezie Românească / 100 Years of Romanian Poetry*, translated by Ioana Deligiorgis (Jassy: Junimea, 1982), pp. 326–329;

Ileana Mălăncioiu

Peste zona interzisă / Across the Forbidden Zone, translated by Dan Duţescu (Bucharest: Eminescu, 1985);

"Pact," translated by Duţescu, and "Hieronymus' Land" and "But Aspens Will Remain," translated by Andreí Bantaş, in *Like Diamonds in Coal Sleep*, compiled by Bantaş (Bucharest: Minerva, 1985), pp. 344–346;

"Alone in a Dark Theatre," "Up to the Limit," "Last Memory," "Love Story," "Serenity," "She Was Dressed like Me," "Two Friends," and "This

Winter Too Will Pass," in *Silent Voices: An Anthology of Contemporary Romanian Women Poets,* compiled and translated by Andrea Deletant and Brenda Walker (London & Boston: Forest, 1986), pp. 111–119;

"Bear's Blood" and "Now There Is So Much Earth, Alas, Between Us," translated by Stavros Deligioris, in *Shifting Borders: East European Poetries of the Eighties,* edited by Walter Cummins (Rutherford, N.J.: Fairleigh Dickinson University Press, 1993), pp. 345–346;

"The Slaughtered Fowl," "Lilies for Her Lady the Bride," "My Sister, the Empress," "Fortepiano," and "Nightmare," translated by Duțescu, in *An Anthology of Romanian Women Poets,* edited by Adam J. Sorkin and Kurt W. Treptow (New York: Columbia University Press, 1994), pp. 61–66;

"Naive and Sentimental Painting," "Somewhere in Transylvania," "Prayers," "The Beginning of the End," "Nightmare," "Samson's Hair," "Pianoforte," "I Can't Complain," "In My Brain," and "The Tower of Babel," translated by Michael Longley, in *When the Tunnels Meet. Contemporary Romanian Poetry,* edited by John Fairleigh (Newcastle upon Tyne, U.K.: Bloodaxe, 1996), pp. 83–90;

Four Contemporary Romanian Poets, 33 Poems, translated by Stavros Deligiorgis (Bucharest: Cartea Românească, 1998), pp. 101–135.

OTHER: Hans Magnus Enzensberger, *Sfîrșitul bufnițelor,* translated by Mălăncioiu and Aurelian State (Bucharest: Univers, 1974);

Emil Botta, *Trîntorul,* edited, with an afterword, by Mălăncioiu (Bucharest: Litera, 1993);

Gabriela Melinescu, *Jurămîntul de sărăcie, castitate și supunere,* edited by Mălăncioiu (Bucharest: Litera, 1993);

Dinu Pillat, *Exerciții de supraviețuire,* edited, with an introduction, by Mălăncioiu (Bucharest: Litera, 1993).

The poet Ileana Mălăncioiu is known for her original and compelling voice. That voice draws its substance from the rich resources of the Romanian language, traditions, and legends; from the poet's firm moral stance; and from a tragic existential vision inspired by the Romanian experience.

Ileana Mălăncioiu was born on 23 January 1940 in the village of Godeni, Arges, the second of four daughters of a peasant couple. Her poetry is deeply rooted in her rural origins. As Gabriela Melinescu puts it, "Mălăncioiu believes in the ancient traditions which teach man to conquer the irrational by creating daily rituals within the frames of nature. . . . [Her poetry] turns into ritual everything that goes by the name of man's existential experience: the yoke of history, love, marriage, mistakes, and the presence of animals."

Mălăncioiu made her literary debut in the cultural weekly *Luceafarul* (The Morning Star) in 1965, when she was a student in philosophy at the University of Bucharest. The publication of her collection *Pasărea tăiată* (The Slaughtered Fowl) in 1967 placed her among the generation of poets, including Nichita Stănescu, Marin Sorescu, Ioan Alexandru, Constanta Buzea, Adrian Paunescu, and Ana Blandiana, that emerged in the 1960s—"the miracle period" of Romanian literature that arose in reaction to postwar Stalinism and its doctrine of proletarian realism. Their works, informed by new moral and aesthetic ideals, aimed to rejuvenate Romanian poetry and to prevent it from becoming an instrument of propaganda. Mălăncioiu's debut went relatively unnoticed; at a time when her colleagues were searching for a new lyric voice, she drew on the old traditions of the epic and on the fantastic and fabulous elements in folklore and in Romanian symbolist and Romantic poetry.

Pasărea tăiată reconstructs the poet's spiritual biography against the background of the Romanian village and its elemental natural rhythms. Resembling a miniature story, each poem starts with a recollection from her childhood of a seemingly ordinary event. The memory occasions a lyric meditation that marks a stage in the making of the future poet.

In the title poem, for instance, the poet's witnessing as a child the killing of a fowl becomes symbolic of her endeavor to turn poetry into a vessel connecting life and death: "I take the head in one hand, the rest in the other / And I change hands when under the weight I sway / Before they die let them be tied together / Through my body, at least in this way." What critic Virgil Ierunca calls the "tragic expressionism" of Mălăncioiu's poetry grows out of her awareness of the extinction of a pastoral way of life built on moral and spiritual values as she draws on folklore and on religious traditions to revive the miraculous, the ritualistic, and the cosmic elements of village existence. This quality of tragic expressionism distinguishes Mălăncioiu among the poets inspired by the Romanian village.

In 1968, the year of the anticommunist upheaval known as the Prague Spring, Mălăncioiu graduated from the university and became an editor with Romanian Television. The tightening of the

Communist Party's control of the media and of literary and artistic creation in the early 1970s prompted her to resign from the national television network, which had become the state's main instrument of propaganda. She accepted the position of editor with *Argesul* (The Arges), a cultural magazine published in Pitesti, but after less than a year she felt forced to resign again to avoid intellectual regimentation.

While most poets of her generation found aesthetic models in the modernist intellectual poetry of Ion Barbu or the mythic-philosophic verse of Lucian Blaga, Mălăncioiu, like Mazilescu, Robescu, and Cezar Ivanescu, was mainly attracted by the poetry of George Bacovia. Especially appealing to her in Bacovia's magical symbolism were the anxiety and neurosis caused by the poet's isolation and alienation, by the decay and disintegration of the world, and by the threat of imminent annihilation. Like Bacovia, she is a poet of oppressive atmosphere; yet, there is in her poetry a mystical and Romantic inspiration that is alien to Bacovia's neorealism. Her atmosphere is primarily created by the recurrence of typically Romantic themes and motifs such as death, suffering, fear, sleep, and painful love, as well as by the accumulation of significant details, especially those related to coldness—corpses, ice, glass, stone, and colors such as white, blue, and black. Several Romantic motifs, like that of the dead queen, are inspired by Mihai Eminescu's poetry. Unlike Romantic poets who juxtapose opposites to reconcile them, Mălăncioiu establishes a permanent flux, a perpetual transformation from one state to another, and structures her work on the principle of communicating vessels.

With the collections *Către Ieronim* (Unto Hyeronimus, 1970), *Inima reginei* (The Queen's Heart, 1971), and *Crini pentru domnişoara mireasă* (Lilies for Her Ladyship the Bride, 1973) the oppressive atmosphere became Mălăncioiu's poetic hallmark. These volumes dramatize the perpetual transfer between life and death, nature and artifice, the real and the imaginary, and the ordinary and the fantastic. They share a set of recurrent symbols from legends and myths, as well as some of Mălăncioiu's creation, and a set of strange characters, such as Hieronymus ("Holy Name"), a Christian ascetic; his son, Nathaniel, named for one of Jesus' disciples; Hierodessa, the wife of King Herod, a popular character in Romanian Christmas carols and the queen of Mălăncioiu's legendary world; and "the dead queen," occasionally identified with Queen Marie of Romania. As several critics have remarked, they

Cover for Mălăncioiu's 1980 collection of elegies, inspired by the death of her sister

resemble characters in a chivalric story or a medieval engraving.

Către Ieronim is a book of poems about love, suffering, and pain. As in Eminescu's Romantic poetry, ideal love exists only in death. Love is substantiated only in the moment of separation and becomes real only through absence in "Noapte aproape albă" (translated as "An Almost White Night," 1985) and in the title poem (translated as "Unto Hieronymus," 1985). Hieronymus, the speaker's lover, is a surrealistic creation: his bones are "smashed up"; his right arm is longer than the left; his eye is "of blue glass," bearing a vague resemblance to the ascetic martyr saints in old Byzantine icons ("Your left temple is askew / Like the old icons . . ."). Intense erotic feeling suffuses "Ursul" (translated as "The Bear," 1985), which is based on an ancient popular belief about the healing power of a bear's touch. Images of violence, torture, and blood occur in "Săbiile" (The Swords) and "Ghorghe cu roata" (translated as "George with His Wheel," 1985).

The limiting effect of the speaker's masochistic devotion to Hieronymus, who exists only as a projection of her imagination, is counterbalanced by the richness of the mythical world inhabited by figures taken from Romanian folktales and legends, from Scandinavian mythology (in the poem "Ondine"), from Greek mythology (the myth of Orpheus), and from Roman history (in the poem "Aurelian Imparatul" [Aurelian the Emperor]). They all become symbolic characters in Mălăncioiu's own mythology and are subject to continual metamorphoses. They are representations of the spiritual legacy of the past that the speaker tries desperately to recover and appropriate, as in "Eden" (translated as "Eden," 1985): "Thus we all talk to one another our voices calm / For none of us knows whose might be / The bone that we behold/ As a body in another eternity."

In *Inima reginei,* just like as in *Către Ieronim,* the magic spell of the surreal is reinforced by the strong ritualistic, incantatory quality of the verse; the bizarre images of beasts and birds such as the strange Sphinx in "Doamna pasăre" (Her Ladyship the Bird); and recurrent images of snakes, glass eyes, and birds underlying such prevailing motifs as "the flight" and "the eye"—"the icy glass eye" as opposed to "the good eye" in "Ochiul tau cel bun" (Your Good Eye), "Talismanul" (translated as "The Talisman," 1985), and "Ca ochiul moartei tale" (translated as "Like Your Dead One's Eye," 1985).

There is, nevertheless, an important difference between the two volumes. In *Către Ieronim* Mălăncioiu is still trying to find her own poetic voice; in *Inima reginei* she has experienced the awakening of her poetic consciousness and cautiously introduces the political subversive dimension that becomes more visible in her poetry after the mid 1970s. Existential fear, which is hardly mentioned in *Către Ieronim,* is a dominant theme in *Inima reginei.* As the poet declares in the opening poem of *Inima reginei,* "Cîntec" (Song), she sings "out of fear"—a fear provoked by the loss of the past, represented by the Romanian fairy-tale figures of the King (Hieronymus) and the Queen (Hierodessa).

Crini pentru domnişoara mireasă further explores the symbolism of the earlier volumes—the dead bride, the lover, Hierodessa, the lamb, the snake, and the horse—and continues to draw on eclectic mythological sources. "Şi dacă" (translated as "And If," 1985), for instance, with its theme of the wedding as death ritual, is inspired by the Romanian folk ballad "Miorița" (The Ewe Lamb). The bride is dead, and the bridegroom is imaginary; but disappointment in love brings forth the

song and nurtures poetry. *Crini pentru domnişoara mireasă* departs from the fluid universe of the earlier volumes by introducing the idea of division in "Din două părţi" (Made of Two Parts), of boundaries in "Hotar" (translated as "Boundary," 1985), and of the toll one has to pay to cross the border in "Vămile" (Custom Duties) and "Pierderea banilor de vamă" (Losing the Duty Money).

Crini pentru domnişoara mireasă received the 1973 Poetry Prize of the Romanian Academy. In the same year Mălăncioiu submitted for publication another book of poems, suggestively titled "Exodul" (The Exodus) in reference to the growing numbers of Romanians who were defecting from the country. By then her uncompromising attitude and her two resignations had made her politically suspect. The censors delayed publication of the volume for three years; it finally came out under the title *Ardere de tot* (Burnt Offering, 1976).

Ardere de tot inaugurates a new stage in Mălăncioiu's poetry. The legendary characters of the previous volumes are replaced by a strange population of souls; the place of nature is taken by closed spaces; and the atmosphere becomes more oppressive as negative categories—ugliness, demonic evil, darkness, violence, and terror—point to the devastating effects of living under totalitarianism. In a search for salvation the poet undergoes the sacrificial ritual of the recovery of the soul: purification by the sacred fire of asceticism and renunciation. The soul sets out on the great journey along the well-traveled road between two worlds in the poem "Arată-mi-te acum" (translated as "Appear to Me Now," 1985): "My soul released from the body like an infant before its time / will wander naked along the way of souls. . . ." The "two opposite poles" mentioned in "Vai, cît pămînt este acum între noi" (translated as "Oh, How Much Earth There Is Now between Us," 1985) reinforce the idea of the border that must be crossed on the way of purification in "De-am trece" (If Only We Could Cross the Border), "De spaima unei clipe" (translated as "For Fear of an Instant," 1985), and "Iarăçi mă tem" (I Am Frightened Again).

Mălăncioiu defended her Ph.D. dissertation at the University of Bucharest in 1975 and published it under the title *Vina tragică* (Tragic Guilt) in 1978. Using examples from the Greek tragedians, William Shakespeare, Fyodor Dostoyevsky, and Franz Kafka, she defines guilt as the crossing of the borders set by sacred or human law and, in the case of Shakespeare's tragic heroes, by the hero's own moral law.

In 1977, after five years of unemployment, Mălăncioiu took a job as an editor with Animafilm Studios. But she had not been there a year when, after refusing to cooperate with the secret police, she resigned.

In 1979 Mălăncioiu published *Peste zona interzisă* (The Forbidden Zone), in which she explores in poetic form the ideas developed in *Vina tragică*, most notably in "Cîntec de bucurie" (translated as "A Song of Joy," 1985) and "Rugă" (translated as "Prayer," 1985). The poet identifies with tragic biblical figures in "Daniel" (translated as "Daniel," 1985), "Salomeia" (Salome), and "Ghetsimani" (translated as "Gethsemane," 1985); she finds correspondences with tragic literary heroes such as Hamlet and Ahab in "Bufonul" (translated as "The Jester," 1985), "Cucuta" (translated as "Hemlock," 1985), and "Pe cînd călătoream" (translated as "While Sailing," 1985). In the latter poem, she willingly takes on herself the burden of the existential tragic in the poem that reenacts Ahab's story: "for I was at the same time ship and waters / and the crew that had agreed to my folly / and the whale which was swallowing us up wholly." The theme of the soul's escaping the prison of the body and finding salvation and purification is replaced here by that of the tragic human condition, which includes death. The soul now is completely alone, vulnerable, and frightened.

Fear is a dominant theme in the volume. Nurtured by the darkness and violence of reality, pain grows into torment and fear into terror in "A intrat în odaie pe întuneric" (She Stole Into the Room at Night) and "Salvatorul" (The Savior). Violent images, including knives, blood, violent deaths, executioners, butterfly eaters, killer spiders, and biting ants and dogs, are juxtaposed to the butterfly metaphor of the poet's soul and to the symbol of the mountain. Life turns into a "frightful, endless night" in "O noapte lungă" (A Long Night); natural landscapes are replaced by closed spaces—dark rooms, musty walls, and crumbling houses— in "Nu știam cum se poate prăbuși o casă" (I Didn't Know How a House Could Collapse) and "Sînt" (I Am); fear becomes "perfect" in "Ghetsimani" and "universal" in "O noapte lungă" and is accompanied by loss of faith. The Savior is a fantastic animal resembling a dog in "Salvatorul," and the rituals of Resurrection and Ascension are performed by a worm that is "a butterfly with broken wings" in "Intunecata zare" (Dark Skies).

At the end of 1979 Mălăncioiu became an editor at the leading literary magazine *Viața Românească* (The Romanian Life). In her next volume, *Sora mea de din-colo* (My Sister Beyond, 1980), the fear of death has been conquered. The poems in this book, occasioned by the death of Mălăncioiu's sister Dorina at the age of thirty-three, rank among the most beautiful elegies in Romanian poetry. They achieve their cathartic effects in a poetic vision of death that is subtly connected with Greek Orthodox rituals but is, at the same time, perfectly integrated into the natural order. The poems are also purged of subjective and biographical elements; the intensity of Mălăncioiu's pain is kept under strict aesthetic control by her conviction, shared with T. S. Eliot, who stated that "the emotion of art is impersonal."

Mălăncioiu's next volume, *Linia vieții* (The Line of Life, 1982), which was awarded the Poetry Prize of the Bucharest Association of the Writers' Union, marks yet another turn in her poetic career: as her focus shifts from death to the social, political, spiritual, and moral aspects of life under totalitarianism, she abandons the metaphysical concerns of her poems of the 1970s. The supreme manifestation of the human condition in the last decade of the communist dictatorship was the loss of the free will, resulting in total resignation and an apathetic acceptance of regimentation. The poems in *Linia vieții* depict a life that is emptied of significance, that is accepted as it is laid down by a supreme power that is like an implacable destiny. The climbing of a mountain represents the opposite attitude, with the mountain standing for the aspiration to moral uprightness, existential awareness, and redemption and resurrection through accepted sacrifice. In *Linia vieții* climbing the mountain is still an option, but nobody except the Christ-like figure of the poet in "Cîntec de primăvară" (translated as "Spring Song," 1985) wants to take it. The atmosphere created by poem after poem is that of a wasteland inhabited by impassive, docile bodies ("Cîntec de dor" [translated as "Love Song," 1986]) or a "boundless, terrifying desert" where "millions of people" are transformed into sand grains, and the lovers are "two dromedaries in search of each other / . . . / Aware that the desert we are crossing / Is our only way" ("Peste acest nisip" [translated as "Over This Sand," 1985]). The restrictions imposed by totalitarianism are suggested by such images as a narrow hospital corridor, a dark room, an elevator, a shabby apartment building, a tunnel, and a concentration camp. Language has been emptied of meaning in "Turnul Babel" (translated as "The Tower of Babel," 1985); the old myths have been forgotten in "Legendă" (translated as "A Legend," 1985) and "Părul lui Samson" (translated as "Samson's Hair,"

Cover for the 1992 edition of Mălăncioiu's poetry collection, which includes several poems that were deleted from the 1985 edition at the insistence of the censors

1985); Jesus has become a "nobody" in "Cîntec despre nimeni" (translated as "A Song for Nobody," 1985), and, according to "Ce frumoasă grădină" (translated as "What a Lovely Garden," 1985), there is no Resurrection: "I was looking at the smiling faces on the crosses / No resurrection. / . . . / They no longer need nutriment / They stay in a row just out of habit / Or by mere accident."

Despite her desire to "climb the mountain," the poet remains a helpless observer; she is tormented by tragic guilt in "Ca un iepure" (translated as "Like a Hare," 1985) for her failure to act and in "Ultima amintire" (translated as "The Last Memory," 1985) for her failure to conquer her fear: "I was sitting face to face with the inventor / of my daily dread." Her pain is rendered in images of physical torment augmented by the anguish caused by her incapacity to choose between living among the "half-dead" in "Amiaza" (Midday) and the temptation of the other world in "Mi s-a întins o mînă de ajutor" (translated as "A Hand Has Been Stretched Out to Me," 1985) and "Pradă visului meu" (translated as "A Prey to My Dream," 1985).

The poet's tragic guilt reaches its apex in the poems of *Urcarea muntelui* (Climbing the Mountain, 1985), a powerful poetic vision of a new Apocalypse brought about by totalitarianism, an epic of death and extinction with the poet as protagonist. Locked in their houses during an endless winter, the "half-dead," bereft of will and hope, watch impassively as their city is invaded by the grotesque, merry parade of the dead ("Coşmar" [translated as "Nightmare," 1985]). Dying a slow death, they will soon join the parade ("Semne de primavara" [Signs of Spring]). By failing to unmask the crimes, the poet has become an accomplice ("O crima savirsita pe strada principala" [Murder on the Main Street]). When her poetry finally "climbed down into the street" and "took once more its place on the barricades," there was no one left to hear it; the streets were deserted ("Cîntec"). The poet's plight is rendered more vivid by reference to other tragic heroes: while Oedipus and Lear found comfort in the love of Antigone and Cordelia, respectively, the poet is left all alone in her ordeal.

As had been the case with Mălăncioiu's previous volume, the publication of *Urcarea muntelui* was delayed by the censors until she agreed to leave out poems that were considered too "politically transparent." Those poems, and others banned from publication, were incorporated in the enlarged edition of *Urcarea muntelui*, which came out in 1992, after the overthrow of communism.

Urcarea muntelui was the most subversive book of poetry published in Romania in the 1980s, and the fact that the book was allowed to be published is astonishing. One of the most compelling pieces of evidence of the communist nightmare and a perfect example of what is called "literature of resistance," *Urcarea muntelui* is also a great poetic achievement. The book brought Mălăncioiu the 1985 Poetry Prize of the Writers' Union; but the authorities soon declared her persona non grata, and she was put under surveillance by the secret police.

In the seven years between the two editions of *Urcarea muntelu*, no book of poetry by Mălăncioiu could be found in print; in 1987, however, in an effort at self-clarification, Mălăncioiu published a volume of prose pieces. *Călătorie spre mine însămi* (Journey into Myself) is a collection of fantastic and moral stories, recollections of childhood, critical readings, portraits of writers (Bacovia is her favorite), and short critical essays that center on two main concerns: the writer's intellectual condition and moral responsibility, and the question of death and extinction.

Two years later, following the banning from publication in *Viaţa Românească* of such writers as Constantin Noica, Mircea Eliade, E. M. Cioran, and Ana Blandiana, Mălăncioiu and four 'other well-known Romanian intellectuals addressed protest letters to the highest communist authorities. Mălăncioiu also submitted her resignation from the magazine. After the collapse of Nicolae Ceauşescu's regime in December 1989 she was appointed one of the chief editors of *Viaţa Românească*, and in 1992 she became chief editor of the Litera publishing house.

A comprehensive anthology of Mălăncioiu's poetic work under the title *Ardere de tot* came out in 1992. The volume comprises 369 poems, 43 of them previously uncollected works written from 1982 to 1991. In the same year she published a new edition of *Sora mea de dincolo,* which was awarded the Vacaresti Prize as the best book of poetry of the year.

Deeply engaged as a writer and editor in the post-1989 democratic changes taking place in Romania, Mălăncioiu advocates the exposure of the communist crimes against humanity. She has participated in international conferences and poetry in Spain (1990), Italy and France (1990 and 1991), Sweden (1993), and Greece and Ireland (1996) and has written regular articles for the cultural and political weekly *22,* the literary journal *România literară* (Literary Romania), and the national daily *România liberă* (Free Romania). In 1993 she collected her political essays in the volume *Crimă şi moralitate* (Crime and Morality), a bitter critique of what she regards as the neocommunism that was installed in Romania after 1989. The book was awarded the Writers' Union Prize and the Slobozia Cultural Center Prize for Excellency. *Poezii* (Poems), another poetry collection, came out in 1996, and in the same year Mălăncioiu was one of ten Romanian poets whose works were translated by ten Irish poets in the volume *When the Tunnels Meet,* published in the United Kingdom. In 1996 she also was awarded the "Mihail Eminescu" National Grand Prize for her literary oeuvre. Mălăncioiu is currently writing mostly political essays and fantastic prose. She believes that the crucial historical period Romania is crossing in its transition to a democratic society is not the most propitious time for writing poetry.

Mălăncioiu is widely recognized in her country as one of the most original and compelling of contemporary poets. Nevertheless, despite the economy of language, absence of metaphors, and narrative quality of her verse, her poetry is hard to translate, as it is imbued with Romanian spirituality and bases much of its effect on the use of popular traditions and Greek Orthodox rituals and symbols. But her poetry of witness is a devastating document of the spiritual traumas produced by totalitarianism, while her lyricism touches on the universal in human nature, the perennial in human values, and the magic in the primordial rhythms of life.

Interviews:

Carlos Garcia-Osuna, "Ileana Mălăncioiu," *El Independiente,* 308 (10 May 1990): 53;

Isabel San Sebastian, "Ileana Mălăncioiu," *ABC* (Madrid), 11 May 1990, p. 39;

Liliana Stoicescu, "Revoluţia continuă," *România liberă,* 19 May 1990, p. 2;

Gabriela Adameşteanu, "Intre criza cuvîntului şi criza instituţiilor culturale," *22,* no. 10 (9 March 1994): 8–9;

Marta Petreu, "Conversaţii cu Ileana Mălăncioiu," *Apostrof,* nos. 1, 2 (1998): 10–14;

Victoria Milescu, "De vorbă cu Ileana Mălăncioiu," *Universal Cărţii,* no. 4 (2000): 12.

References:

Valeriu Cristea, "Ileana Mălăncioiu: *Catre Ieronim; Inima reginei,*" in his *Un an de poezie* (Bucharest: Cartea Românească, 1974), pp. 206–210;

Cristea, "Motive si orientari poetice" in his *Modestie si orgoliu* (Bucharest: Eminescu, 1984), pp. 62–65;

Cristea, "Sufletul ce n-a capitulat," in his *Faptul de a scrie* (Bucharest: Cartea Românească, 1980), pp. 141–144;

Cristea, "The Utopias of Survival," translated by Dan Duţescu, in Mălăncioiu's *Peste zona interzisa / Across the Forbidden Zone* (Bucharest: Editura Eminescu, 1985), pp. xvii–xxx;

Ovid S. Crohmalniceanu, "Spatiul magic al Ilenei Mălăncioiu," in his *Al doilea suflu* (Bucharest: Cartea Românească, 1989), pp. 51–58;

Andreea Deciu, "Poeta anului," *România Literară,* no. 3 (12–18 January 1993): 4;

Daniel Cristea Enache, "Ileana Mălăncioiu: linia poeziei," *Adevărul Literar şi artistic,* nos. 529, 530, 531 (2000): 5;

Victor Felea, "Ileana Mălăncioiu: *Ardere de tot; Peste zona interzisă,*" in his *Aspecte ale poeziei de azi,* volume 2 (Cluj-Napoca: Dacia, 1980), pp. 165–172;

Felea, "Ileana Mălăncioiu: *Către Ieronim; Inima reginei,*" in his *Sectiuni* (Bucharest: Cartea Românească, 1974), pp. 199–207;

Gheorghe Grigurcu, "Ileana Mălăncioiu," in his *Poeti romani de azi* (Bucharest: Cartea Românească, 1979), pp. 206–212;

Grigurcu, "Poezia Ilenei Mălăncioiu," *România Literară*, no. 13 (2000): 5, 14;

Virgil Ierunca, "Autobiografia Antigonei," *22*, no. 47 (December 1992): 14–15;

Ierunca, "Ileana Mălăncioiu," *Familia*, 9 (September 1992): 4–5;

Mircea Iorgulescu, "Ileana Mălăncioiu," in his *Scriitori tineri contemporani* (Bucharest: Eminescu, 1978), pp. 98–100;

Dan Laurentiu, "Imaginaţia şi memoria," in his *Eseuri asupra stării de graţie* (Bucharest: Cartea Românească, 1976), pp. 149–155;

Florin Manolescu, "Poeme cenzurate: Ileana Mălăncioiu, *Urcarea muntelui*," *Luceafărul*, no. 43 (1992): 5

Nicolae Manolescu, "Poezia marilor simboluri," *România Literară*, no. 8 (20 February 1986): 9;

Gabriela Melinescu, "Poezie si mit," *România Literară*, no. 28 (17–23 July 1996): 11, 12;

Dumitru Micu, "Neoromantisme," in his *Limbaje moderne în poezia românească de azi* (Bucharest: Minerva, 1986), pp. 270–279;

Ion Negoitescu, "*Linia vieţii şi Urcarea Muntelui*," *Familia*, 3 (March 1991): 7, 9;

Eugen Negrici, "Ileana Mălăncioiu," in his *Introducere în poezia contemporana* (Bucharest: Cartea Românească, 1985), pp. 133–153;

Alexandru Niculescu, "Un limbaj liric autohton," *România Literară*, no. 8 (2–8 March 1994): 11;

M. Nitescu, "Biografie si şimbol," in his *Poeţi contemporani: Sinteze critice* (Bucharest: Cartea Românească, 1978), pp. 233–242;

Mihail Petroveanu, "Ileana Mălăncioiu," in his *Traiectorii lirice* (Bucharest: Cartea Românească, 1974), pp. 314–318;

Alexandru Pintescu, "Ars doloris sau poezia Ilenei Mălăncioiu," *Poesis*, 6 (1990): 1, 15;

Alexandru Piru, "Ileana Mălăncioiu," in his *Poezia românească contemporană*, volume 2 (Bucharest: Cartea Românească, 1975), pp. 273–275;

Cristian Tudor Popescu, "Sora mea de dincolo," *Adevarul*, no. 226 (October 1992): 2;

Lucian Raicu, "Ardere de tot," in his *Printre contemporani* (Bucharest: Cartea Românească, 1980), pp. 127–135;

Raicu, "Fervoarea incisiva," in his *Fragmente de timp* (Bucharest: Cartea Românească, 1984), pp. 255–260;

Raicu, "Guillaume şi Administratorul (II)," *România Literară*, no. 11 (15 March 1990): 8;

Raicu, "Ileana Mălăncioiu—Forţa născută în tăcere," in his *Critica, formă de viaţă* (Bucharest: Cartea Românească, 1976), pp. 352–356;

Raicu, "Poezia neliniştită," *România Literară*, no. 6 (8 February 1990): 9;

Von Dieter Roth, "Uber Grenzen: Das Verstehen von Gedichten und die Wirklichkeit des Lesers," *Rhein-Neckar-Zeitung*, 13 (17–18 January 1987): 49;

Eugen Simion, "Ileana Mălăncioiu," in his *Scriitori români de azi*, volume 3 (Bucharest: Cartea Românească, 1984), pp. 376–393.

Dan Stanca, "Modalităţile lecturii," *Jurnalul Literar*, nos. 7–8 (2000): 3;

Alex. Ştefănescu, "La o nouă lectură: Ileana Mălăncioiu," *România Litereră*, no. 3 (26 January 2000): 12–13;

Dorin Tudoran, "Fojgăieli doctrnare," *România Literară*, no. 7 (24 February 1999): 12–13.

Norman Manea

(19 July 1936 –   )

Virgil Nemoianu
Catholic University of America

BOOKS: *Noaptea pe latura lungă* (Bucharest: Editura pentru literatura, 1969);

Captivi (Bucharest: Cartea Românească, 1970);

Atrium (Bucharest: Cartea Românească, 1974);

Primele porţi (Bucharest: Albatros, 1975);

Cartea fiului (Bucharest: Eminescu, 1976);

Zilele şi jocul (Bucharest: Cartea Românească, 1977);

Anii de ucenicie ai lui August Prostul (Bucharest: Cartea Românească, 1979);

Octombrie, ora opt (Cluj: Dacia, 1981); translated by Cornelia Golna and others as *October, Eight O'Clock* (London: Quartet, 1992; New York: Grove, 1992);

Pe contur (Bucharest: Cartea Românească, 1984);

Plicul negru (Bucharest: Cartea Românească, 1986); translated by Patrick Camiller as *The Black Envelope* (New York: Farrar, Straus & Giroux, 1995; London: Faber & Faber, 1996);

Fericirea obligatorie (Cluj: Biblioteca Apostrophe, 1989); translated by Alain Paruit and Andre Vornic as *Le bonheur obligatoire* (Paris: A. Michel, 1991); translated from the French by Linda Coverdale as *Compulsory Happiness* (New York: Farrar Straus & Giroux, 1993; London: Faber & Faber, 1994);

On Clowns: The Dictator and the Artist (New York: Grove, 1992; London: Faber & Faber, 1994); Romanian version published as *Despre clovni. Dictatorul şi artistul* (Cluj: Biblioteca Apostrof, 1997);

Casa Melcului (Bucharest: Hasefer, 1999).

Editions in English: "Empty Theaters?," translated by Adriane Paran, *World Policy Journal*, 10 (Spring 1993): 79–82;

"Writers and the Great Beast," translated by Tess Lewis, *Partisan Review*, 61 (Winter 1994): 46–54;

"Epitaph as Prologue (Literature at the End of the Century)," translated by Camiller, *TriQuarterly*, 94 (Fall 1995): 161–169;

Norman Manea *(photograph by Josef Sudek; from the dust jacket for* October, Eight O'Clock*)*

"Blasphemy and Carnival," translated by Camiller, *World Policy Journal*, 13 (Spring 1996): 71–82;

"Cioran," translated by Camiller, *Conjunctions*, no. 3 (1998);

"The Incompatibilities," translated by Camiller, *New Republic*, 218 (April 1998): 32–37;

"The Jewish Writer," *Partisan Review* (April 1998);

"A Hooligan's Return," translated by Camiller, *Salmagundi*, nos. 121/122 (Winter/Spring 1999): 82–131;

"The Walser Debate," translated by Susan Bernofski, *Partisan Review* (Summer 1999): 392–403;

Dust jackets for the U.S. editions of English translations of a short-story collection (1992) and a novel (1995) by Manea

"Made in Romania," translated by Camiller, *New York Review of Books*, 47 (10 February 2000): 44–46.

Norman Manea represents both the modernist vocation of Romanian prose writing and the well-established tradition and inclination of this literature toward the expressionist style. He stands for a specific Romanian mode of opposition to totalitarianism: an aesthetic one, mild, yet tenacious. He is also a good example of the way in which the Romanian literary language was able to benefit from the influx of various ethnic influences, in this case the Jewish one.

Norman Manea was born on 19 July 1936 in the city of Suceava in northern Romania. His father, Marcu Manea, was an accountant, and his mother, Janeta (née Braunstein), was a bookseller. Soon the family fell victim to the atrocities of World War II: in 1941 Manea, his parents, and grandparents were transported to a concentration camp in Ukraine. He spent four years there and saw part of his family perish, an experience that indelibly marked his later life. He graduated from high school in 1954 in his native town and thereafter studied hydrotechnology at the Construction Institute in Bucharest, earning a master's degree in 1959.

Manea practiced engineering until 1974, but he started writing soon after graduation, making his prose debut in 1966 in the small avant-garde journal *Povestea Vorbei* (Narrative Rumors) under the auspices of Miron Radu Paraschivescu, an erratic and heretical Communist poet. In 1969 Manea married Josette-Cella Boiangiu, an art conservator. His modernistic writing style, as well as the many allusions in his texts critical of the social and political system, slowed down his public recognition. Moreover, his references to Jewish persecution (past and present) irritated the Romanian Communist authorities, who regarded him with suspicion. Nevertheless, after the publication of two volumes of short stories, *Noaptea pe latura lungă* (Night on the Long Side, 1969) and *Primele porți* (The First Gates, 1975), and two novels, *Captivi*

(Captive, 1970) and *Atrium* (1974), he felt confident enough to dedicate himself exclusively to writing. These early works, while still somewhat tentative and juvenile, managed nevertheless to break the mold of the servile "realist" or "mimetic" style recommended or imposed by cultural authorities.

Some of Manea's best works of fiction, notably *Octombrie, ora opt* (1981; translated as *October, Eight O'Clock,* 1992) and *Plicul negru* (1986; translated as *The Black Envelope,* 1995), appeared in the 1980s, albeit with great difficulty and marred by cuts imposed after long struggles with censors. The passages eliminated were interpreted as satirical allusions to the state of things in a society shaped by communist totalitarianism. Manea comments on these incidents in "The Censor's Report," included in the volume *On Clowns: The Dictator and the Artist* (1992). In 1979 he was awarded the Literary Prize of the Association of Bucharest Writers, and in 1984 he won the National Prize of the Romanian Writers' Union for fiction (only to see the latter promptly withdrawn by the Communist authorities).

In 1986 Manea exiled himself, living first in West Berlin as recipient of the DAAD Berliner-Künstlerprogramm fellowship, and then in the United States, where he was awarded a Fulbright fellowship (1988–1989). Manea's first residence was in Washington, D.C., but in 1989 he moved to New York. Since 1989 Manea has been associated with Bard College in Annandale-on-Hudson, where he has been an International Academy fellow (teaching courses on Eastern European writers and on "Holocaust and Literature"), and writer in residence. In 1996, Manea received an endowed chair at Bard College, the Francis Flourney Professorship in European Studies and Culture.

Manea's international recognition came without much delay. He obtained an impressive number of prominent awards, perhaps most notably a Guggenheim fellowship in 1992 and the five-year MacArthur Award, also in 1992. He was granted the National Jewish Book Award and the "Literary Lion" Award of the National Library of New York in 1993. Major literary figures such as Philip Roth and Heinrich Böll, and writers such as Louis Begley and Paul Bayley, have praised Manea as one of the most original voices coming out of Eastern Europe. His works have been translated into German, French, Spanish, Italian, and Dutch and have appeared in Mexico, Norway, and Israel.

Manea uses a narrative discourse of indirection; he is a master of oblique suggestion and insinuation. His novels are not eventful or packed with exciting action. Rather they tend to point toward dramatic or anguishing realities through small occurrences, apparently secondary and devoid of great moment. Manea's writing has often been placed in the Central European tradition of Bruno Schulz, Franz Kafka, and Robert Musil, in which philosophical skepticism and a melancholy, subdued kind of satire intermingle. However, it should not be forgotten that Manea does come from a Romanian background and that he continues to write in Romanian. Thus, he can also be placed in the tradition of the poet George Bacovia and of M. Blecher, both writers who dwelt on the sad uncertainties and disappointments of human life in the provincial and stagnant parts of Romania.

What makes Manea different from his predecessors is the way in which his life experiences obliged him to respond to the double dictatorship of fascism and communism. Human efforts (always only partly successful) to maintain identity and interiority, indeed sometimes simply to survive, are foregrounded in his work, but in quiet, soft, almost apologetic tones. *Octombrie, ora opt* is a collection of heart-wrenching short stories set in the deportation wastelands of Ukraine that obliquely suggest the conditions of bare survival and the emotional suffering of the Jewish inhabitants. By contrast, the novel *Plicul negru* is set in the 1970s and includes grotesque scenes of human manipulation by an ever-present controlling regime.

Once displaced in the West, Manea continued writing in Romanian but published his writings in adaptations in other languages, often participating in the translation. He developed a highly original mode of writing, based on coherent groupings of prose fragments in which the lyrical, the essayistic, and political and ideological polemics are interwoven. Five pieces—"Romania: Three Lines with Commentary," "On Clowns: The Dictator and the Artist: Notes to a Text by Fellini," "Censor'd Report: With Explanatory Notes by the Censored Author," "Felix Culpa," and "The History of an Interview"—collected in the volume *On Clowns* are particularly representative: they juxtapose the dangers and weaknesses of human consciousness under different forms of totalitarian pressure. The title piece is one of the best critiques of Nicolae Ceaușescu's dictatorship and of the oppositional role of literature during that period. A kind of gray, subdued form of fear and depression are masterfully described in "Trenciul" (translated as "The Trenchcoat") as well as in "O fereastră spre clasa muncitoare" (translated as "A

475

Motivatia adversitatii nu era aceeasi ca la Verona. Clasica era,
insa, si aceasta meschina tragi-comedie de ghetto.

La citeva saptamini dupa ritualul fara ritual al eliberarii de
virginitate, Julieta se izolase de parinti si frati si surori,
retrasa in camera ei, isi pregatea examenul de admitere la
universitate. Era vara, perioada vacantelor si concediilor. Romeo
plecase la mare, unde cutreiera, insingurat, tarmul si
restaurantele.

La intoarcere, fiul ratacitor nu fusese recompensat pentru
infidelitatea fata de iubita. Curind dupa plecarea sa in concediu,
familia primise, un impertinent mesaj telefonic, o voce care se
pretindea martora comunica de pe litoral ca fericitul cuplu se afla
in perfecta stare de functionare si adoratie. Provocarea ar fi
putut veni de la neconsolata doamna de pe strada Armeneasca,
umilita de scandalul erotic al junelui Romeo pe care tocmai il
reparase. Stupide incidente ale unei lumi stupide, de nu ar fi
fost mai adinca patologia si mai dramatica. Lamentatia milenara,
ura veche fata de asupritorii dintotdeauna temerari in
capcana erotica a Shiksei. "Nu a mai intilnit de multe generatii o
fata atit de inteligenta" repeta isterica mama evreica
caracterizarea prin care varul nostru, profesorul Riemer, isi
onorase eleva. Elogiul intors, spontan, in derivate degradate:
inteligenta adversarului nu insemna decit siretenie, smecherie,
ipocrita desteptaciune, intentiile perfide dinsa stiute.

Comicul vira imperceptibil in maladiva angoasa, turmentarea
nevrotica nu putea fi separata de reflexia ei amara, repulsia si

Page from the typescript for Manea's novel "The Return of the Hooligan," written during the summer of 2000 and scheduled to be published in 2001 (Collection of Norman Manea)

Window on the Working Class"), both included in *Compulsory Happiness*, published in 1993.

Through his international career and his self-invention in a kind of temperate, suggestive, and pervasive language, Manea has emerged as one of the most original figures of contemporary Romanian literature. The success of Manea's work in the international literary world contributed to a better and more rounded understanding of his significance for Romanian society and culture.

Interviews:

Marta Petreu, "An Interview with Norman Manea," *Partisan Review*, 62 (Winter 1995): 28–35;

Marco Cugna, "Interview with Norman Manea," translated by Patrick Camiller, *TriQuarterly*, 97 (Fall 1996): 21–42.

References:

Paul Bailey, "The Archive of Truths," *Times Literary Supplement*, 10 May 1996, p. 22;

Stanisław Barańczak, "The Gulag Circus," *New Republic* (1 June 1992): 44;

John Bayley, "Treading the Edge of a Nightmare," *New York Times Book Review*, 21 June 1992, p. 3;

Louis Begley, "A Matter of Survival," *New York Review of Books*, 24 September 1992, p. 6;

Eva Behring, "The Fate of an Exiled Writer," translated by Edith Kurzweil, *Partisan Review*, 64 (Fall 1997): 630–634;

Matei Càlinescu, "On Clowns: The Dictator and the Artist," *World Literature Today*, 68 (Winter 1994): 111–112;

Càlinescu, "Totalitarianism's Mad Mysteries," *Boston Sunday Globe*, 11 June 1995;

Adrei Corbea, "Exilul dianinte si dupa exil," *Observatorul Cultural*, no. 14 (2000);

Valeriu Cristea, "Atrium," *Romania literara* (25 April 1974);

Ov. S. Crohmanliniceanu, "Octombrie, ora opt," *Romania literara* (16 September 1984);

Crohmaliniceanu, "Plicul negru," *Romania literara* (11 September 1986);

Richard Eder, "Where Everyone Wears a Trenchcoat," *Los Angeles Times*, 23 May 1993, p. 3;

Rad Enescu, "Captivi," *Familia* (May 1971);

Al. George, "Pe contur," *Romania literara* (7 June 1984);

Paul Georgescu, "Octombrie, ora opt," *Romania libera* (20 February 1982);

Georgescu, "Variante la un autoportret," *Romania literara* (13 January 1977);

Mircea Iorgulescu, "Norman Manea," *Romania literara* (24 July 2000);

Virgil Nemoianu, "Norman Manea: A Profile," *Steaua*, 47 (July–August 1996): 7–8, 20–21;

Liviu Petrescu, "Alegoria Prudentei," *Steaua*, no. 10 (1986);

Lucian Raicu, "Anii de Ucenicie," *Romania literara* (31 July 1980);

Raicu, "Octombrie, ora opt," *Romania literara* (8 March 1984);

Salmagundi, special Manea issue (Winter 1997).

Michael Shafir, "The Man They Love to Hate," *East European Jewish Affairs* (Summer 2000).

Justinas Marcinkevičius

(10 March 1930 –   )

Indrė Žekevičiūtė-Žakevičienė
Kaunas Vytautas Magnus University

BOOKS: *Prašau žodžio* (Vilnius: Valstybinė grožinės
literatūros leidykla, 1955);
Daina prie laužo (Vilnius: Valstybinė grožinės
lieratūros leidykla, 1955);
Dvidešimtas pavasaris (Vilnius: Valstybinė grožinės literatūros leidykla, 1956);
Grybų karas (Vilnius: Valstybinė grožinės lieratūros
leidykla, 1958);
Kraujas ir pelenai (Vilnius: Valstybinė grožinės lit-
eratūros leidykla, 1960);
Laukinė kriaušė (Vilnius: Valstybinė grožinės
lieratūros leidykla, 1960);
Publicistinė poema (Vilnius: Valstybinė grožinės lit-
eratūros leidykla, 1961);
Pušis, kuri juokėsi (Vilnius: Valstybinė grožinės lit-
eratūros leidykla, 1961);
Duoną raikančios rankos (Vilnius: Valstybinė grožinės
literatūros leidykla, 1963);
Donelaitis (Vilnius: Valstybinė grožinės literatūros
leidykla, 1964);
Baladė apie Ievą (Vilnius: Vaga, 1965);
Siena (Vilnius: Vaga, 1965);
Mediniai tiltai (Vilnius: Vaga, 1966);
Liepsnojantis krūmas (Vilnius: Vaga, 1968);
Mindaugas (Vilnius: Vaga, 1968);
Greitoji pagalba (Vilnius: Vaga, 1968);
Sena abėcėlė (Vilnius: Vaga, 1969);
U-ti-ti-ti, šalta (Vilnius: Vaga, 1969);
Katedra (Vilnius: Vaga, 1971);
Ungnies poema (Vilnius: Vaga, 1972);
Devyni broliai (Vilnius: Vaga, 1972);
Poemos, 2 volumes (Vilnius: Vaga, 1972);
Mažosios poemos (Vilnius: Vaga, 1973);
Šešios poemos (Vilnius: Vaga, 1973);
Heroica, arba Prometėjo pasmerkimas (Vilnius: Vaga,
1973);
Po aukšta aja žvaigžde (Vilnius: Vaga, 1975);
Mažvydas (Vilnius: Vaga, 1977);
Poemos (Vilnius: Vaga, 1977);
Gyvenimo švelnus prisiglaudimas (Vilnius: Vaga, 1978);
Pažinimo medis (Vilnius: Vaga, 1979);

Justinas Marcinkevičius

*Skrendančios pušys. Eilėraščiai, 1962–1977. Vyresniam
mokykliniam amžiui* (Vilnius: Vaga, 1979);
Būk ir palaimink (Vilnius: Vaga, 1980);
Voro vestuvės (Vilnius: Vaga, 1980);
Dienoraštis be datų (Vilnius: Vaga, 1981);
Tokia yra meilė/Love Is Like This, translated by Liongi-
nas Pažūsis (Vilnius: Vaga, 1983);
Vienintelė žemė (Vilnius: Vaga, 1984);
Už gyvus ir mirusius (Vilnius: Vaga, 1988);
Lopšinė gimtinei ir motinai (Vilnius: Vaga, 1992);

Prie rugių ir prie ugnies (Vilnius: Lituanus, 1992);
Eilėraščiai iš dienoraščio (Kaunas: Spindulys, 1993);
Tekančios upės vienybė (Kaunas: Santara, 1994);
Daukantas (Kaunas: Santara, 1997);
Žingsnis (Kaunas: Santara, 1998);
Carmina minora (Vilnius: Tyto Alba, 2000).
Editions: *Raštai*, 4 volumes (Vilnius: Vaga, 1975–1978);
Raštai, 5 volumes (Vilnius: Vaga, 1982–1983);
Poezija, 2 volumes, edited by J. Riškutė (Vilnius: Vaga, 2000).
Editions in English: "Father's Winter" and "Green Crab," translated and edited by Jonas Zdanys, in *Selected Post-War Lithuanian Poetry*, edited by Zdanys (New York: Manyland Books, 1978), pp. 249–254;
"Landscape with Apparition" and "Nemunas," translated by Irene Pogoželskyte Suboczewski, and "Father's Winter," translated by Zdanys, in *Contemporary East European Poetry*, edited by Emery George (Ann Arbor, Mich.: Ardis, 1983), pp. 81–83;
"Like Letters," "Unity of Grass and Stone," "Evening: Atom-Bomb Fright," "Wooden Bridges," "Potato-Picking," "Night," "August," "'I have the feeling now that not your hands . . . ,'" "Love Is Like This," "Confession," "Creation," "Carrying My Homeland," "'Suppose all the roads should vanish . . . ,'" and "Punishment," translated by Lionginas Pažūsis, in *Songs of Life and Love*, edited by Pažūsis (Vilnius: Vaga, 1989), pp. 129–159.

PLAY PRODUCTIONS: *Krintančios žvaigždės*, Klaipėda Drama Theatre, 1968;
Mindaugas, Academic Drama Theatre of Lithuania, 1969;
Katedra, Vilnius, Academic Drama Theatre of Lithuania, 1970;
Mažvydas, Vilnius, Academic Drama Theatre of Lithuania, 1978;
Prometėjas. Ikaras, Vilnius, Academic Drama Theatre of Lithuania, 1981;
Daukantas, Vilnius, Vilnius Youth Theatre, 1985;
Voro vestuvės, Vilnius, Vilnius Puppet Theatre, 1994.

TRANSLATIONS: Adam Mickiewicz, *Gražina* (Vilnius: Valstybinė grožinės literatūros leidykla, 1955);
Aleksandr Pushkin, *Bachčisarajaus fontanas* (Vilnius: Valstybinė grožinės literatūros leidykla, 1955);
Mickiewicz, *Vėlinės (Dziady)* (Vilnius: Valstybinė grožines literatūros leidykla, 1958);
Mickiewicz, *Meilės sonetai* (Vilnius: Valstybinė grožinės literatūros leidykla, 1961);
Sergej Jesenin, *Baltoji obelų pūga* (Vilnius: Valstybinė grožinės literatūros leidykla, 1961);
Kalevo sūnus (Vilnius: Valstybinė grožinės literatūros leidykla, 1963);
Mikhail Lermontov, *Demonas* (Vilnius: Vaga, 1964);
Kalevala (Vilnius: Vaga, 1972);
Mickiewicz, *Ponas Tadas*, translated by Marcinkevičius and Vincas Mykolaitis-Putinas (Vilnius: Vaga, 1974).

Justinas Marcinkevičius emerged on the Lithuanian literary scene in the post–World War II era as a spokesman for the revival of national consciousness. Depicting examples of social truths, morality, and ethics, Marcinkevičius's writing drives toward visions of equality and fraternity. His poetry and drama convey the joys and sorrows of his homeland. From Marcinkevičius's point of view, the mission of a writer is to protect and preserve the life of the nation; thus, as he explores the emotional attitudes of Lithuania, he portrays the totality of a community of human beings who are participants in the historical process. As one of the most popular contemporary Lithuanian poets and dramatists, Marcinkevičius became a symbol of the nation's sufferings under the Soviet regime as well as a symbol of integrity and hope for the nation's future. His books have been translated into at least twenty other languages, including German, English, Norwegian, and Russian, and his plays have been staged not only in several Lithuanian theaters but also in such countries as the Czech Republic, Hungary, Latvia, and Uzbekistan.

Justinas Marcinkevičius was born on 10 March 1930 in the village of Važatkiemis, an area of Prienai, into a large family of peasants. As a child he was charmed by the change of seasons and the different cycles of peasant work, which seemed to him to be some mysterious ritual. He states in volume two of Jonas Lankutis's *Lietuvių literatūros istorija* (1982) that "such labor seemed to be not only merely episodes of daily life; rather, it expressed great vitality in a peculiar spiritual mood of the people." Marcinkevičius was heavily influenced by the provincial arts of ceramics and wood carving as well as by traditional folk songs, tales, proverbs, and riddles. He believed that the simple arts of the common people constantly support and nourish the spirit of the nation.

However, the pastoral simplicity of childhood was distorted for Marcinkevičius by both the encroachment of war and of personal loss. "It was in

Scene from the 1978 production of Marcinkevičius's play
Mazvydas *at the Academic Drama Theatre in Vilnius*

my young years," declared Marcinkevičius in Kudirkienė's history, "when I had the opportunity to learn that a human being is not important at all, that his heart is under the shadows of falsehood, compulsion, and terror all the time." Thus, his poetry attempts to reach his readers with a message relating the necessity of maintaining the eternal values of truth, generosity, sincerity, and love. With the death of his mother in 1944, Marcinkevičius's creative consciousness was further shaken, and the portrait of his mother became one of the most prominent images within his work. As Marcinkevičius later said of his mother: "She has become a certain standard of beauty and goodness, an idea of love and truth, a synonym for my homeland, and the epitome of femininity."

In 1947, while still in high school at Prienai, Marcinkevičius was arrested for taking part in student anti-Soviet activities. In 1949 Marcinkevičius began his studies in Lithuanian language and literature at Vilnius University. In 1954, the year he graduated, he began working in the editorial offices of *Genys* (The Woodpecker), a magazine for children, and *Pergalė* (Victory), a literary journal. In 1957 he became a member of the Communist Party, which he left in 1990, and in 1959 became a member of the board of the Writers' Union of Soviet Lithuania.

Heavily influenced by love for his country, his people, and particularly for his family, Marcinkevičius managed to balance his creative works with his family life. In 1955 he married Genovaitė Kalvaitytė, a high-school teacher, and he claims that his most beautiful and perfect creative works are their two daughters, Ramunė (born in 1957) and Jurga (born in 1964). In *Tekančios upės vienybė* (The Unity of the Flowing River, 1994) he expresses the importance of maintaining a healthy family life: "The writer is the same as anyone else; therefore, he has the right to experience life, to feel the joy and troubles of a family. He must find the time and energy to express love for his home. . . . Having a family is a certain way of life, so I don't think that it should be like a stone that pulls you down. In many ways, raising a child is far more difficult and more important than writing a book."

Marcinkevičius's works are extremely lyrical. He was heavily influenced by the poetry of Vincas Mykolaitis-Putinas, Salomėja Nėris, Jonas Maironis, Kazys Binkis, and Kristijonas Donelaitis. Together with poets such as Algimantas Baltakis, Alfonsas Maldonis, and Janina Degutytė, he initiated a new period in the development of Lithuanian poetry: the poem itself became more connected to human experience as authors returned to authentic self-expression. His poetry expresses archaic Lithuanian attitudes toward life as well as the tragedies of the twentieth century. Marcinkevičius is a poet of great philosophical insights, attempting to embrace the whole of existence through references to Lithuanian customs that often center around natural phenomena. For example, the poet recalls in *Tekančios upės vienybė*, "During summer thunder storms our mother used to kneel us down to pray. Then she used to burn consecrated bunches of yew, and with the help of the smoke, tried to protect our home from lightning and fire." Marcinkevičius believes that the most important and interesting genre is epic poetry because through this form he can delve into the past, portray the present, and create visions of the future.

Marcinkevičius's creative career can be divided into three periods; the first is the decade from 1953 to 1963. During this period, Marcinkevičius formulated his world outlook, breaking through his peasant nature and beginning to accept the premise of socialism and its concept of history. In 1953 his first printed poems appeared in the journal *Jaunimo gretos* (Ranks of the Youth). In 1955 his first book of lyrics, *Prašau žodžio* (Let Me Speak), appeared. In this work Marcinkevičius expresses the highest possible moral regulations.

Although his language is simple, it leads to various associations. Within this book, it appears that life has stopped, and rather than seeing the present moment, the poet is capable of perceiving only the darkness of the past and the uncertainty of the future. In 1956 Marcinkevičius's epic *Dvidešimtas pavasaris* (The Twentieth Springtime) was published. There were also some serious conflicts with the authorities: in 1957 a publishing house refused to bring out a book of his lyrics, "Šventoji duona" (The Sacred Bread), because it included some criticism of the realities of those days. That same year, an entire issue of the newspaper *Literatūra ir menas* that included several of his poems was halted by censorship.

Marcinkevičius's well-known epic *Kraujas ir pelenai* (Blood and Ashes), which told of German atrocities committed in 1944 in the village of Pirčiupis, was published in 1960. In 1961 he published *Publicistinė poema* (Publicist Poem) and his narrative *Pušis, kuri juokėsi* (The Laughing Pine Tree). Within *Pušis, kuri juokėsi* Marcinkevičius began poeticizing the basic elements of a socialist world attitude. He was quite methodical in his rejection of the individualism inherent in Western lifestyles. Indeed, he presented Western mass culture as if it were treasonous to humanism as well as to his nation.

Marcinkevičius's second book of lyrics, *Duoną raikančios rankos* (The Bread-Slicing Hands, 1963), presents a much wider vision of the world than *Prašau žodžio*. In this book the poetic language is depersonalized. The author attempted to create a logical system of universal values that would not collide with the present socialist order; rather, he sought to justify this order in terms of the global development of humankind and its moral principles. Thus, this first period of Marcinkevičius's creative work is marked by a naive vision of Lithuania's future prosperity and a belief in an historical movement toward world communism and subsequent universal happiness that, although appearing somewhat pathetic, was sincere.

The second period of Marcinkevičius's creative work encompasses the decade beginning in 1964. This period is marked by a new maturity in his lyrics. In 1966 Marcinkevičius's collection of verse *Mediniai tiltai* (Wooden Bridges) was published, and two years earlier his major epic *Donelaitis* was also published. Although his tone remained the same, this work expressed the problems of the poet's mission. Indeed, as he attempted to grasp the role of historical time, the issues of the continuation of national culture became problematic. However, the poet managed to apprehend some truths: *Donelaitis* preserves the Lithuanian language, the greatest treasure of his nation. Marcinkevičius manages to create a poetic personality, original in its expression of the natural formulation of the duties of an artist. The work consists of seven chapters in which Donelaitis becomes a symbol of the struggle for the life of the tribe. The theme of the death of the nation becomes clearer within each chapter. The last chapter appears to synthesize a vision of Donelaitis and the people that resembles the traditional Lithuanian mythological creation story, in which the Lithuanian word gains the power of the sword.

In 1968 Marcinkevičius experienced a change in his attitude toward the world. He lost the illusions connected with the ideas of socialism; instead, he attempted to find new means of expressing an original poetic vision. In this same year he published *Liepsnojantis krūmas* (The Burning Bush), in which he formed a new model for his poetic language based on metaphors of nature and human beings. Indeed, *Liepsnojantis krūmas* expresses the essence of the second period of his creative work. It marked the beginning of his trajectory toward philosophical lyrics through his acute attention to existential problems. In this work the author achieved a new spiritual state, expressing himself as a bard of the common being of all people. During this period he also published his well-known dramas in verse, *Mindaugas* (1968) and *Katedra* (The Cathedral, 1971).

In 1972 *Ungnies poema* (Poem about the Fire) was published, while another epic, *Devyni broliai* (Nine Brothers), also appeared. This epic is somewhat different from his previous ones. The author attempts to depict the days of postwar resistance struggles, and Marcinkevičius reflects on the destiny of his generation and of his nation. He makes use of the image of nine brothers from traditional folktales, although there are no other allusions to particular fairy tales, and there is no traditional plot. Rather, the work is made up of several separate lyrical fragments, similar to the ballad form. Nonetheless, the ballad is not the basis of the work; the main element is a lyrical meditation in which fragmented images are connected through a shared experience rather than a plotline, and the center is not based on dramatic events but on reflection. In his reflections on the fate of the nation, Marcinkevičius invoked biblical images and grotesque intonations from the genre of laments.

In 1975 *Po aukšta aja žvaigžde* (Under the High Star) was published. The main elements of Marcinkevičius's poetic view during this period

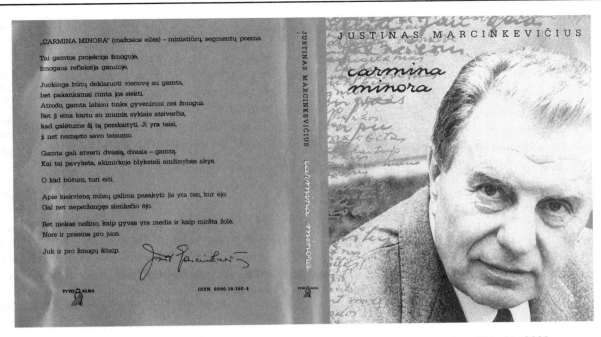

Dust jacket for Marcinkevičius's most recent book, Carmina minora *(Minor Songs), published in 2000*

were the details of the everyday life of peasants, which often carried symbolic value. Marcinkevičius suggests that the world is mythological in its essence. In 1996 one of Lithuania's prominent literary critics, Vytautas Kubilius, clearly defined the state of the poet as he attempted to change his inner world through the writing of original, mature verses: "Marcinkevičius is a poet of dramatic nature. When his inner contradictions, suppressed by utopian illusions, fight through to expression within his poems, a psychological process of acute breakage occurs, and this process is full of the existential uncertainty of the postwar generation."

The third period of Marcinkevičius's creative career is the decade between 1977 and 1988, during which he wrote several books of lyrics: *Gyvenimo švelnus prisiglaudimas* (Tender Touch of Life, 1978), *Būk ir palaimink* (Live and Bless, 1980), *Vienintelė žemė* (The Only Land, 1984), and *Už gyvus ir mirusius* (For the Living and the Dead, 1988). He also published his poetic drama *Mažvydas* (1977), his epic *Pažinimo medis* (The Tree of Knowledge, 1979), and his book of autobiographical essays *Dienoraštis be datų* (The Diary without the Dates, 1981). Marcinkevičius perceived this period as a time of new ideas and of new poetic projects free from any ideological perspectives. He was attempting to help his nation rise to new spiritual levels while focusing on traditional ideals and attitudes of his culture.

The new ethical background he was searching for found its center in goodness and love. In *Gyvenimo švelnus prisiglaudimas* Marcinkevičius searched for answers to the questions of his roles and duties in life. Biblical symbols, images, situations, and motifs of language and culture coalesce in the vision of the poet's native land. Marcinkevičius represents the homeland as the most important guide through which individuals define themselves as participants in national history, culture, and traditions. Indeed, Marcinkevičius wrote in *Tekančios upės vienybė:* "Sometimes people reproach me for using the word 'Lithuania' too often. I try to change this word into various synonyms (homeland, native land, motherland) and sometimes, especially in my lyrics, I try to manage with epithets (my kindest of all, my dearest one); nevertheless, I need to make myself stop . . . but rather often it seems to me that I cannot get enough of pronouncing this word, no matter how many times I repeat it."

In *Už gyvus ir mirusius* Marcinkevičius's poetic language is highly metaphorical, and object and subject merge within the poetic scene, a principle often used within traditional Lithuanian folklore. The poet attempts to be laconic since he is certain that laconic poetic language will make the poem perfect.

Pažinimo medis commemorates the four hundredth anniversary of Vilnius University. The genesis of this work was rather interesting: the anniversary celebrations included a competition for epic writings. Although Marcinkevičius did not take part in the competition, he was asked to write a scenario for a movie about the university; instead, he created the epic, in which the narrative focus is, in effect, the Lithuanian language. Marcinkevičius believes that history cannot be separated from the experience of human beings, from individual drama. Similarly, Marcinkevičius's trilogy of dramatic verse, *Mindaugas*, *Mažvydas*, and *Katedra*, creates a vision of the three main elements of the historical destiny of Lithuania: the formation of the state, the publication of the first Lithuanian book, and the cathedral of spiritual values. The romantic concepts within this trilogy suggest that the past never dies; rather it has its continuation in the present. Presented as an elegy of the rise and fall of the main institutions of the nation, which are interpreted as existing in eternal contradiction, the trilogy made the model of Lithuanian drama in verse more intellectual and more modern. In addition, it consolidated Marcinkevičius's authority and popularity, even though he had already gained a reputation as the spokesman of national values and propagator of national consciousness.

In 1993 Marcinkevičius published *Eilėraščiai iš dienoraščio* (Poems from the Diary). In this volume the poet proved once again that his work is an act of compassion and love. The word has no power; rather, it carries compassionate fragility. The culmination of images present a heightened emotional experience in which one's individual existence merges into the landscapes of the native country, into its historical destiny and culture. Thus, Marcinkevičius continues to pursue his perceived mission as an artist: to preserve and care for the life of the nation.

Although best known as a poet and dramatist, Marcinkevičius is also one of Lithuania's most productive translators. He translated the works of Adam Mickiewicz and the poetry of Sergej Jesenin, Aleksandr Pushkin, and Mikhail Lermontov, as well as the Estonian epic *Kalevipoeg* (as *Kalevo sūnus*, 1963) and the Finnish national epic *Kalevala* (1972), both titles taken from the main hero in Estonian epic. Marcinkevičius has been awarded several national and international prizes (such as the Herder Prize in Germany and Austria and the PEN Center Prize in Poland) and honorary titles. In 1972 he received the honorary title of National Poet of Soviet Lithuania, and in 1990 he was elected a member of the Lithuanian Academy of Sciences. Lithuanian readers believe in his vision, and this belief was supported most heartily in the days of Lithuanian national revival in 1988, when Lithuania started the process of separating from the Soviet Union. In 1988 Marcinkevičius opened the constitutive congress of the Lithuanian movement and was one of its most active members.

In 1994 Marcinkevičius published *Tekančios upės vienybė*, which includes various speeches, interviews with the press, and new essays. These texts reveal the depth of Marcinkevičius's personality and show the importance of his social activities for the spiritual revival of the nation. In Lankutis's history, Marcinkevičius defined the gift of writing as the ability to recognize that "everything is hidden in ourselves in suffering and love, heroism and cowardice, faithfulness and treason . . . all this is like some seeds, waiting for a time or a suitable climate to grow and turn green."

References:

Vitas Areška, *Lietuvių tarybinė lyrika* (Vilnius: Vaga, 1983), pp. 367–391;

Vilius Gužauskas, "Žodžio atmintis," *Pergalė*, 10 (1981): 139–149;

Dovydas Judelevičius, "Kai pareiga virsta jausmu," *Literatūra ir menas* (5 February 1977);

J. Knipovič, "Mindaugas," *Literatūra ir menas* (12 June 1975);

Vytautas Kubilius, "Lyrika-tylioji sesuo," *Pergalė*, 5 (1979): 121–127;

Kubilius, *XX amžiaus literatūra* (Vilnius: Alma Litera, 1996), pp. 533–538;

Jonas Lankutis, *Justino Marcinkevičiaus draminė trilogija* (Vilnius: Vaga, 1970);

Lankutis, ed., *Lietuvių literatūros istorija*, volume 2 (Vilnius: Vaga, 1982), pp. 361–384;

Lankutis, "Rimties ir susikaupimo programa," *Pergalė*, 5 (1982): 142–148;

Ričardas Pakalniškis, *Justinas Marcinkevičius* (Kaunas: Šviesa, 1984);

Pakalniškis, "Nuo poemos į dramą," *Literatūra ir menas* (1 February 1969);

Pakalniškis, *Poezija, asmenybė, laikas: Justino Marcinkevičiaus kūryba* (Vilnius: Vaga, 1969);

Algis Samulionis, "Kai dramaturgai kalba eilėmis," *Poezijos pavasaris* (1973): 162;

Rimvydas Šilbajoris, introduction to *Fire and Night. Five Baltic Plays*, edited by Alfreds Straumanis (Prospect Heights, Ill.: Waveland Press, 1986): 147–153;

Valentinas Sventickas, "Vaizdas ir kontekstas," *Pergalė*, 9 (1984): 133–144;

Aleksandras Žalys, "Šiuolaikinė žanro viršūnė," *Pergalė*, 12 (1987): 126–134.

Miklós Mészöly
(Miklós Molnár)
(19 January 1921 –   )

Péter Szirák
Lajos Kossuth University, Debrecen

BOOKS: *Vadvizek* (Pécs: Batsányi Társaság, 1948);
Hétalvó puttonyocska (Budapest: Ifjúsági, 1955);
Sötét jelek (Budapest: Magvető Könyvkiadó, 1957);
Fekete gólya (Budapest: Móra Könyvkiadó, 1960);
A hiú Cserép-királykisasszony (Budapest: Móra, 1964);
Az elvarázsolt tűzoltózenekar: Mesék Kicsiknek és nagyoknak (Budapest: Móra Könyvkiadó, 1965);
Mort d'un athlète: Roman, translated by Georges Kassai and Marcel Couralt (Paris: Éditions du Seuil, 1965); republished as *Az atléta halála* (Budapest: Magvető, 1966);
Jelentés öt egérről (Budapest: Magvető Könyvkiadó, 1967);
Csodacsupor, by Mészöly, György Bella, and Mária Foris (Budapest: Móa Könykiadó, 1968);
Saulus (Budapest: Magvető, 1968);
Pontos történetek, útközben (Budapest: Magvető Könyvkiadó, 1970);
Alakulások (Budapest: Szépirodalmi Könyvkiadó, 1975);
Film (Budapest: Magvető, 1976);
A pipiske és a fűszál (Budapest: Móra, 1977);
A tágasság iskolája (Budapest: Szépirodalmi Könyvkiadó, 1977);
Kerti hangverseny (Budapest: Móra, 1977);
Bunker; Az ablakmosó (Budapest: Magvető, 1979);
Szárnyas lovak (Budapest: Szépirodalmi Könyvkiadó, 1979);
Jelentés egy sosevolt cirkuszról és más mesék (Budapest: Móra, 1980);
Érintések (Budapest: Szépirodalmi Könyvkiadó, 1980);
Esti térkép. Kiemelések (Budapest: Szépirodalmi, 1981);
Megbocsátás (Budapest: Szépirodalmi Könyvkiadó, 1984); translated by Ferenc Takács as *Forgiveness*, in *A Hungarian Quartet: Four Contemporary Short Novels*, selected by Maria Korosy (Budapest: Corvina, 1991);

Miklós Mészöly

Merre a csillag jár (Budapest: Szépirodalmi Könyvkiadó, 1985);
Sutting ezredes tündöklése (Budapest: Szépirodalmi Könyvkiadó, 1987);
Volt egyszer egy Közép-Európa (Budapest: Magvető, 1989);
A pille magánya (Pécs: Jelenkor Irodalmi és Művészeti Kiadó, 1989);

Wimbledoni jácint (Budapest: Szépirodalmi Könyvkiadó, 1990);

A negyedik út: Esélyek és kockázatok az ezredvég küszöbén (Szombathely: Életünk Szerkesztőosége/Magyar Írók Szövetsége Nyugat-Magyarországi Csoportja, 1990);

Ballada az úrfiról és a mosónő lányáról: Végleges változatok a hagyatékból (Budapest: Szépirodalmi Könyvkiadó, 1991);

Az én Pannóniám (Szekszárd: Babits, 1991);

Elégia (Budapest: Helikon, 1991);

Bolond utazás: Történetek (Budapest: Századvég, 1992);

Lassan minden (Budapest: Századvég, 1994);

Otthon és világ (Bratislava: Kalligram, 1994);

Hamisregény: Változatok a szép reménytelenségre (Pécs: Jelenkor, 1995);

Idegen partokon: Elbeszélések (Pécs: Jelenkor, 1995);

Családáradás: Beszély (Bratislava: Kalligram, 1995);

Pannon töredék irodalmi forgatókönyv, by Mészöly, András Sólyom, and János Gulyás (Budapest: Odeon Art Video, 1997);

Az ember, akit megölt esszék (Budapest: Pont, 1998);

Mesék történetek–kicsiknek és nagyoknak, illustrated by Zsuzsa Szenes (Pécs: Jelenkor/Bratislava: Kalligram, 1998);

Érintések 1942–1992 (Pécs: Jelenkor/Bratislava: Kalligram, 2000).

Collection: *Az atléta halála; Saulus; Film* (Budapest: Magvető,1977).

Edition in English: *Once There Was a Central Europe: Selected Short Stories and Other Writings,* translated by Albert Tezla (Budapest: Corvina, 1997).

OTHER: László Karsai, ed., *Kirekesztők antiszemita írások, 1881–1992,* preface by Mészöly (Budapest: Aura, 1992);

Géza Csáth, *Egy elmebeteg nő naplója Csáth Géza elfeledett orvosi tanulmánya,* edited by Mihály Szajbély, preface by Mészöly (Budapest: Magvető, 1994);

Katalin Sebes, *Ha minden jól megy antológia,* preface by Mészöly (Budapest: Balassi Soros Alapítvány, 1994).

With a long and distinguished career, Miklós Mészöly is acknowledged as one of the most important figures of twentieth-century Hungarian literature. Known primarily as a short-story writer and novelist, Mészöly is also an accomplished essayist, dramatist, and poet. Among the few Hungarian writers during the postwar era to resist the aesthetics of socialist realism imposed by the political regime, Mészöly was instrumental in maintaining a standard of artistic integrity in Hungarian literature. His art effectively links Hungarian short fiction as modernized in the first decades of the twentieth century, mainly through the work of Dezső Kosztolányi, with the postmodernist short fiction that became prevalent in the last decades of the twentieth century. Mészöly was not only a forerunner of but also an active participant in the literary trends of the 1980s and 1990s. He has exerted a significant influence on the prose works of the younger generation that includes Péter Nádas, Péter Esterházy, Ádám Bodor, and Lajos Grendel, and his novels and short stories have been translated into English, French, German, Danish, Czech, Slovak, Polish, Estonian, Finnish, Spanish, and Italian.

Born Miklós Molnár on 19 January 1921 to Sándor Molnár, a dike protection engineer, and Jolán Szászy in Szekszárd, the seat of Tolna County by the Danube, in the eastern corner of the "Pannon region" often described in his works, Mészöly later took his paternal grandmother's maiden name as his pen name. Mészöly's ancestry reflects a broad spectrum of Eastern European history. The paternal, Protestant line of the family derives partly from the southern region of pre-1920 Hungary (now Vojvodina, the northern territory of Yugoslavia) whereas the maternal line comes from Transylvania (now part of Romania). He received his early education in Szekszárd at the primary school of the Sisters of Mercy, where he immersed himself in his studies. In addition to the writers of Hungarian classical literature, his favorite authors included Fyodor Dostoevsky, Emile Zola, and, later, Nikolai Gogol and Anton Chekhov. His piano teacher was Márta Ziegler, the first wife of world-famous composer Béla Bartók. From 1938 to 1942 he studied law at Péter Pázmány University in Budapest, and when he graduated summa cum laude, his professors urged him to remain at the university as a faculty member. Although he refused this offer, his university years had a major impact on his way of thinking, and he has several times confessed that his economical style and disciplined approach to writing are primarily due to his studies in law. Later, when in financial need, he wrote works in the field of legal philosophy as a freelance writer. After graduation he wanted to study at the Sorbonne in France, but World War II changed his plans. Following the German invasion of the Soviet Union in 1941, the Hungarian government reluctantly entered the war on the side of the Axis, hoping that by sending a token force in sup-

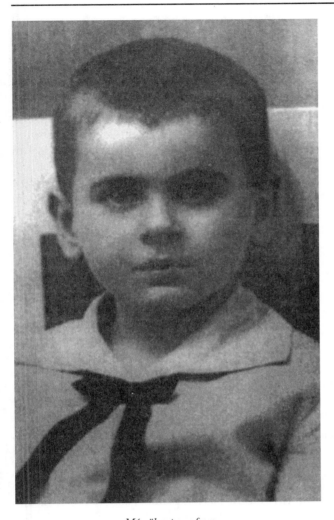

Mészöly at age four

port of the German offensive, Hungary could avoid further entanglement in the war.

In 1942 Mészöly became apprenticed to an attorney in Szekszárd, and in the following year he published his first short story "Bridzs és nyúl" (Bridge and Rabbit) in the Pécs journal *Sorsunk* under the name of Miklós Molnár. The government, eager to extract Hungary from the war, had begun secretly negotiating surrender terms with the Allies. Learning of these negotiations, the Germans sent military forces to occupy Hungary in March of 1944, seizing all military assets and impressing Hungarians into the German military. Mészöly lived with his parents until the spring of 1944 when—after the German occupation—he was conscripted into the army. After a short period of military training, he was ordered to northern Germany where he fought against the Soviet forces. After surviving a large-scale tank attack, he and

five of his comrades-in-arms deserted and wandered around Germany with forged documents as the Third Reich edged closer to final collapse. In early 1945 Mészöly returned to Hungary, where he was detained by the authorities and court-martialed. Later, he was captured by Russian and Bulgarian troops and taken to Bor in Serbia. After several attempts, he finally managed to escape and returned home to a Hungary devastated by war. As a retaliation for the devastation that the Germans had wreaked, the Swabians (ethnic Germans) living in his hometown were relocated and replaced by homeless ethnic Hungarians displaced from communities beyond the border. Working as an inspector of mills and commissioner of Soviet compensation deliveries, Mészöly became an eyewitness to the struggle of provincial Hungary to recover from the horrors of war. In 1947 he launched a political-literary weekly in Szekszárd in which he published several sketches and short stories. At the time of the Communist takeover in the spring of 1949, he "voluntarily" stopped publishing the democratic weekly and escaped from arrest to Budapest.

His first collection of short stories, *Vadvizek* (Marshy Tracts), appeared in 1948, and in that same year Mészöly married psychologist and writer Alaine Polcz, who is an author of both important psychiatric studies and literary works. In the late 1940s Mészöly worked as a proofreader and freelance writer doing hackwork under a variety of pseudonyms. During the repressive dictatorship of Mátyás Rákosi he was only allowed to publish fairy tales and other writing intended for children. Mészöly became involved with a Budapest puppet theater, writing plays as a means to defy the authorities. He also made the first of his trips to Transylvania, which formed the basis of his book titled *Pontos történetek, útközben* (Punctual Stories, On the Way), published in 1970. In the early 1950s Mészöly was named a playwright at the State Puppet Theater but was summarily dismissed for what the authorities called anticommunist behavior. As a result, he was again forced to do pseudonymous hackwork in order to survive.

Politically involved with the reform Communists opposing Rákosi's dictatorship, Mészöly did not take part in the armed resistance in the uprising of October and November 1956 but had a role in the Writers' Union movement and in formulating the declaration of the writers' revolutionary demands. Consequently, the publication of his second collection of short stories, *Sötét jelek* (Dark Omens), was delayed until 1957, one year after the suppression of the revolution and nine years after the appearance of his first book. Further complicating his situation, however, the so-called review published in the official Communist Party newspaper was essentially a political denunciation, and Mészöly was once again denied an active role in Hungarian literary life. When the French author Albert Camus offered a substantial amount of money to support endangered Hungarian writers, the list of writers who benefited included Mészöly, who was provided with food parcels for several months and with books and journals for a period of years. As a result of his role in the revolution and his definite rejection of any compromise, he had to fear arrest even as late as 1958. He was under surveillance, followed in the streets, and his phone was tapped. To escape from police harassment, he moved to a small village in southern Hungary, where he lived for one and a half years. Although in 1960 he was allowed to publish *Fekete gólya* (Blackball), a juvenile novel, in the early and mid 1960s several of his books were banned. In addition, he was forced into silence for periods and seriously limited in his travels, compelling him to reject invitations from abroad. In 1963, because of publishing Mészöly's absurdist drama *Az ablakmosó* (The Window-Cleaner), the chief editor of the Pécs journal *Jelenkor* (Period) was replaced and the production of the play in Miskolc was banned.

Despite the imposed limitations that severely restricted the publication of his work, Mészöly, nonetheless, developed as a masterful short-story writer of immense talent and creativity, as evinced in the stories collected in *Vadvizek* and *Sötét jelek*. Written in the 1940s and early 1950s, the stories are characterized by a clear description of situations, disciplined structure, and the ability to represent psychological motivation, relating crucial moments in people's lives during and after the war with a dramatic atmosphere and in an objective and nondidactic manner that contrasted with the expected schematism of Social Realism. From the beginning, mainstream literary critics in Hungary looked upon Mészöly's activity with suspicion on political grounds, and his refusal to meet the requirements of the prevailing monolithic political and literary system made it impossible for his works to receive an unbiased critical assessment.

In 1965 Mészöly traveled to Western Europe for the first time and became reacquainted with members of the Hungarian literary community who had gone into exile following the failed 1956 revolution. In Paris he met Endre Karátson and Pál Albert, the authors of the émigré publication *Magyar Műhely*, as well as Ferenc Fejtő, labeled a "dangerous

enemy" by the Communist authorities, and while in London he came into contact with leading figures of the Szepsi Csombor Literary Society, notably Zoltán Szabó, Győző Határ, László Cs. Szabó, and István Siklós. While in Paris, Mészöly signed a contract with Éditions du Seuil to publish his novel *Az atléta halála* (The Death of an Athlete), which had been banned in Hungary prior to publication. The work appeared in French in that same year as *Mort d'un athlète: Roman*. As a result, after his return to Hungary, Mészöly experienced renewed harassment by the authorities and was prevented from attending the premiere of his play in Augsburg. Nonetheless, the Hungarian publication of *Az atléta halála* appeared in 1966, followed in the next year by a collection of short stories titled *Jelentés öt egérről* (Report on Five Mice).

Both *Az atléta halála* and *Jelentés öt egérről* reflect Mészöly's ability to link the social and political conditions of contemporary existence with the dimensions of existential life experience, while simultaneously rejecting the prevailing ideology of socialist realism. *Az atléta halála* is a biographical account—told by his widow—of a celebrated athlete, Bálint Őze, a free-spirited and independent-minded distance runner who has died under mysterious circumstances. Representing the ideal of unreachable human integrity and interdependence, Őze is portrayed as a singular man forced to confront the reality that social and political repression make true freedom impossible. The thematic concerns of *Az atléta halála* are further explored in the stories of *Jelentés öt egérről*, especially in the title story, written in 1958, in which Mészöly reports on the fate of a mouse family escaping from the cold of winter through a hole into a pantry. The couple living in the flat discover the "parasites" fleeing from the basement to their pantry and systematically exterminate them.

In 1967 Mészöly was selected for the prestigious Kossuth Prize but refused the award in protest of what he considered an attempt by the government to use the award to manipulate him. He became further outspoken in his political opposition following the Soviet invasion of Czechoslovakia in 1968 that brutally repressed the burgeoning reform movement. That same year Mészöly published the introspective novel *Saulus*, in which the title character, the first-century Saul of Tarsus, who became St. Paul the Apostle, plays several roles, including those of persecutor and persecuted. Reflecting the condition of present-day society, the standstill image of the "road to Damascus" at the end of the novel suggests the open interpretation of personal history rather than the certainty of conversion. Multifaceted and open to differing interpretations, the novel was highly influential in the development of postmodern Hungarian literature.

In the late 1960s Mészöly formed a close friendship and working relationship with Ervin Szederkényi, then chief editor of *Jelenkor*, whom he supported and provided with advice to preserve the independent spirit of the journal. He persuaded new authors, such as Nádas and Esterházy, to write for *Jelenkor* rather than the more politically controlled and manipulated journals of the capital. During this same period he also frequently visited the city of Novi Sad (called Újvidék in Hungarian), a partly ethnic Hungarian cultural center of Vojvodina, Yugoslavia, and established contact with the editors of *Híd* (Bridge), the Hungarian-language journal of the region, and with the young and avant-garde writers around *Új Symposion*. Then in 1969, together with Nádas, Miklós Fogarassy, and Béla Horgas, Mészöly attempted to launch a literary journal called *Eszmélet* but was denied permission to do so by the authorities.

Beginning in the early 1970s Mészöly simultaneously developed two techniques in his writing: an objective form of narration reducing the role of the narrator, as exemplified by *Pontos történetek, útközben* (1970), and a fragmented organization of the text, as can be seen in the 1973 story "Térkép Aliscáról" (A Map of Alisca) and "Alakulások" (Transformations), both collected in *Alakulások* (1975). *Pontos történetek, útközben*, based on Mészöly's memories of his travels in Transylvania, with a narrative form that focuses on landscape description and de-emphasizes conventional narrative techniques, constitutes an important innovation in Hungarian fiction writing. This innovation can be seen as even more important if one considers that while Mészöly's early works, influenced by the writings of Camus and Samuel Beckett, tend to describe human existence with a high level of symbolism and abstraction, in *Pontos történetek, útközben* there is an attempt to suppress the methods of abstraction. The technique of depersonalizing the narrator creates the illusion of the absence of a narrator, suggesting that things can be read without commentary.

Published in 1976, *Film* allows for more complex nonfigurative methods of this kind of reading technique. The novel is about the last day in the life of an elderly man. Landscape description connects it to *Pontos történetek, útközben*, whereas the reflected camera-eye technique gives a different meaning to the "poetics of punctuality." While in the earlier work the narrator is part of the story but does not advance the plot, in the later work the metafictional techniques of the narrator become an organizing principle. This interdependence between the actual story and how the story is narrated demands a reading technique that is aware of the uncertainty of textual meaning.

According to critic Beáta Thomka, the author of a 1995 monograph on Mészöly, the accelerated change in Mészöly's fiction took place after the appearance in 1968 of *Saulus*. The most important feature of this new trend is its nonlinear form. According to other critical opinions, the decisive change was signaled by *Alakulások*, since in this work Mészöly's fiction seems to cross the literary boundaries from modernism to postmodernism in Hungarian prose writing. In the short stories in this collection Mészöly combines an essentially modernist perspective with postmodernist self-referentiality and self-questioning. In such stories as "Térkép Aliscáról," "Alakulások," "Nyomozás" (Investigation), and "Fakó foszlányok nagy esők évadján" (Pale Shreds during Rainy Seasons), the reader encounters a postmodernist form of writing that implicitly criticizes modernist principles of intention and unity; yet, in each of these stories Mészöly seems intent on creating a unified modernist vision from postmodern, nonlinear fragments. The nonlinear discourse evident in these texts is also an organizing principle in Mészöly's later works. Parallel with this use of nonlinear structure, however, Mészöly, even if skeptically, has continued to search for conventional storylike frameworks that interpret human existence. Examples of this combination can be seen in *Szárnyas lovak* (Winged Horses, 1979), *Megbocsátás* (1984; translated as *Forgiveness*, 1991), *Sutting ezredes tündöklése* (The Glory of Colonel Sutting, 1987), *Wimbledoni jácint* (Hyacinth of Wimbledon, 1990), and *Ballada az úrfiról és a mosónő lányáról: Végleges változatok a hagyatékból* (Ballad of the Young Master and the Washerwoman's Daughter, 1991). In addition, through his brief short stories—that is, by rewriting the Hungarian tradition of fragmentation—Mészöly has become one of the originators of a specific genre of postmodernist Hungarian short fiction, as typified by "Falusi terepismertetés" (A Review of A Village Ground), "Riportok" (Interviews), "Kiemelések" (Emphases), and "Negyvenhat videoklip" (Forty-Six Video Clips).

Mészöly broke new ground by incorporating older texts within his own work. For instance, the intertextual source of "Fakó foszlányok nagy esők évadján" is István Wesselényi's early-eighteenth-century diary titled *Sanyarú világ* (Miserable World). Mészöly deconstructs the formal order of the antecedent text by replacing the continuity of the original with a discontinuous structure, and the fragments of the original text are imbued with new meanings imparted by the twentieth-century context.

Mészöly has used his own work as intertexts. Passages within stories are linked by self-citations, and segments are used and reused. The variable repetition of some passages in "Anno," one of the short stories in the 1979 collection, *Szárnyas lovak*, allows the reader to read the work within the context of the works preceding it. This kind of repetition was often used by Mészöly throughout the 1970s and 1980s. His *Volt egyszer egy Közép-Európa* (Once Upon a Time There Was Central Europe, 1989) includes previously published texts maintaining its limits, at least formally, but *Hamisregény: Változatok a szép reménytelenségre* (False Novel, 1995) creates a special textual universe by totally dissolving formal limits.

"Térkép Aliscáról," "Anno," and "Pannon töredék" (Pannonian Fragment) demonstrate the relativity of history through their mingling of historical periods. In the first story Mészöly rewrites the preconceived form of the travelogue by unifying narrative time and giving prominence to the spatial aspect. The temporal and narrative layers in "Anno" are similar to the epic world of "Pannon töredék," in which—despite its timescale that covers several centuries—the constant interruptions in the narrative seem to argue that history should be interpreted as a series of accidents rather than the realization of certain rules. One of the most typical aspects of Mészöly's later narratives is also one of the most postmodern—the seeming denial of any possibility of differentiating between history and fiction.

In another group of his works Mészöly tries to reinterpret the connection between autobiography and fiction, as evidenced in "Térkép repedésekkel" (A Map with Cracks)," "Nyomozás 1–4" (Investigation), "Lesiklás" (Downhill), "Magyar novella" (A Hungarian Short Story), and "A kitelepítő osztagnál" (In the Relocating Squad). As early as the 1950s and 1960s Mészöly wrote memorable first-person narratives evoking the themes of the war and postwar period (which have been constantly present in his works), notably in "Képek egy utazás történetéből" (Pictures from the Story of a Journey), "Agyagos utak" (Clayey Roads), "A stiglic" (The Goldfinch), "A három burgonyabogár" (The Three Colorado Beetles), and "Film, az Emkénél" (Film, at the Emke). In the 1970s and 1980s Mészöly turned this type of evocative first-person narrative into a form

Mészöly with his wife, the psychologist and writer Alaine Polcz, in 1959

in which he addresses issues of verisimilitude and temporality. These later stories may be generally characterized by the neutralization of the principle of purpose, the distortion of causal and chronological relations, and the deconstruction of narrative structure as applied later by Esterházy and Garaczi. Naturally, all these aims are realized in different ways and to different degrees in the various individual works. By breaking off continuity, "Magyar novella," and "Lesiklás" primarily create a sense of aimlessness, "Térkép repedésekkel" builds up "parallel worlds" beside one another while "Nyomozás 1–4" makes narrative knowledge insecure by treating memory and imagination as relativistic.

In the novella *Sutting ezredes tündöklése*, both the protagonist, Colonel Sutting, and the narrator are in hiding. The voice of the chronicler is interrupted by insertions and passages from Colonel Sutting's speech. The minute details provided by the colonel are relativized by the narrator, who always refers to the secret meanings behind the visible things. His knowledge, however, is diffuse and insecure, and he views the world in terms of uncertain outlines and mosaics, "not knowing" the beginning and end of the story. As in *Saulus* and other works, the topos of the journey is realized in terms of being on the road forever and waiting forever. First published in that same year, the title story of *Bolond utazás: Történetek* (Crazy Journey: Stories, 1992) is one of Mészöly's typical works in which there is a "shifting" interplay between "deconstructed" narrative structures and individual readings.

The collection *Ballada az úrfiról és a mosónő lányáról* is one of the most complex creations in Mészöly's fiction. The narrator keeps the elements of the crime story in the background, and the ballad techniques used—omission, dramatic character, obscurity—deprive the reader of the antecedents of the crisis and the background of Baracs, the central character. Presented in this way, however, the traditional romantic story of the protagonist and the gypsy girl gains a mythic perspective and special emphasis in the narrator's hierarchy of values. The meeting of the two characters is framed by the special chronicling-informing tone of the narrator and a narrative structure that also includes landscape descriptions, historical digressions, as well as anticipatory and metafictional passages. The symbolism and allegorical nature of the work is realized through several layers in terms of the reader's experience of narrative indeterminancy. Inasmuch as the work challenges the validity of traditional literary principles of unity, analogy, and identity by evoking and destroying preconditioned expectations, it is typical of postmodernist literature of the 1980s and 1990s, notably in the stories of suffering or crime and parables of individual and collective freedom.

In "Pannon töredék," as in *Sutting ezredes tündöklése, Volt egyszer egy Közép-Európa* (1989), and *Az én Pannóniám* (My Pannonia, 1991), the regionalism or the awareness of regional identity allows for multiple interpretations. In Mészöly's writing, Pannonia, historically the area east of the Adriatic Sea and west of the Carpathian Mountains that was conquered by the Romans in the first century B.C., is the mythicized setting of things happening in the world, a symbolic space-time with a frequently emphasized connection to the nineteenth century. He preserves late modernist literary discourse and its more or less homogeneous nature but looks at the possibility of identifying meanings with doubts: "only to give space to the imagination and magic of facts. We are so vulgarly dumb but not careless," Mészöly writes in *Családáradás: Beszély* (Family Flow, 1995).

In the early 1970s Mészöly began living in Kisoroszi, north of Budapest on the Danube, where he devoted himself to his work in almost total isolation. His retirement was interrupted by his journey to London and Paris in 1971 and by a one-year grant in West Berlin in 1973–1974. He was one of those few Hungarian writers who, taking a great personal risk, signed Charter 77, the declaration by Czechoslovakian intellectuals protesting against the failure of their government to adhere to the principles of intellectual freedom and human rights to which it had purportedly agreed in signing the Helsinki Accord. Also in 1977, three of his novels, *Az atléta halála, Saulus,* and *Film,* were collected in one volume as part of the gold-cover series of fiction of the previous thirty years published jointly by Szépirodalmi and Magvető Presses. *Film,* first published the previous year, generated a serious and undeserved ideological attack on Mészöly by cultural politicians. By the 1980s, however, Mészöly had become a widely recognized, canonized, and celebrated author of Hungarian literature as well as a symbolic figure of intellectuals consistently adhering to their independence. In addition to accepting several foreign invitations and giving public readings abroad—in the United States, Poland, Germany, the Netherlands, France, Austria, and elsewhere—he became more and more active in the struggle against the János Kádár regime. In 1984 he became a member of the Committee on Doing Justice to History, whose purpose was to rehabilitate the reputations of the political martyrs of 1956. In 1985 he was elected president of the League Against Conscription, and in 1989 that of the Hungarian Helsinki Committee; the Hungarian Democratic Charter, established in the same year, elected him as spokesman. From the 1980s on, his writing has been consistently honored: in 1986 he was awarded the Déry Tibor Prize, in 1988 the Örley Prize, and in 1990—on the eve of the democratic change of power—he received the Kossuth Prize. In 1991 he was elected president of the Széchenyi Academy of Arts.

Throughout his career Mészöly has remained an uncompromising and innovative literary practitioner possessed with an understanding of the purpose of art and the role of the writer in society. A forerunner of postmodernist fiction, Mészöly experimented with a variety of narrative forms and techniques to produce a body of writing of singular importance in maintaining the vitality and integrity of postwar literary activity. In many ways the moral conscience of his generation, Miklós Mészöly is acknowledged both as a master craftsman and one of the most influential figures in contemporary Hungarian literature.

Interviews:

Alexa Károly, "Alexa Károly beszélgetése Mészöly Miklóssal," *Jelenkor* (1981): 1;

Sándor Mészáros, "Nincs rés, nincsutolsó ablak?" *Alföld*, 9 (1996): 46–56.

Bibliography:

László Jeney, ed., *Mészöly Miklós irodalmi munkássága* (Miskolc: II. Rákóczi Ferenc Megyei Könyvtár, 1989).

Biography:

Beáta Thomka, *Mészöly Miklós* (Bratislava: Kalligram, 1995).

References:

Pál Albert, "A búntudat évszaka," *Új Látóhatár* (Munich), 1968: 6;

Albert, "Egy (mifelénk) korszakos regényről," *Új Látóhatár* (Munich), 1975: 6;

Károly Alexa and László Szörényi, eds., *"Tagjai vagyunk egymásnak." A Tarzuszi szavaival köszöntik a hetvenéves Mészöly Miklóst barátai* (Budapest: Szépirodalmi, 1991);

Péter Balassa, "Passió és állathecc. Mészöly Miklós filmjéről és művészetéről; A cselekmény rejtélye mint anekdotikus forma," in his *Észjárások és formák* (Budapest: Tankönyvkiadó, 1985), pp. 37–127;

Miklós Béládi, "A tények parabolája; Az elbeszélő illetékessége; Az epika megtisztítása és felvezetése," in his *Válaszutak* (Budapest: Szépirodalmi, 1983), pp. 288–323;

Béládi, "Jelentés egy íróról: Elbeszélés vagy 'szöveg,'" in his *Érintkezési pontok* (Budapest, 1974);

Imre Bori, "Írók a 'pálya szélén,'" *Híd* (Novi Sad), 1967);

Bori, *"Jelentés öt egérről." Huszonöt tanulmány a huszadik századi megyar irodalomról* (Novi Sad, 1984);

Miklós Csúrös, "A tágasság pátosza. Az esszéíró Mészöly Miklós," in his *Színképelemzés* (Budapest, 1984);

Csúrös, "The Pathos of Spaciousness: On the Essayist Miklós Mészöly," *Acta Litteraria Academiae Scientiarum*, 28 (1986): 365–372;

Miklós Fogarassy, "A lappangó történetek közös természete. [Volt egyszer egy Közép-Európa]," *Jelenkor*, 1 (1990): 86–91;

Ernő Kulcsár Szabó, "Mészöly Miklós," in his *A magyar irodalom története 1945–1991* (Budapest: Argumentum, 1993), pp. 102–105;

Sándor Mészáros, "Tabló és töredék. (Mészöly Miklós újabb prózájáról.) Keresztury," in *Szövegkijáratok*, by Tibor Keresztury and Mészáros (Budapest: Széphalom Kvműhely, 1992), pp. 103–111;

Béla Pomogáts, "Mészöly Miklós parabolai," *Kritika*, 6 (1968): 51–56;

Sándor Radnóti, "Az elmaradt apoteózis. Mészöly Miklós Saulusáról," in his *Recrudescunt vulnera* (Budapest, 1991), pp. 129–134;

Mihály Szegedy-Maszák, "A múlás elpusztíthatatlansága," *Kortárs*, 4 (1986): 145–150;

Péter Szirák, "Nincs pont, csak folytatás," in his *Az Úr nem tud szaxofonozni* (Budapest: JAK Balassi, 1995), pp. 43–69;

László Szörényi, "Saját halál, saját élet," *Jelenkor*, 16 (1973): 644–645;

Beáta Thomka, ed., *Tanulmányok. Mészöly Miklós művészete* (Novi Sad: A Magyar Nyelv, Irodalom és Hungarológiai Kutatások Intézete, 1986);

Gábor Tolcsvai Nagy, "Állat, ember, szolidaritás. Mészöly Miklós állatmotívumairól," *Pannonhalmi Szemle* (1994).

Sławomir Mrożek

(29 June 1930 –   )

Halina Stephan
University of Florida

This entry originally appeared in Concise Dictionary of World Literary Biography:
South Slavic and Eastern European Writers.

BOOKS: *Opowiadania z Trzmielowej Góry* (Warsaw: Czytelnik, 1953);

Półpancerze praktyczne. Opowiadania satyryczne (Kraków: Wydawnictwo Literackie, 1953);

Maleńkie lato (Kraków: Wydawnictwo Literackie, 1956);

Polska w obrazach (Kraków: Wydawnictwo Artystyczno-Graficzne, 1957);

Słoń. Opowiadania (Kraków: Wydawnictwo Literackie, 1957); translated by Konrad Syrop as *The Elephant* (London: Macdonald, 1962; New York: Grove, 1963);

Wesele w Atomicach. Opowiadania (Kraków: Wydawnictwo Literackie, 1959);

Postępowiec. Organ Sławomira Mrożka (Warsaw: Iskry, 1960);

Ucieczka na południe. Powieść satyryczna (Warsaw: Iskry, 1961);

Deszcz. Satyry (Kraków: Wydawnictwo Literackie, 1962);

Utwory sceniczne (Kraków: Wydawnictwo Literackie, 1963)—comprises *Policja, Męczeństwo Piotra Oheya, Indyk, Na pełnym morzu, Karol, Striptease, Zabawa,* and *Kynolog w rozterce;*

Opowiadania (Kraków: Wydawnictwo Literackie, 1964; enlarged edition, Kraków: Wydawnictwo Literackie, 1974);

Przez okulary Sławomira Mrożka. Żarty rysunkowe (Warsaw: Iskry, 1968);

Dwa listy i inne opowiadania (Paris: Instytut Literacki, 1970)—comprises *Moniza Clavier, Ona, We młynie, we młynie mój dobry panie, Nocleg,* and *Ci, co mnie niosą;*

Vatzlav: A Play in 77 Scenes, translated by Ralph Manheim (New York: Grove, 1970; London: Cape, 1972); Polish version published in *Vatzlav. Ambasador* (Paris: Instytut Literacki, 1982);

Sławomir Mrożek (photograph by Simone Oppliger)

Ambasador, translated by Mrożek and Manheim as *The Ambassador* (New York: Institute for Contemporary Eastern European Drama and Theatre, 1984);

Utwory sceniczne (Kraków: Wydawnictwo Literackie, 1973)—comprises *Czarowna noc, Śmierć porucznika, Tango, Testarium, Drugie danie, Woda,* and *Dom na granicy;*

Dwa listy (Kraków: Wydawnictwo Literackie, 1974);

Utwory sceniczne nowe (Kraków: Wydawnictwo Literackie, 1975)—comprises *Rzeźnia, Emigranci,* and *Wyspa Róż;*

Wybór dramatów i opowiadań (Kraków: Wydawnictwo Literackie, 1975);

Amor (Kraków: Wydawnictwo Literackie, 1979)—comprises *Amor, Krawiec, Garbus, Polowanie na lisa, Serenada, Lis filozof,* and *Lis aspirant;*

Opowiadania (Kraków: Wydawnictwo Literackie, 1981);

Małe listy (Kraków: Wydawnictwo Literackie, 1982);

Rysunki (Warsaw: Iskry, 1982);

Donosy (London: Puls, 1983);

Pieszo (Warsaw: Czytelnik, 1983);

Alfa (Paris: Instytut Literacki, 1984);

Miłość na Krymie. Komedia tragiczna w trzech aktach (Warsaw: Noir sur Blanc, 1994);

Dziennik powrotu (Warsaw: Noir sur Blanc, 2000).

Editions and Collections: *Moniza Clavier* (Kraków: Wydawnictwo Literackie, 1983);

Tango, Woda (Kraków: Wydawnictwo Literackie, 1984);

Wybór dramatów (Kraków: Wydawnictwo Literackie, 1987);

Wybór opowiadań (Kraków: Wydawnictwo Literackie, 1987);

Rysunki (Kraków: Oficyna Literacka, 1990);

Dramaty (Kraków: Oficyna Literacka, 1990);

Małe prozy, edited by Tadeusz Nyczek (Kraków: Oficyna Literacka, 1990);

Maleńkie lato (Poznań: SAWW, 1993);

Słoń (Warsaw: Noir sur Blanc, 1994);

Wesele w Atomicach (Warsaw: Noir sur Blanc, 1994);

Dzieła zebrane, 9 volumes (Warsaw: Noir sur Blanc, 1994–1998);

Rysunki zebrane, 2 volumes (Gdańsk: Wydawnictwo Slowo/Obraz Terytoria, 1997–1998)—comprises volume 1, *Od służby do "Postępowca";* volume 2, *Polska w obrazach i inne polskie cykle.*

Editions in English: *At Sea,* translated by Ewa Markowska, *East Europe,* 10 (October 1961): 27–35;

Striptease, translated by I. A. Langnos and Robert O'Brien, *Odyssey Review,* 3 (June 1963): 53–72;

Striptease, translated by Edward Rothert, *Polish Perspectives,* no. 10 (1965);

Home on the Border, translated by Rothert, *Polish Perspectives,* nos. 8–9 (1967);

Six Plays, translated by Nicholas Bethell (London: Cape, 1967; New York: Grove, 1967)—comprises *The Police, The Martyrdom of Peter Ohey, Out at Sea, Charlie, The Party,* and *Enchanted Night;*

Tango, translated by Bethell and adapted by Tom Stoppard (London: Cape, 1968);

Tango: A Play in Three Acts, translated by Ralph Manheim and Teresa Dzieduszycka (New York: Grove, 1968);

The Ugupu Bird, translated by Konrad Syrop (London: Macdonald, 1968);

Striptease, Repeat Performance, and The Prophets: Three Plays, translated by Lola Gruenthal, Dzieduszycka, and Manheim (New York: Grove, 1972);

"Taking a Fall," *Polish Perspectives,* 12 (1973): 24–31;

"He Who Falls," *Poland,* 5 (1974): 34–35;

"Letters by the Way," *Polish Perspectives,* 3 (1975): 35–39;

"The Tailor," *Polish Perspectives,* 5 (1978): 49–57;

"Three Stories," *Polish Perspectives,* 2 (1979): 49–60;

Striptease, Tango, Vatzlav: Three Plays (New York: Grove, 1981);

The Emigrants, translated by Henry Beissel (New York: S. French, 1984).

PLAY PRODUCTIONS: *Profesor,* Gdańsk: Teatr Studencki Bim-Bom, 16 March 1956;

Policja, Warsaw: Teatr Dramatyczny, 27 June 1958;

Męczeństwo Piotra Oheya, Kraków: Teatr Groteska, 20 December 1959;

Na pełnym morzu, Lublin: Teatr im. Osterwy, 1 June 1961;

Indyk, Kraków: Stary Teatr, 25 July 1961;

Karol, Sopot: Teatr Wybrzeże, 31 December 1961;

Striptease, Sopot: Teatr Wybrzeże, December 1961;

Zabawa and *Czarowna noc,* Wrocław: Teatr Polski, 30 March 1963;

Kynolog w rozterce, Wrocław: Teatr Kameralny, 30 March 1963;

Śmierć porucznika, Kraków: Teatr Kameralny, 24 October 1963;

Tango, Belgrad: Jugoslovenske Dramsko Pozorište, 21 April 1965;

Racket-baby, Darmstadt, June 1965;

Jeleń, Berlin: Vagantenbühne, 9 October 1965;

Poczwórka, Sopot: Teatr Wybrzeże, 8 February 1968;

Testarium, Düsseldorf: Schauspielhaus, 28 September 1968;

Drugie danie, Düsseldorf: Schauspielhaus, 28 September 1968;

Vatzlav, Zürich: Theater am Neumarkt, 11 February 1970;

Mrożek, age thirteen, in Kraków during the Nazi occupation
(Archiwum Sławomira Mrożka)

Szczęśliwe wydarzenie, Düsseldorf: Schauspielhaus, 30 October 1971;

Emigranci, Paris: Petit Théâtre d'Orsay, 24 October 1974;

Rzeźnia, Warsaw: Teatr Dramatyczny, 21 March 1975;

Garbus, Łódź: Teatr Nowy, 14 December 1975;

Serenada, Zabrze: Teatr Nowy, 11 December 1977;

Lis filozof, Zabrze: Teatr Nowy, 11 December 1977;

Polowanie na lisa, Zabrze: Teatr Nowy, 11 December 1977;

Lis aspirant, Zabrze: Teatr Nowy, 11 December 1977;

Krawiec, Warsaw: Teatr Współczesny, 23 February 1979;

Pieszo, Kraków: Wyższa Szkoła Dramatyczna, 8 December 1980;

Ambasador, Warsaw: Teatr Polski, 22 October 1981;

Letni dzień, Stockholm: Kungl. Dramatiska Teatern, 17 March 1984;

Alfa, New York: La Mama Theater, 16 October 1984;

Kontrakt, Warsaw: Teatr Polski, 15 March 1986;

Portret, Warsaw: Teatr Polski, 14 November 1987;

Wdowy, Warsaw: Teatr Współczesny, 30 December 1992;

Miłość na Krymie, Kraków: Stary Teatr, 25 March 1994.

PRODUCED SCRIPTS: *Wyspa Róż,* television, Deutsches Fernsehen (ARD), 13 April 1976;

Amor, also directed by Mrożek, television, Deutsches Fernsehen (ARD), 22 March 1978;

Powrót, also directed by Mrożek, television, Deutsches Fernsehen (ARD), 19 March 1980.

Sławomir Mrożek is perhaps the best-known and the most widely performed contemporary Polish dramatist. His work is also often staged in Western European theaters. Mrożek's early dramas written in Poland dealt with the socialist experience in the manner of the Theater of the Absurd. They appealed to such a wide audience that the phrases "straight from Mrożek" or "Mrożek himself could not invent that" were colloquially used to describe real-life situations. His later work, written during the thirty years he spent abroad, is more universal in orientation and ranges from commentaries on the experience of exile and contrasting studies of Western and Eastern European mentalities to attempts to analyze the human factor in the historical process. Since his return to Poland in 1996, he has continued his career there as a leading dramatist, widely read feuilletonist, and author of popular satirical drawings.

Born on 29 June 1930 to a postmaster family with a peasant background, Mrożek spent his earliest years in the village of Borzęcin, in southern Poland, and in Kraków—that is, in the part of the country that until 1917 belonged to the Austro-Hungarian empire. His adolescence was overshadowed by the turmoil of World War II, the German occupation, and the subsequent devastation of his country. He went to a village grammar school but could not continue his education, because schooling in Poland under German occupation was restricted to the elementary level. After the war he entered the prominent Nowodworski gymnasium in Kraków and eventually began studying architecture. Mrożek's mother, Zofia (née Kędzior), to whom he was quite close, died when he was nineteen. In those years his relationship with his father, Antoni Mrożek, was distant. Left for the most part alone, conscious of his provincial background and of the volatility of the postwar situation, he soon abandoned his studies and found employment as a journalist, satirist, and cartoonist.

Like many of his generation, Mrożek emerged from the war searching for order and stability, for optimism and a way to rebuild his belief in reason. He found his initial identity in the new socialist ideology. His work as a journalist gave him a purpose and a sense of personal importance. Admittedly, his journalistic activities were limited by the purview of the Kraków newspapers, but from 1950 to 1954 Mrożek conscientiously performed the tasks of a committed reporter and satirist, occasionally also producing cartoons. As early as 1951 he was accepted into the prestigious Writers' Union. His first satirical collections, *Opowiadania z Trzmielowej Góry* (Tales from Bumble Bee Hill) and *Półpancerze praktyczne* (Practical Armor Plates), appeared in book form in 1953. But the relaxation of political controls in Polish cultural life that followed the death of Joseph Stalin in 1953 affected Mrożek's perspective. He gradually freed himself from the communist ideology, began to develop his own personal point of view in feuilletons written for *Dziennik Polski* (Polish Daily), familiarized himself with the elements of Western art and literature that had been banned under socialist realism, and increasingly practiced his skills as satirist and cartoonist. When in 1956 he began to serialize his cartoons in the popular magazine *Przekrój* (Crosscut), the recognition he received as a journalist and cartoonist presaged his later popularity as a writer.

From 1955 to 1957 Mrożek wrote theatrical reviews for a local paper, indirectly preparing himself for his dramatic debut in 1958 with the play *Policja* (translated as *The Police*, 1967). In 1956 he went to the Soviet Union as a tourist and traveled in the south. The following year he published *Słoń* (translated as *The Elephant*, 1962), his first volume of short stories, which established him as an original new satirist confronting the stereotypes of socialist realism and popular myths of Polish culture. His stories constituted a reductio ad absurdum of the principles and consequences of the socialist realist mentality and echoed a widespread longing for the prewar world, which by contrast appeared to be the epitome of humanist values and a form of behavior that respected one's dignity. This anchoring in domestic memories, and the ability to write in a style that echoed the thinking patterns of his contemporaries, made Mrożek a much-liked literary figure.

The staging of Mrożek's comedy *Policja* in 1958 was a signal that the confining aesthetics of socialist realism, superimposed but never internalized in Poland, could be finally discarded. In *Policja* Mrożek created an allegorical satire that brought together the traditions of the political cabaret and the strict logic of the Western European theater of Friedrich Dürrenmatt, Max Frisch, and Harold Pinter, popular in Poland in the late 1950s. This play is based on the premise that the state police has managed to wipe out all crime and to convert all opponents of the totalitarian system into joyfully obedient citizens. To prevent the disbanding of the police, which has achieved its ultimate aim, one of the policemen agrees to be incarcerated for the sake of keeping the police system going. Once in prison, however, the former loyalist reassesses his loyalty and develops into a true opponent of the system. His cry for freedom closes the play as the need for the existence of the police has once again been reconfirmed. Predictably, the play experienced difficulties with censorship in Poland, but immediately enjoyed great popularity in Western Europe.

In 1959 Mrożek married Maria Obremba, a painter whom he met during his Russian trip, and moved from Kraków to Warsaw. The move put him close to the central cultural administration and made him ponder his status as a subversive satirist enjoying the generous support of the socialist cultural establishment. That same year he traveled to Paris and spent two months in Boston as a participant in a program run by Harvard University.

His subsequent plays, *Męczeństwo Piotra Oheya* (1959; translated as *The Martyrdom of Peter Ohey*, 1967), *Na pełnym morzu* (1961; translated as *At Sea*, 1961), *Karol* (1961; translated as *Charlie*, 1967), and *Striptease* (1961; translated as *Striptease*, 1963) develop the theme of a victim manipulated by crude force and use the technique of absurd rationalizing that he had already developed in *Policja*. *Męczeństwo Piotra Oheya* is a farcical story about a father and obedient citizen who is suddenly told that a mysterious tiger has settled in his bathroom. The play presents a gradual invasion of representatives from various institutions who intrude on the hero's life in order to utilize the tiger for their own purposes. In effect, Peter Ohey is finally destroyed as he becomes a victim of "higher causes" for which he has to give up his normal existence. Like *Policja*, the play deals with the complex of martyrdom, the submissive reaction of an individual to the pressures that society, and especially its ruling establishment, impose on him.

Na pełnym morzu presents three shipwreck survivors who run out of food and use the democratic process to select the weakest among them to be eaten by the other two. Similarly, in *Karol* the hero begins as an innocent victim of senseless brutality only to end up as an oppressor, an ideologist of

Scene from the premiere of Mrożek's play Męczeństwo Piotra Oheya *at the Teatr Groteska in Kraków in 1959 (photograph by Juliusz Wolski)*

oppression, and an active participant in a hunt for an innocent victim. Finally, in *Striptease* the system of oppression becomes perfectly mechanized. Two nameless bureaucrats are made to submit to the power of an absurd hand that imprisons them. The play analyzes psychological reactions in the face of coercion, exploring the complex philosophical formulas with which the victims attempt to rationalize their confinement.

Related to the same theme of invisible oppression is the two-act play *Zabawa* (1963; translated as *The Party*, 1967). Here three village boys are obsessed by the idea that somewhere there exists true enjoyment, but somehow they have been left out of it. They find themselves in a cultural limbo, where neither the peasant nor the former aristocratic standards are in operation. Written in the simplest possible idiom, the play revolves around a hopeless quest for fun that becomes transformed into a sad and ineffectual search for the authenticity of existence.

Despite his great popularity in Poland, Mrożek felt confined and unhappy within the sys-

tem of centrally controlled culture. In 1963, under the pretext of a short vacation in Italy, he and his wife left the country. His stay eventually extended into some thirty-three years of expatriate existence. When he left for Italy, he intended to escape from the literary formulae he developed in Poland, from the temptation to continue the same kind of writing that enjoyed great popularity among his home audience. Departure also meant breaking away from the dependence on the all-controlling political and administrative structures that had given him support and recognition but had also watched over his activities—breaking away from the "intellectual and moral demoralization," as he called it in his letters.

The "grotesque" period of his writings, originally inspired by the socialist realist experience, culminated in the tragicomedy *Tango* (1965; translated as *Tango*, 1968), published shortly after he left Poland. *Tango* appeals not only to the Polish audience but—through the framework of a family conflict—is equally effective and meaningful abroad, under altogether different cultural circumstances. The play reflects the Western experience of the decline of tradition, the demise of the upper classes, and the rise of self-centered individualism, as well as the Eastern European experience of the complete destruction of former social structures brought about by the war and postwar political change. *Tango* brought Mrożek international recognition and remains his most frequently performed play.

The self-imposed exile in Italy gave Mrożek an opportunity to reinvent himself as a writer, free of administrative pressures and the demands imposed by the public accustomed to his image of a witty debunker of false cultural consciousness. Indeed, once he found himself abroad, he quickly abandoned his former poetics, which was based on sharing a common subtext with his audience, and began to practice a new kind of drama. The freedom of moving outside the immediate literary and political context gave him a chance to explore a new identity, no longer anchored in the particularities of Polish experience. He tentatively experimented with new forms and new themes ranging from art to emigration, wrote a radio play and movie scenarios, and directed movies.

While abroad, Mrożek chose not to identify with any particular national culture. He and his wife lived first in Chiavari, on the Italian Riviera, and decided in 1968 to move to Paris. That same year, he felt compelled to break off his ties to Poland. Following the invasion of Czechoslovakia by the Warsaw Pact troops, he published a protest letter in the Western press against the participation of Polish troops and was promptly recalled to Poland. He refused to return and applied for political asylum in France. In consequence, Mrożek's plays were removed from the stage in Poland, and a ban on their performance lasted until 1973.

In 1969 Mrożek's wife died of cancer in West Berlin. After her death Mrożek resided primarily in Paris, but traveled extensively and lived for short periods in the United States and in Germany. He remained stateless until 1978 when he received French citizenship. Yet, despite his constant travels, the locations in which he has lived throughout his life do not find their reflection in his writings, nor have the cultural circles in which he moved particularly affected his concept of literature. He has remained a private person, whose public image is restricted to a purely professional role. He valued the isolation offered by his expatriate status and claimed that "emigration is not only an existential condition, but can also be a human disposition. One can be condemned to emigration, but one can also value it and, more or less subconsciously, seek it

out as one kind of antilife." His insistence on maintaining his essentially "homeless" state as one best suited to his identity represented yet another way in which Mrożek attempted to escape entrapment by culture, tradition, and politics.

The first longer drama inspired by his expatriate experience was *Vatzlav* (performed in 1970 and published in 1982; translated as *Vatzlav*, 1970), first staged in Switzerland because Mrożek's work could no longer be performed in Poland. It is an allegorical tale reminiscent of an eighteenth-century moral fable, in which a shipwreck survivor named Vatzlav seeks wealth and fame in the new world. He fails in the pursuit because the new world proves just as imperfect as the one he left behind. With this play Mrożek's work, once regarded as belonging to the theater of the absurd, turns out to be a protest against destroying the traditional order of the world, and he appears as a classical rationalist thrown into an epoch of surrealism, barbarism, and mass destruction. *Vatzlav* is to a certain extent a result of Mrożek's experience in the West; it addresses a general, nonnational audience and deals with themes outside the specific cultural/political context of Eastern Europe.

With his next play, *Emigranci* (1974; translated as *The Emigrants*, 1984), however, Mrożek returned to a theme that is typically Polish. The play has an almost classical simplicity: two characters, who find themselves in a foreign city, face each other, with the outside world practically nonexistent. One of them is a confused and aimless intellectual in search of freedom of self-expression. The other is a worker, a simple man who earns money in order to impress everyone in the village back home. Their dialogue is funny, occasionally intense, as they torment each other with something akin to a Dostoyevskian fury. Commentators have noted that *Emigranci* is Mrożek's first optimistic play, as its characters are no longer threatened by anonymous forces but are shown as the creators of their own fate.

Mrożek's next play, *Rzeźnia* (The Slaughterhouse, 1975), marks his further departure from satire. The theme of the play is art and its function in the twentieth century. *Rzeźnia* is directed against modern art, which destroys all conventions. Mrożek believes that art has been arbitrarily endowed with supreme value, but is in fact incapable of carrying the load of goodness and beauty assigned to it. As a result, the modern world tends to reject art and culture, seeking the ultimate truth in the last absolute of death.

Jerzy Bińczycki and Jerzy Stuhr in a scene from a 1976 production of Mrożek's two-character play Emigranci *at the Kameralny Theater in Kraków (photograph by Wojciech Plewiński)*

In 1978, fifteen years after his departure, Mrożek finally visited Poland and was reinstated as a member of the Polish Writers' Union. Around this time he also worked for a German television studio, where he wrote and directed three movies. In 1980 and 1981 a four-volume edition of his collected works was published in Germany. He visited Poland again in 1981 and was confronted by martial law imposed by the communist government in an attempt to suppress the Solidarity movement. Some of his plays were banned from theaters, and he refused to publish in Poland.

With *Pieszo* (On Foot, 1980), Mrożek returned to a Polish theme. The time of action is the end of World War II; the location is a provincial railway station in Poland. The drama depicts an assorted group of characters displaced by the war, who come together at the station in the hope of getting away and finding a semblance of normal life, which has been irrevocably destroyed by the historical cataclysm. Although not frequently performed, *Pieszo* is considered by critics to be among Mrożek's best plays.

Although Mrożek largely separated himself from his home country, the political struggle in Poland surrounding the rise of the Solidarity movement provoked him to turn to political themes. In 1981 a new play, *Ambasador* (published in 1982; translated as *The Ambassador*, 1984) contrasted two people: a Western ambassador somewhere in Eastern Europe or Russia, and an asylum seeker, a simple worker and a native of the guest country. The relatively brief and simple plot gives much space to philosophical exchanges. The ambassador is faced with the moral problem of protecting or refusing to protect the applicant. The two characters confront each other in a study of cultural differences between the European East and West. The play retains the schematic structure of Mrożek's earlier work, but unlike those plays, it functions as a moral parable.

In 1984 Mrożek wrote a play for Dramaten, a Stockholm theater group with which he frequently collaborated. *Letni dzień* (A Summer's Day, 1984) is based on a simple structure reminiscent of the Theater of the Absurd. It demonstrates two different schemes of perceiving oneself and the world, together with the behavioral patterns that correspond to these perceptions. The message confirms the old truism that a person's view of himself generates his reality and that there is no escape either from failure or from success. *Letni dzień* offers a parable in the style of early Mrożek, although the author no longer sees his characters as victims of cultural patterns manipulated by outside forces, but shows them just as destructively entrapped in their own psychological schemes.

Mrożek's plays were widely staged, and he attended premieres in various countries. In a Mexico City theater that performed his *Emigranci*, Mrożek met Susana Osorio Rosas, a Mexican theater director. They were married in 1987 and lived initially in Paris. Two years later Mrożek decided to move from Paris to Mexico, feeling that Europe had become less interesting to him. While in Mexico, he devoted himself entirely to the life of a recluse on an exotic hacienda. For the next several years he lived on the Rancho La Epifania near the village Tlahuapan, somewhere in the mountains between Mexico City and Puebla.

Despite his efforts to distance himself from the past, the experience of the early 1950s remained a haunting presence in Mrożek's writings. He addressed this period in his autobiographical stories and confronted it on stage in *Portret* (Portrait, 1987), in which he focused on the psychological and moral torments inherited from the Stalinist experience. The protagonists of this play represent Mrożek's own generation born around 1930, one that had the opportunity and the enthusiasm to embrace the socialist utopia offered to them in the late 1940s. The play shows the symbiotic relationship of two middle-aged men connected by their Stalinist past: one as the proponent, the other as the opponent of the system. What Mrożek presents in this work is the heritage of totalitarianism, consisting of pettiness, a provincialism of thoughts and feelings, and a destruction of self-worth in both male and female personalities. As he sees it, entrapment by Stalinist ideology degraded both the supporters and the opponents of the system.

In 1990, on the occasion of Mrożek's sixtieth birthday, his home city of Kraków organized an impressive two-week-long Mrożek Festival. The event included a retrospective of his work staged by Polish and foreign theaters. For the first time Mrożek's appearance in Poland was not confined by a political framework, and his image, which suffered from the disjointed reception caused by political restrictions, could finally be reestablished in its continuity. The festival reconfirmed the great popularity that Mrożek enjoyed in Poland as well as the broad dimensions of his international reception.

Back in Mexico, five years after the political soul-searching performed in *Portret*, Mrożek again changed his dramatic register and wrote a two-act play, *Wdowy* (The Widows), first performed in 1992, in which he returned to the style of the theater of the absurd. The play can be best described as a black comedy in which two women and two men try to avoid a confrontation with death, which is personified as a mysterious, silent, black-clad woman. The theme of death appeared as a reflection of Mrożek's own traumatic experience with a sudden life-threatening illness that he suffered in Mexico and from which he eventually recovered.

Miłość na Krymie (Love in the Crimea, 1994), also written on his Mexican ranch, won a French award for the best play of the year. It presents a panorama of Russian history by focusing on three stages: tsarist Russia (1910), Soviet Russia (1928), and contemporary post-Soviet Russia (circa 1990). The elements unifying these three radically different stages of Russian identity are the Crimean setting of the play—a maritime landscape of permanence and splendor—and the theme of unfulfilled love, which ultimately leads the play into a metaphysical dimension. Despite the apparent historicity of *Miłość na Krymie*, Mrożek does not write about historical Russia but builds, from literary and popular stereotypes, a mythical Russia, whose center is in the spectacular sea and mountain scenery of the semiarid Crimea, and the main concern is not political oppression and suffering but unfulfilled, unabashedly romantic love.

In all those years, Mrożek maintained a steady presence in Western theaters. Beyond the theater, after a relative lull in the reception of his prose in the 1980s, his visibility considerably increased with the appearance of new collected works in both German and French. In 1994 his collected works finally began to appear in Polish. Most significantly, however, Mrożek made an unexpected decision to return to Poland. In 1996 he and his wife settled in Kraków, where he continues working on his dramas and publishing feuilletons and satirical drawings in local papers. In this way he has returned in a circular fashion to the initial point of his literary career.

Letters:
"Listy Sławomira Mrożka do Jana Błońskiego," *NaGłos*, 2 (1991): 153–197.

Interviews:
"'Nie uważam się za pisarza. Po prostu piszę.' Rozmowa ze Sławomirem Mrożkiem," *NaGłos*, 3 (1991): 135–152;

"Mam to, co chciałem: Rozmowa ze Sławomirem Mrożkiem," *Tygodnik Powszechny,* 41 (1993): 1, 7;

"Ja się szybko nudzę: Ze Sławomirem Mrożkiem rozmawia Gabriela Łęcka," *Polityka* (9 October 1993): 23;

Józef Opalski, "Kraków to Uniwersum . . . ," *Teatr,* 11 (1993):17–18;

"Słowo oskarżonego. Rozmowa ze Sławomirem Mrożkiem," *Nowe Książki,* 6 (1994), 1–3;

"Goście Starego Teatru. Spotkanie dziewiąte. Ze Sławomirem Mrożkiem rozmawia Jerzy Jarocki," *Teatr,* 4 (1994): 4–8;

Opalski, "O Miłości na Krymie," *Teatr,* 4 (1994): 9–11;

Opalski, "Konwersacja? Ja się nie nadaję . . . ," *Rzeczpospolita,* 297 (1995);

Opalski, "Na wysokości trzech tysięcy metrów," *Dialog,* 5–6 (1996):169–174.

Bibliographies:

"Sławomir Mrożek," in *Słownik współczesnych pisarzy polskich,* Series II, edited by Jadwiga Czachowska and others (Warsaw: PIW, 1978), volume 2, pp. 122–138;

Szczepan Gąssowski, "Sławomir Mrożek," in his *Współcześni dramatopisarze polscy 1945–1975* (Warsaw: Wydawnictwa Artystyczne i Filmowe, 1979), pp. 242–261;

Utwory Sławomira Mrożka na scenach polskich i zagranicznych, edited by Anna Stafiej (Kraków: Mrożek Festival, 1990).

References:

Jan Błoński, *Wszystkie sztuki Sławomira Mrożka* (Kraków: Wydawnictwo Literackie, 1995);

Maciej Broński (Wojciech Skalmowski), "O twórczości Sławomira Mrożka," *Kultura* (Paris), 9 (1971): 17–37;

Edward J. Czerwinski, "Jester in Search of an Absolute," *Canadian Slavic Studies,* 4 (1969): 629–645;

Drama at Calgary, special "Mrożek and the Polish Absurd" issue, edited by Philip McCoy and others, 3 (1969);

Krystyna Dziewańska and Agata Kubik, *Catalogue of the Exhibit Mrożek!* (Kraków: Muzeum Starego Teatru, 1990);

Daniel Gerould, "Mrożek Revisited," in *Slavic Drama: The Question of Innovation. Proceedings,* edited by Andrew Donskov and Richard Sokoloski (Ottawa: Department of Modern Languages and Literatures, 1991), pp. 27–40;

Marketa Goetz-Stankiewicz, "The Moulding of a Polish Playwright," in *The Tradition of Polish Ideals: Essays in History and Literature,* edited by W. J. Stankiewicz (London: Orbis Books, 1981), pp. 204–225;

Goetz-Stankiewicz, "Sławomir Mrożek: Two Forms of the Absurd," *Contemporary Literature,* 12 (1971): 189–203;

Regina Grol-Prokopczyk, "Sławomir Mrożek's Theatre of the Absurd," *Polish Review,* 3 (1979): 45–46;

Józef Kelera, "A Concise Guide to Mrożek," *Theatre in Poland,* 3 (1990): 8–11;

Kelera, "Mrożek–Dowcip wyobraźni logicznej," in his *Kpiarze i moraliści. Szkice o nowej dramaturgii* (Kraków: Wydawnictwo Literackie, 1966), pp. 86–114;

Jan Klossowicz, *Mrożek,* translated by Christina Cenkalska (Warsaw: Authors Agency/Czytelnik, 1980);

Wolfgang Kroeplin, *Das Groteske. Eine Gestaltungsweise im Drama und Theater. Studien zu Majakowski, Bulgakow, Örkeny, Mrożek,* Material zum Theater 150, Reihe Schauspiel 41 (Berlin: Verband der Theaterschaffenden der DDR, 1981);

Ewa Widota Nyczek and Józef Opalski, eds., *Mrożek i Mrożek. Materiały z sesji naukowej zorganizowanej przez Zakład Teatru Instytutu Filologii Polskiej Uniwersytetu Jagiellońskiego 18–20 czerwca 1990 roku* (Kraków: Mrożek Festival, 1994);

Tadeusz Nyczek, "Obrona tradycji," in his *Emigranci* (London: Aneks, 1988), pp. 70–85;

Alek Pohl, *Zurück zur Form. Strukturanalysen zu Sławomir Mrożek* (Berlin: Henssel, 1972);

Jürgen Serke, "Sławomir Mrożek: Dichter des Weltuntergangs," in his *Das neue Exil. Die verbannten Dichter* (Frankfurt: Fischer, 1985), pp. 224–237;

Anna Stafiej, ed., *Mrożek Festival* (Kraków: Mrożek Festival, 1990);

Halina Stephan, *Mrożek* (Kraków: Wydawnictwo Literackie, 1996);

Stephan, *Transcending the Absurd: Drama and Prose of Sławomir Mrożek* (Amsterdam: Rodopi, 1997);

Małgorzata Sugiera, *Dramaturgia Sławomira Mrożka* (Kraków: Universitas, 1996);

Krzysztof Wolicki, "W poszukiwaniu miary. Twórczość dramatopisarska Sławomira Mrożka," *Pamiętnik teatralny,* 1 (1975): 3–37;

Jacek Żakowski, *Co dalej Panie Mrożek?* (Warsaw: Iskry, 1996).

Kostas Ostrauskas

(5 April 1926 –)

Violeta Kelertas
University of Illinois at Chicago

BOOKS: *Kanarėlė* (Chicago: Lietuvių studentų santara, 1958);

Žaliojoj lankelėj (Chicago: Santara-Šviesa, 1963)—comprises *Pypkė* and *Žaliojoj lankelėj;*

Kvartetas (Chicago: Algimanto Mackaus knygų leidimo fondas, 1971)—comprises *Gyveno kartą senelis ir senelė, Duobkasiai, Kvartetas,* and *Metai;*

Čičinskas (Chicago: Algimanto Mackaus knygų leidimo fondas, 1977)—comprises *Šaltkalvis, Lozorius,* and *Čičinskas;*

Gundymai (Chicago: Algimanto Mackaus knygų leidimo fondas, 1983);

Eloiza ir Abelardas (Chicago: Algimanto Mackaus knygų leidimo fondas, 1988);

Ars amoris: Historiae sacrae et profanae (Chicago: Algimanto Mackaus knygų leidimo fondas, 1991);

Ketvirtoji siena (Chicago: Algimanto Mackaus knygų leidimo fondas, 1996);

Kaliausės mirtis (Vilnius: Lietuvos rašytojų sąjunga, 1996);

Žodžiai ir žmonės: Straipsniai, atsiminimai, laiškai (Vilnius: Vaga, 1997);

Gyveno kartą senelis ir senelė: Triptikas (Chicago: Algimanto Mackaus knygų leidimo fondas, 2000).

Editions in English: *The Pipe,* translated by Rimvydas Šilbajoris, *Arena,* 15 (1963): 78–97;

The Gravediggers, translated by Šilbajoris, *Lituanus,* 4 (1967): 41–67;

Lazarus, translated by Vilius Lukas Dundzila, *Lituanus,* 2 (1986): 14–23;

The Quartet, translated by Violeta Kelertas, *Lituanus,* 4 (1992): 53–81.

PLAY PRODUCTIONS: *Kanarėlė,* Chicago, Lietuvių teatras Atžalynas, 1956;

Pypkė, Sodus, Michigan, Santara-Šviesa, 1961;

Žaliojoj lankelėj, Chicago, Lietuvių teatras Atžalynas, 1964;

Gyveno kartą senelis ir senelė, Chicago, Lietuvių teatras Atžalynas, 1964;

Duobkasiai, Chicago, Lietuvių teatras Atžalynas, 1966;

Lozorius, Sodus, Michigan, Santara-Šviesa, 1971;

Metai, Chicago, Jaunimo teatras, 1972;

Čičinskas, Sydney, Australia, Atžala, 1980;

Lozorius (in English), Chicago, University of Illinois at Chicago, 1983;

Lozorius, Klaipėda, Klaipėdos dramos teatras, 1990;

Šaltkalvis, Chicago, Vaidilutė, 1990;

Eloiza ir Abelardas, Vilnius, Lietuvos televizija, 1990;

Čičinskas, Šiauliai, Šiaulių dramos teatras, 1995;

Vaižgantas, Vilnius, Jaunimo teatras, 1995;

Duobkasiai, Vilnius, Lietuvos televizija, 1996;

Cantra naturem, Kalingrad, Russia, Deutsches Theater Kalingrad, 1998.

OTHER: Antanas Škėma, *Raštai,* volumes 1–2, edited by Ostrauskas and others (Chicago: Santara-Šviesa, 1967–1970);

Julius Kaupas, *Raštai,* edited by Ostrauskas and Alfonsas Nyka-Niliūnas (Chicago: Algimanto Mackaus knygų leidimo fondas, 1997).

One of the major émigré Lithuanian writers of the twentieth century, playwright Kostas Ostrauskas stands out from the rest of the exile writers for his unsentimental attitude toward the fate that befell his nation during World War II and several occupations by the Soviets and the Nazis and for his ability to rise above these inherently dramatic events. With the exception of some historical rewriting and re-creation, usually about centuries other than the twentieth, he has opted to make his thematic concerns more universal problems such as anxiety, fear, boredom, injustice, cruelty, aging, love, and death. Praised as a writer of international importance, he is nonetheless almost unknown outside his own language group. He can be classed as part of a small body of avant-garde Lithuanian writers of all genres for his experiments with language and form, his tendency to abstractionism, his black humor, and

Kostas Ostrauskas in 1997 (courtesy of the author)

his uses of the grotesque and paradox. Coming close to theater of the absurd in his early years, he has progressed to postmodernist invention and economy of language, sometimes bordering on total use of intertext and quotation almost to the exclusion of any "original" text.

Ostrauskas demonstrates a postmodern distrust of words to convey meaning, allowing the context to produce innovation. Sometimes context and texture are suggested through the incorporation of classical music citation or the inclusion of paintings (by Hieronymus Bosch, James Abbott McNeill Whistler, or Edouard Manet) to illustrate the text. These kinds of extensions flesh out the minimalism of the writing. Although almost all his major plays—with the exception of what he calls his "microdramas," as brief as one to four pages—have been staged at least once, his works so far have been mainly read as literary texts, because there has been no professional Lithuanian theater in the West and because his works, for all their universality, were anathema to the Soviet regime they sometimes satirize. Superficially humorous and even farcical, his plays can be

too abstract and serious to mean much to the lay reader and present difficulties of comprehension and accessibility to directors in Lithuania. When they have attempted his plays, directors have confined themselves to the realistic surface structure that may bring out the absurdity of the situations involved but leaves the deeper, more meaningful layers unrecognized.

Kostas (in some early publications, Konstantinas) Ostrauskas was born on 5 April 1926 in Veiveriai, in the county of Marijampolė, Lithuania. He is the only child of Ona Urbaitytė and Kostas (Konstantinas) Ostrauskas, an organist and choir director who made his living in Veiveriai and Vilkaviškis before moving to the then capital of Lithuania, Kaunas. Around 1930 the family settled in the working-class district of Šančiai. There Ostrauskas attended a local high school. School was not difficult for the young Ostrauskas, and he had plenty of time for soccer and reading. He especially favored the *Lithuanian Encyclopedia,* which was just starting publication then, and he read it much like one reads a novel. He recalls with special nostalgia swimming in the Nemunas River and spending summers at an aunt's home in the country at Veiveriai.

Eventually, he discontinued his schooling to join the Young Peoples Theater in Kaunas in 1943. However, this infatuation did not last long; having a good baritone voice, he began to devote more time and effort to a singing career. Ostrauskas escaped from Lithuania in 1944 because both his mother and he were slated to be deported to Siberia in the second wave of deportations when the Soviets returned. Like many political refugees of the period, he ended up in Germany. While still in Lithuania during one of those Veiveriai summers in 1943 he wrote his first piece of dramatic art, of which he will only say facetiously that it was "quite dramatic." The rest of his unpublished juvenilia includes another play written while he was a student at the Lithuanian High School in Lübeck, Germany (from which he graduated in 1946), and some early and unimpressive poems, a few of which actually did appear in print in some of the émigré magazines being published by then in Germany.

In Germany, Ostrauskas studied singing more seriously and began solo concerts, wishing above all to have an operatic career. He matured into a Lieder singer (a singer of German genre art songs), but eventually the enthusiasm for singing left him. He enrolled at the Baltic University in Hamburg, later in nearby Pinneberg, and was engaged in Lithuanian literary studies from 1946 to 1949. Baltic University was a hastily organized joint postwar effort, making use of the many professors from Baltic universities who had ended up in Germany and decided to use their talents and knowledge to educate their young people. There Ostrauskas met his future wife, Danutė Valaitytė, who was then studying medicine. In 1948 he directed and staged a reading of Vincas Krėvė-Mickevičius's *Šarūnas* (1911) and Balys Sruoga's *Baisioji naktis* (Night of Terror, 1935), two Lithuanian classics. But familiarity with the classics did not lead to imitation in Ostrauskas's case— the kind of drama that he eventually wrote was untraditional and innovative, a complete departure from his predecessors.

Ostrauskas came to the United States in 1949 with the second wave of postwar Lithuanian immigrants. While living briefly in Brooklyn, New York, he married Danutė in 1950. In that same year he started graduate studies at the University of Pennsylvania in the Baltic and Slavic department, majoring in Lithuanian literature. In 1952 Ostrauskas received his M.A. degree and in 1958 his Ph.D. with a dissertation on the letters of the famous Lithuanian writer Jonas Biliūnas (1879–1907) to Jurgis

Šaulys, a journalist, political comrade-in-arms, and later a diplomat who was studying in Switzerland at the time. Ostrauskas annotated and edited these letters, held in the University of Pennsylvania Library, while uncovering new manuscript material regarding Biliūnas's life and works. Ostrauskas had started working at the University of Pennsylvania Library in 1952 and continued working there in several capacities until his retirement in 1989. From 1958 to 1978 he was director of its Music Library, where he put his knowledge of music and composers to daily use. In 1955 the couple's only son, Darius, was born. Danutė returned to graduate school and earned her M.A. degree in clinical psychology from Temple University in 1963 and her Ph.D. in clinical and developmental psychology from Bryn Mawr College in 1974. While Ostrauskas was getting established in his career at the Music Library, Danutė continued to work in the field of clinical psychology, from which she retired in 1995.

Ostrauskas was not free to dedicate himself to his writing seriously until after graduate school. His first book, *Kanarėlė* (The Canary), was published in 1958. Generally speaking, two tendencies are apparent throughout the playwright's canon: he either subverts tradition from within or from without. *Kanarėlė* is an example of the former, as it is a seemingly traditional play in many respects. It has characters who are named, psychologically individualized, and motivated; their speech is adapted to their social status and worldview. The theme can be described as the desire for beauty (symbolized by the canary who sings beautifully) among the lowliest of creatures despite the deceit and falsity of their surroundings, which fail to satisfy this human need for aesthetics and goodness. All the characters are rustics, the beggars that drifted around the prewar Lithuanian countryside. Although the play swings between poignancy and awe, comedy and tragedy, there is no romanticization of the rustics, and no platitudes are presented. But it is clear that the author is on the side of the impoverished, the kind and the good, the ones forsaken by man and fate. Through his vision of their essential humanity, regardless of their low calling in life, he manages to raise them to sublimity and makes the reader feel pity and fear.

Written in 1951, Ostrauskas's first play, *Pypkė* (translated as *The Pipe*, 1963), was not published until 1958 in *Literatūros lankai* (Literary Folios) and was included in *Žaliojoj lankelėj* (The Green Meadow) in 1963. It is illustrative of the second concurrent direction in his writing, the attempt to free himself of tradition, and in many ways it anticipates

Ostrauskas in 1963 (courtesy of the author)

interchangeability of laughter and tears, and the presence of death, which mocks all human endeavor.

The title piece in *Žaliojoj lankelėj* is an unusually American play in many ways. "The Green Meadow" refers to a sentimental Lithuanian song, but in the play it is the name of a bar owned by a Lithuanian émigré. The space of the play is set off between the neon sign of the Green Meadow bar, reminiscent of home, and the sign for another dive across the streetcar tracks that flashes "Sam the Crabman" and "Live it up," which is how the Lithuanian émigrés arriving in the United States perceived this society. Setting up a series of paradigmatic oppositions of life and death, Ostrauskas first uses the bar, where a deadly game between the barkeeper and the Man without a Home is played out. Inside this main frame is a sideshow of two shady chessmen also playing a game of life and death, and several poems written by a frequenter of the bar, the Poet, who first describes in traditional rhyme the quintessential fate of the émigré "whose fate not even a dog will mourn." At the end of the drama, drunk, the Poet can only sing surreally and absurdly. Traditional poetry, like traditional drama, does not fit life in America, and old songs in a new setting no longer hold the same meaning.

The play as published is a bilingual edition of sorts—the text includes insertions where the characters speak English. The English text is interesting not only because it shows Ostrauskas's ear for American slang but also because it illustrates how many more slang terms and phrases associated with death (such as "kick the bucket") the English language provides compared to Lithuanian. Writing in two languages at once results in a broken Lithuanian indicative of the mentality of the characters. The barkeeper and the Man without a Home have both left wives and children behind in the old country, except that the Man without a Home treats this situation as tragic, while the barkeeper pretends not to be affected by it. When the barkeeper accidentally pushes the Man without a Home into the path of a streetcar, the Poet remarks, "It is yourself that you have killed," pointing out the parallelism implicit in their fates. Ostrauskas differs from most émigré Lithuanian writers because he rarely treats the nostalgic theme of loss of the homeland that preoccupied the majority of his contemporaries, and when he does, he frames it in a universal setting. *Žaliojoj lankelėj* displays another pattern that can be found in Ostrauskas's writing—confrontation between the strong (the barkeeper) and the weak (the Man without a Home, the Poet). Though his sympathies obvi-

his postmodernist leanings. Even though it shows evidence of a young author still not quite sure of his craft, its theme and form are mature and original in Lithuanian drama. The plot is really a set of reminiscences about buying the pipe from an antique dealer and confronting death, personified by an actress representing the Pipe. There are several features that mark the experimental style of the piece: the temporal line is broken because the play starts by flashing back from the afterlife of the main characters; there are two human characters, the nameless A and Z; the Pipe (feminine in Lithuanian) also has a speaking part; intertextuality is used (liberal quotes from the Bible, a certain vague similarity to Ilya Ilf and Evgenii Petrov's famous 1928 Soviet Russian satire *Twelve Chairs*); and the spectator and the author are referred to openly, thus making a mockery of any attempts to interpret the play as realism. The main targets again are human greed, the haphazard twists and turns in any individual's life, the

ously lie with the latter, as in real life, the strong are the ones who win.

Kvartetas (The Quartet, 1971) consists of four rather short plays: *Gyveno kartą senelis ir senelė* (Once Upon a Time There Lived an Old Man and an Old Woman), *Duobkasiai* (translated as *The Gravediggers,* 1967), *Kvartetas* (translated as *The Quartet,* 1992), and *Metai* (The Seasons). The old man and woman of *Gyveno kartą senelis ir senelė* recur several times in his works. In this play the two old people are mourning the death of their son by taking in other young students and killing them. *Duobkasiai* returns to the theme of death, focusing on two gravediggers, rather different in social status and taste. One is a poetic former actor who quotes William Shakespeare, mostly *Hamlet,* and the other is one of the rustics in Ostrauskas's works who gives the author a chance to include much low-register language, humor, and sometimes smut. Such juxtaposition is a favorite strategy for Ostrauskas. The two are at work digging when a strange, attractive young woman suddenly appears. The naive, poetic gravedigger is quite smitten with her at first; the commonsensical brute is cooler, calling her a whore. The young woman turns out to be death herself flirting with them, then making them fall into the grave, which is meant for them. Ostrauskas comments on the nature of death, man's desire to avoid it, and his refusal to recognize it when it is staring him in the face.

Duobkasiai is dynamic and tightly constructed, with much repartee. Ostrauskas often has a stand-in for himself (the poet figure or some other character) who seems to articulate the author's real views more closely. This stereotypical figure changes over time—becoming the sophisticated, world-weary, and wise Ovid in *Ars amoris: Historiae sacrae et profanae* (The Art of Love: A Sacred and Profane History, 1991), for instance—but he is always present in some shape or form. Another constant in Ostrauskas's texts is the superior position of the reader/spectator, who usually stands above the characters in foresight, knowledge, and understanding.

In the late 1950s Ostrauskas began to participate in a Lithuanian organization called Santara-Šviesa (Concordance and Light), which was more liberal in its thinking in the context of Lithuanians in general, who may be classed as right of center. This group and its press have published and continue to publish all of the author's work in the United States. They have also informally staged some of his plays and supported him in his endeavors. His first play was published in one of the last issues of the émigré group's first journal, *Literatūros*

lankai, and he also began to contribute some literary criticism, especially under the pseudonym Andrius Baltaragis. He used that name in the early years of the Cold War for writing anything politically controversial that might have reverberations in the homeland, then still under Soviet occupation, and that might harm his mother, who continued to reside there until 1969. The Santara-Šviesa group continued with a different journal of the arts and criticism, *Metmenys* (Patterns, 1959–); Ostrauskas has been closely identified with this movement and has served on the editorial board of *Metmenys* since 1971.

In the early 1960s the Santara-Šviesa group lost three of its most prominent writers. Antanas Škėma died in a car accident on the Pennsylvania Turnpike in 1961; Julius Kaupas, a psychiatrist and writer, failed to take his daily dose of insulin and died in March 1964; and Algimantas Mackus was also killed in a car accident in December 1964. Ostrauskas dedicated plays to each of the writers in turn, although he asserts that these dedications were added onto the plays at the time of book publication (as opposed to publication in journals) and that the deaths themselves were not the catalyst for his writing. It is difficult to believe, nevertheless, that they had no impact on Ostrauskas. He was closest to Kaupas and Mackus; Škėma (born in 1910), a playwright of an earlier generation, was representative of the tradition to be reacted against. But these deaths shook up the small community of artists and scholars and may account in some perhaps subconscious way for Ostrauskas's premature interest in the phenomenon of death that figures so prominently in his early work. The later work more often deals with the vagaries of love.

Ostrauskas's involvement with music has been lifelong. He owns an enormous collection of musical recordings and has said that he could more easily live without books than without music. His favorite composer is Wolfgang Amadeus Mozart; and if Shakespeare's plays form an almost invisible background to some of Ostrauskas's work, Mozart and other composers can be heard softly in other texts. *Kvartetas,* for example, incorporates Franz Schubert's "Death and the Maiden" string quartet into its structure. Again, the author claims that the idea of using Schubert was a superimposition on an already existing written text; however, the bond between the two works is close. This play is one of the most abstract that Ostrauskas has written and is often perceived as one of the most obscure. It is a paradigm, a model of how epistemes change and what a painful but inevitable procedure that progress is, especially when it leads to perceived chaos and disorder.

The four players of the string quartet are placed against an apocalyptic background. Panic and fear are the dominant feelings displayed by the musicians, who enter into a convulsive series of arguments and physical violence (the two women roll around on the stage pulling each other's hair out) as they try force as a method for preserving the status quo, symbolized by their attempts to play a work of assonance. Instead, at one point before the denouement, the quartet hears an excerpt from one of Mozart's letters as well as his "Ein musikalischer Spass," which they roundly criticize. Suddenly Béla Bartók appears as an illumination on a screen and shoots Mozart; but after the initial shock the players can play their Schubert piece again.

The play is about not only music and the turning point from assonance to dissonance but also world politics, mainly World War I (several generals' names are mentioned), so the work can be read as a kind of allegory of the decline of the West in musical terms. Along with the horror and fear there is much humor and slapstick in the repartees. Though the characters are identified only by gender and by the parts they play in the string quartet (Woman I, Man II, for example), they still have recognizable character traits and can nonetheless be differentiated. The twists and turns of the plot are more difficult to find a meaning for: all the shenanigans on stage seem absurd and pointless, held together only by the preset parts of the quartet—"Allegro," "Andante," "Scherzo," and "Finale."

The last play in *Kvartetas* is called *Metai*, simultaneously alluding to Antonio Vivaldi's composition and to the most famous poem in the Lithuanian language: Kristijonas Donelaitis's *Metai*, first published in 1818. The main connection is the cycle of time from spring to winter, but the atmosphere is quite different from either of the two models that Ostrauskas is refashioning and updating. "Spring" is the season of love and hope, and in this part a naive, carefree young couple present themselves to be married, only to be given a seemingly absurd speech by the Marriage Performer (deliberately not referred to as a justice of the peace or a man of God), who tries to scare them with what awaits them—dirty diapers, crying babies, discord, and despair. But they are too taken with each other to understand him. Cupid, who runs on and off stage, is supposedly responsible for the mayhem. "Summer," subtitled "The Birds," is labeled a "fantasy-pantomime," a ballet of infidelity. The woman, disguised as a hen, is seduced by a man disguised as

a great condor, who then takes off his mask and reveals himself to be the bridegroom of "Spring"—the woman has yielded to her own husband, bringing the romance of the first part to a bitter end.

"Autumn" continues the same downward spiral in the couple's relations, as age begins to take its physical, sexual, and emotional toll; accusations fly back and forth, and hatred, the reverse side of love, rears its ugly head. The romance of "Spring" and the sexual adventures of "Summer" have disappeared. The old man and the old woman who "lived once upon a time" reappear in the "Winter" episode. During the course of the act they manage to kill off not only their offspring but also the Marriage Performer of the first act and Cupid. Their revenge on the institution of marriage (and on life) is complete, as they sing in English: "Lord, we ain't what we ought to be. / We ain't what we want to be. / We ain't what we gonna be. / But thank God, we ain't what we was."

Ostrauskas seems to have genuine insight into the man-woman relationship and its passages through all the stages, subtly commenting on the trick that nature (or God, if He exists) has played on man in giving him the illusion of love that passes and changes through the course of a couple's living together until the true reason for marriage—procreation and the continuation of the species—is revealed. Everyone has been duped into keeping it going, except that the old man and the old woman decide that enough is enough and break the cycle. They will leave no descendants; they refuse to play the game. Ostrauskas's macabre vision touches on man's relationship to God as well as man's ambiguous, deceptive position in the world camouflaged by illusion and false received ideas that serve the status quo.

In 1977 Ostrauskas published his fourth book, *Čičinskas*, which includes two of his microdramas and one longer piece that gives its name to the book, a play about an infamous seventeenth-century aristocrat known for his debauched and wicked ways. Čičinskas embodied a fantastic, evil, elemental force and had not only captured the imagination of the common folk but also had been the subject of previous works by such writers as Adam Mickiewicz and Jonas Maironis. Ostrauskas depicts him living in an armoire, interacting with representatives of the clergy, Russian officials, and their mistresses, who come to check on rumors that he is still alive. Čičinskas terrifies them and goes on drunken rampages during which he argues with the contents of the legends that have sprung up about him. This work may be classified as a turning point in Ostrauskas's writing. Without giving up his sense of the absurd, and retaining certain features usually associated with theater of the absurd such as humor, slapstick, and physical action on the stage, he begins to consider the differences between historic "truth" and contemporary versions that conflict with this so-called truth. In his later writing he tries out variations on this insight by rewriting "history" more radically than he does in *Čičinskas,* inventing new ways of confronting characters from different eras and allowing them to interact.

One of the microdramas in the volume is titled *Šaltkalvis* (The Blacksmith) and is meant to commemorate the great figure of the first Lithuanian reawakening at the end of the nineteenth century, Vincas Kudirka, author of the Lithuanian national anthem. Kudirka does not appear in the play, but an illiterate blacksmith is ordered by the tsar's authorities to remove the letters of the national anthem from Kudirka's gravestone. Although the drunken blacksmith obeys, he knows he has done something terribly wrong in desecrating this tomb even though he cannot articulate what exactly his sin is. Once again Ostrauskas presents a major historical figure as he must have seemed to his contemporaries, thus reversing the myth of the national hero, who was no hero in his own time and went mostly unrecognized, especially by ordinary people. In time this device became a favorite for the playwright, used to good effect on universally famous figures of Western history and legend.

The other microdrama in that volume, *Lozorius* (translated as *Lazarus,* 1986), is also quite brief. Lazarus, on being brought back to life, is fought over by two sisters, Mary and Martha, with all kinds of innuendos, sexual and otherwise, as to their real motives. Yet, in the end Lazarus refuses to give them the satisfaction of hearing what he has to say about his "near-death experience," uttering only one word—"No"—and returning to his tomb. In other words, he did not ask anyone to raise him from the dead and he prefers whatever state it was that he came from. The reader must draw his or her own conclusions as to whether the play is an existentialist rejection of life or an affirmation of the goodness or beauty of the afterlife.

Published in 1983, *Gundymai* (Temptations) is a political play, a satire obviously based on Soviet army practices well known in Lithuania during the guerrilla war in Czechoslovakia in 1968 and in Afghanistan post-1980. Double-crossing, double-dealing, and double entendres abound in the battle between the inhabitants and the invaders, who are never identified as Soviet but are easily recognizable

Dust jacket for Ostrauskas's 1991 work, in which the Roman poet Ovid escorts Romeo and Juliet through the history of love in the Western world

as such from their actions. Drawings by Bosch are inserted into the text, and aphorisms from a Polish writer, Stanisław J. Lec, are quoted but do not rescue this play from its lack of depth. The humor is flat, and the action can easily be anticipated. Ostrauskas rails against God and man, questioning and criticizing the structure of the universe and identifying new ways in which humanity has been cheated as the inheritor of the earth. *Gundymai* would have had a resonance in Lithuania or even Eastern Europe had the play been staged there at the time of writing. However, the paradox was that Soviet censorship forbade anything so obviously aimed at it, while under conditions of freedom the play becomes a period piece, having lost its former punch.

Eloiza ir Abelardas (Heloise and Abelard, 1988) suggested another new direction for the author. The first part of the play departs from the sentimentality of the age-old story of Heloise and Abelard by showing Heloise to be perversely devout, intellectually brilliant yet naively romantic, and in love with a cynical, debauched Abelard who uses her for his own ends and for his own glory. Ostrauskas, however, explores further, bringing two characters from different periods of time face to face: he confronts the historical Heloise with Simone de Beauvoir to see what they will make of each other. Heloise remains true to her faithful nature, never having given up on her sexuality and having been separated from Abelard by his deception and wish for vainglory. Simone, whose myth as the strong feminist and freethinker is overturned here, appears as not only jealous and perceptive of Jean-Paul Sartre's infidelities but also desirous of being his wife, after all. Her most precious memory in Ostrauskas's version is when Sartre, perhaps already delirious in his final coma, says to her, "You . . . were . . . a . . . wonderful . . . wife . . . to . . . me." Heloise is the superior being; she has remained true to her convictions. Abelard and her uncle Fulbert may have deceived her by marrying her off and then sending her to a convent to preserve Abelard's good name, but Abelard is the one who, after his castration, reneges on their love and acts the hypocrite, while she retains her virtue and her innocence in the face of men's duplicity. These are unusual interpretations that cause the reader to reconstruct old stories and myths of famous lovers and view them from a fresh perspective.

In the same vein but on a larger scale, Ostrauskas constructs what is probably his major work, *Ars amoris: Historiae sacrae et profanae.* The book has a large cast of famous lovers from history and literature, ranging from Romeo and Juliet through Salome and John the Baptist, Francesca and Paolo, Zeus and Hera, Sappho, the Marquis de Sade, and Casanova, ending with a ball at which they intermingle, dance, and converse. Ovid is "the master of ceremonies" who introduces and escorts Romeo and Juliet through the history of love in the Western world, commenting on the characters' self-delusions, their romantic yearnings, their interludes and dallyings, and their inevitable downfall.

Juliet is the ingenue that this voice of experience tries to influence the most by seducing her mind and corrupting her soul; but she is only awed, horrified, and stunned in turn, never really giving up her illusions or her innocence. Romeo is more down-to-earth and accepts the cynicism that often follows in love's wake. The two of them, nevertheless, present a postmodernist perspective because they no longer can relate to the intent of the original texts; they seek a contemporary relevance for these great literary figures and cannot find it. They are children of the end of the twentieth century who find the passions, immoralities, soul-searching, and sins of the earlier lovers incomprehensible, outside their experience, and can only marvel at the consternation and wonder that these lovers provoked in their own time.

Ostrauskas's scope, however, is vast; he surveys not all the varieties of love, because that would be impossible even in 365 pages, but certainly a dizzying variety of kinds—sacred and profane, narcissistic and sadistic, playful and jealous. Each chapter devoted to a pair of lovers is followed by an interlude in which Ovid and the young couple analyze the lesson that could have been learned but never is. The many faces of love are discussed: its blindness, vagaries, exploitation, deceit, and disillusionment. Postmodernist though it is, rewriting and recasting literature into a Hollywood-style extravaganza, *Ars amoris* captivates by the oldest of dramatic means, namely pity and fear leading to catharsis, and it makes the reader question the possibility and nature of love: is it a game, a hoax, a deadly serious self-absorption, or an elaborate scheme of nature to ensure procreation and the continuity of the race? For Ostrauskas it is all of those things and much more.

Ostrauskas continued to write minor dramas and shorter pieces, publishing in his favorite journal, *Metmenys,* and finding a fresh audience in newly liberated Lithuania. In 1996 he published a significant book in Chicago, *Ketvirtoji siena* (The Fourth Wall). In this volume he has incorporated several of his critical articles, some of them (such as "The Writer and Exile," originally written in 1973 and revised in 1992) with a "Post Scriptum" and footnotes that indicate that he has continued to meditate and read about these topics. His attitude to being a writer living in exile is at least twofold: exile can be a blessing in disguise, as it allows the writer to absorb and experience a new environment; and/or all writers of a certain sensibility are "inner" exiles in their own country or elsewhere in any case, so the state of exile is natural and certainly not to be bemoaned as many émigrés are wont to do. In his criticism Ostrauskas remains the objective and impartial observer of reality that he is in his creative writing. This same balanced view prevails in another brief critical article, "On Translation and Translations," in which the author upholds the position that translation is impossible, especially in poetry, where what is lost in the translation is precisely the essence of the poetry. But as a realist Ostrauskas has to admit that translation is a painful necessity that has to be performed and endured.

Scattered throughout *Ketvirtoji siena* are also some interviews selected and edited by Ostrauskas with no attribution to the interviewers. For example, one such piece is a melange of interviews and conversations that took place in 1961, 1964, and 1984 and has two parts separated in the text by material of other genres. Obviously control of the content rests with Ostrauskas and is perhaps part of his facade-building or image-making. On the other hand, this condensed form spares the reader from having to wade through irrelevant or uninspired questions and presents only the best, most revealing questions and answers. Ostrauskas has some perceptive things to say about such topics as how he views theater of the absurd, the role of the director (to whom he allows much freedom), and the relationship between the play as text and as a performance. The interviews thus are most useful in yielding a few insights into the playwright's preferences, goals, likes, and dislikes rather than producing much biographical information.

Ketvirtoji siena also includes a clever play, "The Second 'Paskenduolė,'" a retelling of the 1913 classic Lithuanian short story "Paskenduolė" (The Drowned Girl) by Antanas Vienuolis. Basing the plot on the original, which dealt with a young unwed girl who gets pregnant and eventually drowns herself because the parochial, ostensibly charitable Catholic society will not tolerate her condition, Ostrauskas sets out to have fun with this character, Veronika, and especially the structuralist and feminist critics for whom she has been a gold mine. He modernizes Veronika and gives her various escape routes from her plight; one is to send her off to college. The playwright uses direct quotations from critical texts about Vienuolis's work (albeit out of context) to not only show what and who Veronika might be today but also to demonstrate that the more formal and structuralist these interpretations are, the sillier they appear. Ultimately, his Veronika once again chooses to drown herself even in these "tolerant" times when many options are open to women.

Ketvirtoji siena ends with two mirror pieces in two types of discourse, both titled "Words, Words, Words." One is an essay on words and their importance to the writer, with quotations from what other famous people have said about words, beginning unsurprisingly with "In the beginning was the Word!" The other selection is a one-act play of the same name dealing mainly with the author in front of a blank page—his procrastination, his inspiration,

and his ruminations, some of which mimic the essay. Readers see the playwright alone with no other characters to relieve his loneliness, confronting his own agony and ecstasy, his craft of writing, and the pain and elation it can bring.

In *Kaliausės mirtis* (The Scarecrow's Death, 1996) more microdramas are collected under the rubric "Spec(tac)ulum mundi"—that is, mirror or spectacle of the world. If these microdramas were art, they might be cartoon or caricature; they deliver a strong, succinct punch. Like cartoons, they depend on the reader's "getting it," which is not always easy—there may be some thinking to be done before the delayed reaction occurs. Ostensibly they are humorous but linger in the mind longer than a joke because some deeper truth is revealed or some idiomatic proverb is deconstructed and questioned.

Several of Ostrauskas's later plays are noteworthy for their innovation and skill. In honor of the 125th anniversary of Canon Juozas Tumas-Vaižgantas's birth, Ostrauskas wrote—or as he says in the text, "edited"—a new play titled *Vaižgantas* (published in the journal *Metai* in 1994 and performed in 1995), which in the opening lines he refers to as a "monodrama." Except for several sentences by Ostrauskas inserted in square brackets to delineate the playwright's words and his instructions to the director, the work is composed entirely of Vaižgantas's own words. Vaižgantas was an admirable cultural force in the Lithuania of his time and a prolific literary figure, writing prose fiction and journalism and editing several newspapers. He was especially distinguished by his democratic and tolerant ideas and actions, placing patriotism during this time of national reawakening in Lithuania above his religious convictions and duties as a priest; thus, he was not much liked by the Catholic hierarchy but valued for his writing that strengthened the political activism of his contemporaries. In this play Ostrauskas assembles and rearranges his literary subject's words to reveal more about his character and his national importance.

The play illuminates Vaižgantas from a fresh angle, but clearly Ostrauskas also has the intention to make him relevant again at his own time of writing, immediately after another political rebirth in Lithuania. Some of Vaižgantas's speeches in the play speak to the modern reader/viewer, teaching national unity, democratic values, and tolerance of those who do not fit the regular mold. The fact that Ostrauskas as playwright removes himself from the play only adds to the force of Vaižgantas's thoughts and convictions. The liberties that Ostrauskas takes with rearranging the original author's texts, of

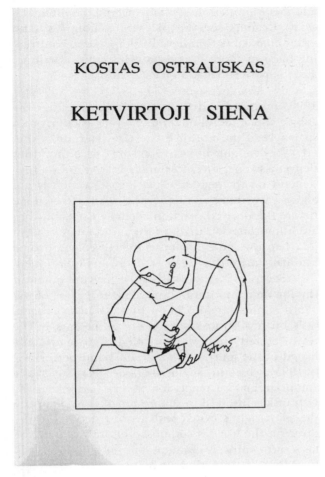

KOSTAS OSTRAUSKAS

KETVIRTOJI SIENA

*Dust jacket for Ostrauskas's collection of miscellaneous pieces,
including critical essays, interviews, and a play,
published in 1996*

course, still place the responsibility for their nuances of meaning on him, so the playwright is not quite as absent as he may seem. On the other hand, the minimalism of his intrusions and the whole concept of allowing the writer to reveal himself make *Vaižgantas* an innovative and even experimental work in Lithuanian letters.

Another of Ostrauskas's plays, *Stasiukas*, appeared in *Metai* in 1996. This work uses a device that is hardly new in world literature, the play within a play; however, Ostrauskas goes further with it, making the internal play extended and complete and giving it the added function of commenting on the exterior play more extensively than is usual. The main character is Stanislovas II Augustas Poniatovskis (known as Stanislaus II Augustus Poniatowski in Polish), the last King of Poland and Grand Duke of Lithuania, affectionately called Stasiukas by Ostrauskas. The action takes place from 1795

through 1797 just as the Commonwealth of Poland and Lithuania, which had endured some two hundred years, was crumbling and being incorporated into tsarist Russia. Traditionally, Poniatovskis has been viewed as a weak, degenerate figure who brought the demise of the Commonwealth. But Ostrauskas, who likes to play with history and character in new-historicist fashion, uses this opportunity to create his own original version of Poniatovskis, making him neither self-deluded nor foolish. Certainly he is still politically weak; however, in Ostrauskas's view he is a triumphant victim, even an ironically heroic figure.

The playwright accomplishes this transformation through the internal play, called "The Furuncle, or the Death of Vytautas the Great," ostensibly written by Poniatovskis—who, though he is being called to St. Petersburg to abdicate, still has enough power over his sycophants and underlings to force them to act out the play that he has composed. They have to perform the parts that correspond to their true natures, while Poniatovskis plays Vytautas the Great, the fifteenth-century Grand Duke of Lithuania, whom the Poles deprived of his crown by stealing it on its way from the Holy See. The historical moments are similar, and by making Poniatovskis the counterpart of Vytautas, a figure much revered by Lithuanians throughout the ages, Ostrauskas raises Poniatovskis to a new level of magnitude that history had not been willing to grant him. The interest of the play lies in seeing the true characters of his court and intimates revealed behind their masks—only Poniatovskis has no mask and thus seems noble and tragic.

Ostrauskas returned once again to the old man and woman of "Gyveno kartą senelis ir senelė" with "Valse Triste," published in *Metmenys* in 1998, which he claims will be his final foray into this topic that has obsessed him since 1968. The old couple, now in their third or fourth incarnation, are killed off in this story; their final dialogues take place from the afterlife. The Author is one of the protagonists of this play, and he is killed off by a blow from the Old Man's hammer, only to reappear in their transformed lives. The dedication of the play is "To my friends who have left never to return (I will catch up with you)." At the end of the play the old couple can no longer strike with the hammer; they cannot even rock in their rocking chairs.

Ostrauskas continues to write. One new tendency is that he favors inverting, quoting, and playing with his own creations and works, citing himself as it were, having left Shakespeare and other favorite allusions behind. His inward turn has not depleted his store of takes on the subjects that interested him most at the beginning of his writing career. He remains distinctive in Lithuanian literature as a universal, objective, unsentimental writer.

Interviews:

"Pokalbis, 1974" and "Iš pokalbių 1961, 1964," *Ketvirtoji siena* (Chicago: Algimanto Mackaus knygų leidimo fondas, 1996); pp. 43–48, 63–69, 94–98;

Ingrida Matusevičiūtė, ". . . esu savo laiko, savo aplinkos sutvėrimas," *Santara,* 28 (1997): 56–61;

"Esu turbūt *homo ludens,*" *Naujasis Židinys/Aidai,* 6 (2000): 301–304.

Bibliographies:

Alfreds Straumanis, ed., *Baltic Drama: A Handbook and Bibliography* (Prospect Heights, Ill.: Waveland Press, 1981), pp. 397–398, 496–498;

Paulė Mikelinskaitė, "Kostas Ostrauskas," *Tarp knygų,* 12 (1991): 22–26.

References:

Živilė Bilaišytė, "Kosto Ostrausko vėlesnioji dramaturgija," *Metmenys,* 47 (1984): 52–69;

Jurgis Blekaitis, "Kostas Ostrauskas ieško savo teatro," *Metmenys,* 10 (1965): 6–28; 11 (1966): 85–106;

Algimantas Bučys, "Žodžių absurdas: apie Kosto Ostrausko lietuvišką avangardizmą," *Literatūra ir menas,* 33 (1992): 5, 12–13;

Petronėlė Česnulevičiūtė, *Dramos pasaulis* (Vilnius: Lietuvos rašytojų sąjungos leidykla, 1996): 36–37, 42–44;

Mieczyslaw Jackiewicz, "Tworca litewskiego teatra absurdu: Uwagi o dramaturgii Kostasa Ostrauskasa," *Studia i Materialy Wyzszej Szkoly Ped. w Olsztynie,* 41 (1992): 109–116;

Vytautas A. Jonynas, "Vingrieji Kosto Ostrausko rašteliai," *Metmenys,* 23 (1972):133–140;

Dovydas Judelevičius, "Dialogas abipus ketvirtosios sienos," *Kultūros barai,* 4 (1997): 71–73;

Violeta Kelertienė, "Savita teritorija: Kostas Ostrauskas—JAV LB Kultūros tarybos 1991 metų literatūros premijos laureatas," *Metai,* 7 (1991): 184–185;

Vytautas Kubilius, *XX amžiaus literatūra,* second edition (Vilnius: Alma littera, 1996), pp. 631–634;

Vladas Kulbokas, *Lietuvių literatūrinė kritika tremtyje* (Rome: Lietuvių katalikų mokslo akademia, 1982–1987): volume 1, pp. 317–319, 423–426; 526–528; volume 2, pp. 93–94;

Jonas Lankutis, "Kosto Ostrausko avangardizmas" in his *Lietuvių egzodo dramaturgija, 1940–1990* (Vilnius: Lietuvių` literatūros ir tautosakos institutas, 1995), pp. 75–92;

Lankutis and Algimantas Bučys, *"Ars amoris," Vilnius,* 1 (1993): 33–38;

Ingrida Matusevičiūtė, "K. Ostrausko *Ars amoris* kaip postmodernistinis tekstas," *Lituanistica,* 2 (1994): 90–96;

Rimvydas Šilbajoris, "Kaliausės veidrodis ir žmogus," *Metmenys,* 74 (1998): 174–182;

Šilbajoris, "Kostas Ostrauskas and the Theater of Death," in his *Perfection of Exile: Fourteen Contemporary Lithuanian Writers* (Norman: University of Oklahoma Press, 1970), pp. 112–134;

Šilbajoris, "Kosto Ostrausko žaidimai," *Kultūros barai,* 7 (1993): 31–33;

Šilbajoris, "Ostrauskas ir autorius," *Kultūros barai,* 10 (1999): 37–41;

Šilbajoris, "Some Structural Principles in the Theater of Kostas Ostrauskas," *Lituanistikos darbai/ Lithuanian Studies,* 3 (1973): 171–197;

Alina Staknienė, "Gyvos bėdos su gyvais lavonais: Kosto Ostrausko vaiduokliškos dramos," *Metmenys,* 38 (1979): 178–190;

Staknienė, "Meilės istorijų intertekstinė mozaika: Kosto Ostrausko postmodernistinė drama," *Metmenys,* 64 (1993): 181–190;

Artūras Tereškinas, "Tekstologija ir tekstideologija Kosto Ostrausko dramoje *Ars amoris:* mušamieji instrumental ir Mozart," *Lituanistica,* 1 (1994): 55–61;

Vincas Trumpa, "Drama istorijoje ir istorinė drama," *Metmenys,* 37 (1979): 34–39;

Undinė Uogintaitė, "Kosto Ostrausko *Gundymai* amerikiečių dramos kontekste," *Gimtasis žodis,* 4 (1996): 17–22;

Bronius Vaškelis, "Kiti žemininkų-lankininkų kartos dramaturgai," in *Lietuvių egzodo literatūra 1945–1990,* edited by Kazys Bradūnas and Rimvydas Šilbajoris (Chicago: Lituanistikos institutes, 1992), pp. 599–607;

Aušra Veličkaitė, "K. Ostrausko *Stasiukas:* Lietuviškoj kontekste," *Metmenys,* 77 (1999): 119–131.

Vladimír Páral

(10 August 1932 –)

Pavel Janoušek
Institute of Czech Literature, Academy of Sciences of the Czech Republic, Prague

BOOKS: *Šest pekelných nocí*, as Jan Laban (Havlíčkův Brod: Krajské nakladatelství, 1964);

Veletrh splněných přání: Příběh pokleslé aktivity (Prague: Mladá fronta, 1964);

Soukromá vichřice: Laboratorní zpráva ze života hmyzu (Prague: Mladá fronta, 1966);

Katapult: Jízdní řád železničních, lodních a leteckých drah do ráje (Prague: Mladá fronta, 1967); translated by William Harkins as *Catapult: A Timetable of Rail, Sea, and Air Ways to Paradise* (Highland Park, N.J.: Catbird Press, 1989);

Milenci & vrazi: Magazín ukájení před rokem 2000 (Prague: Mladá fronta, 1969);

Profesionální žena: Román pro každého (Prague: Československý spisovatel, 1971); translated by Harkins as *The Four Sonyas* (North Haven, Conn.: Catbird, 1993);

Mladý muž a bílá velryba: Malý chemický epos (Ústí nad Labem: Severočeské nakladatelství, 1973);

Radost až do rána: O křečcích a lidech (Prague: Melantrich, 1975);

Generální zázrak: Román naděje (Ústí nad Labem: Severočeské nakladatelství, 1978);

Muka obraznosti (Prague: Československý spisovatel, 1980);

Pokušení A-ZZ (Prague: Melantrich, 1982);

Romeo & Julie 2300 (Prague: Práce, 1982);

Válka s mnohozvířetem: Památce Karla Čapka s pokorou a láskou (Prague: Československý spisovatel, 1983);

Země žen (Prague: Československý spisovatel, 1987);

Dekameron 2000 aneb Láska v Praze (Prague: Československý spisovatel, 1990);

Kniha rozkoší, smíchu a radosti (Litvínov: Dialog, 1992);

Playgirls I (Litvínov: Dialog, 1994);

Playgirls II (Litvínov: Dialog, 1994);

Profesionální muž. Vladimír Páral o sobě a jiných, zajímavějších věcech (Český Těšín: GABI, 1995);

Tam za vodou (Litvínov: Dialog, 1995).

Vladimír Páral (from the dust jacket for Catapult, *1989)*

Edition: *Tři ze Zoo* (Prague: Melatrich, 1977)—comprises *Veletrh splněných přání, Soukromá vichřice,* and *Katapult.*

Vladimír Páral came to the forefront of Czech literature in the late 1960s, at a time when enthusiasm for the communist revolution was waning and turning into self-criticism. Until 1968 there was an attempt to revise communist dogmas, and Páral's first novels surprised readers at home and abroad by the topicality and originality of his subject matter. His tales of life reduced to basics, as manifested in "statistically significant individuals," map out the mechanical lifestyle of certain social classes. At the same time, Páral's stories brought a sharply critical moral judgment to bear on the dull routine of that lifestyle. His individual writing style is a product of his technical education. Páral's method of composition is, for the most part, conjectural, deductive, and synthesizing. His work is on the borderline between pulp-fiction narratives and typically intellectual prose, involving permutations of language and thought.

Many of the ideas and themes recurring in his novels stem directly from the author's life. Páral's father, originally from Moravia, had been in the Czech Legion in France, which was made up of Czech deserters and which fought against Austria-Hungary during World War I. Páral's father was a knight of the Legion of Honor, and between the wars, in the independent democratic Czechoslovakia, he held a high position in the Czechoslovak army. Páral's mother came from a well-to-do aristocratic family from Prague. In spite of her family's going bankrupt, she brought a considerable dowry to the marriage. Páral was born on 10 August 1932 in Prague, but his father was transferred to Brno, and the family soon moved to that city, where they owned a tenement house. Páral, the second son, was reared in a strongly Catholic environment in which the puritanical and moralistic demands of his father existed in sharp contrast with the aristocratic manner of his mother. World War II and particularly the communist coup in Czechoslovakia in 1948 put an end to the affluent, lavish lifestyle of Páral's childhood and adolescence. As a result of the coup, Páral's father was dismissed from the army, and his mother was forced to take care of the house herself. These experiences provided the origins of the frequent social contrasts in Páral's work: the rise of the poor and the fall of the rich, the longing for wealth and fame and the boredom after these aims have been achieved.

Páral's mother wanted him to become a priest; but when he completed his secondary school studies in 1950, at the time of rampant Stalinism in Czechoslovakia, a career in the church was ruled out. He applied to the Faculty of Law; however, Brno University had been changed into a military academy, so he chose instead to study chemistry, first in Brno and later in Pardubice. After graduating in 1954 Páral held several professional and technological posts. Between 1955 and 1956 he worked in Liberec and in Jablonec nad Nisou. In 1956 he was employed in the gasworks in Plzeň, and then he was a researcher and patents officer in Ústí nad Labem. For much of his early career as a writer, the combination of his profession, the environment of the chemical works in the north of Bohemia, and his love affairs provided him with the material for his novels.

In an interview in *Kulturní tvorba* (1967) Páral said that he began writing on New Year's Eve in 1957, but that he did not publish anything until seven years later, when he took second place in a small regional publisher's competition. He published his winning novel, *Šest pekelných nocí* (Six Nights of Hell, 1964), under the nom de plume of Jan Laban, for by then the Prague publishing house Mladá fronta was preparing the publication of his novel *Veletrh splněných přání* (A Tradefair of Fulfilled Desires, 1964), which he considered his proper first work. However, the two novels, the one he disowned and the one that established him as a writer, have much in common. The central character in both is a young man with high aspirations for his love life and his work. In complete contrast to his ordinary, everyday life he creates a fictitious world of adventure. Another point common to both is the protagonist's final reconciliation with everyday life.

On the other hand, the two works represent quite different sets of values. In *Šest pekelných nocí* the author represents conforming to the "normal" as a positive quality, a manifestation of the maturing of a young man who will presumably become successfully integrated into society. In *Veletrh splněných přání* the parallel reconciliation with the "normal" is deemed to be completely negative, a crime committed by the protagonist against the girl he loves and against himself. In this novel the protagonist's stereotyped lifestyle and his dreams and fantasies are part of, and the consequence of, a general social way of life. When the protagonist is offered a chance to escape from dull normality and become involved in a "real human relationship," he does not find enough courage to give his emotions free rein. As a result, he metaphorically "kills" his love and turns his love affair into a mechanized sexual relationship.

In his work Páral tends to be preoccupied with a single theme. His novels are set predominantly in the chemical works in northern Bohemia, and his protagonists are generally of one particular psychological type. He also utilizes a singular method of creating his plots, incorporating different literary or cinematic patterns for variety. In addition, his vision, perception, and judgment of the world has remained more or less consistent throughout his career. What provides the link between his works is his perception of the world as a conflict between two irreconcilable forces: the banality of everyday existence and the desire of the protagonists to lead a different, better, and more meaningful life.

In Páral's view, routine existence is incompatible with authentic life; every aspect of this ordinary living is a priori negative. Authenticity is, on the other hand, a kind of unrealizable ideal, almost attainable for brief moments through love and sex or—as illustrated in his later novels—through yoga and through transcending one's physicality. In the liberalizing, communist Czechoslovakia of the 1960s the relationship between everyday life and the ideal, and also between everyday life and the ruling political dogma, was considered extremely topical. What Páral treated in literary terms in his highly popular work was dealt with on the theoretical level by the Marxist philosopher Karel Kosík in his book *Dialektika konkrétního* (1963; translated as *Dialectics of the Concrete,* 1976) and particularly in the treatise "Každodennost a dějiny" (Everyday Life and History).

From the publication of his first book Páral showed he had not only an original subject but also suitable literary powers with which to present it. Expressive language; factual, almost technical-sounding vocabulary; and above all, the technique of repeated permutations of words, sentences, and complete paragraphs make the reader aware of an existence that is mechanical and stereotyped. At the same time, there is an element of playfully manipulating the reader. Every Páral novel can be interpreted as a kind of laboratory experiment in which the author tries to see how, according to a certain formula, a character or characters will behave in certain preset conditions. Páral said of himself in a 1981 interview with Rudolf Křesťan, "All my life I have been writing one novel." This statement can be taken to mean that, at least in the first decades of his career as a writer, he kept asking one question in a variety of different ways. It is worth noting that these variations form a relatively logical sequence, for as long as the author did not want merely to repeat what he had already written, he had to look for a new way of asking his basic question in every work.

The four novels Páral wrote in the 1960s are among the best in contemporary Czech literature. Although the "sociological sample" examined by Páral in each subsequent work becomes ever larger, at the beginning he appeared to attack the lifestyle of certain passive individuals, satirizing and distanc-

ing himself from them. In *Veletrh splněných přání* Páral passed judgment on a passive, compliant character. In his next novel, *Soukromá vichřice* (A Private Gale, 1966), with the characteristic subtitle *Laboratorní zpráva ze života hmyzu* (A Laboratory Report of Insect Life), he gives several pairs of lovers and married couples the chance to cut loose from the constant repetition of the same old routines. All of these characters achieve authentic life through their new erotic relationships and, for a time, are blissfully happy and fulfilled. Then, however, they realize that the freedom they have gained is none other than the same, or even worse, stereotyped freedom they had before, and that they have gone back to their original lifestyles. *Soukromá vichřice* was the first of Páral's novels to be adapted for the screen; the movie version appeared in 1967, directed by Hynek Bočan.

In his next book, *Katapult: Jízdní řád železničních, lodních a leteckých drah do ráje* (1967; translated as *Catapult: A Timetable of Rail, Sea, and Air Ways to Paradise,* 1989), Páral allows his protagonist—an energetic, competent man with whom the reader can identify—to fail in his futile, tragicomic struggle with everyday life. Inspired by the small personal advertisements that were at that time allowed to be published in daily newspapers, the author depicts a man who answers these ads and meets a succession of women of various ages, professions, and temperaments along the railway line between Ústí nad Labem, Prague, and Brno. Each of them tells him a different story that incorporates a different way of life, a different career, and a different destiny; but ultimately all these tales reflect the same theme: that ordinary, everyday life is a cage from which there is no escape. The protagonist tries in vain to escape the firm grasp of his own family, succeeding only when he finds a bizarre substitute for himself. Then, of course, there is no way back for him, and his attempt to return results in his death. Released in 1983, the movie version of this novel was directed by Jaromil Jireš.

Páral's early novels received significant critical acclaim both in Czechoslovakia and abroad; they were translated into German, Danish, French, Dutch, Polish, Hungarian, and English, and later into Finnish, Estonian, and Romanian. After the success of *Katapult,* Páral became a full-time writer and began working on a long, wide-ranging social novel: *Milenci & vrazi: Magazín ukájení před rokem 2000* (Lovers and Murderers: A Story of Gratifications before the Year 2000, 1969). Páral used his own experiences as a writer and a lover as material for this novel, including the affair he had with an older woman when he was working in Liberec—an affair he referred to several times in his subsequent novels. As in most of his work, Páral turned to earlier literature as a basis for his plots, in particular to Stendhal's *Le rouge et le noir* (The Red and the Black, 1830) and the Bible. The unbridgeable gap between the eternal human desire for meaningful life and the routine of everyday existence is presented with conviction. Gradually, from the portrayal of the lives of individuals, there emerges an archetypal image of the life of several human generations. In this novel the author interprets the entire history of the human race as an eternal duel between Conquerors and Besieged, or Red and Blue people; that is, those who are fighting for something real and those who have already succumbed to a routine life. After the former are victorious, they always inevitably become the latter. According to Páral, nobody can ever escape the commonplace that orders all life; every "red" activity must inevitably finish in a "blue" sterile existence and self-gratification.

At the end of the 1960s, after the occupation of Czechoslovakia by the Warsaw Pact armies that ended the liberalization period, culminating in the 1968 Prague Spring and the introduction of the "normalization" (the return to strict communist rule), this all-embracing negation of everyday life was unacceptable to the official cultural policies of the totalitarian state. *Milenci & vrazi* was subsequently banned; it was included on the list of a large number of works that could not be republished and were removed from public libraries. Although the post-1968 authorities in Czechoslovakia never fully trusted Páral, he managed to successfully negotiate the hazards of the political screenings to which the whole nation was subjected after the Russian invasion. He did not become a completely banned writer. Yet, the question remains whether the changes he made to his writing after 1968 were the result of an attempt to conform to the regime or whether in *Milenci & vrazi* he had taken his subject as far as it could go, and thus could only stop writing, repeat himself, or try to change. Support for the last option comes from Páral's own statement in a 1969 interview with Otakar Brůna that his work until then was part of the "black," negative pathology, and that the "light," positive pathology would follow.

Beginning with *Profesionální žena* (Professional Woman, 1971; translated as *The Four Sonyas*, 1993), Páral began conducting an argument with himself, trying to find a way of combating his concept of "stereotyped everydayness." He was now seeking a compromise. But the new ideological

Dust jacket for the English translation of Páral's novel Katapult *(1967), about a man who futilely searches for independence by meeting a series of women who have placed personal advertisements in the newspaper*

model on which Páral began to build his novels gradually ceases to be convincing, for even from the text of the novels it is obvious that his attempt at a positive solution is at variance with his intrinsic view of the world. Repeatedly, and often at the expense of art and credibility, Páral succumbs to the temptation to make the characters in his novels triumph at all cost over the stereotyped pressure of everyday life. For example, in the most successful novel of this period, *Mladý muž a bílá velryba* (The Young Man and Moby Dick, 1973), Páral brings his protagonist to the pinnacle of fulfillment in work and sex, but only at the cost of dying before his new life ends in the typical pattern of dull normality. New motives appear in his work at this time: his protagonists are able to find themselves in creative work. The preoccupation with sex is counterbalanced with yoga—the desire for pure asceticism and the transcendence of human physicality.

In spite of his partial turnabout, Páral was the most widely read author in Czechoslovakia during the 1970s and 1980s. His novels were also frequently adapted for the stage, although he did not write a single play. In 1974 the banned playwright Milan Uhde, under the pseudonym of Zdeněk Pospíšil, adapted *Profesionální žena*, which was also adapted by Ewald Schorm in 1975 and by Markéta Bláhová in 1996. In 1975 *Mladý muž a bílá velryba* was adapted by Miloš Horanský and Vojtěch Ron, who also adapted *Generální zázrak* (General Miracle, 1978) in 1983 and *Romeo & Julie 2300* (1982) in 1987. Zdeněk Potužil adapted *Mladý muž a bílá velryba* in 1976 under the title *Knedlíkové radosti* (Dumpling Pleasures). In 1983 *Generální zázrak* was also adapted by Jan Vedral; and in 1991 *Milenci & vrazi* was adapted by Zdeněk Potužil. Páral's popularity increased as his novels became more like light literature, and the joy of telling a story gradually became more important than the social content.

The publication of Páral's autobiographical novel *Muka obraznosti* (The Torment of Imagination, 1980) marked the end of the second stage of his development. In this novel the author comes to the conclusion that the gap between human aspirations for a meaningful life and everyday existence as a negative concept was simply a figment of the extravagant imagination of the protagonist, Marek Paar. In this way Páral removes any negative concept of everyday life from the sphere of objective reality to the sphere of subjective impressionism, in fact bringing his development full circle to where he began in his first unacknowledged work. Again his protagonist lives as he does not only because he is forced to do so by society, but also chiefly because his excessive fantasies make him unfit for everyday life. The novel ends with the hero deciding that literature would provide the most suitable outlet for his overdeveloped imagination. *Muka obraznosti* was also adapted for the screen; the movie version, directed by Vladimír Drha, was released in 1989.

In the course of the next few years Páral went on to write science fiction and produced four books that were extremely popular with readers. These works were more entertaining than serious, whether they were concerned with ecological and moral problems—as in *Válka s mnohozvířetem* (A War with the Multibeast, 1983), in which a serious ecological devastation of Northern Bohemia becomes a metaphor for self-indulgent, immoral, and political degeneration—or with feminism, as in *Země žen* (A Women's World, 1987). In *Pokušení A-ZZ* (Temptation A-ZZ, 1982) Páral's characters undergo a test of moral probity during an encounter with an extraterrestrial civilization, which can perhaps be construed as a metaphor for communism.

From the beginning of his career Páral's work was marked by a characteristic tension between the author's fascination with women and sex, and his basically Catholic moral search for absolute unsullied purity. Since the fall of the communist regime and the taboos that went with it, the erotic aspect of Páral's work has become dominant. The author has made no secret of joining the "Independent Erotic Initiative"—a political party working for the "rehabilitation of sex." Soon after the fall of communism, Páral published the omnibus novel he had written some time previously, *Dekameron 2000 aneb Láska v Praze* (Decameron 2000 or Love in Prague, 1990), in which he featured a wide range of examples of lovemaking. The next book, *Kniha rozkoší, smíchu a radosti* (The Book of Delight, Laughter and Joy, 1992), is supposed to be, at least according to its title, an argument against Milan Kundera's *Kniha smíchu a zapomnění*, first published in French in 1979 and translated in the following year as *The Book of Laughter and Forgetting*. From the wild ravings of the emerging Czech capitalist society, the author's alter ego finds release in death and absolute denial of the physical. Then, turning to popular literature, Páral published two explicitly erotic novels, *Playgirls I* (1994) and *Playgirls II* (1994), making full use of the increases in prostitution and the number of sex parlors that sprang up, especially in Northern Bohemia, after the collapse of police control. Both works were made into movies and released in 1995, directed by Vít Olmer.

A novelist of sophisticated technique and complex imagery, Vladimír Páral emerged as one of the most influential Czech authors in the second half of the twentieth century. Through his fiction and the highly successful adaptations of his work for both stage and screen, Páral has enjoyed immense popularity with the Czech public and has since gained increased critical recognition for his contribution to the development of contemporary Czech literature.

Interviews:

Ladislav Kapek, "O lidech živých i mrtvých hovoříme s Vladimírem Páralem," *Kulturní tvorba*, no. 26 (1967): 1;

Otakar Brůna, "Pět minut s Vladimírem Páralem," *Československý voják*, no. 2 (1969) : 19;

Rudolf Křesťan, "Píšu pořád jednu knihu," *Mladý svět*, no. 42 (1981): 20–21.

References:

Jan Čulík, "Integrity, Creativity and Death: Three New Czech Novels," *Irish-Slavonic Studies,* 6 (1985): 133–141;

Jan Čulík Sr., "Multibestia triumphans et incorporata," *Proměny,* 27, no. 4 (1990): 150–152;

Vladimír Dostál, "Mechanický zvěřinec z konce tisíciletí," in his *Zrcadla podél cest. K české próze 1969–1974* (Prague: Československý spisovatel, 1987): 71–84;

Igor Hájek, "Making an Enemy of Man," *Times Literary Supplement,* 7 (1 February 1986): 2;

William E. Harkins, "Vladimír Páral's Novel *Catapult,*" in *Czech Literature Since 1956: A Symposium,* edited by Harkins and Paul I. Trensky (New York: Bohemica, 1980), pp. 62–73;

Pavel Janoušek, "Vladimír Páral, *Katapult,*" in his *Česká literatura 1945–1970. Interpretace vybraných děl* (Prague: Státní pedagogické nakladatelství, 1993), pp. 374–383;

Janoušek, "Vladimír Páral, *Muka obraznosti,*" in his *Český Parnas. Literatura 1970–1990* (Prague: Galaxie, 1993), pp. 223–229;

Milan Jungmann, "Cena za seberealizaci," in his *Cesty a rozcestí, Kritické stati z let 1982–87* (London: Rozmluvy, 1988), pp. 122–145;

Jungmann, "Páralovo teatrum mundi," in his *Průhledy do české prózy* (Prague: Evropský literární klub, 1990);

Pavel Kosatík, "Vladimír Páral," in his *Malá galerie autorů Československého spisovatele* (Prague: Československý spisovatel, 1989);

Karel Kosík, *Dialektika konkrétního.* (Prague: Československá akademie věd, 1963);

Helena Kosková, "Profesionální spisovatel," in her *Hledání ztracené generace* (Toronto: Sixty-Eight Publishers, 1987), pp. 242–260;

Zdeněk Kožmín, "Zvětšeniny z moderní prózy," *Plamen,* 3 (1969): 48;

Karel Milota, "Podivný let inženýra Jošta," *Plamen,* 6 (1968): 44;

Jiří Opelík, "Neo-Balzac z Ústí nad Labem," *Literární listy,* 21 (1968): 3;

Robert B. Pynsent, *Sex Under Socialism. An Essay on the Works of Vladimír Páral* (London: School of Slavonic and East European Studies, University of London, 1994);

David Short, "Páralův *Veletrh splněných přání*—učebnicový vzor překladatelské problematiky," *Proměny,* 19, no. 1 (1988): 35–41;

Josef Škvorecký, "Ecce scriptor!," *Kulturní tvorba,* 3, no. 5 (1965): 14;

Škvorecký, "Páralovo permanentní posvícení," in *Na brigádě,* by Škvorecký and Antonín Brousek (Toronto: Sixty-Eight Publishers, 1979), pp. 213–231;

Škvorecký, "Some Contemporary Czech Prose Writers," *Novel,* 4 (1970): 5–13.

Tadeusz Różewicz

(9 October 1921 –   )

Richard Sokoloski
University of Ottawa

BOOKS: *Echa leśne,* as "Satyr" (N.p., 1944; Warsaw: Państwowy Instytut Wydawniczy, 1985);

W łyżce wody: Satyry (Częstochowa: Słowo, 1946);

Niepokój (Kraków: Przełom, 1947);

Czerwona rękawiczka (Kraków: Książka, 1948);

Pięć poematów (Warsaw: Czytelnik, 1950);

Czas który idzie (Warsaw: Czytelnik, 1951);

Wiersze i obrazy (Warsaw: Czytelnik, 1952);

Kartki z Węgier (Warsaw: Czytelnik, 1953);

Równina (Kraków: Wydawnictwo Literackie, 1954);

Opadły liście z drzew (Warsaw: Państwowy Instytut Wydawniczy, 1955);

Srebrny kłos (Warsaw: Czytelnik, 1955);

Uśmiechy (Warsaw: Czytelnik, 1955);

Poemat otwarty (Kraków: Wydawnictwo Literackie, 1956);

Formy (Warsaw: Czytelnik, 1958);

Przerwany egzamin (Warsaw: Państwowy Instytut Wydawniczy, 1960; enlarged, 1965);

Rozmowa z księciem (Warsaw: Państwowy Instytut Wydawniczy, 1960);

Głos anonima (Katowice: Śląsk, 1961);

Zielona róża: Kartoteka (Warsaw: Państwowy Instytut Wydawniczy, 1961);

Nic w płaszczu Prospera (Warsaw: Państwowy Instytut Wydawniczy, 1963);

Twarz (Warsaw: Czytelnik, 1964; revised, 1966);

Wycieczka do muzeum (Warsaw: Czytelnik, 1966);

Twarz trzecia (Warsaw: Czytelnik, 1968);

Regio (Warsaw: Państwowy Instytut Wydawniczy, 1969);

Śmierć w starych dekoracjach (Warsaw: Państwowy Instytut Wydawniczy, 1970);

Teatr niekonsekwencji (Warsaw: Państwowy Instytut Wydawniczy, 1970);

Przygotowanie do wieczoru autorskiego (Warsaw: Państwowy Instytut Wydawniczy, 1971; enlarged, 1977);

Duszyczka (Kraków: Wydawnictwo Literackie, 1977);

Opowiadanie traumatyczne: Duszyczka (Kraków: Wydawnictwo Literackie, 1979);

Tadeusz Różewicz (photograph by Renate von Mangoldi)

Próba rekonstruckcji (Wrocław: Zaklad Narodowy im. Ossolińskich, 1979);

Tarcza z pajęczyny (Kraków: Wydawnictwo Literackie, 1980);

Pułapka (Warsaw: Czytelnik, 1982); translated by Adam Czerniawski as *The Trap* (New York: Institute for Contemporary Eastern European

Drama and Theatre, 1984; Amsterdam: Harwood Academic Publishers, 1996);

Na powierzchni poematu i w środku (Nowy wybór wierszy) (Warsaw: Czytelnik, 1983);

Płaskorzeźba (Wrocław: Wydawnictwo Dolnośląskie, 1991);

Historia pięciu wierszy (Kłodzko: Witryna artystów, 1993);

Słowo po słowie: Nowy wybór wierszy (Wrocław: Wydawnictwo Dolnośląskie, 1994);

Zawsze fragment (Wrocław: Wydawnictwo Dolnośląskie, 1996);

Zwierciadło: Poematy wybrane (Kraków: Wydawnictwo Literackie, 1998);

Zawsze fragment: Recycling (Wrocław: Wydawnictwo Dolnośląskie, 1998);

Matka odchodzi (Wrocław: Wydawnictwo Dolnośląskie, 1999).

Editions and Collections: *Wybór wierszy* (Warsaw: Państwowy Instytut Wydawniczy, Seria "Biblioteka poetów," 1953);

Poezje zebrane (Kraków: Wydawnictwo Literackie, 1957);

Niepokój: Wybór wierszy 1945–1961 (Warsaw: Państwowy Instytut Wydawniczy, 1963);

Utwory dramatyczne (Kraków: Wydawnictwo Literackie, 1966);

Poezje wybrane, edited by Hieronim Michalski (Warsaw: Ludowa Spółdzielnia Wydawnicza, Seria "Biblioteka poetów XX wieku," 1967);

Wiersze i poematy, edited by Michalski (Warsaw: Państwowy Instytut Wydawniczy, Seria "Biblioteka poetów," 1967);

Opowiadania wybrane (Warsaw: Czytelnik, 1968);

Poezje zebrane (Wrocław: Zakład Narodowy im. Ossolińskich, 1971);

Sztuki teatralne (Wrocław: Zakład Narodowy im. Ossolińskich, 1972);

Proza (Wrocław: Zakład Narodowy im. Ossolińskich, 1973);

Poezja. Dramat. Proza (Wrocław: Zakład Narodowy im. Ossolińskich, 1973);

Wiersze (Warsaw: Państwowy Instytut Wydawniczy, Seria "Biblioteka poetów," 1974);

Białe małżeństwo i inne utwory sceniczne (Kraków: Wydawnictwo Literackie, 1975);

Poezje wybrane (Warsaw: Ludowa Spółdzielnia Wydawnicza, 1984);

Poezja, 2 volumes (Kraków: Wydawnictwo Literackie, 1988);

Teatr, 2 volumes (Kraków: Wydawnictwo Literackie, 1988);

Proza, 2 volumes (Kraków: Wydawnictwo Literackie, 1990);

Dlaczego Różewicz: Wiersze i komentarze, edited by Jacek Brzozowski and Jerzy Poradecki (Łódź: Wydawnictwo Uniwersytetu Łódzkiego, 1993);

Dramaty wybrane (Kraków: Wydawnictwo Literackie, 1994);

Niepokój: Wybór wierszy z lat 1944–1994 (Warsaw: Państwowy Instytut Wydawniczy, 1995).

Editions in English: "The New Philosophical School," translated by Paul Mayewski, in *The Broken Mirror: A Collection of Writings from Contemporary Poland*, edited by Pawel Mayewski (New York: Random House, 1958), pp. 11–29;

"In the Most Beautiful City in the World," translated by Adam Czerniawski, and "The Plains," translated by Mayewski, in *Introduction to Modern Polish Literature: An Anthology of Fiction and Poetry*, edited by Adam Gillon and Ludwik Krzyżanowski (New York: Twayne, 1964), pp. 331–354, 449–459;

"In the Middle of Life," "The Apple," "Playing Horses," "The Wall, "A Voice," "Albumen," "Transformations," "Leave Us Alone," "The Deposition of the Burden," "To the Heart," and "A Sketch for a Modern Love Poem," translated by Czesław Miłosz, in *Postwar Polish Poetry: An Anthology*, edited by Miłosz (New York: Doubleday, 1965), pp. 62–74;

"Playing Horses," "The Wall," "A Sketch for a Modern Love Poem," "In the Middle of Life," and "Leave Us Alone," translated by Miłosz; "To the Heart," translated by Peter Janson-Smith; "Fear," translated by Celina Wieniewska; "Apart," "The Survivor," "Haskiel," "Massacre of the Innocents," and "An Address," translated by Jan Darowski; and "A Monument Raised Under the Occupation," "A Tale of Old Women," and "Unrecorded Epistle," translated by Czerniawski, in *Polish Writing Today*, edited by Wieniewska (Baltimore, Md.: Penguin, 1967), pp. 122–137;

The Card Index and Other Plays, translated by Czerniawski (London: Calder & Boyars, 1969; New York: Grove, 1970);

Faces of Anxiety: Poems, translated by Czerniawski (Chicago: Swallow Press, 1969; London: Rapp & Whiting, 1969);

The Witnesses and Other Plays, translated by Czerniawski (London: Calder & Boyars, 1970);

"Fear," translated by Andrzej Busza and Bogdan Czaykowski; "Knowledge," "Birth of a New Poem," "New Comparisons," "A Tree," and "Poem," translated by Czerniawski; "Chestnut," translated by Geoffrey Thurley; and "A Dithyramb in Honour of the Mother-in-Law,"

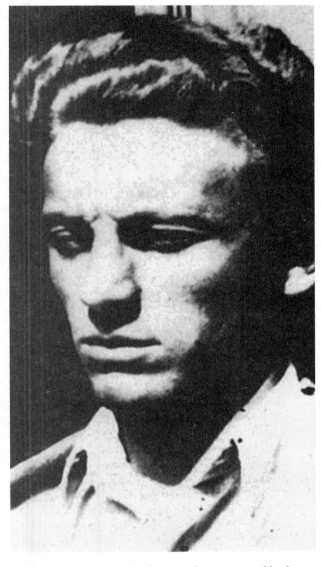

Różewicz's older brother, Janusz, who was executed by the Gestapo in 1944

translated by Miłosz, in *Modern Poetry in Translation: Polish Issue*, edited by Czaykowski, 23–24 (1975): 17–19;

"The Survivor" and Other Poems, translated by Magnus J. Krynski and Robert A. Maguire (Princeton: Princeton University Press, 1976);

Selected Poems, translated by Czerniawski (Harmondsworth, U.K.: Penguin, 1976);

"Birth Rate: The Biography of a Play for the Theatre," translated by Daniel Gerould, in *Twentieth-Century Polish Avant-Garde Drama: Plays, Scenarios, Critical Documents*, edited by Gerould (Ithaca, N.Y.: Cornell University Press, 1977), pp. 269–279;

"The Green Rose," "Lamentation," and "First Love," translated by Krzysztof Zarzecki, in *White Stones and Fir Trees: An Anthology of Contemporary Slavic Literature*, edited by Vasa D. Mihailovich (Rutherford, N.J.: Fairleigh Dickinson University Press, 1977), pp. 146–150, 187–189;

"Lament," translated by Marek Englender; "Who Is a Poet," translated by Janusz Maliszewski; and "My Poetry," translated by Krystyna Kamińska, Maliszewski, and Ela Perepeczko, in *The New Polish Poetry*, edited by Milne Holton and Paul Vangelisti (Pittsburgh, Pa.: University of Pittsburgh Press, 1978), pp. 3–7;

Unease, translated by Victor Contoski (St. Paul, Minn.: New Rivers Press, 1980);

Conversation with the Prince and Other Poems, translated by Czerniawski (London: Anvil Press Poetry, 1982);

Green Rose: Poems, translated by Thurley (Darlington, Australia: John Michael, 1982);

"Boobsie Tootsie or Romantic Love is Already Waiting at the Door," "The Double," "A Discordant Drama," and "What Comes What Goes," translated by Edward J. Czerwinski, *Slavic and East European Arts*, 1 (Spring 1983): 134–149;

Mariage Blanc and The Hunger Artist Departs: Two Plays, translated by Czerniawski (London & New York: Marion Boyars, 1983);

"Moment," "Forms," "Roots," "Talent," "I Build," and "Remembrance from a Dream in 1963," translated by Contoski, in *Contemporary East European Poetry*, edited by Emery George (Ann Arbor, Mich.: Ardis, 1983), pp. 111–115;

"Doors," "The First Is Hidden," "Chestnut," "Photograph," "But whoever sees . . . ," "The Return," "Wood," "Pigtail," "Massacre of the Boys," "A Tree," "The Survivor," "In the Midst of Life," "They Shed the Load," "New Comparisons," "Autumnal," "Laughter," "Death," "Penetration," "Proofs," "Picture," "That rustle . . . ," "Grass," "Tree-felling," and "Description of a Poem," translated by Czerniawski, in *The Burning Forest: Modern Polish Poetry*, edited by Czerniawski (Newcastle upon Tyne: Bloodaxe Books, 1988), pp. 62–83;

They Came to See a Poet: Selected Poems, translated by Czerniawski (London: Anvil Press Poetry, 1991);

Tadeusz Różewicz's Bas-Relief and Other Poems, translated, with an introduction, by Edward J. Czerwinski (Stony Brook, N.Y.: Slavic Cultural Center Press, 1991);

"Laughter," "Pouring," and "The poet grows weaker . . . ," translated by Stanisław Barańczak and Clare Cavanagh, in *Polish Poetry of the Last Two Decades of Communist Rule: Spoiling Cannibals' Fun*, edited by Barańczak and Cavanagh (Evanston, Ill.: Northwestern University Press, 1991), pp. 54–56;

Poezje Wybrane / Selected Poems, translated by Czerniawski (Kraków: Wydawnictwo Literackie, 1991);

"The Tree" and "The Grass," translated by Karen Karleski, in *Shifting Borders: East European Poetries of the Eighties*, edited by Walter Cummins (Rutherford, N.J.: Fairleigh Dickinson University Press, 1993), pp. 273–274;

Forms in Relief and Other Works, bilingual edition, translated and edited by Richard Sokoloski (Ottawa: Legas, 1994);

Reading the Apocalypse in Bed: Selected Plays and Short Pieces, translated by Czerniawski, Barbara Plebanek, and Tony Howard (London: Marion Boyars, 1998).

PRODUCED SCRIPTS: *Trzy kobiety*, motion picture, by Różewicz, Stanisław Różewicz, and Kornel Filipowicz, Film Polski, 1956;

Miejsce na ziemi, motion picture, by Różewicz and Filipowicz, Film Polski, 1959;

Świadectwo urodzenia, motion picture, by Różewicz and Stanisław Różewicz, Film Polski, 1961;

Głos z tamtego świata, motion picture, by Różewicz and Filipowicz, Film Polski, 1962;

Echo, motion picture, by Różewicz and Stanisław Różewicz, Film Polski, 1964;

Piekło i niebo, motion picture, by Różewicz and Filipowicz, Film Polski, 1966;

Mąż pod łóżkiem, motion picture, by Różewicz and Stanisław Różewicz, television, Film Polski, 1967;

Samotność we dwoje, motion picture, by Różewicz and Stanisław Różewicz, Film Polski, 1968;

Drzwi w murze, motion picture, by Różewicz and Stanisław Różewicz, Film Polski, 1973.

RECORDING: *Wiersze wybrane czyta poeta*, read by Różewicz, Seria "Współczesna poezja polska," Muza, N0271, 1965.

OTHER: *Nasz starszy brat*, edited by Różewicz (Wrocław: Wydawnictwo Dolnośląskie, 1992).

SELECTED PERIODICAL PUBLICATIONS— UNCOLLECTED: "Dźwięk i obraz w poezji współczesnej," *Trybuna Literacka*, 19 (1958): 97–100;

Kartoteka [previously unpublished fragments], *Odra*, 11 (1971): 67–75;

Pogrzeb po polsku, *Odra*, 7–8 (1971): 71–78;

Do piachu . . . , *Dialog*, 2, (1972): 5–29;

"Poemat otwarty i dramaturgia otwarta," *Odra*, 15 (1975): 89–90;

O wojnę powszechną za wolność ludów prosimy Cię, Panie, *Dialog*, 9 (1978): 5–26;

"Sztuka nienapisana," *Dialog*, 10 (1991): 70–73.

Tadeusz Różewicz is one of the most original twentieth-century Polish writers. His poetry, drama, and prose works, which have gained him a high reputation at home and abroad, are both innovative and controversial. World War II and its aftermath provide an important point of departure for his early writing; however, his later works address more universal contemporary themes. His invention of new verse strategies as an artistic response to his war experiences constitutes a significant literary achievement. His blending of diverse literary and nonliterary forms, an innovation that pervades all of his creative writing, best conveys the spirit of his principal philosophical concerns: the loss of absolute cultural norms, the destruction of subjective knowledge, and the relativization of truth. Translated into more than thirty languages, his work has received several prestigious national and international awards, and for many years, various groups have lobbied unsuccessfully for Różewicz to receive the Nobel Prize in literature.

Różewicz was born in the city of Radomsko in central Poland on 9 October 1921, the middle son of Stefania Maria (née Gelbard) and Władysław Różewicz, a minor judicial officer. Różewicz's younger brother, Stanisław, eventually became a moviemaker with whom Różewicz collaborated; his older brother, Janusz, a promising poet murdered by the Gestapo in 1944, was an early literary influence. Różewicz began writing in his teens, editing with Janusz a school newspaper in which his first literary attempts appeared. An early play, "Krzywda" (Injustice), written with Janusz and staged at home, dates from this period. His juvenilia, comprising love lyrics, parodistic imitations, and verses with socialist colorings, were published in several minor regional journals. Approaching matriculation, Różewicz hoped to attend a pedagogical institute in nearby Piotrków Trybunalski; his family's financial situation in the economically depressed 1930s, however, prevented his enrollment. Shortly before the out-

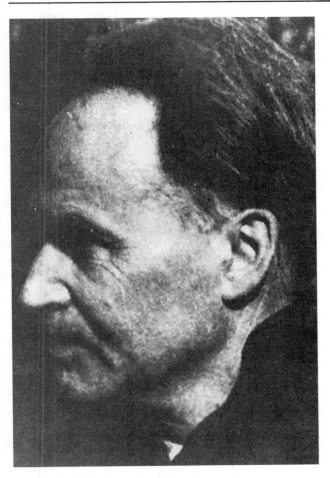

The avant-garde poet Julian Przyboś, who published Różewicz's early poems in the magazine Odrodzenie

November 1944 he served in a peasant battalion of the underground *Armia krajowa* (Home Army), active in the Radomsko-Częstochowa region. While a partisan, in 1944 he published (clandestinely, under the pseudonym of "Satyr") *Echa leśne* (Forest Echoes), a collection of poems and short prose pieces drawn from his daily observations and written for the underground soldiers. Describing the individual exploits of Różewicz's unit in both humorous and serious tones, *Echa leśne* is largely devoid of politics. The collection also includes a poem by his brother Janusz, and another that was written jointly. Różewicz also edited his unit's newspaper, *Głos krzaka* (Voice from the Underbrush). In the forest the young soldier-author profited from his long periods of inactivity by reading intensively the works of William Shakespeare, Fyodor Dostoyevsky, Juliusz Słowacki, and Friedrich Wilhelm Nietzsche.

By 1944 the advances of the Red Army on the Eastern Front had become a source of anxiety for the staunchly nationalist *Armia krajowa*. In February of that year an article by Różewicz titled "Słowo o żołnierzu polskim" (A Word about Polish Soldiers) appeared in an issue of another partisan publication, *Czyn zbrojny* (Armed Action). The article, because of certain perceived leftist themes, may have prompted Różewicz's hasty deactivation from the underground. After the war Różewicz was twice decorated for his military service.

Following the conclusion of hostilities, the twenty-four-year-old survivor registered in a school in Częstochowa, anxious to complete his education. Between studies Różewicz began writing satirical prose for various important journals, including *Szpilki* (Pins). Several of these pieces, along with his poems, eventually appeared in Różewicz's first postwar collection, *W łyżce wody* (In a Spoonful of Water, 1946). Following his discharge from the military, Różewicz moved to Kraków, where he spent the years 1945 to 1949 studying art history at the Jagiellonian University. In Kraków, Różewicz decided to become a professional writer. He published mostly in *Odrodzenie* (Rebirth), which was then edited by Julian Przyboś, a leading avant-garde poet in Poland in the interwar and early postwar periods. Różewicz's relationship with Przyboś, first as a young adept and later as a colleague, proved to be an important creative influence. Aside from Przyboś, however, Różewicz in characteristic fashion shunned the larger literary community of Kraków, preferring instead the company of painters and moviemakers, many of whom, including Tadeusz

break of war, he withdrew from school and was forced to seek work as a physical laborer.

Radomsko, a small provincial town isolated from larger cosmopolitan centers, permanently marked Różewicz as an "outsider," both distant from and impervious to literary trends and coteries. This attitude constantly reemerges in Różewicz's public and personal life. In Poland, where boundaries between power spheres have always been sharply drawn, Różewicz's estrangement from the artistic, political, and religious establishments left him vulnerable to criticism and indeed misunderstandings on all sides. To seek in Różewicz any conventional relationship between the artist, the nature of his art, and the private individual is highly problematic.

Różewicz spent the first years of the war in Radomsko, then under German occupation, at a variety of jobs: as a messenger in a storage depot, a superintendent of apartments, and a laborer in a furniture factory. From 26 June 1943 to 3

Kantor, Andrzej Wajda, Jerzy Nowosielski, and Jerzy Tchórzewski, achieved national and international recognition.

World War II had constituted for Różewicz a new stage in mankind's history. As he noted in "Do źródeł" (To the Sources, 1959), published in *Przygotowanie do wieczoru autorskiego* (Preparation for an Author's Reading, 1971), "the umbilical cord connecting" his poetry to metaphysics "had been torn." Deprived of a metaphysical referent, Różewicz vented his frustration in the first significant volume of verse, *Niepokój* (Anxiety, 1947), a landmark work that brought instant acclaim. As he explained in "Do źródeł," for Różewicz the events of 1939–1945 had exposed a false morality and culture, a value system that had failed to avert the catastrophe: "I felt as if something had ended forever, for me and for all mankind. Something neither religion, science, nor art had managed to preserve."

In *Niepokój*, burdened by shame as a participant and a sense of guilt as a survivor, Różewicz fused his poetic predicament and ethical outrage to formulate a distinctive artistic response. He deliberately rejected the formal conventions of poetry—such as meter, rhyme, imagery, and diction—and attempted to "de-poeticize" poetry, "to create facts instead of verse." The result was a form of expression that reaffirmed the poetic through contrary strategies: poetic asceticism, subversion of conventional syntax, rejection of the limits of traditional form, and silence. Różewicz's stark antipoetry and innovative verse arrangement (later codified by theorists as the "fourth" system of Polish prosody) was recognized as a form of writing "in the aftermath of Auschwitz," as illustrated in the poem "Ocalony" (translated as "The Survivor," 1967):

I am twenty-four
led to slaughter
I survived

The following are empty synonyms:
man and beast
love and hate
friend and foe
darkness and light

The way of killing men and beasts is the same
I've seen them:
truckfuls of chopped-up men
who will not be saved
....
I seek a teacher and a master
may he restore my sight hearing and speech
may he again name objects and ideas

may he separate darkness from light

(translated by Adam Czerniawski)

Much of Różewicz's early verse, which includes the collections *Czerwona rękawiczka* (The Red Glove, 1948), *Pięć poematów* (Five Longer Poems, 1950), *Czas który idzie* (Time Unbound, 1951), *Wiersze i obrazy* (Poems and Images, 1952), *Równina* (The Plain, 1954), *Srebrny kłos* (A Silver Ear of Corn, 1955), and *Poemat otwarty* (An Open Poem, 1956), attempts to bridge the gap between the recent past and contemporaneity. Poetry became for Różewicz an act of naming—devoid of ornament, stripped of form, ordinary and unambiguous, expressively blunt. Juxtaposing the feelings of a victim/survivor and a perpetrator/advocate, Różewicz expressed his war experience in terms of nostalgia and guilt. Shame and guilt resulted from having been an instrument of death, as in "Lament" (translated as "Lament," 1976), published in *Niepokój*: "I am twenty / I am a murderer / a blind tool"—and for having survived when so many did not, as in "Widzę szalonych" (translated as "I See Madmen," 1969), published in *Czerwona rękawiczka*: "I see madmen / who had walked on the sea / believing to the end / and went down / . . . / cruelly alive I push away / those stiff hands / I push them away year after year."

Despite a disdain for the past, nostalgia for an unrealized utopia provided Różewicz with an antidote, both as an individual, as in "Powrót" (translated as "The Return," 1976), published in *Czerwona rękawiczka*, and as an artist, as in "Drzewo" (translated as "A Tree," 1976), published in *Srebrny kłos*: "Happy were / the poets of old / beneath the oak / they sang like a child / But our tree / creaked in the night / with the weight / of a corpse despised." The horrors of war took at times the image of the slaughter of innocents, as in "Rzeź chłopców" (translated as "Massacre of the Innocents," 1967, also translated as "Massacre of the Boys," 1969) and "Warkoczyk" (translated as "Pigtail," 1969), published in *Pięć poematów*, while longing for a lost world of innocence became a form of escape, as in "Kasztan" (translated as "Chestnut," 1975), published in *Czerwona rękawiczka*, and "Wspomnienie dzieciństwa" (translated as "Evocation of Childhood," 1982), published in *Wiersze i obrazy*. Reverence for the constancy of old age—especially of old women, as in "Matka powieszonych" (translated as "Mother of Hanged Men," 1976), published in *Niepokój*, and "Stara chłopka idzie brzegiem morza" (translated as "An Old Peasant Woman Walks Along

Różewicz in 1947 with Wiesława Kozłowska, whom he married two years later

the Beach," 1976), published in *Wiersze i obrazy*—also recurs as a means of refuge from the immediate past. In the years that followed the appearance of *Niepokój* Różewicz's poems were, with few exceptions, studied elaborations on a single formal method. "W środku życia" (translated as "In the Midst of Life," 1976), published in *Poemat otwarty,* may be read as a summing-up of his early *ars poetica.*

Eventually abandoning his formal study of art, in 1949 Różewicz resolved to leave the more urbane Kraków for the gray working-class city of Gliwice in the industrial heart of southern Poland. By August 1950 he had taken up residence in a crowded flat (owned by his mother-in-law) with his new bride, Wiesława Kozłowska, a fellow partisan whom he had married in February 1949. In Gliwice, Różewicz lived in relatively unchanged circumstances for the next two decades. To help support the family, which was frequently faced with insolvency and made larger by the births of two sons, Kamil

(1950) and Jan (1953), his wife took up clerical work. Queried by fellow writers as to what he was doing in Gliwice, Różewicz answered: "living."

The immediate postwar period was not without deviations in his writing, some even harmful. The years 1947 to 1955 were marked by politicization of all spheres of life in Poland. Following the war, the Communist faction, with strong backing from the Soviet Union, consolidated its power by 1948. The mandatory incorporation of communist ideology into all social and political domains, including art, proceeded unabated. Różewicz had written two plays between 1948 and 1950: "Będą się bili" (They Will Fight) and "Ujawnienie" (Coming Out), both inspired by contemporary political realities. Viewed as failures by the author, these plays were neither formally published in their entirety nor performed. At the same time, Różewicz had also begun work on a prose piece titled "Do piachu . . ." (Dead and Buried); dealing with the sensitive subject of the

Armia Krajowa, the text was similarly abandoned, but the idea was later reworked as a play.

While attending a literary convention at Nieborów in 1948 in his capacity as a correspondent for *Trybuna Robotnicza* (Worker's Tribune), Różewicz openly ridiculed the major Marxist journal *Kuźnica* (The Forge) for its blind advocacy of the tenets of socialist realism in art. Subsequently shunned at a convention of the Congress of Polish Writers' Union the following year in Szczecin, where the principles of socialist realism were announced and made binding on Polish writers, Różewicz sought refuge abroad, first in a short trip to Prague in the fall of 1949 and later to Hungary in January 1950, where his eight-month sojourn resulted in his *Kartki z Węgier* (Postcards from Hungary, 1953), short journalistic vignettes based on observations of his stay.

Though not a political writer by inclination, Różewicz wrote certain verses in this period, such as "W związku z pewnym wydarzeniem" (Regarding a Certain Incident), published in *Równina,* and "Rehabilitacja pośmiertna" (translated as "Posthumous Rehabilitation," 1982), published in *Poemat otwarty,* that were interpreted politically both by the communist authorities and the opposition. With his fame constantly growing, Różewicz's ambiguous position in regard to various camps—literary, political, religious, and otherwise—became increasingly uncomfortable.

Dubbed an "internal émigré" for his reluctance to press his writing more forcefully into the service of official policies, Różewicz eventually relented, and for a short time his verse displayed unambiguous political content. A small corpus of poems—such as "Ballada o karabinie" (Ballad of a Rifle), "Nie kładź mi rąk na sercu" (Do Not Place Your Hands on My Heart), "Gwiazda proletariatu" (Proletarian Star), and "Skąd smutek" (Whence Sadness) from the collection *Pięć poematów*—represent a serious though short-lived regression in Różewicz's poetic development. They are steeped in optimism for the better world of communism and are expressed in conventional verse structures (formal rhyme, punctuation, and syntax). Without exception, these particular verses are absent from subsequent collected editions.

Seizing on these poems, the antigovernment opposition found further reason for criticism when in 1955 the author accepted a State Award for poetry (second class) for his collection *Równina.* More sober critical voices at the time were generally divided on the question of Różewicz: those who read his works as a plea for a lost Arcadia

dubbed him a neoclassicist, while to those who attributed his rhetorical stance to anguished moral dislocation, he was a neoromantic. His most virulent detractors, such as Jan Błoński in *Przegląd kulturalny* in 1963, labeled him a "tragic nihilist" who was "living beyond life and the life of his country" and having nowhere to go with his art.

Różewicz was at a creative crossroads. He turned in earnest to other forms, especially to creative prose, following a suggestion by Przyboś that he expand his literary horizons. In 1955 Różewicz published his first collection of short stories, *Opadły liście z drzew* (Leaves Fell from Trees), which, in a manner reminiscent of his stark verse, resumed many of the themes he had already dealt with poetically. A collection of satirical stories, *Uśmiechy* (Smiles, 1955), displaying occasional surrealistic tones, also appeared. A particularly poignant prose work from this period, "Wycieczka do muzeum" (Excursion to a Museum, 1959), which served as the title piece for a subsequent collection of prose works (1966), describes a day trip to Auschwitz by a boorish working-class group hungry for the sensationalism they presume the death camp will offer. Intellectually and emotionally incapable of any appreciation of what they witness, they leave disappointed and angry.

When compared to his poetry and later his drama, Różewicz's prose initially seemed less innovative. However, Różewicz cultivated all three literary forms simultaneously. Though verse predominates in his early (and later) career and drama fills the middle, prose being a rather distant third throughout, undoubtedly Różewicz's most important achievement as an artist, aside from his verse innovations, was the manner in which he gradually fused disparate genres into one idiosyncratic artistic whole—a strategy that critics later came to call "impure form." By the 1950s Różewicz had also begun collaborating with his brother Stanisław on screenplays. Done ostensibly to supplement his income, these efforts testify to Różewicz's lifelong interest in visual art, also evidenced by the frequent presence of painting in his essays and creative writings, not to mention the strong visual elements of his poetry and plays.

In October 1956 there was a brief relaxation of tensions in Poland, and the suppression of the Hungarian Revolution by Soviet tanks "normalized" the situation in the Soviet bloc. Western Europe and North America, emerging from a political and cultural phase of staid conservatism, were set to explode in the creative turbulence of the 1960s. At the age of thirty-six, Różewicz

Manuscript page for Różewicz's poem "Nic w płaszczu Prospera," published in 1963 (from Tadeusz Drewnowski, Walka o oddech: O pisarstwie Tadeusza Różewicza [1990])

became the first Polish writer of his generation to be honored with a collected edition of his poetry, *Poezje zebrane* (Collected Poems, 1957). The accolade not only made his work an instant classic, but also gave a sense of closure to his verse.

Various visits in Europe and to North America encouraged Różewicz's artistic instincts, and in the ensuing two decades he was highly prolific, writing and staging more than a dozen innovative and controversial full-length plays as well as several smaller dramatic works. Różewicz continued his collaborative work on motion picture scripts, many of which were beginning to appear on screen. As his national reputation grew, so did his international reception. Several editions of his verse appeared in English, German, French, Russian, and other European languages, while his dramas were likewise translated and performed throughout Europe and North America. The increase in his international popularity was accompanied by frequent invitations to poetry readings and stagings. Różewicz traveled to Paris in March 1957, Yugoslavia in 1958 (where he enunciated a poetic credo titled "Dźwięk i obraz w poezji współczesnej," Sound and Image in Contemporary Poetry), Italy in 1960 (and later in 1964), Belgium in 1961, Finland in 1963, Copenhagen and Oslo in 1964, Rome and Berlin in 1967, Spain in 1970, London in 1971, Sweden in 1972, and New York in 1975. Further national and international distinctions were accorded him: First Prize of the Ministry of Polish Culture and Art (1962); the Jurzykowski Foundation Prize, New York (1966); the Literary Prize of the Polish periodical *Odra* (1970); the Polish Young Poets' Literary Prize (1971); and an award from the city of Wrocław (1973).

Against a backdrop of mounting tension in the political and cultural life of Poland in the 1960s, Różewicz's strict apolitical stance and the increasingly provocative themes of his writings served to fuel his notoriety. Denounced by his former mentor Przyboś (and a host of others) for self-pity and creative impotence, Różewicz responded with his incisive article "Sezon poetycki—jesień 1966" (Poetry Season—Fall 1966), first published in *Poezja* (Poetry) in 1967, in which he declared poetry "dead." His critics remained unrelenting in their onslaught for the rest of the decade and part of the 1970s. Also joining the attack was the Catholic Church. By the mid 1970s the Polish Primate Stefan Wyszyński, in a sermon decrying the proliferation of immorality in Polish art, publicly labeled Różewicz's work "smut."

Undeterred by the criticism (and frequent censorship), Różewicz began in earnest to develop further his curious synthesis of literary forms. His earlier verse, born of loss and disorientation, had striven to obliterate the boundaries between poetry and nonpoetry through basically reductivist means; his new concept of drama, a response to more universal themes of modernism and postmodernism, sought rather an expansion of existing methods through a merging of dramatic and nondramatic structures. Though Różewicz maintained that his poetry was "a preparation for his dramas," the formulation of his peculiar style of drama was in fact one of continuous interaction. In some instances, his dramas became extensions of his poetic works, as with "Et in Arcadia ego" (translated as "Et in Arcadia ego," 1982), published in *Głos anonima* (Voice of an Anonymous Man, 1961), and *Grupa Laocoona* (The Laocoon Group, 1961). The reverse is also true, as poems occasionally began to resemble dramas in miniature, as illustrated by the entire collection *Poemat otwarty*. Similarly, works written primarily in prose, such as *Śmierć w starych dekoracjach* (Death in Old Stage Sets, 1970), were also successfully performed on stage. Hybrid forms, such as *Przygotowanie do wieczoru autorskiego*, combine elements of the essay, short story, literary memoir, reminiscence, letter, and scholarly treatise with dramatic and lyrical passages to form a curious cohesion of their own.

Różewicz's plays also fuse disparate dramatic and theatrical concepts, seeking new artistic possibilities of transcription and performance. Różewicz's characters often speak both verse and prose, in addition to enunciating all manner of intertextual allusions, quotations, and even deliberate misquotations from both his own works and those of others. Many of his most innovative dramas at this time inspired some of the highest achievements of postwar theater directors, including Jerzy Jarocki and Kazimierz Braun. Invigorating for some, his manner was a bane to editors intent on categorizing his work on the basis of poetry, drama, and prose.

Różewicz's first major dramatic work, *Kartoteka* (translated as *The Card Index*, 1969), which premiered in Warsaw at Teatr Dramatyczny on 25 March 1960, made as profound an effect on the theatrical world as his poetic work *Niepokój* had some thirteen years prior. Różewicz had actually returned to drama in the mid 1950s, transposing the rejected prose work "Do piachu . . ." into a play in 1955 (though it remained incomplete for several years). *Kartoteka*, however, was his first mature attempt at poetic drama, one that opposed both classical and avant-garde traditions. Compositionally, he exploited open forms devoid of traditional action and temporal sequencing, while rejecting plot, psychological characterization, logic, and causality. Physical space is relativized, and the characters are rendered anonymous and multidimensional. Extensive literary and linguistic intertextual passages, often ironic or parodic, include nominal declensions, nursery rhymes, news clippings, quotations from classical works of Polish and non-Polish authors, and occasional hints at an historical setting. Thematically, *Kartoteka* was another attempt by Różewicz to resolve the dilemmas of his generation, morally disenfranchised by war and lost in the chaos and repression of contemporary life. Given its problematic self-defining strategies, the play was not immediately understood, and it closed after only nine performances. It has since, however, become a staple in schools, and has been successfully revived on the stage.

Several plays followed *Kartoteka* in rapid succession. A year later, in *Grupa Laocoona*, Różewicz again used an open-ended structure, this time to parody the Ibsenesque model of the family drama of realistic illusion and psychological disclosure. His implicit message, enunciated through a depersonalized family made up of figures such as Father, Mother, and Son, was that absolute aesthetic norms are themselves a self-perpetuating illusion, one that ultimately becomes anachronistic. Ethical values were similarly critiqued in Różewicz's next play, *Świadkowie, albo nasza mała stabilizacja* (1962; translated as *The Witnesses*, 1970). His real target, however, was the materialistic opportunism and consumer comfort he perceived in a society whose foundations, despite a semblance of normality (political, cultural, and social), had been seriously undermined. Though the play preserves a strong sense of nonreferentiality, dramatic tension proceeds logically through a series of incidents that reinforce the theme: an infant tortures a kitten to death while soothing music plays, and a living creature within touching distance perishes as two men lounge comfortably on chairs.

In *Akt przerywany* (1964; translated as *The Interrupted Act*, 1969) Różewicz made a radical attempt to write a play that would preclude performance. His previous plays, despite their nonillusionistic strategies, had nevertheless used dialogue, albeit of an unconventional manner. Left purposely incomplete by Różewicz, *Akt przery-*

wany offers at best a series of authorial ruminations on the potential for a play, or indeed several plays. Adding a negligible reference to plot—an engineer's conflict with his daughter—Różewicz wrote a nondrama with little more than disjointed stage directions, the value of which can only be determined by a director and cast.

Throughout the 1960s and early 1970s, Różewicz composed a series of shorter-length plays, including *Śmieszny staruszek* (1964; translated as *The Funny Old Man*, 1970), *Wyszedł z domu* (1964; translated as *Gone Out*, 1969), *Spaghetti i miecz* (Spaghetti and the Sword, 1964), *Pogrzeb po polsku* (A Funeral Polish Style, 1971), and *Na czworakach* (On All Fours, 1971), all conceived in less radical form than *Akt przerywany*. In *Śmieszny staruszek* and *Wyszedł z domu*, he traces in tragicomic fashion the failure of ordinary individuals to find a suitable place in contemporary reality. A study in loneliness and delusion, the former work relates the story of a seventy-year-old alleged child-killer, who defends himself in court by means of a rambling monologue. In *Wyszedł z domu*, again parodying the family drama, Różewicz took up several existential concerns relating to reality and the individual. A husband, afflicted by amnesia, returns home lacking an identity, which his wife then proceeds to reconstruct on the basis of sundry philosophical concerns. *Spaghetti i miecz* and *Pogrzeb po polsku* both subvert sacrosanct myths relating to romantic notions of Polish heroism. An evocation of the Faust legend with actors performing on all fours, *Na czworakach* examines the notion of artistic genius in the modern world and the cultural role of the artist in a mass society. The artist, Laurentius the Poet, corrupted by adulation and collective association with the masses, is dispossessed of all creative genius after he assumes the dimensions of an institution.

Continuing to explore longer dramatic forms, Różewicz followed *Akt przerywany* with a more intemperate form of meta-theater in his *Przyrost naturalny: Biografia sztuki teatralnej* (1968; translated as "Birth Rate: The Biography of a Play for the Theatre," 1977). Desultory jottings alongside notes from a dramatist's diary vaguely suggest a few scenes that relate to the theme of overpopulation. Performable as environmental theater, *Przyrost naturalny* offers interesting possibilities for creating dramatic tension through space and movement. Commenting on his intentions, Różewicz stated: "Do you realize how hard I worked not to write 'Birthrate'?"

In *Stara kobieta wysiaduje* (1968; translated as *The Old Woman Broods,* 1970), one of his most disturbing works, Różewicz turned the stage into a poetic metaphor. While an old woman searches for a lost son, the author evokes a complex image of postcatastrophist humanity wallowing in material and ideological refuse. Tension and a sense of menace increase as the stage becomes a wasteland pervaded by madness and imminent death. An orgy of accumulation that shrinks theatrical space in novel ways, the play juxtaposes moods of deprivation and loss with a desire for resolution.

By the end of the 1960s Różewicz was one of the most published and discussed writers in Poland. His financial situation had improved in the interim, and in 1968 he moved his family from Gliwice to Wrocław, a larger, university city in southwestern Poland. The political situation in Poland was again volatile by the end of the decade, as a change in party leadership had been precipitated by student demonstrations in Warsaw and other cities in 1968 and workers' strikes in Gdańsk in 1970. During this time Różewicz continued writing plays. New poems also appeared, though often in collections that included poems that had previously been published (or their revised versions). Four plays—*Do piachu . . .* (Dead and Gone . . . , completed 1972; performed 1979); *Białe małżeństwo* (1974; translated as *Mariage Blanc,* 1983), which, during a slight relaxation in censorship in the early 1970s, managed to arouse wide controversy because of its overt treatment of sexuality; *Odejście głodomora* (1976; translated as *The Hunger Artist Departs,* 1983); and *Pułapka* (1982; translated as *The Trap,* 1984)—at first glance seem to be less extreme in formal experimentation. Employing more or less conventional unities of characterization and plot, the plays nonetheless strive for formal destabilization through less obvious deployment of the author's "impure form" strategies.

Do piachu . . . , finally completed in 1972 and withdrawn from the stage after a brief and vehemently protested run in 1979, is a bold attempt at mythological deconstruction. Różewicz's immediate target was a sensitive subject of recent Polish history—the heroism of the *Armia Krajowa*—and in a broader sense, war and its destruction of the individual. Begun as a work of prose in the late 1940s, recast as a drama in the mid 1950s, shelved in the 1960s, staged and summarily barred from the Polish dramatic repertoire by the end of the 1970s (though later made into a movie in the postcommunist era), the play relates the demise of an *Armia Krajowa* soldier through a disturbing use of historical, social, and religious motifs. An unheroic and simple character, Waluś, a deserter who is suspected of rape, is captured by another unit and eventually led to believe he will be set free. Escorted outside the camp, he abruptly hears a death sentence and is shot, unable to contain his bowels during his final seconds. A brutal exorcism and conscious profanation of a sensitive part of Poland's wartime past, the play continues to arouse heated discussion both inside and outside Poland.

Białe małżeństwo, a turn-of-the-century comedy of manners, is a frank analysis of feminine sexual awakening in a repressive, intrigue-filled rural setting. A form of creative plagiarism that lifts freely and for parodistic purposes from such works of the classical canon as Piotr Skarga's sixteenth-century *Żywoty świętych* (Lives of the Saints) and Adam Mickiewicz's romantic verse epic *Pan Tadeusz* (Master Thaddeus, 1834), *Białe małżeństwo* proved immensely popular with Polish (and non-Polish) audiences, though it was condemned as pornographic by both the establishment and the Church.

In *Odejście głodomora* Różewicz again returned to the relevance of art and the artist in a modern consumer society, an idea previously explored in *Grupa Laocoona* and *Na czworakach.* In this play Różewicz scrutinizes the public's ritualistic view of the artist and those processes by which the creative individual cultivates a role that addresses an inner need for artistic and spiritual sustenance. The work of Franz Kafka, whose short story "Ein Hungerkünstler" (The Hunger-Artist, 1924) was an inspiration for the play, had held an ongoing fascination for Różewicz since the late 1940s, when he started but failed to complete a volume of nonfiction based on Kafka's biography.

Pułapka also derives from Kafka. A family drama for which Różewicz relied extensively on Kafka's diaries and letters, the play traces the life, loves, and death of the artist, focusing primarily on the last element. *Pułapka* is also a metaphor for the demise of artistic creativity, played out against visions of the impending "final" solution. The work is the only dramatic attempt by Różewicz to deal explicitly with the Holocaust. An absorbing piece when read or performed, *Pułapka* is one of Różewicz's most powerful in terms of his analysis of the relationships between art, the gifted individual, and the indiscriminate destruction in recent history.

Although Różewicz's achievements in the dramatic mode overshadowed his poetry for a

Wojciech Siemion as The Funny Old Man in a scene from a production of Różewicz's play Śmieszny staruszek
at the Teatr Polski, Wrocław, in 1968

time, new directions in his poetry were nonetheless emerging, though they were not as radical as during the immediate postwar period. Thematically, the erstwhile victim and survivor from the earlier verse began, like his dramatic counterpart, to address more contemporary and universal issues. Novel themes for Różewicz's poetry during this period include: the abstract illusions of both capitalistic and socialistic notions of progress, as in "Nowy człowiek" (translated as "The New Man," 1982), published in *Rozmowa z księciem* (1960); the subversion of the classical heritage by the growth of mass culture and its consequent denial of the individual, as in "Et in Arcadia ego"; the search for a secular form of ethical/spiritual legitimacy to replace hackneyed, outmoded models, as in "Nic" (Nothing), published in *Twarz trzecia* (1968), and "Zielona róża" (translated as "Green Rose," 1976), published in *Zielona róża* (1961); the place of art and the artist in a changing world, as in "Nic w płaszczu Prospera" (translated as "Nothing in Prospero's Cloak," 1976), published in *Nic w płaszczu Prospera* (1963); the dangers of moral and spiritual relativism, as in "Spadanie" (translated as "Falling," 1976), published in *Twarz trzecia;* the devastating effects of consumerism, as in "Non-Stop

Shows" (title in English; translated as "Continuous Performances," 1976), published in *Twarz trzecia;* and eroticism, as in "Regio" (translated as "Regio," 1982), published in *Regio* (1969).

Różewicz also resumed poetic experimentation during this period. Abandoning his earlier strategy of "naked poetry," Różewicz began to construct longer digressive structures that employ an extreme form of "collage" arrangement, one that conveys the lyric statement through the accelerated and disjointed imagery of a camera eye, often in several idioms simultaneously (as in "Non-Stop Shows"):

> Intermezzo Striptease à la Paris
> Moulin Rouge Bomben Variétéprogramm
> Die Zwiebel Lola Montez Bar Pique Dame
> Gastätte Nürnberger Bratwurstglöckl
> Weiss und Bratwürste Hünergustl
> Schweinswürstl etc Playboys Bierhalle
> Stachelwchwein Schwabing
> On parle français Eve Schöne Frauen
> English spoken kucharze z Czunkingu

The 1960s and 1970s were also characterized by poetic experimentation with strategies that wed verse and prose. The process had first been initiated in Różewicz's *Formy* (Forms, 1958), wherein both genres appeared as interdependent parts of the same text, and later in *Tarcza z pajęczyny* (The Cobweb Shield, 1980), which virtually obliterated all distinctions between the two. Różewicz went to further extremes with *Złowiony* (Caught) in 1969 and *Duszyczka* (Animula) in 1977. In effect, his goal was to turn language and art inward, to the extent that his verse had become deliberately redundant, able only to reduplicate its own past achievement.

The lyric voice of Różewicz's early postwar period—a silent, distanced observer speaking for an entire generation—contrasts with a variety of voices in this subsequent period. The poet's persona assumes a more impersonal stance, at times that of an "anonymous man." Eventually a more intimate tone reasserts itself, replacing anonymity, and the poetic "I" comes closer to Różewicz himself. Just as toward the end of the 1970s a technique of collage and intergenre structuring gave way to a sparse incremental ordering reminiscent of his earlier verse, the use of a more direct voice (often preoccupied with purely individual cares) increased once again the immediacy of Różewicz's lyricism. This latter tendency—which reached a high point in the collections *Opowiadanie traumatyczne* (A Traumatic Tale, 1979) and *Na powierzchni poematu i w środku* (On the Surface of a Poem and in the Middle, 1983)—is illustrated in "Siedziałem w fotelu" (translated as "'I was sitting in an easy-chair . . . ,'" 1982) from the former volume:

> I was sitting in an easy-chair
> I stopped reading
> suddenly I heard
> my heart beating
> it was so unexpected
> as though a stranger had entered into me
> and hammered with a clenched fist
> some unknown creature
> locked inside me
> there was something indecent
> in its battering with no relation
> to me
> to my abstract thought

In the 1980s the widening political crisis in Poland had assumed dramatic dimensions. The entire gamut of cultural life was negatively affected by the imposition of martial law in December 1981. With the exception of some sporadic poems, Różewicz lapsed into an artistic silence, publishing little in the period between 1983 and 1991. An ardent defender of his personal and artistic independence, he doggedly refused to respond publicly or privately to the political and social ferment that was transforming not only Poland but also the whole of Central and Eastern Europe. His short-lived flirtation with socialist themes in the early 1950s had undoubtedly made him wary of placing his art in the service of ideology. In another respect, to what extent Różewicz was merely adhering to his contentions regarding the "death of poetry" is difficult to say. In the wake of the declaration of martial law in Poland, Różewicz also declined the prestigious Juliusz Słowacki Prize (1982). Because of his stature, certain of his poems were heatedly analyzed for cryptic political allusions, such as "Przyszli żeby zobaczyć poetę" (They Came to See a Poet), published in *Na powierzchni poematu i w środku.*

Despite his withdrawal, and in some ways as a consequence, Różewicz continued to remain a subject of discussion in Poland throughout the 1980s. The various arguments put forward at this time to either vilify or defend him did little to further the understanding of his art. At best, Różewicz's status as a "classic" prompted retrospective critical appraisals, as in a special double issue of the journal *Poezja* in 1982, as well as a basic monograph for students of Polish literature, Stanisław Burkot's *Tadeusz Różewicz* (1987), and an impressive six-volume edition of his poetry, drama, and prose (1988–1990). While his standing in Poland remained controversial, his stature outside of Poland continued to grow. In 1980 Różewicz conducted a series of poetry evenings in Austria, where a year later he was awarded the Austrian State Prize for his contribution to European literature. In the same year he was granted membership in the Bavarian Academy of Arts, and in 1987 he became a member of the Berlin Academy of Arts. As if fulfilling his youthful desire to teach, he became writer in residence at the University of Salzburg in 1988. He attended foreign productions of his plays in Athens and Paris (1981), New York (1987), and Toronto (1991). Requests to participate in readings were also plentiful: Prague (1985); Amman, Jordan (1986); Struga, Yugoslavia, where—in the company of W. H. Auden, Pablo Neruda, and Rafael Alberti—he received a Golden Laurel award for his poetry (1987); London (1988); and Toronto (1991). Translations of his poetry appeared in such non-European languages as Chinese and Arabic. In addition to several new

Cover for a 1982 translation of Różewicz's poetry

English-language collections of his verse and dramas, an insightful series of conversations between Różewicz and the noted director Braun, *Języki teatru* (Theater Idioms), was published in 1989.

By 1991, as the repercussions following the collapse of communism in Europe began to subside, Różewicz's self-imposed withdrawal from artistic life ended. The decade also brought a more sober appreciation and reappraisal of Różewicz both within his native country and outside. Several celebrations and honors, coinciding with his seventieth birthday (1991) and a half-century of his writings (1994), were organized. At the invitation of the University of Ottawa, Różewicz made his first trip to Canada in May 1991, where he was featured at a symposium devoted to Slavic drama. There he published an article titled "Sztuka nienapisana" (The Unwritten Play) that praises the failed work as an integral part of the creative process. The article may also be read as

an oblique commentary on his creative frustrations and silence of the previous decade. In 1991 and 1994 conferences devoted to Różewicz's work were staged in Poznań and Katowice; he was also awarded an honorary doctorate by the University of Poznań in 1991. Important literary journals in Poland, including *Dialog* (Dialogue) and *Teatr* (Theater), came out with theme issues, while monographic studies in Poland and the United States added new critical insights.

Różewicz published five collections of poetry in the 1990s, all comprising individual poems that had appeared during the 1980s but also including new verses: *Płaskorzeźba* (Bas-Relief, 1991); *Historia pięciu wierszy* (A History of Five Poems, 1993); *Słowo po słowie* (Word by Word, 1994); *Zawsze fragment* (Ever a Fragment, 1996); *Zawsze fragment: Recycling* (1998), in which several poems of the last volume were reprinted, together with a new work; and *Matka odchodzi* (Mother Departs, 1999). In addition, Różewicz edited a memoir of his executed brother Janusz, *Nasz starszy brat* (Our Elder Brother, 1992), which includes reminiscences, Janusz's poems, and correspondence as well as a section titled "Wiersze o starszym bracie" (Poems about the Elder Brother). Innovative productions of his works were staged in 1993 in Poland, including *Pułapka*, *Złowiony*, and *Kartoteka*, the latter with the author's participation.

Różewicz's poetry of the 1990s represents no radical departures from earlier works; rather, various formal and thematic elements reappear and are realigned, with occasionally novel results. The collections *Płaskorzeźba* and *Historia pięciu wierszy*, which sequentially display the author's handwritten drafts alongside finished versions, further emphasize Różewicz's desire for "impure form." Rejecting "finished" forms, he concentrates rather on process, implying that the true essence of art exists within imperfect variants of itself. Ostensibly atheistic, Różewicz's poetry has at times also incorporated Christian symbolism (the Fall, expulsion from Paradise, redemption).

Several verses from *Płaskorzeźba* again underscore the theme of the death of poetry, as in "Więc czy jednak żyje się za długo pisząc poezję?" (Does One Then Live Too Long Writing Poetry?) and "Do Piotra" (To Peter), while also returning metapoetically to the act of poetic creation, as in "Jeszcze próba" (Further Attempt), "Teraz" (Now), and "Wspomnienie" (Recollection). Also visible is a predilection for writing poems that are transcendental in inspiration and intended to pierce the boundaries of silence, as in ". . . Poezja nie zawsze" (At Times Poetry Needn't . . .):

> at times
> a poem needn't have
> a verse form
>
> after fifty years
> of writing
> poetry
> may appear
> to a poet
> as a tree
> a bird
> lost in sight
> light
>
> it has the shape
> of lips
> nests in silence
>
> or lives in the poet
> unformed
> meaningless

Modernist in his attempt to regain a lost humanity through sundry means of formal experimentation, Różewicz is also one of a few poets and dramatists for whom the term postmodernist also has relevance. Nevertheless, though he exploits such devices as nostalgia and the blurring of traditional cultural and genre boundaries, Różewicz has stubbornly resisted the semantic collapse of postmodernism. Philosophically (through aesthetic denial, demythologizing, and a revalidation of the artist's role) and conceptually (through novel means of versification, a poetization of drama, and a symbiosis of diverse literary forms) Różewicz offers new insight into the anxieties of his times. In a poem from *Zawsze fragment*, "Prognoza do roku 2000" (Prognosis to the Year 2000), Różewicz steadfastly maintains that "things yet uncreated / still await / the poets."

Interviews:

Krystyna Nastulanka, "Dużo czystego powietrza," *Polityka*, 9 (1965): 1, 7;

Konstanty Puzyna, "Wokół dramaturgii otwartej," *Dialog*, 14 (1969): 101–108;

Adam Czerniawski, "Tadeusz Różewicz in Conversation with Adam Czerniawski," *New Review*, 3 (1976): 9–16;

Różewicz and Kazimierz Braun, *Języki teatru* (Wrocław: Wydawnictwo Dolnośląskie, 1989);

Richard Chetwynd, "Ufajcie obcemu przechodniowi," translated by Grzegorz Musiał, *Potop* (1991): 8–10;

Richard Sokoloski, "Tadeusz Różewicz: Records and Recollections," in *Slavic Drama: The Question of Innovation*, edited by Andrew Donskov and Sokoloski (Ottawa: University of Ottawa, 1991), pp. 348–355;

Sokoloski, "Nie chcę nie dbam żartuję . . ." *Odra*, 6 (1993): 33–37.

Bibliography:

Joanna Kisielowa, "Bibliografia edycji książkowych Tadeusza Różewicza," in *Świat integralny, pół wieku twórczości Tadeusza Różewicza*, edited by M. Kisiel (Katowice: Górnośląskie Towarzystwo Literackie, 1994), pp. 111–124.

Biographies:

Henryk Vogler, *Tadeusz Różewicz* (Warsaw: Czytelnik, 1972);

Tadeusz Drewnowski, *Walka o oddech: O pisarstwie Tadeusza Różewicza* (Warsaw: Wydawnictwa Artystyczne i Filmowe, 1990).

References:

Stanisław Barańczak, "Okaleczona twarz Hypnosa," *Twórczość*, 11 (1968): 115–118;

Rhonda Blair, "*White Marriage:* Różewicz's Feminist Drama," *Slavic and East-European Arts*, 3 (1985): 13–21;

Jan Błoński, "Szkic do portretu poety współczesnego," in his *Poeci i inni* (Kraków: Wydawnictwo Literackie, 1956), pp. 219–275;

Tomasz Burek, "Nieczyste formy Różewicza," *Twórczość*, 30 (1974): 99–109;

Stanisław Burkot, *Tadeusz Różewicz* (Warsaw: Wydawnictwa Szkolne i Pedagogiczne, 1987);

Paul Coates, "Gardens of Stone: The Poetry of Zbigniew Herbert and Tadeusz Różewicz," in *The Mature Laurel: Essays on Modern Polish Poetry*, edited by Adam Czerniawski (Brigend: Seren, 1991), pp. 175–188;

Bogdan Czaykowski, "Poetry and Anti-Poetry in Modern Polish Drama," *Slavic Drama: The Question of Innovation*, edited by Andrew Donskov and Richard Sokoloski (Ottawa: University of Ottawa, 1991), pp. 58–68;

Mieczysław Dąbrowski, "Teatr Różewicza—opisanie formy," *Miesięcznik Literacki* 3 [55], (1971): 64–69;

Stanisław Dąbrowski, "Przyboś, Różewicz i . . . (w związku z konfliktem z 1967 roku)," *Poezja* (1982): 74–89;

Andrzej Falkiewicz, "Cztery spojrzenia na Różewicza," *Twórczość*, 8 (1980): 59–82;

Marta Fik, "Teatr Różewicza," *Pamiętnik Teatralny*, 1 (1974): 3–16;

Halina Filipowicz, *A Laboratory of Impure Forms: The Plays of Tadeusz Różewicz* (Westport, Conn.: Greenwood Press, 1991);

Stanisław Gębala, *Teatr Różewicza* (Wrocław: Zakład Narodowy im. Ossolińskich, 1978);

Daniel Gerould, ed., *Twentieth-Century Polish Avant-Garde Drama: Plays, Scenarios, Critical Documents* (Ithaca, N.Y.: Cornell University Press, 1977), pp. 88–95;

E. Guderian-Czaplińska and Elzbieta Kalemba-Kasprzak, eds., *Zobaczyć poetę* (Poznań: Wydawnictwo WiS, 1993);

Wojciech Gutowski, "Aluzje biblijne i symbolika religijna w poezji Tadeusza Różewicza," *Acta Universitatis Nicolai Copernici*, 193 (1989): 77–102;

Jerzy Kwiatkowski, "Antypoezja i Apollińskie gniewy," in his *Remont Pegazów. Szkice i felietony* (Warsaw: Państwowy Instytut Wydawniczy, 1968), pp. 260–268;

Andrzej Lam, "Antypoezja T. Różewicza, czyli potęga nicości," *Z teorii i praktyki awangardyzmu* (Warsaw: Państwowy Instytut Wydawniczy, 1976), pp. 77–98;

Madeline G. Levine, *Contemporary Polish Poetry, 1925–1975* (Boston: Twayne, 1981), pp. 73–91;

Jacek Łukasiewicz, "Trzy kompromisy Tadeusza Różewicza," *Odra*, 5 (1965): 27–34;

Heinrich Olschowsky, "Językowe podstawy poetyki Tadeusza Różewicza," translated by Ryszard Handke, *Pamiętnik Literacki*, 63, no. 2 (1972): 87–116;

Marta Piwińska, "Różewicz albo technika collage'u," *Dialog*, 9 (1963): 85–89;

Poezja, special Różewicz issue, 5–6 (1981);

Przekład artystyczny, special Różewicz issue, edited by Piotr Fast, 1327 (1992);

Ryszard Przybylski, "Rok 1961–Zagłada Arkadii," in his *Et in Arcadia ego: Esej o tęsknotach poetów* (Warsaw: Czytelnik, 1966), pp. 127–186;

Zbigniew Siatkowski, "Wersyfikacja Tadeusza Różewicza wśród współczesnych metod kształtowania wiersza," *Pamiętnik Literacki*, 3 (1958): 119–150;

Jerzy Sito, "Nic albo niewiele w potoku słów," *Współczesność*, 10 (1965): 1, 11;

Rochelle Stone, "The Use of Happenings in Tadeusz Różewicz's Drama," *Pacific Coast Philology*, 11 (1976): 62–69;

Kazimierz Wyka, *Różewicz parokrotnie* (Warsaw: Państwowy Instytut Wydawniczy, 1977).

Paul-Eerik Rummo

(19 January 1942 –   )

Piret Kruuspere
Under and Tuglas Literature Center

BOOKS: *Ankruhiivaja. Luuletusi 1959–1962* (Tallinn: Eesti Riiklik Kirjastus, 1962);

Tule ikka mu rõõmude juurde. Teine vihik luuletusi (Tallinn: Eesti Riiklik Kirjastus, 1964);

Lumevalgus . . . lumepimedus (Tallinn: Perioodika, 1966);

Meestelaulud. Rahvaviisid ja rahvaluule, text by Rummo, music by Veljo Tormis (Tallinn: Eesti Raamat, 1966);

Põõsas ning rändaja said kokku (Tallinn: Eesti Riiklik Kunstiinstituut, 1966);

Tuhkatriinumäng (Tallinn: Perioodika, 1969); translated by Andres Männik and Mardi Valgemäe as *Cinderellagame,* in *Confrontations with Tyranny: Six Baltic Plays,* edited by Alfreds Straumanis (Prospect Heights, Ill.: Waveland Press, 1977), pp. 265–322;

Lugemik lugemiki (Tallinn: Eesti Raamat, 1974);

Kokku kolm juttu (Tallinn: Eesti Raamat, 1975);

Värvilind (Tallinn: Perioodika, 1981);

Ajapinde ajab. Luulet, juhuluulet, laulusõnu ja muud eri aegadest (Tallinn: Eesti Raamat, 1985);

Saatja aadress ja teised luuletused 1968–1972 (Tallinn: Kupar, 1989);

Luuletused (Tallinn: Kupar, 1999).

Editions and Collections: *Luulet 1960–1967* (Tallinn: Eesti Raamat, 1968);

Kass! Kass! Kass! in *Eesti näidendid 1977–1979,* edited by Ülev Aaloe (Tallinn: Eesti Raamat, 1981), pp. 97–161;

Oo et sädemeid kiljuks mu hing: Valitud luulet 1957–1984 (Tallinn: Eesti Raamat, 1985).

Editions in English: *The September Sun,* translated by Ritva Poom, Cross-Cultural Review Chapbook 16 (Merrick, N.Y.: Cross-Cultural Communications, 1981);

"Here You Grew Up," "Again Again Again," "The Sky Bends," and "The World Did Not Force Itself," translated by Ivar Ivask, in *Contemporary East European Poetry,* edited by Emery George (Ann Arbor, Mich.: Ardis, 1983), pp. 30–32;

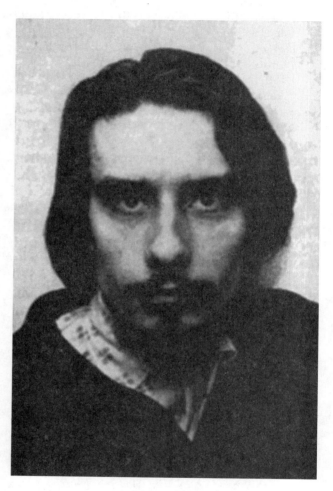

Paul-Eerik Rummo

Cinderellagame, translated by Andres Männik and Mardi Valgemäe (Tallinn: Kupar, 1992);

"Fragments from 'Return Address'" and "We're Here to Hold Fast to Each Other," translated by Elmar Maripuu, in *Shifting Borders: East European Poetries of the Eighties,* edited by Walter Cummins (Rutherford, N.J.: Fairleigh Dickinson University Press, 1993), pp. 42–43.

PLAY PRODUCTIONS: *Tuhkatriinumäng,* Tartu, Vanemuine Theater, 19 February 1969; translated by Andres Männik and Mardi Valgemäe as *Cinderellagame,* New York, La Mama Experimental Theater Club, 7 April 1971;

Sind me ootasimegi, Tallinn, State Youth Theater, 1 March 1973;

Kass! Kass! Kass! Tallinn, Drama Theater, 2 May 1981; New York, Arts Club Theater, 5 April 1985;

Kõrgemad kõrvad, Tallinn, Drama Theater, 29 December 1985;

Kes on kes, Tallinn, Vanalinna Studio Theater, 2 January 1986;

Blind Alley of Light, translated by Valgemäe, Ada, Ohio, Ohio Northern University, 14 October 1992; Scotland, Edinburgh Festival Fringe, 20 August 1993;

Valguse põik, Viljandi, Ugala Theater, 25 November 1993.

PRODUCED SCRIPTS: *Võõrad inimesed,* Estonian Television, 28 May 1963;

Suvi, motion picture, Tallinnfilm, 1975;

Kõrboja peremees, motion picture, Tallinnfilm, 1979;

Kass! Kass! Kass! Estonian Radio, Radio Theater, 1 January 1985;

Globaalkolleegium: valepüüdja, Estonian Radio, Radio Theater, 24 March 1996.

OTHER: Artur Alliksaar, *Olematus võiks ju ka olemata olla,* edited by Rummo (Tallinn: Perioodika, 1968);

Alliksaar, *Luule,* edited by Rummo (Tallinn: Eesti Raamat, 1976);

Alliksaar, *Luuletused,* edited by Rummo (Tallinn: Eesti Raamat, 1984);

Uusien sulkien kasvaminen: Kymmenen nykyvirolaista runoilijaa, edited by Rummo and Pirkko Huurto (Helsinki: Tammi, 1984);

Paul Rummo, *Luuletused,* edited by Rummo (Tallinn: Eesti Raamat, 1985);

Van haast naamloze kusten: Moderne Estische poëzie, edited by Rummo, translated by Mati Sirkel and Marianne Vogel (Leiden: De lantaarn/De Slavische Stichting, 1989).

TRANSLATIONS: *Kõne voolab voolavas maailmas,* translated by Rummo and Ly Seppel (Tallinn: Perioodika, 1967);

Dylan Thomas, *Piimmetsa vilus: Mäng häältele* (Tallinn: Perioodika, 1970);

Thomas, *Surmad ja sisenemised: Valik luuletusi* (Tallinn: Eesti Raamat, 1972);

Joseph Heller, *Me pommitasime New Havenit: Näidend* (Tallinn: Perioodika, 1973);

Ronald David Laing, *Omadega puntras: Luuletused* (Tallinn: Perioodika, 1978);

Aleksander Vampilov, *Näidendid ja lühiproosa,* translated by Rummo and Rein Saluri (Tallinn: Eesti Raamat, 1978);

Tuomas Anhava, Aastad: Luuletusi aastaist 1951–1968 (Tallinn: Eesti Raamat, 1981);

Kümme nüüdissoome luuletajat, compiled by Joel Sang, partly translated by Rummo (Tallinn: Eesti Raamat, 1991);

T. S. Eliot, Ahermaa ja teisi luu letusi (Tallinn: Hortus Litterarum, 1999).

SELECTED PERIODICAL PUBLICATIONS—UNCOLLECTED: *Pseudopus: Näidend kolmeteistkümnes pildis* and *Kotkast-Prometheust: Näidend ühes vaatuses seitsmes pildis,* in *Looming* (September 1980): 1252–1277;

Valguse põik: Kompositsioon kolmes osas, in *Looming* (January 1993): 6–51.

Belonging to the generation that matured in the 1960s, Paul-Eerik Rummo is one of the most outstanding figures in contemporary Estonian poetry and drama. His lyrical poems reflect the moods and images typical of this time, while carrying on the best poetic traditions of Estonian literary heritage and making connections with the work of such previous writers as Juhan Liiv, Gustav Suits, Heiti Talvik, and Henrik Visnapuu. In addition, the first professional production of one of his plays, *Tuhkatriinumäng* (1969; translated as *Cinderellagame,* 1971), changed the theatrical landscape of Estonia almost overnight. For many, Rummo has become a mythical person, a veritable cultural hero in spite—or perhaps because—of his long period of silence in the 1970s and 1980s.

Paul-Eerik Rummo was born on 19 January 1942 in Tallinn as the youngest child (after two older sisters) in the family of the writer Paul Rummo and his wife, Tiio. He began his formal schooling in 1948, but undoubtedly his home environment first influenced the development of his literary interests and experiments. Rummo's first literary attempts appeared in print in 1954, when he was twelve, in the youth periodicals *Säde* (Flame) and *Pioneer,* but he considers the 1957 publication of his poem "Kunstinäitusel" (At the Art Exhibit) in the cultural weekly *Sirp ja Vasar* (Hammer and Sickle) to be his debut.

In 1959, after graduating from a Tallinn secondary school, Rummo entered Tartu University as one of the first students to have the opportunity to follow a special program in the theory of literature. While at the university, Rummo participated in the activities of literary and theater groups, joined the Young Authors' Union, and received various prizes for his work. His play *Võõrad inimesed* (Strangers), depicting the conflict between different attitudes toward life, was staged by the university theater group in 1963 with Mati Unt, later a literary phenomenon in his own right, playing the lead. In the same year the play was also shown on Estonian Television. *Võõrad inimesed*, though never produced on the professional stage, could nevertheless be considered the first sign of the changes to come in dramaturgy and stagecraft that freed the Estonian theater from the fetters of socialist realism. During his university years Rummo also established close contact with one of the boldest experimenters in the poetry of the 1960s, Artur Alliksaar, who was at that time officially excluded from the nation's cultural life because of his individualistic and hence anti-Soviet behavior. Later Rummo compiled several posthumous collections of poems by Alliksaar, who died in 1966.

Two significant events in Rummo's life took place in 1962: he married Karin Uibo, a fellow student (their marriage ended in divorce), and he published *Ankruhiivaja* (The Anchor-Heaver), his first collection of verse. The poems express the spirit of an optimistic youth at the start of his symbolic life-journey, as illustrated in the poem "Algused" (Beginnings). The poet clearly expresses his ethical views, sounding slightly rhetorical and insisting that all compromises are wrong. Rummo emerges in this collection as a talented, self-conscious, and open-minded young man, discreetly lyrical as well as mildly humorous and cautiously intellectual. Critics welcomed him with unusual enthusiasm, declaring in essence that no one entering postwar Estonian literature had ever been so young and so mature at the same time.

Rummo's first daughter, Ingrid, was born in 1963, and in December of that year his mother was killed in a traffic accident. The latter event left deep traces in his poetry, especially in the cycle "Läbi talve: Luulet ema mälestuseks" (Through the Winter: Poems in Memory of My Mother) in his third collection, *Lumevalgus . . . lumepimedus* (Snowlight . . . Snow-Blindness, 1966). In 1964 his second collection of verse was published under the title *Tule ikka mu rõõmude juurde* (Come Always into My Joys), indicating a change in mood from the first volume and displaying a variety of new tonalities. Rummo's earlier optimistic, even somewhat pathetic treatment

of life had become more varied, subtle, and complicated, full of questions and doubts. The poet now sees and perceives more problems and dissonances in the life that surrounds him.

Some poems in this collection, such as "Mõistmisest" (Of Understanding), tend to display moralistic or didactic elements. A second, more aesthetic trend of the volume reveals the poet's search for harmony between people as well as between man and nature and man and society. "Hamleti laulud" (Hamlet's Songs), which was considered one of the best poems written in Estonian during this period, attempts a deeper perception of reality, reflecting in the inner dialogue of the second part a mood of resignation. This collection displays a motif typical of Rummo's poetry as a whole: the desire to return to one's childhood, to be a child again, as a way of escape from the disordered world. The third part of the collection offers lyric verse depicting nature. The cycle "September: Hetked ja meelisklused" (September: Moments and Meditations) synthesizes and sums up the moods and thoughts of the young poet. In this volume Rummo is actively looking for new means of expression, using rhetorical and descriptive as well as lyric elements. Reviewers have also pointed out the poet's intimate relationship with and creative use of Estonian folklore.

In the same year, 1964, while still a student, Rummo was accepted as a member of the Estonian Writers' Union. His acclaimed senior thesis at the university dealt with the work of the poet Visnapuu. After graduation in 1965 Rummo worked briefly as the literary consultant at the Vanemuine Theater in Tartu. Then he had to meet his military obligation, serving from 1965 to 1966. Poems written in the Soviet army were published in his book of verse, *Lumevalgus . . . lumepimedus*. This volume has been viewed as pivotal, fusing the very center of Estonian literature of the 1960s with the nation's literature as a whole. Rummo's most intensive and homogeneous collection reflects above all his increasing internal conflicts, as if he were synthesizing his personal experiences as a poet with the heritage of Estonian poetry.

Lumevalgus . . . lumepimedus, including the cycle in memory of the poet's mother, has been called a collection of distress signals. The inner tensions of the artist and the man, as well as the loss of his mother, issues of sociopolitical/cultural deadlock, the painful conflicts of the times he lives in, and devotion to one's nation and homeland while understanding their fate are here presented in a fresh way. The poems in this volume can be divided into those dealing with broader issues and those

Scene from a performance of Rummo's Tuhkatriinumäng *(1969), a "sequel" to the Cinderella story that revolutionized Estonian drama by breaking with the norms of socialist realism*

dealing more intimately with the mapping of different states of mind. The best example of the first is the cycle "Pööriöömaa" (Land of Equinoctial Night), depicting human life with the metaphor of eternal darkness. This cycle can also be interpreted as a dialogue with the esteemed poet Gustav Suits, especially with the latter's image of "tuulemaa" (land of winds). Concentrating on the fate of Estonia—here more conspicuously than before—and describing it through the key image of equinoctial night, Rummo identifies himself with his homeland. This sense of communion culminates in the poem "Ikka Liivist mõteldes" (Still Thinking of Liiv), for which he was awarded the 1966 Juhan Liiv Prize. The poem juxtaposes individual loneliness and the political stalemate of the Soviet occupation. Though stirring up feelings of unrest and concern, the poet is unwilling to give up his striving for integrity, his personal resistance, and his stoical optimism. All these feelings crystallize in the image of a small lake that is trying to keep itself from freezing over.

While Rummo's vision of the larger universe addresses what could be called social and political issues, poems focusing on the inner world express an impatient fluctuation of various moods and asso-

ciations. Such poems are characterized by subjective and suggestive imagery rich in semantic overtones. At the same time the poet makes use of the images and structural elements of Estonian folk songs. His most accomplished poems, such as "Oo et sädemeid kiljuks mu hing" (O, If Only My Soul Could Flash Forth in Sparks) and "Olla maastik olla maastik suurejooneline" (To Be a Landscape, a Grand Landscape), avoid social allusions and communicate in a highly poetic style the complexities of the human mind.

Since 1967 Rummo has lived in Tallinn as a professional writer. In 1967 and 1968 he wrote critical reviews under the pseudonym of Poor Yorick in the journal *Noorus* (Youth). In 1968 he collected his lyrics into *Luulet 1960–1967* (Verses 1960–1967), which includes a cycle of poems, "Läbi peo mul voolab puu" (Wood Flows Through My Palm), that had not been published earlier and that explores the glory and indeed the sacredness of the physical universe. Of these perhaps the most accomplished is "Maarjaheina kõrreke" (A Tiny Stalk of Vernal Grass), which offers an expressive and suggestive approach to the interdependence of man and nature. The volume also includes a few poems dedicated to the outstanding cultural figures who were the poet's coevals. After 1968 Rummo's poems were printed mainly in periodicals, and for seventeen years he did not publish a new collection of verse.

Also in 1968 a posthumous collection of Alliksaar's poetry, *Olematus võiks ju ka olemata olla* (Nonexistence Could Be Nonexisting), compiled by Rummo, was published. Rummo also wrote a preface to this book. In 1969 a widely shown Estonian motion picture, *Viimne reliikvia* (The Last Relic), directed by Grigori Kromanov, was released by Tallinnfilm; for this movie Rummo had written song lyrics that became well known all over the country. The lyrics spoke of the need to be free: in the words of the most popular of these songs, "Põgene, vaba laps, see on ainus võimalus" (Run away, free child, this is your only chance!).

In 1969 the young Estonian director Evald Hermaküla staged Rummo's play *Tuhkatriinumäng* at the Vanemuine Theater. This work has been considered the turning point in the development of Estonian drama, breaking the rules of traditional (socialist) realism with a vengeance. The play belongs to the genre of more abstract and physical metadrama of the 1960s, based on a new set of conventions and making use of game playing and more visual theater. *Tuhkatriinumäng* is the most outstanding Estonian example of this trend.

The play is an epilogue to the well-known fairy tale of Cinderella, and it follows the neoclassical demand for unity in structure. Taking place nine years after the traditional happy ending, the events focus on the Prince's attempts to find out whether he has in fact gotten the "right" girl. At the same time he endeavors to secure his position as ruler and to identify the hostile forces that face him. The plot maps his journey of self-consciousness, constructing as well a model or a metaphorical picture of the layers of human existence. The action has been turned into archetypal theatrical images and the characters have become players on a cosmic stage. The Prince's search for the truth culminates in his discovery that She Who Represents Omnipotent Life is paradoxically confined to a wheelchair, thus creating an ambivalent image of power that is both infinite and an invalid.

As in the theater of the absurd, Rummo's play is based not on philosophical discussions but on visual stage images, revealing the absurdity of the human condition in a godforsaken world deprived of meaning and purpose. Indeed, commentators on the 1969 premiere spoke of Man as Actor on the stage of *Theatrum Mundi* (the theater of the world). Typical of Rummo, the style of the play is meta-

phoric and rich in associations, subtly philosophical, yet conveying highly subjective conventions. The dialogue is often poetic. Critic Jaak Rähesoo has mentioned that finality and closure have a philosophical meaning not only in this play, but in Rummo's work as a whole. *Tuhkatriinumäng*, dealing with the relationships between the eternal and the temporal, the human and the cosmic, is a distinctive work in Estonian dramatic literature. In April 1971 it was staged at the famed La Mama Experimental Theater Club in New York. In Estonia it has been revived in 1979 at the Pärnu Theater, in 1993 by students at the Tallinn Youth Theater, and in 1996 as a radio play directed by Rummo.

Rummo has acknowledged that 1969 was a turning point in his life. Critic Luule Epner agrees that drama has played an important role in Rummo's personal metamorphoses and that *Tuhkatriinumäng* could be viewed as marking a shift in Rummo's creative work. The other two plays that Rummo wrote during 1968 and 1969, *Pseudopus* (Pseudo-Oedipus) and *Kotkast-Prometheust* (The Eagle and Prometheus), were published in the literary journal *Looming* (Creation) in 1980. These allegorical works are meditations on the stories of Oedipus and Prometheus and view in a satiric mode ethical problems of guilt and salvation, of social memory and hypocrisy. Also from this period is Rummo's poem "Palve" (Prayer), published in *Looming* in 1968 and declaring the need for change. The same sentiment appears in his so-called wag songs that combine elements of the grotesque and jest: "Vettinud peiar" (A Soaked Wag), written in 1968, and "Kuivanud peiar" (A Dried Wag), written in 1970. In these poems previous tensions have subsided, revealing different attitudes ranging from the sarcastic to the elegiac. Rummo's translation of Dylan Thomas's *Under Milk Wood* (1954) as *Piimmetsa vilus* was published in 1970. In the same year he was declared legally married to Viiu Härm, an actress and poet with whom he had been living. They have three daughters, Lilit (born 1968), Tiiu-Liisa (born 1974), and Viiu-Marie (born 1982).

During the next period—the 1970s as well as the beginning of the 1980s—Rummo was mainly occupied with translations, works for theater and motion pictures, and other writing activities except poetry. In 1972 Rummo had assembled a manuscript collection of his poems written between 1968 and 1972, called "Saatja aadress" (Return Address), which remained unpublished at the time because of political censorship. In October 1972 Rummo read these works at two poetry evenings in Tallinn, but they were printed only in 1985 and 1989 as parts of

Cover for Rummo's 1985 collection of poems, for which he won the Juhan Smuul Prize

two later collections. This manuscript could be called the summary as well as a further elaboration of the earlier *Lumevalgus . . . lumepimedus*. Rummo's poetry of the 1970s had undergone a remarkable change: his highly lyric mode of the 1960s was now characterized by simple diction. The poet had obviously accepted the inevitability of socialist routine, and though he remained personally—and ethically—active, his resignation is unmistakable. His style becomes highly subjective, yet at the same time he tries to avoid or at least to subdue emotional outbursts. The poems are now simpler and much shorter and at times are in conversational free verse. His new, realistic verse may be characterized as poetry without passion, for it tends to be rational and objective; some critics have even called it anti-poetry.

At the time the manuscript of "Saatja aadress" was completed, Rummo's translation of Dylan Thomas's *Deaths and Entrances* (1946) appeared as

Surmad ja sisenemised: Valik luuletusi. In this work even Rummo's method of translating differs from his earlier approach. Now he concentrates mainly on the transmission of the semantics of the original language, not paying as much attention to meter and rhythm. In 1972 Rummo was also involved as a scenarist in the Youth Theater staging of *Oliver ja Jennifer,* based on Erich Segal's *Love Story* (1970). The next year, his children's play *Sind me ootasimegi* (Just Waiting for You), a reworking of "Little Red Riding Hood," was staged at the Youth Theater. In 1974–1975 he published two books for children: a collection of poems, *Lugemik lugemiki* (A Prime Primer), in which he plays with the possibilities of language (baby talk, puns); and *Kokku kolm juttu* (Altogether Three Stories), a prose collection offering reversed versions of three well-known tales. Writing for children, Rummo tends to break up traditional relationships and to widen the perception of the world at large.

During the period from 1976 to 1989 Rummo worked as a literary editor at the Tallinn Drama Theater. Since 1977 he has also been a member of the Estonian Theater Union. His contacts with the world of theater, which always have been important to him—in his youth he had even thought about becoming an actor—find expression in such projects as a compilation from the texts of the Estonian writer Anton Hansen Tammsaare, staged under the title *Ramilda Rimalda* at the Youth Theater in 1979, or his dramatization of Jaan Kross's *Rakvere romaan* (Rakvere's Novel, 1982), staged in 1982 by the Rakvere Theater as *Rakvere romanss* (Rakvere's Romance). In 1981 Rummo's play *Kass! Kass! Kass!* (Cat! Cat! Cat!), derived from "Puss in Boots," was staged at the Tallinn Drama Theater; it was published the same year in the collection *Eesti näidendid 1977–1979* (Estonian Plays 1977–1979). In 1985 another play for children, *Kõrgemad kõrvad* (Higher Ears), based on fairy-tale motifs, was staged at the Tallinn Drama Theater. In the first half of the 1980s his translation of poems by the Finnish writer Tuomas Anhava also appeared, and he edited two volumes for the series "Väike luuleraamat" (Small Chapbooks of Poetry) from the works of Alliksaar and Paul Rummo.

In 1985, after a long period of silence, Rummo's new book of poems *Ajapinde ajab* (Time Is a Splinter under the Skin) and the collection *Oo et sädemeid kiljuks mu hing: Valitud luulet 1957–1984* (Oh, If Only My Soul Could Flash Forth in Sparks: Selected Poems 1957–1984) were finally published. For the latter he received the Juhan Smuul Prize. That same year Rummo was awarded the Soviet

Estonian Prize, and the following year he received the title of Merited Writer of the Estonian Soviet Socialist Republic.

Ajapinde ajab looks like a new collection and an anthology at the same time, including various groupings of poems: a great part of the cycle "Saatja aadress," written as an epilogue to Rummo's previous period, the 1960s; the cycle of wag songs; occasional poems imitating the style of his contemporary poets in exile; and songs from the motion picture *Viimne reliikvia*, revealing Rummo's romantic side, which he had given up in the 1970s. In this collection Rummo has avoided chronology; the heterogeneous selection produces an impression of sketchiness and polyphony at the same time. The book was received by critics with interest and caution: they wondered if it was really new at all, or just the author's attempt to break his personal myth. Rummo has remained a skeptical humanist, lacking hope and ideals but impressing the reader by his inner intensity, sensitive perception of ethics, self-irony, and doubts. Formally he favors a fragmentary style, which some critics have labeled as anti-aestheticism. The anthology *Oo et sädemeid kiljuks mu hing* has been composed as a more convincing whole. The title poem has been interpreted as one of Rummo's key verses. The predominant state of mind of the poet—being on the periphery all the time—found a sustained presentation in this volume.

In 1986 Rummo was elected a secretary of the board of the Writers' Union and held this post from 1987 to 1989, becoming vice president of the Union in 1989. That same year Rummo was accepted as a member of the PEN Club and attended the PEN conference in the Netherlands. In 1989 his collection *Saatja aadress ja teised luuletused 1968–1972* (Return Address and Other Poems 1968–1972) was finally published as well—and in its entirety.

As did many other outstanding cultural figures who took part in the liberation movement and the reestablishing of the Estonian Republic, Rummo began an active political career at the end of the 1980s. Since 1989, when the Estonian Liberal-Democratic Party was founded, Rummo has been its president. In the beginning of the 1990s he worked as a cultural adviser at the State Chancellery. In 1990 he was elected a member of the Estonian Congress. Since the restoration of Estonian independence in 1992, he has been a member of the Estonian Parliament, working during the period from 1992 to 1994 as the Minister of Culture and Education.

In 1992 Rummo's play *Blind Alley of Light*, commissioned by Ohio Northern University, was performed by students at the university campus; the following year the production traveled to the Edinburgh Festival Fringe in Scotland. Its Estonian version, *Valguse põik*, was published in 1993 in the journal *Looming* and staged at the Viljandi Cultural College as well as at the Ugala Theater. In this work Rummo maps a series of grotesque and slightly absurd pictures of the abruptly changing economic environment in the Estonia of the late 1980s. *Valguse põik* can be seen as a dramatic parallel to his so-called anti-poetry, for both lack cohesiveness. The play is constructed of episodes of slightly alienated everyday life as well as dramatic ritual scenes that treat such themes as the function of memory, personal as well as social identity, and the question of whether or not you can go home again.

In 1995 the Liberal-Democratic Party joined with other political factions to form the Reform Party, and Rummo became a member of the board and chairman of the party's council of representatives. In the same year he was elected a member of Parliament for a second term, and in 1999 he was reelected to a third. In 1996–2000 Rummo was chairman of the Broadcasting Council. For a short period in 1997 he worked as the editor in chief of the cultural weekly *Kultuurimaa* (Cultureland). In 1992, 1996, and 1997 Rummo published translations of T. S. Eliot's *The Waste Land* (1922), "The Love Song of J. Alfred Prufrock" (1915), and *Four Quartets* (1943) in *Looming*. In the 1990s his literary activities included more translations (of works by Ivar Ivask, Desmond O'Grady, and Czesław Miłosz, for example) as well as critical reviews. He has also translated African, Caribbean, Czech, Russian, Italian, and Finnish poetry and has contributed translations for anthologies of Renaissance, seventeenth-century, and contemporary Russian poetry. His translation of selected poems by T. S. Eliot received the Year's Best Translation Prize for 1999. His own poems have been translated into more than twenty languages—collections have been published in Latvian, Russian, Polish, English, and Lithuanian. Rummo's poetry has been set to music by such Estonian composers as Veljo Tormis, Gustav Ernesaks, Arne Oit, Uno Naissoo, Raimond Lätte, and Rein Rannap.

As a writer conveying an inner intensity and expressing his ethically uncompromising views, Paul-Eerik Rummo represents a remarkable degree of achievement in poetry as well as in drama. His verse has many moods and voices, ranging from the sparse and laconic to the breathtakingly elevated.

His poems and plays, born of painful impulses, have spoken to and of an entire people at an extremely trying moment in their history.

Interviews:
"'Keele ja Kirjanduse' ringküsitlus kirjanikele: Paul-Eerik Rummo," *Keel ja Kirjandus* (September 1974): 484;

Endla Köst, "Kirjanikud räägivad: Paul-Eerik Rummo," in her *Loomine ja lugemine* (Tallinn: Eesti Raamat, 1986), pp. 39–60;

Paul-Eerik Rummo, "Alguse algusest: Intervjuu Sirje Ruutsoole," *Looming* (August 1987): 1113–1125;

Märt Väljataga, "Vestlus Paul-Eerik Rummoga," *Vikerkaar* (January 1992): 54–56.

Bibliography:
Oskar Kruus, ed., *Eesti kirjarahva leksikon* (Tallinn: Eesti Raamat, 1995), p. 483.

References:
Luule Epner, "'Võõrastest inimestest' 'Valguse põiguni': Paul-Eerik Rummo näitekirjanikuna," *Keel ja Kirjandus* (April 1994): 210–224;

Hellar Grabbi, "Paul-Eerik Rummo avaldamata jäänud luulekogu 'Saatja aadress,'" *Mana 56* (1987): pp. 43–45;

Ivar Ivask, "Paul-Eerik Rummo luulemaailm," *Mana 38* (1971): 19–28;

Vytautas Kavolis, "Literature and the Dialectics of Modernization," in *Literary Criticism and Sociology*, edited by Joseph P. Strelka (University Park: Pennsylvania State University Press, 1973), pp. 89–106;

Jüri Kurman, "Eesti keele õnneriigis," *Mana 56* (1987): 44–45;

Toomas Liiv, "Paul-Eerik Rummo," in *Eesti kirjanduse ajalugu: Kirjandus Eestis 1950–1980-ndail aastail*, edited by Maie Kalda (Tallinn: Eesti Raamat, 1991), volume 5, book 2, pp. 415–426;

Karl Muru, "Lauliku lapsepõlv ja noormeheiga," in his *Vaateid kolmest aknast* (Tallinn: Eesti Raamat, 1975), pp. 258–268;

Muru, "Paul-Eerik Rummo luule," in his *Kodus ja külas* (Tallinn: Eesti Raamat, 1987), pp. 88–113;

Jaak Rähesoo, "See maailm ja teised," *Looming* (July 1969): 1086–1093;

Hando Runnel, "Eleegiaid ankruhiivajale ehk Paul-Eerik 1500," *Looming* (January 1992): 107–110;

Mardi Valgemäe, "The Cinderella Skirmish," *Baltic Forum*, 2 (Spring 1985): 70–87;

Valgemäe, "Paul-Eerik Rummo: Tuhkatriinumäng," *Books Abroad*, 43 (1969): 629–630;

Valgemäe, "Paul ja Eerik ja Rummo," *Mana 59* (1999): 18–22;

Valgemäe, "Tuhkatriinu tulevahetus," in his *Ikka teatrist mõteldes* (Stockholm: Välis-Eesti & EMP, 1990), pp. 72–87;

Rein Veidemann, "Kaks mõttekontsentrit Paul-Eerik Rummost," in his *Olla kriitik . . .* (Tallinn: Eesti Raamat, 1986), pp. 75–82;

Veidemann, "Karje," *Keel ja Kirjandus* (September 1988): 513–520.

Mircea Horia Simionescu

(23 January 1928 –)

Monica Spiridon
University of Bucharest

BOOKS: *Dicţionarul onomastic: Ingeniosul bine temperat* (Bucharest: Editura de stat pentru literatură şi artă, 1969);

Bibliografia generală: Ingeniosul bine temperat (Bucharest: Eminescu, 1970);

După 1900 pe la amiază: Proze (Bucharest: Eminescu, 1974);

Răpirea lui Ganymede (Bucharest: Sport-Turism, 1975);

Jumătate plus unu: Alt dicţionar onomastic (Bucharest: Albatros, 1976);

Nesfîrşitele primejdii: Roman (Bucharest: Eminescu, 1978);

Învăţături pentru Delfin: Roman (Bucharest: Albatros, 1979);

Breviarul: Historia calamitatum (Bucharest: Cartea Românească, 1980);

Banchetul: Povestiri (Bucharest: Eminescu, 1982);

Ulise şi umbra (Bucharest: Sport-Turism, 1982);

Toxicologia, sau, Dincolo de bine şi dincoace de rău (Bucharest: Cartea Românească, 1983);

Redingota: Roman (Bucharest: Cartea Românească, 1984);

Licitaţia: Roman (Bucharest: Albatros, 1985);

Trei oglinzi (Bucharest: Cartea Românească, 1987);

Asediul locului comun: Roman (Bucharest: Militară, 1988);

Îngerul cu şorţ de bucătărie (Cluj-Napoca: Clusium, 1992);

Povestiri galante (Bucharest: Minerva, 1994);

Paltonul de vară (Bucharest: Albatros & Universal Dalsi, 1996);

Febra: File de jurnal 1963–1971 (Bucharest: Vitruvia, 1998).

One of the most prominent figures in Romanian literature of the second half of the twentieth century, Mircea Horia Simionescu first gained recognition as part of the so-called Tîrgovişte School, a group of young writers, including Radu Petrescu and Cosache Olăreanu, who emerged in the early 1970s deter-

Mircea Horia Simionescu

mined to renew the creative spirit and originality of Romanian prose by embracing the techniques of European modernism. The Tîrgovişte School resumed the innovative literary experimentation that had characterized Romanian fiction between the two world wars. It also prepared the way for the postmodernist "generation of the 1980s."

Simionescu was born on 23 January 1928 in Tîrgovişte in the hilly area of Muntenia, the first of two sons of Nicolae and Irina Popescu Simionescu. His father was an infantry officer, his mother a post office clerk. Simionescu attended the local primary school and then Ienachita Vărăescu High School, where he met Petrescu and Olăreanu. Between 1943 and 1948 the three composed avant-garde literary magazines and poetry booklets that they circulated in manuscript form.

In 1948 Simionescu was admitted to the Faculty of Letters at the University of Bucharest, where he studied with some of the leading intellectuals of the time, including the critic George Călinescu. The atmosphere at the institution became increasingly stifling under the communist regime, however, and Călinescu was among the professors who were dismissed from the faculty. Consequently, Simionescu abandoned his studies after two years and became a journalist with the Communist Party newspaper *Scînteia* (Sparks). While working there he amassed a body of unpublished fiction, including the first volumes of his tetralogy *Ingeniosul bine temperat* (The Well-Tempered Ingenious, 1969–1983).

Because he needed a diploma in order to make some more money as a titled journalist, Simionescu resumed his studies while continuing his career. Simionescu completed his degree in 1964 with a graduation paper on Călinescu's poetry. In 1968 he made his debut in the literary magazine *Luceafărul* (The Morning Star) with a short story, "Cum l-am trădat pe Pascal" (How I Betrayed Pascal.) The following year Simionescu's former editor in chief at *Scînteia* became secretary of the Central Committee of the Romanian Communist Party and appointed his former colleague cabinet chief, a vaguely defined position that afforded Simionescu some protection from censorship. In addition, Simionescu and others benefited from a period of relaxation of the regime-imposed doctrine of socialist realism in the aftermath of the "Prague Spring": the Romanian government was critical of the brutal suppression by Soviet forces of the emerging reform movement in Czechoslovakia, and, as a result, the intellectual community experienced a cultural thaw that lasted until 1971. During this period Simionescu published the first two volumes of *Dicționarul onomastic: Ingeniosul bine temperat* (The Onomastic Dictionary, 1969) and *Bibliografia generală: Ingeniosul bine temperat* (The General Bibliography, 1970).

The first volume is a whimsical, parodic dictionary—ending at the letter *I*—of biographies of fictitious individuals; the avowed source of the list is the phone book. The author pretends to refute the notion that personal names are arbitrarily assigned; often, identities emerge from the shocking conjoining of a resonant Christian name—heroic, sacred, or legendary—with a prosaic family name: Napoleon Gătej, Hercule Frîncu, Byron Luca, Absalon Pop. The dictionary constitutes a vast human comedy of literature. For example, the entry on "Elizarie Dascălu" identifies him as a professional writer who extracts from the most important novels in Romanian literature tips on living a carefree and adventurous life. Sometimes the characters are mere pretexts for improvisations in which Simionescu parodies standard narrative styles, themes,

genres, techniques, typologies, and literary clichés. One critic called the book a "Flaubertian dictionary of literary ready-made ideas." At a time when most Romanian literature had ossified into the canon of socialist realism, Simionescu and the other members of the Tîrgoviște School marketed a radically different type of writing that disrupted routine reading habits.

The second volume of the *Ingeniosul bine temperat* cycle is a huge bibliography of writers and literary works—all of them invented. Often compared by Romanian literary critics to the Argentine writer Jorge Luis Borges's "La Biblioteca de Babel" (1941; translated as "The Library of Babel," 1961), Simionescu's *Bibliografia generală* seems at first glance to be a systematic and authoritative literary study; the work is, in fact, a contrived assemblage of metaphysical and linguistic chaos. The expert and serious nature of the fictitious author of the book—a bibliographer as industrious as he is humble—is contradicted by his selection of literary works such as *Cățelul în manuscrisele literaturii secolului XIX* (The Puppy in the Literary Manuscripts of the Nineteenth Century), *Textile și incertitudini* (Fabrics and Uncertainties), *Nudismul sub Mihai Vodă Viteazul* (Nudity under Michael the Great), *Revolțiile se fac sîmbăta* (Revolutions Always Start on Saturdays), *Papa Clement al XII-lea și lovitura după ceafă* (Pope Clement XII and the Blow on the Nape of the Neck), and *Principii morale la întemeietorii fanfarei Regimentului 85 infanterie* (The Moral Principles of the Founders of the Band of the Eighty-Fifth Infantry Regiment). Many of the titles play on the absurdity of the surreal associations of words, and well-known authors are endowed with fictitious works. The pageantry of literature is thus reduced to a joke.

Repression of the Romanian literary community resumed in 1971, and Simionescu was demoted to the position of assistant director of the music department of the recently created National Council of Culture. He was appointed director of the Romanian Opera in January 1972 but soon met with official disfavor, and he resigned in 1974. That same year, however, he was awarded the Prize of the Writers' Union for the volume of short stories *După 1900 pe la amiază* (After 1900 in the Afternoon). He withdrew to his house at Pietrosita, fifty miles from Tîrgoviște, to devote himself to writing.

In 1975 Simionescu published *Răpirea lui Ganymede* (Ganymede's Abduction), a literary "travelogue" in which genuine travel impressions become the pretext for an imaginary journey with the most varied itineraries. It is a "voyage among words"—part of the "Odyssey in the Papersphere" that the Tîrgoviște writers attempted to create in their literary exploits. Simionescu also violates the canons of the traditional

Romanian travelogue by meditating on his own creative insights and methodology. This work was followed the next year by *Jumătate plus unu* (Half Plus One), carrying the *Dicționarul onomastic* through the end of the alphabet. While generally acknowledged as less successful than the first volume, *Jumătate plus unu* received the prestigious Ion Creangă Prize of the Romanian Academy.

Reality and fantasy merge in *Nesfîrșitele primejdii* (The Endless Dangers, 1978), a novel about the writing of a novel. An engineer named George Pelimon writes an autobiographical novel titled *Nesfîrșitele primejdii*, in which the circumstances of his life fuse with the most fabulous invented elements. The main character of the fictitious novel, also named George Pelimon, is a daring journalist who is adored by women and given to flights of eccentricity. His identity and those of his wife, Despina, and his mistress, Helga, multiply; tenses are superimposed on one another; and events contradict each other. Moreover, the narration is filled with reflections by the fictitious characters on the techniques of producing a novel and on the aesthetic condition of the novel form. The conclusion reached by the novel within the novel is that novels are an unfolding of banality similar to that of real life.

Simionescu continued to experiment with narrative form in *Învățături pentru Delfin* (Teachings for the Dolphin, 1979). A young man named Dolphin Protopoescu seeks to uncover how his mentor, a typist, managed to compose a sham biography of a common Budapest swindler, Gri Macedoneau, that becomes a model and, at the same time, a parody of heroic and sensational literary writing. Characters from Simionescu's other works appear in *Învățături pentru Delfin*, as do writers bearing his name and those of his literary friends, such as Petrescu. The adventure and the detective novel, as well as the biography, are denounced as instruments by means of which literature falsifies reality. Simionescu inventories the stock literary formulas, themes, motifs, clichés, and stereotypes that writers have at their disposal in the so-called creative process: it is not an accident that the anonymous chronicler of Gri Macedoneau's life is a typist—that is, a mere copyist. The novel serves as a warning against the superperfected literary mechanisms that jeopardize an author's identity.

In the early 1980s censorship in Romania intensified. Fearing that the generic title *Ingeniosul bine temperat* would be too provocative, Simionescu published the third volume of his tetralogy in 1980 as *Breviarul: Historia calamitatum* (The Breviary: History of a Calamity), in which the animal fable, the parable, and the satirical utopia coexist in a convoluted structure that resembles a scholarly edition, with several layers of

Cover for Simionescu's 1984 novel, about a German professor who travels and dies in Romania during World War II

comments, explanations, and notes. The book opens with a series of digressive discourses and pseudophilosophical dissertations by animals, insects, and birds with names such as Lepidus, Procopius, Rara Avis Avicena, and Myriapodus Tancredini. They speak of their past human lives, prior to the metamorphosis through which, by their own will, they turned into what they are now. A series of footnotes by an anonymous author supplements the animals' discourses with absurd comments; the "publisher" of the book adds, in a supplementary series of notes, that the anonymous author once wrote a *Dicționarul onomastic* and a *Bibliografia generală*. Finally, the reader witnesses a discussion in a mental asylum by paranoid schizophrenics who are convinced that they are mutants. Simionescu's book is a symbolic allusion to the completely alienated state of communist Romania.

In 1982 Simionescu published in a collection of short stories, *Banchetul* (The Banquet), and a volume of travel notes, *Ulise și umbra* (Ulysses and the Shadow). Both works are in the playful and erudite tradition of the previous texts.

The tetralogy was completed with the publication in 1983 of an unconventional autobiography titled *Toxicologia, sau, Dincolo de bine și dincoace de rău* (Toxicology, Beyond Good and on the Side of the Devil). As always in Simionescu's writings, appearances are deceiving. At the beginning the book complies with the rules of the autobiographical genre: the reader is provided with information about the author's family, his childhood in Tîrgoviște, his high-school and university friends, and his time in the editorial offices of *Scînteia* and other communist cultural institutions. His statements are authenticated by witnesses whose statements are inserted into the text; among them, however, are some of the novelist's fictitious characters. Through multiple deviations and distortions, the autobiography ends up as pure fantasy. Included in the text is a short novel, *Intoarcerea Fiului Risipitor* (The Return of the Prodigal Son), in which Felix Iacob becomes addicted to writing and produces a series of bizarre texts, such as *Metafizica Pentru Biciclisti* (Metaphysics for Bicyclists), *Istoria Ingerilor* (The History of Angels), and *Poezia Ca o Știință Fatala, Imprecisa și Ocazională* (Poetry as a Fatal, Imprecise and Occasional Science), before his father forces him to lead a dull life as a pharmacist in the remote village of Vintu de Jos. Felix, the author explains, was always a good boy, but books drove him crazy. He liked to concoct unusual tales and tie them to actual facts, to add stories from his exuberant dreams, and to bind them all in a gaudy and flashy bunch—a parodic description of Simionescu's own oeuvre—and he ended up believing everything he had fabricated. Inserted under various pretexts, as in all the volumes of the tetralogy, are the author's opinions regarding the status and the production of literature, the inertia of its norms, and the pressure of tradition.

Simionescu's novel *Redingota* (The Riding Coat, 1984) appeared on the fortieth anniversary of the so-called Liberation—the Soviet invasion of Romania—and the publisher created a cover in the colors of the national flag and included an inscription linking the publishing of the book to the anniversary. As a result, the public and the critics mistook the work for a piece of propaganda, and interest in it was minimal. During World War II, Erich vol Vogelbach, a Munich professor, is writing a novel about the Thirty Years' War. In the course of his research he takes a perilous trip to Romania and, after wandering through diverse social milieus, he dies at Tîrgoviște. Adrian, one of his Romanian friends, has had premonitory visions of vol Vogelbach's death: somewhere behind the professor

Cover for Simionescu's complex 1985 novel, about an author who returns from the dead to write one more book

someone is sitting at a table, pen in hand, writing vol Vogelbach's destiny until he runs out of paper and must put an end to the story.

In the five years that preceded the fall of communism in Romania, Simionescu seldom left his retreat at Pietrosity. During those years increased censorship forced writers to create works with subtle and multilayered themes, and in 1985 Simionescu published *Licitația* (The Auction), a labyrinthine novel in which the anonymous narrator, needing money to settle the debts of his estate, returns from the afterlife and writes a novel that is to be included in the public auction of his works. The finished product is an epic of grandiose verbal architecture incorporating oneiric divagations, mini-essays, parodies of love stories and detective adventures, and theoretical dissertations on the novel. *Licitația* was followed by another piece of writing strategically adapted to the circumstances: *Trei oglinzi* (Three Mirrors, 1987) includes fragments transcribed from a diary Simionescu kept in 1947. The work is his way of escaping from the suffocating reality of communist censorship into memories of an adolescence full of literary projects.

The last book published by Simionescu during the communist period, *Asediul locului comun* (The Siege of the Commonplace, 1988), is set in the Fagetel Castle in the Carpathian Mountains, reputed to have been a residence of the fifteenth-century Walachian prince Vlad Tepes (Vlad the Impaler), the model for the title character in Bram Stoker's novel *Dracula* (1897). The chapter titles—"Asediul" (The Siege), "Releveuri" (Observations), "Preparative" (Preparations), "Tatonări" (Probings), and "Tactică generală" (General Tactics)—are taken from military terminology. The castle is the temporary refuge of a group of amateur writers on history and military strategy and tactics who intend to publish a magazine. Instead, they write texts with titles similar to those listed in *Ingeniosul bine temperat*, such as *Cum sa Tai Nodul Flamand* (How to Tie the Flemish Knot), *Eroarea Tîrgovişteană* (The Tîrgovişte Error), and *Două Case, Un Copac* (Two Houses, One Tree). At the end of the book the reader discovers that the whole thing was a theatrical performance.

The fall of communism in Romania in 1989 was followed by a period during which literature was dominated by journalism and the memoir. After a short period of silence Simionescu made his comeback in 1992 with *Îngerul cu şorţ de bucătărie* (The Angel Who Wore a Kitchen Apron), seven miniature prose pieces incorporating elements of fantasy. In 1996 he published the highly acclaimed novel *Paltonul de vară* (The Warm Summer Coat), written in the manner and style of *Ingeniosul bine temperat* but without the additions that had been necessary to deceive the censors. The narrator receives a visit from a bizarre character who claims to travel on a regular basis between this world and the afterlife and to know the customs officers quite well. The stranger suggests that the narrator prepare a package of items that will be indispensable in his postearthly existence. For an initially reasonable sum, which gradually increases, the stranger promises to slip the package through the celestial customs. Happy to be able to secure himself a comfortable afterlife, the narrator starts to inventory his needs. He comes to the conclusion that he will have to take with him not only things but also persons, memories, feelings, meanings, experiences, options, and values, a "picture frame in whose perimeter appears a portrait laughing with one eye and weeping with the other. It is our own portrait, of a fidelity that will never cease to trouble us."

Evaluated adequately only during the postcommunist period, Simionescu's oeuvre has played an essential role in the shift of the paradigms of contemporary Romanian literature. Combining intellectual experimentation with cultural allusion, he created a canon of mystifying texts that distorted traditional narrative forms. For Simionescu the creative process is an act of subversion, converting erudition into a means of challenging and questioning reality.

References:

Ion Buzera, *Literatura română faţă cu postmodernismul Studiu critic despre Şcoala de proză de la Tîrgovişte* (Craiova: Scrisul Românesc, 1996), pp. 7–22, 110–143;

Al. Călinescu, "Un jurnal cît toate zilele," *Cronica,* 14 (1987): 10;

Barbu Cioculescu, "Piatra oceanică de Atlantic," *Luceafărul,* 2 (1997): 8–9;

Marcel Cornis-Pope, "The Disobeying Apprentice as Storyteller," in his *The Unfinished Battles: Romanian Postmodernism before and after 1989* (Iasi: Polirom, 1996), pp. 149–159;

Mihai Dragolea, *În exerciţiul ficţiunii: Eseu despre şcoala de la Tîrgovişte* (Cluj: Dacia, 1992);

Mircea Iorgulescu, "Maşina de scris poveşti," in his *Prezent* (Bucharest: Cartea Românească, 1985), pp. 219–221;

Iorgulescu, "Romanele dintr-un roman," in his *Firescul ca excepţie* (Bucharest: Cartea Românească, 1979), pp. 197–201;

Ion Bogdan Lefter, "Un pionnier: Mircea Horia Simionescu," *Euresis: Cahiers Roumains d'Études Littéraires,* 1–2 (1995): 263–267;

Nicolae Manolescu, "Comedia literaturii," in his *Arca lui Noe,* volume 3 (Bucharest: Minerva, 1983), pp. 216–242;

Eugen Negrici, "Expansiunea clişeului," in his *Figura Spiritului creator* (Bucharest: Cartea Românească, 1978), pp. 201–205;

Virgil Nemoinau, "Simionescu şi posibilul," in his *Utilul şi plăcutul* (Bucharest: Eminescu, 1973), pp. 39–45;

Eugen Simion, "Jurnalul intim," *România literară,* 27 (1987): 5;

Simion, "Mircea Horia Simionescu," in his *Scriitori români de azi,* volume 4 (Bucharest: Cartea Românească, 1989), pp. 272–273;

Monica Spiridon, "Les ages de la modernite roumaine," *Euresis: Cahiers Roumains d'Etudes Litteraires,* 1–2 (1995): 202–206;

Spiridon, "Scrisul ca voinţa şi reprezentare," *Revista de istorie şi teorie literară,* 1–2 (1987): 277–281;

Spiridon, "Sinceritatea sintaxei," in her *Apărarea şi ilustrarea criticii* (Bucharest: Didactică şi pedagogică, 1996), pp. 34–44.

Ion D. Sîrbu
(28 June 1919 – 17 September 1989)

Virgil Nemoianu
Catholic University of America

BOOKS: *Concert* (Bucharest: Editura Tineretului, 1956);

De ce plînge mama? (Craiova: Scrisul Românesc, 1973);

Povestiri petrilene (Iaşi: Junimea, 1973);

Teatru (Craiova: Scrisul Românesc, 1976);

Hateg '77 (Rapsodie transilvana) (Bucharest: Consiliul Culturii şi Educatiei Socialiste, Institutul de Cercetari Etnologice şi Dialectologice, 1977);

Arca bunei speranţe (Bucharest: Eminescu, 1982);

Şoarecele B si alte povestiri (Bucharest: Cartea Românească, 1983);

Bieţii comedianţi (Craiova: Scrisul Românesc, 1985);

Dansul ursului: Roman pentru copii şi bunici (Bucharest: Cartea Românească, 1988);

Jurnalul unui jurnalist fără jurnal, 2 volumes, edited by Marius Ghica (Craiova: Scrisul Românesc, 1991, 1993);

Adio, Europa! 2 volumes (Bucharest: Cartea Românească, 1992, 1993);

Lupul şi catedrala, edited by Maria Graciov (Bucharest: Casa Şcoalelor, 1995);

Intre Scylla si Carybda: Din insemnarile unui secretar literar, edited by Dumitru Velea (Petrosani: Editura Fundatiei Culturale "Ion D. Sirbu," 1996).

PLAY PRODUCTIONS: *La o piatră de hotar*, Craiova, Teatrul Naţional, 2 March 1968;

Frunze care ard, Craiova, Teatrul Naţional, 2 November 1968;

Arca bunei speranţe, Piatra-Neamt, Teatrul Tineretului, 4 April 1970;

Pragul albastru, Craiova, Teatrul Naţional, 1974;

Iarna lupului cenuşiu, Timişoara, Teatrul National, 27 April 1977;

Legenda naiului, Craiova, Teatrul de Păpuşi, 29 March 1979;

Covor oltenesc, Craiova, Teatrul Naţional, 27 April 1979;

Simion cel drept, Craiova, Teatrul Naţional, 12 June 1981.

Ion D. Sîrbu

Although he started writing and publishing early in his life, Ion D. Sîrbu emerged as a major literary figure only after 1989, when his previously unpublished works came to be known by a wider public. He combined the genteel and cultivated tradition of his generation of friends with an earthier, simpler, and grosser kind of carnivalesque humor and pessimism. This hidden work of the 1980s propelled Sîrbu into the first ranks of Romanian writing.

Ion Dezideriu Sîrbu was born on 28 June 1919 in the village of Petrila (Hunedoara County) in central Romania. His father, Ioan Sîrbu, was a miner, and his mother, Ecaterina Glaser, was of German-Czech background. Sîrbu was decisively influenced by the ways of life and thinking of the mining subculture in the Jiu Valley. He still found many rural traditions there, blended with trade-union, working-class ethics; an ideology in which ethnic hostility disappeared in the face of socioeconomic class solidarity; and an emphasis on values such as industrial progress and political equality. These left-wing values and modes of thinking were by no means common among the Romanian intellectuals of his day.

Sîrbu studied at the local village grade school and was an apprentice industrial worker for one year (1934–1935) but eventually managed to graduate in 1939 from the high school in Petroşani, the chief mining center of his native region. In that same year Sîrbu became an undergraduate student in literature and philosophy at the University of Cluj, which was moved to the city of Sibiu in southern Transylvania during World War II because of military occupation. Drafted into the military as a reserve noncommissioned officer, Sîrbu served as an artillery sergeant on the eastern front three times: from September 1941 to January 1942, September 1942 to April 1943, and March 1944 to July 1944. These war experiences left a deep imprint in Sîrbu's mind and strengthened his pacifist and internationalist inclinations.

Returning to his studies, Sîrbu obtained his master's degree (magna cum laude) in 1945 with a dissertation comparing the archetypes of the Swiss philosopher and psychologist Carl Jung to the "deep-structure categories" of Romanian philosopher and poet Lucian Blaga, who was also one of Sîrbu's chief professors and inspirations. This work was a study in aesthetics, psychology, and the philosophy of culture. During this same period (1945–1946) Sîrbu obtained his teaching credentials from the pedagogical department of the university. He was admitted to a program for doctoral studies, choosing as a dissertation topic "the epistemological function of metaphor"; he worked on it for more than a year but never completed his dissertation. Between 1946 and 1949 Sîrbu was first an assistant professor, then an associate professor at the University of Cluj and later at the Institute for Drama in Cluj. In 1949 he was fired as part of a general political cleansing of higher education initiated by the Communist authorities. Thus, Sîrbu's academic career came to an abrupt end.

Almost as soon as he enrolled in college, Sîrbu had become active in the Cercul Literar de la Sibiu (Sibiu Literary Circle), a group of students under the influence of Blaga and other professors such as Liviu Rusu and Victor Iancu; yet, under the leadership of future writers such as Ion Negoiţescu and Radu Stanca, Sîrbu started writing plays and short stories, some of which were published in *Revista Cercului* (Circle Review) in 1945. He not only forged lifelong friendships but also began to gain a formidable reputation as a master of oral and comic narrative and of witty, cutting barbs and puns.

After the collapse of his academic career, Sîrbu taught from 1950 to 1955 in high schools in the towns of Baia de Arieş and Cluj. Between 1955 and 1957 he held editorial positions in the capital city of Bucharest—first at the Pedagogical Institute there, and later with the monthly journal *Teatru* (Theater). Sîrbu managed in 1956 to publish *Concert*, his first collection of short stories.

In September 1957 Sîrbu was arrested and indicted for failing to denounce to the authorities private conversations that were deemed antigovernmental. The Bucharest Military Tribunal sentenced him in December 1958 to seven years in prison. He spent time in the notorious penitentiaries of Jilava and Gherla, as well as the forced labor camps of Periprava, Grindu, and Salcia. He was given an early release in February 1963 after a general amnesty for political prisoners was instituted in the early 1960s.

From September 1963 to August 1964 Sîrbu was a blue-collar worker in the Petrila mines, near his birthplace, as well as a stagehand in the Petroşani theater. By 1964 he was appointed dramatic secretary of the theater of Craiova, in southern Romania. In October 1973 Sîrbu retired for medical reasons (nervous depression and mild diabetes), but he received a writer's retirement pension and remained active as a writer. He died of throat cancer on 17 September 1989 in Craiova.

Sîrbu was married twice. From 1948 to 1959 he was married to Maria Ardeleanu, holder of a law degree from the University of Cluj; although the divorce was made final while Sîrbu was

*Sîrbu in 1942, a time when his pacifist and internationalist
convictions were strengthened by his experiences
in World War II*

tion from the rural-industrial folklore of his native area, or from the life of animals, such as *Dansul ursului* (Dance of the Bear, 1988). He also published several plays (some of them symbolic-fantastic and inspired by Romanian folklore) that were well received by audiences and gained several prestigious awards after subsequent stagings and republications (twice in 1983, once in 1985, once in 1988). *Pragul albastru* (The Blue Threshold), written in 1966 and staged in 1974, is steeped in dreamy folklore visions, and *Iarna lupului cenuşiu* (The Winter of the Gray Wolf), staged in 1977, is placed at the outset of the Romanian War of Independence (1877–1878). Sîrbu was proud of these plays; yet, they are far from representing his best literary achievements. Better than these are the short stories collected in *Şoarecele B si alte povestiri*, in which a sardonic and pessimistic view of human existence sometimes surfaces.

At another level Sîrbu, who used to complain that time was running short on him and that he missed about seven years of his life (presumably the years he spent in prison), wrote massively "for the drawer." Sîrbu's private and unpublishable works were openly opposed to the Communist totalitarian dictatorship, whereas what he could publish during his lifetime was toned down, censored, or self-censored. These private works came to be published soon after the political changes of 1989. They include notably *Jurnalul unui jurnalist fără jurnal* (The Journal of a Journalless Journalist, 1991, 1993), an aphoristic and political diary written during the 1980s, of which two volumes have been published, as well as his correspondence with friends in exile (also written during the 1980s). The latter, though subject to censorship and partly incomplete, shows the author's courage, intellectual ebullience, and independence of spirit. Two volumes of correspondence have come out: *Traversarea cortinei* (Crossing the Curtain, 1994) and *Scrisori către bunul Dumnezeu* (Letters to the Good Lord, 1996).

Most important are the two posthumous novels. *Lupul si catedrala* (The Wolf and the Cathedral, 1995), written in the 1980s, tries to be a kind of bildungsroman, the ambiguous and uncertain reconstructing of a young man under the stifling circumstances of communism by an eccentric network of odd, marginalized intellectuals. The novel also tries symbolically to suggest a reinvention of Romanian civilization using in equal measure the nativist, savage, local traditions ("the wolf") and the Western strains of

imprisoned, the marriage had already broken down by 1955, well before his arrest. In 1965 he married Elisabeta Afrim, a clerical employee in several cultural institutions such as the Craiova radio station and the local Artists's Union. The rescue of Sîrbu's unpublished manuscripts and their posthumous publication are largely because of Afrim's efforts.

After his release from prison, Sîrbu wrote ceaselessly and energetically on two different levels. On one level there were the works intended for prompt publication. Some of these were short novels or long short stories, as in *Şoarecele B si alte povestiri* (Rat B and Other Stories, 1983), which in a coded way satirized social manipulation by totalitarian forces. A few of these were intended for a younger audience and drew their inspira-

beauty, spirituality, and smooth cleanliness ("the cathedral"). By contrast, the two-volume *Adio, Europa!* (Adieu, Europe, 1992, 1993), probably written between 1985 and 1986, is perhaps the most powerful dystopian novel ever written in Romanian. It begins in an ironic mode, depicting the petty political conflicts and interdependencies in a small Balkan town under a communism transparently and jocularly disguised as stooping under an Ottoman yoke. However, soon the tones become darker, and the whole country is seen as subjected to a ludicrous system bent on the destruction of any kind of individual identity or independent initiative. The protagonist ends up in an insane asylum.

The belated discovery of Sîrbu's value and hidden dimension came as a tremendous surprise to the Romanian public. To be sure, he had been somewhat known and had enjoyed some esteem. However, after the revolutionary events of 1989, when freedom of the media and of expression were gained, Sîrbu's hitherto unpublished writings were perceived as the record of an honest, radical writer and thinker struggling to maintain his integrity under totalitarian oppression. His own experiences and changes (not always for the better: toward the end of his life Sîrbu became more embittered and misanthropic) were seen as typical for a broader category of intellectuals. He thus gained an unexpected stature in Romanian letters.

Letters:

Traversarea cortinei: Corespondenta lui Ion D. Sîrbu cu Ion Negoiţescu, Virgil Nemoianu, Mariana Sora, edited by Virgil Nemoianu and Marius Ghica (Timişoara: Editura de Vest, 1994);

Scrisori către bunul Dumnezeu, edited by Ion Vartic (Cluj: Apostrof, 1996).

References:

Caiete critice, special Sîrbu issue, 10–12 (1995);

Maria Graciov, "Prezentare," *Contrapunct* (1991): 35;

Dan C. Mihăilescu, "Singuratatea histrionului," *22,* 2 (1995): 15;

Marin Mincu, "Ion D. Sîrbu," *Paradigma,* 2 (1994): 1–2;

Virgil Nemoianu, "Surse romantice la I. D. Sîrbu," *Orizont,* 7 (24 January 1996): 6;

Zigu Ornea, "I. D. Sîrbu epistolier," *Romania literară* (November 1994): 9;

Sorina Sorescu, *Jurnalistul fără jurnal. Jocurile semnăturii* (Craiova: Aius, 1998).

Jan Skácel

(7 February 1922 – 7 November 1989)

Jiří Trávníček
Masaryk University, Brno

BOOKS: *Kolik příležitostí má růže* (Prague: Československý spisovatel, 1957);

Co zbylo z anděla (Prague: Československý spisovatel, 1960);

Jak šel brousek na vandr (Prague: Státní nakladatelství dětské knihy, 1961);

Pohádka o velikém samovaru (Prague: Státní nakladatelství dětské knihy, 1961);

Hodina mezi psem a vlkem (Prague: Československý spisovatel, 1962);

Jedenáctý bílý kůň (Brno: Blok, 1964; revised, 1966);

Smuténka (Prague: Československý spisovatel, 1965);

Metličky (Prague: Československý spisovatel, 1968);

Tratidla (Brno: Privately printed, 1974);

Chyba broskví (Prague: Edice Petlice [samizdat edition], 1975; Toronto: Sixty-Eight Publishers, 1978);

Oříšky pro černého papouška (N.p. [samizdat edition], 1976; Hamburg: Svato Verlag, 1980);

Dávné proso (Brno: Blok, 1981);

Básně (1976–1978) (Munich: Poezie mimo domov, 1982);

6 básní (Prague: Privately printed by Karel Majer, 1982);

Naděje s bukovými křídly (Prague: Mladá fronta, 1983)—comprises *Naděje s bukovými křídly* and *Oříšky pro černého papouška* in bowdlerized form;

Uspávanky (Prague: Albatros, 1983);

Odlévání do ztraceného vosku (Brno: Blok, 1984);

Kam odešly laně (Prague: Albatros, 1985);

Kdo pije potmě víno (Brno: Blok, 1988);

Proč ten ptáček z větve nespadne (Prague: Albatros, 1988);

Hřbitov vinařů (Třebíč: Privately printed by Emanuel Ranný, 1989);

A znovu láska (Brno: Blok, 1991);

Třináctý černý kůň, edited by Jiří Opelík (Brno: Blok, 1993);

Na koni páv a smrt a moruše, edited by Opelík (Brno: Blok, 1997).

Editions and Collections: *Vítr jménem Jaromír* (Prague: Československý spisovatel, 1966)—comprises *Kolik příležitostí má růže, Co zbylo z anděla*, and *Hodina mezi psem a vlkem;*

Krajina s kyvadly (Třebíč: Privately printed by Emanuel Ranný, 1985);

Kdo se vejde na housle (Třebíč: Privately printed by Ranný, 1986);

Druhá tratidla (Třebíč: Privately printed by Emanuel Ranný, 1987);

Píseň o nejbližší vině (Třebíč: Privately printed by Emanuel Ranný, 1988);

Poslední žízeň (Třebíč: Privately printed by Emanuel Ranný, 1990);

Noc s Věstonickou venuší (Prague: Československý spisovatel, 1990);

Stracholam (Prague: Mladá fronta, 1993);

Básně, 3 volumes, edited by Jiří Opelík (Brno: Blok, 1995–1996).

Editions in English: "What's Left of the Angel," "Rain," "Proverbs," "Contract," and "Sheep," translated and edited by George Theiner, in *New Writing in Czechoslovakia*, compiled by Theiner (Baltimore, Md.: Penguin, 1969), pp. 168–170;

"The Counsel of Princess Chiau," translated by Káča Poláčková, in *White Stones and Fir Trees: An Anthology of Contemporary Slavic Literature*, edited by Vasa D. Mihailovich (Rutherford, N.J.: Fairleigh Dickinson University Press, 1977), p. 230;

"Second Poem for the Moon and the Man" and "Sonnet about Love and Poets," translated by E. J. Czerwinski and Stana Dolezal, in *Shifting Borders: East European Poetries of the Eighties*, edited by Walter Cummins (Rutherford, N.J.: Fairleigh Dickinson University Press, 1993), pp. 204–205.

TRANSLATIONS: T. M. Plautus, *Lišák Pseudolus* (Prague: Dilia, 1988);

Sophocles, *Oidipus*, as Milan Pásek (Prague: Dilia, 1988).

Jan Skácel

Jan Skácel is generally acknowledged as one of the most significant Czech poets of the second half of the twentieth century. In the 1960s he became well known as the author of a highly characteristic genre of poetry, poetry that was based on myth and tradition but that at the same time dealt with the predicament of contemporary man. Skácel also played an important role in Czech literary life as the editor in chief of *Host do domu* (A Guest in the House), a significant literary and cultural periodical, from 1963 to 1969. Following the Prague Spring of 1968, Skácel was among the many writers whose work was banned from publication in Czechoslovakia, and not until the mid 1980s was he allowed to reemerge in part into Czech literary and cultural life.

Skácel was born on 7 February 1922 in the South Moravian village of Vnorovy to Emil Skácel and Anna (née Raná) Skácelová. His father was a teacher who exchanged letters with writers, including Romain Rolland, and published several peda-

gogical treatises as well as a collection of poems, *Bude vojna, bude?* (Will There Be War? 1936). Skácel's mother was also a teacher, and his grandmother's brother was František Herites, a well-known South Bohemian Czech writer of the second half of the nineteenth century. Skácel's brother, Petr, born in 1924, was a graphic artist and a well-known teacher who greatly influenced several generations of Czech painters.

Skácel spent his childhood in South Moravia, in Poštorná and Břeclav, where he began attending secondary school. In 1938 he moved to Brno-Královo Pole. He lived in Brno, the second largest Czech city, for the rest of his life. In *Odlévání do ztraceného vosku* (1984) he devoted a cycle of poems to the city, which he called "Město které musím" (The City which I Must). After completing secondary school in 1941, Skácel became an usher in the Brno "Modera" cinema. During the Nazi occupation of Czechoslovakia, the Germans closed down Czech universities, and there was no possibility of further study. Like many other young Czechs, in 1942 Skácel was sent by the Nazis to *Totaleinsatz* (forced labor) in the Third Reich; he worked at the Hermann Goering-Werke in St. Valentin in 1942 and 1943, at the Beton Morier Bau in Wiener Neustadt in 1943, and at the Beton Morier Bau in Ebensee in 1944 and 1945. He was sent to Ebensee as a punishment, since he had tried several times to run away from the *Totaleinsatz*. Skácel later said in his interview with Antonín J. Liehm that Ebensee was one of the worst *Vernichtungslager* (destruction labor camps) in the whole of the Third Reich.

In 1945 Skácel registered as a student at the Arts Faculty of Brno University, where he studied Czech and Russian. In 1946 he transferred to the newly founded Pedagogical Faculty but then left the university in 1948. In that year, poet and lifelong friend Oldřich Mikulášek found Skácel a job writing the cultural section for the *Rovnost* (Equality) daily in Brno. While working for *Rovnost*, Skácel used the pseudonyms SK and J.S. to sign his pieces. In 1949 Skácel was attacked for writing and publishing a poem titled "Pětiletka" (The Five-Year Plan), and under pressure by the ideologues from the Central Committee of the ruling Czechoslovak Communist Party was transferred from the arts section to the farming section of the paper, where he wrote articles on agriculture for two years. Also in 1949 he married Božena Mikulášková (née Hanzlíková), who was divorced from Mikulášek. From 1952 to 1953 Skácel worked as a maintenance man at Závody přesného strojírenství (Precise Engineering Works) in Brno-Líšeň.

In 1948 Czechoslovakia became a part of the Soviet bloc, and a pro-Soviet "dictatorship of the proletariat" was created in the country. The Czechoslovak Communist Party, with the help of Soviet advisers, assumed absolute power. The years 1948 through 1953 were a period of rampant Stalinism, characterized by show trials, social upheavals—in which large numbers of people in white-collar jobs were moved to factories and vice versa—and sustained political propaganda campaigns in the media. Skácel's journalism published during this period reflects the revolutionary fervor of the times as well as the official enthusiasm for the building of the "glorious (communist) future." Nevertheless, even in the most servile journalistic forums of the time Skácel always remained independent. His journalism is characterized by a detailed, concrete knowledge of the environment as well as by his interest in individual people. Skácel transgresses against the stereotyped norms of the poetry of socialist realism by including in his poems concrete

experiences of the senses. His journalism on farming is never pedestrian; Skácel developed an individual style, and his articles often border on poetry.

On 1 April 1953 Skácel joined the literary and dramatic department of Czech Radio in Brno and worked there until 31 August 1963. The radio experience influenced Skácel's writing: he learned to be concise and to write texts that would be read easily on the air. During this period Skácel created his own idiosyncratic genre *malé recenze* (small reviews, or short prosaic texts), which made him as well known as his poetry. The point of departure in these small reviews was a brief anecdote or a minor observation that Skácel placed in a startling new context. He wrote these comments on such topics as contemporary city life, literature, the fine arts, forgotten words, meetings with ordinary people, and the way children see things.

In 1957 the thirty-five-year-old Skácel published his first volume of poetry, *Kolik příležitostí má růže* (How Many Opportunities a Rose Has). This collection was partially influenced by the then-fashionable interest in ordinary, everyday things—a reaction to the bombastic, mythologizing, ideological literature of the previous, Stalinist era. At this time, while most poets interested in the everyday existence of people wrote about urban life, Skácel found his inspiration in the countryside. He used many of his childhood experiences, emphasizing the lasting validity of fundamental, unchangeable, timeless values.

Skácel's next two collections, *Co zbylo z anděla* (What Has Remained of the Angel, 1960) and *Hodina mezi psem a vlkem* (The Hour between the Dog and the Wolf, 1962), confirm, however, that Skácel cannot be regarded as a "poet of the countryside," as someone who merely preaches a nostalgic return to an obsolete way of life. These two collections show that Skácel's poetry is based on the eternal values of order and myth, and it aims at re-creating the integrity that has disintegrated in the modern world. The author was influenced by folk poetry as well as by sophisticated literature. There are references to the Czech nineteenth-century Romantic poet Karel Jaromír Erben, for example. Skácel was further influenced by the work of poets close to his vision of the world, such as František Halas; in his poetry he also reacted, sometimes polemically, to poetry by other authors. In *Smuténka* (Little Sadness, 1965), Skácel's fourth volume of poetry, the poet looks back. He evaluates the worth of poetry and weighs the value of words. He began frequently to use expressions associated with lan-

Skácel with fellow Czech writer Bohumil Hrabal

guage; some of his poems are titled "Přísloví" (translated as "Proverb," 1969), "Verše" (Verse), "Smlouva" (translated as "Contract," 1969), and "Dopis" (A Letter). Skácel also strove in this volume to be as terse as possible. Silence and open-ended statements gain in importance.

The monthly periodical, *Host do domu,* had been founded in 1953, and Skácel began publishing his poetry in that periodical in 1958, using the pseudonym SK to sign some of his published pieces. Five years later he became editor in chief. In March 1969 Skácel left the editorial post, and it was taken over by his colleague Jan Trefulka. In 1970 *Host do domu* was closed down by the communist authorities as part of the political clampdown that followed the Warsaw Pact–led invasion in August 1968.

Skácel helped make *Host do domu* into one of the most remarkable literary and cultural periodicals of the time. He set up an editorial team highly capable of searching out interesting new texts and stimulating authors to write them. *Host do domu* equally published original work, criticism, Czech fiction, and translations from foreign literatures. The periodical featured a section for young authors, "Zelený host" (The Green Guest); a firm, although not inflexible structure of thematic sections, such as "Drzý interview" (The Insolent Interview); and the column "Sami proti sobě" (Against Themselves), in which *Host do domu* printed various howlers made by journalists writing on the arts. Although *Host do domu* was subject to state censorship, which was abolished in Czechoslovakia only briefly in 1968, it occasionally published critical political pieces. Skácel edited the poetry section and the last page of the periodical, on which his small reviews appeared.

After the banning of *Host do domu*, Skácel, like some four hundred other contemporary Czech writers, suffered a complete publication ban. He became, as he said in his poem, "básníci zakázaní za živa," from *A znovu láska* (1991), one of the "poets, banned while alive." What followed was twenty years of so-called normalization, a neo-Stalinist backlash that became the worst period of Skácel's life. He and his wife were forced to depend on a single salary, and at first they lived off their savings. Skácel suffered from depression; his health deteriorated; and soon he did not have enough money to live on. He was also followed and harassed by the secret police. In one of his notebooks he wrote: "I have never had enough money to buy what I wanted. Now I do not even have money to buy what I badly need."

Skácel continued writing poetry, which his friends copied out on the typewriter. In the 1980s some of his poetry was published by Czech émigré publishing houses abroad. Two cycles of four-line poems—*Chyba broskví* (The Flaw of the Peaches, 1975) and *Oříšky pro černého papouška* (Nuts for a Black Parrot, 1976), each of them comprising a hundred poems in Czech—were published in the West (an official publication in Czechoslovakia did not follow until 1983). In these poems Skácel attempts to reach the limits of terseness, as though what really mattered took place before and beyond the existence of the poems. The four-liners, as they are called, are filled with child-like playfulness: the poet toys with the meanings of words and with the way they sound. He again reflects upon the meaning of poetry, and again nature remains an important theme.

Circles of friends, often made up of students, formed around Skácel, and on Saturdays he went on trips with them. He also secretly collaborated with certain theaters, doing translations and editing scripts. For instance, in 1988 Skácel translated Sophocles's *Oedipus Rex* (circa 429 B.C.).

In 1981, after many arguments with the ruling Communist Party and the Writers' Union bureaucracy, Skácel's collection *Dávné proso* (Ancient Millet) was published. In this volume the poet concentrates on memory and on looking back. With great urgency the landscape of childhood opens up before the poet, and there is a sense of death, not as something that comes at the end of one's days but as something that is permanently present. Skácel's favorite theme, although often obliquely expressed returns in a more profound variation: the poet again reflects on the nature of time.

The 1980s were slightly more bearable for Skácel than the 1970s. Under his own name, as a result of the personal courage of his friends in the editorial offices—who risked their livelihoods to publish a semibanned author—he was occasionally allowed to print some of his new small reviews in *Brněnský večerník* (The Brno Evening News). He also managed to publish two more collections of poetry and three collections of verse for children—of these, *Uspávanky* (Lullabies, 1983), includes some of the most original Czech poetry for children. He was now able to work regularly for the theater, and the Brno Divadlo Na provázku (Theater on a String) put on a program of his poetry. His verse was put to music by popular balladeers. Although Skácel suffered from both asthma and emphysema, he took part in an increasing number of unofficial events, lectures, and poetry readings; he was frequently invited to speak, especially to students. The official proregime Writers' Union offered him membership several times, but Skácel turned down these offers.

In 1989 Skácel received two major European prizes: the Italian Petrarca Prize and the Slovenian Vilenica Prize. These occasions also meant that for the first time in twenty years he was allowed to travel abroad. In Florence the official "laudatio" over Skácel's work was read by Peter Handke, who placed Skácel in the European context near Georg Trakl and Wolfgang Amadeus Mozart. When Skácel traveled to Slovenia in September 1989, his asthma had seriously worsened, and for a part of his stay in Slovenia, he was confined to bed. Skácel could neither descend into the Vilenica cave for the prize-giving ceremony nor take part in the planned news conference. On 7 November 1989, ten days before the fall of communism in Czechoslovakia, Skácel died of emphysema.

Jan Skácel has a place among the most widely read twentieth-century Czech poets. Perhaps one reason his poetry has been highly popular is because in materialist times it offers a spiritual and transcendental alternative without looking for shelter within a concrete religious denomination. Both "ordinary" readers and connoisseurs of poetry loved Skácel, who had a following in the German-speaking world as well as in Czechoslovakia. Skácel knew how to merge opposing themes: the popular and the sophisticated, the countryside and the urban, tradition and modernity, adulthood and childhood, image and reflection, history and mythology, and words and silence.

Interview:

Antonín J. Liehm, *Generace* (Prague: Československý spiśovatel, 1990), pp. 242–262.

References:

Václav Černý, "Hrst úvah nad Janem Skácelem," in *Tvorba a osobnost I*, edited by Jaroslav Kabíček and Jan Šulc (Prague: Odeon, 1992), pp. 821–831;

Milan Hamada, "O pravde, kráse a Janovi Skácelovi," in his *Básnická transcendencia* (Bratislava: Slovenský spisovatel, 1969), pp. 91–101;

Peter Handke, "Das plötzliche Nichtmehrwissen des Dichters: Laudatio auf Jan Skácel," *Die Zeit*, 44, no. 25 (1989): 61;

Vladimír Karfík, "Z mladší poezie," in *Jak číst poezii*, edited by Jiří Opelík, second edition (Prague: Československý spisovatel, 1969), pp. 221–261;

Zdeněk Kožmín, "Eros holanovský a skácelovský," *List pro literaturu*, 1, no. 7 (1990): 30–31;

Kožmín, *Skácel* (Brno: Jota, 1994);

Kožmín, *Umění básně* (Brno: K22a, 1990);

Jiří Kudrnáč, "Dva básníci a tradice. Nad novými sbírkami Jana Skácela a Oldřicha Mikuláška," *Sborník prací filozofické fakulty brněnské univerzity*, Literary Historical Series (D 32), 30 (1983): 53–61;

Ludvík Kundera, "SK–," in his *Řečiště bz L. K.* (Brno: Rovnost, 1993), pp. 116–119;

Vlastimil Maršíček, "Jan Skácel," in his *Nezval, Seifert a ti druzí . . .* (Brno: Host, 1999), pp. 131–136;

Petr Musil, "Jan Skácel, básník tiché poezie," *Malovaný kraj*, 28, no. 3 (1992): 8;

Jiří Opelík, "Skácel," in *Jak číst poezii*, edited by Opelík (Prague: Československý spisovatel, 1963), pp. 249–255;

Emanuel Ranný, ed., *Bílá žízeň* (Třebíč: FiBox, 1993);

Sylvie Richterová, "Krajina proměn a tvary ticha. 2x100 čtyřverší Jana Skácela," in her *Slova a ticho* (Munich: Arkýř, 1986), pp. 93–105;

ROK, special Skácel issue, 3, no. 1 (1992);

Šlépěje kultury západní Moravy, special Skácel issue, no. 3 (1992);

Oleg Sus, "Od moudrosti k ironickému humoru," in *Cesty k dnešku*, edited by Sus (Brno: Blok, 1964), pp. 167–194;

Jiří Trávníček, "Moravská inspirace v poezii Oldřicha Mikuláška a Jana Skácela," *Česká literatura*, 38 (1990): 337–346;

Vilém Trávníček, "Jan Skácel a jeho svět," *Malovaný kraj*, 6, no. 1 (1970): 12–15.

Josef Škvorecký

(27 September 1924 –)

Martin Pilař
University of Ostrava

and

Jan Čulík
University of Glasgow

This entry originally appeared in Concise Dictionary of World Literary Biography:
South Slavic and Eastern European Writers.

BOOKS: *Zbabělci* (Prague: Československý spisovatel, 1958); translated by Jeanne W. Němcová as *The Cowards* (New York: Grove, 1970; London: Gollancz, 1970);

Vražda pro štěstí, by Škvorecký and Jan Zábrana (Prague: Mladá fronta, 1962);

Legenda Emöke (Prague: Československý spisovatel, 1963);

Sedmiramenný svícen (Prague: Naše vojsko, 1964);

Vražda se zárukou, by Škvorecký and Zábrana (Prague: Mladá fronta, 1964);

Táňa a dva pistolníci, by Škvorecký and Zábrana (Prague: Svobodné slovo, 1965);

Ze života lepší společnosti: Paravanprózy z text-appealů (Prague: Mladá fronta, 1965);

Nápady čtenáře detektivek (Prague: Československý spisovatel, 1965);

Smutek poručíka Borůvky: Detektivní pohádka (Prague: Mladá fronta, 1966); translated by Rosemary Kavan, Káča Poláčková, and George Theiner as *The Mournful Demeanour of Lieutenant Boruvka* (London: Gollancz, 1973);

Babylónský příběh a jiné povídky (Prague: Svobodné slovo, 1967);

Konec nylonového věku (Prague: Československý spisovatel, 1967);

Vražda v zastoupení, by Škvorecký and Zábrana (Prague: Mladá fronta, 1967);

O nich–o nás (Hradec Králové: Kruh, 1968);

Lvíče: Koncové detektivní melodrama (Prague: Československý spisovatel, 1969); translated by Peter

Josef Škvorecký (photograph by Phill Snel)

Kussi as *Miss Silver's Past* (New York: Grove, 1975; London: Bodley Head, 1976);

Farářův konec: Podklad pro celovečerní tragikomedii, by Škvorecký and Evald Schorm (Hradec Králové: Kruh, 1969);

Hořkej svět: Povídky z let 1946–1967 (Prague: Odeon-Státní nakladatelství krásné literatury, hudby a umění, 1969);

Tankový prapor (Toronto: Sixty-Eight Publishers, 1971); translated by Paul Wilson as *The Republic of Whores: A Fragment from the Time of the Cults* (Toronto: Knopf Canada, 1993; Hopewell, N.J.: Ecco Press, 1994; London: Faber & Faber, 1994);

All the Bright Young Men and Women: A Personal History of the Czech Cinema, translated by Michal Schonberg (Toronto: Peter P. Martin Associates, 1971); published in Czech as *Všichni ti bystří mladí muži a ženy: Osobní historie českého filmu* (Prague: Horizont, 1991);

Mirákl: Politická detektivka, 2 volumes (Toronto: Sixty-Eight Publishers, 1972); translated by Wilson as *The Miracle Game* (Toronto: Lester & Orpen Dennys, 1990; New York: Knopf, 1991; London: Faber & Faber, 1991);

Hříchy pro pátera Knoxe: Detektivní divertimento (Toronto: Sixty-Eight Publishers, 1973); translated by Káča Poláčková-Henley as *Sins for Father Knox* (Toronto: Lester & Orpen Dennys, 1988; New York: Norton, 1989; London: Faber & Faber, 1989);

Prima sezóna: Text o nejdůležitějších věcech života (Toronto: Sixty-Eight Publishers, 1975); translated by Wilson as *The Swell Season: A Text on the Most Important Things in Life* (Toronto: Lester & Orpen Dennys, 1982; London: Chatto & Windus, 1983; New York: Ecco Press, 1986);

Konec poručíka Borůvky: Detektivní žalozpěv (Toronto: Sixty-Eight Publishers, 1975); translated by Wilson as *The End of Lieutenant Borůvka* (Toronto: Lester & Orpen Dennys, 1989; New York: Norton, 1990; London: Faber & Faber, 1990);

Příběh inženýra lidských duší: Entrtejnment na stará témata o životě, ženách, osudu, snění, dělnické třídě, fizlech, lásce a smrti, 2 volumes (Toronto: Sixty-Eight Publishers, 1977); translated by Wilson as *The Engineer of Human Souls: An Entertainment on the Old Themes of Life, Women, Fate, Dreams, the Working Class, Secret Agents, Love and Death* (New York: Knopf, 1984; Toronto: Lester & Orpen Dennys, 1984; London: Chatto & Windus, 1985);

Samožerbuch–Antinostalgicum, by Škvorecký, Zdena Salivarová, and Ota Ulč (Toronto: Sixty-Eight Publishers, 1977);

Na brigádě, by Škvorecký and Antonín Brousek (Toronto: Sixty-Eight Publishers, 1979);

Velká povídka o Americe (Toronto: Sixty-Eight Publishers, 1980);

Bůh do domu: Fraška o čtyřech dějstvích (Toronto: Sixty-Eight Publishers, 1980);

Nezoufejte! Zpěv první (Munich: Poezie mimo domov, 1980);

Dívka z Chicaga a jiné hříchy mládí: Básně z let 1940–45 (Munich: Poezie mimo domov, 1980);

Návrat poručíka Borůvky: Reakcionářská detektivka (Toronto: Sixty-Eight Publishers, 1980); translated and adapted by Wilson as *The Return of Lieutenant Borůvka* (Toronto: Lester & Orpen Dennys, 1990; London: Faber & Faber, 1990; New York: Norton, 1991);

Jiří Menzel and the History of the Closely Watched Trains (Boulder: East European Monographs, 1982);

Scherzo capriccioso: Veselý sen o Dvořákovi (Toronto: Sixty-Eight Publishers, 1984); translated by Wilson as *Dvořák in Love: A Light-hearted Dream* (Toronto: Lester & Orpen Dennys, 1986; London: Chatto & Windus, 1986; New York: Knopf, 1987);

Ze života české společnosti (Toronto: Sixty-Eight Publishers, 1985);

Talkin' Moscow Blues, edited by Sam Solecki (Toronto: Lester & Orpen Dennys, 1988; New York: Ecco Press, 1990; London: Faber & Faber, 1990); revised and published in Czech as *Franz Kafka, jazz a jiné marginálie* (Toronto: Sixty-Eight Publishers, 1988);

Hlas z Ameriky (Toronto: Sixty-Eight Publishers, 1990);

Čítanka Josefa Škvoreckého (Prague: Společnost Josefa Škvoreckého, 1990);

Divák v únorové noci (Prague: Společnost Josefa Škvoreckého, 1991);

Leading a Literary Double-Life in Prague (Toronto: Ontario Institute for Studies in Education, 1991);

Slovo má mladý severovýchod (Prague: Společnost Josefa Škvoreckého, 1991);

O anglické literatuře (Prague: Společnost Josefa Škvoreckého, 1991);

Ožehavé téma; Jsou Kanaďané politicky naivní?; Divné události v Lisabonu (Prague: Společnost Josefa Škvoreckého, 1991);

Blues libeňského plynojemu (Plzeň: Bibliophile Print, 1992);

Jak jsem se učil německy (Prague: Společnost Josefa Škvoreckého/Městský úřad v Náchodě, 1992);

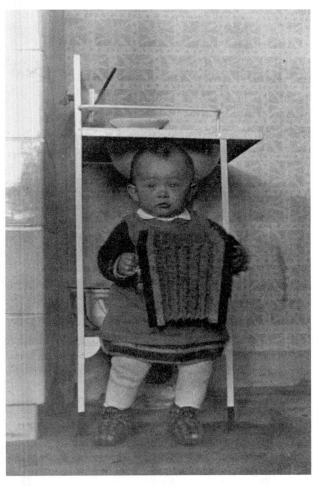

Škvorecký, age two, in a photograph taken by his father

Jaká vlastně byla Marilyn? (Prague: Společnost Josefa Škvoreckého, 1992);

Vladimíra v Territorio libre, as Vladimíra Burke (Prague: Společnost Josefa Škvoreckého, 1992);

Dvě neznámé povídky. Pravda. Panta rei. (Prague: Společnost Josefa Škvoreckého, 1992);

Věci (Prague: Společnost Josefa Škvoreckého, 1992);

Nevěsta z Texasu: Romantický příběh ze skutečnosti (Toronto: Sixty-Eight Publishers, 1992); translated by Káča Poláčková-Henley as *The Bride of Texas: A Romantic Tale from the Real World* (Toronto: Knopf Canada, 1995; New York: Knopf, 1996; London: Faber & Faber, 1996);

Věk nylonu: Fragment románu (Prague: Společnost Josefa Škvoreckého, 1992);

Povídky tenorsaxofonisty (Toronto: Sixty-Eight Publishers, 1993); translated by Caleb Crain, Poláčková-Henley, and Kussi as *The Tenor Saxophonist's Story* (Hopewell, N.J.: Ecco Press, 1997);

In the Lonesome October (Toronto: Harbourfront, 1993);

Slovo má mladý severovýchod 2 (Prague: Společnost Josefa Škvoreckého, 1994);

Povídky z Rajského údolí (Prague: Ivo Železný, 1996).

Editions and Collections: *Dvě legendy* (Toronto: Sixty-Eight Publishers, 1982)—comprises *Bassaxofon, Legenda Emöke,* and "Red Music";

Spisy Josefa Škvoreckého—comprises volume 1, *Prima sezóna, Zbabělci, Konec nylonového věku* (Prague: Odeon, 1991); volume 2, *Příběhy o Líze a mladém Wertherovi a jiné povídky* (Prague: Ivo Železný, 1994); volume 3, *Nové canterburské povídky a jiné příběhy* (1996); volume 4, *Neuilly a jiné příběhy* (1996), translated by Káča Poláčková-Henley as *Headed for the Blues* (Hopewell, N.J.: Ecco Press, 1996); volume 5, *Lvíče* (1996); volume 6, *Dvě vraždy v mém dvojím životě* (1996), translated as *Two Murders in My Double Life: A Crime Novel in Two Interlocking Movements* (Toronto: Key Porter Books, 1999); volume 7, *Příběh neúspěšného tenorsaxofonisty* (1997); volume 8, *Mirákl* (1997); volume 9, *Nápady čtenáře detektivek a jiné eseje* (1998); volume 10, *Tankový prapor* (1998); volume 11, *Nevysvětlitelný příběh aneb Vyprávění Questa Firma Sicula* (1998); volume 12, *. . . na tuhle bolest nejsou prášky* (1999); volume 13, *Krátké setkání, s vraždou,* by Škvorecký and Zdena Salivarová (1999); and volume 14, *Podivný pán z Providence a jiné eseje* (1999);

Josef Škvorecký–život a dílo, CD-ROM (Prague: Vyšší odborná škola a Soukromé gymnasium Josefa Škvoreckého, Společnost Josefa Škvoreckého, 1999).

Editions in English: "Oh My Papa!" translated by George Theiner, in *Seven Short Stories,* edited by Dušan Kužel and others (Prague: Orbis, 1965, 1967), pp. 77–101;

"The Great Catholic Water Fast," translated by Jeanne W. Němcová, in *Czech and Slovak Short Stories,* edited and translated by Němcová (London & New York: Oxford University Press, 1967), pp. 199–212;

"Song of the Forgotten Years," translated by Theiner, in *New Writing in Czechoslovakia* compiled by Theiner (Baltimore: Penguin, 1969; Harmondsworth, U.K.: Penguin, 1969), pp. 70–80;

Oh, My Papa! edited by Itaru Iijima and Minoru Miyata (Tokyo: Asahi Press, 1972);

"Eine Kleine Jazzmusik," translated by Alice Denesová, in *White Stones and Fir Trees: An Anthology of Contemporary Slavic Literature,* edited by Vasa D. Mihailovich (Lewisburg: Bucknell University Press, 1977), pp. 351–364;

The Bass Saxophone. Emöke, translated by Káča Poláč-ková-Henley (Toronto: Anson-Cartwright Editions, 1977; London: Chatto & Windus, 1978—comprises *The Bass Saxophone, Emöke,* and "Red Music"; New York: Knopf, 1979);

Headed for the Blues, a Memoir with Ten Stories, translated by Poláčková-Henley, Caleb Crain, and Peter Kussi (Toronto: Knopf Canada, 1997; London: Faber & Faber, 1998)—comprises *Headed for the Blues* and *The Tenor Saxophonist's Story.*

TRANSLATIONS: Ray Bradbury, *451 stupňů Fahrenheita,* translated by Škvorecký and Jarmila Emmerová (Prague: Melantrich, 1957);

Ernest Hemingway, *Sbohem armádo* (Prague: Státní nakladatelství krásné literatury, hudby a umění, 1958);

Henry James, *Listiny Aspernovy,* translated by Škvorecký and Lubomír Dorůžka (Prague: Československý spisovatel, 1958);

William Faulkner, *Báj,* translated by Škvorecký and Dorůžka (Prague: Státní nakladatelství krásné literatury, hudby a umění, 1961);

Americká lidová poezie, translated by Škvorecký and Dorůžka (Prague: Státní nakladatelství krásné literatury, hudby a umění, 1961);

Sinclair Lewis, *Babbitt* (Prague: Státní nakladatelství krásné literatury, hudby a umění, 1962);

Dashiell Hammett, *Skleněný klíč* (Prague: Mladá fronta, 1963);

Warren Miller, *Prezident krokadýlů,* as Jan Zábrana (Prague: Státní nakladatelství krásné literatury, hudby a umění, 1963);

Tvář jazzu, translated by Škvorecký and Dorůžka (Prague: SHV, 1964);

Raymond Chandler, *Dáma v jezeře* (Prague: Mladá fronta, 1965);

Alan Sillitoe, *Osamělost přespolního běžce* (Prague: Státní nakladatelství krásné literatury, hudby a umění, 1965);

William Styron, *Dlouhý pochod* (Prague: Státní nakladatelství krásné literatury, hudby a umění, 1965);

Martina Navrátilová and George Vecsey, *Já jsem já: Martina Navrátilová* (Toronto: Sixty-Eight Publishers, 1985).

PRODUCED SCRIPTS: *Zločin v dívčí škole,* script by Škvorecký, Ivo Novák, Ladislav Rychman, and Jiří Menzel, motion picture, Filmové studio Barrandov, February 1966;

Zločin v šantánu, script by Škvorecký, Menzel, and Jiří Suchý, motion picture, Filmové studio Barrandov, December 1968;

Farářův konec, script by Škvorecký and Evald Schorm, motion picture, Filmové studio Barrandov, January 1969;

Flirt se slečnou Stříbrnou, screenplay by Škvorecký and Zdeněk Mahler, motion picture, Filmové studio Barrandov, September 1969;

Poe a vražda krásné dívky, story and screenplay by Škvorecký, television, Česká televize, 11–12 December 1996.

OTHER: "An Eastern European Imagination?" in *The Eastern European Imagination in Literature,* edited by Robert G. Collins and Kenneth McRobbie, New Views: A Mosaic Series in Literature, no. 16 (Winnipeg: University of Manitoba Press, 1973), pp. 101–105;

"The East European Émigré as Writer: Some Personal Observations," in *Studies in Ethnicity: The East European Experience in America,* edited by Charles E. Ward, Philip Stasko, and Donald E. Pienkos (Boulder, Colo.: East European Monographs / New York: Columbia University Press, 1980), pp. 225–231;

"Franz Kafka, Jazz, the Anti-Semitic Reader, and Other Marginal Matters," in *Cross Currents: A Yearbook of Central European Culture,* volume 2 (Ann Arbor: Department of Slavic Languages and Literatures, University of Michigan, 1983), pp. 169–182;

"The Big Insult. An Essay on Literature and Culture in Czechoslovakia and in Eastern Europe," in *Cross Currents: A Yearbook of Central European Culture,* volume 5 (Ann Arbor: Department of Slavic Languages and Literatures, University of Michigan, 1986), pp. 123–135;

"Reception: An Authorial Experience," by Škvorecký and Celia Hawkesworth, in *Literature and Politics in Eastern Europe: Selected Papers from the Fourth World Congress for Soviet and East European Studies, Harrogate, 1990,* edited by Hawkesworth (New York: St. Martin's Press, 1992), pp. 5–10.

SELECTED PERIODICAL PUBLICATIONS—UNCOLLECTED: "The President Wrote Absurdist Plays," *World & I* (March 1990): 418–428;

"Bohemia of the Soul," *Daedalus,* 119, (Winter 1990): 111–139.

As one of the few internationally appreciated modern Czech authors, Josef Škvorecký has a special position in the cultural context of his native country. From his earliest literary attempts he has been writing about the Czech national traumas of

Škvorecký playing the tenor saxophone, circa 1940

the twentieth century, but he has done so in a way that does not adhere to the prevailing and recommended traditions of Czech literature. Škvorecký's love for jazz and for the classics of modern American literature makes his work different from the bulk of Czech literature in the period between the National Revival in the nineteenth century and World War II, because local cultural trends were inspired mostly by either Russian or French traditions in order to separate the newly revived Czech culture from the "fatal" German influence, which cannot be avoided in Central Europe.

Škvorecký's ability to enjoy writing fiction about the most serious problems of his time and to write texts that seem to be created mainly for entertainment has only a few predecessors in Czech literature, notably Jan Neruda, Jaroslav Hašek, and Karel Čapek. His balancing act between serious and popular literature makes his work reminiscent of the Anglo-Saxon literary tradition. Škvorecký's deep-rooted belief in democratic principles caused him—together with his wife, Zdena Salivarová—to found a small, independent subscription publish-

ing house, "Sixty-Eight Publishers," in Toronto. It became one of the main Czech émigré publishing houses that helped independent Czech literature to survive the two decades of totalitarian political and cultural oppression following the Soviet invasion of Czechoslovakia in 1968. More than 220 original titles were brought out by Sixty-Eight Publishers between 1971 and 1989; their last book was published in 1993, and the house was officially closed in 1994.

Škvorecký was born on 27 September 1924 to Josef, a bank clerk, and Anna (Kurážová) Škvorecký in Náchod, a small provincial town in northeastern Bohemia. Its streets and houses can be easily recognized in his fictional town called Kostelec, where Danny Smiřický, Škvorecký's literary hero and alter ego, falls in love with jazz and girls and as a teenage witness to World War II meets eternal paradoxes, both Czech and generally human. In 1943 Škvorecký graduated from the local secondary school and was then forced by the occupying German troops to work at the local Messerschmitt factories, which made parts for German airplanes. Immediately after the postwar reopening of Czech universities, Škvorecký left Náchod for Prague and began studying medicine at Charles University. After completing one term, he decided to study philosophy and English philology. For his diploma thesis (1949) he discussed Ernest Hemingway, and for his dissertation (1951) he researched Thomas Paine.

During his studies Škvorecký wrote a few early literary works that he later called "the sins of my youth" and that were only published many decades afterward. The first was a Whitmanesque free verse composition, *Nezoufejte!* (Don't Despair, 1980). This work attracted the interest of the great poet František Halas; references in Halas's diaries to Škvorecký and his then-unpublished manuscripts brought the young author to the attention of important personalities from the nonofficial cultural milieu, notably avant-garde literary and art theoretician Jindřich Chalupecký and world-renowned artist and poet Jiří Kolář. Another collection of poems, *Dívka z Chicaga* (A Girl from Chicago, 1980), in spite of its title, shows Škvorecký's close connection with the tradition of Czech modernism. The short-story collection *Nové canterburské povídky* (The New Canterbury Tales, included in his collected works in 1996) won the Prague University literary contest in 1948 and seems most typically to anticipate the future development of its author. The characters, members of a Dixieland band, are clearly early versions of characters in subsequent books.

In 1947 Škvorecký produced his first novel, "Věk nylonu" (The Nylon Age), the surviving fragment of which was published in 1992. An episode from it became the basis of Škvorecký's short story "Babylonský příběh" (The Babylonian Story, 1967). Soon after the Communist coup in February 1948, Škvorecký wrote his first mature novel, *Zbabělci* (1958; translated as *The Cowards,* 1970). In the following years the writer experienced extremes of political stupidity and absurdity—at first as a young teacher, but especially during his two years of military service with the elite Tank Division. This chapter of his life provided him with a considerable amount of material that he later successfully used in his fiction. In 1954 Škvorecký wrote the comic novel *Tankový prapor* (The Tank Corps, 1971; translated as *The Republic of Whores,* 1993).

Determined to go on writing and living his own way, Škvorecký started to work as editor of a Prague publishing house specializing in foreign literatures and art. He soon became a recognized essayist writing on modern classics of American and English literature. As a result of this work he was appointed deputy editor in chief of the magazine *Světová literatura* (World Literature) in 1956. In the same year he submitted for publication his novel *Konec nylonového věku* (The End of the Nylon Age, 1967), which takes place at a dance given by the American Institute of Prague in February 1949. The work did not appear until eleven years later and was initially banned by the censors. Nevertheless, literary fame soon followed.

From the late 1940s to the early 1950s Škvorecký's literary activity was more or less hidden because of the strict cultural dictatorship of the Communist Party. Škvorecký was allowed to publish his first book—*Zbabělci*, written ten years earlier—only in 1958, in the atmosphere of the incipient political thaw. (In that same year, on 31 March, Škvorecký married Salivarová.) *Zbabělci* caused one of the biggest scandals in the Czech literary world. Initially, *Zbabělci* received several lukewarm reviews, but then a strong anti-Škvorecký campaign was started in the media. Ideological critics saw *Zbabělci* as a "slap in the face of the living and the dead," as "worm-infested fruit," and as "spit, hurled in the face of all those whose graves were scattered all over the republic after the war." The work was banned and confiscated. The official campaign directed against *Zbabělci* was used as a pretext for a general clampdown; publishing houses were forced to cancel the printing of several other liberal-minded titles.

Zbabělci describes the last days of World War II in Kostelec as seen through the eyes of Danny Smiřický, a young jazzman and unsuccessful lover who unmasks the mediocrity of the last-minute war "heroes." The account of the end of the war is casual, unpretentious, and subjective, which is why the novel provoked a fierce reaction from the communist authorities when it was first published. It was a direct assault on the official heroic interpretation of the end of the war as well as some of the less pleasing aspects of the Czech middle-class, small-town mentality. Smiřický does not consciously analyze the twists and turns of history to which he is subjected, but he strongly feels the impact of historical events. He witnesses the useless deaths and cruel murders committed by local "patriots" in the final days of the war. At the end of the novel, Smiřický has a foreboding about the forthcoming era, marked by the arrival of the Red Army. Yet, throughout the novel, the war events are not in the center of his attention. The most important things for Smiřický are jazz and courting girls. As top communist literary ideologist Ladislav Štoll put it in *Literární noviny* (7 March 1959), *Zbabělci* is a

> work which is thoroughly alien to our beautiful democratic and humanist literature because it is artistically dishonest, mendacious and cynical. The author's ideological standpoint is the greatest cause of concern. A great event of our national history has been used as a garish backdrop for the depiction of an amorous campaign by a hooligan. The provocative cumulation of coarse expressions, along with erotic exhibitionism, shows that the work is not artistically original, but it is a cheap scandalous sensation, a kind of Czechoslovak bestseller.

Zbabělci should also be seen as an important milestone in jazz literature: Škvorecký's use of colloquial speech, together with his ability to express jazz rhythms in prose, is matched by hardly anyone else in Central Europe.

After the publication and the subsequent suppression of *Zbabělci* Škvorecký lost his post as deputy editor in chief of *Světová literatura* and survived for almost five years in official disfavor in his earlier position as a book editor. Škvorecký was not taken off the list of banned authors until 1963. He translated American fiction into Czech and wrote detective stories, first under the name of his collaborator, the poet and translator Jan Zábrana. For the rest of his literary career he remained faithful to detective literature.

Škvorecký's devotion to cultivated popular literature has embarrassed a certain type of Czech lit-

Škvorecký as a sergeant in the Czechoslovakian tank corps in the early 1950s, an experience that he used in his comic novel Tankový prapor. *Written in 1954, the work was not published until 1971.*

erary critic, in spite of the fact that Škvorecký's writing became highly popular in Czechoslovakia in the 1960s. It cannot be denied that Škvorecký wrote many of his stories primarily for fun. Some of his comic texts, such as *Ze života lepší společnosti* (From the Life of High Society, 1965), were deliberately written to be read aloud in fringe theaters. Written in the stilted school-essay prose of a nine-year-old who is under the influence of his pedantic teachers, these texts parody middle-class life in prewar Czechoslovakia. Later, Škvorecký complemented this work with "Ze života socialistické společnosti" (From the Life of Socialist Society), school essays of a "Young Pioneer" parodying life under communism, and with "Ze života exilové společnosti" (From the Life of Exile Society), texts by a young son of Czech émigrés that liberally mix Czech and English vocabulary, idioms, and syntactic structure, to strong comic effect. All these pieces were finally gathered together as *Ze života české společnosti* (From the Life of Czech Society, 1985). Škvorecký sees him-

self primarily as a raconteur who knows that the act of narration can be entertaining both for the author and for his readers (or listeners). Humor and lyricism are significant elements of his writing, as are linguistic parody and experimentation, which is often comic.

In the 1960s Škvorecký published two collections of short stories dealing with the predicament of his Jewish fellow citizens during World War II and with life after the war: *Sedmiramenný svícen* (The Menorah, 1964) and *Babylónský příběh* (The Babylonian Story, 1967). He also wrote two lyrical novellas, *Legenda Emöke* (The Legend of Emöke, 1963) and *Bassaxofon* (included in *Babylónský příběh;* translated as *The Bass Saxophone*, 1977). *Legenda Emöke* is a lyrical monologue about a brief encounter between two young people on a dreary work-sponsored holiday and how their incipient love is destroyed by a primitive. The narrator, a Prague employee of a publishing house, is attracted by a mysterious and beautiful girl, Emöke, from Eastern Slovakia. Emöke had been brutalized by a crude husband. After the breakdown of her marriage she became a follower of theosophism. She believes that the material world and the human body are evil and that people should free themselves and dissolve in "mystical divine love." The narrator is gently trying to persuade her to return to earth and at the same time is attracted by her search for transcendence. Their dialogue is disrupted by another participant in the holiday, a coarse teacher who tries to seduce Emöke. She leaves prematurely, and the magic bond is broken. During the return journey of the company to Prague, the narrator revenges himself on the teacher by exposing his primitivism. The novella highlights a clash between nobility and baseness and bitterly attacks the philistinism and coarseness created by the communist regime. While working on *Legenda Emöke*, Škvorecký was translating William Faulkner's *A Fable* (1954) into Czech, and the style of the novella is influenced by Faulkner's writing.

Bassaxofon is another lyrical, highly poetic text: it is an homage to music, especially jazz, which serves as a metaphor for the ultimate in human creativity. This creativity lifts human beings from their second-rate, earthly existence and unites them with the divine. *Bassaxofon* tells the story of an unnamed youth, a jazz player from Smiřický's home town of Kostelec. During World War II the young man reluctantly agrees to stand in for the ill saxophonist in a touring German orchestra to play in a concert for local German luminaries—officials from the Nazi occupying authorities. He only does so in an effort to get close to a rare instrument, the bass saxophone, of which he has heard but which he has never seen. Each of the German musicians is deformed or scarred in some way, but music lifts all of them from their imperfect human existence. The young man overcomes his prejudice against the Germans and realizes that what unites people regardless of nationality or class is the creative divine spark within them.

Škvorecký's literary reputation was rising in the second half of the 1960s: his writing was praised; his short stories and scripts were made into successful movies (in which he even played cameo roles); he had a regular jazz-music radio program; and in 1966 Gallimard published *La Légende d'Emöke* in French. Together with many well-known authors, who had by that time become public figures in Czechoslovakia, Škvorecký took an active part in the Prague Spring of 1968, a movement that attempted to democratize the Czechoslovak communist regime, although his political thinking had always been more radical than the reformism that prevailed at that time. The Warsaw Pact invasion of Czechoslovakia on 21 August 1968 cut short the high hopes of the reformers, and Škvorecký and his wife left their native country for Canada on 31 January 1969. On the North American continent, Škvorecký spent some time at Cornell and Berkeley universities, but in the end he settled in Toronto, where he became writer in residence at the University of Toronto and later joined the department of English as a full-time member.

Excerpts from his satirical novel *Tankový prapor* had been published by the Czech literary periodical *Plamen* (The Flame) in 1967. The whole work, scheduled to be published in book form, was printed and immediately destroyed in Prague in 1969, because it was regarded as deeply subversive: it portrayed the "great," "heroic," socialist Czechoslovak army as an absurd, funny, muddled organization and a source of slapstick and often scatological humor. Even if the work had been innocent, it would have been baned as a result of Škvorecký's emigration.

This suppression gave Salivarová the idea of founding a publishing house for independent Czech literature in Canada and putting together a list of subscribers, connecting Toronto with the Czech diaspora throughout the world. Salivarová and Škvorecký's Sixty-Eight Publishers was not the first Czech publishing house to be set up outside Czechoslovakia. There is a long history of outside Czech publishing, especially on the American continent in the nineteenth century, and several small

Czech publishers were founded throughout the noncommunist world soon after the communist takeover of power in Czechoslovakia in 1948 and the installation of a totalitarian regime there.

The liberalization movement of the 1960s was, however, primarily a cultural phenomenon. When the movement was halted by the Warsaw Pact invasion in August 1968, several hundred thousand Czechs and Slovaks emigrated from Czechoslovakia to the West. They were accustomed to the vibrant cultural activity from the 1960s in their home country and thus formed a relatively receptive audience to the new émigré publishing ventures that were set up in the West in the early 1970s. Of these, the Škvoreckýs' publishing house in Toronto was perhaps the most important. Czech émigré publishing played a major role in Czech literature until the fall of communism in 1989, since the postinvasion neo-Stalinist regime in Czechoslovakia had imposed a total publication ban on some four hundred Czech authors. Škvorecký became one of the main authors and also a joint editor and reader for Sixty-Eight Publishers. *Tankový prapor* (1971) was the first title brought out by this small publishing house.

Written in 1954, *Tankový prapor* can be seen as a variation on the theme of Hašek's *Osudy dobrého vojáka Švejka za světové války* (1921–1923; translated and expurgated as *The Good Soldier: Schweik*, 1930; also translated as *The Good Soldier Švejk and His Fortunes in the World War*, 1973), although Škvorecký had not read the Švejk stories when he wrote the novel. Like folksy simpleton Josef Švejk in the Austrian army in World War I, Škvorecký's hero, Daniel Smiřický—now an intellectual with a Ph.D., doing his national service in the Czechoslovak army amid rampant Stalinism in 1951—also finds that there are two primary factors in his life: compulsion and prohibition. Švejk and his successors in the communist army around Smiřický react to the oppressive power of the military machine with humor, which is predominantly verbal. The military life in *Tankový prapor* is a metaphor for the enslavement of the whole of Czechoslovak society by the absurd Stalinist ideological dogma. The book centers around the conflict between uncriticizable dogma, as represented by the primitive military machinery and its officers, and natural reality, which is unsuppressable. People can retain human dignity only if they display passive resistance that borders on animality, and one is only free in the army of a totalitarian state if one pretends to be an idiot. The comedy in *Tankový prapor* is primarily linguistic and situational. In this novel Škvorecký

Škvorecký as deputy editor in chief of the magazine Světová literatura (World Literature) in 1957

often mocks, caricatures, and plays with soldiers' speech, peppered with vulgarisms.

After settling in Canada, Škvorecký pursued a wide range of literary activities—he produced many detective stories, wrote essays on Czech and American literature (for twenty years he regularly reviewed American literature for the Czechoslovak Service of the Voice of America), and published his most important work, which included his four major novels. In the 1970s Škvorecký wrote two of these novels, Mirákl (1972; translated as The Miracle Game, 1990) and Příběh inženýra lidských duší (1977; translated as The Engineer of Human Souls, 1984). These works have many things in common, including the character of Smiřický, who is much less naive than he was in Zbabělci. In his middle age Smiřický has developed a slightly cynical streak as a detached, helpless observer of the absurdities of the times. Both novels have a mosaic-like structure and a multilayered plot that interconnects different time levels and different events from Czechoslovak national history as well as from Škvorecký's/Smiřický's past. Both Mirákl and Příběh inženýra

lidských duší simultaneously develop several narrative strands, constantly intercutting from one story to another. This weaving creates a strong impression of synchronicity—at the same time, the narrated episodes acquire a generalized meaning. In both novels there is tension between documentary events and their fictional rendition, thereby warning that much of what people regard as authentic news might be a fictionalized version of reality. There is also tension between the act of narration and existing literary texts (both by Škvorecký and by other authors) as well as tension between various styles of written and spoken language.

The plot of Mirákl focuses on two "miraculous" events. Allegedly, a statue of St. Joseph in a Czech country church had miraculously moved in 1949. Such a miracle-trick was in fact widely reported by the communist media in the first months of fierce persecution in Czechoslovakia by the authorities, not long after the communist takeover of February 1948. This "miracle" was politically misused by the Czechoslovak secret police as a pretext for the persecution of the clergy. The second "miracle" is the rise of the Czechoslovak reform movement during the Prague Spring and its failure. Smiřický's demystifying reminiscences of 1968 and his critical attitude to revolutionary illusions can be to some extent compared to Milan Kundera's antilyrical stance in his novel Život je jinde (published first in English as Life Is Elsewhere, 1974), although most of the criticism of the Prague Spring is attributable to Smiřický's middle-age cynicism and is a part of Škvorecký's indirect characterization of his hero. Both of these miracles are witnessed by Smiřický, who works as a teacher at a secondary school for girls in Kostelec in the 1950s after his graduation from university, and by his girlfriend, one of the pupils at the school. In 1968 Smiřický is also a witness to unsuccessful attempts by a Czech investigative journalist to uncover the truth behind the miracle from 1949 and the subsequent persecution and murder of the parish priest by the Czechoslovak secret police.

Mirákl is yet another of Škvorecký's "demythologizing" works that approaches reality casually and with a critical detachment, thus provoking charges of being "sacrilegious." Just as Zbabělci was criticized by the communist establishment for being subversive, Mirákl was seen by some in Czechoslovakia during the 1970s as an unfair attack on the liberalizing reforms of the 1968 Prague Spring, written at the time of a fierce official communist backlash against this period of liberalization. Škvorecký's work entered Czechoslovakia in the 1970s, however, only in a few secretly smuggled copies, which then went hastily from hand to hand. The critical reaction of some readers in Czechoslovakia may have been the result of reading without full concentration. People in Czechoslovakia often had a copy of *Mirákl* at their disposal only overnight and had to read the voluminous work within a matter of hours. Thus, misunderstandings of the text arose. Not many people noticed that the somewhat mocking, almost cynical attitude toward the events of the Prague Spring was not the attitude of the author, but of the narrator (who actually only poses as a cynic). Škvorecký indirectly but powerfully characterizes Smiřický by displaying his critical attitude toward modern Czechoslovak history, including the 1968 Prague Spring. Smiřický's attitude, however, does not say anything about Škvorecký's own attitude toward the 1968 events in Czechoslovakia. If Škvorecký did not regard the Prague Spring as a special period in modern Czechoslovak history, he would hardly have given his publishing house the name Sixty-Eight Publishers.

Mirákl is a graphic account of the first twenty years of communism in Czechoslovakia, with all its injustices, cruelty, absurdity, and black comedy. The novel includes several unforgettable anecdotes that capture the atmosphere of the times. In one episode, for instance, Soviet author Arashidov meets a left-wing British "angry young" author at a literary congress in Vienna and during a drunken session explains to the absolutely stunned Westerner the incredibly complex strategy necessary to persuade the literary powers in Moscow to allow the British author's novella to be published in Russian translation. There are many comic episodes from the secondary school where Smiřický starts his teaching career under Stalinism. The main theme of *Mirákl* is noetic: the work is a bitter intellectual game arguing that human beings are incapable of understanding the world around them and gaining true insight about their existence ("The worst thing was that it was not possible ever to learn anything for sure"). Human predicament is not only tragic but also banal. The motif of a puppet theater recurs: "I had a feeling that I was watching a Shakespearean drama staged by an amateur puppet master," says Smiřický.

Příběh inženýra lidských duší, Škvorecký's second long novel from this period, is often understood as a synthesis of the main topics and techniques of Škvorecký's work. The novel belongs to the genre of Czech émigré literature. This type of writing primarily describes the clash of an immigrant's experiences and value system with the civilization of a new country and the process of integration with the new

Škvorecký and Zdena Salivarová on their wedding day,
31 March 1958

environment. According to some critics, the structure of *Příběh inženýra lidských duší* is tighter than that of *Mirákl.* In *Příběh inženýra lidských duší* Smiřický becomes a skeptical university professor in Canada, trying to look back through the kaleidoscope of the various personal histories of his compatriots. The scope of the novel is much wider than that of *Mirákl,* juxtaposing events and experiences from the Nazi occupation of Czechoslovakia in the 1940s, life in Czechoslovakia under the communists in the 1950s and the 1960s, and the carefree existence of people on the North American continent in the 1970s. The main theme of the novel is the nontransferability of human experience. The bitter lessons learned by Central Europeans in the twentieth century are impossible to communicate to the generation of often indolent, carefree youngsters in Canada. The novel includes several comic conflicts based on misperceptions that are the result of different life experiences by different characters. The author's knowledge of both the Czechoslovak and the Canadian environment makes it possible for him to highlight certain typical features of human behavior that recur regardless of a particular political situation.

The title of the novel comes from a quotation from Joseph Stalin, repeated in a speech by the Czech Communist leader Klement Gottwald to

Czech writers: "Be engineers of the souls of our people." Writers under communism were seen as propaganda workers: it was their task to fictionalize the main tenets of communist ideology. The presented mosaic of personal histories in the novel is again complex—readers are offered the tragic love story of young Smiřický and a working-class girl during World War II; a less serious love affair between Smiřický as a middle-aged Canadian professor and his affluent, beautiful student Irena Svensson; the story of Smiřický's naive attempt at war sabotage in an armament factory in Kostelec; and a commentary on the various predicaments of Czech émigrés living in Canada. Again, Škvorecký uses linguistic caricature to great effect. One larger-than-life comic character is Blběnka (Dotty) Cabicarová, a flirtatious young woman with a rich Czech-Canadian fiancé and an unforgettable linguistic mixture of low-style Czech and American English. Through letters from people from his Czechoslovak past, Smiřický is able to follow the grotesque and tragic story lines of their lives even after his departure from Czechoslovakia. This contact enables him to compare the quality of life in his democratic exile with that under a totalitarian regime.

The postmodern *Příběh inženýra lidských duší* wavers openly between two literary contexts. The main characters and most of its plots are Czech, but the general frame of each of the seven chapters is derived from the Anglo-Saxon literary tradition. The chapters are given the names of the authors read and analyzed by Smiřický and his students in class: Edgar Allan Poe, Nathaniel Hawthorne, Mark Twain, Stephen Crane, F. Scott Fitzgerald, Joseph Conrad, and H. P. Lovecraft. Smiřický as a university lecturer projects many of his experiences into his seminars on literature. These classroom discussions with his students are just as important as the concrete personal histories of the characters: in these classes the difference between the American and European understanding of history is highlighted. Many of Škvorecký's Czech characters have experienced the worst aspects of European history at first hand, but Smiřický's students are carefree and lucky enough to regard history as just an academic exercise that does not concern them personally.

In 1975, with *Prima sezóna: Text o nejdůležitějších věcech života* (translated as *The Swell Season: A Text on the Most Important Things in Life,* 1982), Škvorecký returned again, nostalgically, to his student days in the small North Bohemian town under the German occupation. The collection of six short stories is a series that grew from an earlier twenty-page text from the 1960s. These playful, often comic stories

detail Smiřický's unsuccessful attempts to seduce various Kostelec girls. The comedy is based on the emergence of sudden unexpected, unsolvable problems, the absurdity of which the author develops further with the help of his imagination. The backbone of the texts is formed by colloquial conversational variations, "teenage chatting," which is seemingly free-wheeling and laid-back, but has a sophisticated underlying structure. The stories center on human decency and have a strong lyrical streak. The comedy is thrown into sharp focus by the fact that free and easy teenage life exists on the fringe of omnipresent Nazi brutality, which intrudes upon the scene only rarely and implicitly.

Scherzo capriccioso: Veselý sen o Dvořákovi (1984; translated as *Dvořák in Love,* 1986) was a new departure for Škvorecký: in this novel and his next, *Nevěsta z Texasu* (1992; translated as *The Bride of Texas,* 1995), he left Kostelec and Smiřický behind in order to write about Czechs who played a certain role in American history. *Scherzo capriccioso* is an historical and a biographical novel about the stay of Czech composer Antonín Dvořák in the United States. The novel is introduced with a motto ascribed by some, as Škvorecký says, to Franz Kafka and by others to W. B. Yeats: "Man may embody truth, but he cannot know it." The novel is about the mysterious and unknowable essence of the creative genius, about love, and about death. At the same time, it is an homage by Škvorecký to the United States.

Again, Škvorecký moves on the precarious borderline between fact and fiction. He uses documentary material, which he transforms thematically and stylistically with his imagination. At the same time, he is trying to create the illusion that he is telling a story that really happened. Apart from objective narration, the twenty-six chapters of the novel include "personal testimonies" by various individuals who knew Dvořák. The objective narrative is often interrupted by passages written in various formal techniques and language styles such as the tall tale, epistolary form, or spontaneous narratives in slang or macaronic Czech-English. The "documentary" aspect of the novel is emphasized by period engravings and photographs. Gradually, a complex image of the United States and Bohemia at the end of the nineteenth century arises from these testimonies. The novel primarily deals with the part of Dvořák's life that the composer spent in New York in the 1890s as the director of the American National Conservatory, but the memories of individual protagonists broaden the scope of the novel far into the past and into the future.

Škvorecký's wife and their cat in the garden of their home in Toronto (courtesy of the author)

Scherzo capriccioso is primarily an affectionate portrait of the United States, written by an immigrant. Škvorecký, nevertheless, does not hesitate to mock American crassness and narrow-mindedness whenever he comes across it. He also takes a spirited stand against injustice. Yet, Škvorecký likes the United States because there, as he sees it, ordinary people always achieve what they set out to do. Sometimes the author gently caricatures this tendency, for instance when describing the long struggle of the Czech beer-loving immigrants against alcohol prohibition. One Czech settler speaks thus:

> "As our great President Lincoln once said, you can hoodwink all of the people some of the time, and some people you can hoodwink all of the time, but you can't go on hoodwinking all of the people for ever. And as it turned out, the will of the people won out, and it's so wet now, Professor, that it almost makes you want to turn prohib, just to preserve your health."

Scherzo capriccioso is also written using the method of mosaic-like intercutting, jumping from one story to another. It is even more lyrical and experimental than Škvorecký's earlier work.

One of Škvorecký's major themes is the inseparable connection between the highbrow and the lowbrow. It is impossible, in his view, to intellectualize about art: the only thing one can do is to show one's humility before its incomprehensible mystery and magic. It seems that for Škvorecký genuine art is always closely associated with the ordinary and the banal—the dividing line between them is quite thin. The divine spark of talent may occur in any person, regardless of his or her social circumstances—the erstwhile butcher's apprentice Dvořák is a prime example. Škvorecký is proudly plebeian and deeply democratic. The most bitter stories in the book are those of gifted blacks who find it impossible to develop and cultivate their talents because of the prevailing racial prejudice, while the establishment heaps its privileges on limited people with the right social background.

Nevěsta z Texasu is a large historical novel that is set during the American Civil War and again uses the well-tried Škvorecký technique of intercutting stories from different places and backgrounds into a multifaceted collage. Critic Milan Jungmann remarked in *Literární noviny* (1992) that Škvorecký seems to have taken as his model the patterning of a war–which may seem like chaos and confusion to those on the ground but which is, nevertheless, the outcome of several rival plans, one of which (usually the most flexible) will eventually prevail. The themes of *Nevěsta z Texasu* are still love, loss, exile, liberty, and the parody of Czechs abroad; but rather than dealing with his own era, Škvorecký concentrates on the life and times of Czechs who came to America a hundred years before him. "When I was doing research for *Scherzo capriccioso*, I came across some brief memoirs printed in the nineteenth-century Czech calendars, as they are called, so I became interested and then I went deeper into it and found out that there were quite a few Czechs in very interesting positions who marched with Sherman," says Škvorecký. The book is a myriad of jokes, anecdotes, and arguments that overwhelm and amuse the reader.

Škvorecký not only draws famous personalities (such as Generals William Tecumseh Sherman and Hugh J. Kilpatrick) but also pays special attention to the inconspicuous and mostly forgotten "little men" of history–the Czech immigrants wearing the Union uniforms. Škvorecký has tried to defeat the national caricature of Švejk, which seems to perpetrate the myth that the Czechs are not good soldiers. "The Czechs were great warriors in the Middle Ages," says Škvorecký, "but in modern times they never fought for their own cause. But in every major war there was a contingent of Czechs who fought against Austria or Germany–the Czech airmen, for instance, who took part in the Battle of Britain distinguished themselves very much indeed. There was such a contingent in the Civil War in the Union army." Škvorecký celebrates them.

In 1985 the English translation of *Příběh inženýra lidských duší* was awarded the Canadian Governor General's Award for Fiction in English, the first time the award had been given to a translation. Five years earlier, Škvorecký had been awarded the Neustadt Prize for Literature at the University of Oklahoma. To a large degree, this prize was for the achievement of *Bassaxofon*, which for a time came to be hailed in the United States as an important contribution to jazz literature.

In May 1990, six months after the fall of the Iron Curtain, Škvorecký and his wife visited Czechoslovakia for the first time in almost two decades. It was a glorious return. The creative and publishing activities of the couple (who had been deprived of their Czech citizenship by the Communist regime) were acknowledged with the highest state award for foreigners–the Order of the White Lion. Škvorecký's books flooded bookshops after having been banned

for twenty years, and a multitude of viewers watched the 1992 television version of Škvorecký's detective stories *Hříchy pro pátera Knoxe* (1973; translated as *Sins for Father Knox*, 1988) and the nostalgic look at young Smiřický's unsuccessful courtships in *Prima sezóna*, broadcast in 1994 on weekend evenings. These television series were a huge success, and the name of Škvorecký again became synonymous with sophisticated entertainment in his homeland. Also in 1990 the Společnost Josefa Škvoreckého (the Josef Škvorecký Society) founded an archive of his works, located in Prague, and offered publications including Škvorecký's lesser-known texts. Volumes of *Spisy Josefa Škvoreckého* (The Collected Works of Josef Škvorecký) have been gradually coming out since 1991. As a result several hitherto unpublished texts by Škvorecký have become available in print. There is also a CD-ROM available: *Josef Škvorecký–život a dílo* (Josef Škvorecký–Life and Work, 1999) includes biography, bibliography, Škvorecký's almost complete works, photographs, documents, video sequences, sound recordings, and references. Although thus the return of Škvorecký's work to his native country seems to be complete, the experience from the late 1990s indicates that Škvorecký's writings no longer universally chime in with people's experiences. Some members of the younger generation in the Czech Republic seem to find it difficult to identify with Škvorecký's work, which seems to bear witness to a different, now extinct, era. Paradoxically, for some young people in the Czech Republic, Škvorecký has apparently become far too much of an "establishment" figure. Maybe unfairly, these young people see Škvorecký now as an "ideological" writer, one of the official "heroes of the struggle against communism." Observers comment that this work might well be rediscovered later, when people are ready to reflect properly on the traumatic experience of communism.

In 1991 Škvorecký and his wife became the subject of two controversies. First, in an article in *Literární noviny* (Literary Gazette) Škvorecký argued that several texts that had been ascribed to Jan Zábrana were written in collaboration. The two friends plotted the books together; then Škvorecký wrote them, and Zábrana edited and typed them up. Škvorecký revealed this collaboration after the Velvet Revolution that ended the Communist regime, and proved it by means of an acrostic: the first letters of the first words in the consecutive chapters of the third novel in the series, *Vražda v zastoupení* (Murder by Proxy, 1967) form the sentence "Škvorecký et Zábrana fecerunt ioculum" (Škvorecký and Zábrana made this joke). The incident is

Page from the manuscript for Škvorecký's 1992 novel Nevěsta z Texasu (from The Paris Review, 31 [Fall 1989])

described in detail in "Spor o autorství" in *Danny* (no. 96/97), a member's magazine published irregularly by the Společnost Josefa Škvoreckho. One Czech critic attacked Škvorecký for allegedly stealing Zábrana's Czech translation of Warren Miller's *The Cool World* (1959), but Škvorecký's supporters proved convincingly that the novel had been translated by Škvorecký. The decisive proof of Škvorecký's authorship of the translation was revealed by Michal Schonberg, who discovered in the University of Toronto library some forgotten letters written by Zábrana to Škvorecký. The letters establish that Zábrana was acting as a front for Škvorecký.

Second, as part of the relatively fierce anticommunist campaign in Czechoslovakia in the early 1990s, the name of Zdena Salivarová had—incorrectly—appeared on one of the blacklists of Czechoslovak secret police collaborators, published in Czechoslovakia and also available on the Internet. In an atmosphere when true perpetrators of political crimes under communism remained unpunished while ordinary people, blackmailed by the communist secret police into various types of "collaboration," were scandalized, the revelations about Salivarová somewhat damaged the reputation of Sixty-Eight Publishers. The accusation against Salivarová was especially welcomed by those people in the Czech Republic who feel distrust toward Czechs living abroad, as well as against dissidents—because dissident anticommunist activity showed up the political inactivity of the majority of the Czechoslovak population in the 1970s and the 1980s.

Škvorecký and Salivarová reacted by publishing *Osočení* (The Unjustly Accused, 1993). This volume, brought out by Sixty-Eight Publishers as publication no. 226, is a six-hundred-page report compiled by Salivarová and consisting of personal testimonies of some one hundred people included in the unofficially circulated lists of alleged secret police informers, documenting that these were not informers but people persecuted by the communist authorities. Salivarová "charged the Ministry of Interior for spreading false rumors about herself and she won the trial in Prague. So she was cleared of that suspicion, but it did terrible things to her. It impaired her health and everything and I don't think she will ever fully recover from that wound," says Škvorecký.

The next novel by Škvorecký, *Dvě vraždy v mém dvojím životě* (Two Murders in My Double Life, 1996), appeared first as volume 6 of his collected works. This detective story was written early in 1996 and is a semifictional reaction to his wife's being accused of collaboration with the Czechoslovak secret police. The main story line revolves around a Czech émigré publisher,

Sidonie, who has been unjustly accused of cooperation with the communist secret police and drinks herself to death in despair. As Viktor Šlajchrt, a Prague literary critic, remarked in the Czech Internet daily *Neviditelný pes* (The Invisible Dog) in 1996:

> We are glutted with information and so we live in a world of lists. Every day, the media compile lists of news-items whose informational value is minimal. Their purpose is to make readers, listeners and television viewers participate in information rituals, created by the news media, and absorb the required portion of advertising. The information from the media must be short and titillating. Names and slogans are the most concise. But the heroine of Škvorecký's latest novel was unable to bear the publication of her name on the secret police list. People living in the Czech Republic have been hardened over the years by the nastiness of the conditions, prevailing locally, and so they can ignore post-communist dirt quite successfully. Decent Czech exiles however have lost this immunity. The poison of the secret police list has hit one of the greatest Czech writers and his wife quite murderously.

In his later years, despite a hip replacement operation in 1995 and the removal of kidney stones, Škvorecký has still been busy writing. "Writing is like a sickness," he says. "I won't get rid of it." In the mid 1990s he wrote a movie based on Poe's story "The Mystery of Marie Rogêt" (1842–1843) that was broadcast on Czech television on 11 and 12 December 1996.

For Salivarová, Canada is a stepmother that treated her more kindly than her motherland; for Škvorecký it is a promised land where most of his dreams have been fulfilled. As scholar Sam Solecki writes, "Škvorecký is now a Czech presence in Anglo-American culture, before 1968 he was perceived as an 'Americanist' in Czechoslovakia." Škvorecký's importance should be viewed in light of his success in surmounting narrow national literary clichés and bridging different cultural contexts.

Interviews:

Vladimír Justl, "Rozhovor s Josefem Škvoreckým," *Červený květ*, 9, no. 10 (1964): 289–292;

Karel Hvížďala, "Josef Škvorecký," in his *České rozhovory ve světě* (Cologne: Index, 1981), pp. 165–197;

Geoff Hancock, "An Interview with Josef Skvorecky," *Canadian Fiction Magazine*, no. 45 (1983): 63–96;

Kerry Regier, "An Interview with Josef Škvorecký," *West Coast Review*, 21 (Winter 1987): 40–51;

Antonín J. Liehm, "Josef Škvorecký," in his *Generace* (Cologne: Index, 1988), pp. 67–89;

John A. Glusman, "The Art of Fiction CXII: Josef Škvorecký," *Paris Review*, 31 (Fall 1989): 117–159;

Sam Solecki, "An Interview with Josef Škvorecký," in *Other Solitudes*, edited by Linda Hutcheon (Toronto: Oxford University Press, 1990);

Václav Krištof, ed., *Josef Škvorecký vypráví* (Prague: Společnost Josefa Škvoreckého, 1992);

Hvížďala, *Opustíš–li mne, nezahyneš* (Prague: Ivo Železný, 1993);

Antonín Přidal, "Josef Škvorecký," in his *Antonín Přidal: Z očí do očí* (Prague: Ivo Železný, 1994), pp. 102–115.

Bibliographies:

Jana Kalish, *Josef Škvorecký: A Checklist* (Toronto: University of Toronto Library, 1986);

Ilja Matouš, *Bibliografie Josefa Škvoreckého I.–doma* (Prague: Společnost Josefa Škvoreckého, 1990);

Matouš, *Bibliografie Josefa Škvoreckého II.–ve světě* (Prague: Společnost Josefa Škvoreckého, 1992);

Matouš, *Bibliografie Josefa Škvoreckého III.–ohlasy ve světě* (Prague: Společnost Josefa Škvoreckého, 1992);

Matouš, *Bibliografie Josefa Škvoreckého IV.–rejstřík* (Prague: Společnost Josefa Škvoreckého, 1994).

Biography:

Václav Krištof and Zdena Krištofová, *Knížka o Josefu Škvoreckém* (Prague: Společnost Josefa Škvoreckého, 1990).

References:

Bohuš Balajka, "Bořitel a tvořitel mýtů," *Plamen*, 11, no. 2 (1969): 124–127;

Přemysl Blažíček, *Škvoreckého "Zbabělci"* (Prague: Oikúmené, 1992);

Květoslav Chvatík, "Josef Švejk a Danny Smiřický," in his *Pohledy na českou literaturu z ptačí perspektivy* (Prague: Pražská imaginace, 1991), pp. 61–71;

Chvatík, "Velký vypravěč Josef Škvorecký," in his *Melancholie a vzdor* (Prague: Československý spisovatel, 1992);

Edward L. Galligan, *The Truth of Uncertainty: Beyond Ideology in Science and Literature* (Columbia: University of Missouri Press, 1998), pp. 84–107;

Mojmír Grygar, "Proměny spisovatele v exilu," *Listy*, 18, no. 3 (1988): 93–101;

Aleš Haman, "Člověk a mýtus," *Tvář*, no. 5–6 (1964): 65–69;

Zdeněk Heřman, "Próza džezem křtěná," *Plamen*, no. 6 (1964): 156–158;

Milan Jungmann, *O Josefu Škvoreckém* (Prague: Společnost Josefa Škvoreckého, 1993);

Helena Kosková, "Bořitel falešných mýtů Josef Škvorecký," in her *Hledání ztracené generace* (Toronto: Sixty-Eight Publishers, 1987), pp. 109–152;

Václav Pletánek, "Jazyk a styl Škvoreckého Zbabělců," *Proměny*, 17, no. 1 (1980): 75–86;

Michal Přibáň, "Nápady čtenáře Miráklu," *Rok*, 2, no. 4 (1991): 33–39;

Přibáň, ed., *Zbabělci . . . a co bylo dál* (Prague: Společnost Josefa Škvoreckého, 1992);

Jiří Rambousek, "Básník Josef Škvorecký," *Sborník prací filosofické fakulty Slezské univerzity v Opavě*, 1, Řada literárněvědná (A), no. 1 (1991): 74–81;

Review of Contemporary Fiction, special Škvorecký issue, 17 (Spring 1997);

Michal Schonberg, "Průzkum o přátelství, odvaze a intelektuálním disentu a (snad už) přesvědčivá tečka za otázkou, kdo přeložil Prezydenta Krokadýlů," *Kritická příloha Revolver Revue*, no. 11 (1998): 69–86;

Sam Solecki, *Prague Blues: The Fiction of Josef Škvorecký* (Toronto: ECW Press, 1990);

Solecki, "Writing West/Looking East," *Cross Currents: A Yearbook of Central European Culture*, 9 (1990): 163–172;

Solecki, ed., *The Achievement of Josef Škvorecký* (Toronto: University of Toronto Press; 1994);

Paul I. Trensky, *The Fiction of Josef Škvorecký* (New York: St. Martin's Press, 1991; London: Macmillan, 1991);

World Literature Today, special Škvorecký issue, 54, (Autumn 1980);

Gleb Žekulin, "The Intellectuals' Dilemma: The Hero in the Modern Czech Novel," *Canadian Slavonic Papers*, 14, no. 4 (1972): 634–642.

Papers:

An archive of Josef Škvorecký's works is kept at the Josef Škvorecký Literary Academy, a private secondary school in Prague. There are also manuscripts in the Thomas Fisher Rare Book Library at the University of Toronto, and correspondence at the Hoover Institution in California.

Nichita Stănescu

(31 March 1933 – 13 December 1983)

Monica Spiridon
University of Bucharest

BOOKS: *Sensul iubirii* (Bucharest: Editura de Stat pentru Literatură şi Artă, 1960);
O viziune a sentimentelor: Versuri (Bucharest: Editura pentru Literatură, 1964);
Dreptul la timp (Bucharest: Tineretului, 1965);
11 elegii (Bucharest: Tineretului, 1966); translated by Roy MacGregor-Hastie as *11 Elegies* (Bucharest: Eminescu, 1970);
Roşu vertical (Bucharest: Militară, 1967);
Oul şi sfera: Versuri (Bucharest: Editura pentru Literatură, 1967);
Laus Ptolemai (Bucharest: Tineretului, 1968);
Necuvintele (Bucharest: Tineretului, 1969);
Un pămînt numit România (Bucharest: Militară, 1969);
În dulcele stil clasic (Bucharest: Eminescu, 1970);
Belgradul în cinci prieteni / Beograd u pet prijatelja, edited by Adam Puslogić (Vršac, Yugoslavia, 1971);
Cartea de recitire (Bucharest: Cartea Românească, 1972);
Măreţia frigului: Romanul unui sentiment (Iaşi: Junimea, 1972);
Clar de inimă (Iaşi: Junimea, 1973);
Starea poeziei (Iaşi: Junimea, 1975);
Epica magna: O iliadă de Nichita Stănescu (Iaşi: Junimea, 1978); translated by Stavros Deligiorgis as *Unfinished Work* (Bucharest: Cartea Românească, 1979; Iowa City: Corycian, 1979);
Operele imperfecte (Bucharest: Albatros, 1979);
Respirări (Bucharest: Sport-Turism, 1982);
Noduri şi semne: Recviem pentru moartea tatălui (Bucharest: Cartea Românească, 1982);
Oase plîngînd (Pancevo: Lumina, 1982);
Antimetafizica: Convorbiri cu Aurelian Titu Dumitrescu (Bucharest: Cartea Românească, 1985);
Amintiri din prezent, edited by Gheorghe Tomozei (Bucharest: Sport-Turism, 1985);
Argotice: Cîntece la drumul mare. Versuri, edited by Doina Ciurea (Bucharest: Românul, 1992);

Nichita Stănescu

Cartile sibiline: Poezii inedite o editie tardiva, edited by Constantin Crisan (Bucharest: Editura "Grai şi Suflet—Cultura Nationala," 1995).
Editions and Collections: *Cinci degete* (Piteşti: Argeş, 1969);
Poezi (Bucharest: Albatros, 1970);
Belgradul în cinci prieteni (Cluj: Dacia, 1972);
O literă în oglindă (Piteşti: Argeş, 1972);
Ordinea cuvintelor: Versuri, 2 volumes (Bucharest: Cartea Românească, 1985);
Poezii: Antologie, edited by Stefania Mincu (Bucharest: Albatros, 1987);

Poezii, edited by Cristian Moraru (Bucharest: Minerva, 1988);

Fiziologia poeziei: Proza si versuri, 1957–1983, edited by Alexandru Condeescu (Bucharest: Eminescu, 1990);

Leoaica tînara, iubirea: Poeme, edited by Dumitru Udrea (Bucharest: InterCONTEMPress, 1991);

Colinda de inima: Poeme de dragoste, edited by Condeescu (Galati: Porto-Franco / Bucharest: Muzeul Literaturii Române, 1991);

Leoaica tinara, iubirea: Poezii de dragoste, edited by Condeescu (Bucharest: Muzeul Literaturii Române, 1995).

Editions in English: "Second Elegy" and "March Rain," translated by Roy MacGregor-Hastie, in *Anthology of Contemporary Romanian Poetry,* edited by MacGregor-Hastie (Chester Springs, Pa.: Dufour, 1969), pp. 148–149;

The Still Unborn about the Dead: Selected Poems, translated by Petru Popescu and Peter Jay (Iowa City: International Writing Program, University of Iowa, 1974; London: Anvil Press Poetry, 1975);

"Food Stones" and "After the Battle," translated by Ioana Deligiorgis, in *100 de ani de poezie Românească / 100 Years of Romanian Poetry* (Jassy: Junimea, 1982), pp. 252–255;

"Second Elegy, Getic," "Homo plangens," "Marina," "Winter Ritual," "Adolescents on the Sea," "Engagement," "Evocation," and "Song," in *Contemporary East European Poetry,* edited by Emery George (Ann Arbor, Mich.: Ardis, 1983), pp. 324–328;

Ask the Circle to Forgive You: Selected Poems, 1964–1979, translated by Mark Irwin and Mariana Carpinisan (Cleveland: Globe, 1983);

Bas-Relief with Heroes: Selected Poems, 1960–1982, translated by Thomas C. Carlson and Vasile Poenaru (Memphis: Memphis State University Press, 1988);

Sentimental Story, translated by Bogdan Stefanescu (Bucharest: Athena, 1995).

OTHER: *Alfa,* edited by Stănescu (Bucharest: Tineretului, 1967);

Adam Puslojić, *Pasărea dezaripată,* translated by Stănescu (Bucharest: Minerva, 1972).

Nichita Stănescu is generally recognized as the preeminent Romanian poet of the post–World War II period. His charismatic personality cast a spell over the Romanian audience, and for many he came to assume almost mythical status. Stănescu belonged to the generation of poets that emerged in the 1960s and included Cezar Baltag, Ana Blandiana, Ioan Alexandru, Ileana Mălăncioiu, Grigore Hagiu, Petre Stoica, Constanţa Buzea, and Adrian Păunescu. Determined to rejuvenate Romanian poetry with a renewed sense of artistic purpose, this generation revived the creative impulse that had been interrupted by the Soviet occupation of the country and a decade of the Moscow-imposed doctrine of socialist realism. Emulating the nineteenth-century Romantic poet Mihai Eminescu, Stănescu remained faithful to his national identity but nonetheless created a poetry that was independent of Romanian literary traditions.

Born on 31 March 1933 in Ploiesti in southern Romania, Stănescu was the first of seven children of Nicolai, a tailor, and Tatiana Cereaciukin Stănescu. In 1940 he enrolled in the elementary school in his native town; but after two years the family became refugees because of World War II, and Stănescu finished the last two grades in Busteni and Vălenii de Munt. In 1944 he continued his studies in Ploiesti at the Petru and Pavel High School, later renamed the Ion L. Caragiale High School, where he established a reputation for his rebellious nature and for his orally improvised nonconformist poetry. Graduating in 1952, Stănescu went to Bucharest, ostensibly to study at the Polytechnic Institute; instead, he took and passed the entrance examination for the Faculty of Letters of the University of Bucharest.

While studying at the university from 1952 to 1957 Stănescu was introduced to the work of Eminescu and Caragiale, as well as that of the major modern Romanian poets Tudor Arghezi, Ion Barbu, George Bacovia, and Lucian Blaga, and he also made two lifelong friends: the poets Grigore Hagiu and Petre Stoica. He married Magdalena Petrescu, but the marriage lasted less than a year. After orally circulating among his fellow students a cycle of unconventional parodies and paraphrases titled "Argotice" (Poems in Slang), Stănescu made his debut in the spring of 1957 in two prestigious magazines: *Tribuna* and the most important Romanian literary periodical, *Gazeta literară* (now *România literară*). The three poems he published in *Tribuna*– "Au fost oameni mulţi" (There Were Many Men), "La lemne" (Chopping Wood), and "Pămînt" (The Land)—and "Ardea spitalulcu bolnavi cu tot" (The Hospital Was Burning and the Sick with It) in *Gazeta literară* were inspired by the fiftieth anniversary of the peasant revolts of 1907.

Throughout the late 1950s and early 1960s Stănescu led a rootless bohemian life, staying with friends and sometimes lacking a roof over his head altogether. In 1960 he published his first poetry col-

Stănescu and his future second wife, Doina Ciurea, as students at the University of Bucharest

lection, *Sensul iubirii* (The Meaning of Love). The pieces vary in artistic merit; some militant poems—odes to labor, to peace, and to the Communist Party—were written on command. Nevertheless, most of the poems are characterized by an exuberant sense of vitality. The dominant emotion is candid wonder in the face of reality, as in "Dimineață marină" (Marine Dawn), "Cîntec de iarnă" (Winter Song), and "O călărire în zori" (Riding at Dawn), all of which are dedicated "lui Eminescu tînăr" (To Eminescu as a young man). Other notable poems include "Cîntec" (translated as "Song," 1983), "Viața mea se iluminează" (My Life Lights Up), and "Amfion constructorul" (Amphion the Builder). The volume was favorably received and established Stănescu as an important new poetic voice.

Stănescu continued to publish conformist poetry glorifying communism in various magazines. In 1962, after a ten-year romance, he married Doina Ciurea, whom he had met at the university. In 1964 he published his second volume of poetry, *O viziune a sentimentelor* (A Vision of Sentiments), which was awarded the Prize of the Writers Union. Here the poet begins to explore a new theme: eroticism. Love is seen as the path of the spirit into the essence of life and into the mythical beginnings of the world, particularly in "Vîrsta de aur a iubirii" (The Golden Age of Love).

In 1964 Stănescu became involved with the poet Gabriela Melinescu. His relationship with Ciurea rapidly deteriorated, and the marriage was eventually dissolved in 1966.

In 1965 Stănescu published *Dreptul la timp* (The Right to Time), in which poetic ecstasy is replaced by grave aphoristic meditations. That year he became a full member of the Writers Union and began participating in international poetry festivals in Czechoslovakia, Finland, and Yugoslavia and was awarded the Quadriga prize at the Struga Festival in 1965 in Yugoslav Macedonia.

The publication in 1966 of *11 elegii* (translated as *11 Elegies*, 1970) confirmed Stănescu's reputation as one of the most original voices in contemporary Eastern European poetry and initiated the "Nichita Stănescu vogue." Originally, the volume was to comprise twelve poems, but the ninth elegy was censored by the editor. One critic noted that the entire book could bear as a motto some verses of the final elegy: "Everything is so simple, / so simple that / it becomes incomprehensible." The eleven texts are almost hermetic, requiring attentive decoding. In them the protagonist of Stănescu's lyrical universe becomes a spirit endowed with vast knowledge, a maker of new worlds, and a creator of poetic language. Poetry, being, and knowing become synonymous, rendering any fracture impossible, and the spiritual and material planes of existence are conceived of as inseparable. The instrument of this communion is a totality of perception: "I am ailing with something between hearing and seeing, / with a kind of eye, with a kind of ear / undevised by the ages." Here Stănescu is building a poetic philosophy based on a Romantic aspiration for the absolute.

In 1967 Stănescu traveled to Austria and France, where he met the authors Jacques Prčvert and Francis Ponge. That year he also edited an anthology of poetry, *Alfa*, and published two more books of his own verse: *Roșu vertical* (Vertical Rose) and *Oul și sfera* (The Egg and the Sphere). These volumes retain the tone of the elegies, with symbolic expression that borders on the absurd: "Naturally, I am an eye, / But in whose socket?"

The next three years were among the most productive in Stănescu's career and mark the zenith of his creativity; much of his poetry during this period was born out of the intensity of his relationship with Melinescu. In *Laus Ptolemai* (A Eulogy of Ptolemy, 1968) the effigy of the second-century Alexandrian astronomer Ptolemy signifies the poet's internal conflict between the rationalist vision—the Euclidian tradition of a linear, geometric, and transparent world, as in "Certarea lui Euclid" (Euclid's Scolding)—on the one hand, and, on the other, the incapacity of words, worn out with too much use, to relate humans to the universe, as in "Împotriva cuvintelor" (Against the Words) and "Trecerea de la noțiuni la poezie" (The Passage from Notions to Poetry). Stănescu's confrontation with language continues in *Necuvintele* (The Unwords, 1969), for which he received the Writers' Society Award. If the book points out the crisis of poetic language as a whole, it also marks a turning point in Stănescu's poetry: the philosophical lyric is beginning to lose its appeal for the poet. Also in 1969 Stănescu became assistant editor in chief of *România literară*, publishing *În dulcele stil clasic* (In the Sweet Classical Style) the following year, another instance of the rebuking of the word by the creator. The oscillations and fragmentation in poems in the volume reveal the fierce battle that the poet is waging—first and foremost against himself.

In the early 1970s Stănescu continued to gain recognition at home and also throughout Eastern and Western Europe as his works began to be translated first in Romania, in bilingual editions such as a Romanian and French version of *11 elegii* in 1970, and later in Czechoslovakia and Serbian Yugoslavia. The Serbian poet and translator Adam Puslogić published Stănescu's collection *Belgradul în cinci prieteni* (Belgrade in Five Friends) in Yugoslavia in a bilingual edition in 1971; the book did not appear in a Romanian edition until the following year.

By 1972 Stănescu had ended his relationship with Melinescu. He traveled that year to Italy and then went to London to take part in the Poetry International Festival, where his charismatic personality attracted the attention of the international media. Also in 1972 he published a collection of essays, *Cartea de recitire* (A Book for Rereading), which won the Writers Union Award, and a volume of poetry, *Măreția frigului: Romanul unui sentiment* (The Glory of Cold: The Novel of a Feeling).

Following the publication of *Măreția frigului* Stănescu entered a period of apparent creative stagnation that lasted nearly five years, but he continued to maintain a public presence that perpetuated his popularity and celebrity status. English, Hungarian, Swedish, Polish, Serbo-Croatian, and Latvian translations of his poetry were published, and his poems appeared consistently in European literary magazines. He traveled to France and West Germany. In 1975 he began working as a columnist and reviewer at *România literară* and moved into a small apartment in downtown

Bucharest that became a mecca for his admiring public. At any time of the day—and especially the night—Stănescu received friends and acquaintances, as well as beginning poets who idolized him. In 1975 the Austrian Academy presented Stănescu with the International Gottfried von Herder Award for his oeuvre. Stănescu spent the money from the award on black tulips that he spread on the Vienna street where Eminescu had lived.

Stănescu regained his momentum as a writer with the publication of two volumes of poetry, *Epica magna: O iliadă de Nichita Stănescu* (The Big Book of Prosaic Poetry, 1978; translated as *Unfinished Work*, 1979), winner of the Mihai Eminescu Academy Award, and *Operele imperfecte* (Imperfect Works, 1979), both of which caused controversy and critical disputes. In these works Stănescu changed his approach once more, rejecting the idea of poetry as the depiction of a universe of law and order and adopting the "epic" or antipoetic mode, to which he attributed a special significance and mission. He considered the epic mode the only possible reaction to the irreparable loss of the unity of the world and of the self, making the point particularly vividly in "Anatomia" (The Anatomy), "Fiziologia și spiritual" (The Physiology and the Spirit), and "Contemplarea lumii din afara ei" (The Contemplation of the World from Beyond), all of which are in *Epica magna*. Time, which naturally metamorphoses living matter, is responsible for instituting the law of multiplicity in the world; this idea is expressed most vividly in "Metamorfozele" (The Metamorphoses) and "Luptătorul obosit" (The Weary Warrior). The poet surprises his readers with variations in expression, as well, ranging from clarity to obscurity to complete opacity. Intertextual references to Romanian and world literature are another innovation.

In 1979 Stănescu was a finalist for the Nobel Prize in literature, along with Max Frisch, Leopold Sedar Senghor, Jorge Luis Borges, and the Greek poet Odysseus Elitis, who was awarded the prize. Shortly thereafter, Stănescu's health began to deteriorate, and in 1981 he suffered a serious attack of cirrhosis. That year he began to write a column of cultural essays and poetic prose in the literary magazine *Luceafărul* (The Morning Star); the columns were collected in 1982 as *Respirări* (Breathings). Also in 1982 Stănescu published a volume of poems, *Noduri și semne: Recviem pentru moartea tatălui* (Knots and Signs), the message of which is that poetry is a means of salvation from death. The book consists of an ars poetica placed between thirty-three poems titled "Noduri" and another twenty-three titled "Semne." The geometrical purity of the poems was enhanced by the illustrations by the painter Sorin Dumitrescu. With this book Stănescu once again bewildered and divided the critics. Some saw the volume as a leap into postmodernist linguistics and metapoetry, given the abundant references to the great literature of the world, to Eminescu, and to Stănescu's own earlier verse. Others considered the poems a slide into self-pastiche and mannerism. Finally in 1982 Stănescu received the prestigious Golden Crown at the international festival in Struga.

In his final years Stănescu's poetry was published in anthologies and magazines and translated into Hungarian, Serbo-Croatian, Macedonian, Hebrew, French, Spanish, English, and Bulgarian. In addition, he began dictating *Antimetafizica* (The Antimetaphysics), a series of conversations with the poet Aurelian Titu Dumitrescu, which was published posthumously in 1985. He also married his third wife, Dora Târîță, in 1982. In the spring of 1983 Stănescu's fiftieth birthday was celebrated nationally. With his health declining, however, the poet became consumed with the preparation of the definitive edition of his works, *Ordinea cuvintelor* (The Order of Words). Refusing to submit to his illness, he traveled to Bulgaria and Yugoslavia, but after several increasingly serious attacks he died on 13 December 1983 in the Emergency Hospital in Bucharest. He was buried in Bellu Cemetery, near the grave of Eminescu.

More than any other Romanian writer of his generation, Nichita Stănescu embodied the post-Stalinist revival of the modernist tradition. An artistic visionary who challenged himself to create a poetry of originality and intrinsic value, Stănescu remains one of the most imposing figures in twentieth-century literature and an influential voice in the development of contemporary Romanian poetry.

References:

Sanda Anghelescu, ed., *Nichita Stănescu* (Bucharest: Eminescu, 1983);

Ioana Bot, "Mitul Nichita Stănescu," *Steaua*, 5 (1983): 12–13;

Corin Braga, *Nichita Stănescu: Orizontul imaginar* (Sibiu: Imaga, 1993);

Matei Călinescu, *Aspecte literare* (Bucharest: Editura pentru Literatură), pp. 289–300;

Constantin Crişan, ed., *Frumos ca umbra unei idei: Album memorial* (Bucharest: Albatros, 1985);

Valeriu Cristea, "Sinele fugar," in his *Interpretări critice* (Bucharest: Cartea Românească, 1974), pp. 82–87;

Ov. S. Crohmălniceanu, "Poetul ca toreador, Grammatici certant," in his *Pîinea noastră cea de toate zilele* (Bucharest: Cartea Românească, 1981), pp. 94–104;

Gabriel Dimisianu, "Lirismul cunoaşterii," in his *Opinii literare* (Bucharest: Cartea Românească, 1970), pp. 56–65;

Ştefan Aug. Doinaş, "Despre moda poetică," in his *Poezie şi modă poetică* (Bucharest: Eminescu, 1972), pp. 151–216;

Doinaş, "Poezia şi poetica lui Nichita Stănescu," in his *Lectura poeziei* (Bucharest: Cartea Românească, 1980), pp. 193–202;

Paul Georgescu, "Nichita Stănescu: *Sensul iubirii*," in his *Păreri literare* (Bucharest: Editura pentru Literatură, 1964), pp. 207–215;

Gabriel Liiceanu, "Necuvintele şi neconceptele," *Transilvania*, 12 (1984): 19–20;

Nicolae Manolescu, *Despre poezie* (Bucharest: Cartea Românească, 1987), pp. 232–235;

Manolescu, "Moştenirea liu Nichita Stănescu," *România literară*, no. 44 (1985): 9;

Manolescu, "Nichita Stănescu î critică," *România literară*, 11 (1984): 9;

Solomon Marcus, "Nodurile lui Nichita Stănescu," in his *Paradoxul* (Bucharest: Albatros, 1984), pp. 129–131;

Mircea Martin, "Nichita Stănescu: *11 Elegii*, oul şi sfera, Obiecte cosmice," in his *Geraraţie şi creaţie* (Bucharest: Editura pentru literatură, 1969), pp. 11–23:

Ştefania Mincu, *Nichita Stănescu: Intre poiesis şi poieîn* (Bucharest: Eminescu, 1991);

Romul Munteanu, "Nichita Stănescu," in his *Jurnal de cărţi*, volume 3 (Bucharest: Eminescu, 1981), pp. 493–495;

Eugen Negrici, "Nepăsarea suverană," in his *Figura spiritului creator* (Bucharest: Cartea Românească, 1978), pp. 55–90;

Marian Papahagi, "Poezia lui Nichita Stănescu," in his *Exerciţii de lectură* (Cluj-Napoca: Dacia, 1977), pp. 178–185;

Ioana Em Petrescu, "Ochiul cu dinţi," in her *Eminescu şi mutaţiile poeziei româneşti* (Cluj-Napoca: Dacia, 1989), pp. 151–232;

Al. Piru, "Nichita Stănescu," in his *Istoria literaturii române* (Bucharest: Univers, 1981), pp. 493–495;

Ion Pop, *Nichita Stănescu–spaţiul şi maştile poeziei* (Bucharest: Albatros, Monografii, 1979);

Eugen Simion, "Poezia poeziei: Criza de identitate. Un poet al transparenţei," in his *Scriitori romani de azi* (Bucharest: Cartea Românească, 1978), pp. 164–188;

Alex. Ştefănescu, *Introducere în opera lui Nichita Stănescu* (Bucharest: Minerva, 1986);

Gheorghe Tomozei, ed., *Nichita Stănescu: Album memorial* (Bucharest: Viaţa Românească, 1984).

Wisława Szymborska

(2 July 1923 –   )

Stanisław Barańczak
Harvard University

This entry was updated by Professor Barańczak from his entry in DLB Yearbook 1996.

BOOKS: *Dlatego żyjemy* (Warsaw: Czytelnik, 1952);

Pytania zadawane sobie (Kraków: Wydawnictwo Literackie, 1954);

Wołanie do Yeti (Kraków: Wydawnictwo Literackie, 1957);

Sól (Warsaw: Państwowy Instytut Wydawniczy, 1962);

Sto pociech (Warsaw: Państwowy Instytut Wydawniczy, 1967);

Wszelki wypadek (Warsaw: Czytelnik, 1972);

Lektury nadobowiązkowe (Kraków: Wydawnictwo Literackie, 1973);

Wielka liczba (Warsaw: Czytelnik, 1976);

Lektury nadobowiązkowe, cz. 2 (Kraków: Wydawnictwo Literackie, 1981);

Ludzie na moście (Warsaw: Czytelnik, 1986);

Koniec i początek (Poznań: Wydawnictwo a5, 1993);

Życie na poczekaniu: Lekcja literatury z Jerzym Kwiatkowskim i Marianem Stalą (Kraków: Wydawnictwo Literackie, 1996).

Editions and Collections: *Wiersze wybrane* (Warsaw: Państwowy Instytut Wydawniczy, 1964);

Poezje wybrane (Warsaw: Ludowa Spółdzielnia Wydawnicza, 1967);

Wybór poezji (Warsaw: Czytelnik, 1970);

Poezje (Warsaw: Państwowy Instytut Wydawniczy, 1970);

Wybór wierszy (Warsaw: Czytelnik, 1973);

Wieczór autorski (Warsaw: Anagram, 1992);

Lektury nadobowiązkowe (Kraków: Wydawnictwo Literackie, 1992);

Widok z ziarnkiem piasku (Poznań: Wydawnictwo a5, 1996);

Wiersze wybrane (Kraków: Wydawnictwo a5, 2000).

Editions in English: "I Am Too Near," translated by Czesław Miłosz; "Four in the Morning" and "The Women of Rubens," translated by Celina Wieniewska; and "Starvation Camp Near Jaslo" and "Hannah," translated by Jan

Wisława Szymborska

Darowski, in *Polish Writing Today,* edited by Wieniewska (Baltimore: Penguin, 1967), pp. 138–142;

"Landscape" and "Innocence," translated by Darowski; and "I am Too Near," "Movement," "Hunger Camp Near Jaslo," and "Monologue for Cassandra," translated by Leonora Mestel,

Modern Poetry in Translation: Polish Issue, edited by Bogdan Czaykowski, 23–24 (1975): 22–24;

"Babel" and "Words," translated by Krzysztof Zarzecki, in *White Stones and Fir Trees: An Anthology of Contemporary Slavic Literature,* edited by Vasa D. Mihailovich (Lewisburg, Pa.: Bucknell University Press, 1977), pp. 217, 407;

"The Two Apes of Brueghel" and "The Joy of Writing," translated by Barbara Rejak, and "The Cave" and "Station," translated by Iwona Gleb, in *Z nowej polskiej poezji / The New Polish Poetry,* compiled and edited by Milne Holton and Paul Vangelisti (Pittsburgh: University of Pittsburgh Press, 1978), pp. 24–33;

Sounds, Feelings, Thoughts: Seventy Poems, translated by Magnus J. Krynski and Robert A. Maguire (Princeton: Princeton University Press, 1981);

"I Am Too Near," "A Great Number," "The Joy of Writing," "Utopia," "Autonomy," "Letters of the Dead," "Every Case," and "Laughter," translated and edited by Czesław Miłosz, in *Postwar Polish Poetry,* third edition (Berkeley: University of California Press, 1983), pp. 109–120;

"Preparing a Curriculum Vitae," "View with a Grain of Sand," and "Tortures," translated by Krynski and Maguire; "The Joy of Writing," translated by John and Bogdana Carpenter; and "Interview with a Child," "Words," and "Born," translated by Tadeusz Sławek, in *Contemporary East European Poetry,* edited by Emery George (Ann Arbor, Mich.: Ardis, 1983), pp. 125–133;

"Portrait of a Woman," "Lot's Wife," "In Praise of My Sister," "Homecoming," "A Contribution on Pornography," "In Praise of Dreams," "Wrong Number," "Perfect," "Theatrical Impressions," "The Terrorist, He Watches," "Funeral," "Miracle Mart," "People on a Bridge," "Utopia," and "Unwritten Poem Reviewed," translated and edited by Adam Czerniawski, in *The Burning Forest: Modern Polish Poetry* (Newcastle upon Tyne: Bloodaxe, 1988), pp. 89–104;

People on a Bridge: Poems, translated by Czerniawski (London: Forest Books, 1990);

"Stage Fright," "Surplus," "Archaeology," "View with a Grain of Sand," "Clothes," "On Death, without Exaggeration," "The Great Man's House," "In Broad Daylight," "Our Ancestors' Short Lives," "Hitler's First Photograph," "The Century's Decline," "Children of Our Age," "Tortures," "Plotting with the Dead," "Writing a Résumé," "Funeral," "An Opinion on the Question of Pornography," "A Tale Begun,"

"Into the Ark," "Possibilities," "Miracle Fair," and "The People on the Bridge," translated and edited by Stanisław Barańczak and Clare Cavanagh, in *Polish Poetry of the Last Two Decades of Communist Rule: Spoiling Cannibals' Fun,* edited by Barańczak and Cavanagh (Evanston, Ill.: Northwestern University Press, 1991), pp. 64–88;

"Hitler's First Photograph," translated by Karen Kovacik, in *Shifting Borders: East European Poetries of the Eighties,* compiled and edited by Walter Cummins (Rutherford, N.J.: Fairleigh Dickinson University Press, 1993), pp. 275–276;

View with a Grain of Sand: Selected Poems, translated by Barańczak and Cavanagh (New York: Harcourt Brace, 1995); Polish version published as *Widok z ziarnkiem piasku* (Poznań: Wydawnictwo a5, 1996);

Nic dwa razy / Nothing Twice: Selected Poems, translated by Barańczak and Cavanagh (Kraków: Wydawnictwo Literackie, 1997);

Poems, New and Collected, 1957–1997, translated by Barańczak and Cavanagh (New York: Harcourt Brace, 1998).

The fourth Polish author honored with the Nobel Prize in literature (1996) after Henryk Sienkiewicz in 1905, Władysław Reymont in 1924, and Czesław Miłosz in 1980—Wisława Szymborska is also the second Polish poet awarded the prize in a mere sixteen years. Along with Miłosz, Zbigniew Herbert, Tadeusz Różewicz, and Miron Białoszewski, Szymborska has been one of the dominating figures in the rich and lively arena of Polish poetry of the second half of the twentieth century. She is both a successor and a leading representative of a strong literary tradition.

Wisława Szymborska was born on 2 July 1923 in the small town of Kórnik (actually Bnin, which later merged with Kórnik to form a joint township bearing the latter's name) near the city of Poznań, the industrial and cultural center of the western part of Poland. She was one of two daughters of Wincenty Szymborski and Anna (née Rottermund); her father served as the steward of Count Władysław Zamoyski's family estate. When Szymborska was eight, her family moved to the historic city of Kraków—as much an informal capital of the southern part of Poland as Poznań is of the western one—to settle down for good. Since then, Szymborska's entire life, except for her infrequent and usually short travels, has been spent in Kraków. There she attended high school

(a private lycée of the Ursulan Sisters) before 1939 and continued her education in a clandestine study group during World War II and the Nazi occupation. Also during the war years she made her living by working as a clerk at the railway office and doing other odd jobs. She studied from 1945 to 1948 at the ancient Jagellonian University in Kraków, majoring in sociology and Polish literature. After graduation, she worked for a while as an assistant editor in publishing houses until 1953, when she became the editor of the poetry section of the Kraków-based weekly *Życie Literackie* (Literary Life), a position she held until 1968. She remained on the board as a regular contributor until 1976; in the wake of the brutally suppressed workers' demonstrations, she found herself unable to accept the pro-regime stance of the periodical and severed all her ties with *Życie Literackie.*

Over the years, her column, *Lektury nadobowiązkowe* (Non-Compulsory Reading), offered brief, often humorous essay-reviews of mostly nonliterary books dealing with subjects as diverse as ancient history, ornithology, the life of Casanova, gardening, jazz, home repairs, and hatha yoga. Collected in three book editions, these reviews (which after Szymborska's breach with *Życie Literackie* continued to appear in other periodicals) constitute her entire literary work other than poetry or poetic translation (she is an excellent, if not prolific, translator of French poetry from Agrippa d'Aubigné to Charles Baudelaire). Despite her aversion to public activities and nonliterary statements, during the late 1970s, and particularly after the imposition of martial law in 1981, she lent her support on several occasions to the protest actions and educational initiatives sponsored by human rights groups such as KOR (Workers' Defense Committee); she was also one of the founding members of the Association of Polish Writers, an independent professional organization that sought to continue the venerable traditions of the Polish Writers' Union after its forcible dissolution by the military regime in 1982. On a more private note, in 1948 Szymborska married Adam Włodek, a poet and editor, whom she divorced in 1954. She has no children. In the late 1980s much personal happiness was brought into her life by the companionship of the prominent fiction writer and poet Kornel Filipowicz, who died after prolonged illness in 1990.

There is not much more to say about Szymborska's life, since up to the Nobel Prize it was, except perhaps for literary awards and other tokens of public appreciation, almost totally uneventful, mostly by her deliberate choice. Szymborska is known for her quiet way of life and unwillingness to embrace the status of a celebrity; she shuns public gatherings, rarely travels abroad, hates being photographed or interviewed, and, except for her human rights and democratic reform activities, refuses to be involved in partisan politics. She is nevertheless quite involved in the cultural landscape of Kraków and maintains lively contacts with a small circle of friends who admire her conversational brilliance and quick sense of humor, which can be seen in her extemporized limericks and her famous homemade postcards—pasted newspaper cuttings of words and images combined in the manner of the quasi-surrealistic collage to a hilarious effect. Her dislike of being in a public spotlight is by no means a sign of antisocial inclinations; rather, it stems from her recognition that the larger part of writers' public functioning is an empty ritual and an unnecessary waste of their inner resources.

Szymborska's literary production has been quite sparse. As the septuagenerian author of just about two hundred individual poems, she is among the least prolific major twentieth-century poets; it is likely that there has been no Nobel Prize–winning poet who has written less verse. Over the three pre-Nobel decades of her career, she published just a few poems a year in the Polish literary press, and her slim collections came out at seven- to ten-year intervals. Her small output is not a result of either laziness or writer's block: rather, she publishes deliberately little because she holds the highest standards for herself. In an interview for *Gazeta Wyborcza* right after receiving the Nobel Prize, when asked what secret reason lurks behind her reluctance to publish more poems, she gave a typically brief and concrete answer: "I have a wastebasket in my study."

Szymborska has actually renounced her first two collections of original verse, and she has never let those poems be reprinted. It is not hard to understand why. The year of her debut in the literary press, 1945, was probably as bad a moment as any in recorded history for young poets in Poland to start learning their trade. The pull of the socialist-realist temptation was almost irresistible, and not just because of the prosaic fact that under Communist rule the writing of propagandistic verse naturally facilitated the poet's career. Another and no less important reason was that the traumatic experiences of the

Szymborska in 1954

just-ended war pushed the typical young idealist to embrace impulsively the ideology that seemed—particularly when set against the backdrop of the "decayed liberalism" of Western democracies—to provide the only efficient way of preventing the moral failure of humankind from happening again.

All these notions find their rather naive but also quite sincere expression in Szymborska's early verse. She made her debut on 14 March 1945—that is, in the final weeks of World War II—with a poem titled "Szukam słowa" (Searching for a Word) published in "Walka" (Struggle), the literary supplement of the Kraków-based *Dziennik Polski* (Polish Daily). In a sense, the title is symbolic of what her early writing was all about: a desperate search for a language and style strong enough to carry the burden of twentieth-century experience. The reason why the search was, at that stage, largely unsuccessful was that the poet

was unable yet to grasp the basic paradox out of which her art soon evolved: in the poetry of this age, the source of such strength is the author's ability to doubt rather than believe, to be skeptically ironic rather than blindly positive, to ask questions rather than make assertions.

This point is evident in the contrast between the title of Szymborska's first collection, *Dlatego żyjemy* (That's What We Live For, 1952), and that of her second, *Pytania zadawane sobie* (Questions Put to Myself, 1954). In the semantic gap between these two titles is the first glimpse of the fully original voice that emerged with Szymborska's third collection, *Wołanie do Yeti* (Calling Out to Yeti, 1957). The youthful self-confidence of the first title gives way to mature self-questioning and doubt; perhaps most significant, the plural "we" is replaced with the singular "myself."

In one of the few interviews Szymborska has given in the course of her career, she said that in her early writing her chief mistake was to try to love humankind instead of human beings. One might add that the doctrine of socialist realism demanded love for nothing less than humankind while at the same time narrowing the multidimensionality of human life down to just one social dimension; in contrast, Szymborska's focus on the individual allows her to view human reality in all its troublesome complexity. The breadth and depth of her vision of human existence, with its inescapable entanglement in several different orders of being at once, can hardly be explained by interpreting it in the light of existentialist philosophy, as some of the Polish critics in the late 1950s and the 1960s were fond of doing. Szymborska reveals more affinity with the ironic vision of Michel Eyquem de Montaigne than with any of the twentieth-century existentialists, if only because of the latter's notorious lack of any sense of humor. For her the result of the realization of the human being's simultaneous involvement in so many different dimensions of existence—from the biological to the civilizational, from spatial to temporal, from social to historical, from distinctive to universal—cannot be restricted to the revelation of the tragic; it also, perhaps first of all, includes the sense of awe, amazement, and amusement with the dissonant and yet somehow harmonious complexity of it all.

Irony and humor are the poet's means to gain a distance to the human predicament, a distance that has nothing to do with detached indifference; rather, it is a position necessary to see things more clearly. Characteristically, even

though the focus of Szymborska's poetry is decidedly anthropocentric, she often employs a lyrical voice that belongs to a nonhuman speaker, regardless of whether the place he or she occupies on the ladder of evolution is inferior to humanity, as in the case of an animal, or superior, as in the case of an imagined extraplanetary observer, as illustrated in two poems from *Sto pociech* (No End of Fun, 1967):

> I, a tarsier,
> sit living on a human fingertip.
> . . . .
> My good lord is gracious,
> my good lord is kind.
> Who else could bear such witness if there were
> no creatures unworthy of death?
> You yourselves, perhaps?
> But what you've come to know about yourselves
> will serve for a sleepless night from star to star.
>
> "Tarsjusz" (Tarsier)

> Carry on, then, if only for the moment
> that it takes a tiny galaxy to blink!
> One wonders what will become of him,
> since he does in fact seem to be.
> And as far as being goes, he really tries quite hard.
> Quite hard indeed—one must admit.
> With that ring in his nose, with that toga, that sweater.
> He's no end of fun, for all you say.
> Poor little beggar.
> A human, if ever we saw one.
>
> "Sto pociech" (No End of Fun)

There has been no shortage of profound poets and multidimensional worlds created by their imaginations in the twentieth century; yet, what makes Szymborska's position in world literature distinctive is that her work remains accessible. Since 1957 her popularity in Poland has been growing steadily and reached staggering proportions with her volume *Koniec i początek* (The End and the Beginning, 1993). Some of her poems, such as "Kot w pustym mieszkaniu" (Cat in an Empty Apartment), from *Koniec i początek*—in which the absence of someone who is dead is presented from the perspective of the house pet he left behind—have acquired the status of cult objects among Polish readers. Moreover, even though her stylistic inventiveness makes her poems difficult to translate in spite of their clear logic and transparent construction, she has successfully crossed the language barrier in several translations, and her work has been enjoyed and admired by non-Polish audiences for many years. Szymborska

manages to be complex yet comprehensible, ambitious yet approachable, individualistic yet involved.

Early in Szymborska's career she realized that what attracts people to modern poetry is not its potential for making statements but rather its art of asking questions. The situation of the individual mind's uncertainty is clearly the single most powerful mechanism of generating lyrical action in her work; correspondingly, the model of inquiry or self-inquiry, of asking "questions put to myself" as well as others, appears frequently throughout her entire body of work. The crucial point of her individual method is the apparent naïveté of the questions asked, as in "Schyłek wieku" (translated as "The Century's Decline," 1991) from *Ludzie na moście* (People on a Bridge, 1986):

> "How should we live?" someone asked me in a letter.
> I had meant to ask him
> the same question.
> . . . .
> the most pressing questions
> Are naïve ones.

Significantly, the uncertainty as to the most basic dilemmas of existence is shared here by the poet and her imagined reader. One fundamental reason for the accessibility of Szymborska's poetry is that the "pressing questions" she keeps asking are, at least at first sight, as "naive" as those of the man in the street. At the same time, the brilliance of her poetry lies in pushing the inquiry much farther than the man in the street ever could or would. Many of her poems start provocatively, with a question, observation, or statement that seems downright trite, only to surprise the reader with an unanticipated yet logical continuation. What can sound more banal than proclaiming, at the outset of "Nic dwa razy" (Nothing Twice) in her book *Wołanie do Yeti*, that "nothing can ever happen twice," that one cannot reenter the Heraclitean river? Yet, the next three lines, by pursuing this thought to its end, offer a complex view of human existence:

> Nothing can ever happen twice.
> In consequence, the sorry fact is
> that we arrive here improvised
> and leave without the chance to practice.

Similarly, the title poem of *Koniec i początek* opens with a statement that sounds so disarmingly trivial that it seems not to contain any potential for revelation at all:

> After every war
> someone has to tidy up.

Things won't pick
themselves up, after all.

Yet, it soon turns out that the "naive question" implied in this poem (namely, the question of how the human race can carry on at all if it is doomed to move within the vicious circle of destruction and reconstruction) concerns no less pressing an issue than the meaning of human history—or perhaps the senselessness of it. What makes this poem typically Szymborskian is that its initial naïveté almost imperceptibly moves to another plane. The action of "cleaning up the mess" turns, by metaphoric equation, into the process of forgetting. Just as one must remove the rubble after the war, one must remove the remembrance of human evil; otherwise, the burden of living would be unbearable. But this point means that people never learn from history. People's ability to forget makes them, at the same time, repeatedly commit the same tragic blunders.

Szymborska's "naive questions" would not perhaps be posed with such force, if not for the fact that they are actually reactions to statements. The assertive statement that provokes her inquiry may not be included in the poem, at least not directly; nevertheless, it is always there, if only concealed in the question itself and waiting to be guessed by the reader. Such a statement is usually a widely shared opinion on an issue, and the "naive question" is supposed to raise doubt about its validity. The opinion not only reflects some common belief or is representative of some widespread mind-set but also, as a rule, has a certain doctrinaire ring to it: the outlook behind it is usually speculative, antiempirical, prone to hasty generalizations, collectivist, dogmatic, and intolerant. The poet's function as seen in Szymborska's poems is to burst the balloons of such self-confidence and blatant oversimplification by simply registering the fact that he or she forms an exception from the supposedly all-binding rule, an individual case that contradicts the supposedly universal law. The natural role for poets, then, is to be eternal spoilsports. And that is precisely why, to quote the concluding sentence of Szymborska's Nobel lecture, "It looks like poets will always have their work cut out for them."

Biography:

Anna Bikont and Joanna Szczęsna, *Pamiątkowe rupiecie, przyjaciele i sny Wisławy Szymborskiej* (Warsaw: Prószyński i Ska, 1997).

References:

Stanisław Balbus, *Świat ze wszystkich stron świata: O Wisławie Szymborskiej* (Kraków: Wydawnictwo Literackie, 1996);

Balbus and Dorota Wojda, eds., *Radość czytania Szymborskiej: Wybór tekstów krytycznych* (Kraków: Znak, 1996);

Edward Balcerzan and others, *Szymborska: Szkice* (Warsaw: OPEN, 1996);

Małgorzata Baranowska, *Tak lekko było nic o tym nie wiedzieć . . . : Szymborska i świat* (Wrocław: Wydawnictwo Dolnośląskie, 1996);

Urszula Biełous, *Szymborska* (Warsaw: Interpress, 1974);

Krzysztof Karasek, "Mozartian Joy: The Poetry of Wisława Szymborska," in *The Mature Laurel: Essays on Modern Polish Poetry,* edited by Adam Czerniawski (Bridgend: Seren Books, 1991), pp. 191–198;

Anna Legeżyńska, *Wisława Szymborska* (Poznań: Rebis, 1996);

Tadeusz Nyczek, *22 x Szymborska* (Poznań: Wydawnictwo 25, 1997);

Barbara Sienkiewicz, ed., *Poznańskie Studia Polonistyczne: Wokół Szymborskiej* (Poznań: Wydawnictwo WiS, 1995);

Anna Węgrzyniakowa, *Nie ma rozpusty większej niż myślenie* (Warsaw: Towarzystwo Zachęty Kultury, 1997);

Dorota Wojda, *Milczenie słowa: O poezji Wisławy Szymborskiej* (Kraków: Universitas, 1997).

Dezső Tandori
(8 December 1938 –   )

Anna Menyhért
University of Miskolc

BOOKS: *Töredék Hamletnek* (Budapest: Szépirodalmi, 1968);

Egy talált tárgy megtisztítása (Budapest: Magvető, 1973);

A mennyezet és a padló (Budapest: Magvető, 1976);

"Itt éjszaka koalák járnak" (Budapest: Magvető, 1977);

Medvék minden mennyiségben (Budapest: Móra, 1977);

Miért élnél örökké? (Budapest: Magvető, 1977);

Még így sem (Budapest: Magvető, 1978);

A meghívás fennáll (Budapest: Magvető, 1979);

Baranyai (Budapest: Képzőművészeti Alap, 1979);

A zsalu sarokvasa: Irodalmi tanulmányok (Budapest: Magvető, 1979);

Medvetalp és barátai (Budapest: Móra, 1979);

Medvetavasz és medvenyár (Budapest: Móra, 1979);

"Kedves Samu" (Hatvan: Hatvany Lajos Múzeum, 1980);

Madárlátta tollaslabda: Ifjúsági regény (Budapest: Móra, 1980);

Nagy Gombfocikönyv. A Liverpool a Vízivárosban. Ifjúsági regény (Budapest: Móra, 1980);

Nem szeretném, ha fáznál, as Nat Roid (Budapest: Magvető, 1980);

Valamivel több. A Kis Koala Kártyabajnokság Első-Nagy-Különtornája (Budapest: Magvető, 1980);

Az erősebb lét közelében (Budapest: Gondolat, 1981);

Most vagy soha, as Roid (Budapest: Magvető, 1981);

Játékmedvék verébdala (Budapest: Móra, 1981);

Túl jól fest holtan, as Roid (Budapest: Magvető, 1981);

Afrika, India: Vadállatok őshona. Verses képeskönyv (Budapest: Móra, 1981);

Mint egy elutazás (Budapest: Magvető, 1981);

Helyből távol (Budapest: Kozmosz könyvek, 1981);

Ne lőj az ülő madárra! (Budapest: Kozmosz könyvek, 1982);

Azt te csak hiszed, bébi! as Roid (Budapest: Magvető, 1982);

. . . de maradj halott; Plusz-minusz senki. Bűnügyi regények, as Roid (Budapest: Magvető, 1983);

Sár és vér és játék (Budapest: Magvető, 1983);

Dezső Tandori (photograph © by Maria Ziegelböck)

A feltételes megálló: Versek 1976–1980 (Budapest: Magvető, 1983);

Celsius (Budapest: Magvető, 1984);

Mesélj rólam, ha tudsz: Versek és mesék (Budapest: Móra, 1984);

Medvék minden mennyiségben (és még verebek is) (Budapest: Móra, 1984);

363

Egyre kisebb gyilkosságok (Kéz a szemet elfedi; A gondviselés akarata nélkül), as Roid (Budapest: Magvető, 1984);

A Stevenson-biozmagória. A Xyget. Steve éve. Tudományos-fantasztikus regény; A hét űrbűn. Tudományos-fantasztikus elbeszélések, as H. C. G. S. Solenard (Budapest: Kozmosz fantasztikus könyvek, 1984);

Bízd a halálra; Külön Kijárás; . . . fényeskedjék neked! as Roid (Budapest: Magvető, 1985);

Új nagy gombfocikönyu. A Liverpool (és a többiek!) ismét a Vízivárosban (Budapest: Kozmosz könyvek, 1985);

Madárnak születni kell, by Tandori and Ágnes Tandori (Budapest: Natura, 1986);

Meghalni és megszeretni; Valakit valamiért; Neki, aki nincs? as Roid (Budapest: Magvető, 1986);

Holtteste éltesse: Bűnügyi regények, as Roid (Budapest: Magvető, 1987);

A becsomagolt vízpart (Budapest: Kozmosz könyvek, 1987);

A megnyerhető veszteség (Budapest: Magvető, 1988);

Meghalni késő, élni túl korán; tandori . . . ? nat roid . . . ? tradoni . . . ? (Budapest: Magvető, 1988);

Vigyázz magadra, ne törődj velem: Válogatott versek 1959–1987 (Budapest: Zrínyi, 1989);

Egy regény hány halott– ? tandori . . . ? nat roid . . . ? tradoni . . . ? (Budapest: Magvető, 1989);

A legújabb kis-nagy gombfocikönyv: Ifjúsági regény (Budapest: Kozmosz könyvek, 1989);

Walton Street/Underlord "T": A tizedik név (Budapest: Holnap, 1990);

A felhúzható medveorr (Békéscsaba: Tevan, 1990);

Erdei nagytakarítás: Lapozó (Budapest: ILKV, 1990);

Koppar Köldüs: Versek, 1970-es és nyolcvanas évek, es konkretan 1990 majus (Budapest: Holnap, 1991);

Sancho Panza deszkakerítése (Budapest: Z-füzetek, 1991);

Szent Lajos lánchídja (Budapest: Zrínyi, 1991);

Döblingi befutó (Budapest: Magvető, 1992);

Hosszú koporsó: H. K. (Budapest: Balassi, 1994);

Kísértetkent a Krisztinán (Budapest: Cserépfalvi, 1994);

A dal változásai (Budapest: Anonymous, 1994);

A vízre írt név–Name Writ on Water (Budapest: Liget, 1995);

Madárzsoké (Budapest: Pesti Szalon, 1995);

Vagy majdnem az (Budapest: Balassi, 1995);

A Semmi Kéz (Budapest: Magvető, 1996);

Az evidencia történetek (Budapest: Magvető, 1996);

Medvék és más verebek (Budapest: Littera Nova, 1996);

Főmű (Budapest: Littera Nova, 1997);

Kész és félkész katasztrófák (Budapest: Magvető, 1997);

Pályáim emlékezete: Napló és önéletrajz, aforizmák (Budapest: Jövendő, 1997);

És megínt messze szállnaki (Budapest: Liget Műhely Alapítvány, 1997);

Jatek-tortenet (Budapest: Liget, 1998);

Utolsó posta Budapest (Budapest: Liget Műhely Alapítvány, 1998);

Keletbe-fúlt kísérletek (Budapest: Terebess, 1999);

Kolárik légvárai: eset-tanulmányok (Budapest: Magvető, 1999).

Editions: *Töredék Hamletnek* (Szeged: Q. E. D., 1995);

Egy talált tárgy megtisztítása (Budapest: Enigma, 1995).

Editions in English: *Birds and Other Relations: Selected Poetry of Dezső Tandori,* translated by Bruce Berlind (Princeton: Princeton University Press, 1986);

"The Christmas of Long Walks," "Tradoni, Stress on an Abandoned Place," "What Gets Lost in the Light," and "The No-Hand," translated by Berlind, in *Shifting Borders: East European Poetries of the Eighties,* edited by Walter Cummins (Rutherford, N.J.: Fairleigh Dickinson University Press, 1993), pp. 253–258.

TRANSLATIONS: Sylvia Plath, *Az üvegbura* (Budapest: Európa, 1971);

Virginia Woolf, *Mrs. Dalloway* (Budapest: Magyar Helikon–Európa, 1971);

Samuel Beckett, *Murphy* (Budapest: Magvető, 1972);

Graham Greene, *Utazás térkép nélkül* (Budapest: Gondolat, 1972);

Franz Werfel, *Cella* (Budapest: Gondolat, 1973);

Thomas Bernhard, *Fagy* (Budapest: Európa, 1974);

Georg Wilhelm Friedrich Hegel, *Esztétika* (Budapest: Gondolat, 1974);

Hans Magnus Enzensberger, *Honatyák és ponyvahősök: Esszék* (Budapest: Európa, 1975);

György Lukács, *A heidelbergi művészetfilozófia és esztétika–A regény elmélete: Ifjúkori művek* (Budapest: Magvető, 1975);

Robert Musil, *A tulajdonságok nélküli ember* (Budapest: Európa, 1977);

Karl Kraus, *Az emberiség végnapjai* (Budapest: Európa, 1977);

Föld és vadon. Válogatott versfordítások (Budapest: Európa, 1978);

Arnold Hauser, *A művészettörténet filozófiája* (Budapest: Gondolat, 1978);

Bernhard, *A mészégető* (Budapest: Magvető, 1979);

Seamus Heaney, *Versei* (Budapest: Európa, 1980);

Wallace Stevens, *Pasziánsz a tölgyek alatt: Versek* (Budapest: Európa, 1981);

Thomas de Quincey, *Egy angol ópiumevő vallomásai* (Budapest: Európa, 1983);

Johann Wolfgang von Goethe, *Wilhelm Meister ván-*
dorévei avagy a lemondók (Budapest: Európa,
1983);

Lombos ágak szívverése. Versek madarakról és fákról.
Műfordítások (Budapest: Kozmosz könyvek,
1983);

Jürgen Theobaldy, *Versek* (Budapest: Európa, 1985);

Hart Crane, *Versei* (Budapest: Európa, 1989);

Amy Clampitt, *Válogatott versek* (Budapest: Európa,
1990);

Műholdas rózsakert: Versfordításregény-töredék (Budapest: Orpheusz, 1991);

Arthur Schopenhauer, *A világ mint akarat és képzelet*
(Budapest: Európa, 1991);

Carl Gustav Jung, *Válasz Jób könyvére* (Budapest:
Akadémia, 1992).

Dezső Tandori is one of the most original
voices within contemporary Hungarian literature.
His works include poems, novels, detective fiction,
children's books, and essays on literature and the
fine arts. Responsible for initiating a paradigm
shift in the poetry of the 1970s, Tandori is also recognized as a leading translator, mainly of works
from English and German. Beyond his literary
endeavors, Tandori is a well-known artist and popular figure within Hungarian society. His lifestyle,
including his attachment to his pet sparrows and
his interest in horse racing, is frequently mentioned not only in literary papers and magazines
but also on television and among the general public. Throughout his career, Tandori's critical reception has generated heated debate; nevertheless, he
is a formidable presence.

Dezső Tandori was born in Budapest on 8
December 1938 to Lenke Nádor, a civil servant, and
Dezső Tandori, commercial director of Hungarian
Railways and an economic consultant before World
War II. Tandori decided to be a writer at the age of
ten, and it was of great importance to him that he
was taught literature in secondary school by the
esteemed poet Ágnes Nemes Nagy. Through her,
Tandori became acquainted with the major writers
belonging to the *Újhold* (New Moon) literary circle,
notably János Pilinszky, Géza Ottlik, Zoltán Jékely,
Iván Mándy, and Miklós Mészöly. Between 1957 and
1962 Tandori studied at Loránd Eötvös University
of Budapest. Having written his thesis on the poetry
of Pilinszky, he received his degree in Hungarian
and German in 1962. After graduating he worked
for a year as a resident assistant for boarding students, and in 1964 he became a college language
teacher. In 1967 he married Nagy, who since then
has been a partner in all of his occupations, whether

translating, writing, or looking after their birds.
They live in Budapest, and their windows overlook
the Chain Bridge, which frequently appears as a
motif in Tandori's books.

Tandori's career as a writer officially began in
1968 with the publication of his first book, *Töredék*
Hamletnek (A Fragment for Hamlet), a collection of
poems written between 1958 and 1968. The original
title of the book was "Egyetlen" (Single), but the
publisher considered that title inappropriate and
decided in favor of *Töredék Hamletnek*. Tandori was
thirty at the time and had been writing verse for
more than a decade. Beginning in 1960, several of
his poems appeared in different literary papers, at
first in the weekly *Élet és Irodalom* (Life and Literature), and some were included in an anthology for
young poets, *Első ének* (First Song), published in
1968. His belated entry into the world of book publication was primarily because of political circumstances; young writers were not easily granted the
opportunity to publish their first books. Although
access to official publication was postponed, Tandori had clearly established a reputation for his
experimental poetry well before the appearance of
Töredék Hamletnek. He had won the award of the
International PEN Club in 1966, and Sándor
Weöres, one of the major poets of the time, had
dedicated a poem to him, thus raising the expectations of Hungarian readers.

Töredék Hamletnek is generally considered to
represent the first period of Tandori's literary
career. It is a continuation of the intellectual poetic
traditions of Attila József and the hermetic tendencies of the *Újhold* circle, and it also bears the influence of objective verse. At the same time, the work
strives to show the impossibility of the very continuity it evokes. This point is made in the first poem of
the book, "Hommage," which is an end and a beginning, both thematically and in terms of its poetic
properties. *Töredék Hamletnek* is essentially both a
tribute to the traditions of Hungarian literature and
the first step in the formulation of Tandori's own
poetic principles.

Critical response to the book was extremely
favorable, emphasizing the elements of disclosure,
silence, and fragmentation that have since become
central in Tandori's poetry. These elements are perhaps most obvious in "Koan III," which questions
the ability and meaning of speech: "Némaság a hang
helyett. / De a némaság mi helyett?" (Numbness
instead of the voice. / But the voice instead of what?).
Perhaps what has not been taken into account by
those critical of Tandori are the consequences of
the paradoxical question, the point of which is not

the emphasis on the inability to find an adequate answer but the fact that it is unnecessary to find one. For Tandori the koan is an invitation to think, not to resolve. Perhaps more in this sense, Tandori's first book can be considered to have initiated a shift in Hungarian poetics, since the problem of the inability to express wholeness is more characteristic of modern poetic traditions than of those leading to postmodern tendencies.

Since 1971 Tandori has been a freelance writer. His second book, *Egy talált tárgy megtisztítása* (The Cleaning of a Found Object, 1973), which initiated the second period of his career, is often said to be the first book of the "real" Tandori. As he writes in the preface of the second edition (1995), the title originally was to be that of the poem "A. Rimbaud a sivatagban forgat" (A. Rimbaud is Filming in the Desert). "Egy talált tárgy megtisztítása" is an allusion to a line in József's poem "Eszmélet" (Consciousness); thus, it was more suitable for the purposes of the cultural policy of the 1970s.

The complex and experimental quality of the book invited reactions ranging from total disapproval to unconditional praise. Rejecting the traditional currents of Hungarian poetry in favor of the neo-avant-garde, the volume includes concrete poems and caligrams, as well as texts that are poems mainly because they are declared to be poems. The best example is "Koratavasz" (Early Spring), a piece of sports news in the form of a poem, which forces the reader to reconsider his or her own image of poetry. Another example is "Pasziánsz. Mottók egymás elé" (Solitaire. Mottoes in Front of One Another), which juxtaposes some fragments of a well-known Hungarian poem—Dezső Kosztolányi's "Csáth Gézának" (To Géza Csáth), written on the death of another writer, Géza Csáth—with fragments from a first-aid handbook. As the poem includes no original text, it is not surprising that it elicited responses that questioned its lyric nature; the notion of lyric poetry dominant in the 1970s was derived from romantic aesthetics, according to which the main features of lyrics are subjectivity and statements about the poetic "I."

In 1974 Tandori was given the Kassák Award, the most prestigious in Hungarian letters, and in 1975 he received the Milán Füst Prize. The following year his third book of verse, *A mennyezet és a padló* (The Ceiling and the Floor), was published. In this book several of the poems from *Egy talált tárgy megtisztítása* were reprinted, which accentuated the continuity of the two books. Tandori attempts to undermine the reading habits of his audience. His numbered sonnets show the impos-

sibility of writing a traditional sonnet; they emphasize the fact that the relationship between genre and single text is not static, that the reader's notion of genres changes through each text. *A mennyezet és a padló* also marks the third period in Tandori's career up until the 1990s. In this book the elements of the lyric subject's everyday life take on extraordinary importance, in a kind of new subjectivity in which the unimportant details of a person's life overwhelm the poems. Yet, in a cunning way the huge quantity and lack of selection of the details make the impression that what is important is not the details themselves but the lyric subject who is writing about them.

The element of writing is important in these poems, and Tandori often includes thoughts about the process of writing. For example, a frequent topic is the making of mistakes when typing. When Tandori makes such a mistake during the creation of a poem, he will leave it as it is and continue the poem with some remark about the existence and significance of the mistake.

Figures of bears, particularly koalas, appear in *A mennyezet és a padló* for the first time and have remained a consistent element in many of Tandori's later books. The collection *"Itt éjszaka koalák járnak"* ("Koalas Go About Here at Night," 1977) consists of eleven short prose pieces on koalas. The characters of the book are the writer and his newspaper-cutting koalas. The koalas think, talk, and discuss theoretical problems with the writer in a childish and repetitive style. The short piece "Egy délelőtt: Alacsony meg én" (One Morning: Alacsony and I) depicts the writer running some errands in the city with his bear Alacsony (Short) beside him. As they walk and look at shop windows, they talk about the possible implications of their relationship and about the subject of birds. Tandori introduces "serious" topics stealthily. For instance, he compares sparrows to other birds and says in his babbling style that while "other birds chase each other away and thus live the 'matters' or 'history,' sparrows live only 'life.'" This roundabout way of expressing thoughts is characteristic of Tandori and becomes increasingly significant in his work throughout the 1980s and 1990s.

In his first novel, *Miért élnél örökké?* (Why Would You Live Forever?), also published in 1977, the character D'Oré, a writer, appears for the first time. The name D'Oré is derived from Tandori's name. Throughout the book the reader becomes familiar with D'Oré's daily occupations and problems. The novel develops a special technique of building up a dialogue between D'Oré and the narrator, who cites D'Oré's words and then explains them, so as to approach everything from both perspectives. He thus gives the impression of always talking around something and never really getting to the expected point. This property of the narrative once again illustrates the inadequacy of language to express things, a tenet of late modernism as it was understood by contemporary criticism. However, from a different point of view, it is not necessary to assume some hidden essence behind the words, and thus the novel is often considered a forerunner of postmodernism.

The elements of *Miért élnél örökké?* are those that the reader finds in most of Tandori's fiction: the bears from the previous book; the championships of "gombfoci," a game similar to tiddlywinks, played according to the rules of football, about which Tandori has written several children's books, such as *Nagy Gombfocikönyv* (The Big Book of Tiddleywinks, 1980); the problems of the writing process and translation chores; the watering of his "Kaktuszka" (nickname of a cactus); and the feeding of sparrows on the windowsills of his flat, initiating a long-term identification with these pets.

Tandori's fourth book of verse, *Még így sem* (Not Even in This Way), appeared in 1978, the same year he was given the Attila József Award. The most interesting poems are the dated sonnets, the titles of which are given in an unusual format: for example, "1976712/j—Koala, koalább, legkoalább" is the "j" poem, probably the tenth poem, written on 12 July 1976, titled "Koala, more koala, most koala." The book includes more than two hundred of these sonnets, beginning with the cycle "Próbálj meg úgy írni, mintha nem írnál" (Try to Write As If You Were Not Writing). "1976712/j" is an interesting example, for in it Tandori reflects on some of the problems cited by his critics. In this book Tandori's poems acquire a quasi-epic character based on remembering and storytelling.

In the second half of the 1970s Tandori radically altered both his lifestyle and working habits. Between 1958 and 1976 he published only three books; but since 1977 he has produced several books per year. The change is apparently connected to a specific incident of symbolic importance to Tandori: he found a sparrow, which died a few days later, but the arrival of another sparrow on that same day seemed to him a spiritual sign. The second sparrow—called Szpéró—lived with him for more than a decade. Prior to this "adoption" he had been feeding birds, and from 1977 on he developed a lifestyle completely subordinated to his birds. They became a dominant thematic element in his writing, illustrated in a series of novels; a collection

Tandori Dezső

VAGY
MAJDNEM
AZ

BALASSI KIADÓ
BUDAPEST, 1995

Title page for a collection of poems in which Tandori returns to the atmosphere of his work of the mid 1970s

of plays, *Mint egy elutazás* (Like a Journey, 1981); the poems in the book *Celsius* (1984); children's books, notably *Mesélj rólam, ha tudsz* (Tell a Story About Me If You Can, 1984); and a book on popular science, *Madárnak születni kell* (One Has To Be Born a Bird, 1986), written with his wife.

The novels in the series include *A meghívás fennáll* (The Invitation Is Valid, 1979), *Valamivel több* (A Bit More, 1980), *Helyből távol* (From Here Far Away, 1981), *Ne lőj az ülő madárra!* (Don't Shoot at the Sitting Bird!, 1982), and *Sár és vér és játék* (Mud and Blood and Game, 1983). Perplexing and disorienting, the novels have elicited a manifold critical response; there are many readers who find them unreadable, and many who consider them brilliant. The rather lengthy novels have the same narrow topic—the daily events of the protagonist's and his wife's life together with the lives of their birds—and the same narrative strategy. In each book, however, the main character has a different name, derived from the name Tandori, and each protagonist "knows" his predecessor and his books, and reflects on them. The situation is complicated further by the dates of publication: some books, written earlier, came out later than others.

The books have a strange atmosphere, a mixture of accurately noted details and deliberately confused dates. The reader is partially assisted by the "biographies" of the different birds—the dates when they arrived at the writer's flat and when they left (for various reasons) are occasionally given in the books, making it possible to measure time. For example, *A meghívás fennáll*, written in the autumn of 1977 and published in 1979, hints at events mentioned in two other books (*Ne lőj az ülő madárra!* [1982] and *Helyből távol* [1981]). The three books thus present different versions of the same set of events: Tandori's journey to "the Island," during which he left his two birds in the care of friends who allowed one of the birds, Némó, to escape. The story of Némó is not recounted in *A meghívás fennáll*, but the text alludes to it from time to time, in a rather secretive manner, as if the protagonist (named D'Array in this volume) were investigating a case, searching for clues. The main topic is D'Array's relationship with his sparrow, Szpéró. The reader becomes familiar with their daily routine: feeding and sunbathing of the bird, the dangers awaiting the tiny bird in the flat, and the writer's efforts to avoid dangerous situations such as treading on the bird, shutting it in the door jamb, or capturing it in the keyboard of the typewriter. D'Array and his wife also play cards with teams of fantasy bears and anthropomorphized objects, and the reader learns the results from charts and descriptions.

Valamivel több, according to its subtitle, is a book about *A Kis Koala Kártyabajnokság Első–Nagy–Különtornája* (The First–Great–Exclusive Tournament of the Small Koala Card Championship). It was published in 1980, but it had been written earlier, in the spring of 1977, before the birds appeared in Tandori's life and books. Thus the protagonist, Rot Esq, in a manner characteristic of Tandori's novels, speaks to the reader about D'Array in the first chapter, titled "Egy év múlva. Utószó a történet utóéletéhez" (A Year Later. Epilogue to the Afterlife of the Story) to build up continuity between the two books and the recounted events. Rot Esq mentions that the reader (the constituted, apostrophized reader who obviously is supposed to be familiar with the full range of the Rot Esq–D'Array–D'Oré books) probably would expect to learn what happened to Szpéró since the previous book, but these expectations will not be fulfilled, as now (in the spring of

1978) Rot Esq is editing D'Array's book, written a year before, and he can only add footnotes and remarks to it.

Tradoni, the main character of *Ne lőj az ülő madárra!*, follows a similar practice when, in the summer of 1980, he puts together the fragments of his notebooks from summer 1978 into a new book. Consequently, the events of 1978 are written from yet another perspective, under different circumstances, in the presence of a new bird, Samu, in the house. During the process Tradoni comments on the act of compiling and again writes about the events of his daily life. In this book the death of Tili, a green finch, is mentioned, and the reader also learns that the writer had already written about it elsewhere—probably in the first drafts of *Sár és vér és játék*.

Sár és vér és játék (1983), which at nearly eight hundred pages is the longest of the so-called bird novels, has the most tense atmosphere. It was written between the autumn of 1981 and the spring of 1982, compiled from the notebooks of the spring of 1980, the time of Tili's death. The text is full of quotation marks, which makes it rather difficult to read; critics usually leave these out when they cite the text. The novel is devoted to the story of Tili's death, to the protagonist's (Tradoni) and his wife's mourning and guilt because they—and the ornithologist expert—had not been able to diagnose and cure Tili's ailment. Tradoni repeatedly recalls the events, accuses himself of negligence, and tries to find some explanation. At the time of writing they have new birds, among them Pipi néni, the blind sparrow, and the reader becomes acquainted with them as well.

Perhaps in this book a primary characteristic of Tandori's novels is most apparent: the meticulous preciseness with which the narrator strives to distinguish the different time layers, following the theory that it is not the same person who writes down the first drafts and the final version because the time that has elapsed changes him, and he is forced to reflect on the changes. Tandori's theory of repetition, expounded in several of the novels, implies that events have to be recounted several times, in different modes and voices of narration, and this process is what gives the events their meaning, which alters from narrative to narrative. The writer characters of these novels are often considered the masks or disguises of the author; however, it is always firmly established that the protagonist is a character, and is not identical with Tandori, or with the narrator, and not even with his predecessor.

Tandori published two collections of essays in 1979 and 1981. In the first, *A zsalu sarokvasa* (The Hinge of the Shutters), he collected his pieces on the poetry of Dezső Kosztolányi, Lajos Kassák, and Sándor Weöres, and he wrote about writers whose books he had translated: Henry David Thoreau, Franz Kafka, Karl Kraus, Robert Musil, J. D. Salinger, Thomas Bernhard, Peter Handke, and Sylvia Plath. In *Az erősebb lét közelében* (Close to Stronger Being) he discusses the semi-long poem, a type common in twentieth-century Hungarian poetry, and analyzes several poems belonging to this category; Milán Füst, Endre Ady, Kosztolányi, Mihály Babits, Árpád Tóth, Ernő Szép, József, Jenő Dsida, Nagy, Pilinszky, Lőrinc Szabó, and László Nagy. These collections of essays are important not only because Tandori is an interesting essayist with a firm literary taste and inspiring ideas but also because the choices he makes reveal his affinity toward the traditional Hungarian literary canon. The inclusion of Szép's poetry brought about considerable debate in academic circles, since it is generally not valued as highly as it is by Tandori.

Between 1980 and 1987 Tandori wrote seven detective novels under the pseudonym Nat Roid. The plots are set in an imaginary America, and the characters have Italian-American-sounding names that are puns on Hungarian and English words. These are not detective stories in the strict sense of the category; they are larded with philosophical problems and thoughts familiar from Tandori's other works. During the recounting of investigations the emphasis is on the characters' attempts to establish connections with past events in order to explain why certain things happened.

In 1983 the book of poetry *A feltételes megálló* (The Request Stop) appeared. It comprises poems written between 1976 and 1980, including poems about specific paintings by artists such as Vincent Van Gogh, Claude Monet, Edouard Manet, Paul Gauguin, Pierre-Auguste Renoir, Georges Seurat, Camille Pissarro, Maurice Utrillo, and Paul Cézanne, as well as the "Hérakleitosz" poems. The concrete poem "Hérakleitosz-emlékoszlop" (Heraclitus-Monument) consists of one sentence in which the letters are composed in a vertical order on the page. The request of the sentence—"Próbáljuk meg első olvasásra megmondani hány sor" (Let's try to tell at the first reading how many lines)—is impossible to comply with, since by the time the reader understands what he or she is to do, the first reading has already been accomplished. Consequently, the poem makes the reader realize that without his

participation the aesthetic process would not come into being.

In 1986 Tandori received the Áprily Award and the Tibor Déry Prize, and in that same year a collection of his poems was published in English, translated by Bruce Berlind. In 1988, on the occasion of his fiftieth birthday, the journal *Tiszatáj* dedicated an issue to him. In 1989 a selection of poems written between 1959 and 1987 was published under the title *Vigyázz magadra, ne törődj velem* (Take Care of Yourself, Don't Mind Me), and in the same year he won the Ernő Szép Award.

After Szpéró's death in 1988, Tandori began to travel more extensively in Europe. The change in his lifestyle also brought about changes in his books: during the 1990s his main topic became traveling, especially visiting horse races. *Koppar Köldüs*, published in 1991, is the most interesting of Tandori's books published in that decade. Its title comprises abbreviations of the names of four major European cities—Copenhagen, Paris, Cologne, and Düsseldorf—yet, it also evokes the Hungarian words "kopár koldus," meaning "barren beggar." It is a book of poetry in which the speaker travels around the mentioned cities, meditating on his dead bird, Szpéró.

The most striking feature of the book is the language: it is a language that consists of mistakes and errors made during typing that are left in the text. At first sight it makes the impression that not a single word is typed the way it should be in ordinary Hungarian. Consequently, the reader has to unravel the meaning of each group of letters, thus deciphering the text. The only part of the text that is written in "normal" language is the last poem of the book: "Londoni Mindszentek" (All Saints' Day in London), which is a beautiful poem about Szpéró. As is frequently mentioned in the reviews of this book, this language seems at least as radical and original as that of Tandori's first two books. Thus, again the critical reception of the book was dominated—apart from the experience of novelty—by the experience of provocation, as in the case of *Töredék Hamletnek* and *Egy talált tárgy megtisztítása*. Reading these books requires extraordinarily active participation on the part of the reader.

The novel *Döblingi befutó* (Arrivals in Döbling), which appeared in 1992, is also organized around the topic of traveling. Its connection with *Koppar Köldüs* is strengthened by the inclusion of "Londoni Mindszentek" in it. There are two main differences from the "bird novels" of the 1980s: one is length (*Döblingi befutó* is around 130 pages) and the other is the simplification of the narrative structure, as the novel is written in first-person singular. The apparent and explicitly expounded interest in socio-political factors is also a novelty. The story recounts the experiences of the main character at the racecourses of Europe. Horses have only partly taken the place of birds; the protagonist's relationship to horses is always affected by the memory of his birds. In fact, he usually places bets on horses that have names that he can connect to the names of the birds; thus, it is more of a linguistic game. The act of betting and learning the results is significant in the sense that it can serve as a justification for the protagonist's actions. To him, the results tell at once whether he had been acting rightly, whether the risk he had taken when backing a horse had to be taken or whether it was useless and unnecessarily foolhardy.

In 1994 the collection *A dal változásai* (The Changes of Song) was published. The book is the text of four lectures delivered at Loránd Eötvös University of Budapest as part of a series of lectures held annually in commemoration of the birthday of the nineteenth-century poet János Arany. In the following year both the collection of short prose pieces *Madárzsoké* (Bird-Jockey) and the collection of poems *Vagy majdnem az* (Or Almost That) were published. In both books the figure of the bird-jockey is relevant. Many poems of *Vagy majdnem az* use more traditional rhymes, and their linguistic humor (even in relation to the topic of the birds) and irony is a kind of return to the atmosphere of the poems of the mid 1970s.

Dezső Tandori enjoys a distinct and multifaceted reputation within contemporary Hungarian literature. Apart from his books and translations, he publishes extensively in literary journals and magazines and reads his poems in performances. He is, in addition, an accomplished graphic artist and has organized exhibitions of his work in Hungary, Austria, Germany, and France. Throughout his career Tandori has maintained a commitment to his craft and artistic vision and continues to exert a considerable influence on younger generations of Hungarian writers, as evinced by the republication in 1995 of his first two collections of poetry. In addition, Tandori was the subject of a documentary directed by Gábor Zsigmond Papp and released in 1996. Whether readers like him or not, Tandori is a writer of originality and importance.

References:

Miklós Almási, "Köznyelvi élmények," *Kortárs*, 1 (1979): 152–157;

Eszter Babarczy, "A szent melengetett helye. Tandori Dezső vállalkozásáról," *Alföld*, 1 (1996): 64–79;

Péter Balassa, "A felnőtt D'Oré szenvedései. Tandori Dezső: 'Miért élnél örökké,'" *Jelenkor*, 7–8 (1978): 669–672;

Imre Bata, "A koalák könyve," *Új Írás*, 9 (1977): 112–114;

Miklós Béládi, "Az elbeszélés hitelessége," *Jelenkor*, 7–8 (1978): 672–676;

Endre Bojtár, "Értékelés és értelmezés. Tandori Dezső: 'Hommage'" and "A mű-szubjektum metamorfózisai. Tandori Dezső: 'Godot-ra várva: 11 aero-mobil,'" in his *Egy kelet-européer az irodalomelméletben* (Budapest: Magvető, 1983), pp. 87–104, 106–128;

Miklós Csűrös, "Tandori Dezső: 'Még így sem,'" in his *Színképelemzés* (Budapest: Szépirodalmi, 1984), pp. 220–236;

Julianna Deréky, "Nachwort," in *Startlampe ohne Bahn*, by Tandori (Graz: Literaturferlag Droschl, 1994), pp. 101–114;

Gyula Doboss, *Hérakléitosz Budán. Tandori Dezső munkásságáról 1983-ig* (Budapest: Magvető, 1988);

Edit Erdődy, "Szerkezet és jelentés Tandori Dezs: 'A mennyezet és a padló' című kötetében," *Literatura*, 1 (1977): 127–133;

Zsolt Farkas, "Az író ír. Az olvasó stb. A neoavantgarde és a minden-leírás néhány problémája Tandori műveiben," in his *Mindentől ugyanannyira* (Budapest: Pesti Szalon, 1994), pp. 136–195;

Győző Ferenc, "Tandori. Vázlat a pályaívhez," *Holmi*, 4 (1994): 503–514;

László Ferenczi, "Recent Poetry. György Rába, László Nagy, Dezső Tandori," *New Hungarian Quarterly* (Autumn 1974): 183–186;

Miklós Fogarassy, *Tandori-kalauz* (Budapest: Balassi, 1996);

Lóránt Kabdebó, "A létezés változatai. Tandori Dezső költészetének alaphelyzetei," in his *Versek között* (Budapest: Magvető, 1980), pp. 504–541;

István Király, "Egy befogadói élmény nyomában," *Tiszatáj*, 12 (1988): 71–94;

Csaba Könczöl, "A hallgatás szinonimái," *Életünk*, 5 (1975): 427–440;

Könczöl, "Az 'antiköltészet' versei," *Jelenkor*, 6 (1974): 565–568;

Könczöl, "Vizsgálat egy minden gyanú felett álló szabályrendszer ügyében. Tandori Dezső: 'A mennyezet és a padló,'" in his *Tükörszoba* (Budapest: Szépirodalmi, 1986), pp. 270–278;

Ernő Kulcsár Szabó, "Antimetaforizmus és szinkronszerűség. A líra mint esztétikai hatásforma a konkrét költészetben," in his *Műalkotás–szöveg–hatás* (Budapest: Magvető, 1987), pp. 354–381;

Kulcsár Szabó, "Tandori Dezső," in his *A magyar irodalom története 1945–1991* (Budapest: Argumentum, 1993), pp. 140–143;

István Margócsy, "Tandori Dezső: 'Két krimi,'" "Tandori Dezső: 'Koppar Köldüs,'" and "Tandori Dezső: 'Madárzsoké,'" in his *"Nagyon komoly játékok"* (Budapest: Pesti Szalon, 1996), pp. 221–244;

Győző Mátyás, "'Helyett.' Tandori Dezsőről a 'Celsius' ürügyén," *Jelenkor,* 9 (1985): 797–807;

János Ősi, "Szerző, elbeszélő, utazó. Tandori Dezső 'Egy talált tárgy megtisztítása' című verséről," *Nappali Ház,* 4 (1994): 27–29;

Lajos Parti Nagy, "Tandori Dezső. 'A megnyerhető veszteség,'" *Kortárs,* 8 (1988): 163–165;

Sándor Radnóti, "Talált tárgyak költészete. Tandori Dezső második kötetéről," "Tandori szonettjeiről," and "'Lösz vögösz,'" in his *Mi az, hogy beszélgetés* (Budapest: Magvető, 1980), pp. 212–254;

Mihály Sükösd, "Mi az, hogy Tandori," *Mozgó Világ,* 8 (1994): 125–128;

Klára Széles, "Tandori Dezsőről—többféleképpen," *Kortárs,* 6 (1974): 1001–1005;

Csaba Szigeti (Xygeti), "A saussure-i anagrammatikáról és Tandori Dezső szigetéről" *Jelenkor,* 4 (1989): 383–390;

Szigeti, "Transz. Tandori Dezső szonettváltozatai," *Tiszatáj,* 12 (1988): 29–40;

Márton Szilágyi, "Halálgyakorlatok. Tandori Dezső újabb pályaszakaszáról," in his *Kritikai berek* (Budapest: Balassi, 1995), pp. 74–84;

Tamás Tarján, "Matt, három lépésben. Tandori Dezső 'sakk-trilógiájáról,'" ". . . ők én vagyok már — avagy a tényleg becsomagolt vízpart," "N, mint Nulla kilométerkő. Tandori Dezső, a kortalan," "Az angyalok és a lovak" and "Két köntös. A szonett és a haiku," in his *Egy tiszta tárgy találgatása* (Budapest: Orpheusz, 1994), pp. 9–83;

Tarján, "Tizennyolc centi próza. Tandori Dezső, az epikus," *Kortárs,* 7 (1981): 1158–1162;

Szabolcs Várady, "Két költő," *Valóság,* 2 (1972): 89–95;

István Vas, "Egy tenyér csattanása. Tandori Dezső" and "A ragasztás diadala—Egy Tandori-versről," in his *Az ismeretlen isten. Tanulmányok 1934–1973* (Budapest: Szépirodalmi, 1974), pp. 861–863, 975–989.

Mati Unt
(1 January 1944 –   )

Luule Epner
University of Tartu

BOOKS: *Hüvasti, kollane kass,* Tartu VIII Keskkooli almanahh *Tipa-Tapa,* no. 6 (Tartu: Kevad, 1963); revised as *Tere, kollane kass!* (Tallinn: Kupar, 1992);

Võlg (Toronto: Eesti Üliõpilaskond Torontos Vilkogu, 1966); translated by Ritva Poom as "The Debt," *Literary Review,* 24 (Summer 1981): 461–513;

Elu võimalikkusest kosmoses (Tallinn: Perioodika, 1967);

Mõrv hotellis. Phaethon, Päikese poeg (Tallinn: Perioodika, 1969);

Kuu nagu kustuv päike: Valik aastatest 1964–1970 (Tallinn: Eesti Raamat, 1971);

Mattias ja Kristiina (Tallinn: Eesti Raamat, 1974);

Via regia (Tallinn: Perioodika, 1975); translated by Mardi Valgemäe as "Via Regia," *Literary Review,* 36 (Winter 1993): 191–237;

Must mootorrattur (Tallinn: Eesti Raamat, 1976);

Sügisball: Stseenid linnaelust (Tallinn: Eesti Raamat, 1979); translated by Mart Aru as *The Autumn Ball: Scenes of City Life* (Tallinn: Perioodika, 1985);

Räägivad (Tallinn: Perioodika, 1984);

Valitud teosed, 2 volumes (Tallinn: Eesti Raamat, 1985);

Räägivad ja vaikivad (Tallinn: Eesti Raamat, 1986);

Kuradid ja kuningad: Teatri ja filmikirjutisi aastaist 1965–1980 (Tallinn: Eesti Raamat, 1989);

Ma ei olnud imelaps (Tallinn: Eesti Raamat, 1990);

Öös on asju (Tallinn: Eesti Raamat, 1990);

Doonori meelespea (Tallinn: Kupar, 1990);

Argimütoloogia sõnastik: 1983–1993 (Tallinn: Kupar, 1993);

Vastne argimütoloogia (Tallinn: Vagabund, 1996);

Brecht ilmub öösel = Brecht bricht ein in der Nacht (Tallinn: Kupar, 1997);

Huntluts: Teosid Oskar Lutsu motiividel (Tallinn: Kupar, 1999).

Mati Unt

Editions in English: *Doomsday,* translated by Maire Jaanus and Mardi Valgemäe, *Modern International Drama,* 10 (Spring 1977): 43–64;

"The Fish's Revenge," "The Black Motorcyclist," "He Translated," and "Tantalus," translated by Ritva Poom, in *Estonian Short Stories,* edited by

Kajar Pruul and Darlene Reddaway (Evanston, Ill.: Northwestern University Press, 1996), pp. 57–91;

"We, Actors and Writers" and "The Everdying Farm," translated by Jaanus and Valgemäe, *Literary Review,* 39 (Summer 1996): 519–522.

PLAY PRODUCTIONS: *See maailm või teine,* Tartu, "Vanemuine" Theater, 12 June 1966;

Phaethon, päikese poeg, Tartu, "Vanemuine" Theater, 28 January 1968;

Kolm põrsakest ja hea hunt, Pärnu, Draamateater, 3 March 1973;

Good-bye, baby, Tallinn, Noorsooteater, 31 October 1975; New York, Kunstiklubi Teater, 29 March 1991;

Peaproov, Tallinn, Noorsooteater, 3 November 1977;

Kollontai, Tallinn, Noorsooteater, 6 November 1977;

Doktor Noormanni kirjasõprade kokkutulek, Pärnu, Draamateater, 3 March 1979;

Gulliver ja Gulliver, Tallinn, Nukuteater, 14 April 1979;

Vaimude tund Jannseni tänaval, Pärnu, Draamateater, 6 October 1984;

Keiser Nero eraelu, Viljandi, "Ugala" Theater, 8 October 1990;

Doomsday, translated by Maire Jaanus and Mardi Valgemäe, New York, Arts Club Theater, 28 August 1991.

PRODUCED SCRIPTS: *Surma hinda küsi surnutelt,* motion picture, Tallinnfilm, 1977;

Saja aasta pärast mais, motion picture, Tallinnfilm, 1987;

Nõid, motion picture, Tallinnfilm, 1988.

TRANSLATIONS: Gottfried August Bürger, *Wabahärra von Münchhauseni imepärased reisid ja seiklused merel ning maal, nii nagu ta ise nendest sõprade ringis veiniklaasi juures pajatas* (Tallinn: Eesti Raamat, 1974);

Carl Gustav Jung, *Tänapäeva müüt: Asjadest, mida nähakse taevas,* translated, with a preface, by Unt (Tallinn: Vagabund, 1995);

Eugenio Barba, *Paberlaevuke: Sissejuhatus teatri-antropoloogiasse,* translated, with a preface and commentary, by Unt (Tallinn: Eesti Teatriliit, EMA Kõrgem Lavakunstikool, 1999).

SELECTED PERIODICAL PUBLICATIONS— UNCOLLECTED: *Imperaator Nero eraelu,* in *Vikerkaar* (June 1991): 3–26;

Memuaare, in *Teater. Muusika. Kino* (December 1993): 12–18;

Unt in 1961 (courtesy of the author)

Minu teatriglossaarium, in *Thespis: Meie teatriuuendused 1972/73,* edited by Vaino Vahing (Tartu: Ilmamaa, 1997), pp. 117–158.

Mati Unt is a prominent prose writer, as well as a playwright, and has more recently become active as a stage director. He arrived on the literary scene in the early 1960s and was instrumental in introducing modernism into Soviet Estonian letters. In the 1970s Unt became one of the initiators of postmodernist writing in Estonia.

Unlike most Estonian writers of his generation, Unt grew up not in an urban setting but in a secluded forest village. He was born on 1 January 1944 in the village of Linnamäe in Voore Parish, Tartumaa, the only child of August and Linda (née Busch) Unt. His father was a bookkeeper at a dairy, and his mother was a clerk on a collective farm. Unt attended the Leedimäe primary school until he was fourteen, when he moved to Tartu to continue his studies at High School Number 8. Fortunately for him, the period of his intellectual awakening coincided with Soviet leader Nikita Khrushchev's "thaw," which allowed the reestablishment of contacts with Western culture and loosened some of the restraints of the Stalinist period. As a result, the works of Ernest Hemingway, Erich Maria Remarque, and Vassili Aksjonov became popular among young people; Unt was strongly influenced by J. D. Salinger's *The Catcher in the Rye* (1951), which was translated into Estonian in 1961. Unt was also fortunate in his mentors. His literature teacher, Vello Saage, a legendary figure who inspired many of his pupils, encouraged Unt to write. Unt, however, was much more interested in art. He took drawing lessons and intended to enter the local art school, but, caught up in the excitement that literature was generating among his friends and influenced by his teacher, he began to write, as he later said, "quite accidentally."

Unt's first attempts at fiction appeared in his high-school literary journal; later, four prose miniatures were published in a youth magazine. At eighteen, just before graduating from high school, Unt wrote his first novel, *Hüvasti, kollane kass* (Goodbye, Red Cat), which was published in 1963 as a hardcover volume of 302 pages in the school's *Tipa-Tapa* (First Steps) series. The work is an episodic bildungsroman; the main conflict is between the youthful protagonist and the petty-bourgeois mentality represented by his aunt and symbolized by a red cat. *Hüvasti, kollane kass* earned Unt a reputation as a sincere and sensitive writer. The novel appeared in a Russian translation in 1967 and was then translated into Latvian, Lithuanian, Ukrainian, Moldavian, Georgian, and Byelorussian. In 1969 a movie version of the novel was produced in Lithuania. Unt himself had second thoughts about the work and published a revised version in 1992.

In 1962 Unt entered the University of Tartu, where he majored in Estonian language and literature, specializing in journalism. Several writers and critics who made up the core of the so-called generation of the 1960s, including Paul-Eerik Rummo, Jaan Kaplinski, Andres Ehin, Marju Lauristin, and Jaak Rähesoo, were also studying at Tartu at that time, and Unt joined their circle. They exchanged books and ideas, held seminars in their rooms, and read papers on various subjects.

Unt quickly became known as the most perceptive member of his generation of writers because of his ability to understand and to express the dominant ideas, emotions, and attitudes of the period. He did so convincingly in his second work, the novella *Võlg* (translated as "The Debt," 1981), which

was first published in the literary magazine *Looming* (Creation) in September 1964. The narrator, a young man, meets a girl who represents what he considers perfection but has to give up the ideal for the sake of the demands of real life. In depicting the experiences and thoughts of his youthful protagonist with unprecedented frankness, Unt broke several ideological and moral taboos. Reception of the novella ranged from enthusiastic approval to furious denunciation, but there was no denying that *Võlg* was a persuasive work of art. The novella was published in book form by the Estonian émigré community Toronto in 1966; that same year Unt was accepted as a member of the Soviet Estonian Writers' Union. A televised version of *Võlg* was produced in 1967. The work was translated into Finnish and Latvian in 1968.

In 1965 Unt married Ela Tomson, a fellow student. That year he also traveled abroad for the first time, visiting Poland. While still at the university he wrote movie criticism for newspapers and became interested in the theater; he had participated in amateur productions both in high school and at the university, and in 1966 he wrote his first play. *See maailm või teine* (This World or Another) was directed by Heikki Haravee at the "Vanemuine" in Tartu, one of the leading Estonian theaters. Based on an actual incident, the play presents the inner struggle of a young man who has come under the influence of criminals. Instead of adhering to the officially approved mode of socialist realism, which dominated Estonian theater at the time, Unt makes use of the Brechtian technique of epic theater. That year Unt was employed as a literary consultant at "Vanemuine."

In 1967 Unt published the novel *Elu võimalikkusest kosmoses* (On the Possibility of Life in Outer Space), depicting the search for love and self-knowledge against a backdrop of eternity and cosmic chance. The plot concerns a young rationalist who commits suicide. The author's awareness of the brevity and insecurity of human existence creates an emotionally strained atmosphere in which sensitive and spiritually independent individuals resist everyday routines and generally accepted truths, yearning for something higher.

In 1967 Unt and his wife staged a reading at the "Vanemuine" Theater of the poems of various authors. Poetry reading was a new phenomenon in Estonia and the rest of the Soviet Union, and the production generated much discussion in the university newspaper. Unt graduated from Tartu University in 1967. In 1968 he traveled to Germany. His wife left him that year, and he married the actress Mare Puusepp. Their son, Indrek, was born in 1969.

In the late 1960s revolutionary changes were occurring at the "Vanemuine" Theater, where the young directors Evald Hermaküla and Jaan Tooming were modernizing the staging of plays under the influence of Antonin Artaud, Jerzy Grotowski, Peter Brook, and the American Off-Off Broadway theater. Unt collaborated with these directors and championed the avant-garde theater in articles. During this time he became acquainted with Carl Gustav Jung's analytical psychology, which deeply influenced his work. His literary models were the French existentialists (Albert Camus, in particular), Franz Kafka, and Mikhail Bulgakov. Mythic features add an aspect of universality to Unt's work, but the main stress is on the problems of individual existence. Unt puts his characters into extreme situations and depicts their ethical and cognitive crises as they strive to understand their deeper, truer "selves." They search desperately for a balance between order and chaos, between the rationality that restricts feelings and the irrationality that becomes destructive. Motifs of choice and self-awareness are closely intertwined with those of love: Unt's protagonists know that they can make contact with themselves only through the Other.

Unt's next drama, *Phaethon, Päikese poeg* (Phaëthon, Son of Helios), was produced at the "Vanemuine" in 1968; it was directed by Kaarel Ird, with the author as assistant director. Unt uses the Greek myth of the death of Phaëthon to comment on the realpolitik of the 1960s. His characters represent generalized attitudes; only the title figure is given a psychological dimension. Unt's Phaethon, unlike the Greek original, is no seeker of celestial thrills; he aims to change the social order. He drives the sun chariot, which symbolizes power, without mishap, but he fails to withstand the might of Death, and the chariot is destroyed on Hades's orders. Though *Phaethon, Päikese poeg* deals with existential and metaphysical anxiety, many theatergoers correctly interpreted the work as an allegory of the Soviet system. Officially there was silence; only one periodical, the university's *Tartu Riiklik Ülikool* (Tartu State University), reviewed it. In a paradoxical way characteristic of the period, the university Komsomol (Young Communist) Committee, which in many respects opposed the official establishment, proposed a prize for *Phaethon, Päikese poeg,* but Unt did not receive it. In 1969 *Phaethon, Päikese poeg* was one of the plays discussed by the critic Jaak Rähesoo in a seminal article on the new Estonian drama in *Looming.*

Cover for the high-school publication in which Unt's first novel, Hüvasti, kollane kass, *appeared in 1963*

Phaethon, Päikese poeg was published in 1969 together with the short novel "Mõrv hotellis" (Murder in a Hotel), a quintessential text of modernist Soviet Estonian prose. The narrator lives in a huge, labyrinthine hotel that is emblematic of civilization and of his own consciousness. He witnesses a murder and, pursuing the unknown killer despite the indifference of the other residents, he assumes the role of the savior of the hotel. He fails to accomplish his task and, in an ironic conclusion, turns out to be himself both a victim and a murderer. The reception of the work was unenthusiastic; critics considered it derivative of Kafka. "Mõrv hotellis" achieves, however, a highly sensory—particularly visual—style as Unt uses language to create a subtle medium of perception. Besides impressions from the external world, he depicts dreams and fantastic visions, creating a psychic reality and revealing archetypal images that hide in the unconscious. This originality is counterbalanced by a web of allusions, quota-

Mezzotint engraving of Unt by Kaljo Põllu, 1973

tions, and parallels from literary and philosophical texts.

Unt's style is most effective in short prose, and he published many prose miniatures in the 1960s and 1970s. In these works he usually concentrates on a single emotion or impression or elaborates mythological plots. His stories often show unknown forces or strange accidents interrupting everyday life, creating an atmosphere of insecurity and angst. Unt has collected these works into volumes that also include plays and longer prose fictions, such as *Kuu nagu kustuv päike: Valik aastatest 1964–1970* (The Moon like a Fading Sun: Selections from the Years 1964–1970, 1971), *Mattias ja Kristiina* (Matthias and Christina, 1974), and *Must mootorrattur* (The Black Motorcyclist, 1976).

Unt's second marriage broke up in 1971, as did his circle of friends and colleagues in the theater. Unt went through a deep personal crisis, and the following year he left the "Vanemuine" Theater and Tartu and moved to the capital, Tallinn. The break was total; later, when he prepared his selected works for publication, he divided his writings into those written in Tartu and those written in Tallinn.

One of Unt's best-known novellas, "Tühirand" (Empty Beach), was published in *Looming* in May 1972 and collected in *Mattias ja Kristiina*. In Unt's opinion it is an "ecstatic and complete" work, and it is one of the few that he has never revised. In an inner monologue, which occasionally becomes

stream of consciousness, the protagonist tells about the seven days he spent on an island with his wife and her lover. During that week his marriage breaks up, he loses his illusions about love, and his universe collapses—in short, his intense striving for the ideal collides painfully with reality. He finally escapes from the island and is left with a sense of emptiness. The text is an associative stream of reminiscences and fantasies, impressions and sensations, punctuated by allusions and by quotations in capital letters that are often in a foreign language. The mixture of highly personal feelings with formulaic clichés is meant to reveal a painfully split consciousness.

In March 1972 Unt's play *Viimnepäev* (translated as *Doomsday,* 1977) appeared in *Looming;* it was collected in *Mattias ja Kristiina* and republished, with minor revisions, in his *Valitud teosed* (Selected Works, 1985). It has never been produced in the author's homeland, but in 1991 Linda Pakri's Arts Club Theater staged it in English in New York. The play depicts in an absurdist manner the release of repressed fears and complexes brought on by violence that turns out to be not what it seemed: soldiers in Nazi uniforms, who turn out to be actors, interrupt the retirement party of a Soviet Estonian worker and molest the guests. Also in 1972 Unt wrote the novella "Mattias ja Kristiina," which was first published in *Looming* in January 1973. Once more, he depicts the flight of a sensitive autobiographical protagonist from the brutality of everyday philistine life, this time together with an ideal beloved. The escape, however, turns out to be illusory.

From 1972 to 1982 Unt lived with Kersti Kreismann, an actress at Tallinn's Drama Theater. He returned to theater criticism, published portraits of actors, and worked on dramatizations for the theater in Pärnu. In 1972–1973 he collaborated with the psychiatrist and writer Vaino Vahing in editing a samizdat theater periodical, *Thespis*. Since 1973 he has also written literary criticism. He traveled to Poland in 1974, 1975, and 1977 and visited Finland in 1976.

The 1970s were a period of significant artistic change for Unt. He began to distance himself from his characters, who were no longer autobiographical; his style became less subjective and more ironic; and historical rather than mythological motifs began to dominate his writings. These changes can be illustrated by the two versions of the story "Ja kui me surnud ei ole, siis elame praegugi" (And If We Haven't Died, We Are Still Alive), about the disintegration of a middle-class family when father and son become enamored of the same mysterious girl. In the first version, published in *Looming* in October and December 1973, the characters are depicted subjectively and realistically, whereas in the revised version in the collection *Must mootorrattur* they are named abstractly (Father, Mother, Son) and viewed from a distance by an omniscient narrator.

The short novel *Via regia* (The Royal Road, 1975; translated as "Via regia," 1981) is based on Unt's experiences at the "Vanemuine" Theater. The earliest rough draft of the novel, a collection of fragments titled "Minu teatriglossaarium" (My Theater Glossary), was "published" in the manuscript journal *Thespis*, where the characters appeared under their real names. This hybrid of fact and fiction caused conflicts between Unt and his former colleagues, and in *Via regia* a veneer of fiction covers the reality. Though the novel is narrated in the first person, the action is now seen from an outsider's point of view: the story is told to the narrator by his intellectual and "eminently reasonable" friend. Also, Unt adds in the finished novel the motif of the national inferiority complex: Soviet Estonia is shown as a backwater where noble ideas come to naught and where attempts to improve society by putting on plays lead to tragicomic results. Unt's style in the work is sharply ironic. *Via regia* was well received and garnered the Tuglas Prize for best short fiction in 1976.

In 1975 Unt became a dramaturge at the Tallinn Youth Theater; the following year he became secretary of the Estonian Writer's Union. He held both posts until 1981. Unlike the avant-garde stage directors in Tartu, Kalju Komissarov, who headed the Tallinn ensemble, saw the theater as having a social and political role. Consequently, Unt turned to political subjects and wrote plays about revolutionaries. At the same time, however, he gave vent to his more subjective impulses in short stories published in *Looming*, such as "Ratsa üle Bodeni järve" (The Ride across Lake Constance, January 1976) and "Unbewusste Ängste" (Unconscious Fears, August 1979), both of which were republished in *Valitud teosed*. In 1975 Unt's play *Good-bye, baby* was staged by Komissarov at the Youth Theater; it was not published in its entirety until it appeared in *Valitud teosed* in 1985. The thirteen scenes of the play differ in subject matter as well as in form, including rhetorical monologues, mythological situations, humorous vignettes, scenes modeled on various theatrical styles, and two documentary fragments involving Chilean communist president Salvador Allende's and Cuban revolutionary Ernesto "Che" Guevara's final writings. In 1991 a selection of scenes from *Good-bye, baby* was produced in Estonian in New York.

In 1977 Kaljo Kiisk directed a motion picture, *Surma hinda küsi surnutelt* (Let the Dead Set the Price of Death), with a screenplay by Unt based on the story of Viktor Kingissepp, a Communist underground leader who was executed in 1922. In his drama *Peaparoov* (Dress Rehearsal, 1977), about the making of a movie similar to *Surma hinda küsi surnutelt*, Unt sets up ironic contrasts between historical and artistic truths. Revolutionary themes are also treated in Unt's next play, *Kollontai* (1977), which presents various views of the first female Russian diplomat, Alexandra Kollontai. Unt received several prizes for *Surma hinda küsi surnutelt* and *Kollontai*. Unt visited Sweden in 1978 and Bulgaria in 1979.

One of Unt's most widely read works, *Sügisball: Stseenid linnaelust* (1979; translated as *The Autumn Ball: Scenes of City Life*, 1985), introduced postmodernism into Estonian literature. The novel depicts simultaneous and interconnecting episodes in the lives of six urban characters: a poet, an architect, a hairdresser, a sex maniac, a boy, and the boy's mother, each of whom represents a different way of thinking and living. *Sügisball* was awarded the Juhan Smuul Prize in 1980 and brought Unt international fame: it has been trans-

Helle Kuningas as Lydia Koidula and Siina Üksküla as Aino Kallas in a scene from a performance of Unt's play Vaimude tund Jannseni tänaval *at the Draamateater in Pärnu in 1984*

lated into at least eleven languages, including Finnish, Russian, Bulgarian, Swedish, Hungarian, Polish, German, Czech, Norwegian, Slovak, and English.

In spite of his success as a novelist, Unt began to concentrate more and more on the theater. He had begun to direct in 1978 with a compilation of Estonian poetry of the 1960s titled *Hamleti laulud* (Hamlet's Songs). Later he staged readings of Estonian texts and directed world classics by such authors as Johann Wolfgang von Goethe, Friedrich Schiller, Mikhail Lermontov, and August Strindberg. As a rule, he did not direct his own plays. He wrote two new dramas during this period: *Doktor Noormanni kirjasõprade kokkutulek* (The Reunion of Doctor Noormann's Pen Pals), produced in Pärnu in March 1979, focuses on the sexual problems of teenagers; *Gulliver ja Gulliver* (Gulliver and

Gulliver), produced at the Tallinn Nukuteater (Puppet Theater) the following month, is an allegory about political power.

In 1980 Unt received the title Merited Writer of Soviet Estonia. Such official recognition, however, did not prevent him from confronting the communist power structure that same year. In the autumn of 1980 youth protests opposing the Soviet policy of Russification were brutally suppressed. In response, a group of Estonian intellectuals composed the "Letter of the Forty," condemning the government's and Communist Party's nationality policies. Unt was one of the signatories; as a consequence, he was interrogated by the authorities and, for a time, was forbidden to publish.

In 1981 Unt was appointed a director of the Youth Theater, and staging plays became his main activity. In 1982 he visited Italy. In 1983 he married Lii Lomp, a makeup artist at the Youth Theater who later became a journalist and novelist. Unt continued to write literary criticism, essays, and short fiction and tried his hand at poetry.

In 1984 Unt published two stories and a play treating the psychology and social roles of women. "Kuuvarjutus" (Lunar Eclipse), which appeared in *Looming* in January 1984 and was republished in Unt's *Räägivad ja vaikivad* (They Talk, They Are Silent, 1986), is one of his most intriguing works. It takes the form of a diary of a woman without a memory or a name who is married to a newscaster who is fascinated by history. The woman's mysterious past is hinted at by repeated references to a cat as Unt develops a contrast between the natural and animal aspects of human existence, on the one hand, and the cultural and historical aspects, on the other. *Räägivad* (They Talk, 1984) tells the story of a woman who is afraid of a taxi driver and presents a strange intertwining of trivial and metaphysical facets of contemporary urban life. The only one of his own plays Unt has directed, *Vaimude tund Jannseni tänaval* (The Spirits Meet in Jannsen Street), was commissioned by the theater in Pärnu, where it opened in 1984. It depicts an imaginary meeting between Lydia Koidula (1843–1886), the legendary songstress of the Estonian national awakening, and Aino Kallas (1878–1956), Koidula's Finnish biographer. The dialogue reveals their common concerns as women: whether to pursue their art or to be wives and mothers.

Unt's *Valitud teosed* was published in two volumes in 1985. A collection of his more recent work, *Räägivad ja vaikivad*, appeared in 1986. During this period he was mainly preoccupied with his directorial assignments, including staging plays at the Finnish National Theater in Helsinki in 1988, 1990, and 1991. Two movies based on his screenplays were also released at this time: *Saja aasta pärast mais* (A Hundred Years Later in May, 1987) and *Nõid* (Witch, 1988). Unt traveled to Greece in 1985, to Sweden in 1987, and to the United States in 1989.

In 1988 Unt was one of the founders of the publishing house Kupar, created to break the state monopoly. He brought out two collections of his articles, *Kuradid ja kuningad: Teatri ja filmikirjutisi aastaist 1965–1980* (Devils and Kings: Theater and Film Writings 1965–1980) and *Ma ei olnud imelaps* (I Was Not a Prodigy) in 1989 and 1990, respectively. Two works of fiction that appeared in 1990—*Öös on asju* (Things in the Night) and *Doonori meelespea* (A Donor's Memo)—can hardly be called novels, because Unt deconstructs the plots, characters, and practically everything else in them. The texts are compilations of heterogeneous fragments in which time, space, form, and subject matter constantly change; they include comments on the author's intentions, doubts, private life, and so forth. But the chaotic textual world is held together by myth. In *Öös on asju* the myth is that of electricity viewed as an incomprehensible power hiding unknown dangers. A kind of subplot takes shape in the final part of the work, involving a mysterious power failure in the dead of winter that threatens to bring an end to civilization and an equally mysterious way out of this dilemma brought about by a real person, the writer Lennart Meri, who later became president of Estonia. Such a mixture of fictional and real persons and events, as well as of different styles, is characteristic of Unt's later writing. In *Doonori meelespea* the myth is that of vampires, which links up with the legend of Lydia Koidula and is deconstructed to throw light on the dissolution of Soviet rule in Estonia.

In 1990 a tragic farce, *Imperaator Nero eraelu* (Emperor Nero's Private Life), projected as early as the late 1960s but rejected by the Soviet censors, was staged by Komissarov in Viljandi as *Keiser Nero eraelu*. By transposing the Roman tyrant and his age into the world of *commedia dell' arte*, Unt's play about absolute power became an allegorized examination of Soviet totalitarianism as well as a metatheatrical exercise. In 1992 Unt revised his first novel as *Tere, kollane kass!* (Hello, Red Cat!), striving for deeper psychological truths and strengthened symbolism by developing the red cat into a multifaceted and ambivalent image. Also in 1992 Unt joined the Estonian Drama Theater of Tallinn, the Estonian national theater. He is one of its leading directors and a member of the board that controls the the-

Cover for a 1986 collection of Unt's recent works

ater. Since 1991 he has had a regular column in various newspapers, airing cultural, historical, political, mythological, and even personal matters, and he has compiled two collections of these essays: *Argimütoloogia sõnastik, 1983–1993* (Dictionary of Trivial Mythology, 1983–1993, 1993) and *Vastne argimütoloogia* (New Trivial Mythology, 1996). The international popularity of his works is also growing: in 1993 "Mõrv hotellis" appeared in Finnish, and in 1997 a collection of his stories was published in German. In 1995 Unt visited the United States for a second time.

In 1997 Unt published *Brecht ilmub öösel = Brecht bricht ein in der Nacht* (Brecht Appears at Night). The novel draws parallels between Bertolt Brecht's stay in Finland as the guest of the Estonian-born wealthy socialist Hella Wuolijoki and the annexation of Estonia by the Soviet Union, both of which occurred in 1940. Within this historical framework Unt develops some of his favorite themes, such as the ambiguity of human relationships and the danger of ideological or emotional extremes. The novel includes a multitude of authentic documents and foreign texts; it also includes metafictional explications and commentary on the techniques used by the author.

Throughout his career Mati Unt has occupied a central position in Estonian literature. His predominant themes include a close examination of the vagaries of human existence, the nuances of love and betrayal, the calculus of role-playing, and the problems of self-realization. Despite the inner unity of his works, as reflected by repeated image clusters and leitmotifs, Unt's style has undergone clearly marked changes. After a lyrical and sentimental start he passed through a deep personal crisis that resulted in some of the most intense and emotionally profound works in Estonian literature. Thereafter, he became rather skeptical and ambiguous in his seemingly carefree attitude toward life, and irony, self-parody, and intertextuality came to dominate his prose. Unt then largely withdrew from prose fiction and began a successful career as a theater director, a move foreshadowed by his lifelong association with the stage as a dramatist. As his position at the top of the Estonian literary hierarchy remains unchanged, his works are attracting more and more attention abroad.

Interviews:

Jaak Allik, "Kaheksa küsimust premeeritud Mati Undile," in *Kirjanduse jaosmaa '78*, edited by Endel Mallene (Tallinn: Eesti Raamat, 1980), pp. 137–141;

Joel Sang, "Küsimisi ja kostmisi," *Looming* (July 1985): 958–965;

Reet Neimar, "Vastab Mati Unt," *Teater. Muusika. Kino* (April 1990): 5–14, 76–77;

Marika Mikli, "Vestlus Mati Undiga," *Vikerkaar* (November 1992): 82–86;

"Kaks intervjuud Jan Blomstedtiga," *Vikerkaar* (December 1993): 53–57;

Tõnis Kahu, "49-ne Unt," *Favoriit* (January 1994): 64–68;

Jüri Pino, "Mati Unt: Miks olla vana, loll ja viriseja?" *Postimees-Extra*, no. 22 (17 June 1995): 3–4;

Maris Balbat, "'Mulle ei meeldi äärmised äärmused,'" *Kultuurileht*, no. 29 (16 August 1996): 8–9.

Bibliographies:

Maie Kalda, ed., *Eesti kirjanduse ajalugu*, volume 5, book 2 (Tallinn: Eesti Raamat, 1991), pp. 477–478;

Oskar Kruus, ed., *Eesti kirjarahva leksikon* (Tallinn: Eesti Raamat, 1995), pp. 631–632.

References:

Irina Belobrovtseva, "Mati Unt na fone rõzhego kota," *Raduga* (March 1996): 72–77;

Luule Epner, "Mati Untin Viro-Euroopan provinssi lännen ja idän välillä," in *Itä ja länsi: Suomen, Viron ja Unkarin kirjallisuus idän ja lännen vaikutuskentässä*, edited by Pekka Lilja (Jyväskylä: Jyväskylän yliopisto, 1994), pp. 96–109;

Ivar Grünthal, "Mati Undi moondumised," *Mana* 53 (1984): 47–49;

Tiit Hennoste, "Mati Unt: Mälestused ja lootused," *Vikerkaar* (December 1993): 60–63;

Ivar Ivask, "Window-Complex and Street-Labyrinth: The Prose of M. Unt and E. Vetemaa," *Lituanus*, 16 (Summer 1970): 29–37;

Maire Jaanus, "Modernism Eestis: Mati Undi proosa," *Vikerkaar* (April 1990): 55–60;

Hasso Krull, "Unt, jäljendamise jäljendaja," *Vikerkaar* (December 1993): 63–68;

Piret Kruuspere, "Mati Undi dramaturgilised tekstid. Tallinna-periood: Empiiriline katse," *Keel ja Kirjandus* (January 1988): 31–36;

Maire J. Kurrik [i.e., Maire Jaanus], "Mati Unt's *Via Regia*: Form and Praxis," *Journal of Baltic Studies*, 8 (Fall 1977): 214–222;

Kurrik, "Tradition and Loss: Mati Unt's *Doomsday*," *Lituanus*, 24 (Summer 1978): 21–25;

Marju Lauristin, "Mati Unt," in *Eesti noori kunstimeistreid*, volume 1, edited by Jaak Allik (Tallinn: Perioodika, 1980), pp. 52–56;

Marika Mikli, "Mati Undi tundelise tegelase teekond," *Keel ja Kirjandus* (July 1977): 385–391;

Jaak Rähesoo, "See maailm ja teised," *Looming* (July 1969): 1086–1093;

Hando Runnel, "Mati Unt ja mood (Close reading)," *Keel ja Kirjandus* (February 1980): 115–120;

Ülo Tonts, "Mati Unt," in *Eesti kirjanduse ajalugu*, volume 5, book 2, edited by Maie Kalda (Tallinn: Eesti Raamat, 1991), pp. 463–478;

Jaan Undusk, "Meie Unt. Kiites ja kahetsedes," *Looming* (January 1985): 958–965;

Mardi Valgemäe, "'Kollase kassi' metamorfoos," *Keel ja Kirjandus* (November 1995): 757–762.

Ojārs Vācietis

(13 November 1933 – 28 November 1983)

Dace Marauska
University of Latvia

and

Kārlis Račevskis
Ohio State University

BOOKS: *Tālu ceļu vējš* (Riga: Latvijas Valsts izdevniecība, 1956);

Ugunīs (Riga: Latvijas Valsts izdevniecība, 1958);

Tās dienas acīm (Riga: Latvijas Valsts izdevniecība, 1959);

Krāces apiet nav laika (Riga: Latvijas Valsts izdevniecība, 1960);

Dziesmas par . . . (Riga: Liesma, 1965);

Viņu adrese–taiga (Riga: Liesma, 1966);

Elpa: Dzejoļi, 1960–1964 (Riga: Liesma, 1966);

Sasiesim astes (Riga: Liesma, 1967);

Dzegužlaiks: Dzejoļi (Riga: Liesma, 1968);

Aiz simtās slāpes: Dzejoļi (Riga: Liesma, 1969);

Melnās ogas (Riga: Liesma, 1971);

Punktiņš, punktiņš, komatiņš (Riga: Liesma, 1971);

Visāda garuma stundas: Dzejoļi (Riga: Liesma, 1974);

Gamma (Riga: Liesma, 1976);

Kabata (Riga: Liesma, 1976);

Antracīts: Dzejoļi (Riga: Liesma, 1978);

Klavierkoncerts (Riga: Liesma, 1978); translated as *Piano Concerto: Poems*, compiled by Laima Vinonen (Moscow: Radiga, 1983);

Zeme: Dzejoļi (Riga: Liesma, 1979);

Zibens pareizrakstība: Dzejoļi (Riga: Liesma, 1980);

Si minors (Riga: Liesma, 1982);

Ar pūces spalvu: Raksti, apceres, intervijas (Riga: Liesma, 1983);

Izlase (Riga: Liesma, 1983);

Astoņi kustoņi (Riga: Liesma, 1984);

Nolemtība: Dzejoļi (Riga: Liesma, 1985);

Partijas piederība (Riga: Liesma, 1985);

Rītam ticēt: Dzeja (Riga: Liesma, 1986);

Ex libris: Dažādu gadu dzejoļi (Riga: Liesma, 1988);

Sveču grāmata (Riga: Liesma, 1988);

Starp dzejoļi un dzejoļi (Riga: Preses nams, 1993);

Putns ar zīda asti (Riga: Likteņstāsti, 1997);

Ojārs Vācietis in 1965

Uz putnu lielceļa (Riga: Zvaigzne ABC, 1998).

Editions and Collections: *Kopoti raksti desmit sējumos*, 7 volumes (Riga: Liesma, 1989–1995);

Es protu noņemt sāpes: Dzejas izlase (Riga: Grāmatu apgāds "Teātra Anekdotes," 1993).

Editions in English: *Selected Poems*, translated by Ruth Speirs (Riga: Liesma, 1979);

"Burning Leaves," "Sunday," "Horse Dream," and "Of Nights," translated by Ināra Cedriņš, in *Contemporary East European Poetry*, edited by Emery George (Ann Arbor, Mich.: Ardis, 1983), pp. 55–58;

"Burning Leaves," translated by Cedriņš; "But I Dare Not Withdraw . . . ," "Didn't You Stop . . . ," and "I Charged Into the Undergrowth . . . ," translated by Speirs; "Autumn Coolness," "Sunday," "Horse Dream," "Aster, Beginning in Peony," "Black Bee," "Don't Cry," "Butterfly Wedding," "Clouds," "Lightning Draws," and "What Childhood Is to Us," translated by Cedriņš, in *Contemporary Latvian Poetry*, edited by Cedriņš (Iowa City: University of Iowa Press, 1984), pp. 129–140.

OTHER: Mikhail Bulgakov, *Meistars un Margarita*, translated by Vācietis (Riga: Liesma, 1979).

Ojārs Vācietis is generally considered one of Latvia's most talented poets of the second half of the twentieth century. He almost single-handedly revived interest in poetry in Latvia following World War II and played a key role in maintaining the vitality of the genre during the decades of Soviet occupation.

Ojārs Vācietis was born on 13 November 1933 in the northeastern county of Trapene to farm workers Oto Vācietis and Berta Vācietis. He acquired at an early age a maturity and self-sufficiency that allowed him to take care of himself as well as his younger brother, Imants. His father's stern and highly principled personality left a profound impression on him and probably accounts for the antagonism he manifested toward both of the great powers—Germany and the Soviet Union—whose struggle enveloped his country. World War II, which robbed his generation of its childhood, left an indelible mark on his psyche and was a theme to which he frequently returned in his writing.

After elementary school in Trapene, Vācietis attended high school in Gaujiene, about twelve miles from his hometown. The nearby river Gauja exerted a powerful attraction on the future poet and became a recurrent motif in his poetry. In school Vācietis excelled in art, choral singing, dramatic recitation, and sports; he also published his first poems at this time. Impressions that he gained in school and through his participation in Communist Party youth organizations contributed to the development of a romanticized view of communism in the budding poet.

Vācietis's first publications attracted the attention of critics and other poets, and he was invited to attend the Young Authors' Seminar in Riga. That experience led him to enroll in the department of Latvian language and literature at the University of Latvia. There he met his future wife, the poet and translator Ludmila Azarova, who was a student in the Russian department.

In 1956 Vācietis published his first book of poems, *Tālu ceļu vējš* (The Wind of Faraway Roads, 1956). While the tone is still declamatory and moralizing, the poetry is a clear departure from the loud pathos, heroic machismo, and flag-draped patriotism that were the norms of the day; it addresses the reader directly, simply, and familiarly.

Also in 1956 Vācietis was elected to the Latvian Writers' Union. That same year he began writing a libretto for an opera, *Pazudušais dēls* (The Prodigal Son), with a score by Romualds Kalsons, based on the 1893 play by the Latvian author Rūdolfs Blaumanis. He never completed the work; after his death his lifelong friend, the motion-picture director Jānis Streičs, finished the libretto, using Vācietis's poetry, and the opera premiered in September 1996.

Deciding that he did not wish to pursue an academic career, Vācietis left the university without a degree in 1958, took the first of a series of jobs in publishing and journalism, and began to write critical reviews. That year he also published his second book of poetry, *Ugunīs* (In Fires). The title symbolizes the inner turmoil and contradictions besetting the Romantic hero; this psychological drama is played out especially vividly in the cycle "Grūtā stundā" (In a Difficult Hour), commemorating the crushing of the 1956 Hungarian Revolution by Soviet tanks. Vācietis's only major work of prose, *Tās dienas acīm* (Through That Day's Eyes), was serialized in 1958 and then published in book form in 1959. Described by Vācietis as "almost a diary," it is a highly personal and emotionally charged account of his high-school years in the late 1940s.

In early 1960 Vācietis and his wife moved into an apartment at 19 Lielā Altonava Street (now O. Vācietis Street), near Māra Lake in a suburb of Riga. They enjoyed taking walks in the rural surroundings, especially the nearby Arkādija Park. Eventually, their favorite activity became what they called walks "no govīm līdz govīm" (from cows to cows), which took them all over Riga. The fresh air was particularly beneficial for Vācietis, who suffered several bouts of pneumonia at this time. The treks, which were accomplished at a brisk pace and covered from six to twelve miles, also served as his "workshop": as he walked, poems took shape in his mind that were written down the following morning at an equally rapid pace. Once the poems were put in writing, Vācietis generally refused to edit or change them in any way.

The poems in the collection *Krāces apiet nav laika* (No Time to Go around the Rapids, 1960) call for honest work and truthfulness and condemn hypocritical, demagogic, and totalitarian thinking. The work elicited a large number of reviews; the majority were by critics of an older generation who attacked the poet for his lack of precision and clarity. Vācietis elaborated on the themes of the collection in "Partijas piederība" (Party Membership), which appeared in the newspaper *Cīņa* (Combat) on 1 January 1963 and was later included in the collection *Elpa* (Breath, 1966), and in the satirical "Potjomkina sādža" (Potemkin's Village), which was published in the magazine *Liesma* (The Flame) in 1965 but did not appear in collections for some years because of the furor it caused among government and party officials.

The poem "Einšteiniāna" (The Einsteinian Epic), published in the 17 November 1962 issue of the newspaper *Literatūra un Māksla* (Literature and Art), marks the beginning of a phase in Vācietis's work that had a profound influence on the development of Latvian literature. Promoting a new perception of reality, the poem calls for a widening and deepening of the artistic experience of time and space in poetry. The poem is notable, as well, for an expressiveness and intellectual power not found in his earlier work. "Einšteiniāna" is a sweeping survey of the contradictions, indifference, apathy, and cowardice that characterize a totalitarian society. The poet recalls past persecutions, citing such victims of ignorance as Giordano Bruno, Galileo, and Federico García Lorca in an effort to forestall the repetition of such mistakes. The poem is addressed to the reason and conscience of his readers, enjoining them to respect the genius of those who can see beyond the limits of the commonplace.

The first reviews of the poem, by authors of Vācietis's generation, were appreciative; but they were followed by a deluge of condemnations. The censure was particularly severe after meetings between the Communist Party leadership and representatives of the artistic and literary communities in Moscow in December 1962 and March 1963. In a similar meeting in Riga the head of the Latvian Communist Party declared some Latvian authors and artists guilty of obscurantism, egotism, and rejecting the ideals of collectivism; Vācietis was singled out for particularly strong condemnation. This diatribe was followed by a publication ban that lasted for several years.

Except for the children's book *Dziesmas par . . .* (Songs about . . . , 1965), Vācietis remained silent until the publication in 1966 of two new

Cover for Vācietis's first book of poems, published in 1956

works: *Viņu adrese–taiga* (Their Address—The Taiga) and *Elpa*. The first is a relatively short collection of poems composed during a visit to Siberia. The distance from his homeland makes the poet turn inward and reconsider his relationship to his society and events around him. Using the poetic figures that are by now trademarks of his art, Vācietis again addresses the question of humanity's place in the world and the problems of truth and responsibility. Although *Elpa* comprises the creative output of six years and is, therefore, varied in subject matter, it is uniform in structure, consisting of a series of dialectical oppositions. In 1967 a selection of the poems in *Elpa*, including "Partijas piederība" and "Einšteiniāna," was presented in a dramatic stage format. Later that year the book was awarded the National Prize of Literature. The waning influence of Moscow, changes in leadership, and Vācietis's growing popularity are all possible factors in his eventual reacceptance.

Vācietis's former home at 19 O. Vācietis Street in suburban Riga. It is now a museum devoted to the author.

In 1968 critics welcomed the collection *Dzeguzlaiks* (The Time of Cuckoos) as a work marking yet another phase in Vācietis's development. They noted that his previous, largely critical outlook had given way to a more harmonious and optimistic perspective sustained by a growing faith in humanity's basic goodness. The work also gives evidence of a thematic and stylistic evolution: the emphasis on the global and universal has been replaced by a concern for the ordinary and the everyday, and inner conflicts have taken the place of struggles with the outside world.

Aiz simtās slāpes (Beyond the Hundredth Thirst, 1969) reinforces these tendencies and demonstrates a lyrical self seeking and finding inner peace in harmony with nature and away from the struggles and strife of social existence. This serenity allows the poet to engage in a meditation on the role of the writer and the artist in the modern world.

The collection *Melnās ogas* (Blackberries, 1971) calls for a new understanding of the world, to be gained through a more intense examination of events and things. The book also develops further the theme of suffering that had appeared in earlier works. The anguish evoked in these poems is not narrow and personal but takes a universal and cosmic

dimension that echoes the drama of George Gordon, Lord Byron's or Mikhail Lermontov's poetic visions. In 1972 Vācietis was honored for his cultural contributions by being named "Latvijas PSR Nopelniem bagātais Kultūras darbinieks" (Latvian SSR's Meritorious Cultural Worker).

The poetry Vācietis wrote during the mid 1970s is so rich and varied that it encompasses all of the topics to be found in the work of any Latvian poet of the time. His stylistic virtuosity is evident in the vast range of tonalities he affects, from lyrical and heroic to satirical and journalistic. *Visāda garuma stundas* (Hours of Every Length, 1974) is largely philosophical in orientation; Vācietis returns here to some of his favorite themes, among which, as the title suggests, the notion of an inner psychological time is of particular interest. The contrast between two opposing attitudes—a love of life and the natural versus a mechanical and utilitarian outlook—structures the collection *Gamma* (Musical Scale, 1976); the ecological issues raised in the volume echo concerns found in the work of other poets of the period. In 1977 Vācietis was awarded the title "Author of the Latvian SSR," a distinction his enormous popularity and his love of his country fully justified. His poetry readings invariably drew full houses, and his books quickly sold out even when the printings reached as high as thirty-three thousand copies.

While the poems in *Gamma* call for a harmonious coexistence with nature, the next collection, *Antracīts* (Anthracite, 1978), voices similar concerns in the context of human relationships, recognizing that interpersonal contact has been trivialized and made shallow by the rapid pace and materialistic concerns of modern life.

In 1979 Vācietis's translation of Mikhail Bulgakov's *The Master and Margarita* was published. The poet noted that he had learned much about the polyphonic quality of poetry from this task and that he found highly instructive the manner in which the novel combines poetry, prose, and drama.

Critics described *Zibens pareizrakstība* (The Orthography of Lightning, 1980) as the embodiment of a people's and an era's conscience, an awakening call that speaks to the souls of all those willing to listen and defines the values that justify human existence. The collection is marked by a harsh and bitter tone that contrasts with the expressions of profound love the poet manifests for his people and his time.

Vācietis's final collection published in his lifetime, *Si minors* (Ti Minor), appeared in 1982. Written in the form of a diary, it talks frankly and openly about its author and includes observations about his daily life as well as meditations on the process of creativity. Although the title, which refers to a minor musical key, suggests a melancholy mood, despair alternates with bursts of energy and the joy of victory in the struggle to find meaning in life.

In addition to his works for adults, Vacietis published several collections of poetry for children. Such compendia as *Dziesmas par . . .*, *Sasiesim astes* (Let's Tie Tails, 1967), *Punktiņš, punktiņš, komātiņš* (Period, Period, Comma, 1971), and *Kabata* (The Pocket, 1976) depict paradoxical, ironic, even absurd situations that valorize family, friendship, and responsibility. Like the poems for grownups, these compositions seek to energize young readers to find out more about the world and about themselves.

Vācietis died on 28 November 1983 and was buried in the cemetery of Carnikava, near Riga, next to the estuary where his beloved Gauja flows into the Baltic Sea. His poetry has been translated into some thirty languages; when he received the PSRS Valsts prēmija, the Soviet Union's most prestigious literary award, in 1982, his works were available in nearly all of the languages of the U.S.S.R.'s constituent nations. Thanks to these translations, he came to be recognized as one of the great Soviet and Eastern European poets of his time. His work and influence enjoy a status comparable to those of Robert Rozhdestvensky, Yevgeny Yevtushenko, and Andrey Voznesensky in Russia, Justinas Marcinkevičius and Algimantas Baltakis in Lithuania, Vitali Korotic and Ivan Drac in Ukraine, Pimen Pacanka in Belarus, and Zdravko Kisjov in Bulgaria.

Bibliography:

M. Garda, ed., *Ojārs Vācietis–50: Pers. bibl. rad.* (Riga: Latvijas PSR Valsts Bibliotēka, 1983).

Biographies:

Ojāra Vācieša Piemiņas grāmata (Riga: Liesma, 1984);

Jānis Plotnieks, *Pērkoņu rātais . . .* (Riga: Plotnieks, 1992);

Ildze Kronta, ed., *Visums, sirds un tāpat . . .* (Riga: Karogs, 1993).

References:

Reinis Admīdiņš, *Dzejas darbdiena* (Riga: Liesma, 1977), pp. 37–84;

Imants Auziņš, *Visas pasaules tapums* (Riga: Liesma, 1979), pp. 16–42, 177–181;

Vizma Belševica, "Nepārprotamība," *Padomju Jaunatne*, 30 November 1982, pp. 17–35;

Māris Čaklais, *Nozagtā gliemežnīca* (Riga: Liesma, 1980), pp. 64–70;

Čaklais, *Saule rakstāmgaldā* (Riga: Liesma, 1975), pp. 65–82;

Viktors Hausmanis, ed., *Latviešu rakstniecība biogrāfijās* (Riga: Latvijas Enciklopēdija, 1992), pp. 335–336;

Valdis Ķikāns, *Kur cilvēks sācies* (Riga: Liesma, 1974);

Ķikāns, *Tevī kāpj mīļums . . .* (Riga: Liesma, 1989);

Ildze Kronta, *Gadi. Darbi. Personības* (Riga: Liesma, 1986), pp. 305–340;

Anda Kubuliņa, *Kontūras* (Riga: Liesma, 1981), pp. 85–101;

Jānis Peters, *Kalējs kala debesīs . . .* (Riga: Liesma, 1981), pp. 132–139;

Mārtiņš Poišs, "Es esmu tas, kurš visu var," *Varavīksne* (1969): 166–194;

Vitolds Valeinis, *Latviešu lirikas vēsture* (Riga: Zvaigzne, 1979), pp. 305–332.

Papers:

Ojārs Vācietis's home in Riga, which is now a museum, houses many of his manuscripts and papers.

Ludvík Vaculík

(23 July 1926 –   )

Jan Čulík
University of Glasgow

BOOKS: *Na farmě mládeže: Črta ze státního statku*
(Prague: Státní nakladatelství politické literatury, 1958);
Rušný dům (Prague: Československý spisovatel, 1963);
Vidět svět novýma očima, edited by Josef Branžovský (Prague: Studijní ústav Československého rozhlasa, 1965);
Sekyra (Prague: Československý spisovatel, 1966); translated by Marian Šling as *The Axe* (London: Deutsch, 1973; New York: Harper & Row, 1973);
Morčata (Prague: Edice Petlice [samizdat], 1973; Toronto: Sixty-Eight Publishers, 1977; Prague: Československý spisovatel, 1991); translated by Káča Poláčková as *The Guinea Pigs: A Novel* (New York: Third Press, 1973);
Český snář (Prague: Edice Petlice [samizdat], 1981; Toronto: Sixty-Eight Publishers, 1983; Brno: Atlantis, 1990); excerpts translated by Michael Henry Heim as *A Czech Dreambook*, in *Cross Currents: A Yearbook of Central European Culture*, 3 (1984): 71–86;
Jaro je tady. Fejetony z let 1981–1987 (Prague: Edice Petlice [samizdat], 1981; Cologne: Index, 1988; Prague: Mladá fronta, 1990);
Milí spolužáci! volume 1, *Kniha indiánská* (Prague: [samizdat] Edice Petlice, 1981; Cologne: Index, 1986); volume 2, *Kniha dělnická* (Prague: [samizdat] Edice Petlice, 1986; Cologne: Index, 1986); both volumes republished, together with volume 3, *Kniha studentská*, as *Milí spolužáci! Výbor písemných prací 1939–1979* (Prague: Mladá fronta, 1995);
Nové vlastenecké písně Karla Havlíčka Borovského (Prague: Edice Petlice [samizdat], 1989; Prague: Scéna, 1990);
Srpnový rok. Fejetony z let 1988–1989 (Prague: Mladá fronta, 1990);
Stará dáma se baví (Prague: Lidové noviny, 1991);
Jak se dělá chlapec (Brno: Atlantis, 1993);

Ludvík Vaculík (photograph by Friedrich Rentch; from the dust jacket for The Axe, *1973)*

Nad jezerem škaredě hrát: Výbor z publicistiky 1990–1995, edited by Jaromír Slomek (Prague: Ivo Železný, 1996);
Nepaměti (1969–1972) (Prague: Mladá fronta, 1998).
Editions in English: "A Spokesman Funeral," "Genie," "How Bad News Turned Better," "Spring is Here," and "Sunspots," translated by Káča Poláčková, and "The First of May," translated by W. E. Harkins, in *The Writing on the Wall: An Anthology of Contemporary Czech Literature*, edited by Peter Kussi and Antonín J. Liehm (Princeton: Karz-Cohl, 1983), pp. 220–252;

A Cup of Coffee with My Interrogator: The Prague Chronicles of Ludvík Vaculík, translated by George Theiner (London: Readers International, 1987).

OTHER: Speech at the June 1967 Congress of Czechoslovak Writers, in *Čtvrtý sjezd Svazu československých spisovatelů, Prague 27.–29. června 1967. Protokol* (Prague: Československý spisovatel, 1968), pp. 141–151; published separately as *The Relations between Citizen and Power: Contribution at the Czechoslovak Writers' Conference 1967* (London: Liberal International, British Group, 1968);

"Pokus pro čtrnáct milionů," in *O čem bych psal, kdybych měl kam: (Tak pišu vám, pane Hrabal!)*, compiled by Vaculík (Prague: [samizdat], 1974), pp. 80–89;

"Dopis Ludvika Vaculíka generálnímu tajmníkovi OSN," in *Hlasy z domova 1975*, edited by Adof Mueller (Cologne: Index, 1976), pp. 63–68;

"O třech pachatelích," in *Die Zauberwurzel* (Munich: Blanvalet, 1978), pp. 172–194; published in Czech as *Uzel pohádek*, edited by Ivan Klíma (Prague: Lidové noviny, 1991), pp. 77–88;

Čára na zdi. Československé fejetony 1975–76, edited with contributions by Vaculík (Cologne: Index, 1977; Prague: Novinář, 1990);

Hodina naděje. Almanach české literatury 1968–1978, edited with contributions by Vaculík, Jiří Gruša, Milan Uhde, and Jan Lopatka (Prague [samizdat], 1978; Toronto: Sixty-Eight Publishers, 1980);

Hlasy nad rukopisem Vaculíkova Českého snáře, edited by Vaculík (Prague [samizdat], 1981);

Sólo pro psací stroj. Československý fejeton 1976–1979, edited, with contributions by Vaculík (Cologne: Index, 1984);

. . . a co si o tom myslíte vy? edited by Lenka Procházková (Munich: Poezie mimo Domov, 1986), pp. 91–92;

Jaro 1968: Čítanka pro děti a mládež, contributions by Vaculík (Cologne: Index, 1988);

Benefice, Rozhovor přes oceán, edited by Karel Hvížd'ala and Zdena Salivarová (Toronto: Sixty-Eight Publishers, 1990), pp. 263–271.

Ludvík Vaculík played a major role in the life of postwar Czechoslovakia as a journalist and a writer. Starting out as an idealistic communist, he helped to promote socialism in his country in the 1950s. As an energetic and active journalist, he gradually discovered the limitations of the political system he had helped to build and started rebelling against it. In the 1960s Vaculík was an important member of the movement of intellectuals and writers who tried to reform the communist system by reintroducing democracy to Czechoslovak public life.

The Warsaw Pact armies invaded Czechoslovakia in August 1968. During the two decades of the postinvasion political clampdown in the 1970s and the 1980s, Vaculík became a banned writer and was regarded as a dangerous subversive and a "reactionary." In the 1960s Vaculík became a major independent writer and journalist and in the early 1970s an important organizer of samizdat publishing. He took an active part in the defense of human rights in Czechoslovakia during the 1970s and 1980s. Since the fall of communism he has provided commentaries on Czech public life, mostly in newspaper articles and on radio.

Ludvík Vaculík was born on 23 July 1926 to Anna (née Lysáčková) and Martin Vaculík, a carpenter in the Moravian village of Brumov (near the town of Valašské Klobouky), in an area where a relatively strong local dialect was spoken. This background has given Vaculík's writing a special idiosyncratic quality: the language of his prose sometimes differs slightly from standard literary Czech. Vaculík has always been able to use his linguistic background as a point of departure when examining the roots of the Czech language. He has produced insights by creating linguistic paradoxes, often using seemingly illogical statements that lead to revelations because they illuminate, at a stroke, those aspects of human communication that are normally hidden by conventional speech.

Vaculík attended *obecná škola* (elementary school) and three years of *měšťanská škola* (junior technical school) in Brumov; he attended the fourth and final year of *měšťanská škola* in Valašské Klobouky. Vaculík's father was often unemployed in the period between the two world wars and was forced to seek employment abroad. For a time he worked in Persia. After World War II and the victory of communism in Czechoslovakia in 1968, Vaculík's father became a local Communist Party official.

After completing school Vaculík became one of the "Young Men" who worked for Tomáš Baťa, an early American-style entrepreneur in interwar Czechoslovakia. Baťa was a shoe manufacturer who pioneered conveyor-belt work and other modern methods of management in his large industrial shoemaking complex in Zlín, southern Moravia. Baťa's works were, in effect, a state within a state in Czechoslovakia. For instance, employees were at least partially paid in special Baťa coupons, which they could use to buy "cheap and cheerful" products from Baťa's own shops. Baťa also provided inexpensive housing for his employees and training for selected members of the younger generation. Vaculík became one of the "Young Men" in Baťova škola práce (Baťa's School of Labor). In the volumes of his diaries, *Milí spolužáci!* (My Dear Fellow Pupils! 1981, 1986, 1995), he writes at some length about the ethos in the Baťa environment, which influenced him deeply at the outset of life. Vaculík worked in Baťa's shoeworks in Zlín and in Zruč nad Sázavou from 1941 to 1946. Concurrently he studied at a specialized two-year shoemakers' school from 1941 to 1943 and a foreign-trade business academy from 1944 to 1946.

In 1946 Vaculík began studying in the political and journalism department at Vysoká škola politická a sociální v Praze (The School of Political and Social Sciences in Prague), from which he graduated in 1950. Toward the end of his studies and for some time afterward he worked as an instructor at boarding schools for the apprentices of Sdružené bavlnářské závody (Joint Cotton Works) in Benešov nad Ploučnicí (from 1948 to 1949) and at Československé závody těžkého strojírenství (Czechoslovak Heavy Engineering Works) in Prague (from 1950 to 1951). He used these experiences in writing his first novel, *Rušný dům* (A Busy House, 1963). In line with the prevailing fashion of the day, *Rušný dům* was an attempt to provide an ordinary, unpretentious account of everyday life. At the same time, the work criticized some insensitive communist practices in education and training for young people.

Vaculík's main profession in the 1950s and the 1960s was that of a journalist and a social commentator. His literary work from all periods is substantially influenced by his journalistic practice. Vaculík's first literary articles were published in the magazines *Květen* (May) and *Květy* (Blossoms) in the middle of the 1950s. After completing his two-year military service, Vaculík first worked as an editor in the political literature department of the Rudé právo (Red Rights) publishing house from 1953 to 1957 and then on the staff of a farming weekly, *Beseda venkovské rodiny* (Discussion within a Country Family) from 1957 to 1958. In 1959 he began working as a journalist for the youth programs of the state-run Czechoslovak Radio and wrote several features about the life of teenagers for radio series such as *Mikrofon mladých* (The Young Microphone) and *Včera mi bylo patnáct* (I Was Fifteen Yesterday). As a journalist, he increasingly found areas that were out of bounds, even for a communist. These programs were designed to tackle issues associated with the political and moral upbringing of the young peo-

ple. Vaculík and his colleagues created a new genre of "problem programming"—radio programs that dealt with difficult and controversial issues. These programs were often highly praised and rewarded by the authorities, but sometimes their authors were punished for making them. Thus in 1964, in the evening of the same day when Vaculík officially received a state decoration "For Outstanding Achievement," a program of his was broadcast for which Vaculík was suspended from Czechslovask Radio and sent to work in a factory for a month as a punishment.

In the 1960s Vaculík published many articles in the increasingly liberal and prodemocratic periodicals such as *Host do domu* (A Guest in the House), *Orientace* (Orientation), and *Filmové a televizní noviny* (The Film and TV Gazette). In September 1965 he joined the staff of what was becoming a rather outspoken cultural and political weekly, *Literární noviny* (Literary Newspaper), published by the Czechoslovak Writers' Union. In the second half of the 1960s *Literární noviny* became an important platform for liberal intellectuals who pushed for political reform. After the open conflict between Czechoslovak writers and intellectuals and the Communist Party leadership, which came to a head during the rebellious Fourth Congress of Czechoslovak Writers in June 1967 (where Vaculík, Václav Havel, and Milan Kundera gave important and hard-hitting speeches), *Literární noviny* was closed down by the communist authorities.

Vaculík gave a courageous speech at the Congress. He expressed his frustration over the fact that although he had hoped to create a society of free individuals, he and his fellow citizens still considered themselves subjugated: "Although we have caught the bull by the horns and we are holding him, somebody is still kicking our backsides and there seems to be no end to it." In Vaculík's view, basic democratic procedures cannot be regarded either as "communist" or "capitalist"; they are simply needed in any society if people are not to be enslaved by absolutist rule.

In 1966 Vaculík published an experimental novel, *Sekyra* (1966; translated as *The Axe*, 1973), which was at the time hailed as one of the most important works of the period, on a par with Kundera's *Žert* (1967; translated as *The Joke*, 1969; complete version translated as *The Joke*, 1982) and Josef Škvorecký's *Zbabělci* (1958; translated as *The Cowards*, 1970). *Sekyra* is a novel of disillusionment, a major work that helped demythologize the communist regime.

Sekyra is openly autobiographical. Although experimental and marked by occasional use of Moravian dialect, it is influenced by journalistic practice. Everything takes place in the narrator's mind simultaneously as he examines his life, the lives of those nearest to him, and the state of his society, from the vantage point of a midlife crisis. Following the idealism of his father, a carpenter who suffered unemployment and had to seek work abroad in Persia in the interwar period, the narrator becomes an ardent communist after World War II, trying to create a communist utopia. Gradually, he discovers that this vision is impossible, that his and his father's idealistic efforts are in vain, that the communist ideology is a lifeless construct that enslaves individuals and is used by unscrupulous people for personal gain. The novel looks for a way out of the traumatic realization that the enthusiastic supporters of the communist dream had wasted almost twenty years of their lives. But unlike Ludvík Jahn, the protagonist of *Žert,* the hero of *Sekyra* is never crushed by the realization that all that he had believed in had turned to dust. The hero's midlife crisis serves as a spur to further energetic activity. As scholar Aleš Haman remarked in *Plamen* (The Flame) in 1968, Vaculík's hero is in the very center of social and political developments in his own country, yet he always remains a proud outsider. When the narrator looks for the roots of his own identity, he finds a certain solace in his return to the traditions of his native, sturdy, and idiosyncratic Moravian region.

During the unprecedented period of freedom in 1968 *Literární noviny* resumed publication, appearing in February under a slightly changed name, *Literární listy* (The Literary Gazette). During the 1968 Prague Spring, *Literární listy* became a major voice of political reform, reaching a print run of three hundred thousand copies in June 1968. At that time Vaculík wrote a political manifesto, "Dva tisíce slov" (Two Thousand Words), which was simultaneously published by *Literární listy* (27 June 1968) and by several daily newspapers and was quickly signed by many supporters of political liberalization, by well-known individuals as well as ordinary people. Until the publication of "Dva tisíce slov," the liberal reforms were being carried out in Czechoslovakia by reformist communists. Noncommunists were regarded as second-class citizens: communists had assumed the right to make all the political decisions in the country because they felt that by embracing Marxist philosophy they had an infallible key to human development, and they saw themselves as the avant-garde of society. Vaculík's

manifesto was different because it called on ordinary people to take matters into their own hands, regardless of what communist rulers might think:

> Let us demand that the meetings of the local authority councils be open to the public. Let us set up our own civic committees in order to deal with problems that nobody wants to touch. It is simple: a few people will get together, they will elect a chairperson, they will take proper minutes, they will publish what they have found, they will demand a solution, they will not be intimidated.

There was a danger that popular reforms might far exceed the moderate changes envisaged by the reformist-minded Communist Party rulers, especially since many of the communist reformers came to be seduced by the spirit of general euphoria, going along with the reforms, relishing the hitherto unknown pleasures of suddenly finding themselves at the top of the opinion polls. But the rulers of the Soviet Union found the demand that ordinary people in Czechoslovakia should take matters into their own hands deeply disconcerting. "Dva tisíce slov" was quoted by the Russian leaders to the Czechoslovak Communist leadership as evidence of "subversion" and "counterrevolution" in Czechoslovakia. One of the main reasons the Warsaw Pact armies invaded Czechoslovakia on 21 August 1968 was to put a stop to the reforms.

The editors of *Literární listy* had planned to launch a separate daily newspaper, *Lidové noviny* (The People's Newspaper), wishing to resume the tradition of the interwar political daily that had included the writer Karel Čapek among its staff. As a result of the Warsaw Pact invasion, all these plans had to be scrapped. *Literární listy* resumed publication in the autumn of 1968 under a shortened title, *Listy* (The Gazette), using the remaining few months of relative freedom to continue disseminating reformist ideas. The newspaper was finally closed down in the spring of 1969, and the editorial staff was disbanded.

The postinvasion regime took firm root in Czechoslovakia from early 1970 onward. It was a period of hysteria and intolerance. Screening interviews, to which all adult citizens in the country were subjected, were carried out in all places of work. Individuals associated with the previous liberal regime (or people who refused to praise the Warsaw Pact invasion as an instance of "fraternal help" by other communist countries against "counterrevolution") lost their jobs. The whole reformist intellectual elite of the 1960s was turned into nonpersons. Some four hundred Czech and Slovak authors were

Dust jacket for the English translation (1973) of Vaculík's Kafkaesque novel Morčata *(1973), about the employees of a mysterious bank*

Czech or in translation by publishers in the West. In the 1970s and 1980s Vaculík was continually harassed by the communist authorities for his samizdat publishing and frequently interrogated by the communist secret police. In 1977 Vaculík was one of the first signatories of the human rights manifesto Charta (Charter) 77, which demanded that the Czech communist government should observe the international covenants on human rights that it had signed. Signatories of the Charter 77 manifesto were seriously persecuted by the communist authorities and isolated from the rest of Czechoslovak society by a wall of fear.

In the 1970s and 1980s Vaculík continued his journalism in samizdat. His feuilletons, terse literary pieces of some one thousand words in length, commenting on "how we live now," circulated in typewritten copies among the informed public and were often reprinted by Czech emigré periodicals such as *Proměny* (Metamorphoses) in New York, *Svědectví* (Testimony) in Paris, and *Listy* in Rome. In the 1980s Vaculík was also a frequent contributor to the samizdat literary monthly *Obsah* (Contents). All of his longer works written in these two decades were first published in samizdat.

In 1973 Edice Petlice brought out a samizdat edition of Vaculík's Kafkaesque novel *Morčata* (translated as *The Guinea Pigs: A Novel*, 1973). The novel, which has been translated into eleven languages, takes place in a phantasmagoric Czechoslovakia, distantly reminiscent of the oppressive atmosphere of Czechoslovakia in the 1970s. Its hero is a bank clerk, employed in a strange financial institution in the center of Prague. The task of the employees of this bank is to count banknotes and register their numbers. The clerks are regularly searched every day at the end of their work shifts to make sure that they are not smuggling any money out of the bank. Smuggled money that is confiscated never returns into circulation and is one of the unsolved mysteries of the novel: is it an assault on the national economy of the country? An old bank specialist, who still remembers the "capitalist" banking system, knows something about it but will not tell. The bank is enveloped in an atmosphere of fear. Everything is run mysteriously and impersonally from the background.

On the advice of one of his colleagues, the protagonist, a rather authoritarian father of two boys, buys them several guinea pigs. Thus the novel acquires a new, disconcerting dimension. The timid and passive animals fascinate the bank clerk. In an attempt to find out how they might react, he starts subjecting them (often in the middle of the night)

banned. Many thousands of individuals were fired from jobs in the media, in industry, in diplomatic service, and in education.

Some of the banned reformist authors continued to meet informally and exchange their now-unpublishable literary texts. Gradually, an independent, alternative, samizdat culture developed from these meetings. In the precomputer age, samizdat publishing (the word is of Russian origin, meaning "self-publication") was produced on the typewriter. Typists secretly copied banned books in the privacy of their homes, producing up to sixteen carbon copies each time. These typed copies on thin copying paper were then bound and circulated.

Vaculík became one of the main organizers of samizdat publishing in the 1970s. In 1973 he founded one of the most important samizdat publication series, Edice Petlice (The Padlock Series), which brought out some four hundred original titles before the fall of communism in 1989. Many of these titles were printed in proper book form in

to various experiments. Many of these experiments are tantamount to torture. The protagonist fully succumbs to his sadistic instincts, and some other employees of the mysterious bank do the same. It turns out that the relationship between the guinea pigs and the bank clerk is practically the same as the relationship between the bank clerk and the impersonal social system in which he lives; therefore, the protagonist's limited ability to understand his environment parallels that of the guinea pig.

Český snář (1981; excerpts translated as *A Czech Dreambook,* 1984) is another experimental work, on the borderline between fiction and journalism. It is a voluminous, highly readable, diary-like semi-autobiographical account of the life of Vaculík and the community of his dissident friends from 22 January 1979 to 2 February 1980. This community is a helpless one, a ghetto under siege, isolated from the rest of society and continually harassed by the police. Vaculík's testimony of life in the dissident ghetto is authentic; yet, it is not 100 percent documentary: the experimental text veers into fiction, memory, and essayistic comment. It is difficult to say how much of the work is documentary and how much is fiction. The text oscillates between a factual record and a fictional "dream." It relies on the tension that arises from the intertwining of the two genres. As Sylvie Richterová pointed out in *Svědectví* (1983–1984), the smaller the shift between fact and fiction, the greater the impression that reality itself, as described in the work, is a fantasy. Richterová also argues that the identity of man is the main theme of *Český snář:* the narrator's ego is realized on various levels of the subjective and objective consciousness. Vaculík says, "I do not pretend that my ideas are the truth about what I think: they are the truth about my mind." The publication of *Český snář* (which has also been translated in four languages) produced a lively debate among Czech dissidents at the time: some of them felt that Vaculík had betrayed too much about the inner workings of the dissident community to the secret police.

At the beginning of *Český snář* Vaculík returns to his diaries from his childhood and student years and comes to the conclusion that "I have written everything that is important." He feels that the diaries include the most important ideas and experiences relating to his life. The three volumes of *Milí spolužáci! Kniha indiánská* (The Red Indian Book, 1981), *Kniha dělnická* (A Worker's Book, 1986), and *Kniha studentská* (A Student's Book, 1995)—seem primarily a documentary record of the author's experiences from his younger years. These diaries also sit uneasily on the borderline

between fiction and fact, although this time the factual line is probably much stronger than in Vaculík's earlier works. The first volume deals with the author's childhood during the German occupation at the time of World War II—the atmosphere does not differ much from the post-1968 period of subjugation. The author ignores politics, as though he had subconsciously felt, even as a boy and a young man, that one can get nearest to the essence of life if one deals with ordinary, everyday events: what the countryside looked like around his village, who his friends were, whom the boys fought with, where they took their goats to pasture. The later volumes include several insightful contemplations on general themes such as friendship, Czech identity, what one may or may not sacrifice when building a career, nationalism, and God.

The novel *Jak se dělá chlapec* (How a Boy is Made, 1993) is a literary polemic with the work *Smolná kniha* (The Black Book, 1991) by Lenka Procházková, with whom Vaculík lived for several years in the 1980s after temporarily leaving his wife, Marie (née Komárková). In *Smolná kniha* Procházková records the end of her relationship with Vaculík; in *Jak se dělá chlapec,* which originated before Procházkova's book was published, Vaculík reacts to the catastrophic end of this relationship in his own way, maps out his attempts to keep in contact with his son, who was born of this union, and is quite deeply traumatized by the finite nature of human existence.

Since the 1960s onward Vaculík has written feuilletons commenting on topical issues of Czech social and political life. These works have been gathered in the volumes *Jaro je tady* (Spring is Here, 1981), *Srpnový rok* (A Year like August, 1990), *Stará dáma se baví* (The Old Lady is Enjoying Herself, 1991), and *Nad jezerem škaredě hrát* (Playing Horribly above the Lake, 1996). In the 1970s and 1980s Vaculík's feuilletons were sharply critical of the post-1968 communist regime. Generally though, these texts are not overtly political: they are short, personal contemplations on current issues, written from the point of view of common sense. Recurringly, the natural order of things is for Vaculík an anchor and a touchstone by which to measure the human concerns of the day.

Starting his analysis of Czech society as a journalist, Ludvík Vaculík has made an important social and literary contribution to the life of his country in the second half of the twentieth centry, not only as a writer and commentator but also as a political and cultural organizer. His work is closely connected with the effort of the Czechs to emancipate themselves from totalitarian oppression, but its meaning reaches beyond politics: it is an original testimony to the condition of modern man.

Letters:
Vaculík and Ivan Kadlečík, *Poco rubato* (Bratislava: F. R. & G., 1994).

Interviews:
Antonín J. Liehm, "Ludvík Vaculík," translated by Peter Kussi, in Liehm's *The Politics of Culture* (New York: Grove Press, 1972), pp. 183–201; Czech version published in Liehm's *Generace* (Index: Cologne, 1988), pp. 91–108;

Friedrich Rentsch, "Rozhovor s Ludvíkem Vaculíkem," *Listy*, no. 2 (1973): 32–36;

Jiří Lederer, *České rozhovory* (Cologne: Index, 1979), pp. 5–22;

Jana Červenková, "Jak se dělá Vaculík," *Nové knihy*, no. 13 (1995): 10;

Michael Špirit, "V životě jsem hrdinou nebyl, tak jsem si to aspoň zapisoval," *Kritická příloha Revolver Revue*, 1 (1995): 44–50; published in English as "Postscript: A Discussion with Ludvík Vaculík," *Trafika: An International Literary Review*, no. 3 (Summer 1994): 71–75.

References:
František Benhardt, "Dřevo má být ze dřeva," *Tvorba*, no. 27 (1991): 8–9;

Václav Černý, "Dva romány téměř veliké," in his *Tvorba a osobnost I* (Prague: Odeon, 1992), pp. 836–848;

Josef Chuchma, "Fejetonový fenomén Vaculík," *Tvar*, no. 4 (1990): 14;

Aleš Haman, "Romanopisci v půli cesty na strom," *Plamen*, 10, no. 7 (1968): 28–32;

Karel Hrubý, ed., "Diskuse o Vaculíkově *Snáři*," *Proměny*, 22, no. 2 (1985): 73–85;

Pavel Janoušek, "Román proti románu: Vaculík v. Procházková" in *Literatura v literatuře: Sborník referátů z literárněvědné konference 37. Bezručovy Opavy 13.–14.9. 1994*, edited by Daniela Hodrová (Prague & Opava: Ústav pro českou literaturu/Slezská univerzita, 1995), pp. 137–143;

Janoušek, "Vaculíkova smolná nesmrtelnost," *Tvar*, no. 5 (1994): 1;

Milan Jungmann, "Dva romány z doby přechodu," in his *Obléhání Tróje: Literární kritiky a listy ze zápisníku z let 1958–1968* (Prague: Československý spisovatel, 1969), pp. 151–165;

Vladimír Karfík, "Deník jako román," *Česká literatura*, 38 (1990): 255–266;

Ivan Klíma, "*Žert* a *Sekyra*," *Orientace*, 2 (1967): no. 1, pp. 84–90; no. 2, pp. 71–76;

Antonín J. Liehm, "Ludvík Vaculík and his novel *The Axe*," in *Czech Literature since 1956: A Symposium*, edited by William E. Harkins and Paul I. Trenky (New York: Bohemica, 1980), pp. 91–102;

Jan Lopatka, "Předpoklady tvorby," in his *Předpoklady tvorby: Výběr kritických článků a recenzí z let 1965–1969* (Prague: Československý spisovatel, 1991), pp. 57–62;

Jan Lukeš, "Jaký režim jsem pomáhal stvořit," *Literární noviny*, no. 27 (1995): 7;

Kees Mercks, "The Semantic Gesture in the Guinea Pigs," in *Vozmi na radosť: To Honour Jeanne von der Eng-Liedmeier* (Amsterdam, 1980), pp. 309–322;

Jiří Opelík, "Hromádka nových českých románů," in his *Nenáviděné řemeslo: výbor z kritik 1957–1968* (Prague: Československý spisovatel, 1969), pp. 186–189;

Jiří Pechar, "Ještě k Vaculíkovým *Morčatům*," *Literární noviny*, no. 6 (1992): 5;

Pechar, "Pokračování experimentu," *Literární noviny*, no. 6 (1994): 6;

Pechar, "Překvapivý Ludvík Vaculík," "Vaculíkovy básně v próze," and "Vaculíkův další experiment," in his *Nad knihami a rukopisy* (Prague: Torst, 1996), pp. 75–99, 223–242;

Pechar, "Vaculíkova konfrontace s vlastní minulostí," *Literární noviny*, no. 27 (1995): 6–7;

Sylvie Richterová, "Co psát a k čemu to vést," in her *Slova a ticho* (Munich: Arkýř, 1986), pp. 106–125;

Richterová, "Milí spolužáci," in *Svědectví*, 20, no. 80 (1987): 937–939;

Vladimír Svatoň, "*Český snář*–deník nebo román?" *Tvar*, no. 30 (1991): 5–6;

Michael Špirit, "Vaculíkova nelítostná analýza," *Kritický sborník*, no. 4 (1994): 68–70;

Milan Suchomel, "Čas románu," in his *Literatura z času krize. Šest pohledů na českou prózu 1958–1967* (Brno: Atlantis, 1992), pp. 134–139;

Josef Vohryzek, "*Morčata*," *Literární noviny*, no. 47 (1991): 4;

Vohryzek, "*Morčata* do třetice," *Literární noviny*, no. 10 (1992): 4;

Vohryzek, "Problematická spolehlivost světa," *Respekt*, no. 17 (1994): 15;

Miloslav Žilina, "Svět z Brumova: Brumovské vzpomínky," *Kritická příloha Revolver Revue*, no. 3 (1995): 44–51.

Judita Vaičiūnaitė

(12 July 1937 –   )

Indrė Žekevičiūtė-Žakevičienė
Kaunas Vytautas Magnus University

BOOKS: *Pavasario akvarelės* (Vilnius: Valstybinė grožinės literatūros leidykla, 1960);
Kaip žalias vynas (Vilnius: Valstybinė grožinės literatūros leidykla, 1962);
Per saulėtą gaublį (Vilnius: Vaga, 1964);
Vėtrungės (Vilnius: Vaga, 1966);
Po šiaurės herbais (Vilnius: Vaga, 1968);
Pakartojimai (Vilnius: Vaga, 1971);
Spalvoti piešiniai (Vilnius: Vaga, 1971);
Klajoklė saulė (Vilnius: Vaga, 1974);
Balkonas penktame aukšte (Vilnius: Vaga, 1976);
Neužmirštuolių mėnesį (Vilnius: Vaga, 1977);
Mėnulio gėlė (Vilnius: Vaga, 1979);
Pavasario fleita (Vilnius: Vaga, 1980);
Šaligatvio pienės (Vilnius: Vaga, 1980);
Karuselės elnias (Vilnius: Vaga, 1981);
Smuikas (Vilnius: Vaga, 1984);
Nemigos aitvaras (Vilnius: Vaga, 1985);
Žiemos lietus (Vilnius: Vaga, 1987);
Šešėlių laikrodis (Vilnius: Vaga, 1990);
Gatvės laivas (Vilnius: Vaga, 1991);
Pilkas šiaurės namas (Vilnius: Vaga, 1994);
Žemynos vainikai (Vilnius: Vaga, 1995);
Vaikystės veidrody (Vilnius: Baltos lankos, 1996);
Kai skleidžiasi papirusas (Kaunas: Orientas, 1997);
Seno paveikslo šviesa (Vilnius: Vaga, 1998).

Editions in English: "Twenty Million," "Circe," "Calypso," "Nausicaa," "Penelope," "Museum Street," translated by Jonas Zdanys, in *Selected Post-War Lithuanian Poetry,* edited by Zdanys (New York: Manyland Books, 1978), pp. 264–277;
"Nausicaa" and "Penelope," translated by Irene Pogoželskye Suboczewski; "Botticelli," translated by M. G. Slavėnas; and "Museum Street," translated by Zdanys, in *Contemporary East European Poetry,* edited by Emery George (Ann Arbor, Mich.: Ardis, 1983), pp. 83–85;
"Juodkrantė (The Black Shore)," translated by Rimvydas Šilbajoris, in *Shifting Borders: East European Poetries of the Eighties,* edited by Walter

Judita Vaičiūnaitė

Cummins (Rutherford, N.J.: Fairleigh Dickinson University Press, 1993), p. 123;
Selected Poems of Judita Vaičiūnaitė in Lithuanian and English: Fire Put Out by Fire, translated by Viktoria Skrupskelis and Stuart Friebert (Lewiston, N.Y.: Edwin Mellen Press, 1996).

PLAY PRODUCTIONS: *Skersgatvio pasaka,* Kaunas, Lithuanian Youth Theater, 1972;
Klouno koncertas, Vilnius, "Lėlė" Theater, 1974;
Mėnulio gėlė, Lithuanian Youth Theater, 1975.

OTHER: "Judita Vaičiūnaitė," in *Tarybinės lietuvių autobiografijos,* edited by Kazys Ambrasas and others, volume 2, (Vilnius: Vaga, 1989), pp. 707–709.

TRANSLATIONS: Semyon Kirsanov, *Poezija* (Vilnius: Valstybinė grožinės literatūros leidykla, 1963);

Anna Achmatova, *Poezija* (Vilnius: Vaga, 1964);

Lewis Carroll, *Alisa veidrodžių karalystėje* (Vilnius: Vaga, 1965);

Giorgi Leonidzė, *Poezija* (Vilnius: Vaga, 1966);

Frantisek Hrubin, *Poezija* (Vilnius: Vaga, 1968);

S. Mogilevskaja, *Violančelė Santa Tereza* (Vilnius: Vaga, 1973);

Vladislav Krapivin, *Pažvelk į tą žvaigždę* (Vilnius: Vaga, 1976);

O. Bergolo, *Blokados kregždė* (Vilnius: Vaga, 1979);

Desanka Maksimovič, *Nebėra daugiau laiko* (Vilnius: Vaga, 1983).

Judita Vaičiūnaitė emerged in the latter half of the twentieth century as one of Lithuania's most prominent women poets. Filled with vibrant personal reflections, her poetry expresses the complicated structure and evolution of human emotions. Free from the ideological thinking and declarative intonations so prevalent in postwar Lithuanian poetry, Vaičiūnaitė's work explores a broad spectrum of thematic concerns ranging from erotic love to the complexities of urban existence. The main characteristics of her poetry include explorations of femininity, shifting emotional attitudes, and descriptions of physical sensations. Her poetry challenged traditional Lithuanian lyricism through its impetus toward spontaneous dynamics, visual perception, and fragmentary composition.

Judita Vaičiūnaitė was born on 12 July 1937 in Kaunas. Her father, a doctor, and her mother, a nurse, met while working together in Kaunas. Her father was affiliated with several neurological clinics in Riga, Helsinki, Karaliaučius, Berlin, Munich, Vienna, Prague, and Milan, and was well known; in an autobiographical sketch published in 1989 Vaičiūnaitė remembers her parents as always being dressed "in white doctor's smocks." She also recalls the many hours her mother spent telling Vaičiūnaitė and her younger sister various tales and legends about their relatives. Her mother's tales created a panoramic view of the family, their travels, and her love and longing to return to Lithuania. Vaičiūnaitė remembers this childhood folklore with a nostalgia for the "unknown towns, streets under ancient titles, yards near the factories, and interiors of flats," and she expressed to Viktorija Daujotytė in 1992 how the "clothes of her childhood, her godfa-

ther and godmother, the Germans, Polish schools, Russian and Ukrainian playmates" remained vivid memories throughout her life.

Raised in a well-educated family, Vaičiūnaitė early in life developed agile associative thinking and rather refined aesthetic sensitivities. In the 1989 sketch she recalls the atmosphere of her childhood as both joyful and stimulating, "where everybody aspired to something more than everyday life." Vaičiūnaitė's close relationship with her younger sister molded much of her childhood years. They shared dreams, fantasies, and childhood aspirations. Indeed, her sister was her closest friend, and Vaičiūnaitė later commented, "we loved each other as twins."

In 1954 Vaičiūnaitė enrolled at Vilnius University, where she studied Lithuanian language and literature. Two years later, while still a student, she began publishing her poems in youth newspapers and magazines. She received her degree in 1959 and began working in the editorial office of the cultural magazine *Literatūra ir menas* (Literature and Art). In 1960 her first book of poetry appeared under the title *Pavasario akvarelės* (Watercolors of Spring). In her search for precise artistic words to express complicated feelings and sensations, Vaičiūnaitė delved into the sphere of cultural symbolism. In *Pavasario akvarelės* Vaičiūnaitė's open, melodious lyricism is reminiscent of the work of Salomėja Neris, one of the most popular Lithuanian writers of the first half of the twentieth century, who clearly influenced Vaičiūnaitė's early development as a writer.

Vaičiūnaitė's later poetry, collected in *Kaip žalias vynas* (As Green Wine, 1962), *Per saulėtą gaublį* (Through the Sunny Globe, 1964), *Vėtrungės* (Weathercocks, 1966), *Po šiaurės herbais* (Under Northern Arms, 1968), *Pakartojimai* (Repetitions, 1971), *Neužmirštuolių mėnesį* (In the Month of Forget-me-nots, 1977), and *Šaligatvio pienės* (Sidewalk's Dandelions, 1980), was based on multifaceted emotional experiences. Vaičiūnaitė's poetry is not simply composed as lyrical melodies of feelings, however; rather, her poetry achieves its preternatural angle through its myriad leaps and metaphoric parallels. Vaičiūnaitė rejects the simple and naive forms of traditional Lithuanian lyricism in her attempts to make her poetry address modern life. The capricious wanderings of her feelings—expressed in twitching rhythms, sudden exclamations, and deep pauses—along with her mellifluous repetitions, asymmetrical stanzas, and scattered metaphors, create a torrent of free speech. Her style is much more complicated, refined, and expressive than traditional Lithuanian poetry.

Vaičiūnaitė's perception of the world is dominated by visual images that are clearly influenced by modern art. Her imagery consists of geometric lines, intensive colors, and clearly delineated details. Although the images appear fragmentary and capable of blocking the reader's perception of her inner emotions, her emotional energy is so strong that it can be felt beyond the impressionistic pictures her words create.

Vaičiūnaitė's use of words and rhythm express extreme feminine sensitivities; even straightforward descriptions of journeys turn into metaphors of a "naked heart." She is capable of expressing the heat of feminine passion through pure images as well as concealing erotic moments behind original and mysterious nature metaphors, as illustrated in these lines from "Asiūklieu" (Horse-tails), written in 1968 and collected in *Klajoklė saulė* (1974):

> Galvotrūkčiais krintančios žalios sūpuoklės.
> Asiūkliai. Aistra. Atskalūniškas aukštis,
>   kurį tu pasiūlei.
> Asiūklieu.
>
> (The green swing falling headlong,
> Horse-tails. Passion. Apostative height,
> thy suggestion.
> Horse-tails.)

Vaičiūnaitė combines oppositional associations and creates short-lasting, poignant moments blurring the divisions between illusion and reality. Her poetry is filled with beautiful objects—roses, marble, silver, amber, mother-of-pearl, a gypsy's hair, china teapots with small blue flowers—so that the many characteristics of the real world connect with individual emotions. The harmony of existence, which can be felt only within the moment of creative acts, is portrayed through the power of her sensory descriptions; this power boldly reforms the elements of reality that were often employed in traditional Lithuanian poetry.

Vaičiūnaitė employs different motifs of culture from intellectual poetry so that her images attempt to address the universal human experience. Drawing from situations elicited from antique, epic heroes within historical chronicles and biographies of various writers, Vaičiūnaitė creates her own myth of burning passion and fantasy, a myth of love that is stronger than death. This element is particularly vivid in her "Keturi portretai" (Four Portraits), "Orfėjas ir Euridikė" (Orpheus and Eurydice), and "Kanonas Barborai Radvilaitei" (Canon for Barbara

Radvilaitė), all of which are included in *Klajoklė saulė*. In these poems Vaičiūnaitė attempts to juxtapose the fragility and subtlety of feminine sensations with a generalization of the masculine situation in the modern world.

In her book of short lyrical plays, *Pavasario fleita* (Flute of Spring, 1980), Vaičiūnaitė again refused the traditional symbols that were characteristic of Lithuanian poetical dramas and retained the ephemeral images existent within her previous works. The plays include no rigid, logical progressions; only the performance of each particular moment is important. Thus, the pieces are incompatible with stage performance. The fragmentary images express not only particular emotions but also the sense of life she wished to communicate—short, sudden flashes of enlightenment and insight into the nature of existence. The protagonists of the plays—Cassandra, Achilles, and Narcissus—have no relation to the ancient Greek heroes; rather, they are participants in the emotional experience of being alive in the midst of the uncertainties of the imagination. They represent the vortices of various human emotions. Vaičiūnaitė's fragmentary world is based on opposites—pieces of antique texts juxtaposed with contemporary jazz music, and the mythology of the past as a stable, unchanging world contiguous with the shifting, constantly changing modern world. The oppositions within each poetical drama reveal a necessary strain of conflict that expresses Vaičiūnaitė's perspective on the modern human condition.

The dominant motif of her work is the joy of living, as in these lines from *Per saulėtą gaublį:*

> Ateis sekmadienis. And duonos tepsim bučinius ir sviestą,
> Ir cirko afišas skaitysim padrikai.
> Ir klaidžiosim po margaspalvį, saulėtą, triukšmingą miestą.
>
> (Sunday will come. We'll butter our bread with kisses,
> We'll read the circus posters over and over.
> We'll wander through the city, alive, bright, exuberant.)

Vaičiūnaitė attempted to express an all-encompassing love for humanity rendered through a personal and heartfelt vision. In her later books Vaičiūnaitė expresses the joy of a young girl as her emotions grow into the deep, intense sensitivities of a mature woman who experiences the pleasure of motherhood. Vaičiūnaitė connects varied images—the sun, fire, and night—to the concept of motherhood, thus rendering motherhood itself into a cosmic as well as an earthly power. The image of mother is one who nurtures, warms, and protects the entire world.

Vaičiūnaitė's poems appear to be rather confined in their expressions of spatial dimensions—a poem might depict one little room with a window opened and curtains fluttering—but there are many details that evoke deep emotional responses, such as a red gown draped over a chair, a small teapot on the table, or scattered yellow beads. These details expand the spatial dimensions of the poem through their ability to create various imaginative associations as well as enable the reader to create a new poetical reality or draw his or her conclusions. Thus, the expansion of space rendered through the use of concrete images often implies a boundless reality, where beauty is the key to elevating one's existence. Within Vaičiūnaitė's poetry, beauty is also the key to the world of culture as it relates to reminiscences of positive emotions that never fade and that can remind one of beloved individuals or treasured moments.

Color and light also play an important role in Vaičiūnaitė's poetry. She uses color imagery and metaphors of light, which, in turn, are associated with different emotional expressions of human beings. This correlation between color and light is often vividly portrayed: "Ir maišosi begalė laimių, likimai kaip šviesoforai / čia žaibiškai keičia spalvą—raudoną, geltoną zailą" (And endless ways of being happy are intertwined, and fortunes like traffic lights / are changing their colors with lightning speed—red, yellow and green). Thus, the reader grasps the poetic notion of colors having their beginnings in light. This use of color and light also tends to extend the spatial dimensions of Vaičiūnaitė's poetry, which renders interior and exterior space simultaneously visible, as evident particularly in her poem "Nežinomai Kabirijai" (To Unknown Kabiria), collected in *Kaip zalias vynas*. In some of her earlier works, color and light are used to express the properties of different powers and forces that have an effect upon human existence and destiny.

The concentration of different colors in her more important images—the sun, amber, loaves of bread, candles, flames, beeswax, bees, and honey—turn exterior pictures into visions of an inner world. More often than not, personal experience and biographical confessions of the poet are hidden behind these metaphors of color and light, as they express passion, intensity, and sensuous physical experiences.

Vaičiūnaitė's poem "Juodkrantė" (translated as "Juodkrantė [The Black Shore]," 1993), first pub-

lished in *Po šiaurės herbais* (1968), reveals a transitional stage in her writing: the light is still hidden in objects, but the sense of these objects appears to be a continuation of a peculiarly Lithuanian mythological consciousness that has existed for centuries. Vaičiūnaitė's poetry also uses time in an original way. She tends to embrace thousands of years within the span of one short poem. She penetrates the past to prehistoric times or to an imaginary mythological land. Thus, the linear progression of hours within the present appears to expand, rendering a different conception of the self, of states of being, and of the nation as parallel realities, coexisting one within the other. "Juodkrantė" illustrates this peculiar yearning and reaching for the primal self as a characteristic of contemporary existence and as a key to an emotional code that connects the past to the present. In general, Vaičiūnaitė's use of the themes and motifs of folklore and mythology is an attempt to find a stronger connection with the reality of her country and to recognize and express its sense of spiritual continuity with the past, which fosters the continuation of a national consciousness.

Within Vaičiūnaitė's work, two sides of femininity exist: the passionate and sensual and the nourishing and loving. For Vaičiūnaitė, however, the nourishing and loving image of femininity appears to be ambiguously defined, as if there are obstacles that hinder the opening of the feminine heart. Vaičiūnaitė expressed this ambiguity when she discussed with Daujotytė her feelings about the genesis of her lyrical drama "Kasandra," in *Pavasario fleita*:

> I don't know why, but my favorite work up to now is 'Kasandra,' though I understand that it is not alive enough and there are no biographical facts there. And why is it so dear to me? Maybe because of that, that I was writing it after the birth of my baby, trying to save in my subconscious the essence of my own creativity, to save it from this everyday routine and from this tremendous feeling of love for my baby; I was saying good-bye to something.

In many ways the experience of motherhood altered the way in which Vaičiūnaitė understood and portrayed women and femininity: the love for her child made it difficult for her to devote herself only to poetry. For her entire life, creative work was the highest level of emancipation; it was her "victory against the everyday routine of women, against fatigue and heartache." The birth of her child, however, forced Vaičiūnaitė into succumbing to the traditional feminine role of mother; although she attempted to be assertive in her creative works, this assertion of self never completely liberated her from her feminine role.

One of the most significant women writers of contemporary Lithuanian literature, Vaičiūnaitė is a poet of deep personal commitment and emotional intensity. Uninhibited by the boundaries of time and place, she creates in her poetry a distinctive vision of the world in which myth and reality merge into a moment of pure harmony and perfection. Transforming the urban landscape of modern existence through language and metaphor, Vaičiūnaitė finds peacefulness and purpose that reveals both the meaning of self and the essence and beauty of womanhood.

References:

Algimantas Baltakis, "Spalvingai, nuoširdžiai, natūraliai," in *Poetų cechas* (Vilnius: Vaga, 1975), pp. 174–184;

Viktorija Daujotytė, "Moteriškųjų prasmių kūrimas," in her *Moters dalis ir dalia* (Vilnius: Vaga, 1992), pp. 213–230;

Vytautas Kubilius, "Lyrinis herojus ir lyrinės akimirkos," *Pergalė*, 10 (1962): 159–162;

Kubilius, *XX amžiaus literatūra* (Vilnius: Alma Literra, 1996), pp. 541–545;

J. Lankutis, ed., *Lietvių literatūros istorija*, volume 2 (Vilnius: Vaga, 1982), pp. 409–413;

Kestutis Nastopka, "Tarp dviejų erdvių," in his *Šiuolaikinės poezijos problemos* (Vilnius: Vaga, 1977), pp. 342–354;

Ričardas Pakalniškis, "Mieste žuvėdros ir kovarniai," *Pergalė*, 2 (1969): 154–160;

Rimvydas Šilbajoris, "Šviesa ir spalvos Juditos Vaičiūnaitės poezijoje," in his *Netekties ženklai* (Vilnius: Vaga, 1992), pp. 424–443.

Adam Zagajewski

(21 June 1945 –   )

Tadeusz Witkowski
Saint Mary's College

BOOKS: *Komunikat* (Kraków: Wydawnictwo Literackie, 1972);

Świat nie przedstawiony, by Zagajewski and Julian Kornhauser (Kraków: Wydawnictwo Literackie, 1974);

Sklepy mięsne (Kraków: Wydawnictwo Literackie, 1975);

Ciepło, zimno (Warsaw: Państwowy Instytut Wydawniczy, 1975);

Drugi oddech (Kraków: Znak, 1978),

List (Poznań: Od Nowa, 1978);

List: Oda do wielości (Kraków: Półka Poetów, 1982);

Cienka kreska (Kraków: Znak, 1983);

Jechać do Lwowa i inne wiersze (London: Aneks, 1985);

Solidarność i samotność (Paris: Zeszyty Literackie, 1986); translated by Lillian Vallee as *Solidarity, Solitude: Essays* (New York: Ecco, 1990);

Płótno (Paris: Zeszyty Literackie/Cahiers Litteraires, 1990); translated by Renata Gorczynski, Benjamin Ivry, and C. K. Williams as *Canvas* (New York: Farrar, Straus & Giroux, 1991; London: Faber & Faber, 1993);

Dwa miasta (Paris: Zeszyty Literackie / Kraków: Oficyna Literacka, 1991); translated by Vallee as *Two Cities: On Exile, History, and the Imagination* (New York: Farrar, Straus & Giroux, 1995);

Ziemia ognista (Poznań: Wydawnictwo a5, 1994);

W cudzym pięknie (Poznań: Wydawnictwo a5, 1998); translated by Clare Cavanaugh as *Another Beauty* (New York: Farrar, Straus, & Giroux, 2000);

Pragnienie (Kraków: Wydawnictwo a5, 1999).

Editions and Collections: *Dzikie czereśnie* (Kraków: Znak, 1992);

Późne święta (Warsaw: Państwowy Instytut Wydawniczy, 1998).

Editions in English: *Tremor: Selected Poems*, translated by Renata Gorczynski (New York: Farrar, Straus & Giroux, 1985);

Adam Zagajewski (photograph by Virginia Schendler; from the dust jacket for Two Cities: On Exile, History, and the Imagination*)*

Mysticism for Beginners, translated by Clare Cavanagh (New York: Farrar, Straus & Giroux, 1997; London: Faber & Faber, 1998);

Trzej aniołowie–Three Angels (Kraków: Wydawnictwo Literackie, 1998).

International recognition of Adam Zagajewski, one of the most talented Polish writers belonging to the "Generation of 1968," is chiefly owing to his achievements in verse. His poems—along with poems by his older Polish colleagues, Czesław Miłosz, Zbigniew Herbert, Tadeusz Różewicz, and Wisława Szymborska—are among the most frequently translated and most popular contemporary poetic works. They have been published in English,

French, German, Swedish, Norwegian, Italian, Serbo-Croatian, Slovak, Slovenian, Russian, Dutch, and Hungarian.

Adam Zagajewski was born on 21 June 1945 in Lwów (then U.S.S.R., now Ukraine), the second child of Ludwika and Tadeusz Zagajewski. In October of the same year, his family moved to the Silesian city of Gliwice in Poland, where his father became a professor at the local technical university. In Gliwice, Zagajewski completed his elementary and high school education. After his graduation from high school in 1963, he moved to Kraków and began to study philosophy and psychology at the Jagiellonian University. During his student years in the late 1960s, he started his literary activities. In 1968, two years before graduating, he was offered a teaching assistantship in the Academy of Mining and Metallurgy, where he continued to teach academic courses in philosophy until 1975. Concurrently, for several years, he remained an editor of the weekly *Student*.

Like many young intellectuals of his generation, Zagajewski became a witness to several important events in the history of East Central Europe: the anti-Jewish purge in communist parties and at institutions of higher learning begun in the Moscow bloc after the Arab-Israeli war in 1967, the Polish student protests in March 1968, the invasion of Czechoslovakia by the Soviet army and its allies in August of the same year, and the bloody suppression of the Polish workers' demonstrations in December 1970. All these events were devastating to the young writers who had previously striven to believe in the slogans of the left. In this atmosphere Zagajewski began his literary career. His name was noticed by Polish literary critics in 1969 in connection with the Kraków group of poets calling themselves "Teraz" (Now), and, from the beginning, he was associated with the literary New Wave and with the idea of "plain speaking" in poetry.

This idea was, first and foremost, directed not only against the concepts of poetry (current in the early 1960s), devoid of "here and now," and utilizing literary allusions and abstract symbolism, but also against the official language of social realism in general. According to Zagajewski, "plain speaking" was a matter of representing reality as openly as possible and directly communicating human experiences in their richness and complexity. The idea was developed in a series of articles published in the student literary press and subsequently included in the collection of essays *Świat nie przedstawiony* (Unrepresented World, 1974), written with Julian Kornhauser. In his article "Walka konkretu z symbolem" (The Struggle

of the Concrete with the Symbolic), Zagajewski explained that "to speak plainly is to express an experience directly, to consider the spontaneity of the persona experiencing the world in various ways and at the same time to contradict a concept of historicism which notices history only on the level of great structures and not on the level of man's elementary experiences."

In 1972 the first volume of Zagajewski's poetry, *Komunikat* (The Communiqué), appeared in print, followed by *Sklepy mięsne* (Meat Shops, 1975). Both collections were attempts at representing reality and, and at the same time, were documents of the poet's struggle with communist censorship. A similar attempt at implementing programmatic ideas from *Świat nie przedstawiony* was also characteristic of Zagajewski's first novel, *Ciepło, zimno* (Warm and Cold, 1975). The whole program, however, could hardly be implemented under the circumstances prevailing in the mid 1970s, when the press and book publishing were strictly controlled by the state, and a writer had little opportunity to say anything critical regarding the abusive system of power. At the time of its debut, the Generation of 1968 had no alternative but to publish in the official media or not to publish at all; hence, many of Zagajewski's and his colleagues' postulates may have seemed naive and their poems impudently moralistic and utopian. In Zagajewski's poem "Prawda" (Truth), for example, readers could find the following counsels:

> Get up open the door untie these ropes
> Make your way out of the nets of nerves
> you are Jonah who is digesting the whale
> Refuse to shake that man's hand
> Straighten up dry the tampon of your tongue
> Leave your cocoon tear the membrane
> Breathe the deepest layers of air
> and slowly while remembering the rules of syntax
> speak the truth this is your purpose in your left hand
> You hold love and in your right hatred

In practice, both the choice of an ethical attitude and selection of the topics that could facilitate a true representation of reality were drastically limited by censorship. A poet could, at most, sarcastically smash linguistic stereotypes or make merciless parody of the official rhetoric and journalist style. At the same time, the concept of literary persona implied in the poetry of the New Wave and the image of the author projected in critical articles and manifestos written by Zagajewski and some of his colleagues were built upon the basis of a unified view of ethics, aesthetics, and politics. Their common denominator included opposition to the system of values promoted by communist politicians and writers profiting from the patronage of the communist state, as well as an opposition to manifestations of evil in the everyday life of an average Polish citizen.

In 1973 and 1974 clear signs of a new policy toward the New Wave appeared in the literary press. The rebellious poets were accused of nihilism, destructiveness, and a lack of a positive program. Censors also began to expurgate the names of some writers. In response, several writers of the Generation of 1968, including Zagajewski, became more openly involved in opposition activities (such as protests against the proposed changes to the Constitution in 1975) and subsequently, after the workers' protests in Ursus and Radom and the establishment of KOR (Workers' Defense Committee) in 1976, made the decision to publish their works beyond the reach of censorship. In 1977 the first issue of the underground quarterly *Zapis* (Record), edited by Zagajewski, Stanisław Barańczak, Ryszard Krynicki, and several older writers, came out in Warsaw. Also outside official channels Zagajewski published a new collection of poems, *List* (A Letter, 1978). *Zapis* was a journal that, by definition, was to print items subjected to the interventions of the censor, items that would not have had a chance of appearing in official circulation; but the publishers emphasized that they intended to record everything that could be considered testimony of truth, in both the cognitive and psychological senses of this term.

In 1979 Zagajewski was offered a fellowship by the Internationale Künstlerprogramm and spent two years in Berlin. In 1981 he became a fellow of the MacDowell Artists Colony in Peterborough, New Hampshire. On a trip to Poland in September 1981 he witnessed the activities of the newly created independent trade union Solidarity and the imposition of martial law. Allowed to leave Poland again in 1982, he established his residence in Paris, France. Since then, he has been a permanent contributor to the Paris-based journal *Zeszyty Literackie* (Literary Notebooks) and a member of its editorial board. In January 1986 Zagajewski became a guest of honor at the international PEN congress held in New York. In the spring of 1988 he began to teach a semester a year at the University of Houston Creative Writing Program, and four years later (1992) he became a fellow of the John Simon Guggenheim Foundation.

Changes visible in Zagajewski's artistic philosophy after he finally decided to stay in the West actually began before the declaration of martial law in Poland. They are clearly reflected in the cycle

"Oda do wielości" (Ode to Plurality) published in the volume *List: Oda do wielości* (A Letter: Ode to Plurality, 1982). Some of his new poems included in this collection, especially those written shortly after the imposition of martial law, bring to mind other dissident texts of that period and are a manifestation of moral support for people remaining under oppression. "Oda do wielości," however, is much closer to Zagajewski's later volumes, *Jechać do Lwowa i inne wiersze* (To Go to Lwów and Other Works, 1985), *Płótno* (1990; translated as *Canvas*, 1991), and *Ziemia ognista* (Land of Fire, 1994). All of those volumes reflect an essential evolution of Zagajewski's artistic sensitivity and articulate a viewpoint clearly different from the majority of views expressed in the Polish underground publications. That viewpoint was expressed in both a poetic and a discursive manner in some of Zagajewski's poems and in his three collections of essays *Solidarność i samotność* (1986; translated as *Solidarity, Solitude*, 1990), *Dwa miasta* (1991; translated as *Two Cities: On Exile, History, and the Imagination*, 1995), and *W cudzym pięknie* (1998; translated as *Another Beauty*, 2000).

In some of the articles included in the first collection, Zagajewski argues that the New Wave was, at its inception, an immature current because it was based on a critique of totalitarianism from an ethical standpoint. This critique led not only to mistaking justice for beauty and to an impoverished view of the world but also to the formation of a "negative spirituality." In place of moral resistance, the author proposed another form of struggle against the totalitarian standardization of reality, one that would stem from an ecstatic affirmation of all existence in its abundance, complexity, and variety. Initially, he considered this affirmation a means of opposing the totalitarian homogenization of life (as in the article titled "1983"), but Zagajewski's need to explain his motives in terms of the social situation disappeared almost completely from his articles published in the mid and late 1980s. In the short statement titled "Co mam do zarzucenia tzw. Nowej Fali" (translated as "What I Have Against the So-Called New Wave," 1995) he discoursed on his own poetic roots:

> The New Wave: I am not thinking of the poets—friends of mine that I respect and admire—who make it up, but of that nauseous concept of the New Wave, the construct it has become, produced and imposed, like a mask, on its living visage . . . derived from one basic tone of opposition, rebellion. A discovery of the value and strength of the word "no" has long designated the direction of development for this poetry. Now I see more and

more clearly that it leads to serious limitations in a writer's music. . . . It grows and can threaten that other tone, that other (how much more important and mighty) word, "yes," whose addressee is no political or ideological, historical or economic system, nor Hegel's philosophy or policemen on horseback; nothing but the wide, living world.

After the collapse of communism in Poland, Zagajewski went even further: he questioned the very principle of making art from collective emotions. In another short article, "O Nowej Fali piosenka . . ." (A Song about the New Wave . . .), he wrote:

> I do not speak from the position of aestheticism, according to which historical, political, and social topics do not have anything in common with art. I am still convinced that everything, including social life, especially if it is full of sense and passion, may be an object of artists' or poets' attention. But this shred of shame which I have felt since long ago in the moments when big emotions left me, did not stop me from deliberating about the origin of artistic affection. More and more I am inclined to admit that poems, essays, or short stories should be derived from emotions, observations, ecstasy, or sadness that are not national, but my own. They should be born in myself, not in a crowd, even if I loved this crowd and passionately identified with it.

Those statements clearly correspond with changes in Zagajewski's poetics. In his early collections Zagajewski chiefly focused on the Polish *hic et nunc*, often examined domestic affairs from political and moral angles, and frequently used vocabulary and syntax typical of utilitarian forms rather than poetry (forms such as headline news, short press communiqué, or the personal letter). In volumes published in the 1980s and 1990s his repertory of poetic genres, themes, and devices underwent essential changes. The poet rediscovered the cyclical nature of human experiences. He began paying attention to instances from general history in addition to the events connected with Polish affairs. Two stanzas from the poem "Uchodźcy" (translated as "Refugees," 1997) provide an illustration:

It could be Bosnia today,
Poland in September '39, France
eight months later, Thuringia in '45,
Somalia, Afghanistan, Egypt.

There's always a wagon or at least a wheelbarrow
full of treasures (a quilt, a silver cup,
the fading scent of home),
a car out of gas marooned in a ditch,

Dust jacket for the English translation (1995) of Zagajewski's essay collection Dwa miasta *(1991)*

a horse (soon left behind), snow, a lot of snow,
too much snow, too much sun, too much rain.

Zagajewski's poetry is frequently characterized by semantics rich in anthropomorphism and syntax full of extended enumerations of details and repetitions. He perceives the world surrounding him in all its richness and multiplicity and increasingly focuses on topics that release the existential wonder and sense of mystery surrounding humankind.

It is hard to pinpoint the main factor contributing to Zagajewski's popularity among critics in the West, but he has received several important international literary prizes. These include the Kurt Tucholsky Prize of the Swedish PEN Club (1985), the New York-based Echoing Green Foundation prize (Zagajewski became its first recipient in 1987), the Jurzykowski Prize, granted by the Alfred Jurzykowski Foundation in New York (1989), the Jean Malrieu Prize (received together with his translator, Maya Wodecka, for a volume of poetry published in French in 1990), and the international Vilenica Prize (Slovenia, 1996).

Since his poetic debut, Zagajewski's approach to the question of creativity and writers' social obligations has evolved steadily. Burdened with Polish historical and literary experiences, Zagajewski has been better able to understand universal history, develop literary language attractive to non-Polish speakers, and create poetry that will stand the test of time.

References:

Stanisław Barańczak, "Alone but Not Lonely," in his *Breathing under Water and Other Eastern European Essays* (Cambridge, Mass.: Harvard University Press, 1990), pp. 214–218;

Barańczak, "Powiedz prawdę, do tego służysz," in his *Etyka i poetyka* (Paris: Instytut Literacki, 1979), pp. 169–176;

Barańczak, "Szukając miary możesz tworzyć miarę," in his *Przed i po* (London: Aneks, 1988), pp. 144–148;

Sven Birkerts, *The Electric Life: Essays on Modern Poetry* (New York: Morrow, 1989), pp. 423–431;

Madeline G. Levine, "Adam Zagajewski, *Jechać do Lwowa i inne wiersze. Tremor: Selected Poems* (trans. by Renata Gorczynski)," *Polish Review,* 32 (1987): 113–115;

Tadeusz Nyczek, "Kot w mokrym ogrodzie," in his *Emigranci* (London: Aneks, 1988), pp. 86–110;

Nyczek, *Powiedz tylko słowo. Szkice literackie wokół, "Pokolenia 68"* (Warsaw: Przedświt, 1985), pp. 11–32, 47–56;

Małgorzata Szulc Packalén, *Pokolenie 68. Studium o poezji polskiej lat siedemdziesiątych* (Warsaw: Instytut Badań Literackich, 1997);

Tadeusz Witkowski, "Adam Zagajewski: In Praise of Multiplicity," *Studium Papers,* 14 (1990): 168–169;

Witkowski, "Between Poetry and Politics: Two Generations," *Periphery: Journal of Polish Affairs,* 2 (1996): 38–43;

Witkowski, "Etyka i okoliczności," *Nowy Wyraz,* no. 2 (1975): 37–42;

Witkowski, "The Poets of the New Wave in Exile," *Slavic and East European Journal,* 33 (Summer 1989): 204–216;

Witkowski, "Politics for Art's Sake," *Periphery: Journal of Polish Affairs,* 3 (1997): 62–68.

Māra Zālīte
(18 February 1952 –   )

Inta Ezergailis
Cornell University

BOOKS: *Vakar zaļajā zālē: Dzejoli, 1970–1975* (Riga: Liesma, 1977);

Rīt varbūt: Dzejoli, 1975–1978 (Riga: Liesma, 1979);

Nav vārdam vietas: Dzejoli, 1979–1983 (Riga: Liesma, 1985);

Deviņpuiku spēks (Riga: Liesma, 1985);

Divas dramatiskas poēmas (Riga: Liesma, 1987);

Pilna Māras istabiņa (Riga: Liesma, 1987);

Tiesa (Riga: Liesma, 1987);

Debesis, Debesis: Dzejoli, 1978–1988 (Riga: Liesma, 1988);

Brīvības tēla pakājē: Runas un raksti (Engadine, N.S.W.: Latviešu preses biedrības Austrālijas kopa, 1990);

Lācplesis: Rokopera, libretto by Zālīte, music by Zigmars Liepins (Riga: Sprīdītis, 1991);

Vai tu vēl turies?: Dzejoli no līdzsinējiem krājumiem (Riga: Liesma, 1992);

Dziedināsana: Komponēti dzejoli un dziesmu teksti (Riga: Liktenstāsti, 1996);

Apkārtne (Riga: Preses nams, 1997);

Kas ticībā sēts: Runas un raksti Latvijas atmodai 1979–1997 (Riga: Karogs, 1997).

Collection: *Dzejas izlase* (Riga: Zvaigzne ABC, 1997).

PLAY PRODUCTIONS: *Pilna Māras istabiņa*, Riga, 1983;

Tiesa, Riga, 1985;

Dzīvais ūdens, Riga, 1988;

Lāčplēsis, libretto by Zālīte, music by Zigmars Liepins, Riga, 1988;

Eža kažociņš, Riga, Valmiera Theater, 1991;

Meža gulbji, libretto by Zālīte, music by Raimonds Pauls, Riga, Daile Theater, 1995.

OTHER: *Dzīvs priedes čiekurs: Dzeja, publicistika*, edited by Zālīte and D. Avotiņa (Riga: Liesma, 1979);

Acis: Jauno dzeja, edited by Zālīte and Ugis Segliņš (Riga: Liesma, 1987);

Māra Zālīte

Karogs rokrakstos, edited by Zālīte (Riga: Karogs, 1992).

SELECTED PERIODICAL PUBLICATION– UNCOLLECTED: "Pilna Māras istabiņa jeb tautas- dziesmu Māras meklējumos," *Varavīksne* (1985): 118–154.

Māra Zālīte represents the generation of Latvian writers that matured as artists under Soviet occupation. There are signs of political and intellectual malaise with the constraints of that regime in her own early poetry as well as in her commentaries on Latvian authors, such as Austra Skujiņa, who were lauded by the socialist realist critics for the wrong reasons. For Zālīte, folklore is an important source of potential liberation, as evidenced most strongly in her play *Pilna Māras istabiņa* (Māra's Room Is Full, 1983), which depicts the pagan nature goddess Māra. Since Latvia regained its independence in 1991, Zālīte has remained an active force in Latvian culture as a poet, playwright, librettist, and editor.

Zālīte was born on 18 February 1952 in Krasnojarsk in the former Soviet Union into a family of political exiles. After her family returned to Latvia in 1956, she spent her childhood in the countryside. In 1975 she graduated with a degree in language and literature from the philology department of the University of Latvia. She began working in the field of literature early, starting out as a technical secretary at the Writers Union, presiding over the Young Writers Studio, and, from 1977 to 1990, serving as poetry consultant for the journal *Liesma* (Flame). Since 1989 she has been the editor in chief of the prestigious literary magazine *Karogs* (Banner).

Like some other Baltic writers, in the early 1980s Zālīte participated in and furthered the movement for Latvian independence. In 1983 she wrote *Pilna Māras istabiņa*, the play that, perhaps more than any of her other works, captured the imagination and interest of readers. Before that, she had published poetry in periodicals as well as in the collections *Vakar zaļajā zālē* (Yesterday in the Green Grass, 1977) and *Rīt varbūt* (Maybe Tomorrow, 1979), a portrait of contemporary youth, with its alienated and nihilistic tendencies.

Although the theme of *Pilna Māras istabiņa* may not seem as contemporary and politically relevant as the poetry, a careful reading will quickly disabuse one of that impression. The central situation is that of motherlessness. Madara, the central female figure in the play, laments: "Where shall I find the source? / They're looking to me, all of them. / But I—where is my source? / My god, my god, / None of us has a mother." The text uses the folktale plot of gifts wished for, received, and mostly misused, and it is written partly in the mode of a folk song. Three brothers do not know how to use the gifts they receive from the goddess Māra, while Madara works hard to fathom the meaning of her

gift of "writing." Writing, in Latvian, also refers to embroidery, the traditional female means of access to ethnic culture.

Māra is, as she herself says, "the mother of all mothers," a goddess of pre-Christian wholeness. There is some hope in this play for the continuing of a feminine tradition, and perhaps even more importantly, some hope for that feminine tradition to lead to a new society built on values and ideas beyond those that motivated the brothers. The men's brutalized use of their gifts stems from a dull, earthbound literalness on the one hand and a vacuous, unthinking borrowing of symbolic values on the other. The tablecloth fosters untrammeled greed; the boots facilitate a foolish transcendence, ignoring all the actuality of life; and the hat provides the covering of denial and unconsciousness for the aggression of a hireling fighting for others' causes. For those who are left at the end of the play, living myth and an active "working through" of folk tradition may eventually provide an answer, but that remains beyond the limits of the play.

Another play, *Tiesa* (Trial), first performed in 1985 and published in 1987, mixes history and allegory in an examination of social conditions and their origin, the meaning of truth and lies in a social context, and the meaning of freedom and human happiness. The play includes among the varied characters Garlieb Merkel, the Baltic German enlightener who wrote an early and influential work on the Latvians at the end of the eighteenth century, and Zālīte uses many quotations from that work. As in *Pilna Māras istabiņa*, there is a female presence at the center, and she is again connected with the word. In this play she is a *vārdotāja*, a sorceress. Toward the end of the play, this "witch" cautions against mere hedonism:

> That is all I will tell you.
> Don't be surprised if some morning
> Your arm feels strong.
> Don't be afraid if suddenly
> wounds heal from your words.
> Don't fear it. It happens to those
> Who have looked me in the eye.
> Just don't forget one thing—
> To assuage pain—is not the end.
> Pain gives birth to words of happiness.

In the play *Dzīvais ūdens* (Living Water, 1988), first performed in 1988, situations of moral conflict in various areas of life are explored, and myth again informs the plot and the characters. In 1988 there was also a performance of the rock opera *Lāčplēsis* (The Bearslayer), based on the national heroic epic, for which Zālīte wrote the libretto. Her musical drama *Eža kažociņš* (The Porcupine Fur) was produced by the Valmiera Theater in 1991, and her musical epic *Meža gulbji* (Wild Swans) was performed by the Daile Theater in Riga in 1995, with a score by the prominent Latvian composer Raimonds Pauls.

Even though Zālīte increasingly turned to drama in the 1980s, she did publish two powerful collections of poetry. The 1985 volume *Nav vārdam vietas* (No Words Needed) celebrates motherhood, from the individual to "the Mother of all Life." It also emphasizes, again, the strong ethical strand of Zālīte's work. One poem addresses that insistence on what seems to be the collective level:

When you lift your helpless
arms, again,
you remember all—the fire, and the night,
make the sun rise again
over the ruin of power,
when you lift your helpless
arms, again.

That this poem is addressed to the Latvian collectivity can be seen most clearly in the mention of "fire and night," a hidden reference to a national monument, the play *Uguns un nakts* (Fire and Night, 1907) by the Latvian poet Jānis Rainis.

Zālīte has an ongoing interest in folklore and myth; she has also written an essay, "Pilna Māras istabiņa jeb tautasdziesmu Māras meklējumos" (The Goddess-Figure Māra in Folk Songs), published in the literary journal *Varavīksne* (Rainbow) in 1985. Yet, this interest is never merely antiquarian. Rather, she uses the archetypal figures and materials in lively and provocative ways. As she writes in an untitled poem about "the native hearth," published in the anthology *Māju svētība*, edited by Anna Rancāne:

We cannot learn from the snail,
for Home is not our shelter.
We will be Home's shelter.

In other words, culture, tradition, and ethnicity do not constitute a ready-made easy recourse, but have to be constructed ever anew. It is humankind's

responsibility to do that; considering it as shelter would wrongly relieve people of that responsibility.

Zālīte, like many writers whose native language is threatened by exile or imperial colonial power, feels a protective love for language even stronger than that of poets generally, as illustrated in her poem "Valoda" (Language), published in *Jaunā Gaita* in 1987:

Language, you are blood and flesh
for my godknowshence flowing thoughts.
I love you, and everyone who
touches my hearing
through you, glimmering river.
In you only do I sense the eternal,
stepping into the same place as always,
where everyone always, everyone and always.
. . . .
Glimmering river.
See—I am.
You alone
can affirm that.

In the wake of Latvian independence, Zālīte, in her capacity as editor in chief of *Karogs*, was responsible for supervising the complex privatization process of the journal and managed, in addition, to continue writing drama as well as poetry. Her collection *Vai tu vēl turies?* (Are You Still Holding On?), published in 1992, was followed by the publication in 1997 of *Apkārtne* (Environment). In that same year, Zālīte published a collection of speeches and editorials in a volume titled *Kas ticībā sēts: Runas un raksti Latvijas atmodai 1979–1997* (What Has Been Sown in Faith: Speeches and Writings for Latvia's Reawakening 1979–1997).

References:

Viktors Hausmanis, ed., *Latviešu rakstnieku biogrāfijas* (Riga: LE, 1992);

Anita Liepiņa, "Par Māras Zālītes lugām: *Pilna Māras istabiņa un Tiesa,*" *Jaunā Gaita*, 31 (July 1986): 3, 49;

Dzidra Vārdaune, "Māras Zālīte," in *Latviešu literātu portreti*, edited by Viktors Hausmanis and others (Riga: Zvaigzne, 1994);

Aina Vāvere, "Par Māras Zālītes drāmatisko poēmu," *Jaunā Gaita*, 156 (February 1986): 47–48.

Imants Ziedonis

(3 May 1933 –   )

Ieva Kalniņa
University of Latvia

and

Kārlis Račevskis
Ohio State University

This entry originally appeared in Concise Dictionary of World Literary Biography:
South Slavic and Eastern European Writers.

BOOKS: *Zemes un sapņu smilts: Dzeja* (Riga: Latvijas
Valsts izdevniecība, 1961);
Sirds dinamīts: Dzeja (Riga: Latvijas Valsts izdev-
niecība, 1963);
Dzejnieka dienasgrāmata: Ceļojuma apraksts (Riga:
Liesma, 1965);
Motocikls: Dzeja (Riga: Latvijas Valsts izdevniecība,
1965);
Pa putu ceļu: Ceļojuma apraksts (Riga: Liesma, 1968);
Es ieeju sevī: Dzeja (Riga: Liesma, 1968);
Kurzemīte: 1. grāmata. Publicistika (Riga: Liesma,
1970);
Dzejas diena, edited by A. Balodis and others (Riga:
Liesma, 1971);
Epifānijas: Proza, 1. grāmata (Riga: Liesma, 1971);
Kā svece deg: Dzeja, 1967–1970 (Riga: Liesma, 1971);
Perpendikulārā karote: Publicistika, by Ziedonis, Vitalii
Korotyc, and Gunārs Janaitis (Riga: Liesma,
1972);
Krāsainās pasakas: Literārās pasakas (Riga: Liesma,
1973);
Epifānijas: 2. grāmata (Riga: Liesma, 1974);
Kurzemīte: 2. grāmata (Riga: Liesma, 1974);
Caurvējš: Dzeja (Riga: Liesma, 1975);
Garainis, kas veicina vārīšanos: Raksti, runas, studijas
(Riga: Liesma, 1976);
Lāču pasaka: Literārā pasaka (Riga: Liesma, 1976);
Poēma par pienu (Riga: Liesma, 1977);
Man labvēlīgā tumsā: Dzeja (Riga: Liesma, 1979);
Blēņas un pasakas: Literārās pasakas (Riga: Liesma,
1980);
Re, kā: Dzejoļi (Riga: Liesma, 1981);

Imants Ziedonis

Maize, Liviu Damianu (Riga: Liesma, 1982);
Kas tas ir—kolhozs? (Riga: Liesma, 1983);
Visādas pasakas (Riga: Liesma, 1983);
Māte: Dzejoli, by Ziedonis and Grigore Vieru (Riga:
Liesma, 1984);
Pasāžas, by Ziedonis and Kurts Fridrihsons (Riga:
Zinātne, 1985);

Tik un tā: Grāmata par Madlienu (Riga: Liesma, 1985);

Sākamgrāmata (Riga: Zvaigzne, 1985);

Taureņu uzbrukums: Dzeja (Riga: Liesma, 1988);

Mūžības temperaments: Studijas par Raini (Riga: Liesma, 1991);

Tutepatās (Riga: Preses nams, 1992);

Mirkļi. Foreles: Dzeja (Riga: Teātra anekdotes, 1993);

Viegli: Dzeja (Riga: Preses nams, 1993);

Epifānijas: 3. grāmata (Riga: Preses nams, 1994);

Es, cilvēks, pasaulē (Riga: Preses nams, 1996);

Es skaitīju un nonācu pie Viena: Ievads, dzejoļi, lūgšanas (Riga: Svētdienas Rīts, 1996);

Pasaka par Bizi (Riga: Jumava, 1997);

Tāpēc jau, ka nevar zināt, kāpēc (Riga: Likteņstāsti, 1997).

Editions and Collections: *Ar tikko grieztu ķeizarkroni rokā: Dzejas izlase* (Riga: Liesma, 1979);

Izlase: Dzejas izlase (Riga: Zvaigzne, 1980);

Ceļmallapas: Dzejas izlase, 1957–1981 (Riga: Liesma, 1983);

Raksti 12 sējumos, 7 volumes, edited by Andra Konste (Riga: Nordik, 1995–1997).

Editions in English: *Selected Poems and Prose,* translated by Ruth Speirs (Riga: Avots, 1980);

Thoughtfully I Read the Smoke: Selected Poems, translated by Dorian Rottenberg (Moscow: Progress, 1980);

"How the Candle Burns," "Inevitability," "That Is Her Memorial," and "That Was a Beautiful Summer," translated by Ināra Cedriņš, in *Contemporary East European Poetry,* edited by Emery George (Ann Arbor, Mich.: Ardis, 1983), pp. 59–61;

"Through Evening Twilight," "Such a Fine Hum," "My Inscriptions," "When Cats," "May," "August," "I Love an Apple," "Small Window," "First," "Try to Find," "That's Only a Rattling of Shell," "The Moon Shines," "Prayer," and "How the Candle Burns," translated by Cedriņš; "We Uncovered a Mystery," "Fall When Still Shining . . . ," and "Hairpins," translated by Speirs; and "Don't Eat," "I Grow Ripe," "A Little Ship," "Bridge Feeling," "Sometimes I Feel," and "Fish Rot," translated by Juris Rozītis, in *Contemporary Latvian Poetry,* edited by Cedriņš (Iowa City: University of Iowa Press, 1984), pp. 151–168;

Flowers of Ice, translated by Barry Callaghan (Riverdale-on-Hudson, N.Y.: Sheep Meadow Press, 1990);

"Through Evening Twilight," "I Love an Apple," "First," "Small Window," and "Try to Find," translated by Cedriņš, in *Shifting Borders: East* *European Poetries of the Eighties,* compiled and edited by Walter Cummins (Rutherford, N.J.: Fairleigh Dickinson University Press, 1993), pp. 103–105.

PRODUCED SCRIPTS: *Uz intensifikācijas ceļa,* motion picture, Rīgas kinostudija, 1964;

Gada reportāža, motion picture, by Ziedonis and Hercs Franks, Rīgas kinostudija, 1965;

Pūt vējiņi! motion picture, based on Jānis Rainis's play, Rīgas kinostudija, 1973;

Puika, based on Jānis Jaunsudrabiņš's *Baltā grāmata,* motion picture, Rīgas kinostudija, 1977;

Zaļā pasaka, television, Latvijas televīzija, 1977;

Suns funs un vējš, television, Latvijas televīzija, 1978;

Kas ir kolhozs? television, Latvijas televīzija, 1981;

Man vienai māsiņai, television, Latvijas televīzija, 1984.

RECORDING: *Epifānijas,* read by Ziedonis, Matrix, 38127–38128, 1976.

OTHER: *Kas jāzina meitiņām: Latviešu tautas dziesmas,* edited by Ziedonis (Riga: Liesma, 1981);

Puisīts augu: Latviešu tautasdziesmas, edited by Ziedonis (Riga: Liesma, 1984);

Tu dzīvoji dižu darbu: Manas tautasdziesmas, edited by Ziedonis (Riga: Liesma, 1985).

SELECTED PERIODICAL PUBLICATION— UNCOLLECTED: "Kungs un kalps: Dzejoļu cikls," *Karogs,* 1 (1988).

The literary productions, journalistic writings, and political activism of Imants Ziedonis make him one of the most important personalities on the twentieth-century Latvian cultural scene. Central to his multifaceted creativity is the idea of tending: applying oneself to the care, preservation, and development of the world of ideas, of the self, and of society. In outlining this motif, Ziedonis effectively blends his love of Latvian folklore and his appreciation for values fortified by centuries of history with an experimental search for new forms and modes of poetic expression.

The son of a fisherman, Ziedonis was born on 3 May 1933 on the Courland seashore, in the village of Ragaciems, county of Sloka. In 1952 he completed his secondary education at the high school of Tukums. His principal interests at the time were agriculture, mathematics, and literature; he was especially drawn to the Scandinavian authors Knut Hamsun, Henrik Ibsen, Selma Lagerlöf, and Sigrid Undset, and to the Estonian A. H. Tammsaare. Following graduation, he first worked on a road crew, then as a teacher and a librarian. He began a correspondence course with the departments of history and Latvian literature at the University of Latvia, which he completed in 1959. By this time he had begun writing poetry, and he published his first poem, "Dzejniekam" (To the Poet), in the magazine *Dadzis* (Thistle). His literary beginnings took place at a time when Latvian literature was moving away from Stalinist ideology following Nikita Khrushchev's dramatic critique of the dictator. Ziedonis's creative output, together with those of Ojārs Vācietis and Vizma Belševica, profoundly influenced the development of twentieth-century Latvian literature.

Ziedonis's first collection of poems, *Zemes un sapņu smilts* (The Sand of Earth and Dreams), appeared in 1961. The main theme is the beauty and importance of physical work. The description of a harsh nature and of ordinary working people—the fishermen and women of his native village—brings out an appreciation of everydayness that was new in postwar Latvian literature. While the glorification of work and worker was an ideological commonplace in Soviet society, Ziedonis innovates by rejecting the declamatory and monumental tone. He also considers the work ethic in the contexts of a tradition represented by earlier generations and of a sense of pride and responsibility in the individual who refuses to be a simple cog in a vast mechanism.

His next collection, *Sirds dinamīts* (Heart's Dynamite, 1963), is ideologically more in tune with the official party line. In this volume he rejects the legacy of the past and presents the notion of an inner dynamism as the force needed for opening the way to a bright new era. This publication drew widespread criticism; the poet was reproached for what was taken to be an arrogant, superior tone and for ignoring the quandaries presented by the fundamental complexity of life.

In 1962 Ziedonis became a member of the Latvian Writers' Union, and the following year he was admitted to the Gorky World Institute of Literature in Moscow, where he completed his studies in 1964. On his return to Latvia, he worked as an editor at the publishing house "Liesma" and became the secretary of the Writers' Union. *Motocikls* (The Motorcycle), a collection published in 1965, marks a break with the poet's earlier idealism. The enthusiastic striving promoted by *Sirds dinamīts* is now counterbalanced by a thematic pattern of stillness and peace; this dialectic interplay allows the poet to develop a more penetrating analysis of the relationship between the individual and his or her world. In 1967 the poetry of *Motocikls* achieved considerable success in the form of a dramatization staged at the Dailes Theater in Riga by Pēteris Petersons.

Ziedonis is also well known for his prose works and, in particular, his travel journals. The first such publication, *Dzejnieka dienasgrāmata* (The Poet's Diary, 1965), was composed during a trip to the Altai mountains in 1963. In certain regards it follows the standards of the genre by offering colorful descriptions of people and places, and it fulfills the political requirement of the time by praising the friendship uniting all peoples of the Soviet Union. But the writing also marks an innovative departure from the genre: it is structured less by chronology than by the thematic sequence of the author's thoughts and experiences, and the observations of the traveler are filtered through the prism of a Latvian viewpoint, intermingling with philosophical and historical reflections on the people and their land. This approach became even more marked in subsequent reports: *Pa putu ceļu* (On the Trail of Foam, 1968), about a trip to Karelia, and *Perpendikulārā karote* (The Perpendicular Spoon, 1972), covering travels in Tadzhikistan. The latter trip was undertaken on behalf of the magazine *Druzhba narodov* (Peoples' Friendship), and Ziedonis was accompanied by photographer Gunārs Janaitis and Ukrainian poet Vitalii Korotych. The book resulting from these travels is organized in terms of questions the author raises that elicit reflections on the distinctiveness of a people's ethnic and cultural characteristics, on the importance of these qualities in the context of the achievements of civilization, and on the need to preserve them.

Toward the end of the 1960s expressions of dynamism and polemical intent were gradually replaced in Ziedonis's work by an appreciation of the intractable guises of reality. This shift is especially evident in the poems of *Es ieeju sevī* (I Go into Myself, 1968), in which the poet examines the paradoxes of both inner and outer worlds but does not seek to resolve the antithetical pairings of courage and cowardice, purity and degradation, resolve and surrender. The period of the late 1960s and early 1970s was marked by sociocultural processes that undermined all notions of self-determination and autonomy in Latvia and other Soviet Republics. While these processes were no longer the brutal coercive methods of the Stalinist era, their effect was to destroy all cultural and moral ties linking individuals to their community. For Ziedonis, the resulting feelings of dread, solitude, and alienation could be resisted only by means of a counter-strategy that valorized the profound meaning of an individual's ethnic and cultural being. He thus undertook an intensive study of Latvian folklore, especially the *dainas* (folk songs); of Eastern philosophy; and of the writings of Jānis Rainis and Aleksandrs Čaks. The collection *Kā svece deg* (Burns Like a Candle, 1971) brings out the poet's maturing insights about an alienation aggravated by a sense of lost ethical bearings as well as by the realization of a looming ecological crisis. At the same time, this pessimism is thwarted by assertions of the individual's right to be different, of the will to resist and to search for new values.

In 1970 Ziedonis published *Kurzemīte* (Little Courland), a work that achieved immense popularity. In this prose volume the author writes about his beloved native province of Courland, describing its people, customs, and traditions, and narrating its history. Following the publication of a second volume in 1974, the work was adapted for the stage. Both books have prompted a series of discussions and conferences inspired by the questions and problematic issues they have raised. What interests Ziedonis above all is the inner character and strength of his people, traits that become manifest in certain colorful personalities. He also considers the ties that link individuals to their land, to its nature and history. In describing the contemporary situation, he points out the contradictions between what has been inherited and what has been imposed, thus invalidating, in effect, the rhetoric of progress and accomplishment that constituted the official party line at the time.

The first volume of *Epifānijas* (Epiphanies) came out in 1971. As the title indicates, the volume of short prose pieces is the record of privileged moments of intellectual revelation when the ordinary and the banal reveal themselves as something new and unexamined. A variety of stylistic and linguistic forms of expression, such as the liberal use of paradox, hyperbole, and catachresis, are all aimed at disrupting commonplace and stereotypical thinking by way of the illogical, the absurd, and the grotesque. The success of the new work was indicated by its many translations: into Romanian, Russian, Swedish, Estonian, Moldavian, Slovak, Uzbek, Polish, and German. Two more volumes of *Epifānijas* appeared, the second in 1974 and the third in 1994.

The poetry of *Caurvējš* (A Draft of Air, 1975) is dominated by themes of weariness and futility, to which the poet opposes the countervailing force of cultural values. Similarly, the tragic tone of some poems contrasts with the ironic and playful mood of others. The sense of new poetic and philosophical possibilities drawn from folklore and mythology is evoked powerfully in the full-length poem *Poēma par pienu* (A Poem about Milk, 1977) and the collection *Man labvēlīgā tumsā* (In a Darkness that Favors Me, 1979). In *Poēma par pienu* Ziedonis turns to the fundamental values inherent in love of mother, family, homeland, nation, and work. The poem incorporates a multiplicity of perspectives; it has the form of a collage that includes poems, prose fragments, and excerpts taken from chronicles and dictionaries. Woman is the central figure of the poem; she becomes, in effect, the thematic

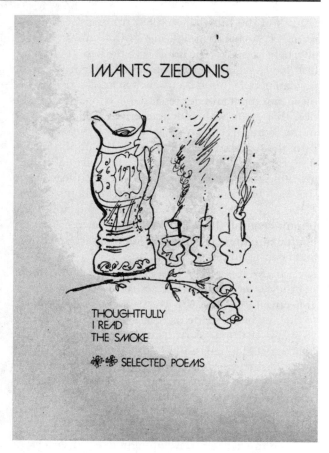

Title page for an English translation of Ziedonis's poetry published in 1980

point of intersection for all the important ethical problems concerning the present situation as well as the historical past. By contrast, in the unfinished poem "Viddivvārpā" (In "Middoubleearofwheat"), included in *Maize* (Bread, 1982), the stress is on the necessary role of the masculine, represented by the figure of the man who tends the earth and makes bread—thus ensuring the survival of humanity. *Man labvēlīgā tumsā* is a collection reinforcing the poet's meditative turn; it elaborates on the meaning of human life in the context of the animate and inanimate forms of being in the world and of the rhythms informing their existence. Pursuing this line of thought, the collection *Re, kā* (That's How, 1980) displays the poet's sense of wonder at the world and at the complexity of the relationships constituting the universe.

The poetry written at this time thus reveals a profound change in the poet's representation of the individual: the ideals of a strong will or purposeful resolve have been replaced by a trusting acceptance of order in the world, as well as an opening to the thought of a divine purpose, made manifest by the symbolism of light and of the sun. The poems in *Taureņu uzbrukums*

(Attack of the Butterflies, 1988) present the world in terms of a dynamic, pulsating rhythm in which highs alternate with lows, the noble with the base. The collection *Viegli* (Lightly, 1993) appeared at a time when the Latvian people found themselves in a collective state of disillusionment and depression following the exhilaration that came with independence. The work, once more, is dual in nature; while depicting the social reality of the day, the author brings out the importance of the realm of the sacred and of the spiritual, which gives meaning to the world of human endeavor and striving. The book *Mirkļi. Foreles* (Moments, Trout, 1993) is a collection of short poems and aphorisms reminiscent of the Japanese haiku style. They are mainly attempts at capturing momentary sensations and fleeting thoughts.

In the 1980s Ziedonis began a project documenting the careers and methods of successful directors of collective farms, the activity of which has contributed to the well-being of the nation. The result was *Tik un tā* (Anyway, 1985), a book detailing the struggle of the kolkhoz of Madliena and its director. Similarly, in 1992 he published *Tutepatās* (You Right Here), a work in which he pays tribute to a group of individuals who have worked to preserve Latvia's parks, natural sites, and most ancient trees.

Over the course of his career, Ziedonis has contributed much to the development of children's literature. In the 1970s he began writing literary fairy tales, and in the 1980s he began to write regularly for children—fairy tales as well as educational works meant to explain the world to them. Thus, *Kas tas ir—kolhozs?* (What Is a Kolkhoz? 1983) presents the principles of collective farming, and *Es, cilvēks, pasaulē* (I, a Human in the World, 1993) is the first part of a projected eight-volume encyclopedia for children.

Lastly, Ziedonis has always manifested an interest in other forms of artistic expression and has been involved in cinematic arts in particular. He has written screenplays for four movies, two based on classics in Latvian literature—*Pūt vējiņi!* (Blow, Wind, Blow, 1973), based on a 1913 play by Jānis Rainis, and *Puika* (The Boy, 1977), based on *Baltā grāmata* (The White Book, 1927) by Jānis Jaunsudrabiņš—and two documentaries, *Uz intensifikācijas ceļa* (On the Road to Intensification, 1964) and *Gada reportāža* (A Year's Reporting, 1965). He has also been involved with theater and opera: he dramatized his own work *Motocikls*, as well as the poetry of Aleksandrs Čaks for the play *Spēlē, spēlmani!* (Make Music, Musician! written in 1944 and published in 1972), and he wrote the libretto for composer Imants Kalnins's opera *Spēlēju, dancoju* (I Played, I Danced), based on a 1919 play by Rainis. In addition, Ziedonis has had an active part in several important political and cultural groups. While he has been forced to curtail some of his activities for reasons of health, he remains one of the more influential creative minds in Latvia and still contributes in important ways to the ongoing process that is shaping the new cultural and political identity of his country.

Interviews:

Kurts Fridrihsons, "Divsaruna," *Māksla*, 4 (1981): 11–12;

Māra Zālīte, "Katram ir savs smilšu pulkstens," *Liesma*, 4 (1983): 4–5;

Gunārs Janaitis, "Pirms nesadegu es, jūs mani nepazināt," *Literatūra un Māksla*, 6 May 1983;

Baiba Petersone, "Latvietis un reliģija," *Karogs*, 8 (1994): 188–194;

Ieva Lešinska, "Kad Dievi smejas, es smejos līdzi," *Rīgas Laiks*, 4 (1995): 32–37.

Bibliography:

Imants Ziedonis (Riga: Latvijas Valsts bibliotēka, 1983).

References:

Uldis Bērziņš and Atners Huzangajs, "Es jūtu, jūtu, jūtu šo zemi . . . ," *Kritikas gadagrāmata*, 16 (1988): 145–159;

Inta Čaklā, "Paradokss dzejā," *Grāmata*, 7 (1990): 55–59;

Čaklā, ed., *Promatnākt, šurpaiziet: Raksti par I. Ziedoņa daiļradi* (Riga: Liesma, 1983);

Valdis Ķikāns, "Imanta Ziedona dzejas tris valzivis," *Kritikas gadagrāmata*, 11 (Riga: Liesma, 1983): 167–178;

Ķikāns, "Mēs būsim lieli tik, cik mūsu griba," in his *Pieci* (Riga: Liesma, 1980), pp. 55–107;

Osvalds Kravalis, "Tautas dzejnieks Imants Ziedonis," in *Mūsdienu latviešu padomju literatūra: 1960–1980* (Riga: Zinātne, 1985), pp. 144–159;

Anda Kubuliņa, "Darbs piedzimstot tiek līdzi dots," in *Ērkšķu kronis katram savs* (Riga: Liesma, 1987), pp. 42–80;

Jolanta Mackova, "No dieva uz Dievu," *Karogs*, 8 (1994): 144–155;

Mackova, "Pasakas darbs," in her *Mūžīgie jautājumi* (Riga: Liesma, 1989), pp. 67–77;

Valda Melngaile, "Vizmas Belševicas un Imanta Ziedoņa dzejas ceļi uz patiesību," *Jaunā Gaita*, 84 (1970): 15–18;

Jānis Peters, "Piena gaismā, sev labvēlīgā tumsā," *Liesma*, 4 (1979): 5–6;

Mārtiņš Poišs, "Dzīvības soļi," in his *Atskaites punkts* (Riga: Liesma, 1971), pp. 101–177;

Laimonis Stepiņš, "I. Ziedoņa darbi ārzemēs," *Karogs*, 5 (1983): 199–201.

Books for Further Reading

Andrups, Jānis, and Vitauts Kalve. *Latvian Literature: Essays.* Stockholm: Goppers, 1954.

Anerauds, Jānis. *Fifty Encounters: Short Information about Fifty Latvian Soviet Men of Letters,* translated by J. Cērps. Riga: Liesma, 1973.

Bălan, Ion Dodu. *A Concise History of Romanian Literature.* Bucharest: Academy of Social and Political Sciences, 1981.

Bantas, Andreí, ed. *Like Diamonds in Coal Asleep: Selections from 20th Century Romanian Poetry,* translated by Bantas, Dan Dutescu, and Leon Leviţchi. Bucharest: Minerva, 1985.

Baranczak, Stanisław. *Breathing under Water and Other East European Essays.* Cambridge, Mass.: Harvard University Press, 1990.

Baumanis, Arturs, ed. *Latvian Poetry.* Augsburg: A. Baumanis, 1946.

Beissinger, Margaret H. *The Art of the Lautar: The Epic Tradition of Romania.* New York: Garland, 1991.

Beza, Marcu. *Papers on the Rumanian People and Literature.* London: McBride, Nast, 1920.

Birnbaum, Henrik, and Thomas Eekman, eds. *Fiction and Drama in Eastern and Southeastern Europe: Evolution and Experiment in the Postwar Period. Proceedings of the 1978 UCLA Conference.* Columbus, Ohio: Slavica, 1980.

Bojtár, Endre. *East European Avant-Garde Literature,* translated by Pál Várnai. Budapest: Akadémiai Kiadó, 1992.

Călinescu, George. *History of Romanian Literature,* translated by Leon Leviţchi. Paris: UNESCO / Milan: Nagard, 1988.

Carlton, Charles Merritt, Thomas Amherst Perry, and Stefan Stoenescu. *Romanian Poetry in English Translation: An Annotated Bibliography and Census, 1740–1996.* Iaşi, Romania: Center for Romanian Studies, 1997.

Catanoy, Nicholas, ed. *Modern Romanian Poetry.* Oakville, Ont.: Mosaic Press, 1977.

Cedrins, Inara, ed. *Contemporary Latvian Poetry.* Iowa City: University of Iowa Press, 1984.

Ciopraga, Constantin. *The Personality of Romanian Literature: A Synthesis,* translated by Stefan Avadanei. Iaşi, Romania: Junimea, 1981.

Close, Elizabeth. *The Development of Modern Rumanian: Linguistic Theory and Practice in Muntenia 1821–1838.* London & New York: Oxford University Press, 1974.

Collins, R. G., and Kenneth McRobbie, eds. *The Eastern European Imagination in Literature.* Winnipeg: University of Manitoba Press, 1973.

Cummins, Walter, ed. *Shifting Borders: East European Poetries of the Eighties.* Rutherford, N.J.: Fairleigh Dickinson University Press / London & Cranbury, N.J.: Associated University Presses, 1993.

Deletant, Andrea, and Brenda Walker, trans. *Silent Voices: An Anthology of Romanian Women Poets.* London & Boston: Forest, 1986.

Deligiorgis, Stavros, trans. *Romanian Poems.* Iowa City: Corycian Press, 1977.

Drăgan, Mihai, comp. *46 Romanian Poets in English,* translations, introductions, and notes by Stefan Avadanei and Don Eulert. Iaşi, Romania: Junimea, 1973.

Dutescu, Dan, ed. and trans. *Romanian Poems: An Anthology of Verse.* Bucharest: Eminescu, 1982.

Ekmanis, Rolfs. *Latvian Literature under the Soviets, 1940–1975.* Belmont, Mass.: Nordland, 1978.

Fairleigh, John, ed. *When the Tunnels Meet: Contemporary Romanian Poetry.* Newcastle upon Tyne: Bloodaxe, 1996.

George, Emery, ed. *Contemporary East European Poetry: An Anthology.* New York: Oxford University Press, 1993.

Harris, E. Howard. *Estonian Literature in Exile.* London: Boreas, 1949.

Harris. *Literature in Estonia.* London: Boreas, 1943.

Hawkesworth, Celia, ed. *Literature and Politics in Eastern Europe: Selected Papers from the Fourth World Congress for Soviet East European Studies, Harrogate, 1990.* New York: St. Martin's Press, 1992.

Hawkesworth, ed. *Writers from Eastern Europe.* London: Book Trust, 1991.

Hosking, Geoffrey A. and George F. Cushing, eds. *Perspectives on Literature and Society in Eastern and Western Europe.* Basingstoke: Macmillan in Association with the School of Slavonic and Eastern European Studies, University of London, 1989; New York: St. Martin's Press, 1989.

Kääri, K. *A Glimpse into Soviet Estonian Literature,* translated by U. Lehtsalu. Tallinn: Eesti Raamat, 1965.

Kangro, Bernard. *Estonian Books Published in Exile: A Bibliographical Survey, 1944–1956.* Stockholm: Eesti Rahvusfond, 1957.

Katzenelenbogen, Uriah. *The Daina: An Anthology of Lithuanian and Latvian Folk-songs, with a Critical Study and Preface.* Chicago: Lithuanian News, 1935.

Kelertas, Violeta, ed. *Come into My Time: Lithuania in Prose Fiction, 1970–90.* Urbana: University of Illinois Press, 1992.

Landsbergis, Algirdas, and Clark Mills, eds. *The Green Linden: Selected Lithuanian Folksongs.* New York: Voyages Press, 1964.

Landsbergis and Mills, eds. and trans. *The Green Oak: Selected Lithuanian Poetry.* New York: Voyages Press, 1962.

Lankutis, Jonas. *Panorama of Soviet Lithuanian Literature,* translated by V. Vladyko. Vilinus: Vaga, 1975.

MacGregor-Hastie, Roy, ed. and trans. *Anthology of Contemporary Romanian Poetry.* London: Owen, 1969; Chester Springs, Pa.: Dufour Edtions, 1969.

Mägi, Arvo. *Estonian Literature: An Outline,* translated by Elgar Eliaser. Stockholm: Baltic Humanitarian Association, 1968.

Mallene, Endel. *Estonian Literature in the Early 1970s: Authors, Books, and Trends of Development,* translated by G. Liiv. Tallinn: Eesti Raamat, 1978.

March, Michael, ed. *Description of a Struggle: The Vintage Book of Contemporary Eastern European Writing.* New York: Vintage, 1994.

Martin, Aurel. *Romanian Literature.* New York: Romanian Library, 1972.

Matthews, W. K., ed. and trans. *Anthology of Modern Estonian Poetry.* Gainesville: University of Florida Press, 1953.

Nirk, Endel. *Estonian Literature: Historical Survey with Bibliographical Appendix,* translated by Arthur Robert Hone and Oleg Mutt. Tallinn: Perioodika, 1987.

Oras, Ants. *Estonian Literature in Exile: An Essay. With a Bio-bibliographical Appendix by Bernard Kangro.* Lund: Eesti Kirjanike Kooperatiiv, 1967.

Pârvu, Sorin. *The Romanian Novel.* Boulder, Colo.: East European Monographs in Cooperation with the Romanian Cultural Foundation Publishing House / New York: Columbia University Press, 1992.

Pavlyshyn, Marko, ed. *Glasnost in Context: On the Recurrence of Liberalizations in Central and East European Literatures and Cultures.* New York: St. Martin's Press, 1990.

Popa, Eli, ed. and trans. *Romania Is a Song: Sampler of Verse in Translation.* Cleveland: America, 1966.

Pranspill, Andres, ed. and trans. *Estonian Anthology: Intimate Stories of Life, Love, Labor, and War, of the Estonian People.* Milford, Conn.: Andres Pranspill, 1956.

Pynsent, Robert B., and S. I. Kanikova, eds. *Reader's Encyclopedia of Eastern European Literature.* New York: HarperCollins, 1993.

Rubulis, Aleksis. *Baltic Literature: A Survey of Finnish, Estonian, Latvian, and Lithuanian Literatures.* Notre Dame, Ind.: University of Notre Dame Press, 1970.

Rubulis and Marvin J. Lahood, eds. *Latvian Literature.* Toronto: Daugavas Vanags, 1964.

Šilbajoris, Rimvydas. *Perfection of Exile: Fourteen Contemporary Lithuanian Writers.* Norman: University of Oklahoma Press, 1970.

Sorkin, Adam J., and Kurt W. Treptow, eds. *An Anthology of Romanian Women Poets.* Boulder, Colo.: East European Monographs in Cooperation with the Romanian Cultural Foundation Publishing House / New York: Columbia University Press, 1994.

Speirs, Ruth, trans. *Translations from the Latvian.* Exeter: Exeter University, 1968.

Steinberg, Jacob, ed. *Introduction to Rumanian Literature.* New York: Twayne, 1966.

Stoica, Ion, ed. *Young Poets of a New Romania: An Anthology,* translated by Brenda Walker and Michaela Celea-Leach. London & Boston: Forest, 1991.

Tappe, E. D. *Rumanian Prose and Verse: A Selection with an Introductory Essay.* London: Athlone Press, 1956.

Terry, Garth M. *East European Languages and Literatures: A Subject and Name Index to Articles in English-Language Journals, 1900–1977.* Oxford & Santa Barbara, Cal.: Clio Press, 1978.

Terry. *East European Languages and Literatures II: A Subject and Name Index to Articles in English-Language Journals, Festschriften, Conference Proceedings and Collected Papers in the English Language, 1900–1981 and Including Articles in Journals 1978–1981.* Nottingham: Astra Press, 1982.

Terry. *East European Languages and Literatures III: A Subject and Name Index to Articles in English Language Journals, Festschriften, Conference Proceedings and Collected Papers, 1982–1984.* Nottingham: Astra Press, 1985.

Terry. *East European Languages and Literatures IV: A Subject and Name Index to Articles in English-Language Journals, Festschriften, Conference Proceedings and Collected Papers, 1985–1987.* Nottingham: Astra Press, 1988.

Terry. *East European Languages and Literatures V: A Subject and Name Index to Articles in English-Language Journals, Festschriften, Conference Proceedings and Collected Papers, 1988–1990.* Nottingham: Astra Press, 1991.

Terry. *East European Languages and Literatures VI: A Subject and Name Index to Articles in English Language Journals, Festschriften, Conference Proceedings and Collected Papers, 1991–1993.* Nottingham: Astra Press, 1994.

Terry. *East European Languages and Literatures VII: A Subject and Name Index to Articles in English-Language Journals, Festschriften, Conference Proceedings and Collected Papers, 1994–1996.* Nottingham: Astra Press, 1997.

Terry, *A Subject and Name Index to Articles on the Slavonic and East European Languages and Literatures, Music and Theatre, Libraries and the Press, Contained in English-Language Journals, 1920–1975.* Nottingham: University Library, University of Nottingham, 1976.

Vaiciulaitis, Antanas. *Outline History of Lithuanian Literature.* Chicago: Lithuanian Cultural Institute, 1942.

Weber, Harry B., George J. Gutsche, and Peter Rollberg, eds. *The Modern Encyclopedia of East Slavic, Baltic, and Eurasian Literatures,* 10 volumes. Gulf Breeze, Fla.: Academic International Press, 1977–1996.

Yakstis, Frank, comp. *Translations of Lithuanian Poetry.* Ozone Park, N.Y.: Association of Lithuanian Workers, 1968.

Zdanys, Jonas, ed. and trans. *Selected Post-War Lithuanian Poetry.* New York: Manyland Books, 1978.

Contributors

Stanisław Barańczak . . . . *Harvard University*

Andrzej Busza . . . . *University of British Columbia*

Magda Carneci . . . . *Institute of Art History, Bucharest*

Bogdana Carpenter . . . . *University of Michigan*

Marcel Cornis-Pope . . . . *Virginia Commonwealth University*

Jan Čulík . . . . *University of Glasgow*

Bogdan Czaykowski . . . . *University of British Columbia*

Rolfs Ekmanis . . . . *Arizona State University*

Luule Epner . . . . *University of Tartu*

Inta Ezergailis . . . . *Cornell University*

András Görömbei . . . . *Kossuth University, Debrecen*

Aleš Haman . . . . *South Bohemia University, České Budějovice*

Iain Higgins . . . . *University of British Columbia*

Jiří Holý . . . . *Charles University, Prague*

Pavel Janoušek . . . *Institute of Czech Literature, Academy of Sciences of the Czech Republic, Prague*

Václav Kadlec . . . .

Ieva Kalniņa . . . . *University of Latvia*

András Kappanyos . . . . *MTA Institute of Literary Studies*

Violeta Kelertas . . . . *University of Illinois at Chicago*

Õnne Kepp . . . . *Under and Tuglas Literature Center*

Piret Kruuspere . . . . *Under and Tuglas Literature Center*

Maire Liivamets . . . . *The National Library of Estonia*

Dace Marauska . . . . *University of Latvia*

Anna Menyhért . . . . *University of Miskolc*

Rodica Mihaila . . . . *University of Bucharest*

Edward Możejko . . . . *University of Alberta*

Virgil Nemoianu . . . . *Catholic University of America*

Martin Pilař . . . . *University of Ostrava*

Kārlis Račevskis . . . . *Ohio State University*

Roman Sabo . . . .

Richard Sokoloski . . . . *University of Ottawa*

Monica Spiridon . . . . *University of Bucharest*

Halina Stephan . . . . *University of Florida*

Ele Süvalep . . . . *University of Tartu*

Péter Szirák . . . . *Lajos Kossuth University, Debrecen*

Broņislavs Tabūns . . . . *University of Latvia*

Jiří Trávníček . . . . *Masaryk University, Brno*

András Veres . . . . *Institute of Literary Studies, Hungarian Academy of Sciences*

Tadeusz Witkowski . . . . *Saint Mary's College*

Indrė Žekevičiūtė-Žakevičienė . . . . *Kaunas Vytautas Magnus University*

Cumulative Index

Dictionary of Literary Biography, Volumes 1-232
Dictionary of Literary Biography Yearbook, 1980-1999
Dictionary of Literary Biography Documentary Series, Volumes 1-19

Cumulative Index

DLB before number: *Dictionary of Literary Biography,* Volumes 1-232
Y before number: *Dictionary of Literary Biography Yearbook,* 1980-1999
DS before number: *Dictionary of Literary Biography Documentary Series,* Volumes 1-19

B

Cumulative Index

J

L

ISBN 0-7876-4649-0

90000